Global Tourism

Global Tourism

Third edition

Edited by William F. Theobald

LONDON AND NEW YORK

First published 2005 by Elsevier

This edition published 2012 by Routledge
2 Park Square, Milton Park, Abingdon, Oxon, OX14 4RN
711 Third Avenue, New York, NY 10017

Routledge is an imprint of the Taylor & Francis Group, an informa business

Library of Congress Cataloging-in-Publication Data

Global tourism / William F. Theobald.—3rd ed.
    p. cm.
    Includes bibliographical references (p.).
    ISBN 0-7506-7789-9 (alk. paper)
    1. Tourism. I. Theobald, William F., 1934–

  G155.A1G49 2004
  338.4ʹ791—dc22

                2004050270

British Library Cataloguing-in-Publication Data
A catalogue record for this book is available from the British Library.

ISBN: 978-0-750-67789-9

Contents

Foreword

Tourism is one of the most remarkable success stories of modern times. The industry, which began on a massive scale only in the 1960s, has grown rapidly and steadily for the past 30 years in terms of the income it generates and the number of people who travel abroad. It has proved to be resilient in times of economic crisis and shows no signs of slowing down, despite the uncertainty, caused by the events such as September 11, other terrorist threats, and even unexpected new illnesses like SARS in the beginning of the new century.

According to World Tourism Organization data, more than 715 million people were travelling internationally in 2002, generating more than US$472 billion in earnings. The outlook for the first decades of the next century is even more astounding. Our forecasts predict 1.6 billion international tourists by the year 2020, spending more than US$2 trillion annually—or US$5 billion every day.

As more and more governments recognise the important role that tourism can play in generating badly needed foreign exchange earnings, creating jobs, and contributing to tax revenues, the competition for tourist spending is becoming ever more intense.

Pressure on national and local governments to rapidly develop their tourism potential to meet demand and produce benefits, makes it more essential than ever to plan carefully and consider the human and environmental impacts of tourism development.

That is why, as Secretary-General of the World Tourism Organization, I am pleased to see the serious analysis of the problems and prospects of the tourism sector as presented in this third edition of *Global Tourism: The Next Decade.*

Tourism is an extremely complex endeavour. Not only are huge amounts of money at stake, we are providing economic incentives for protecting the natural environment, restoring cultural monuments, and preserving native cultures. We are, in a small but important way, contributing to understanding among peoples of very different backgrounds. But, above all, we are in the business of providing a break from the stress of everyday routine and fulfilling the dreams of leisure travellers.

This book goes a long way toward increasing our understanding about those dreams and complexities that make up the tourism industry.

Francesco Frangialli
Secretary-General,
World Tourism Organization

Preface

This book was the result of a need for such a collection that the editor personally experienced when attempting to teach a seminar in tourism where no traditional source books were available. It is intended for anyone who is or will be engaged in the tourism industry, regardless of his or her particular field of interest. The work is planned on original lines because the editor has found in his experience as teacher and author that the needs of students and practitioners, whether in university or graduate school, in government or in the private sector, are not met by the usual 'Introduction to Tourism' book. Rather, the need is for a new view of the subject that ordinary textbooks tend to separate.

This volume draws together the insights of 39 observers commonly concerned with the effects of tourism on contemporary society. The chapters represent various viewpoints from leading educators and practitioners from such disciplines as anthropology, economics, environmental science, geography, marketing, political science, psychology, public administration, sociology, and urban planning.

The purpose of this book is to present critical issues, problems, and opportunities facing the tourism industry. Tourism problems are complex and interrelated and they suggest myriad crises such as overcrowding of tourist attractions; overuse and destruction of natural resources; resident–host conflicts; loss of cultural heritage; increased crime and prostitution; inflation and escalating land costs; and a host of other political, sociocultural, economic, and environmental problems that may be brought about or exacerbated by tourism development.

The approach taken by this book is not on a particular subject, but rather the exploration of issues facing those involved in the tourism domain. The scope of the book provides each chapter as a mini-treatise on tourism, from an *international* perspective. Individual chapters scrutinise, reflect upon, and question the changes and transformations needed. Each chapter provides an exploration of concerns, issues, assumptions, values, and perceptions, and the reasoning for a view taken by individual authors. The issues raised in the book will hopefully bring about much needed thought, discussion, reflection, argumentation, and, perhaps, debate.

It would be patently absurd to claim that this book encapsulates all that might or should be said about tourism. It should be discerned, however, that an attempt has been made to present the viewpoints of both those who look with optimism at tourism and those who scrutinise it with some skepticism. It has not been a goal to prove any individual point of view as the 'right' one, but rather to examine the phenomena of tourism as fully as possible.

The impetus for this third edition came in large measure from the extremely helpful and highly positive reviews of the first book from the following individuals and publications: Derek Hall, *Tourism Management*; Paul F. Wilkinson, *Annals of Tourism Research*; Jonathan Goodrich, *Journal of Travel Research*; J.R. McDonald, *Choice Magazine*; John Joseph Courtney, *Journal of Vacation Marketing*; and reviewer unknown, *Future Survey*. Now, allow me turn to those whose special individuals whom I sincerely wish to recognise and thank.

It would not be possible to have undertaken this project without the love, support, and total commitment of my wife, Sharon. Thank you for being by my side through the years. To my children, Gregg and Amanda, may your lives be filled with as much happiness as you have given me over the years.

As editor I wish to acknowledge the contribution of Brian Archer, who not only provided encouragement to undertake this project, but also initially recommended it to the publisher, Butterworth-Heinemann. Thanks are also extended to my colleagues at Purdue University (U.S.), the Universities of Surrey (U.K.), and Waterloo (Canada) for the many opportunities they provided that helped expand my view of tourism as an international phenomena.

Acknowledgement is made of both the World Tourism Organization (WTO) and the Travel and Tourism Research Association (TTRA) who granted permission to reproduce selected portions of previously published materials. The editor is indebted to Francesco Frangialli, Secretary-General of the WTO, who generously agreed to write the introduction to the book and to Rok V. Klancnik, Chief, Press & Communications, of the WTO, for his kindness and logistical assistance.

This book has been translated into three additional languages: Japanese, Portugese, and Chinese. I wish to thank Professor Kazuhiko Tamamura of Doshisha University for his excellent translation into Japanese (by Koyo Shobo), the China Travel and Tourism Press for the Chinese edition, and Editora Senac for the Portuguese translation.

The editor wishes to thank Kathryn Grant, Publishing Director (Business Books), and Sally North and Jane MacDonald, editors at Butterworth-Heinemann, for their enthusiastic support of the idea underlying this book and their cogent suggestions throughout its compilation. In addition, the publisher's editorial staff is acknowledged for their help with the completed manuscript.

The editor wishes to acknowledged the contribution of those individuals who having adopted the book for their classes so generously provided constructive criticism of the text in order to strengthen this the third edition.

Finally, a specific note of appreciation is extended to the contributors to this volume for their wholehearted efforts in bringing their knowledge, ability, experience, and expertise to the task at hand. It was an exhilarating experience working with them. I am indebted to them, and I am also quite proud to count them as colleagues.

William F. Theobald
Purdue University
West Lafayette, Indiana

List of Contributors

Brian Archer is Professor Emeritus and former pro-Vice-Chancellor at the University of Surrey (U.K.), where previously he was Head of the Department of Management Studies for Tourism and Hotel Industries. Prior to joining the University of Surrey in 1978 he was Director of the Institute of Economic Research at the University College of North Wales, Bangor. He has degrees in Economics (University of London), Geography (University of Cambridge), and a Ph.D. (University of Wales), and is a Fellow of the Tourism Society and of the Hotel, Catering and Institutional Management Association

Gurhan Aktas is a Researcher in the Department of Tourism Management, Faculty of Business, T.C. Dokuz Eylul University, Izmir, Turkey, and is also a Ph.D. candidate at Bournemouth University (U.K.), working on a thesis titled, *Marketing Cities for Tourism: Developing Marketing Strategies for Istanbul with Lessons from Amsterdam and London*. His main research interests lie in tourist destinations with a particular focus on urban tourism, visitor attractions, tourism marketing, and tourism development and planning. He has written articles and conference papers on topics including tourism and environmental issues, tourist attractions in urban areas, the importance of lifetime education in tourism, and marketing city destinations.

Bill Bramwell is Reader in Tourism at the Centre for Tourism and Cultural Change at Sheffield Hallam University (U.K.). He has a Masters Degree in Geography from Cambridge University and a Ph.D. from the University of London. He formerly worked for the English Tourist Board, where he developed local tourism development programmes in various parts of England and he was responsible for the Board's rural tourism policies. Author of many articles in academic tourism journals, Dr. Bramwell is cofounder and coeditor of the *Journal of Sustainable Tourism*. He is coeditor of the books *Rural Tourism and Sustainable Rural Development* (1994), *Sustainable Tourism Management: Principles and Practice* (1998), and *Tourism Collaboration and Partnerships: Politics, Practice and Sustainability* (2000), as well as sole editor of *Coastal Mass Tourism: Diversification and Sustainable Development in Southern Europe* (2003). His research interests include the relations between tourism and growth management, local communities, actor networks, politics and governance, discourses of sustainability, and globalisation.

Peter M. Burns is the Director of the Center for Tourism Policy Studies (CENTOPS), University of Brighton, and Professor of International Tourism and Development. He has published on a wide range of social and planning matters including a book on tourism and anthropology. His teaching and research interests include the social dynamics of tourism with a burgeoning interest in the use of visual evidence in analysing tourism. As well as his academic work, Dr. Burns holds an active tourism planning consultancy portfolio with both public and private sector clients including the United Nations Development Program (UNDP), the WTO, and the European Union (EU). Dr. Burns sits on the WTO Education Council and is Founding Chair of the Association of Leisure and Tourism Studies (ATLAS) Social Identities Group.

Nancy E. Chesworth is Assistant Professor in the Department of Business and Tourism and Hospitality Management, Mount St. Vincent University. She holds a Masters in Tourism Planning and Administration from the George Washington University and received her doctorate in Man-Environment Relations from the Pennsylvania State University. Her diverse background includes studies in business, psychology, history, and education. She teaches graduate level planning and development, contemporary tourism issues, and international tourism. Her research interests include ecotourism, travel styles, tourist/host relations, and behaviour and marine and community tourism. She has conducted an ecotourism assessment of Mount Makiling in the Philippines, fieldwork on several Caribbean Islands, and community tourism development projects in Nova Scotia. Her consulting activities include involvement in a quality service assessment of resorts and visitor information centres for the province of Nova Scotia, and the impact of a historical reenactment event at Fortress Louisbourg.

Tim Coles is Business Research Fellow in Tourism and Lecturer in Human Geography in the School of Geography, Archaeology and Earth Resources at the University of Exeter in the United Kingdom. He is currently the Honorary Secretary of the Geography of Leisure and Tourism Research Group of the Royal Geographical Society (with Institute of British Geographers). His principal research interests surround the relationships between tourism production and consumption and the restructuring of society, economy, and polity, not least in central and Eastern Europe where he has worked extensively. His recent publications include (with Dallen Timothy) *Tourism, Diasporas and Space* (London: Routledge, 2004), and he is currently working (with Andrew Church) on a volume dealing with the connectivities between *Tourism, Power and Place* (London: Routledge, 2004).

Chris Cooper is Foundation Professor of Tourism Management in the School of Tourism and Leisure Management, Faculty of Business Economics and Law, The University of Queensland, Australia. He has an honours degree and Ph.D. from University College London and before beginning an academic career he worked in market planning for the tourism and retail sectors in the United Kingdom. Chris Cooper has authored a number of leading textbooks in tourism and worked closely with the WTO in developing the status of tourism education on the international stage. He is coeditor of *Current Issues in Tourism*, editor for a leading tourism book series, *Aspects of Tourism*, author of many academic papers in tourism and has worked as a consultant and researcher in every region of the world.

Graham M.S. Dann is Professor in Tourism at the University of Luton (U.K.). A native of Edinburgh, he obtained his doctorate from the University of Surrey (U.K.) and lectured in sociology at the University of the West Indies (Barbados). Professor Dann is the author of seven books and over seventy refereed articles. He is an associate editor of *Annals of Tourism Research*, a founding member of the International Academy for the Study of Tourism, and President of the Research Committee on International Tourism of the International Sociological Association. His research interests in tourism focus principally on motivation and the semiotics of promotion, brought together in his latest book, *The Language of Tourism* (1996).

Thomas Lea Davidson was, until his death, Principal and CEO of Davidson-Peterson Associates, Inc., a company he founded with Karen Ida Peterson. A full-service marketing research and strategic planning consulting company based in York, Maine (U.S.), they specialise in the travel, tourism, accommodations, meetings and conventions, entertainment, and recreation marketplace. Formerly, he was Executive Vice President of Davidson-Lasco, and Oxtoby-Smith, Inc. He was an adjunct faculty member at several universities including Northwestern and Connecticut (U.S.) where he was also Associate Director of Graduate Studies in Business. Mr. Davidson was a member of the editorial board of the *Journal of Travel Research*, and the U.S. Department of Commerce Task Force on Assessment Research Methods (Performance Accountability). A past national chairperson, board member, and committee chair of the Council of American Survey Research Organizations (CASRO), he also chaired the Certification Committee of the Association of Travel Marketing Executives.

Sara Dolnicar is a Senior Lecturer at the School of Management, Marketing & Employment Relations at the University of Wollongong. She completed her Masters degree in Psychology at the University of Vienna and her Masters/Ph.D. degree in Business Administration at the Vienna University of Economics and Business Administration, where she worked as an Assistant Professor at the Institute for Tourism and Leisure Studies. During this period she also acted as Secretary General of the Austrian Society for Applied Research in Tourism. In her Ph.D. thesis she compared neural networks with traditional algorithms for behavioural market segmentation. Her subsequent contributions include conceptual and methodological contributions in the area of *a posteriori* market segmentation, development of perceptions-based market segmentation (PBMS), and investigation of specific market segments among tourists and critical reviews of cluster–analysis–based segmentation studies. Most of these contributions resulted from interdisciplinary teamwork in the Research Centre 'Adaptive Modelling and Information Systems in Economics and Management Science,' a joint endeavour of three Viennese universities funded by the Austrian Research Foundation.

David Timothy Duval is a Lecturer in the Department of Tourism at the University of Otago in New Zealand. A formally trained archaeologist (having worked in the Caribbean in the early 1990s), David holds graduate degrees in Anthropology and Tourism and Development. David's primary research interests incorporate the social aspects of international migration and return migration, including the resulting transnational social relations, networks of cultural ties, and the impact of technology on movement and identity. Following ethnographic fieldwork conducted in Toronto, he has written extensively on migration from the Eastern Caribbean to Canada. He is the editor of *Tourism in the Caribbean: Trends, Development, Prospects* (London: Routledge, 2004) and is coeditor (with C.M. Hall and D.J. Timothy) of *Safety and Security in Tourism: Relationships, Management, and Marketing* (Haworth Press, 2004).

Larry Dwyer is Qantas Professor of Travel and Tourism Economics at the University of New South Wales. He publishes widely in the areas of tourism economics and tourism management with over 150 publications in international journals, government reports, chapters in books, and monographs. Dr. Dwyer maintains strong links with the tourism industry internationally and domestically. He has worked with the WTO in tourism strategy development in India and the National Centre for Development Studies in researching the economic impacts of tourism in the Pacific. He has also served as contracted consultant to the Australian government advising on the economic impacts of government policies on the tourism industry and has recently provided expert testimony to the tourism industry in its submission to the Australian government's Ten Year Plan for the tourism industry. Dr. Dwyer is on the Editorial Board of six international tourism journals.

Bill (H.W.) Faulkner was until his untimely death the Director of the Centre for Tourism and Hotel Management Research at Griffith University, Gold Coast (Australia). Former positions held included founding Director of the Australian Bureau of Tourism Research, senior policy research positions in the Australian Government's tourism and transport administrations, and an academic position at Wollongong University. Dr. Faulkner served on the editorial boards of several international tourism research journals, including *Tourism Management, Journal of Tourism Studies, Pacific Tourism Review, Turizam,* and *Anatalia.* His doctoral research was conducted in the Research School of Pacific Studies at the Australian National University, while undergraduate studies were completed at the University of New England.

Xavier Font is Principal Lecturer in Tourism Management at Leeds Metropolitan University. He has degrees in tourism management and marketing from the University of Girona (Spain) and Surrey (U.K.). Formerly he lectured at Buckinghamshire Chilterns University College and was Project Officer for an EU project on forest tourism. His research focusses on standard setting and certification of sustainable tourism and hospitality. He has coauthored and coedited four books and published in a variety of academic journals, including recent papers in *Annals of Tourism Research, Tourism Management, Journal of Sustainable Tourism,* and *Corporate Social Responsibility and Environmental Management.* In the last five years he has undertaken research and consultancy for UNEP, WTO, Ford Foundation, Travel Foundation, and WWF International, Germany and Netherlands.

Alan Fyall is Senior Lecturer in Tourism Marketing at the International Centre for Tourism & Hospitality Research, Bournemouth University. His interests are in heritage tourism and visitor attractions, tourism marketing, and interorganisational collaboration in tourism. He has published widely in journals, written a large number of book chapters, and has contributed to a number of professional publications. In addition, Alan was lead editor of the book *Managing Visitor Attractions: New Directions* and has recently completed authoring the book *Tourism Marketing: A Collaborative Approach* with Brian Garrod. Alan is a consultant editor for the *International Journal of Tourism Research* and resource editor for *Annals of Tourism Research,* both in the area of tourism marketing. Alan has travelled widely and has worked as a consultant for a number of large organisations including, in the United Kingdom, the former British Tourist Authority and the London Development Agency.

Brian Garrod is Senior Lecturer in Rural Economics and Tourism at the Institute of Rural Sciences, University of Wales, Aberystwyth. He holds a

Ph.D. from the University of Portsmouth. His interests are in sustainable tourism, visitor attractions, and tourism marketing, and he has published numerous journal articles and book chapters in these areas. He has also written a number of books, including most recently *Managing Visitor Attractions: New Directions*, published by Butterworth-Heinemann (with Alan Fyall and Anna Leask) and *Marine Ecotourism: Issues and Experiences*, published by Channel View (with Julie C. Wilson). He is an associate editor of the *Journal of Ecotourism* and an editor of *Tourism in Marine Environments*. He has worked as a consultant on tourism and environmental management issues to the WTO, the OECD, and the Countryside Agency.

Donald Getz is Professor of Tourism and Hospitality Management, Haskayne School of Business, at the University of Calgary. Previously he was on the faculty at The University of Waterloo, and early in his career he worked as a city and regional planner in Ontario. He holds degrees from the University of Waterloo, (Bachelor of Environmental Studies in Urban and Regional Planning), Carleton University (Master of Arts, Geography), and the University of Edinburgh, in Scotland (Ph.D. in Social Sciences–Geography). His books include *Festivals, Special Events, and Tourism* (1991), *Event Management and Event Tourism* (1997), and *Explore Wine Tourism* (2001). He has also coedited *The Business of Rural Tourism* and recently completed a new book to be published by CABI titled, *The Family Business: Tourism and Hospitality*. Dr. Getz cofounded, and until recently was Editor-in-Chief of *Festival Management and Event Tourism: An International Journal,* and recently was renamed Event Management. He also serves on the editorial board of several international tourism journals including *Tourism Management.*

Alison Gill is a Professor in the Department of Geography at Simon Fraser University and is also a member of the Centre for Tourism Policy and Research. Her research interests are closely aligned to the study of single industry and small community development processes and issues. Dr. Gill currently focusses her research in areas related to the planning and development processes used in resort communities.

Frank M. Go currently holds the Bewetour Chair of Tourism Management at the Rotterdam School of Management at the Erasmus University, the Netherlands. Prior to that he served within business faculties at universities in Canada and Hong Kong. He received his doctorate from the University of Amsterdam where his dissertation concentrated on strategy and structure. His current research interest is on the coevolution of tourism marketing and information and communication management.

Ebru A. Gunlu is a Research Fellow at the Department of Tourism Management, Faculty of Business, T.C. Dokuz Eylul University, Izmir, Turkey, where she has recently completed her Ph.D. thesis titled *The Interaction Between Conflict Management and Organizational Culture in the Hospitality Industry*. Her main research interests lie in the application of managerial issues and behavioural sciences to the hospitality industry. She has written articles and conference papers on topics including barter as a means to increase sales in the hospitality industry, importance of time management in the hospitality industry, and factors affecting communication in the hospitality industry. She is currently cowriting a book on convention management.

C. Michael Hall is a Professor in the Department of Tourism, School of Business, University of Otago, New Zealand, and Honorary Professor, Department of Marketing, University of Stirling, Scotland. His Doctorate was from the University of Western Australia and Masters from the University of Waterloo, Canada. As at the time of writing he was also coeditor of the journal *Current Issues in Tourism* and Chairperson of the International Geographical Union's Commission on Tourism, Leisure and Global Change. He has published widely on topics related to tourism, regional development, heritage, wilderness, food, and wine.

Simon Hudson is an Associate Professor in the Tourism Management Area at the University of Calgary. Prior to working in academia, he spent several years working for U.K. tour operators, and also ran his own successful business for eight years. He has lectured and consulted in many aspects of tourism, but specialises in the marketing of tourism. His research is focussed on sports tourism, and he has published numerous journal articles and book chapters from his work. He has written three books, the first two titled *Snow Business* and *Sport & Adventure Tourism*. His latest book titled *Tourism & Hospitality Marketing: A Canadian Perspective* was published by Nelson Thomson in 2004. He is on the editorial boards of the *International Journal of Tourism Research, Journal of Teaching in Travel & Tourism,* and the *Journal of Travel Research*.

Donald V.L. Macleod is a Research Fellow and Director of the Crichton Tourism Research Centre at the University of Glasgow, Scotland Previously he was a Research Associate at the University of Oxford, and Visiting Professor in Cultural Anthropology at Macalester College, U.S. He has also tutored Social Anthropology at both Oxford and London Universities. He graduated from the University of Oxford in 1993 with a D.Phil. in Social Anthropology. It was during research for his doctorate that he developed an interest in tourism whilst working in the Canary Islands. Dr. Macleod has coedited *Tourists and Tourism: Identifying With People and Places,* and recently he edited *Niche Tourism in Question,* and authored *Tourism, Globalisation and Cultural Change,* both published in 2003. He has also published widely in academic journals and contributed numerous chapters to edited collections on the issues of identity, power, culture, change, national parks, and branding, based in different regions including the Dominican Republic, the Canary Islands, and Scotland.

David Mercer has degrees from Cambridge University and Monash University in Melbourne, Australia. He is currently Associate Professor in the School of Social Science & Planning, RMIT University, in Melbourne where he coordinates the Master of Social Science (International Urban and Environmental Management) Program. Prior to moving to RMIT in 2002 he was Associate Professor in the School of Geography & Environmental Science at Monash University, where he taught for more than 30 years. Dr. Mercer is an elected Fellow of the Environment Institute of Australia and New Zealand and is the author of over 130 publications on many issues in the general area of social science and natural resource management, mainly with a focus on Australia. His most recent book (2000) is *A Question of Balance: Natural Resource Conflict Issues in Australia* (Sydney: The Federation Press). Recent papers have appeared in such journals as *Citizenship Studies*, *The Australian Geographer*, *Urban Studies*, and *Annals of Tourism Research*.

Graham Miller is a lecturer in management at the University of Surrey, England. His primary research and teaching interests lie in sustainable tourism and in particular, assessing the reasons why tourism organisations adopt a sustainability agenda. This has led to examinations of the attitudes of tourism experts to indicators of sustainable tourism, tourism companies to corporate responsibility, consumers to sustainable tourism products, and the role of financial institutions in promoting greater sustainability in the companies they invest in. In addition, Dr. Miller has also considered the moral approach to sustainable tourism through research into the level of ethical awareness and orientation of tourism practitioners. Related research has explored the accessibility of tourism establishments in the United Kingdom for the disabled consumer and the adherence of the industry with the recent Disability Discrimination Act, also to consider the role of charities within the tourism industry.

Michael Morgan is a Senior Lecturer in Tourism Marketing at Bournemouth University, U.K., where he is Course Tutor of the M.A. in European Tourism Management. He is the author of *Marketing for Leisure and Tourism* (1996) and has published articles on resort management, tour operations, and tourism education. Before becoming an academic, he worked in marketing management and tour operations for cross-channel ferries.

Peter E. Murphy is the foundation professor and Head of the La Trobe University School of Tourism and Hospitality. He is a recipient of the Roy Wolfe Award for research in tourism in North America and is a member of the International Academy for the Study of Tourism. He has published or edited 7 books and over 60 articles relating to tourism. Professor Murphy was an active member of the Tourism B.C. strategic plan task force and was the facilitator and chairperson for the creation of Tourism Victoria, the destination association for Victoria, B.C., Canada. He later was elected to the Board of Tourism Victoria, B.C., where his principal functions were to chair its development committee and to conduct its annual visitor exit surveys. He has assisted Tourism Victoria, Australia, in the development of its new strategic plan and he currently serves on the board of Bendigo Tourism. Dr. Murphy' books include *Strategic Management for Tourism Communities: Bridging the Gaps* (Clevedon: Channel View Press), forthcoming book (with Ann Murphy) and *Tourism: A Community Approach* (London: Routledge, 1985).

Philip L. Pearce holds a Doctorate from the University of Oxford, U.K., and is the Foundation Professor of Tourism at James Cook University, Townsville, Queensland, Australia. He has held a Fulbright scholarship to Harvard University and is the Editor of *The Journal of Tourism Studies*. He has long-standing interests in tourist behaviour and has authored numerous articles and several books including *The Social Psychology of Tourist Behaviour* (1982), *The Ulysses Factor* (1988), *Tourism Community Relationships* (1996), and *Tourism: Bridges Across Continents* (1998). He is currently working on a new book on tourist behaviour. He is a Foundation member of the International Academy for the Study of Tourism, a founding Vice-President of the Asia Pacific Tourism Association, and an Honorary Professor of X'ian International studies, University, X'ian, China.

Stanley C. Plog has more than 35 years of experience in travel and tourism research. He founded Plog Research and currently directs his own consulting service (SPC Group) and has completed assignments for virtually every segment of the travel industry. With a doctorate from Harvard University, he began his professional career at UCLA as Academic Director of the Social Psychiatry programme and later founded a research centre focussing on urban social problems. He has written or coauthored seven books, including *Leisure Travel: A Marketing Handbook* (Prentice Hall, 2003), *Vacation Places Rated* (Fielding, 1995), and *Leisure Travel: Making It a Growth Market Again* (John Wiley & Sons, 1991). He has written regular columns for industry publications such as *Travel Weekly*, *ASTA Agency Management*, and *Travel Counselor*. He has written numerous articles for academic books and professional journals on travel and tourism, and also on research methods and procedures. Dr. Plog is an editor of the *Cornell Hospitality & Restaurant Administration Quarterly* and a past editor of the *Journal of Travel Research.*

Garry G. Price is a lecturer in the School of Tourism and Hospitality at La Trobe University, Victoria, Australia. His research interests include nature-based tourism, entrepreneurship, environmental education, tourism policy and planning, and cultural and heritage tourism. Prior to joining La Trobe University Garry owned and operated an ecotourism business (Top Country Nature Tours). His publications include a chapter titled Ecotourists' Environmental Learning Opportunity as a Source of Competitive Advantage: Are Ecotourism Operators Missing the Boat with their Advertising? in *Consumer Psychology of Tourism, Hospitality and Leisure,* Vol. 3 (Wallingford: CABI, 2004) and (with K.W. Hopkins) Ecotourism's Competitive Advantage? Environmental Education in *Tourism and the Environment: Sustainability in Tourism Development* (Dublin: Dublin Institute of Technology, 2002).

Linda K. Richter is professor of political science at Kansas State University where she teaches public policy, gender, and politics and a variety of public administration courses. She has lectured in 18 countries on gender, American government, and tourism public policy and was a Visiting Research Associate of the University of the Philippines. On a Fulbright Scholarship, Dr. Richter wrote *Land Reform and Tourism Development: Policy-Making in the Philippines.* She wrote *The Politics of Tourism in Asia* on an Alumni in Residence Fellowship at the East-West Center in Hawaii. Dr. Richter coauthored *Tourism Environment.* She has conducted extensive field research in the Philippines, India, and Pakistan and has twice testified before Congress on aid to the Philippines. She is an associate editor of *Annals of Tourism Research,* serves on the editorial board of *Tourism Recreation Research,* is a member of the International Academy for the Study of Tourism, served four years on the National Travel and Tourism Advisory Board, and was an associate editor of the *Encyclopedia of Tourism.* She has authored more than 80 articles and book chapters.

Lisa Ruhanen is a Research Assistant with the School of Tourism and Leisure Management, Faculty of Business Economics and Law at the University of Queensland, Australia. She has an honours degree from James Cook University and is currently undertaking a Ph.D. at the University of Queensland. Her research interests are in strategic tourism planning and destination visioning.

Chris Ryan is Professor of Tourism at the University of Waikato, is editor of *Tourism Management,* author of a number of books including *Sex Tourism: Marginal People and Liminalities* (London: Routledge, 2001), *The*

Tourist Experience (Continuum, 2002), and *Recreational Tourism: Demands and Impacts* (Channel View, 2003). He has published work in all the leading journals including *Tourism Management, Annals of Tourism Research, Journal of Travel Research,* and *Journal of Sustainable Tourism*—having published over 80 refereed journal articles. He is a member of the Special Projects Committee of the New Zealand Ministry of Tourism, and sits on the Advisory Board of Tourism, Waikato. His research interests lie in tourist behaviour and their various forms and impacts.

Gordon D. Taylor has been a tourist consultant since his retirement in 1988 from Tourism Canada where he was Manager, Special Research Projects. Formerly, he was Director, Research and Planning, Manitoba Department of Tourism, Recreation and Cultural Affairs and a research officer with both the National Parks Service and British Columbia Provincial Parks. He served as an Adjunct Professor of Geography at Carleton University for 15 years prior to his retirement. Mr. Taylor was the president of the Travel and Tourism Research Association in 1976, and served of the Board of Directors of the Canada Chapter, TTRA, from 1988 to 1994. His published articles have appeared in *Tourism Management, Journal of Travel Research, Journal of Travel and Tourism Marketing, Tourismo y Sociedad,* and *Tourism Reports.* Mr. Taylor was president of the British Isles Family History Society of Greater Ottawa in 1997 and 1998. He was recently named to the Hall of Fame of that Society.

William F. Theobald is Professor and Chairman Emeritus of both the Interdisciplinary Graduate Program in Travel & Tourism, and the Leisure Studies Division at Purdue University (U.S.) where he taught tourism and recreation management. Formerly, Professor and Head of the Recreation & Leisure Studies Department at the University of Waterloo (Canada), he has also served as Visiting Professor at The George Washington University (U.S.) and the University of Surrey (U.K.). Dr. Theobald's research interests are tourism planning and development. He has contributed to a variety of social science and professional journals, and is editor of *Global Tourism: The Next Decade* (1994, 1998, and 2004), author (with H.E. Dunsmore) of *Internet Resources for Leisure and Tourism* (2000), *The Evaluation of Human Service Programs* (1985), *Evaluation of Recreation and Park Programs* (1979), and *The Female in Public Recreation* (1976). He has served as an associate editor or reviewer for *Tourism Economics, The Journal of Leisure Research,* and *Leisure Sciences,* and has conducted numerous studies and reports on tourism planning and development for private corporations and various branches of government.

Seldjan Timur is a Ph.D. candidate in Tourism Management in the Haskayne Business School, University of Calgary. She holds an MBA from

Radford University in Virginia, as well as a B.S. in Business Administration from Hacettepe University of Ankara, Turkey. Ms. Seldjan's research focusses on sustainable tourism development and urban tourism management.

Birgit Trauer is currently completing her doctoral studies at the University of Queensland, and tutors in adventure tourism. Her research interests lie in concepts of continuing involvement and tourist behaviours. She completed her postgraduate Diploma at the University of Waikato, having gained her first degree in Leisure Management at Griffith University. Her publications include work in *Tourism Management, The Journal of Sports Tourism, Australian Parks and Recreation*, and *International Tourism Review*. She has undertaken research on behalf of the Department of Environment and Heritage, Queensland, Australia, the Department of the Environment Australia on developments at Fraser Island, and Brisbane International Airport. Ms. Trauer has also lectured at Lakehead University, Canada, in sports and adventure tourism.

Stephen Wanhill is Professor of Tourism Research in the School of Services Management at Bournemouth University (U.K.). His post at Bournemouth has received sponsorship from Travelbag, a leading direct sell tour operator in the United Kingdom with whom the School of Services Management has a close association. His work in tourism goes back more than 30 years with his involvement in airport planning. His main research interests lie in destination development and project planning. He has previously held Professorships at the University of Surrey and the University of Wales, Cardiff, and has recently completed tourism research programmes at the Centre for Regional and Tourism Research, Bornholm, Denmark. He has also been a Tourism Advisor to the U.K. House of Commons and a Board Member of the Wales Tourist Board. He is the editor of the journal *Tourism Economics*.

Peter W. Williams is a Professor in the School of Resource and Environmental Management at Simon Fraser University. He is also Director of University's Centre for Tourism Policy and Research where his work centres on issues related to creating more sustainable forms of tourism development. Dr. Williams is particularly involved with research addressing such issues in mountainous regions.

Part One

Clarification and Meaning: Issues of Understanding

Introduction

Tourism has grown significantly since the creation of the commercial airline industry and the advent of the jet airplane in the 1950's. By 1992, it had become the largest industry and largest employer in the world. Together with this growth there have emerged a number of extremely critical issues facing the industry in terms of the impacts it has already had on destination areas and its residents, and the future prospects for people and places into the coming decades.

One of the major issues in gauging tourism's total economic impact is the diversity and fragmentation of the industry itself. **Theobald** (Chapter 1) suggests that this problem is compounded by the lack of comparable tourism data since there has been no valid or reliable means of gathering comparable statistics. He proposes that the varying definitions of tourism terms internationally, and the complex and amorphous nature of tourism itself have led to difficulty in developing a valid, reliable, and credible information system or database about tourism and its contribution to local, regional, national and global economies.

The author provides an introduction to the context, meaning and scope of tourism beginning not simply with basic definitions, but also a discussion on the derivation of those definitions. This leads to sections on how tourism data is gathered, measures of tourism, basic tourism units, and classification of both tourism supply and demand. Finally, he chronicles the major international developments that have occurred between 1936 and 1994 whose objectives were to reduce or eliminate the incomparability of gathering and utilizing tourism statistics.

Davidson (Chapter 2) links the question of whether tourism is really an industry to the misunderstanding, resistance and hostility that often plague proponents of travel and tourism as worthy economic forces in a modern economy. He questions the common practice, especially as suggested in the literature of referring to tourism as an industry. He contends that such a designation may not be correct, and that tourism is not an industry at all. He states that much of the current misunderstanding, resistance and even hostility plaguing proponents of tourism may be due to its mistakenly being called an industry. Three arguments for tourism's designation as an industry are: it needs to gain the respect it now lacks among other competing economic sectors; it needs sound, accurate and meaningful data in order to assess its economic contribution, and; it needs to provide a sense of self-identity to its practitioners.

Similar to the previous chapter, the author decries the difficulty in defining the terms tourist and tourism among others. He contends that tourism is not an industry at all and suggests that rather than a production activity or product, tourism should be viewed as a social phenomenon, an experience or a process. Therefore, defining tourism as an industry is incorrect and demeaning to what it really is. While the editor agrees with the author that tourism is largely a social phenomenon and experience, and the tourism industry is complex and difficult to define precisely, nevertheless, he believes the preponderance of evidence supports the position that tourism can be industrially classified and measured, and therefore, can indeed be counted as an industry. The debate continues.

For many people, much time and effort is expended by looking back to an earlier time in their lives, perhaps in an attempt to recapture a past that for them was happier or more rewarding than what the future might hold. The past has always been more orderly, more memorable, and most of all, safer.

A provocative insight on the meaning and substance of tourism is provided by **Dann** (Chapter 3), striking at the heart of the motivation for so much travel: nostalgia. The Western drive of escapism to the numerous outlets of yesteryear are enhanced by the 'evocation of the past as a promise to the future'. The author states that tourism is the nostalgia industry of the future. He suggests that tourism has employed nostalgia for its own financial advantage. A strong connection between nostalgia and tourism is explored, especially as related to historical figures, accommodations, attractions and cultural institutions. In addition, it is pointed out that tourists often have a strange fascination for tragic, macabre or other equally unappealing historical sites.

Nostalgia is grounded in dissatisfaction with social arrangements, both currently and likely continuing into the future. Nostalgia tourism that provides an alternative to the present does so by recourse to an imagined past that people often believe is fact. The author suggests that nostalgia tourism is really the antithesis of reality tourism.

Natives in Third World countries living for generations in one village could not comprehend the concept of nostalgia. On the other hand, today's dislocated Western tourist often travels in order to experience nostalgia. Tourism collateral literature and publicity which is based upon nostalgic images of the past promote glamour and happiness, provide something to be envied, and return love of self to the reader. Nostalgia is big business, and when it is associated with the world's leading industry, tourism, it offers unlimited financial possibilities.

Although collaboration is now commonplace in most industrial sectors, **Fyall** and **Garrod** (Chapter 4) suggest that for years, the tourism industry was (and remains in some instances) highly fragmented and independent. With the accelerating pace of technological innovation and the continuing trend toward globalization, traditional competitive and adversarial relationships between competing business organizations is giving way to collaborative arrangements between them.

For many tourism organizations, performance is dependent on establishing collaborative relationships in order to better serve the customer. The message this chapter conveys is that due to economic, social and political pressures, the primary concern of tourism organizations must shift from an individual and competitive focus to an inter-organizational, collaborative domain. The authors provide examples of tourism collaboration and suggest that it is becoming increasingly more difficult for organizations to survive in competitive isolation in tourism.

1 The meaning, scope, and measurement of travel and tourism

William F. Theobald

Background

Travel has existed since the beginning of time when primitive man set out, often traversing great distances, in search of game that provided the food and clothing necessary for his survival. Throughout the course of history, people have travelled for purposes of trade, religious conviction, economic gain, war, migration, and other equally compelling motivations. In the Roman era, wealthy aristocrats and high government officials also travelled for pleasure. Seaside resorts located at Pompeii and Herculaneum afforded citizens the opportunity to escape to their vacation villas in order to avoid the summer heat of Rome. Travel, except during the Dark Ages, has continued to grow, and throughout recorded history has played a vital role in the development of civilizations.

Tourism as we know it today is distinctly a twentieth-century phenomena. Historians suggest that the advent of mass tourism began in England during the industrial revolution with the rise of the middle class and relatively inexpensive transportation. The creation of the commercial airline industry following World War II and the subsequent development of the jet aircraft in the 1950s signaled the rapid growth and expansion of international travel. This growth led to the development of a major new industry: tourism. In turn, international tourism became the concern of a number of world governments because it not only provided new employment opportunities, but it also produced a means of earning foreign exchange.

Today tourism has grown significantly in both economic and social importance. The fastest growing economic sector of most industrialised countries over the past several years has been in the area of services. One of the largest segments of the service industry, although largely unrecognised as an entity in some of these countries, is travel and tourism.

According to the World Travel & Tourism Council (2003) (WTTC), travel and tourism is the biggest industry in the world on virtually any economic measure, including gross output, value added, capital investment, employment, and tax contributions. In 2003, the industry's gross output was estimated to be in excess of US$4.5 billion of economic activity (total demand), more than 10 percent of the total gross national product spending. The travel and tourism industry is one of the world's largest employers, with nearly 195 million jobs, or 7.6 percent of all employees. This industry is the world's leading industrial contributor, producing 10.2 percent of the world gross domestic product, and accounting for capital investment in excess of US$685 billion in new facilities and equipment. In addition, it contributes more than US$650 billion in direct, indirect, and personal taxes each year. As indicated by Table 1.1, research conducted by the World Tourism Organization (WTO) show the almost uninterrupted growth of tourism since 1950.

Frechtling (2001) suggests that Futurist John Naisbitt in his best-selling book, *Global Paradox*, subscribes to the concept that tourism will be one of the three industries that will drive the world economy into the twenty-first century. Reinforcing Naisbitt's concept is data provided for the WTTC suggesting that there will continue to be significant increases in tourism in the coming years (Table 1.2).

Table 1.1 World Tourism Growth: 1950–2002

Year	International Tourist Arrivals (millions)	International Tourist Receipts[a] (billions in US$)
1950	25.3	2.1
1960	69.3	6.8
1970	165.8	17.9
1980	286.0	105.3
1985	327.2	118.1
1990	457.3	263.4
1995	552.3	406.5
1996	596.5	435.6
1997	618.2	439.6
1998	626.4	442.5
1999	652.2	456.3
2000	696.7	474.4
2001	692.7	462.2
2002[b]	715.6	478.0

[a] International transport receipts excluded.
[b] Estimates.
Source: World Tourism Organization. 2003. *World Tourism in 2002: Better than Expected* Madrid: WTO News Release.

Table 1.2 WTTC Research Projections for Economic and Employment Growth (world estimates 1996–2006)

Category	1996	2006	Real Growth
Jobs	255 million	385 million	50.1%
Jobs (%)	10.7%	11.1%	—
Output	US$3.6 trillion	US$7.1 trillion	48.7%
Gross Domestic Product	10.7%	11.5%	49.6%
Investment	US$766 billion	US$1.6 trillion	57.3%
Exports	US$761 billion	US$1.5 trillion	51.2%
Total Taxes	US$653 billion	US$1.3 trillion	49.6%

Source: World Travel & Tourism Council, Research & Statistical Data. 1997. Worldwide Web page, *http://www.wttc.org/*.

The WTTC (2003) predicted that during the next decade, world travel and tourism is expected to achieve annualized real growth of:

- 4.6 percent in total travel and tourism demand to US$8.939 billion in 2013;
- 3.6 percent for the industry directly to US$2.279 billion and to US$6.461 billion for the travel and economy overall in 2013;
- 2.2 percent in travel and tourism employment to 83,893,600 jobs directly in the industry, and 2.4 percent to 247,205,000 jobs in the travel and tourism economy overall in 2012;
- 7.1 percent in visitor exports, rising to US$1.308 billion in 2013;
- 4.3 percent in terms of capital investment, increasing to US$1.308 billionin 2013; and
- 3.0 percent in terms of government expenditures to US$378.2 billion in 2013.

However, one of the major problems of the travel and tourism industry that has hidden or obscured its economic impact is the diversity and fragmentation of the industry itself. The travel industry includes hotels, motels, and other types of accommodation; restaurants and other food services; transportation services and facilities; amusements, attractions, and other leisure facilities; gift shops; and a large number of other enterprises. Because many of these businesses also serve local residents, the impact of spending by visitors can easily be overlooked or underestimated. In addition, Meis (1992) points out that the tourism industry involves concepts that have remained amorphous to both analysts and decision makers. Moreover, in all nations, this problem has made it difficult for the industry to develop any type of reliable or credible tourism information base in order to estimate the contribution it makes to regional, national, and global economies. However, the nature of this very diversity makes travel and tourism an ideal vehicle for economic development in a wide variety of countries, regions, or communities.

Once the exclusive province of the wealthy, travel and tourism have become an institutionalised way of life for most of the world's middle-class population. In fact, McIntosh, Goeldner, and Ritchie (1995) suggest that tourism has become the largest commodity in international trade for many world nations, and for a significant number of other countries it ranks second or third. For example, tourism is the major source of income in Bermuda, Greece, Italy, Spain, Switzerland, and most Caribbean countries.

In addition, Hawkins and Ritchie (1991), quoting from data published by the American Express Company, suggest that the travel and tourism industry is the number one ranked employer in Australia, the Bahamas, Brazil, Canada, France, [the former] West Germany, Hong Kong, Italy, Jamaica, Japan, Singapore, the United Kingdom, and the United States. Because of problems of definition that directly affect statistical measurement, it is not possible with any degree of certainty to provide precise, valid, or reliable data about the extent of worldwide tourism participation or its economic impact. In many cases, similar difficulties arise when attempts are made to measure domestic tourism.

The Problem of Definition

It is extremely difficult to define precisely the words *tourist* and *tourism* because these terms have different meanings to different people, and no universal definition has yet been adopted. For example, *Webster's New University Dictionary* defines tourism as 'traveling for pleasure; the business of providing tours and services for tourists,' and a tourist as 'one who travels for pleasure.' These terms are inadequate synonyms for travel, and their use as such adds further confusion when the field of travel is variously referred to as the *travel industry*, the *tourism industry*, the *hospitality industry*, and most recently, the *visitor industry* (see Chapter 2 for a different view of whether or not they should be so named).

Why is so much attention given to these definitions? According to Gee, Makens, and Choy (1997), the concern is from both an academic and a practical perspective. 'First, travel research requires a standard definition in order to establish parameters for research content, and second, without standard definitions, there can be no agreement on the measurement of tourism as an economic activity or its impact on the local, state, national or world economy.' Therefore, comparable data are necessary requisites, and identical criteria must be used in order to obtain such data. For example, in North America, the U.S. Census Bureau and the U.S. Travel Data Center's annual travel statistics consider only those trips taken that are 100 miles or more (one-way) away from home. However, Waters (1987) argued that this criteria is unreasonably high, and proposed instead in his annual compendium on travel that similar to the U.S. National Tourism Resources Review Commission's guidelines (1973), distances of 50 miles or more are a more realistic criteria. On the other hand, the Canadian government specifies that a tourist is one who travels at least 25 miles outside his community. Therefore, each of these four annual data sets is quite different, and which (if any) contains the most accurate measurement of tourism activity?

The United Nations (UN) was so concerned about the impossible task of compiling comparative data on international tourism that they convened a Conference on Trade and Development, which issued guidelines for tourism statistics (UNCTAD Secretariat, 1971). The ensuing report suggested that the functions of a comprehensive system of national tourism statistics could serve:

1. To measure from the demand side the volume and pattern of foreign (and domestic) tourism in the country (as well as outgoing tourism),
2. To provide information about the supply of accommodation and other facilities used by tourists, and
3. To permit an assessment to be made of the impact of tourism on the balance of payments and on the economy in general.

Therefore, accurate statistical measurement of travel and tourism is important in order to assess its direct, indirect, and induced economic impacts; to assist in the planning and development of new tourist facilities and resources; to determine current visitor patterns and help formulate marketing and promotional strategies, and to identify changes in tourist flows, patterns, and preferences.

The Derivation of Definitions

Etymologically, the word *tour* is derived from the Latin 'tornare' and the Greek 'tornos,' meaning 'a lathe or circle; the movement around a central point or axis.' This meaning changed in modern English to represent 'one's turn.' The suffix *-ism* is defined as 'an action or process; typical behavior or quality' whereas the suffix *-ist* denotes one that performs a given action. When the word *tour* and the suffixes *-ism* and *-ist* are combined, they suggest the action of movement around a circle. One can argue that a circle represents a starting point, which ultimately returns back to its beginning. Therefore, like a circle, a tour represents a journey that it is a round trip, i.e., the act of leaving and then returning to the original starting point, and therefore, one who takes such a journey can be called a tourist.

There is some disagreement as when the word *tourist* first appeared in print. Smith (1989) suggests that 'Samuel Pegge reported the use of "tourist" as a new word for traveller c. 1800; England's *Sporting Magazine* introduced the word "tourism" in 1911.' Feifer (1985) proposes that the word tourist 'was coined by Stendhal in the early nineteenth-century [1838].' Mieczkowski (1990) states that 'The first definition of tourists appears in the *Dictionnare universel du XIX siecle* in 1876,' defining tourists as 'persons who travel out of curiosity and idleness.' Kaul (1985) argues that even though the word *tourist* is of comparatively recent origin, nevertheless invaders were commonly referred to as tourists in the hope that one day they would leave. In addition, Kaul points out that:

> In the 17th and early 18th centuries, the English, the Germans and others, traveling on a grand tour of the continent, came to be known as 'tourists.' . . . In 1824, Scott, in *San Roman's* stated thus, 'it provoked the pencil of every passing tourist.'

Leiper (1979) relates that the word *tourism* appears to have first been used in England to describe young male British aristocrats who were being educated for careers in politics, government, and diplomatic service. In order to round out their studies, they embarked on a customary three-year grand tour of the European continent, returning home only after their cultural education was indeed completed. According to Inskeep (1991), the first guidebook for this type of travel was Thomas Nugent's *The Grand Tour*, published in 1778. Far from the traveler of 1778, today's tourist tends to connote a singularly negative image, one who is a bargain hunter, who travels en masse, and according to Eliot (1974), is one who is sought out for his cash, but despised for his ignorance of culture.

In addition, tourism has been variously defined (or refined) by governments and academics to relate to such fields as economics, sociology, cultural anthropology, and geography. Economists are concerned with tourism's contributions to the economy and economic development of a destination area, and focus on supply/demand, foreign exchange and balance of payments, employment, and other monetary factors. Sociologists and cultural anthropologists study the travel behaviour of individuals and groups of people, and focus on the customs, habits, traditions, and lifestyles of both hosts and guests. Geographers are concerned with the spatial aspects of tourism, and study travel flows and locations, development dispersion, land use, and changes in the physical environment.

It is generally recognised that there are two different types of tourism definitions, each with its own rationale and intended usage. Burkart and

Medlick (1981) suggest that there are *conceptual* definitions that attempt to provide a theoretical framework in order to identify the essential characteristics of tourism, and what distinguishes it from similar, sometimes related, but different activity.

Examples of such a conceptual definition would include that proposed by Jafari (1977) who states that 'tourism is a study of man away from his usual habitat, of the industry which responds to his needs, and of the impacts that both he and the industry have on the host socio-cultural, economic, and physical environments.' In addition, Mathieson and Wall (1982) conclude that 'Tourism is the temporary movement of people to destinations outside their normal places of work and residence, the activities undertaken during their stay in those destinations, and the facilities created to cater to their needs.'

There are also *technical* definitions that provide tourism information for statistical or legislative purposes. The various technical definitions of tourism provide meaning or clarification that can be applied in both international and domestic settings. This later approach, technical definitions, can be seen in the actions taken to help standardize comparative international tourism data collection.

Finally, Leiper (1979) postulated that there are three approaches in defining tourism: economic, technical, and holistic. Economic definitions view tourism as both a business and an industry. Technical definitions identify the tourist in order to provide a common basis by which to collect data. Holistic definitions attempt to include the entire essence of the subject.

Dimensions of Travel

Although technical definitions such as suggested previously should be applicable to both international and domestic tourism, such definitions are not necessarily used by all countries with respect to domestic tourism. However, most have adopted the three elements of the international definition: (1) purpose of trip, (2) distance travelled, and (3) duration of trip. In addition, two other dimensions or elements are sometimes used to define travellers. One that is often used is (4) residence of traveller, and one that is used less often is (5) mode of transportation.

1. *Purpose of trip*: The notion behind this tourism dimension was to include the major components of most travel today. However, there are a number of destination areas that only include nonobligated or discretionary travel in defining tourists. They view only leisure travellers as tourists, and purposely excluded travel *solely* for business purposes. However, one might well argue that business travel is often combined with some amount of pleasure travel. In addition, business travel to attend meetings or conferences should be included because

it is considered to be discretionary travel rather than part of the normal, daily business routine.

2. *Distance travelled*: For statistical purposes, when measuring travel away from home (nonlocal travel), a number of national, regional, and local agencies use total round-trip distance between place of residence and destination as the distinguishing statistical measurement factor. As indicated earlier, these distances can and do vary from zero to 100 miles (0 to 160 kilometers). Therefore, attractions that are less than the minimum prescribed distance(s) travelled are not counted in official estimates of tourism, thereby creating both artificial and arbitrary standards.

3. *Duration of trip*: In order to meet the written criteria for defining travellers, most definitions of tourists and/or visitors include at least one overnight stay at the destination area. However, this overnight restriction then excludes many leisure-related one-day trips that often generate substantial business for attractions, restaurants, and other recreation resources.

4. *Residence of traveller*: When businesses attempt to identify markets and associated marketing strategies, it is often more important for their business to identify where people live than to determine other demographic factors such as their nationality or citizenship.

5. *Mode of transportation*: Used primarily for planning purposes, a number of destination areas collect information on visitor travel patterns by collecting information on their mode of transportation, such as air, train, ship, coach, auto, or other means.

Finally, according to Williams and Shaw (1991):

> Each national tourist organization may record different types of information. For example, duration of stay, mode of travel, expenditure, age, socio-economic group, and number of accompanying persons are all important aspects of tourism but these are not recorded in all tourist enumerations.

Major Definition Developments

The growth of world receipts from international tourism that occurred between the two world wars led to the need for a more precise statistical definition of tourism. An international forum held in 1936, The Committee of Statistical Experts of the League of Nations, first proposed that a 'foreign tourist' is one who 'visits a country other than that in which he habitually lives for a period of at least twenty-four hours.' In 1945, the UN (which had replaced the League of Nations) endorsed this definition, but added to it a maximum duration of stay of less than six months. Other international bodies have chosen to extend this to one year or less.

A UN Conference on International Travel and Tourism held in Rome in 1963 and sponsored by the International Union of Official Travel Organizations (IUOTO) (now the WTO) recommended that a new word, 'visitor' be adopted, which would define tourists as 'any person visiting a country other than that in which he has his usual place of residence, for any reason other than following an occupation remunerated from within the country visited.' Visitors included two distinct categories of travellers: (1) tourists: temporary visitors staying at least 24 hours in the country visited, and whose purpose was for leisure, business, family, mission, or meeting; and (2) excursionists: temporary visitors staying *less* than 24 hours in the destination visited and not staying overnight (including cruise ship travellers). Since 1963, most world nations have accepted the definitions of *visitor, tourist,* and *excursionist* that were proposed by the UN Conference and many of the revisions made subsequently.

At their 1967 meeting in Geneva, the UN Statistical Commission recommended that a separate class of visitor be established. Tourists stay at least 24 hours, but because some visitors take excursions then return back to their place of residence the same day, they were to be called, 'excursionists.' This group included daily visitors with purposes other than employment, cruise passengers, and visitors in transit. Excursionists could be easily distinguished from other visitors because there was no overnight stay involved.

The definition of the term *visitor,* refined in 1963, refers to only international tourism. However, although it is more difficult to measure, it is quite obvious that it is also applicable to national (domestic) tourism as well. For example, in 1980, the WTO's Manila Declaration implicitly extended the definition to all tourism. According to BarOn (1989), the Working Party on Tourism Statistics of the WTO Commission for Europe agreed that recommendations on domestic tourism, although narrower than international tourism, were nevertheless compatible. These definitions have undergone subsequent refinements, and it would appear that the WTO/UN definition of tourism should have created a uniform basis for collection of standardized tourism data. Although the majority of countries use these definitions, unfortunately, not all adhere to them.

Incomparability of Tourism Statistics

The principal difficulty in measuring the extent of tourism demand is the basic incomparability of tourism statistics. Such incomparability exists not only when attempting to compare data from various nations, but also creates problems when regions, provinces, states, or cities within a country attempt to compare with one another data on tourism demand. At the international level, there are a number of reasons for this incomparability.

The definitions of a *tourist* and a *visitor* vary, especially at frontiers where statistics are collected. Not all countries have adopted the UN Statistical Commission's definitions, whereas others use their own definitions. Even when the UN definitions are used, data collection methods vary widely so that some countries may not gather information on the purpose of a visit or whether or not the visitor will be (or has been) remunerated. In addition, although most countries gather statistical data at their frontiers, others rely on information provided by hotel registrations. In this case, even though the same definitions may be used, the two data sets are not comparable.

Some countries do not even count the arrivals of foreign nationals from bordering countries, especially if there is a unique or special relationship between the countries. Often, in some world nations visitors who are travelling for business or other similar purposes are not regarded as tourists, and therefore they are not recorded as such. In addition, students who spend most of the academic year studying abroad in foreign countries are also often overlooked when compiling statistical data.

Excursionists and other day visitors are included in the statistical data of some countries, but are excluded in others. Special situation visitors such as cruise ship passengers are often not counted in some countries because they are considered to be transients. Flight crews and other visitors in transit are often treated likewise.

Frechtling (1992) suggests that of the 184 nations in the world, 166 report tourism data to the WTO each year, and:

> [o]f these 166 countries, four do not have a measure of international visitors or tourists. Thirteen countries have no recent measure of international tourism receipts, and 46 do not estimate international travel expenditures. More than one-half (84) have no measure of international departures, and two-thirds (113) do not count visitor nights in all accommodation establishments.

At the subnational level, similar situations also exist. For example, in the United States, there is no standard definition valid throughout the country. As a result, definitions of tourism vary from state to state. Gee, Makens, and Choy (1989) suggest that in Florida, 'a tourist is an out-of-state resident who stays at least one night in the state for reasons other than necessary layover for transportation connections or for strictly business transactions.' In Alaska, 'a tourist is a nonresident traveling to Alaska for pleasure or culture and for no other purpose.' Massachusetts defines a tourist as 'a person, not on business, who stays away from home overnight.' For Arizona, 'a tourist is a nonresident traveller in the state, while a traveller is used to identify Arizona residents traveling within the state.' In Utah, 'a tourist will participate in some activity while in the state, while a traveller simply passes through on their way to another state.'

Finally, in Nevada, 'tourists are residents of states other than Nevada who visit the state or stop somewhere in the state while en route through and without regard for trip purpose.'

The confusion in terminology is by no means limited to the United States. A review of any of the statistics published by the WTO/UN points out the innumerable footnotes to the data indicating national variations, differences in data collection methodology, and significant diversity in terminology standards. Indeed, one of the important tasks of the WTO is to work systematically to improve and help develop definitions and classifications of tourism that are of worldwide application and that emphasize both clarity and simplicity in their application.

Throughout Europe, Wöber (2000) suggests that 'unfortunately, city tourism office managers have very little influence on the local authorities who are usually responsible for conducting national and regional tourism research studies.' Although in 1995 the Federation of European Cities Tourist Offices (FECTO) attempted to establish a common database of primary city tourism statistics among their members, nonetheless it has proved unworkable because of the lack of uniform reporting and definitional differences.

Common Measures of Tourism

In June 1991, 250 individuals representing 90 countries participated in a landmark meeting held at Ottawa, Canada, and cosponsored by the WTO and Tourism Canada. This meeting, The International Conference on Travel and Tourism Statistics (1991) had three primary aims:

1. Development of a uniform and integrated definition and classification system of tourism statistics,
2. Implementation of a strict methodology for determining the economic impact of tourism and the performance of various sectors of the industry, and
3. Establishment of both a means of dialogue between governments and the tourism industry and a coherent work program for collecting tourism statistics and information.

The Conference was successful in agreeing on approaches to standardize tourism terminology and industrial classifications, as well as indicators of market growth, economic impact, and overall industry development. All delegates to the Conference endorsed the concepts, measures, and definitions that were proposed in the resolutions that came out of the meetings. In 1993, the UN accepted the report of the WTO and adopted the recommendations of the UN Secretariat's Statistical Division pertaining to tourism statistics.

One of the principal findings that came out of the conference resolutions (WTO, 1991) recommended that tourism be defined as:

> the activities of a person travelling to a place outside his or her usual environment for less than a specified period of time and whose main purpose of travel is other than the exercise of an activity remunerated from within the place visited . . .

In addition, tourism was further defined as the activities of people travelling for leisure, business, and other purposes to places outside their usual environment and staying for no more than one consecutive year. BarOn (1996) has compiled a helpful list of those WTO/UN-adopted definitions as shown in Table 1.3.

The Ottawa Conference further recommended the development and implementation of a system of performance measures and indicators, which could help measure trends and provide forecasts for the industry as a whole, thereby maximizing tourism's economic contribution to national benefits. They recommended that the concept of satellite accounting systems that derive their principle aggregates and basic concepts from the United Nations System of National Accounts be supported, and that all countries introduce such accounting systems into their analytic base for tourism data on an incremental basis.

In an effort to measure modern service sectors, such as travel and tourism, in this system of national accounts, the UN and WTO (1994) approved the delineation of the Standard International Classification of Tourism Activities (SICTA). In March 2000, the United Nations Statistical Commission (UNSC) approved the Tourism Satellite Account (TSA): Methodological References, together with modifications presented by the WTO, the Organization for Economic Co-operation and Development (OECD), and the Statistical Office of the European Communities (EUROSTAT).

The purpose of this system is to classify all elements of tourism economic activity in a consistent and comprehensive manner. In order to be useful, such a classification system for tourism that was based on supply-side economic activity had at some level to be consistent with, and allow the identification of, the primary activities or products of tourism as traditionally identified from the demand-side. Therefore, if the travel and tourism sector were evaluated as economists measure other industries, its total economic impact would be substantially larger than the traditional estimates of visitor arrivals and tourist expenditures. It would appear that past comparative statistical instability within the tourism industry may come to an end because of the adoption and implementation of two key elements, the WTO/UN tourism definitions and the SICTA classification system.

Table 1.3 Travel and Tourism Definitions

(1) *Visitor* (V): Any person travelling to a place *other than that of his/her usual environment for up to 12 months* and whose main *purpose of trip* is leisure, business, pilgrimage, health, etc., other than the exercise of an activity remunerated from within the place visited or migration.

  Transport Crew and Commercial Travellers (even those travelling to different destinations over the year) may be regarded as travelling in their usual environment and excluded from visitors (Transport Crew are usually excluded from Frontier Control), also those travelling year round (or most the year) between two places of residence (e.g., weekend homes, residential study).

(2) *Tourist* (T, stay-over/overnight): A visitor staying at least one night in the place visited (not necessarily in paid accommodation).

(3) *Same-day visitor* (SDV, Excursionist, Day-visitor): A visitor who does not stay overnight in the place visited, e.g.:
  (a) *Cruise Visitor* (CV), who may tour for one or more days, staying overnight on the ship (includes foreign naval personnel off duty).
  (b) *Border Shopper* (BS), who may have high expenditures on purchases of food, drink, tobacco, petrol, etc.; excluding border workers.

(4) *Travellers:* Visitors and
  (a) *Direct Transit Travellers* (DT, e.g., at an airport, between two nearby ports);
  (b) *Commuters*, routine travel for work, study, shopping, etc.;
  (c) *Other Noncommuting Travel* (ONT), e.g., occasional local travel, transport crew or commercial traveller (to various destinations), migrants (including temporary work), diplomats (to/from their duty station).

(5) *Passengers* (PAX, Revenue): Travellers excluding crew, nonrevenue (or low-revenue) travellers e.g., infants, free or travelling on a discount of up to 25%.

(6) *Tourism*: The activities of visitors, persons travelling to and staying in places outside their usual environment for up to 12 months for leisure, business, pilgrimage, etc.
  (a) *International*: (i) Inbound, (ii) Outbound: may include overnight stay(s) in country of residence,
  (b) *Domestic* (in country of residence).

(7) *Tourism Industry*: Establishments providing services and goods to visitors, including:
  (a) *Hospitality* (hotels, restaurants, etc.),
  (b) *Transport*,
  (c) *Tour Operators* and *Travel Agents*, Attractions,
  (d) Other branches of the economy supplying visitors (some of these may also provide a significant volume of services and goods to nonvisitors, and the proportion of revenue etc. due to visitors is important in estimating receipts from tourism).

(8) *The Travel and Tourism Industry* (TTI): The tourism industry (and receipts from tourism, etc.) together with the provision of goods and services by establishments to other noncommuting travelers occasional local travelers, etc.[a]

[a] WTTC. 1995. *Travel and Tourism's Economic Perspective 1995, 2005*, WTTC: Brussels.
Source: Based on UNSTAT, *Recommendations on Tourism Statistics, op cit.*

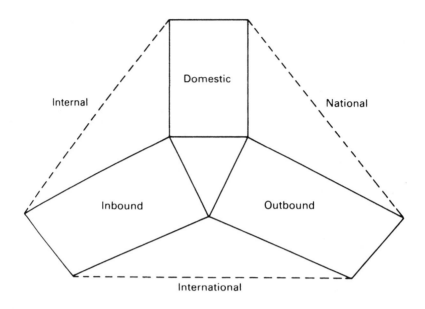

Figure 1.1:   Forms of tourism.
Source: World Tourism Organization.

Basic Tourism Units

As indicated by Figure 1.1, for a given country, three basic forms of tourism were first identified, then defined as:

1. *Domestic tourism*: residents visiting their own country,
2. *Inbound tourism*: nonresidents travelling in a given country, and
3. *Outbound tourism*: residents travelling in another country.

These forms can be combined in a number of ways in order to derive the following categories of tourism:

1. *Internal tourism*: involves both domestic and inbound tourism,
2. *National tourism*: involves both domestic and outbound tourism, and
3. *International tourism*: involves both inbound and outbound tourism.

It should be noted that although this figure refers to a country, it could be applied to any other geographic area(s).

Basic tourism units refer to individuals/households that are the subject of tourism activities and therefore can be considered as statistical units in surveys. 'Travellers' refers to all individuals making a trip between two

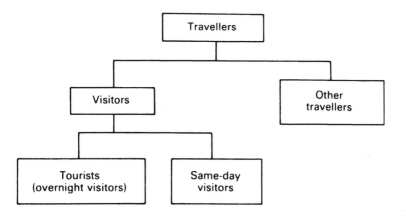

Figure 1.2:   Traveller typology.
Source: Travel and Tourism Research Association.

or more geographic locations, either in their country of residence (domestic travellers) or between countries (international travellers). However, as can be seen in Figure 1.2, there is a distinction made between two types of travellers, *visitors* and *other travellers.*

All travellers who are engaged in the activity of tourism are considered to be 'visitors.' The term 'visitor' then becomes the core concept around which the entire system of tourism statistics is based. A secondary division of the term 'visitor' is made into two categories:

1. Tourists (overnight visitors) and
2. Same-day visitors (formerly called 'excursionists').

Therefore, the term 'visitor' can be described for statistical purposes as 'any person travelling to a place other than that of his/her usual environment for less than twelve months and whose main purpose of trip is other than the exercise of an activity remunerated from within the place visited.'

Classification of Tourism Demand

An extended classification system of tourism demand delineating the main purpose(s) of visits or trips by major groups was developed based on that first proposed by the UN (1979) (Figure 1.3). This system was designed to help measure the major segments of tourism demand for planning and marketing purposes. The major groups include:

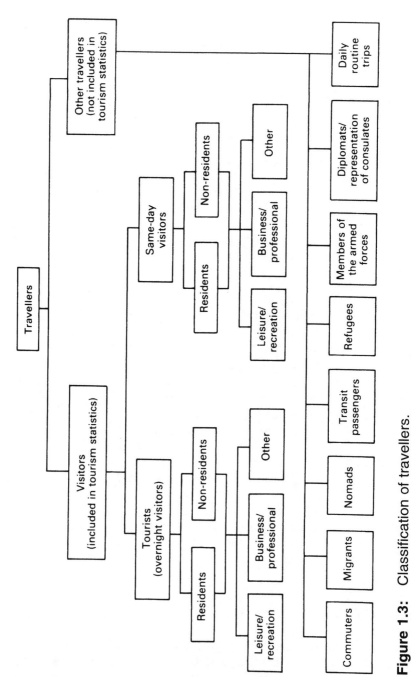

Figure 1.3: Classification of travellers.

Source: World Tourism Organization and the Travel and Tourism Research Organization.

1. Leisure, recreation, and holidays;
2. Visiting friends and relatives;
3. Business and professional;
4. Health treatment;
5. Religion/pilgrimages; and
6. Other (crews on public carriers, transit, and other or unknown activities).

Other measures of tourism demand enumerated were:

1. Duration of stay or trip,
2. Origin and destination of trip,
3. Area of residence or destination within countries,
4. Means of transportation, and
5. Tourism accommodation.

Each of these demand measures was first defined, then where possible, specific examples of each were indicated.

Paci (1992) argued however, that not only tourism demand should be considered, but more importantly, tourism 'must seek to more clearly delineate a supply-based conceptual structure for its activities because that is the source of most national economic statistics.' When incorporated into supply-based statistics, the relationship and relative importance of tourism to other economic sectors can be more easily recognised. In addition, Paci pointed out that because such a system would not only foster and provide for greater comparability among national tourism statistics, but would also 'provide statistical linkage between the supply side of tourism and the demand side.'

Classification of Tourism Supply

Tourism expenditure data are one of the most significant indicators used to monitor and evaluate the impact of tourism on an economy and on the various representative tourism industry segments. The Conference has defined *tourism expenditure* as 'the total consumption expenditure made by a visitor or on behalf of a visitor for and during his/her trip and stay at destination.'

It has been proposed that tourist expenditures be divided into three broad categories, depending on the specific periods the visitor makes those expenditures. The first, advanced spending that is necessary to prepare for the trip (trip purpose); second, expenses while travelling to, and those at the travel destination (trip location) and; third, travel-related spending made at home after returning from the trip (trip conclusion).

It has also been recommended that tourism consumption expenditures should be identified by a system of main categories, and should include:

1.   Packaged travel (holidays and prepaid tour arrangements);
2.   Accommodations (hotels, motels, resorts, campgrounds, etc.);
3.   Food and drinking establishments (restaurants, cafes, taverns, etc.);
4.   Transport (airplane, rail, ship, bus, auto, taxi, etc.);
5.   Recreation, culture, and sporting activities;
6.   Shopping; and
7.   Other.

The fundamental structure of the TSA relies on the existing balance within the economy of the demand for goods and services generated by visitors and other consumers, and the overall supply of these goods and services. Therefore, TSA will be able to measure the following:

- Tourism's contribution to gross domestic product,
- Tourism's ranking compared with other economic sectors,
- The number of jobs created by tourism in an economy,
- The amount of tourism investment,
- Tax revenues generated by tourism industries,
- Tourism consumption,
- Tourism's impact on a nation's balance of payments, and
- Characteristics of tourism human resources.

Summary

For too long, the tourism industry, both international and domestic, has had great difficulty making statistical comparisons with other sectors of the economy. In all nations, this has led to difficulty in developing valid, reliable, and credible information or databases about tourism and its contribution to local, regional, national, and global economies.

A number of individuals throughout the world who are involved in the travel and tourism industry have long recognised the interdependent nature of travel and tourism statistical systems at all levels of government. Further, they realized the need for ongoing reviews and revisions of both concepts and working definitions of travel and tourism that are used internationally. The various Conference recommendations that have been adopted by the UN Statistical Commission laid the foundation for new, expanded, and modified international definitions and standards for travel and tourism. Those principles and guidelines provide for the harmonious and uniform measurement of tourism among world nations.

Now that such an international definition/classification system for the tourism sector does exist, there is finally a universal basis for the collection of standardized data on tourism activity. The implementation of the TSA system has now been placed with the National Statistical Offices throughout the world. The credibility and legitimacy of this statistical system will be based on the joint cooperation of both the National Statistical Offices and the National Tourism Administrations in each world country.

However, although there has been significant progress in reaching consensus on what constitutes *international* tourism, there is no such consensus in *domestic* tourism terminology. Therefore, caution must be exercised because a clear distinction must be made between basic definitions of tourism and those elements that describe tourists themselves, and their demographic and behavioral characteristics. Because the tourist is the principal component of tourism, it is therefore unrealistic to develop uniform tourism data without first deciding the types of variables and the range of phenomena that should be included in data collection efforts.

The WTO will be largely responsible for reviewing and revising the definitions, classifications, methodologies, data collection, and analysis of international tourism proposed by the Ottawa Conference. However, the ultimate success or failure of gathering and using comparable tourism statistical data lies with their acceptance and implementation by the entire world community.

References

Bar-On, Raymond. 1989. *Travel and Tourism Data: A Comprehensive Research Handbook on the World Travel Industry*. London: Euromonitor Publications.

——. 1996. Databank: Definitions and Classifications. *Tourism Economics* 2(4): 370.

Burkart, A. J., and S. Medlik. 1981. *Tourism: Past, Present and Future*. London: Heinemann.

Conference The. 1991. *International Conference on Travel and Tourism Statistics: Ottawa (Canada), 24–28 June 1991 Resolutions*. Madrid, World Tourism Organization, p. 4.

Eliot, E. 1974. Travel. *CMA Journal*. February 2: 271.

Feifer, Maxine. 1985. *Tourism in History: From Imperial Rome to the Present*. New York: Stein and Day Publishers.

Frechtling, Douglas C. 1992. International Issues Forum: World Marketing and Economic Research Priorities for Tourism. Tourism Partnerships and Strategies: Merging Vision with New Realities. *Proceedings of the 23rd Travel and Tourism Research Association Conference*. Minneapolis, June 14–17.

——. 2001. *Forecasting Tourism Demand*. Oxford: Butterworth-Heinemann.

Gee, C., C. Makins, and D. Choy. 1997. *The Travel Industry*, 3rd ed. New York: Van Nostrand Reinhold.

Hawkins, Donald E., and J. R. Brent Ritchie, eds. 1991. *World Travel and Tourism Review: Indicators, Trends and Forecasts*, Vol. 1. Wallingford, England: C.A.B. International.

Inskeep, Edward. 1991. *Tourism Planning: An Integrated and Sustainable Development Approach*. New York: Van Nostrand Reinhold.

International Conference on Travel and Tourism Statistics. 1991. *International Conference on Travel and Tourism Statistics: Ottawa (Canada), 24–28 June 1991 Resolutions*. Madrid, World Tourism Organization.

Jafari, Jafar. 1977. Editor's Page. *Annals of Tourism Research*. V (Special Number October/December): 8.

Kaul, R. N. 1985. *The Dynamics of Tourism, Volume 1: The Phenomenon*. New Delhi, India: Sterling Publishers Private Limited.

Leiper, Neil. 1979. The Framework of Tourism: Towards a Definition of Tourism, Tourist, and the Tourist Industry. *Annals of Tourism Research* 6(4): 391, 394.

Mathieson, Alister, and Geoffrey Wall. 1982. *Tourism: Economic, Physical and Social Impacts*. London: Longman Group Limited.

McIntosh, Robert W., Charles R. Goeldner, and J. R. Brent Ritchie. 1995. *Tourism Principles, Practices, Philosophies*, 7th ed. New York: John Wiley & Sons.

Meis, Scott. 1992. International Issues Forum: Response. Tourism Partnerships and Strategies: Merging Vision With New Realities. *Proceedings of the 23rd Travel and Tourism Research Association Conference*, Minneapolis, June 14–17.

Mieczkowski, Zbigniew. 1990. *World Trends in Tourism and Recreation*. New York: Peter Lang Publishing.

Paci, E. 1992. *Collection and Compilation of Tourism Statistics*. Technical Manual No. 4. Madrid, World Tourism.

Smith, Stephen L. J. 1989. *Tourism Analysis: A Handbook*. London: Longman Scientific & Technical.

United Nations. 1971. UNCTAD Secretariat, Conference on Trade and Development. *Guidelines for Tourism Statistics*. New York: United Nations, p. 6.

——. 1979. Statistical Division. *Provisional Guidelines on Statistics of International Tourism*. Statistical Papers, Series M, No. 62. New York: United Nations.

United Nations and World Tourism Organization. 1994. *Recommendations on Tourism Statistics*. Department for Economic and Social Information and Policy Analysis, Statistical Division, Series M, No. 83. New York: United Nations.

Waters, Somerset. 1987. *Travel Industry World Yearbook: The Big Picture* (annual). New York: Child and Waters, p. 21.

Williams, Allan M., and Gareth Shaw, eds. 1991. *Tourism and Economic Development: Western European Experiences*, 2nd ed. London: Belhaven Press.

Wöber, Karl. 2000. Standardizing City Tourism Studies. *Annals of Tourism Research* 27, no. 1: 65.

World Tourism Organization. 2003. *Executive Summary, Travel and Tourism: A World of Opportunity: The 2003 Travel & Tourism Economic Research*. Worldwide Web Pages, 2 March and undated, http:www.wttc.org/measure/PDF/Executive%20Summary.pdf and http://www.wttc.org/News7.htm.

2 What are travel and tourism: are they really an industry?

Thomas Lea Davidson

Introduction

Common practice, at least among those who are involved in the development and marketing of tourism, is to refer to (travel and) tourism as an industry. In fact, considerable effort has been devoted to creating the impression that tourism is a legitimate industry, worthy of being compared with other industries such as health services, energy, or agriculture. The importance of tourism is underscored by referring to it as 'one of the top three industries in most states,' 'largest or next to largest retail industry,' or 'largest employer (industry) in the world.'

The intent of this chapter is to suggest that this designation may not be correct. In fact, I will contend that tourism is not an industry at all. At best, it is a collection of industries. Furthermore, I will suggest that referring to tourism as an industry may be a major contributor to the misunderstanding, resistance, and even hostility that often plague proponents of travel and tourism as worthy economic forces in a modern economy.

Background

By way of preface, let us consider why so much effort has been devoted toward making tourism an industry. Historically, tourism has not been taken seriously by economists, economic developers, or even government. Tourism is seen as fun and games, recreation, leisure, unproductive. Under this view tourism is just the opposite of the traditional work ethic. Residents see tourists as crowds, enemies of the environment, undesirable, the 'ugly visitor' from wherever he or she may have come. Too bad tourists spend money or there would be no redeeming virtue to hosting tourists in one's community.

This negativism culminated in the early 1970s when petrol sales were banned on Sunday as a way to address the fuel crisis. Although this ban crippled tourism, it was not viewed as critical, except by the businesses whose customers could not, or would not, come.

In response, those in the business of tourism undertook to gain respect by defining tourism as an industry and then by measuring the economic impact of the tourism industry in terms that were comparable to those used for other industries. 'Industry' was a positive term connoting work, productivity, employment, income, economic health—all attributes that tourism wanted but did not have.

Tourism as an Industry

Under this 'industry' view, the tourism industry is made up of a clearly defined grouping of firms that are perceived to be primarily in the business of selling to or serving tourists. Hotels, restaurants, transportation, and amusements are examples of the types of firms that comprise the tourism industry. The United Nations identifies 7 industrial areas, whereas the U.S. Travel Data Center includes some 14 types of businesses as defined by the Standard Industrial Classification (SIC) system.

What are the advantages of designating tourism as an industry? Let me suggest three.

1. The first advantage is the need to gain respect, respect based on understanding the contribution that tourism makes to economic health. Tourism has an image problem. It is not really perceived as a legitimate part of economic development. For some, tourism is not even a legitimate part of government and in today's budget crises, not worthy of funding. If tourism can argue that it really is an industry worthy of being considered on the same terms as other recognized industries, then the image of and the support for tourism will improve.
2. The next advantage is the need for a sound framework to tabulate, analyse, and publish data about tourism—data that are accurate, meaningful, and believable. Historically, economists have used the 'industry' as the basis for measurement and study. If tourism wants to be measured and studied seriously, it follows then that tourism must be an industry. Only by treating tourism as an industry can tourism be compared with other industries in the world economy.
3. There is a need among some in 'tourism' for a format for self-identity. Being part of an industry is a clear and easy way to achieve identity and the self-esteem that goes with identity.

Tourism is beset by many outside pressures: world events; budget problems and mounting deficits; recession; the staggering need for funds to support education, health care, social needs, and crime prevention; and the maturing, competitive tourism marketplace. In this environment, a great effort has been devoted to legitimizing tourism as a key industry in today's service economy. In great measure, these efforts have been successful. But, is this 'success' really positive? Or has the 'industry' label actually hurt the cause that this designation is supposed to champion. To answer this question we need to define what an industry is, use this definition as a framework to look at tourism, and then consider the ramifications of the difference.

What Is an Industry?

We can look to two sources for an answer:

1. Economics defines an industry as being a group of independent firms all turning out the same product. Whether or not two products are 'the same' is defined in terms of their substitutability expressed as the cross-elasticity of demand. In lay terms, the more that the purchase of Product A replaces (can be substituted for) the purchase of Product B, the more A and B are the same and hence in the same industry.
2. The second source for definitions are the SIC manuals. Such publications suggest that the SIC system was developed to classify establishments by the type of activity in which they are engaged. To be recognized as an industry, a group of establishments must share a common primary activity and be statistically significant in size.

It is clear that the focus of 'industry' is:

- Individual business establishments grouped together,
- The revenue received by these economic units, and
- Producing and selling a common product, i.e., the product of one firm is a substitute for the product of any other firm in the same industry.

And it is equally clear that the 'manufacturing' sector provides the framework for this focus. Thus, to the extent that tourism is an industry, economists and others will position tourism in terms of these factors—individual businesses, revenues of those businesses, and a common product.

But Just What Is Tourism?

But what is travel and tourism? Do they fit this industry mould? To answer these questions we need to define a tourist and tourism and then relate this phenomenon to an industry as defined above.

Clearly, there is confusion and controversy surrounding the definitions of travel and tourism. Are they the same or are tourists only seeking pleasure whereas travellers may also be on business? How far must one travel from home to be a tourist/traveller? Does paying for a room make one a tourist? . . . And so forth.

From the viewpoint of economic development and/or economic impact, a visitor, nominally called a tourist, is someone who comes to an area, spends money, and leaves. We employ an economic framework to be comparable with the concept of 'industry,' which is an economic term. The reasons for the visit, length of stay, length of trip, or distances from home are immaterial.

Thus, we define a tourist as *a person travelling outside of his or her normal routine, either normal living or normal working routine, who spends money.* This definition of visitor/tourist includes:

- People who stay in hotels, motels, resorts, or campgrounds;
- People who visit friends or relatives;
- People who visit while just passing through going somewhere else;
- People who are on a day trip (do not stay overnight); and
- An 'all other' category of people on boats, who sleep in a vehicle of some sort, or who otherwise do not fit the above.

For purposes of this definition a resident (or someone who is not a tourist) is defined as a person staying longer than 30 days.

Note that visitors/tourists can:

- Be attending a meeting or convention;
- Be business travellers outside of their home office area; be on a group tour;
- Be on an individual leisure or vacation trip, including recreational shopping; or
- Be travelling for personal or family-related reasons.

In today's world there are three problems with this definition:

1. Some people travel considerable distances to shop, especially at factory outlets. They may do so many times a year. They are difficult to measure. Technically they are not tourists; their shopping has become routine.
2. Some people maintain two residences—a winter home and a summer home. Their stay in either one usually exceeds one month and these people are *not* classified as tourists. Again, their travel is routine. However, short-stay visitors to their homes whether renting or not *are* tourists.

3. When people live in an area just outside of a destination and have friends or relatives visit them, how are these visitors classified when they visit the destination? Actually, the problem here is not whether they are tourists; those visiting friends or relatives clearly are. Rather, the question is which area gets the credit? Or, how should the people they are visiting be classified? Again, although measurement is difficult, the destination area should be credited for money spent therein.

Tourism, then can be viewed as:

- A social phenomenon, *not* a production activity;
- The sum of the expenditures of all travellers or visitors for all purposes, *not* the receipt of a select group of similar establishments; and
- An experience or process, *not* a product—an extremely varied experience at that.

To underscore this view of tourism, let us focus on the economic impact of tourism on the economic health of a community. The best measure of this economic impact is not the receipts of a few types of business. Rather, the economic impact of tourism begins with the *sum total of all expenditures by all tourists*. Yes, this impact includes some of the receipts of accommodations, restaurants, attractions, petrol (gas) stations—the traditional tourism-orientated businesses. (We might note that these are vastly dissimilar businesses.) However, it also includes retail purchases that often amount to more than the money spent for lodging. These include services (haircuts, car repairs), highway tolls in some countries, church contributions, and so forth. In fact, visitors spend money on just about everything that residents do. Thus, any and every 'industry' that sells to consumers is in receipt of cash from tourism. Clearly, the criteria of similar activity or common product or production process are *not* met in tourism!

Further, the requirement of substitution is not met either. More often than not, most of these expenditures go together as complementary or supplementary purchases. Thus, food is not competitive with lodging. A visitor buys both.

Seen this way, travel and tourism—the movement of people outside their normal routine for business, pleasure, or personal reasons—is much, much more than an 'industry' in the traditional sense. As an economic force, it is the impact of everything the visitor or tourist spends. Thus, we really have an expenditure-driven phenomenon, not a receipts-driven one.

So What? Why Raise the Issue at All?

With so much effort to sell tourism as an industry, specifically an 'export industry,' what is the purpose of questioning this designation? Are not many of these people just going to fight for their viewpoint? Won't this conflict be a problem?

These are legitimate questions. However, I believe that there are several important, and negative, ramifications in attempting to make tourism an industry when, in fact, it is not an industry in the traditional sense. Let me comment on three such negative ramifications.

The first negative ramification comes from the disbelief that is created. Somehow, whether it is conscious or subconscious, people know that tourism does not fit the traditional definition of an industry. This disbelief tends to discredit the arguments supporting the importance of tourism and the level of support that tourism and tourism growth deserve. How often do we hear economic development proponents say that tourism is not an industry and, therefore, not economic development?

In essence, this ramification says that when people recognize—correctly—that tourism does not fit the classic definition of an industry, then they discredit the argument that tourism deserves the benefits that accrue to a *legitimate industry*.

The second negative ramification is subtler. It says that the attempt to define tourism as an industry has led to attempts to employ traditional methods of measurement and analysis to the study of tourism. But traditional methods just do not work well. One result has been inaccurate results that often understate the size, impact, or benefits to a community of the tourism phenomenon. Let me offer two examples:

1. The issue of business receipts versus total tourism expenditures. Receipts of specific businesses are the traditional method for measuring an industry. Usually, the total receipts of all of the relevant business units are summed. Yet few businesses receive all of their receipts from tourists and few consumer businesses receive no money at all from tourists. Thus, tourist expenditure is the better measure of the size, scope, and impact of tourism.
2. The issue of substitute or competitive goods versus supplementary or complementary goods. Traditionally, members of an industry compete on some level for the same money. If a visitor stays tonight in Hotel A, he or she does not spend tonight in Hotel B, and hotels are an industry. However, many expenditures of tourists are complementary. When spending the night in Hotel A, the tourist travels, eats, pays for entertainment, and may buy a gift to take home. Taking one action does not necessarily exclude taking another action. It is more probable that all are done during the course of the stay.

The third negative ramification relates directly to the disadvantage tourism faces for public funding. When tourism—an industry made up of individual business firms seeking their own benefit—comes up against education, public health, crime prevention, infrastructure repair or development, etc. (all seen as serving society as a whole), the problem before the appropriations committee is clear. Why should government use limited funds to support one industry—and a 'frivolous' one at that—when there are so many social ills that demand attention? As an industry, tourism is often seen as self-serving when, in fact, it is a key ingredient in the economic health of the community. Thriving tourism can be key to attending to these other issues.

Thus, the question raised by this issue is, 'Does the "industry" designation make it harder to argue, and win, the broader implication?' Frankly, as one who has been intimately involved in these confrontations, I believe that it does. The net of this argument is that to truly understand, measure, analyse, and sell tourism we need to go beyond traditional thinking. We need to 'think outside of the box.'

- If we are to study tourism to expand it or to control it, is it not better to have an accurate understanding and definition?
- If we are to communicate the value of tourism, is it not more effective to reflect the totality of tourism and not just champion a few industries?

In sum, I believe that *defining tourism as an industry is incorrect*; and further, *this definition demeans what tourism really is.* Tourism is a social/economic phenomenon that acts both as an engine of economic progress and as a social force. Tourism is much more than an industry. Tourism is more like a 'sector' that impacts a wide range of industries. Tourism is not just businesses or governments—it is people. Supporting rational tourism growth and development needs to be viewed in this broader context.

Given today's economic conditions, environmental concerns, evil, turmoil, and strife, positioning tourism properly takes on added importance. Maybe now is the time to rethink the 'industry' classification and find a way to communicate more clearly just how important tourism's health is to our economy.

3 Nostalgia in the Noughties

Graham M.S. Dann

Introduction

One September evening in 1999, in Ormonds Restaurant, London, the unheralded birth took place of *School Disco*. Here 50 young people were gathered for the modest celebration of what was to become something of a phenomenon. After several months of trial and error in various clubs throughout the British capital, in April 2001 the company launched at the Po Na Na, Hammersmith. On this occasion, however, 3000 persons were in attendance. By December of that year, its London Arena Dance had sold 10,000 tickets in just 25 days. The following February, its *Spring Term* album shot to number one, and in July 2002 its third disco rock album entered the charts at number two. *School Disco* quickly spread—opening in Dublin (October 2001), Manchester (December 2001), Ibiza (June 2002), and Sydney (October 2002). Plans are in the pipeline for Toronto.

Now, since May 2003, every Friday in London, 10 p.m. to 3 a.m. sessions are held at Heavens, Villiers Street (entrance £10 in advance, £12 at the door). On Saturdays the action moves to the Hammersmith Palais (9 p.m. to 3 a.m., £12.50 in advance and £15 at the door), with upwards of 2500 *aficionados* present at these venues. 'Boys' are required to be attired in white/grey/blue/brown shirts, short or long dark trousers, and stripy ties, and 'girls' must have skirts or pinafores to match. Both sets of wear are obtainable from the 'tuck-shop.' The Head of English, Mr. Chapman, is also there, testing pupils on their 'speling [sic] and grammer [sic].' Corporate events (minimum 70 guests) are also available. They comprise school dinners (e.g., bangers and mash or fish and chips, followed by jam roly-poly or jelly and ice cream), party dances, and games (including the headmaster giving detention).

But how was the movement inspired and what was the secret of its runaway success? According to its founder, Bobby Sanchez (*School Disco*, 1999–2002), everything began when he was dismissed from a leading London club for playing Shakin' Stevens's *This Ole House*—a foot-tapping number that brought back memories of his childhood. That same night, he drove to his old school, only to be overwhelmed by fond recollections of football, school dinners, 100 lines, assembly, and *Kumbayah my Lord*— the very antithesis to and escape from his current girlfriend problems, outstanding mortgage, and monotonous 9-to-5 job. In making this confession, he was admitting that schooldays were the best days of his life and that the reason why the past was so good was that it offered a selective, pleasurable alternative to the odious present and dreaded future. In other words, it fulfilled all the conditions of nostalgia.

Clearly Sanchez was not alone in his belief, because several thousand other fans were also ready to acknowledge the superiority of the melodies and lyrics of the 70s, 80s, and 90s, when contrasted with contemporary fare. They also relished the idea of dressing up in school uniforms, break dancing, snogging to smoochy old numbers, and nipping out for a fag (cigarette) in the bogs—politically incorrect pursuits actively encouraged by *School Disco*.

At roughly the same period, a group known as *Friends Reunited* burst on to the London scene. Brainchild of Stephen Pankhurst and his business partner, Jason Porter, it commenced operations in February 2000 with a company known as the Happy Group Ltd. and went online that July. As the moniker suggests, *Friends Reunited* sought to bring together former pupils who had once sat in the same classroom and gambolled on the same playing fields. Like *School Disco*, it too had an Internet presence. In the beginning, *Friends Reunited* was receiving just 20 hits a day on its Web site. After six months, it was obtaining between 2000 and 3000 hits every 24 hours. Two months later, the company was worth roughly £1 million (with subscribers paying £5 per registration). As of April 2003, there are approximately 8.6 million members growing at a rate of 15,000 per day, it has a CD with Universal (with 120,000 copies selling in the first month), and is valued at £30 million (British Broadcasting Corporation, 2003). Roughly 40,000 U.K. educational establishments are included on the system, ranging from primary to tertiary, along with 500,000 workplaces. Links exist with Australia, Germany, Ireland, Italy, New Zealand, South Africa, Spain, and the Netherlands. Opportunities are also provided to look up ancestors via *Genes Connect*, (launched November 2002, currently with more than 3 million names on its data base), participate in a *Friends Reunited* book and *After School Club* second CD, and even to resit past examinations online, as 180,000 have already done (*Friends Reunited,* 2003).

The formula is similar—one of nostalgia—only this time it is based on the assumption that the alienating circumstances of today (where even next door neighbours may not speak to one another) can be alleviated by returning to the presumed warmer relationships of yesteryear. Another point of convergence is that both of these movements are millennial, occurring at the changeover to the twenty-first century, a time of transition *par excellence*.[1] According to leading commentator, Fred Davis (1979), it is in such a situation of change that conditions of acute discontinuity awaken a need for the discovery of self-identity in the past. Indeed, even after entering the new millennium, many people are still worried about the present and apprehensive about the future. Inauspicious events have included the 9/11 assault on New York's Twin Towers; the Iraq war[2]; terrorist attacks in Bali, Kenya, and Saudi Arabia; and the continual and pervasive threat of al-Qaeda. Throughout the brave, new globalised world, powerless citizens remain unconvinced by the political spin of those leaders whose countries possess too little history or those who have too much (but in which they nevertheless crave a place). Many inhabitants of the United Kingdom, for example, are disenchanted with the designation of their kingdom as *Cool Britannia*. They feel this way because they are convinced that nothing works anymore. For them, the postal service is in disarray, the courts are full of gaga judges, the health service is a shambles, and transport is in chaos. No small wonder then that they yearn for the days of an imagined past when their nation was great and ruled the waves.

With today's comedians apparently no longer so funny and much of what passes as entertainment being unnecessarily salacious, violent, and crude, it is not surprising that the audio-visual media are increasingly relying on the past for their more successful programming. Just one week's recent edition of television and radio (*Sunday Telegraph*, 2003) quickly reveals what is happening. The publicly funded BBC television, for instance, is seemingly obliged to turn to old favourites such as *The Good Life*, *What the Tudors Did for Us*, *Fawlty Towers*, *Some Mothers Do 'Ave 'Em*, and *Only Fools and Horses*. Meanwhile, and in similar prime time, ITV offers *Heartbeat* and *Hornblower*. Over on radio, BBC7 thrives on such hardy perennials as *Take It from Here*, *The Goon Show*, *Dad's Army*, *Steptoe and Son*, *Hancock's Half Hour*, *Round the Horne*, the *Navy Lark*, *I'm Sorry I'll Read That Again*, *Yes Minister*, and *The Frankie Howard Show*.[3] It is not just

1 This observation should not imply that there are no other movements of this nature. In fact, a recent 2003 issue of *Saga Magazine* (targeted principally at the over 50 year olds) provides details of 'Saga Circles,' a free online service for its readers. Here they can trace their family trees, contact people with similar interests, and search for former acquaintances from the armed forces, previous workplaces, school, college, and university.
2 This war, whose dilemma of entry was described by the United Kingdom's Channel 4 as 'between Iraq and a hard place' could also be viewed as an exercise in nostalgia for the two principal members of the coalition. For the United States it was an opportunity to prove that it was truly a superpower and for the United Kingdom that it was indeed 'Great' Britain, harking back to the days of Empire.
3 If one turns to extraterrestrial channels, an offer from the History Channel is *inter alia*, *War in the Falklands*, *Elizabeth*, *Crown and Country*, *Battleships*, *Dam-busters: The True Story*, *The Royal Navy* and *The Real Dad's Army*—all guaranteed to evoke patriotism in the viewer. Meanwhile, UK Gold digs up such classics as *It Aint 'Alf 'Ot Mum*, *All Creatures Great and Small*, *The Two Ronnies*, and *Are You Being Served?*

that these programmes of yesteryear are considered better than the fare of today, or that the well-proven recipes of the past cater exclusively to an over-50 audience (they don't!). It is more a realisation that the present crop of entertainment is simply not good enough, the lowest common denominator of a yobbish culture, or at least it is often perceived in such a manner by young and old alike.

Some of these programmes relate to setting up home abroad. With names like *I Want that House* and *A Place in the Sun*, they have a deep resonance with millions of viewers. These expatriates-to-be (having seen the concreting over of the so-called 'green belt,' and having witnessed their country become the refuge of seemingly unchecked droves of asylum seekers and illegal immigrants availing themselves of the hard-earned State benefits due to the resident population) seek a better life elsewhere. Here again the idea is straightforward and based on nostalgia. If born and bred sons and daughters of the soil cannot turn back the clock to a time when their own England was a fair and pleasant land, they will attempt to do so in their quest for premodern climes elsewhere.

From the search for permanent residence in a sun-drenched paradise replete with smiling natives, it is only a matter of degree to limit the extent of their sojourn via tourism. Here there is another raft of TV programmes, such as *Holiday* and *Wish You Were Here?* to cater to their needs. Most of these offerings, too, are nostalgia driven, and come with themes like '50 places to see before you die.' For these viewers, the 'green, green grass of home' has long since surrendered to council houses, industrial estates, and supermarkets; even the romantic hills of Wordsworth's hallowed Lake District are today only alive with the sound of mobiles (Humphrys, 2000). Now is surely the time therefore for them to relocate, however temporarily, from the secular centre of their own degraded society to a pristine and sacred 'centre-out-there' (Cohen, 1991). As Nicolson (1998a) puts it, 'nostalgia is our private version of pastoral, the place in which perfection can at least be imagined. We are all Adam and Eve expelled from Eden making our solitary way in a postlapsarian world.'

The linkages between nostalgia and tourism have already been outlined by the present writer in a number of earlier publications (Dann, 1989; 1994a; 1994b). However, these papers were all authored before the year 2000. Where this account differs, then, is in its focus on nostalgia tourism in the first decade of the new millennium. Thus, although trips are similarly taken back to the 50s, 60s, 70s, 80s, and 90s, their point of departure is now the noughties.[4] Even here, however, it cannot be stressed enough

---

4 The title of this chapter was chosen before the editor introduced this writer to a Web site debating the most appropriate designation of the first decade of the twenty-first century (Brock and Starr, 1999). After dismissing such offerings as 'The Oh-Oh's,' 'The O-Zone,' 'The Dread Noughts,' and 'The Silly Mille,' these authors come down in favour of 'The Noughties.'

that nostalgia is a product rather than a creator of the present, and, for that reason, it can be adequately understood only by reference to the current situation (Davis, 1979). Tourism of this nature is hence no exception to the general observation that 'nostalgia has much less to do with the past than with the present; it is present anxieties, concerns and existential discontinuities that evoke and amplify it' (Davis, 1979). Here it is treated under three inductive headings that somehow represent the spirit of the postmodern era:

- Hostels of history,
- Playful pilgrimage, and
- Theming and dreaming.

Hostels of History

As Buck (1978) pointed out over a quarter of a century ago, there is nothing quite so ego-enhancing as to be pampered in a château by a retinue of fawning servants. This form of conspicuous consumption (Veblen, 1899) is particularly appreciated by those of lowly origin who can thus enjoy the status-inverting experience of being a king or a queen for a day (Gottlieb, 1982). However, what none of these commentators explicitly mentions is the connection between this ancient luxury and feelings of nostalgia for a bygone premodern era when rigid lines of social stratification made this sampling of the lifestyles of the old-moneyed aristocracy possible.[5]

Nevertheless, the tourism industry has been quick to realise the potential of providing hostels of history for its clients. The following illustrative examples include the paradors of Spain, the Udaipur Lake Palace Hotel in India, and the English stately home of Cliveden.

Castles in Spain

According to Paradores (1992), a 'parador,' meaning an 'inn' or 'stopping place' appears in many classic Spanish texts. Yet, it was not until 1926 that the Royal Tourist Commissioner, the Marquis de la Vega-Inclán, persuaded King Alfonso XIII to approve the establishment of state paradors throughout the land. They were to be located in places that were not commercially viable for the private sector to develop and which were spaced at intervals within an easy distance for the motor vehicles of the period. Behind the plan also was the idea of taking advantage of 'ancient monuments—old hospices, palaces, castles and convents.' Soon a national network was established and a star system of grading (ranging from 3 to

5 It is not quite the same to enjoy the lifestyle of the rich and famous, where new-moneyed celebrities are creatures of the media.

5) introduced. Currently top of the range is the 5-star GL Hotel de los Reyes Católicos at Santiago de Compostela, originally constructed in 1499 as a royal hospital for pilgrims to the shrine of St. James (and, as such, the oldest hotel in the world [Paradores, 1992]). There is also a 5-star GL Hotel San Marcos in León. Built originally in 1515 as the Mother House for the Knights of St. James, in 1965 it was converted into a luxury parador (Paradores, 1992).

Even a modestly graded 3-star parador, like the one at Ávila, has so much to offer that it favourably compares with, or even exceeds, the comforts of a traditional 5-star establishment (such as adobe floors and four-poster beds). For example, a former sixteenth-century palace (Piedras Albas) is surrounded by the town's ancient walls, which conserves a monastic, devout and spiritual air that is characteristic of the city (where St. Theresa was born). Leading out from the dining room is a beautiful secluded garden with archaeological remains and an orchard. Inside, patrons of taste savour such local delicacies as roast sucking pig, veal steak, 'judías de el Barco.' 'puncheretes teresianos,' and the famous 'yemas de la Santa' (Parador de Ávila, n.d.).

This is typical of the delights to be had at a parador. Everywhere the language of the general brochure is shamelessly couched in motivational references to nostalgia. The following is a typical example:

> Thus the traveller will discover today, with pleasant surprise, that he can sleep in the same room in the Castle of Jarandilla de la Vera where Carlos V is said to have stayed while he waited for his lodgings in the nearby monastery of Yuste to be made ready; or he can dine in the rooms which belonged to the Alcalá de Henares University founded by Cardinal Cisneros; or even spend a few days in the Castle of Hondarribia against which the Prince of Condé laid a useless siege three hundred years ago (Paradores, 1992).

Here the discovery of today becomes a 'pleasant surprise' precisely because it can turn the clock back hundreds of years ago to a world of kings, castles, and cardinals. All this becomes possible because the contemporary tourist can sleep in the same room and eat in the identical quarters as the leading figures of a glorious past.

Udaipur Lake Palace

Over in India, where colonial times (for the British at least) are synonymous with the days of the Raj and of Empire, visitors can sample the life of a maharajah in one of several lake palaces operated by the prestigious Taj Palace Hotels group.

Here is a year 2003 description of the Lake Palace Hotel, Udaipur:

> The Lake Palace is one of the most beautiful palaces in the world, arising out of the turquoise waters of the Pichola like an elegant fantasy in white

marble. The place was built in the 17th century on a natural foundation of 4 acres of rock. It was initially called Jaginwas after its founder Maharama Jaggit Singh. The Maharama, ruler of Jaipur from 1628 to 1654, was very friendly with Moghul Emperor Shah Jahan, and encouraged his craftsmen to copy some of the glories of his incomparable building at Agra. The successive rulers used this cool haven as a summer resort, holding their regal durbars in its courtyards. These courtyards lined with columns, pillared terraces and fountains, add to its impressive image. The rooms are decorated with cusped arches, inlaid stones of pink and green lotus leaves, and apartments like the Bada Mahal, Kush Mahal, Ajjan Niwas, Phool Mahal and Dhola Mahal.

It is subsequently explained that the Lake Palace Hotel has 84 rooms (ranging in price from $280 [superior, lake view] to $750 [grand royal suite] single, per night). Each room is designed according to a particular theme and is decorated with textiles and handicrafts of the region. Their names are said to conjure up a romantic setting and give a taste of regal splendour of a bygone era. The Amrit Sagar bar is decorated with intricate glass mosaic work on the walls and ceiling, whereas the Neel Kamal restaurant facing a lily pond serves Indian and continental cuisine. There is a complimentary puppet show and Rajasthani folk dance and music.

All the ingredients are here—rulers, emperors, the Taj Mahal, elegant fantasy, romance, servants, and lotus leaves. It just needs the discerning, well-heeled nostalgic tourist to complete the picture.

Cliveden House

Hostels of history would be somehow incomplete without the presence of a stately home. Here Cliveden House in the English county of Berkshire is a good example. As the Web site explains, Cliveden was originally constructed for the second Duke of Buckingham in 1666. It has hosted 'almost every British monarch since George I' **(Cliveden House, 2003)** (Queen Victoria was a frequent visitor), and since becoming the family home of Lord and Lady (Nancy) Astor, has accommodated the likes of President Roosevelt, George Bernard Shaw, Winston Churchill, and Charlie Chaplin.

In 1986 it became a 5-star hotel set on 376 acres of rolling countryside, where patrons can now 'walk in the footsteps of Cliveden's notable past guests' **(Cliveden House, 2003)**. Its individually furnished rooms range from £250 a night (classic) to £1375 a night for a minimum of two nights (Spring Cottage), inclusive of full English breakfast and value added tax (VAT). There are more than four members of staff per bedroom, the house *still* makes its own bread, cakes, biscuits, and confectionery *just as it has always done,* and there are four dining rooms—the Terrace, Waldo's, the French, and the Cellar. The last mentioned is for private functions and run by a team whose 'knowledge of wines and spirits is unsurpassable' **(Cliveden, 2003)**. Boating on the river is said to '*remain* a favourite pastime,' 'and on summer evenings guests are invited to join the *1911* river launch Suzy Ann as she is taken out for a champagne cruise before dinner' (emphases added) **(Cliveden, 2003)**.

However, it is only in a section entitled 'The House Experience' that the full nostalgic links are sketched in:

> From the moment you step across the threshold into a *recaptured* world of style and elegance, you will feel like honoured private guests in a stately home of outstanding beauty and know you are at the beginning of a very special experience (emphasis added).

Having driven up the quarter-mile drive and caught sight of the distinguished pile, at the *porte cochère* one is greeted by uniformed footmen, shown into the Great Hall and led up the grand staircase with its figures on each newel post representing persons from Cliveden's past. Just walking into one's room is said to be an experience like no other hotel can provide—gentle music, a blazing log fire, fresh flowers, and a personal note from the manager.

This is luxury at its most opulent, made all the more wicked by its association with a mysterious past. Strangely no reference is made to one of Lord Astor's friends, John Profumo, or to the latter's lover, Christine Keeler. It was she who, on one infamous occasion in the 1960s, cavorted naked around the pool, thereby initiating an affair that would later rock the British establishment to its foundations and bring down the Tory government of Harold Macmillan (Smyth, 1990). Maybe this is an instance of nostalgia's ability to screen out the unpleasant. Whatever the reason, Cliveden was recently the locale for two episodes of an avidly followed BBC TV programme broadcast in May 2003, *The Antique Roadshow*.

Playful Pilgrimage

From the idea of a stately home and all that it conjures up, it is just one small step to the notion of 'home' itself and its connection with nostalgia. Etymologically, nostalgia means a form of homesickness—the pain experienced by those away from home—a pain alleviated only by a physical return to home (Davis, 1979; Nicolson, 1998a). This *heimweh*, or aching for home, thus turns into an act of regression, a longing for the maternal home of childhood, and ultimately a primeval desire to re-enter the womb. This is the yearning for a reunion with the most significant other of all—mother. Hence the discourse about 'the tourist as child' (Dann, 1989).

However, what is rarely discussed is the possibility of returning to a cultural centre once inhabited by alternative or additional significant others—those who bestow a quasispiritual meaning on the lives of people engaged in a quest of this nature. Such is the case of popular cult figures who fill the void left empty by secularisation—icons of the order of Elvis Presley, Diana Princess of Wales, and Marlene Dietrich that are examined here. This should not imply that there is no longer room or need for traditional pilgrimage to the shrines of saints and martyrs. Rather it signifies that, for many persons, premodern pilgrimage has been replaced by a postmodern equivalent—playful pilgrimage.

Elvis, the King

Although some refuse to believe that Elvis ever passed away, August 16, 1977, is generally acknowledged as the day the 42 year old died. Consequently August is known as 'death month' for those who make the journey to Graceland with floral tributes and teddies at the ready to lay at Presley's grave (Langley, 2000). There is also the more concentrated 'death week,' introduced by Priscilla when opening this home of amazing grace to the public—a shrine visited by more pilgrims than those paying respect to John F. Kennedy, and the most popular home attraction in the United States after the White House (Anon, 1997).

Today's mansion tour (US$16.25 adults, US$6.25 children 7 to 12) includes a new digital guide featuring the voice of Elvis. It takes in the living room, music room, his parents' bedroom, the dining room, kitchen, TV room, pool room, and jungle den. Pilgrims can gaze upon the desk from his office, his collection of stage costumes, gold records, awards, jewellery, and photographs. The tour concludes with a visit to the meditation garden where Elvis and his close relatives are interred (Elvis Presley Official Site, 2003). Here the family grave is surrounded by teddy bears, hearts, and guitars made of roses, and there is a simple plaque that reads, 'It was a precious gift from God we cherished and loved dearly. He became a living legend in our time. God saw that he needed some rest and called him home' (Cohn, 1991).

It is important to recognise that there are several occasions during which visitors can communicate with the King. They can listen to his tape-recorded voice speaking personally to them, sample peanut butter and mashed banana sandwiches (Elvis's favourite snack), purchase spirit portraits from street artists (Cohn, 1991)—the list is endless. At the corporate level, Elvis Presley Enterprises also extends to the Elvis Presley Memphis Restaurant and Heartbreak Hotel, arranging special events such as weddings, issuing news bulletins, organising charities, and a fan collectors' club (Elvis Presley Official Site, 2003). All this commercial activity ensures that the dead King is today worth more than he ever was alive.

Diana, Princess of Wales

In August 1997, Diana Princess of Wales was the fatal victim of a high-speed car crash in a Parisian subterranean tunnel where she perished with her lover, Dodi Fayed, heir to the Harrods' fortune. The outpouring of national grief as her funeral was beamed around the world to the accompaniment of Elton John's *Candle in the Wind* was immense, and the British readily identified with her Tony Blair's New Labour inspired sobriquet, 'the people's princess.' Diana was buried on an island in a lake forming part of her brother's Althorp estate. On July 1, 1998, the home was opened for two months to 2500 visitors a day who had paid £9.50 a head for the privilege, a considerable increase on the previous year, which had a total of just 5000 persons (Gillan, 1998). 'Dianaville,' as it came to be known, was said to be the English Graceland (Nicolson, 1998b). In June 1998, a special concert was arranged at Althorp as a tribute to Diana, and featured such artistes as Cliff Richard, Lesley Garrett, and Chris de Burgh. Fans queued for 10 hours in the rain for the 15,000 tickets on offer at £40 each (Milner, 1998).

Today, Althorp, seat of the Spencer family for nearly 5 centuries and 20 generations, is described as having a warm and welcoming feel of a home with an unbroken link, a 'house with a soul.' There is now a permanent exhibition located in six of the rooms that are dedicated to the life and work of Diana. Relics include her bridal gown, her childhood letters and school reports, and 28 designer outfits (complete with accessories and shoes) that cover the period from the 1980s to her last public engagement (Althorp House, 2003).

However, and in addition to visits to Diana's last resting place, it is now possible to take a 'Diana Memorial Tour.' One organised by the London Tourist Board takes in St. Paul's Cathedral (where she was married) and provides lunch at the Orangery in Kensington Palace. It then proceeds to St. James's Palace, an Earls' Court gym (where she exercised), and her Coleherne flat (an eighteenth birthday present from her parents in 1979). Afterwards, it includes a Pimlico nursery (where she worked), Vacani's School of Dancing (where she had lessons), the Kensington Odeon Cinema, and two South Kensington shops (owned by her designer friend, Catherine Walker). Finally, the tour traces the route of the funeral cortège from Kensington Palace, via Hyde Park and Buckingham Palace, to Westminster Abbey (Leventhal, 1998).

Alternatively, pilgrims can undertake 'The Diana Walk,' a seven-mile trek marked by 90 plaques at a cost of $1.9 million. According to Lucy Moss (2000), it is best to start at the seventeenth-century Kensington Palace, Lady Di's residence from the time of her marriage (1981) to her death (1997), and meander through the state apartments. The gardens are where she used to roller blade and jog incognito. South of the palace are the black and gold Crowther gates where thousands of mourners left flowers, messages, and toys (and some still do), and through which her funeral procession began on September 6, 1997. North of the palace is the $2.5 million Diana Princess of Wales Memorial Playground with a Peter

Pan theme and pirate ship for children. East of Kensington Gardens is Hyde Park. Thereafter, pilgrims can wander to Green Park, the Mall, Buckingham Palace, St. James's Park, St. James's Palace (home to Charles after the 1992 separation), and Clarence House (home of the late Queen Mother, and the place where Diana spent her wedding eve).

Whether devotees of Diana go to Althorp or follow in her footsteps, there is a deep reverence associated with her name. Indeed her death in 1997 completely eclipsed that of the far more saintly Mother Teresa of Calcutta occurring a few days later. The Tate Liverpool's 'Heaven: An Exhibition that will Break Your Heart' (December 1999–February 2000) to mark the transition into the new millennium even had a statue of Diana dressed as the Virgin Mary in which she was clearly treated as a religious figure (Petre, 1999).[6] Here nostalgia conveniently overlooks her serial affairs and instead treats her as all but canonised.

Marlene Dietrich

The year 2001 saw Berlin celebrating Marlene Dietrich's one-hundredth birthday (she died in 1992). Today, *aficionados* can trace her life around the city. According to Cook (2001), they can begin at her birthplace in Leberstrasse 65, located close to the restaurant of the *Blauer Engel* (named after her best known film, *The Blue Angel*). Thereafter, they proceed to her old school in Gasteinerstrasse and to Hildegardstrasse 54, the flat where she lived as a young actress. Next comes the Kaiser Wilhelm Memorial Church where she married Rudolf Sieter, followed by the Komödie Theater (revue performances), Deutsches Theater (classical dramas), Babelsberg studios (where *The Blue Angel* was filmed), and the Zooplast cinema (where it opened on April 1, 1930). Thereafter she left Germany for California, and subsequently Paris where she lived and died, never to reside in Berlin again, although she did return in 1945 attired in American uniform to entertain the allies and in 1960 took part in a postwar tour of the country. Her last resting place is the Stubenrauchstrasse cemetery where a simple plaque announces the name 'Marlene.' Most of the Dietrich memorabilia, purchased with her estate from her daughter in 1993 for £3.6 million, are to be found in the New Film Museum in Potsdammer Platz. They include her love letters, diary, gifts from Ernest Hemmingway and Douglas Fairbanks, Jr., as well as 3000 dresses, 10,000 photographs, and 35,000 documents.

This anti-Nazi icon (who refused several of the Führer's invitations for her to return in a triumphant procession through the Brandenburg Gate) in many ways encapsulates all that is best in the postmodern German psyche, a rags to riches saga based on Weberian hard work. Even with the reconstruction of Berlin all around them, her compatriots do not forget.

---

6 Interestingly, the exhibition also included Elvis Presley.

The future is thus connected to the past via nostalgia. Mother Marlene has at last come home to the fatherland.

Theming and Dreaming

> You know that it's time to take a fad seriously when someone dedicates a film and a theme park to it.
> –Marshall, 2003

According to Swarbrooke (1997), there are four main types of visitor attractions—natural, man-made though not designed primarily to attract visitors (e.g., cathedrals), special events, and man-made and purposely built to attract tourists. The last of these categories comprises 20 subtypes ranging from amusement parks to garden centres and waterfront developments. However, of particular interest here are those subtypes that specifically employ nostalgia in their appeal, notably theme parks, open-air museums, heritage centres, craft centres, factory tours, and shops. In the United Kingdom at least, most of these variants appeared from the 1970s onward and were generally successful in terms of visitor numbers and return on capital. Undoubtedly part of this success was due to their postmodern pastiche and emphasis on the past (e.g., Beamish Open Air Museum, Ironbridge Gorge Museum). As far as theme parks are concerned, the paradigm case is Walt Disney World.

Walt Disney World

Whether the Florida complex (equal in area to San Francisco) comprises four or seven theme parks, depending on how they are counted (Fjellman, 1992), the one that most clearly evokes nostalgia is the Magic Kingdom. Here Main Street USA leaps over two world wars and the Depression to the hazy Victorian era of 1880–1910. It is a microcosm of warm, small town America with its ice cream parlours, apothecary shops, and candy stores, where 'harassed people in a dangerous, impersonal and unfriendly world can symbolically locate friendship, order, intimacy, innocence' (Fjellman, 1992). Under a prevailing collective amnesia, there are no references to messy, unpaved, muddy streets, with their ubiquitous telephone poles and billboards; there are no bars, no jails, no 'other side of the tracks.' The grim reality of these times and places has been filtered out. It is now replaced by a false benign history, or 'distory,' an edited version of history as it should have been, a powerful set of pleasant messages that parents feel compelled to share with their children (Fjellman, 1992). All this fantasy is underlain with the corporate mantra, 'if we can dream it, we can do it.'

The Disney 'product,' with its deodorised, de-sexed version of human relationships, where goodness is always rewarded, suffering is superficial, and we're all nice guys really, is based on a thoroughly sentimentalised vision of life . . . communism, fascism, and socialism have come and gone over the course of the century. Disney has remained and looks well set for the next millennium (Palmer, 1999).

Yet these criticisms cannot negate the fact that 'there's no business like old business' (Morley, 1972). In this connection, although admittedly referring to Disneyland Paris and its 40,000 a day visitors, more than half of whom are adults, Lawson (1998) remarks,

> This, it seems to me, underlines the real reason for the outstanding commercial success of the Disney corporation: it is based on the very simple idea that adults wish above all else to re-attain the happiness which they had— or, more poignantly, wish that they had had—as children.

The Holy Land Experience

Also in Florida (isn't it strange how nostalgia flourishes in one of the most futuristic states of the union?) is another theme park, only this time based on a different ideology—that of religion. This is 'The Holy Land Experience.' First conceived in 1991, and opened on February 5, 2001, it is the brainchild of Baptist minister, Marvin Rosenthal. It occupies some five acres, was designed at a cost of US$16 million by ITEC entertainment, and is run by Zion Hope. The Holy Land, with its 20-minute films shot on location in Jerusalem, covers the whole gamut of biblical history and eschatology from Adam and Eve to the Second Coming. Employees are decked out in period costume from the time of Christ, and a 100-strong cast plays out parts ranging from Roman soldiers to flower girls. Exhibits include a smoke emitting Ark of the Covenant, a Wilderness Tabernacle show featuring the observances of the 12 tribes of Israel in the desert, and laser and dry ice rituals of the High Priest on the Day of the Atonement. There is also a projection of a Nativity scene, a reconstruction of the Temple of the Great King, a first century Jerusalem street market, a Via Dolorosa, the caves of Q'mran, and the rock tomb of Jesus complete with discarded shroud. The gift-retailing emporia are known as Methuselah's Mosaics and The Old Scroll Shop (Langton, 2001).

According to the official Web site, 'it's been 2000 years since the world has seen anything like this' (The Holy Land Experience, 2003). For just US$29.75 adults and US$19.75 children, the stated purpose of the Holy Land Experience is to 'provide answers to life's most important questions: Where am I from? Why am I here? Where am I going? What is life really about?' It claims to be able to achieve this goal by taking people '7,000 miles away and 3,000 years *back* in time' (emphasis added) and by giving them a 'unique experience' in a 'search for enduring truth and the ultimate meaning in life' (Holy Land Experience, 2003). Such an experience is said to be 'educational,' 'inspirational,' 'theatrical,' and 'historical,' one that can be enjoyed outside in 'the beautiful Florida sunshine' and inside in air-conditioned comfort (Holy Land Experience, 2003). Although food and drink cannot be brought on to the premises, the gastronomic delights of the Oasis Palms Café supply this gustatory need in the forms of 'Goliath Burgers,' 'Jaffa Hot Dogs,' 'Oasis Chicken,' 'Bedouin Beef,' 'Tabgha Tuna,' 'Arabian Chicken,' 'Centurion Salad,' 'Shepherd Soup,' and 'Caesar's Delight.'

The underpinning nostalgia message of this theme park seems to be that in a largely atheistic Western world, it is necessary to *return* to biblical times in order to discover authentic personal identity. As such the project is at odds with the predominantly secular message of Walt Disney World (WDW) that celebrates 'Americana' as the true meaning of life for civil religion.

Haw Par Villa

Another themed attraction based on a religious or moral set of ideas is Haw Par Villa in Singapore. Originally a gift in 1937 from the indigenous entrepreneur, Aw Boon Haw, to his brother, Aw Boon Par, to mark their joint success in the Tiger Balm menthol ointment business, it was intended as a Chinese mythological complex, and opened to the public under the name of Tiger Balm Gardens. It featured such terrifying exhibits as 'The Ten Courts of Hell,' a graphic display illustrating the fate of those who misbehaved in this life, and was one of the island's top leisure sites from the 1950s to the 1980s. Subsequently, in 1985 it was acquired by the government, handed over to an offshoot of Disney production, Battaglia Associates, rebranded as 'Dragon World,' and introduced a number of flume rides and multimedia shows. Thus began a rare failure for the corporation who witnessed a decline in visitor numbers from 1.44 million in 1993 to 382,000 in 1997. According to many locals—the main patrons—it was too American and too expensive. As for overseas tourists, they preferred shopping in the new malls. By 1998, the theme park was recording losses of US$17.5 million and in 2001 there was talk of returning it to the Singapore Tourist Board (STB) for demolition. However, there was strong support (more than 80 percent) from Singaporeans to go back to the original and to preserve the Chinese mythology of the prototype for moral, cultural, and historical reasons. Indeed, all the Chinese staff who had remained with the project from the 1990s firmly believed that the statues and figurines had divine power and were inhabited by spirits. They consequently prayed to them, made daily offerings of incense, and erected an altar to appease the Hungry Ghosts. They further decided to give the exhibits their former old look. They painted back the Disney mountains from blue to a more sober brown, and placed a wooden pillar at the entrance with the inscription 'The Spirit of Haw Par,' accompanied by two Chinese notices urging 'perseverance and hard work' and 'remember your benefactor.' In such a manner they were able to preserve their sense

of roots in a rapidly globalising era and to retain the nostalgic philan-
thropy and filial piety of the Haw Par brothers (Teo and Li, 2003).

Viking Museums

Attempts to provide roots experiences and a sense of history can also
be found in Northern Europe, particularly Scandinavia.[7] According to
Halewood and Hannam (2001), they generally fall into one of four types:

> Conventional museums (e.g., Viking Ships' Museum at Bygdøy, Norway,
> where three 19th century ships are housed in an ecclesiastical style edifice
> that helps construct a sense of nationhood and enables people to return to
> the very heart of Norwegian culture)

Heritage centres (e.g., Jorvik Viking Centre in York, England, with its
time car ride, together with sounds and smells of the past)[8];

Reconstructed villages (e.g., Foteviken in Sweden, with handicarft
demonstrations, houses, people working with pottery and tending crops,
Viking markets, and re-enactments of cooking and fighting);

Theme parks (e.g., Tusenfryd, 20 kilometres south east of Oslo,
Norway). The last mentioned contains 'Viking Land,' constructed at a cost
of $4.9 million in 1995. It comprises a mountain hall, a multimedia audi-
torium wherein participants go for a ride in a long-ship to 'Vinland.' On
the way they encounter storms, attacks by pirates, and the intervention
of gods. There are additional facilities for corporate banquets with host
and guests in Viking attire. There is also a re-created village by a lake, a
quay, a ship, a nobleman's house, and a market place filled with staff in
period costume.

---

7 However, an interesting case has recently surfaced elsewhere in Europe. Polls show, for
instance, that more than 40 percent of Ossies (those born in the former German Democratic
Republic [GDR]) are unhappy with life in the unified Germany. 'Ostalgie' parties are held
on a regular basis, participants yearn for Vita Cola (the socialist answer to 'the ultimate imperial beverage'), Trabant cars, and pickled gherkins, and an East German theme park is sched-
uled to open in 2004. Suggested names include Stasi World and the Duetsch Democatische
Republik (DDR). Fun Park, although DDR, Haus der Republik, is reckoned to be the
favourite. It will feature surly border guards, badly stocked department stores, and *bierkeller*
sing alongs. There is even a blockbuster film—*Goodbye Lenin*—in release from July 2003, and
a corresponding Web site where former Ossies can reminisce about the days of no unemployment, no drugs, and no boredom. On a more commercial basis (www.ossi-versand.de)
aficionados may purchase such long lost items as Halberstadter frankfurters, Zetti Crunchi
flakes, and nostalgic videos like *The Legend of Paul and Paula* (Marshall, 2003). It can, of
course, be argued that a desire to return to an inglorious past is not so much a nostalgic
quest as an instance of masochism. However, under the caption 'milking the macabre,' this
writer has provided the counter cases of the former KGB complex in Moscow and the Pudu
Prison in Kuala Lumpur. He maintains that such 'dark tourism' sites can be viewed by those
who have experienced them either really or vicariously, as a harking back to a system of
albeit harsh law and order, and, in that sense, to a past that is superior to the present.
8 For a detailed discussion of the linkages between nostalgia and the sense of smell, see
Dann and Jacobsen (2002; 2003).

In spite of the seemingly contrived nature of some of these displays (e.g., the carnival-like atmosphere of the markets), Halewood and Hannam maintain that there is a strong emphasis on authenticity (albeit in various ways) in all four of these types of Viking experience. There is a validation by expert historians, archaeological evidence, scripting by professional linguists—a meticulous concern for detail—in order to ensure that the past is portrayed accurately. What Halewood and Hannam do not say, but nevertheless imply, is that this open parading of origins for people today may be suggesting to them that the way they were is superior to the way they are. It may be proposing that things were made better in the past, that a sense of community prevailed, and that people could enjoy themselves so much more when they knew exactly who they were.

Discussion

Although acknowledging that there are several more variants that require exploration (e.g., retailing, travelling by train), this chapter has examined three types of tourism nostalgia of the noughties. Yet even based on a limited number of cases, it is possible to evaluate the phenomenon by inducing its essential characteristics. By way of conclusion, this assessment is conducted under the following headings: imagination versus reality, motivational appeal, and millennial moments.

Imagination Versus Reality

Nostalgia tourism that provides an alternative to the present does so by recourse to an imagined past, a version of reality that people carry around in their heads. This observation is true for the Indian palace that screens outside surrounding poverty, for in-the-footsteps tours that are carefully zoned to remove references to contemporary surroundings, or for themed attractions that are instances of hyper-reality.

Nostalgia tourism is thus the very antithesis of reality tourism. It stands at the opposite end of the continuum of the sort of tourism promoted by Global Exchange[9] that takes its clientele into such places as the Gaza Strip,

9 This California-based company that began in 1988 today conducts up to 80 trips a year, each lasting from 7 to 14 days, at prices ranging from US$850 to US$4000. The educational aim is to show its clients via face-to-face confrontation how they contribute to global problems and to suggest ways that they can contribute to positive change. Among its most popular tours, and the only one to an area of the developed world, is that to Northern Ireland. Now in its tenth year, it allows customers to participate in the Orange Order marches, the West Belfast Festival, to meet political representatives of all political parties and released political prisoners, even to take up B&B accommodation with families in the Falls Road (Global Exchange, 2003).

Haiti, and Cuba to witness firsthand the abuse of human rights (Langton, 1998; Purdy, 1998). Nostalgia tourism is not concerned with such matters; in fact, it studiously ignores them.

Motivational Appeal

From what has been seen already, and given the hazards of political labelling, it is clear that nostalgia tourism is more likely to appeal to an ideology that is conservative rather than liberal. By definition, a conservative wishes to preserve all that is wholesome from the past, whereas a liberal is more intent on change. Postmodernism itself is also said to be conservative in outlook, and its pastiche-like touristic theming in Disney and its imitators is indicative of this trend. There is thus a certain indulgence associated with nostalgia tourism, one that approvingly believes that the past is good for you rather than 'a poison that kills by cloying'—a more puritanical disapproving position (Nicolson, 1998a).

It should also be evident that nostalgia tourism appeals more to those who can afford to indulge in it. Although reminiscing is of course a free activity, actual participation in touristic pursuits that evoke the past can be quite expensive. The cost of staying in a stately home or going to a theme park with all the family would be ruled out for most proletarian discretionary incomes. So, too, would be the associated expenses. English Heritage, for instance, reckons that for every £8 million it takes in entrance fees it brings in another £6 million from its gift shops (Leslie, 1998). Nostalgia tourism, like most forms of special interest tourism, may thus be said to be middle-class oriented.

Nostalgia tourism can additionally appeal more to the elderly (Davis, 1979; Swarbrooke, 1997) than to the young, if only because the former has a richer data bank of memories with a longer time span. A loss of status among retirees may also encourage backward glimpses to the past, just as a sense of lack of future may lead to a retrieval of worth from yesteryear (Davis, 1979). Even so, those of more tender years can and do experience nostalgia, particularly in such rites of passage as going to a new school, entry into adolescence, and so on where nostalgia thrives on transition (Davis, 1979). Also related, it is important to realise that it is not so much a question of how long ago an event occurred, as it is how individuals contrast it with present circumstances (Davis, 1979).

Then, too, there is a certain narcissism or *amour propre* (Davis, 1979) connected with nostalgia, one that may appear to the psychocentric personality (Plog, 1977). Here self-approval is cultivated in order to make the present seem less frightening (i.e., an experience of flow as opposed to schizophrenic timelessness) (Davis, 1979).

Arguably, too, because nostalgia thrives where identity is threatened, it may be experienced to a greater degree by men than by women. Male roles and statuses are often more sharply demarcated with respect to occupation, geographical location, reference groups, and lifestyle (Davis, 1979). For that reason, it may not simply have been a *lapsus calami* that the parador brochure addressed itself solely to males.

Millennial Moments

As each year draws to a close and a new year dawns, thoughts turn to change and to the making of fresh resolutions. Such a trend is even more pronounced at the turn of a century and the entry into its first decade. At the same time, however, this can be a period of the greatest anxiety, when the continuity of identity is most threatened. Here, then, it becomes necessary to establish appreciative stances of former selves and to eradicate from memory unpleasant and shameful experiences. It is correspondingly essential to rediscover and rehabilitate 'marginal, fugitive and eccentric facets of earlier selves' in order to assert, 'look how far I've come' and 'how well equipped I am to deal with challenges of the present' (Davis, 1979). Nostalgia responds to this existential tension in the subject.

Tourism can also alleviate such anxiety in its language of promotion. It is not sufficient simply to provide luxury accommodation, playful pilgrimage, and themed attractions. It must strike a resonance with the corresponding personalities of nostalgia prone clients. In such a manner, Croatia is now advertised as 'the Mediterranean as it used to be' (Croatia Tourist Board, 2003) and Scotland is still marketed as a romantic land of mists, glens, landscapes, and castles 'as people want to find it' (Elsworth, 1998a). As for Cool Britannia, well, in the words of a spokesman for the English Tourist Board, Debbie Waite, 'While we are very excited about the production of a new face of Britain, we do need to make sure it goes hand in hand with our history and heritage' (Elsworth, 1998b).

References

Althorp House. 2003. http://www.althorp-house.co.uk. Accessed 05/19/03.

Anonymous. 1997. The King Won't Die. *Sunday Telegraph*, August 3: 27.

British Broadcasting Corporation. 2003. *Profits Reunited, The Money Programme, BBC2 Television*, March 5.

Brock, D., and G. Starr. 1999. What Do We Call the Next Decade? The Noughties! http://www.users.senet.com.au/~gstarr/noughties.html. Accessed 05/27/03.

Buck, R. 1978. Toward a Synthesis in Tourism Theory. *Annals of Tourism Research* 5: 110–111.

Cliveden House. 2003. http://www.clivedenhouse.co.uk. Accessed 05/12/03.

Cohen, E. 1991. A Phenomenology of Tourist Experiences. *Sociology* 13: 179–201.

Cohn, N. 1991. Two for the Show, *Sunday Times*, March 24.

Cook, W. 2001. Falling in Love Again. *Sunday Telegraph Travel*, May 20: 1–2.

Croatia Tourist Board. 2003. Advertisement, CNN, April 7.

Dann, G. 1989. The Tourist as Child. Some Reflections. *Cahiers du Tourisme*, série C, no. 135.

——. 1994a. Tourism and Nostalgia: Looking Forward to Going Back. *Vrijetijd en Samenleving* 12(1/2): 75–94.

——. 1994b. Travel by Train: Keeping Nostalgia on Track. In *Tourism: The State of the Art.* ed. A. Seaton. Chichester: Wiley.

Dann, G., and J. Jacobsen. 2002. Leading the Tourist by the Nose. In *The Tourist as a Metaphor of the Social World.* ed. G. Dann. Wallingford: CAB International.

——. 2003. Tourism Smellscapes. *Tourism Geographies* 5(1): 3–25.

Davis, F. 1979. *Yearning for Yesterday: A Sociology of Nostalgia.* New York: Free Press.

Elsworth, C. 1998a. Scotsman's Home Isn't Always a Castle. *Sunday Telegraph*, January 25.

——. 1998b. Now St George Gets the Re-branding Treatment. *Sunday Telegraph*, April 5.

Elvis Presley Official Site. 2003. http://www.elvis.com. Accessed 05/12/03.

Fjellman, S. 1992. *Vinyl Leaves: Walt Disney World and America.* Boulder, Colo.: Westview Press.

Friends Reunited. 2003. http://www.friendsreunited.co.uk. Accessed 05/23/03.

Gillan, A. 1998. Althorp Visitors Bringing Crime in their Wake. *Sunday Telegraph*, June 21.

Global Exchange. 2003. http://www.globalexchange.org. Accessed 05/19/03.

Gottlieb, A. 1982. Americans' Vacations. *Annals of Tourism Research* 9: 165–187.

Halewood, C., and K. Hannam. 2001. Viking Heritage Tourism: Authenticity and Commodification. *Annals of Tourism Research* 28: 565–580.

Humphrys, J. 2000. Wales, the Best of Britain. *Sunday Telegraph Supplement* 24–25.

Lake Palace Hotel, Udaipur. 2003. http://www.lake-palace-udaipur.com. Accessed 05/12/03.

Langley, W. 2000. The Man who Made Rock and Roll. *Sunday Telegraph Review*, August 27.

Langton, J. 1998. American 'Reality Tourists' Seek Out Misery. *Sunday Telegraph*, April 19.

——. 2001. 'Holy Land' Rival to Disney Angers Florida's Jews. *Sunday Telegraph*, February 4.

Lawson, D. 1998. I'm on Mickey Mouse's Side. *Sunday Telegraph*, June 7.

Leslie, A. 1998. Selling England by the Pound. *Sunday Telegraph Travel*, February 8.

Leventhal, M. 1998. Princess Di's London—A Tacky Tour or a National Treasure? *Sunday Express Travel*, May 31.

Marshall, L. 2003. Good Old Bad Old Days. *Sunday Telegraph Review*, July 6.

Milner, C. 1998. Althorp Concert-Goers Muddy but Unbowed. *Sunday Telegraph*, June 28.

Morley, S. 1972. There's No Business Like Old Business. *Punch*, November 29.

Moss, L. 2000. http://www.travellady.com. Accessed 05/19/03.

Nicolson, A. 1998a. The View from Perch Hill. *Sunday Telegraph Magazine*, December 20.

——. 1998b. The Making of Dianaville. *Sunday Telegraph Review*, March 15.

Palmer, A. 1999. Is He Taking the Mick? *Sunday Telegraph*, April 11.

Parador de Ávila. n.d. Pamphlet in English and Spanish. Paradores, Madrid.

Paradores. 1992. Booklet in Spanish, English, French and German. Gráficas Saldaña, Madrid.

Petre, J. 1999. Outcry Greets Statue of Diana as Madonna. *Sunday Telegraph*, September 12.

Plog, S. 1977. Why Destination Areas Rise and Fall in Popularity. In *Domestic and International Tourism*, ed. E. Kelly. Wellesley, Mass.: Institute of Certified Travel Agents.

Purdy, A. 1998. 'Troubles Tourism' Brings New B & Bs to Falls Road. *Sunday Telegraph*, June 14.

Saga Magazine. 2003. Saga Circles, *Saga Magazine*, June.

School Disco. 1999–2002. http://www.schooldisco.com. Accessed 05/19/03.

Smyth, R. 1990. Away from it All. *Toronto Star*, October 27.

Sunday Telegraph. 2003. TV and radio supplement 11–17 May 2003. *Sunday Telegraph*, May 11.

Swarbrooke, J. 1997. *The Development and Management of Visitor Attractions*. Oxford: Butterworth-Heinemann.

Teo, P., and L-H Li. 2003. Global and Local Interactions in Tourism. *Annals of Tourism Research* 30: 287–306.

The Holy Land Experience. 2003. http://www.theholylandexperience.com. Accessed 05/19/03.

Veblen, T. 1899, reprint 1994. *The Theory of the Leisure Class*. New York: Dover Publications.

4 From competition to collaboration in the tourism industry

Alan Fyall and Brian Garrod

Introduction

> The realisation that individual businesses no longer compete as stand alone entities, but as collaborative networks, has been perhaps one of the most significant breakthroughs in management thinking in recent years. We are now entering the era of 'network competition' where the prizes will go to those organisations that can best structure, coordinate and manage relationships with their partners in a network committed to creating customer and consumer value through collaboration.
> —Christopher, Payne, and Ballantyne, 2002

Collaboration is now commonplace in most industrial sectors. With the accelerating pace of technological innovation and the ever-hastening trend toward globalisation, traditional, 'competitive' adversarial relationships among business organisations are increasingly being swept away and replaced by enduring 'collaborative' relational arrangements (Telfer, 2000). This trend is particularly apparent in tourism, where the fragmented, multisectoral, and interdependent nature of the industry provides a potent catalyst for interorganisational collaboration and decision making. Indeed, for many organisations, performance is critically dependent on the establishment and maintenance of effective collaborative relationships in an effort to serve the customer better. Furthermore, there is now a view emerging that successful collaborative relationships are in fact an essential ingredient of organisational longevity in the tourism industry (Go and Appelman, 2001).

The central message at the core of this chapter is that the focus of concern now needs to shift from the individual, 'competitive' organisation, to the interorganisational, 'collaborative domain' (defined as the configuration of organisations linked to a particular shared problem). This shift is likely to be hastened by the considerable economic, social, and political pressures that are encouraging tourism organisations to relinquish their autonomy and to participate in collaborative decision making. Those interested in the management and marketing of the tourism industry misunderstand the dynamics of collaboration at their peril. Collaboration, in all its various forms, is not only central to the management of tourism, it is arguably the single most important aspect of management in determining the success or otherwise of tourism marketing strategies.

Tourism and Collaboration

Interest in collaboration in tourism has arisen at a time of increasing environmental turbulence and operational complexity for organisations of all kinds. A variety of drivers are behind this trend, the majority being linked in some way to the wider issue of globalisation. There can be little doubt that the predominant force acting on the world's economic systems today is that of globalisation. The process of globalisation has broken down the barriers between economic systems and encouraged them to become progressively more integrated with one another. The result has been the emergence of what can increasingly be described only as a single, global economy. Globalisation has been, and continues to be, driven by an array of converging forces. Advances in information technology, communication methods, and distribution systems, along with continued economic growth in the developing world, have all contributed greatly. Likewise, policy changes in many countries around the world and the emergence of transnational corporations are also reinforcing the trend toward globalisation.

In the specific context of tourism, Wahab and Cooper (2001) suggest that the continuing growth in demand for tourism, the expansion and diversification of travel motivations, and the enlarged expectations of tourists are all contributing to the increasing global presence and significance of tourism in the world economy. Heightened competition among an ever-increasing number of destinations and the gathering trend toward deregulation in many of the world's tourism industries are also contributing to a more globalised environment in which the business of tourism must be conducted. Deregulation is particularly apparent in passenger air transportation, in that the policy of 'liberalisation' has resulted in the emergence of numerous bilateral 'open skies' agreements between international airlines. This policy has undoubtedly contributed to the development of airline hubs and the emergence of 'collaborative' strategic alliances in recent years (World Tourism Organization, 2002). More generally, globalisation is leading to an increasingly borderless and interdependent world, and this serves as the catalytic focus for much collaborative activity.

Given the enormous power and reach of globalisation as a driving force in the business environment, Kanter (1995) argues that the success criteria for tourism organisations in a globalised society are changing. Kanter suggests that in the future, tourism organisations will no longer be judged only on the quality of their concepts and competencies, but also on their connections. The notion of 'connections' relates to the organisation's collaborative networks, that is, the alliances and relationships that lever core capabilities, create value for customers, and remove boundaries.

The benefits of obtaining 'added value' through the creation of integrated networks or alliances can be considerable. Drawing on Porter's (1980) concept of the value chain, Ashkenas and colleagues (1995) argue that in a globalised society, the value chain has come to represent the single most significant concept by which organisations and enterprises are linked together. By integrating the activities along their value chain, organisations can work together to create products and services that have more value combined than separately. The increasingly competitive nature of global markets suggests that cooperation between firms, especially among smaller players, will continue to expand. This collaborative imperative is of particular importance in tourism, where the value chain is central to the creation of products by intermediaries. In this instance, globalisation provides the environment for a new way of thinking in the tourism distribution channel, as individual tourism businesses, intermediaries, and tourists in a channel cease to be adversarial and move to a more relational mode of behaviour (Crotts and Wilson, 1995).

Many collaborative initiatives have already begun to evolve among organisations seeking to serve the increasing growth in tourism demand worldwide. The most notable form of interorganisation collaboration, strategic alliances, offers organisations the flexibility they need to 'deal with globalisation, increased consolidation of economic power, the high cost of keeping up with constantly changing technologies and a highly competitive business environment' (World Tourism Organization, 2002). Participants in such alliances are able to share resources and risks in a relatively cost-efficient manner, thereby combining their strengths and enhancing their ability to achieve economies of scale.

Emerging Collaborative Relational Perspectives of Marketing

Adherence to the marketing concept has served the management and marketing literature well for the past 40 years. However, in view of the above drivers of change, Donaldson and O'Toole (2002) suggest that the traditional orientation of marketing is now insufficient to meet the demands of a more dynamic and complex marketplace, and that the manipulation of former marketing tools is deficient as a vehicle for an organisation to compete effectively in the global marketplace. Marketing conducted at the organisational level in the future that does not make explicit reference to the organisation's relationship with other key stakeholders is therefore unlikely to meet the objectives set for it. If the collaborative dimension is overlooked or ignored, marketing strategies of the future will lack relevance and therefore potency. The suggestion is that the marketing domain is intrinsically one in which collaboration is not just desirable but indispensable.

This migration toward a collaborative relational view of marketing has not simply surfaced overnight. Indeed there have been calls for definitions of marketing to include longer term relational aspects over the past 15 years. For example, authors such as Grönroos (1989) and Morgan and Hunt (1994) suggested that the aim of marketing should ultimately be to establish, maintain, and enhance relationships with customers, and other stakeholders, at a profit, so that the objectives of the parties involved are met. This viewpoint, which provides the definitional basis for this chapter, is underpinned by the philosophy of mutual exchange and the fulfillment of promises.

The winds of collaborative change are now such that this view of business—one that encompasses exchange and relationships, and focuses on collaboration and the needs of different stakeholders—is widely seen to be the way forward. To accommodate the collaborative relational approach to business, however, change is deemed vital. Organisations need to reconfigure in terms of philosophy, organisation and management, development and maintenance of partnerships with a range of stakeholders, and development of ways to secure competitive advantage and deliver superior added value. For example, Christopher, Payne, and Ballantyne (2002) suggest that collaborative arrangements 'satisfy customer needs at a profit more effectively than does a single firm that undertakes multiple value-creating activities.' They go on to argue that the growth of collaborating 'network' organisations has 'profound implications for relationship marketing and may potentially change the whole basis of competitive advantage.'

The question to be addressed, therefore, is the extent to which this emerging collaborative relational orientation to business may be considered consistent with the notion of the marketing concept. The traditional understanding of the marketing concept is based on the notion of business as a system of exchange. A comparison with the emerging collaborative relational approach to business can be viewed in Table 4.1.

The previous discussion might be taken to suggest that there are two polar cases: the 'competitive' transaction and the collaborative relational approaches to business. However, Figure 4.1 shows that, more realistically, a continuum is likely to exist between these two extremes. On the one hand the extreme transaction-based approach indicates that little or

Table 4.1   A Comparison Between the 'Competitive' Transaction and Emerging Collaborative Relational Approach to Business

Transactional Approach	Relational Approach
Transaction focus	Partnership focus
Competition	Collaboration
Organisation induced	Cooperation
Value to the organisation	Value in partnership
Buyer passive	Buyer as an active participant
Organisation as a focus for control	Organisation as part of the process
Organisation as a boundary	Boundary less
Short-term focus	Long-term focus
Independent	Dependence and network led

Source: Adapted from Donaldson and O'Toole, 2002.

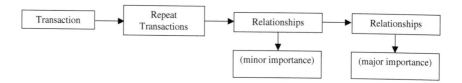

Figure 4.1:   A continuum of business relationships.
Source: Donaldson and O'Toole, 2002.

no joint involvement is necessary or desirable, whereas, at the other extreme, the more significant relationships existing between organisations may be formalised into various forms of collaboration such as partnerships, joint ventures, and strategic alliances. In between these extremes exist two other approaches to business. The first, the repeat transaction scenario, is where some evidence of repetition is in existence (and possibly opportunities for the development of relationships). The second focuses on relationships of minor importance where, although they may be deemed important by organisations, they do not represent a strategic imperative. Perhaps more importantly, a critical issue is the extent to which the traditional view of market orientation is able to incorporate the emerging collaborative relational approach to business. Indeed, this relational view of markets fundamentally questions the appropriateness of the established notion of the marketing concept.

A recent study by Helfert, Ritter, and Walter (2002) has, however, begun to grasp the issue. The study argues that in most cases it is better to understand the organisation's 'surroundings' as a network of interorganisational relationships rather than an anonymous 'market.' The primary conclusion to be drawn from the study is that the existing formulation of the marketing concept needs to be translated to a relationship level in order to be effective. The study also concludes that market orientation on a relationship level can be interpreted in terms of the resources the organisation employs and the activities it undertakes further to the process of relational exchange. For market orientation to be relevant in the collaborative relational sense, Helfert, Ritter, and Walter (2002) argue that four main relationship management 'task bundles' need to be performed. These are:

1. *Exchange activities.* This refers to exchanges that can involve product-service-, problem-, or person-related activities.
2. *Interorganisational coordination.* This refers to the synchronisation of the relationship partners' actions and comprises the establishment, use, and control of formal rules and procedures and the exertion of informal influence.
3. *Conflict resolution mechanisms.* Partners will need to address conflict arising in nonstandard situations, which are bound to occur in every long-term relationship.
4. *Adaptation.* This is a prerequisite to meeting the special needs or capabilities of a partner.

Figure 4.2 provides an overview of this conceptualisation of market orientation at the collaborative relational level. The connection between the above four tasks and the dimensions of market orientation can be summarised as follows:

- With the desire to understand and meet customer needs, a market orientation can serve as an enabler for relational activities.
- With customer satisfaction measures in place, employees can be motivated to fulfill the relationship management tasks in order to satisfy the customer.
- An understanding of competitors and their movements can serve as a basis upon which to build mechanisms to resolve conflict.
- Because most relationships are handled by more than one individual and often require complex exchange, interfunctional coordination is the key to serving customers.

For the previous to be achieved, Helfert, Ritter, and Walter (2002) suggest that informational, physical, human, and financial resources are required for relationship management to be present in market-oriented firms. This conceptualisation will be put to the test at the end of this chapter where

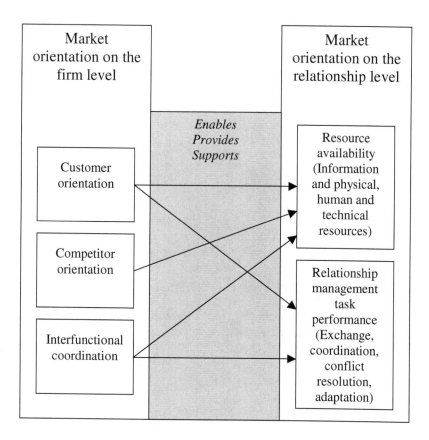

Figure 4.2: A relationship concept of marketing orientation.
Source: Helfert et al., 2002.

the application of collaborative relational marketing strategies within two tourism sectors will be critically explored and examined with regard to their adherence or otherwise to the principles of the collaborative relational concept of market orientation.

Although not perhaps true for all industrial sectors, the collaborative relational concept of market orientation is particularly appropriate for service providers, specifically inasmuch as they are more likely to interact intensively with their customers. As a key component of the wider service industry, tourism is clearly a candidate worthy of investigation. The interdependent nature of tourism and the unavoidable need for contact with a number of other partners and stakeholders, often across the public–private sector divide, in particular, serves as the principal catalyst for the adoption of more collaborative relational approaches to marketing in tourism. It is clear that the vast majority of the industry is no longer able to meet the likely future needs and demands of customers by working independently. By adopting the relational principles advocated by Helfert, Ritter, and Walter (2002), an alternative notion of the marketing concept is therefore proposed as a viable solution to manage and develop tourism to its full potential. The consequences are that in the future, the marketing of tourism conducted at the organisational level, without explicit relevance to the organisation's relationship with other key stakeholders, will be unlikely to meet its objectives fully. If the collaborative dimensions are overlooked or ignored, marketing strategies in the future will lack relevance and hence potency.

Interorganisational Collaboration and Relational Marketing

Collaboration activity has been a key feature of the marketing of tourism for a number of years. For example, airlines, hotels, and local authorities have been working together successfully in a variety of collaborative forms. Whether referred to as alliances, consortia, or partnerships, these are all forms of working together for the achievement of a mutual goal, that is, they are all forms of collaboration. For collaborative relational marketing to succeed interorganisational collaboration, be it vertical, horizontal, or diagonal, is a prerequisite for success. Interorganisational collaboration in the context of tourism marketing can be defined in this instance as:

> a process of joint decision-making among autonomous, key stakeholders of an inter-organisational, tourism marketing domain, to resolve marketing problems of the domain and/or manage issues related to the marketing and development of the domain.

To examine the application and appropriateness of interorganisational activity in pursuing individual and collective goals in the context of tourism marketing, two sector-based case studies will be introduced. However, before exploring the dynamics of such activity, four issues require clarification:

1. The concept of collaborative advantage,
2. The rationale and motives for collaboration,
3. Collaborative forms, and
4. Drivers of collaborative effectiveness.

Each, in turn, contributes to a better understanding of collaborative relational marketing and its application in tourism.

Collaborative Advantage

Consistent with the earlier definition of collaboration, is the term 'collaborative advantage,' first identified by Huxham (1993). Which he defines as:

> ... when something unusually creative is produced—perhaps an objective is met—which no organization could have produced on its own and when each organization, through the collaboration, is able to achieve its own objectives better than it could alone.

This concept focuses on the outcomes of collaboration, which Huxham argues can (but need not necessarily) create synergy between the participating organisations. This means that the joint outcomes of collaboration are in some sense greater than the sum of individual outcomes that could be achieved in the absence of collaboration.

The notion of collaborative advantage has enormous implications for the concept of collaborative relational marketing. Through collaboration, organisations that do not have any significant competitive advantage in a given market environment independently might be able to achieve sufficient collaborative advantage to compensate for this and enable them to out-perform longer established organisations. In an industry where the existence of a large number of relatively small organisations is the norm, the scope for achieving such collaborative advantage can be considerable. Similarly, seeking collaborative advantage rather than competitive advantage might be a particularly effective market-entry strategy where the product is a composite one and the industry highly fragmented, as is often the case in the context of tourism. Such outcomes simply cannot be achieved in a market environment where organisations are operating independently from one another.

Indeed, Huxham argues that the concept of collaborative advantage is in some ways more important than that of collaboration. In particular, the notion of collaborative advantage has enormous potential value in legitimising collaboration as an activity that is worth investing in. Given that it is often necessary to invest substantial organisational and financial resources in order to collaborate, the potential for benefits to be achieved through collaboration, benefits moreover, that would otherwise not be captured by the organisation must form the cornerstone of the rationale for collaboration.

Rationale and Motives for Collaboration

Numerous motives undoubtedly exist to explain why organisations come together to form collaborative arrangements in pursuit of collaboration marketing objectives. Table 4.2 provides a useful overview in that it

Table 4.2   Motives for Collaboration

Market entry and market position-related motives
- Gain access to new international markets
- Circumvent barriers to entering international markets posed by legal, regulatory, or political factors
- Defend market position in present markets
- Enhance market position in present markets

Product-related motives
- Fill gaps in present product line
- Broaden present product line
- Differentiate or add value to the product

Product-/market-related motives
- Enter new product/market domains
- Enter or maintain the option to enter into evolving industries whose product offerings may emerge as either substitutes for, or complements to, the firm's product offerings

Market structure modification-related motives
- Reduce potential threat of future competition
- Raise/erect barriers to entry
- Alter the technological base of competition

Market entry timing-related motives
- Accelerate pace of entry into new product/market domains by accelerating pace of research and product development

Resource use efficiency-related motives
- Lower production costs
- Lower marketing costs

Resource extension and risk reduction-related motives
- Pool resources in light of large outlays required
- Lower risk in the face of large resource outlays required, technological uncertainties, market or other uncertainties

Skills enhancement-related motives
- Learning new skills from alliance partners
- Enhancement of present skills by working with alliance partners

Source: Adapted from Beverland and Brotherton, 2001.

divides the motivations for interorganisational collaboration into eight main groups.

Many of the previous motives are market related. This is particularly true in the context of tourism where motivations related to building the customer base, gaining access to new markets, defending existing markets, and conducting marketing strategies more generally are commonplace. Arguably, the focus on the market benefits of interorganisational collaboration are in no small part due to the increasing globalisation of economic activities in the last quarter of the twentieth-century—a phenomenon that has been felt particularly strongly in service industries. Organisations have typically found the need to collaborate in order to take up better strategic positions in the emerging global marketplace. Internal growth strategies are often impeded by short-term funding constraints, whereas the conventional external growth strategies, which are based on mergers and takeovers, have tended to prove unwieldy and drawn out given the speed of change implied by the globalisation of markets. Collaboration, meanwhile, represents an alternative market-access strategy that can, given the right conditions, steal the march on other external growth strategies.

One issue arising out of the earlier discussion relates to the degree to which organisations work together in a truly relational spirit. Two distinct theoretical standpoints exist on this matter. First, there is the theory of resource dependency. This theory is based fundamentally on the view that interdependencies exist among organisations because individual stakeholders in the domain own or have control over vital resources (be these material, human, political, structural, or symbolic). These, in turn, represent sources of environmental pressure for other firms in that lack of access to these resources may seriously impede the individual organisation in meeting its strategic goals. As such, resource dependency and access to resources may introduce significant uncertainties to the environment in which the organisation is operating.

Under resource dependency theory, organisations seek to reduce these external pressures by gaining control over crucial resource supplies. Traditionally this is achieved through a process of competition, with those organisations most willing and able to pay the highest price for the resources concerned being the most likely to secure access to them. In this way, organisations hope to reduce the uncertainty they experience for themselves, although in many cases this will actually increase it for others operating in the same domain.

The second theoretical standpoint relates to the theory of relational exchange. This theory begins with the assumption that problem domains tend to become more turbulent as they develop and become more densely populated. In this way, organisations become increasingly mutually dependent, so that their central task, which is to solve such problems and reduce the uncertainties encountered in the domain, becomes ever more difficult to achieve if they operate in isolation from one another. Thus, organisations operating within an increasingly complex problem domain are expected to develop interorganisational relationships that will help them solve their problems by working together (i.e., to engage in a process of collaboration).

There is, however, a sharp contrast between relational exchange theory and resource dependency theory. For resource dependency theory, the task for organisations is to enter into such relationships in order to make use of other parties' resources, which would otherwise be unavailable to them, thereby achieving their own objectives more fully. For relational exchange theory, collaboration is the result of organisations recognising the interdependence of problems in their domain and the benefits of developing reciprocal relationships aimed at solving them. It is the latter theory that epitomises the true spirit of collaborative relational marketing as identified in the model developed by Helfert, Ritter, and Walter (2002). For example, relational exchange theory accepts self-interest as the underlying motivation for an organisation to become involved in collaborating with others but argues that collaboration typically involves cases in which this self-interest is best served by the adoption of joint-working strategies. Relational exchange theory also focuses on relationships rather than transactions, in that exchanges are achieved through processes of relational contracting, involving bilateral mechanisms for coordinating the activities of the organisations involved. This forms a management structure with mutuality rather than competition at the core. Consequently, the boundaries between organisations become blurred, so that organisations become progressively linked to others in the form of a network. Finally, unlike resource dependency theory, which focuses on power and control, the key forces driving exchanges under relational exchange theory are trust and commitment. These forces serve to moderate the impact of power within the network of organisations and establish a perception of fairness in the exchange relationship.

Types of Collaboration

As with most aspects of interorganisational collaboration, opinion varies as to how best one categorises collaborative types. For example, directional categorisation, perhaps more commonly used in respect of corporate integration, is one mean in that horizontal collaboration refers to instances where collaboration takes place between organisations that are in other respects in competition with one another. Vertical collaboration, meanwhile, refers to instances of collaboration between suppliers of a product and its buyers. Finally, diagonal integration refers to collaboration between organisations in different sectors or industries.

Another, perhaps somewhat simplistic but nevertheless very useful, typology of collaboration is provided by Terpstra and Simonin (1993). Here, four principal features of collaboration are used to distinguish conceptually between different types of collaboration.

1. Coverage,
2. Form,

3. Mode, and
4. Motive.

The coverage of a collaborative type refers to its extensiveness in terms of the markets, marketing functions, or geographical areas with which it is concerned (Bleeke and Ernst, 1995). Simpler forms of collaboration are likely to be restricted in their activities to specific products or markets, specific components of the marketing mix, and/or close geographical areas. The most basic coverage of a collaboration is thus represented by single-sector collaborations (e.g., among hotels), whose purpose is narrowly defined (e.g., the joint production of promotional brochures). More mature forms of collaboration, on the other hand, will have a more complete coverage in terms of competitive product areas and components of the marketing mix. They may also have a more extensive geographical coverage. By extending its coverage, members of the collaboration will be able to increase their control over the domain; where specific product areas are excluded, control is lessened. Similarly, excluding specific marketing functions will weaken the degree of control that collaborating organisations are able jointly to exert on their external environment.

The form of collaboration refers to the constitutional characteristics of the collaboration. According to Terpstra and Simonin (1993), the least developed form of collaboration is a nonequity arrangement. This involves members agreeing on methods of operation, joint promotion, and so on, but the collaborating organisations do not share financial resources, funding their own contributions to the collaboration independently. A more developed form of collaboration, on the other hand, is the joint venture. This involves the collaborating organisations retaining financial independence but may involve the creation of an 'offspring' through the pooling or exchanging of resources. The most evolved form of collaboration, meanwhile, occurs when members acquire equity stakes in one another, leading to financial interdependency at the organisational level rather than simply at the level of the collaboration.

The mode of collaboration refers to the intrinsic nature of relationships among the members involved. According to Palmer and Bejou (1995), there are two main dimensions to the mode of a given collaboration: the personal characteristics of individuals involved and the cultural characteristics of the organisation each is representing.

Finally, and as discussed in the previous section, there is the issue of motive. The motive for collaboration can, for example, include the desire to internalise the core competencies of other members, achieving economies in advertising and intelligence gathering, joint development of new facilities, making a stronger case for the acquisition of resources. The primary motive for collaboration is likely to differ from participant to participant, and may change as the collaboration evolves.

Drivers of Collaborative Effectiveness

Although opinion varies greatly as to what are the key determinants of collaborative effectiveness, opinion is united in that collaboration is considered to be difficult to implement. One of the problems in commenting on this subject, however, is that although there exists a broad assumption that 'relationships improve performance' (Donaldson and O'Toole, 2002), few measures exist upon which such an assumption can be substantiated. Work by Jamal and Getz (1995), however, provides six overarching propositions relating to the enhancement of collaborative effectiveness, these being based on previous studies conducted by Gray (1985; 1989). The six propositions are as follows:

1. Collaboration requires recognition of a high degree of interdependence in planning and managing the domain.
2. Collaboration requires recognition of individual and/or mutual benefits to be derived from the process.
3. Collaboration requires the perception that decisions arrived at will be implemented.
4. Collaboration will depend on encompassing key stakeholder groups.
5. A convenor is required to initiate and facilitate collaboration.
6. Collaboration requires formulation of a vision statement on desired tourism development and growth, joint formulation of tourism goals and objectives, self-regulation of the planning and development domain through the establishment of a collaborative (referent) organisation to assist with ongoing adjustment of these strategies through monitoring and revisions.

The range of possible factors facilitating collaboration is evidently very wide. However, Jamal and Getz (1995) narrow down the focus considerably by arguing that two particular issues are critical in that they influence every stage of the collaboration process. These relate firstly to the legitimacy of stakeholder process and, secondly, to the power relationships that develop as the collaboration proceeds. Both of these factors can inhibit the initiation and success of collaborative relationships considerably. For example, the exclusion of key stakeholders at the beginning of the collaborative process may lead to problems in implementing decisions made, particularly if this restricts the collaborative group's legitimacy as a valid decision-making body in the problem domain. Meanwhile, the issue of legitimacy of participating stakeholders is also considered to be critical, especially in the context of tourism because of the complications introduced to the collaboration process by the often very large number of actual and potential participants, who may well have highly diverse and opposing interests. In such cases, difficulties experienced in collaboration may be directly related to differences in the value orientations of the various stakeholders.

We will now explore two specific sector-based examples of inter-organisational collaborative relational marketing in contrasting sectors of the wider tourism industry, namely global airline alliances and hotel consortia.

Collaboration in Practice

Global Airline Alliances

Although collaborative alliances among airlines are not a new development, the extent to which truly 'global' alliances have emerged clearly is. Prominent among these is Star, One World, and Sky Team, which include carriers such as Lufthansa, British Airways, and Air France, respectively. By the end of the 1990s global alliances accounted for 63.6 percent of passenger traffic, 55.8 percent of passenger numbers, and 58.4 percent of group revenues (Morrish and Hamilton, 2002). Market factors have been instrumental in driving the development of such alliances, insofar as collaboration represented a suitable means by which airlines were able to combat market turbulence and shift relatively effortlessly between weakening and emerging markets. With a variety of interorganisational arrangements, such as code-sharing arrangements, block space agreements, franchising, and reciprocity between frequent-flyer programmes, alliances continue to present airlines with means of securing access to new markets. In many instances, alliances have in fact helped airlines to extend their reach into areas in which their influence has been limited by government regulation at the national level.

Market factors are not alone, however, in providing the catalyst for change; technological motivations have also been important in some instances. For example, the need to develop common technology so as to achieve efficiencies in aircraft maintenance has served as a primary motivation for collaboration in some cases. Hanlon (1999) identifies a lone instance in which both technological and market motivations have been important in the airline industry: the development of computerised reservation systems (CRSs). In the case of CRSs, few airlines would have been able to muster the financial resources necessary to develop such highly complex systems on their own. However, airlines have been able to cluster together and share the cost of developing them. In doing so, they have developed highly sophisticated CRS systems, which have not only led to efficiencies in booking and the reduction of operational costs, but have also enabled valuable marketing links to be developed between organisations.

In summarising the rationale for the growth in global airline alliances, Oum and Park (1997) identify the following six forces:

1. Consumers tend to prefer airlines serving a large number of cities, so to attract more customers in a more competitive environment airlines need to be able to offer flights to an extensive range of destinations worldwide. As alliance partners link up their networks they can provide a 'seamless' service, thereby expanding their network into new territories.
2. Traffic feed between partners helps increase load factors and achieve economies of density. Partners may also be able to increase flight frequency without actually increasing the number of flights they themselves operate.
3. Alliance members can reduce unit costs by taking advantage of economies of scale, increased traffic density, and economies of scope.
4. Frequency, schedule convenience, and convenience of connections are seen as major features of quality. By coordinating their activities, alliance partners can improve the quality of their services.
5. An alliance can offer far more variety of itinerary and routing choices than a single carrier of a similar size.
6. Members can take advantage of alliance-wide CRSs through the practice of code sharing. Flights sharing the same code are listed more than once on a CRS search. This has the effect of pushing competitor flights off the first booking screen, from which many travel agents prefer to book.

With regard to coverage, alliances now have a much wider remit than was previously the case. For example, collaboration now takes place on a wide range of issues including purchasing, aircraft maintenance, booking and sales, customer incentives, marketing and advertising, and staff training. Hanlon (1999) also points out that although airline alliances are predominantly horizontal and market motivated, vertical and technology-based alliances are not unheard of. British Airways, for example, has extensive vertical linkages with companies in its supply chain, including hotel groups such as Marriott, Hertz for car hire, and Diners Club for charge cards. Meanwhile, a good example of a technology-based alliance in the airline industry is the KLM, SAS, and Swissair (KSS) consortium, wherein through coordinated purchasing decisions, member airlines (KLM, SAS, and Swissair) are able to specialise in different aspects of aircraft maintenance: one in airframes, another in landing gear, another in engines, and so on.

One of the key features of global airline alliances is that they are predominantly of a nonequity form. On the one hand, this arrangement protects individual airlines from the negative consequences of a partner that encounters serious difficulty, such as bankruptcy. On the other hand, alliances are only as strong as their weakest member. Thus, the failure of one member to participate fully may seriously compromise the degree of collaborative advantage an alliance is able to achieve relative to competitor alliances. The current financial problems being encountered by United Airlines, Air Canada, and American Airlines suggest that the current form of interorganisational collaboration among airlines is going to be put to the test in years to come. Much will depend on the extent to which there exists a truly relational exchange 'mode' of collaboration among participating airlines. The influence of individuals and personalities and diversity of cultural characteristics among the three predominant global airline alliances are such that in truth there is a mix of both resource dependence and relational exchange dynamics in each. What is clear is that the future effectiveness and longevity of such interorganisational forms is uncertain in that the degree to which individual airlines have fully been able to reconcile their naturally competitive and emerging collaborative tendencies has yet to be tested fully.

In conclusion, two future scenarios can be envisaged. In the first, further consolidation and concentration of the industry takes place, either through greater merger and acquisition activity or the development and/or creation of further alliance structures. In the second there is an explosion of individual competitive activity in response to the emerging threat from discount airlines and the greater price sensitivity of passengers. In view of the considerable weight of forces driving collaboration that were mentioned at the beginning of this chapter, further collaborative relational marketing alliance activities are viewed as the least destructive choice for the airline industry.

Hotel Consortia

The hotel industry is complex, fragmented, and highly competitive, and over recent decades has witnessed unparalleled growth driven principally by globalisation. Through a combination of mergers and acquisitions, and various forms of collaboration, considerable consolidation and concentration have taken place across the industry, to the extent that the ten largest chains of hotels now account for well over three million rooms. This, however, represents less than one-fifth of the total world supply, with only 26 percent of all hotel rooms being marketed under the brand names of the top 50 global companies (World Tourism Organization, 2002). The vast majority of the hotel industry remains under independent ownership, although the scale and reach of independents varies enormously. Among independent hotel operators, it is widely acknowledged that it is becoming ever more difficult to survive alone.

For independent hotels, three principal options exist to counter the growth among hotel chains and the accompanying threat to their market segment: affiliation with a major hotel group, the exploitation of specific niche markets, and membership of a consortium. The benefits of the first option, affiliation with a major hotel group, can be considerable in that the independent hotel is able to draw from the group's brand image and reputation, and benefit from their increased marketing power, managerial expertise, and ease of financing. However, lack of overall control and strategic inflexibility, a long-term contract, and payment of royalties can represent substantial drawbacks to affiliation with one of the major groups. The second option is to enter and exploit niche markets. Indeed, in spite of the growth of the large hotel chains there remains space in the marketplace for niche operators, as recently evidenced in the United Kingdom by the growth of 'boutique hotels' such as Malmaison. The third option is to join one of the growing number of consortia that currently exist in the marketplace and so pursue a collaborative marketing approach. Consortia represent collaborative arrangements between hotels designed to improve their competencies, advance their market and competitive position while retaining independence of ownership. Such arrangements usually vary in terms of the degree of commitment, control, cooperation, and organisational formality, but they are more often than not referred to as marketing consortia and represent a collaborative survival route for many independently managed hotels around the world.

Slattery, Roper, and Boer (1985) identified five distinct categories of hotel consortia, namely:

1. *Marketing and Purchasing Consortia.* These evolved from the marketing consortia that were committed to increasing membership numbers. With larger numbers they are able to negotiate reduced prices for bulk purchases and generate considerable savings for members. The prospect of such savings and reduction in purchasing costs are a considerable attraction for prospective members. Best Western Hotels and Consort Hotels are representative of this type of consortium.
2. *Referral Consortia.* In this type of consortium, hotels demonstrate a collaborative relationship with airlines whereby the hotels receive bookings through the airlines' reservation systems. This 'diagonal' collaborative form provides international exposure for hotels in travel markets; often these have proved difficult for hotels to penetrate on their own.
3. *Personnel and Training Consortia.* Rather than being driven by revenue generation or cost reduction, such consortia are driven by individual hotels pooling their resources with regard to personnel, training, and the development of skills.

4. *Reservation Systems.* These consortia provide a reservation system network for hotels throughout the range of the market. They provide a wide choice of size, location, and prices for the potential hotel customer. These consortia also provide comprehensive marketing services for its members. The largest of these reservation systems is REZsolutions, with its coverage of approximately 25,000 hotels, 80 brands, and 3 million rooms.

5. The benefits of consortia membership are many and varied. For example, benefits can be of a financial, operational, or marketing nature. Financial benefits include increased income through greater bookings, reduced administrative costs, and reduced investment exposure and risk. Operational benefits include the strengthening of operations through innovative and enhanced processes, managerial control over a horizontally integrated value-added chain, and increased bargaining leverage over suppliers and intermediaries. Marketing benefits typically include the geographic strengthening and widening of market access, shaping competition by providing new and joint market opportunities, and enhanced growth through overcoming barriers to market entry. These advantages are gained through the consortium's provision of access to networking opportunities, economies of scale, technology and distribution networks, and access to a CRS, to name but a few. As with global airline alliances, hotel consortia include elements of both resource dependency and relational exchange, although the short-term (five or fewer years) nature of many consortia agreements suggest that resource dependence is perhaps of greater significance in this instance.

In view of the mentioned benefits, it is clear that many independent hotels view consortium membership as a means of gaining authority in the marketplace through greater marketing muscle and lower purchasing costs. However, there are some costs associated with consortium membership. For example:

- *Financial costs.* These are the costs associated with supporting the coordination, administration, and marketing activity of the consortium.
- *Operational costs.* These may include the reduction in innovation and entrepreneurship of the individual hotel. Vulnerability due to mutual dependency and uncertainty may also be a problem, as can conflict, which may arise from the division of authority and decision-making power. There is always the potential for imbalances between benefits and commitment to arise, for the imposition of a standardised product and trading format, and for intermember conflicts.
- *Marketing costs.* These may include the loss of flexibility and quick response to the needs of the market, the erosion of individual com-

petitive position through the creation of a weakened bargaining position, and suppression of individual identity in order to enhance the
brand image of the consortium.

There is little doubt that the large chains will continue to threaten consortia, especially the smaller players. However, by furthering collaborative marketing strategies, of which consortia membership is a classic
example, there can be little doubt that many can survive provided they
remain adaptable. Independent consortia are moving rapidly and crea-
tively in building their core competencies by representing fine hotels and
developing and maintaining high quality standards for their constituent
properties. Small consortia are also continuing to grow, albeit at a slower
rate than the large chains. One emerging strategy for consortia wishing
to remain competitive is by forming yet further marketing partnerships
and alliances, often in related business areas such as in travel, car hire,
retailing, and online businesses (Chipkin, 2001). The scenario is one in
which the continued existence of collaborative marketing approaches is
achieved through the further expansion of the collaborative relational
marketing agenda.

Conclusion

There can be little doubt that it is becoming increasingly more difficult for
organisations to survive in competitive isolation in tourism. As illustrated
earlier, both the international airline and hotel industries are leading the
way in the adoption of collaborative relational marketing approaches in
tourism. While tourism intermediaries, tourist attractions, and tourism
destinations are also beginning to implement collaborative relational marketing strategies of their own, international airlines and independent
hotels demonstrate very clearly the benefits to be derived from collective
strength in furthering their market positions and economic longevity. For
most collaborative relational marketing strategies that have been implemented to date, however, the long-term outcomes remain unclear. This is
simply because most of these strategies have yet to come fully to fruition.
This chapter argues, however, that alternative approaches to existing
'competitive' marketing theory and practice are required for the future
development of tourism. The foundations upon which existing competitive tourism marketing theory and practice are based are set to be tested
and reconfigured in light of the drivers of collaboration discussed at the
beginning of this chapter, and which are making such a profound impact
on the world we live in and the ways in which we manage ourselves
to accommodate them. The collaborative approaches discussed in this

chapter perhaps offer a road map for the future longevity and prosperity of the global tourism industry.

References

Ashkenas, R., D. Ulrich, T. Jick, and S. Kerr. 1995. *The Boundaryless Organisation*. San Francisco: Jossey-Bass.

Beverland, M., and P. Brotherton. 2001. The Uncertain Search for Opportunities: Determinants of Strategic Partnerships. *Qualitative Market Research: An International Journal* 4(2): 88–99.

Bleeke, J., and D. Ernst. 1995. Is Your Strategic Alliance Really a Sale? *Harvard Business Review* (January–February): 97–103.

Chipkin, H. 2001. Is Independents Day at Hand? *Lodging* 26(11): 44–48.

Christopher, M., A. Payne, and D. Ballantyne. 2002. *Relationship Marketing: Creating Stakeholder Value*. Oxford: Butterworth Heinemann.

Crotts, J., and D. Wilson. 1995. An Integrated Model of Buyer-Seller Relationships in the International Travel Trade. *Progress in Tourism and Hospitality Research* 1(2): 125–140.

Donaldson, B., and T. O'Toole. 2002. *Strategic Marketing Relationships: From Strategy to Implementation*. Chichester: John Wiley & Sons.

Go, F. M., and J. Appelman. 2001. Achieving Global Competitiveness in SMEs by Building Trust in Interfirm Alliances. In S. Wahab and C. Cooper (eds.) *Tourism in the Age of Globalisation*. London: Routledge.

Gray, B. 1985. Conditions Facilitating Interorganizational Collaboration. *Human Relations* 38(10): 911–936.

———. 1989. *Collaborating: Finding Common Ground for Multiparty Problems*. San Francisco: Jossey-Bass.

Grönroos, C. 1989. Defining Marketing: A Market-Orientated Approach. *European Journal of Marketing* 23(1): 52–60.

Hanlon, P. 1999. *Global Airlines: Competition in a Transnational Industry*, 2nd ed. Oxford: Butterworth-Heinemann.

Helfert, G., T. Ritter, and A. Walter. 2002. Redefining Market Orientation from a Relational Perspective: Theoretical Considerations and Empirical Results. *European Journal of Marketing* 36(9 and 10): 1119–1139.

Huxham, C. 1993. Pursuing Collaborative Advantage. *Journal of the Operational Research Society* 44(6): 599–611.

Jamal, T. B., and D. Getz. 1995. Collaboration Theory and Community Tourism Planning. *Annals of Tourism Research* 22(1): 186–204.

Kanter, R. M. 1995. Thinking Locally in the Global Economy. *Harvard Business Review* (September/October): 151–160.

Morgan, R. M., and S. D. Hunt. 1994. The Commitment-Trust Theory of Relationship Marketing. *Journal of Marketing* 58(3): 20–38.

Morrish, S. C., and R. T. Hamilton. 2002. Airline Alliances—Who Benefits? *Journal of Air Transport Management* 8(6): 401–407.

Oum, T. H., and J. H. Park. 1997. Airline Alliances: Current Status, Policy Issues, and Future Directions. *Journal of Air Transport Management* 3(3): 133–144.

Palmer, A., and D. Bejou. 1995. Tourism Destination Marketing Alliances. *Annals of Tourism Research* 22(3): 616–629.

Porter, M. 1980. *Competitive Strategy.* New York: Free Press.

Slattery, P., A. Roper, and A. Boer. 1985. Hotel Consortia: Their Activities, Structure and Growth. *Service Industries Journal* 5(2): 192–199.

Telfer, D. J. 2000. Tastes of Niagra: Building Strategic Alliances Between Tourism and Agriculture. In *Global Alliances in Tourism and Hospitality Management.* eds. J. C. Crotts, D. Buhalis, and R. March. New York: The Haworth Hospitality Press.

Terpstra, V., and B. Simonin. 1993. Strategic Alliances in the Triad: An Exploratory Study. *Journal of International Marketing* 1(1): 4–25.

Wahab, S., and C. Cooper. 2001. *Tourism in the Age of Globalisation.* London: Routledge.

World Tourism Organization. 2002. *Tourism in the Age of Alliances, Mergers and Acquisitions.* Madrid: the World Tourism Organization.

Part Two

Results and Residuals: The Issue of Impacts

Introduction

Throughout recorded history, tourism has impacted in some way everything and everyone that it touched. Ideally, these impacts should have been positive, both in terms of benefits to destination areas and their residents. These positive impacts should include results such as improvements in local economic conditions, social and cultural understanding and protected environmental resources. In theory, the benefits of tourism should produce benefits far in excess of their costs.

Initial studies of tourism impacts dealt mainly with economic aspects since they were more easily quantifiable and measurable. In addition, it was presumed that the income derived from tourism could make up for any negative consequences of tourism. However, over-emphasis on economic benefits have often led to adverse physical and social consequences.

Due to the rising concern for the environment, the concept of 'sustainable tourism development' (defined as the protection and conservation of an area's ecology in order to maintain its useful life over a long period of time) has emerged. **Archer, Cooper** and **Ruhanen** (Chapter 5) review the key elements of the positive and negative impacts of tourism, including economic, political, socio-cultural, environmental and ecological impacts.

Careful planning and management, including the understanding of an area's carrying capacity is essential in order to avoid exploitation and potential destruction of physical and personal resources. The authors conclude that what is needed to avoid the negative impacts of tourism is a shift away from short term to longer-term thinking and planning, and a recognition that exploitation of places and people is not only unethical but unprofitable (in the long run) as well.

Increasingly, both politicians and planners are becoming aware of the longer-term social, economic and environmental consequences of excessive and poorly planned tourism expansion. The authors suggest that planning for the impacts of tourism development requires a firm understanding and acceptance of the respective responsibilities of the public and private sectors as well as the communities where such development is to take place.

The issue of tourist-resident impacts is extended by **Pearce** (Chapter 6) who describes and discusses the social interaction level between travelers, their hosts, other travelers and travelers themselves in various roles and moods.

The experience of being a pleasure traveler often poses a number of unexpected relationship challenges that may arise in many guises for any individual. Travel difficulties as well as rewards might include dealing with oneself or with one's familiar travelling companions, interaction with fellow travelers who are strangers, or attempting to communicate with local residents across cultural divides. The major part of the chapter is given to travellers' experiences with other travelers since this element is the least well described in the existing literature.

The author states that the construction and development of conceptual schemes in order to better understand and interpret the relationships in the tourist experience is needed. He suggests that there are a number of issues to be considered in the next phase of the relationship: conceptualizing tourist relationships as extensions of the ingroup-outgroup approach; concept development of threshold and space limitations for tourist settings; innovative representation and performance accounts, and; theories combining social exchange and representation approaches. What is known however, is that relationships are pivotal and should be a primary goal in tourism management.

The next chapter in this section deals with the elusive character of the term, 'alternative tourism' and its impact. **Macleod** (Chapter 7) suggests that as a concept, alternative tourism is far too broad, it is fundamentally problematic, and is subject to heavily emotional responses. Further, he contends that the content of the term is grossly overstretched and as a result, it is inadequate, hazy and subject to parody. Such terms as 'ecotourism, green tourism, adventure tourism, ethnic tourism' and others have helped fragment the concept of alternative tourism into disparate and often meaningless lexicon subsets.

Defining the concept of alternative tourism is important because of the relationship to basic problems of human society including environmental destruction, inequalities of wealth and irresponsible development. In an ethnographic case study, the author concludes that alternative tourism is largely a contextual creation in terms of space and time, and that in reality, it is a reflection of society's contemporary attitudes and value system.

In terms of impacts, the prevailing values of society are focused predominately on economic impacts of tourism development, thereby often concentrating solely on monetary data and other financial information. Such economic preoccupation neglects often more important factors such as socio-cultural, psychological and environmental factors. Alternative tourism must be used to strengthen linkages between the tourism industry and other forms of local community activity.

The rather uneasy relationship between contemporary western tourism development and native peoples is explored by **Mercer** (Chapter 8). His examination of the Aboriginal, 'outback' population of northern and central Australia focuses on the social appropriateness of tourism development from the native Aboriginal viewpoint. The main focus of the chapter is the inseparability of questions surrounding tourism development and broader social justice issues concerning Aboriginal rights. Two case studies dealing with the concepts of control and choice are explored. Control relates to whether native populations control their own destinies when negotiating decisions regarding tourism development on their land.

Choice relates to their having the freedom to choose to negotiate, or simply refuse to do so.

The central problem addressed revolves around the question of whether or not contemporary tourism development in Australia beyond major urban centers is economically beneficial as well as socially and culturally appropriate from an Aboriginal viewpoint. Growing Aboriginal militancy related to what they viewed as their basic rights had come up against the western practice of eminent domain, i.e., government gaining control of individual (or group) owned land 'for the good of the many,' through a legal process often including condemnation. This practice, together with other denials of land ownership led to what some writers termed, 'the invasion and theft of the Aboriginal nation.' However, in recent years, through a combination of land grants and successful native title claims, the Aboriginal-owned land base has been progressively expanding, now comprising approximately eighteen percent of Australia.

The key problem is related to the principle of equity or fairness, and how today, native peoples including Aboriginals can achieve the most benefits derived from tourism without being overrun and overwhelmed by the excesses that tourism itself often causes.

5 The positive and negative impacts of tourism

Brian Archer, Chris Cooper, and Lisa Ruhanen

Introduction

> In the 1980s, individuals questioned whether tourism was a blessing or blight, but the issue is now essentially academic, given the value of tourism as the world's largest industry and its role as a global employer and customer.
>
> —Smith, 2001

The essence of this quote by Valene Smith is that the activity of tourism creates impacts and consequences; we cannot prevent these, but need to plan and manage to minimize the negative impacts and accentuate the positive impacts of tourism. These impacts occur because tourism, both international and domestic, brings about an intermingling of people from diverse social and cultural backgrounds, and also a considerable spatial redistribution of spending power, which has a significant impact on the economy of the destination. Early work on the impact of tourism on destinations focused primarily on economic aspects. This was not only because such impacts are more readily quantifiable and measurable, but also there was a pervading climate of optimism that these studies would show that tourism was of net economic benefit to host destinations. In many cases, this was indeed true. Yet tourism, by its very nature, is attracted to unique and fragile environments and societies and it became apparent that in some cases the economic benefits of tourism may be offset by adverse and previously unmeasured environmental and social consequences.

The benefits and costs of tourism accrue to two quite distinct groups of people. On the one hand, the visitors themselves receive benefits and

incur costs in taking holidays. On the other hand, the resident populations of the host region benefit from tourism (not only financially) but at
the same time incur costs of various types. Because it is not possible to
deal adequately with both aspects within the limited scope of this single
chapter, attention will be devoted to the positive and negative effects of
tourism from the point of view of the host country or region.

The general issues central to any discussion of the positive and negative impacts of tourism must include notions of carrying capacity and also
of how impacts can be assessed. Carrying capacity is a relatively straightforward concept—in simple terms it refers to a point beyond which
further levels of visitation or development would lead to an unacceptable
deterioration in the physical environment and of the visitor's experience
(Getz, 1983; O'Reilly, 1986; McCool and Lime, 2001). Commentators point
out that operationalising capacity is difficult. Buckley (1999), for example,
mounts a scathing attack on the concept and its utility, stating that
carrying capacity is 'ultimately meaningless.' This is echoed by McCool
and Lime (2001) who state that 'the concept of a tourism and recreation
carrying capacity maintains an illusion of control when it is a seductive
fiction, a social trap, or policy myth.' Yet, despite this debate and discussion in the literature, the basic conceptual framework of carrying capacity remains the same (Saveriades, 2000), and however it is approached,
there is no doubt that any consideration of the impact of tourism must
recognise the pivotal role that carrying capacity plays by intervening in
the relationship between visitor and resource.

Effectively, the impact made by tourism depends on both the volume
and profile characteristics of the tourists (including their length of stay,
activity, mode of transport, and travel arrangement). In this respect, a
number of authors have attempted to classify tourists according to their
impact on the destinations (see, for example, Smith, 1977). The character
of the resource (including its natural features, level of development, political and social structure) is equally important because it determines the
degree of its robustness to tourism and tourism development (Mathieson
and Wall, 1982).

A range of variables, therefore, needs to be taken into account in any
determination of the impact of tourism. Yet determining such impacts also
raises a number of issues. In economics, impact methodology has a long
pedigree, but the measurement of environmental and social impacts has
not progressed anywhere near as far. Indeed, in all forms of impact analysis, it is important to distinguish tourism-induced events from other
agents of change, ensure that secondary and tertiary effects are considered, and have a view as to what the situation was before tourism intervened. All of these points are problematic and the tendency is therefore
to simplify and narrow the scope of investigation to 'contain' the research
into a manageable outcome (Mathieson and Wall, 1982).

In part, the difficulty of quantifying the environmental and social impacts of tourism has delayed the development of impact methodologies. But the rising tide of environmentalism has caught up with tourism and has lent support to the view that in some cases the economic benefits of tourism are more than outweighed by the environmental and social costs of tourism. Concepts such as 'sustainable tourism development' and 'the responsible consumption of tourism' are seen by many as the answer, along with the enhanced planning and management of tourism. These issues are discussed later in this chapter. Nonetheless, the issue of management is closely related to the notion of carrying capacity because a destination can be 'managed' to take any number of visitors. Simply 'hardening' the environment and managing the visitor can accommodate large volumes without an unacceptable decline in the environment or the experience. McCool and Lime (2001) reconceptualise carrying capacity along these lines, suggesting that managers should be looking at the particular conditions that are desired or appropriate at a destination to support recreation and tourism activity—'sustaining these conditions is at the heart of concerns over impacts, saturation and carrying capacities.' The question must therefore be asked, managing and sustaining these conditions for whom? In pluralistic societies, the conflicts and tensions between the stakeholders in tourism—tourists, developers, planners, environmentalists, and communities—will in the end determine levels of tourist development. Butler (1999) then raises the question as to how we judge the notion of the 'satisfaction' of these various stakeholders as one of the key research questions for sustainable tourism. After all, tourism takes place within political and social contexts of power, relationships, and governance. It is, however, heartening that the result of this discussion is a continued pressure for sustainable tourism amongst the various groups in society and that this is changing the perceived balance between the positive and negative effects of tourism. This balance has also been influenced by the events of the early years of the twenty-first century including the terrorist attacks on New York and the bombings in Bali. It could be said that these 'shocks' to the tourism system have acted to reduce the impacts of tourism in some parts of the world because levels of international travel have reduced and tourists have switched to domestic travel or opted for destinations that are perceived as 'safe.'

Economic Effects

The economic advantages and disadvantages of tourism have been extensively documented (see, for example, Bryden, 1973; Archer, 1977; Eadington and Redman, 1991; Tribe, 1999; Tisdell, 2000; and Vogel, 2001).

The Economic Impact of Tourism

International tourism is an invisible export in that it creates a flow of foreign currency into the economy of a destination country, thereby contributing directly to the current account of the balance of payments. Like other export industries, this inflow of revenue creates business turnover, household income, employment, and government revenue.

However, the generation process does not stop at this point. Some portion of the money received by the business establishments, individuals, and government agencies is respent within the destination economy, thereby creating further rounds of economic activity. These secondary effects can in total considerably exceed in magnitude the initial direct effects. Indeed any study purporting to show the economic impact made by tourism must attempt to measure the overall effect made by the successive rounds of economic activity generated by the initial expenditure. The process has been documented with attention drawn to the strengths, weaknesses, and limitations of the various approaches (see, for example, Archer and Fletcher, 1991).

Domestic tourism has somewhat similar economic effects on the host regions of a country. Whereas, however, international tourism brings a flow of foreign currency into a country, domestic tourism redistributes currency spatially within the boundaries of a country. From the point of view of a tourist region within a country, however, domestic tourism is a form of invisible export. Money earned in other regions is spent within the host region creating additional business revenue, income, jobs, and revenue to local government. The process of secondary revenue, income, and employment generation within the host region is then the same as for a national economy. The principal difference during these secondary stages, however, is that individual regions within a country are usually less economically self-contained, and, hence, a far greater proportion of the money is likely to leak out of the regional system into other regions. The secondary effects in individual regions are far lower in magnitude than for the national economy as a whole.

Moreover, tourism seems to be more effective than other industries in generating employment and income in the less developed, often peripheral, regions of a country where alternative opportunities for development are more limited. Indeed, it is in these areas that tourism can make its most significant impact. In such places many of the local people are subsistence farmers or fishermen, and if they become involved in the tourism industry their household incomes increase by a very large amount. The growth of tourism in such areas may provide also a monetary incentive for the continuance of many local crafts, whereas the tourist hotels may create a market for local produce. Indeed, the introduction of a tourism industry into such areas can have a proportionally greater effect on the welfare of the resident population than the same amount of tourism might have on the more developed parts of the same country.

The development of tourism, especially in a previously under-developed part of a country, requires the existence of an infrastructure, as well as hotel accommodation and other facilities specific to tourism. In many cases these utilities are economically indivisible in the sense that, in providing them for the tourism industry, they at the same time become available for the use of local people. Thus, in many countries, highways and airfields, constructed primarily to cater for tourism, now provide an access to wider markets for many locally produced goods. Unfortunately, in many cases the local people still receive little direct benefit from these developments. This in essence is a problem of both physical and economic distribution (i.e., of the extent to which, and the speed at which, these facilities should be made more generally available).

As tourism continues to grow in a region, it makes increasing demands on the scarce resources of that area. Land in particular is required and in consequence land prices rise. Farmers and other local landowners are encouraged to sell, with the result that, although they may obtain short-term gains, they are left landless with only low paid work available. Indeed much of the benefit from higher land prices may accrue to specu-lators who buy land from the previous owners before it has been sched-uled for development. These problems can be overcome, however, if either the land is acquired at an early stage by the government for a fair, market price or if the land is rented rather than sold to the developers. Market forces do not necessarily ensure that development keeps pace with demand. There is a need for realistic planning and the effective enforce-ment of planning regulations to reduce possible conflicts of interest and, where appropriate, to conserve unique and unusual features for the enjoy-ment of future generations of visitors and residents alike. This is a lesson that has been learned rather late in many developed countries.

Superficially at least the economic 'benefits' of tourism seem self-evident. Yet in recent years several writers have expressed reservations about the nature and size of the benefits attributable to tourism and have become increasingly skeptical about the potentialities of tourism as a tool for development and growth and as a means of maximizing the welfare of the indigenous population. For example, Tosun, Timothy, and Öztürk (2003) found that although tourism as an economic development strategy in Turkey has increased the rate of economic development, it has also created inequalities between Turkish regions and social classes. In partic-ular this was caused by the approach of offering economic incentives for mass coastal tourism developments at the expense of rural areas. The problem is essentially one of resource allocation and of whether or not the development of a tourism industry offers the optimum usage of the resources available—in other words an assessment of the costs and benefits of tourism development vis-à-vis alternatives.

Cost-Benefit Analysis

In cost-benefit terms, the economic benefits gained by a recipient country from tourism have been outlined previously. Again, these benefits have to be offset against the economic costs involved. Apart from the purchase of import requirements, the earnings of expatriate workers, and the overseas expenses incurred by the foreign companies concerned during both the construction and operating phases of the development, none of which benefits the resident population, the country itself incurs considerable costs internally. The real cost to society of employing resources and factors of production in any one sector, including the construction and operation of hotels and other associated tourism services, is the value of the output that could have been obtained from their use in other sectors of the economy (Archer, 1996). Because capital and skilled labor are rarely, if ever, abundant in such countries, the development of a tourism industry requires some of these scarce resources to be diverted from their alternative uses. Admittedly, some factors of production might otherwise be unemployed, in which case their use in tourism involves no real cost to society, but in most cases the opportunity cost incurred is the value of the production lost in other sectors.

Whether or not tourism creates greater net benefits to society than other forms of development depends primarily on the nature of the country's economy and what alternative forms of development are practicable. Also, in the interests of diversification, it is sometimes considered desirable to promote several forms of development even though one or more of these may offer relatively lower net benefits.

Issues Requiring Further Research

Despite the plethora of economic analyses undertaken during the last 25 years, economists have not displayed any noticeable propensity to work jointly with specialists from other disciplines in multidisciplinary teams. Their contribution to such work has normally consisted of analyses undertaken in parallel but not jointly with other specialists. There is a need for research in the following areas:

- A more balanced view of the economic effects of tourism demands a deeper understanding of the human issues surrounding the impact made by tourism. This requires joint work by economists, sociologists, political scientists, and others. In particular, economists should work

more closely with sociologists in analysing and quantifying the social costs and benefits of tourism.
- The long-term advantages and disadvantages of tourism can be better understood if economists work more closely with environmentalists as well as specialists in the various humanities.
- The economic analysis of tourism will be improved if more economists apply their efforts to improving the methodology of existing techniques rather than merely replicating them in a succession of case studies. Wagner (1997), for example, employs a social accounting matrix to examine the economic impact of tourism on a Brazilian ecosystem. There is an especial danger that replication of economic impact studies in isolation will simply fuel the call for development in destinations and omit considerations of other costs.

In addition to the economic costs and benefits already mentioned, tourism also imposes political, cultural, social, moral, and environmental changes on the host country. The fact that such costs are rarely quantifiable in money terms has prevented more all-embracing considerations of the impact of tourism on destinations. However, techniques are being developed to allow comparison across impacts utilizing a standard set of variables. For example, Lindberg and Johnson (1997) have developed a framework for measuring social impacts in a metric consistent with economic impacts using contingent valuation to provide a cost-benefit framework.

Political Effects

The Political Costs and Benefits of Tourism

Whereas the virtues of international tourism have been extolled as a major force for peace and understanding between nations (World Tourism Organization, 1980; 1982; Litvin, 1998; Leitner, 1999), the reality is often far removed from this utopian image. Long-haul travel between developed and developing countries is increasing annually and is bringing into direct contact with each other people from widely different backgrounds and with very contrasting lifestyles and levels of income. Where these disparities are very great, the political as well as the sociocultural consequences may be severe.

In extreme cases international tourism has imposed a form of 'neo-colonial' type development on emerging nations (Hall, 1994; Hall and Jenkins, 1995). Quite simply, this neo-colonialism takes power from the local and regional levels and concentrates it into the hands of multinational companies. These companies will negotiate only at the national level and expect any 'problems' to be solved by national governments, otherwise investment will be withdrawn. At the operational level, the higher paid, more 'respectable' posts in hotels and other establishments are sometimes occupied by expatriates who possess the necessary expertise and experience. Although the lower paid, more menial jobs are frequently reserved for the indigenous population, it is possible that such apparent discrimination can foster resentment and can sour international relationships. In extreme cases such development can even inhibit the growth of a national consciousness in a newly dependent country.

Domestic tourism, on the other hand, can act as an integrating force strengthening national sentiment. Peoples in outlying areas are traditionally more preoccupied with local village affairs and, in consequence, sometimes prove easy prey to separatist agitators. If, by travel to other parts of the same country, such people can begin to experience pride in their national heritage, a sense of national unity may help to prevent regional fragmentation.

In the more developed countries, visits to national historical monuments, stately homes, and ancient battlefields form a significant motivation for domestic travel, and similar developments are already taking place in other parts of the world. In many developing countries, students and groups of schoolchildren travel to other regions of their homelands, and such movements of people can do much in the long run to strengthen the political unity of a country. Provided that the individual characteristics and identities of the various regions are not submerged and lost, such travel can benefit both tourists and residents alike.

Unfortunately, contact between peoples of different backgrounds is not always beneficial and may in some cases generate additional cultural, social, and moral stresses. Although the mixing of people from different regions of a country can produce a better understanding of each other's way of life and a better appreciation of problems specific to particular regions, it can at the same time create misunderstandings and even distrust.

Issues Requiring Further Research

So far political scientists have contributed relatively little to the analysis of tourism, and most of the work in this field has been concerned with the situation in particular countries. Noteworthy exceptions include books by Hall (1994), Hall and Jenkins (1995), Hall (2000), and Kerr (2003) and a paper by Mathews and Richter (1991). The books provide a framework for the examination of tourism and politics/policy making, whereas the paper by Mathews and Richter reviews the efforts made by political scientists to apply their special disciplines to the study of tourism. The authors examine first the ways in which many important aspects of tourism involve some of the central concepts of political science and, second, the contribution that political science can make to the study of tourism. Two major issues in tourism can be addressed by political scientists.

1. A fuller understanding of the human impact of tourism on destination areas can be achieved only by a much greater integration of the work of political scientists with specialists in other disciplines and with tourism practitioners.

2. Knowledge of the impact of tourism on many aspects of human life and organization can be improved if more political scientists are willing to use their expertise to study tourism as an independent variable affecting areas of concern in public administration, comparative politics, political theory, international relations, and national politics (Richter, 1983). Specific work is needed in a variety of areas but particularly welcome would be:

   • Studies examining the influence of tourism on the roots of power in communities and the implications for community-based investment and the integration of tourism into the community. A major contribution here would be in terms of examining the many political interests involved in the development of tourism and the role of conflict resolution and consensus models (Jamal and Getz, 1995);
   • Work examining the stage of destination life cycle at which community involvement is most appropriate, and the stages at which communities are most vulnerable to external political and commercial decision making; and
   • Further examination of policy impact analysis within a tourism and event context (Whitford, 2003).

Sociocultural Effects

Although political effects are influential, it is difficult to disentangle them from the social and cultural effects of tourism. For example, Tsartas (2003) examines the influence of local social structures, particularly the family, on both tourism development and policy in the Greek islands and coastal areas. These social influences on policy and planning have led to unplanned and rapid tourism development, partly driven by the pressures of mass tourism and the downgrading of agriculture as an economic sector.

Some Sociocultural Costs and Benefits

Wide cultural differences occur between different countries and some-times between different regions within the same country. Indeed the exis-tence of such differences may be one of the principal stimulants of a tourism industry. In some developing countries such traditional cultural behaviour patterns of particular groups of people form one focus of the tourism industry (Butler and Hinch, 1996). Sometimes, however, differ-ences in physical appearance and, perhaps more importantly, differences in cultural behaviour between visitors and residents, are so great that mutual understanding is replaced by antipathy.

The problem is exacerbated because tourists are, by definition, strangers in the destination. Their dress codes and patterns of behaviour are dif-ferent to the residents and, often, different from those that the tourist would display at home; inhibitions are shed and the consequent problems of prostitution, drugs, gambling, and sometimes vandalism ensue. As strangers, tourists are also vulnerable and fall victim to robbery and crimes perpetrated by the local community who may see these activities as a way to 'redress the balance.' Lindberg, Andersson, and Dellaert (2001) chart the social gains and losses to residential populations as a result of tourism stating that the attitudes of residents are heterogeneous, with this very diversity creating a challenge to decision makers who try to reach consensus. This comes down to recognising that the values of residents, rather than straight demographics, may explain antecedents of opinions on tourism (Williams and Lawson, 2001).

When the cultural distinctions between the residents and tourists from more prosperous countries and regions are strongly marked, local culture and customs may be exploited to satisfy the visitor, sometimes at the expense of local pride and dignity. Here the issue of staged authenticity is an important one where the host destination is able to convince tourists that festivals and activities in the 'front region' of the destination (e.g., public areas such as hotel lobbies or restaurants are authentic and thus they protect the real 'back region', i.e., residents' homes and areas where life continues) (McCannell, 1973; Ingles, 2002). Tourists are increasingly motivated by a quest for authenticity, and one of the problems of 'alter-native tourism' is that the tourists are encouraged to penetrate the 'back region.' With good management and planning, however, tourism can provide an impetus for the preservation of ancient cultures, but too often the local way of life degenerates into a commercially organized effigy of its former self. The traditional dances and the skilled craftwork give way to cheap imitations to satisfy the needs of the visitor and to obtain money with the least possible effort. Here, Medina (2003) recounts that Mayan indigenous peoples even access new channels (such as archaeologists) to research and revive their traditional practices. In some cases this is merely an initial response and, later, tourism can stimulate high quality revivals of crafts in particular. Nonetheless, there is a constant tension in countries wishing to be part of the global tourism movement but also to retain their cultural authenticity (Brunet, et al., 2001).

In primitive and isolated areas, the arrival of too many visitors can even cause local people to leave their settlements and move to new areas where they can remain undisturbed. To combat this in vulnerable areas such as North American Indian reservations, 'governing rules' for visitors have been formulated. In more developed areas, in extreme cases, tourism has disrupted completely the way of life of the local people. The institution of the national park system in some parts of Africa, although justifiable on the grounds of wildlife conservation and tourism, has in some cases seriously affected the hunting and nomadic existence of the local people. The problem is not confined, however, to developing countries. In Canada, for example, the creation of parks of outdoor recreation and domestic tourism at Forillon and Gros Morne necessitated the eviction of previous residents and in consequence aroused considerable local opposition.

Insufficient research has been carried out so far to disentangle the social and cultural side effects of tourism development. Where the cultural and socioeconomic backgrounds of the tourists are very different from those of the local population, the results of their intermingling may be favourable but it can be explosive. The so-called demonstration effect of prosperity amid poverty may create a desire among local people to work harder or to achieve higher levels of education in order to emulate the way of life of the tourists. On the other hand, in many cases the inability of the local people to achieve the same level of affluence may create a sense of deprivation and frustration, which may find an outlet in hostility and even aggression.

The merit of social intercourse between tourists and the indigenous population as a means toward fostering better understanding and goodwill between nations has been extolled as a major social benefit obtained from tourism. Although this is true in many cases, particularly in those countries where tourists are still comparatively rare, it is certainly not true in many countries where tourists' tastes and habits have proved offensive to particular sectors of the local population. Because of factors such as these, some writers have rejected the term 'demonstration effect' and substituted the term 'confrontation effect.'

Perhaps the most significant and one of the least desirable by-products of this confrontation is the effect on the moral standards of the local people. In extreme cases, crime, prostitution, gambling, and drug traffic may be imported into the holiday areas from other regions. Many of the social conventions and constraints imposed on tourists in their home areas are absent when they visit another region, and in consequence their moral behaviour can deteriorate without undue censure. As a result, many local people find that by catering to the several needs of their visitors they themselves can achieve a relatively high level of prosperity. Although the credit or blame for developments such as red light districts can be attributed more to the growth of international tourism than to an increase in domestic tourism, the latter must bear its share of responsibility.

A critical issue here is the form of contact between host and guest. In the 'enclave' tourism model, so berated by proponents of 'alternative forms of tourism,' contacts are controlled and minimal, mainly confined to 'culture brokers' who speak the language of both host and guest and who understand both cultures. It is when the tourist penetrates into the daily lives and homes of the hosts, the back region, that real exposure of cultural and social differences between the two groups emerge, and problems may occur.

Tourists have been blamed for assisting the spread of sexually transmitted diseases and AIDS in many countries, but their contribution is probably very small in relation to the part played by the local population. Indeed, visitors themselves do not always emerge unscathed from their interaction with the local community (Petty, 1989; Cliff and Grabowski, 1997; Wilks and Page, 2003). Poor hygienic conditions in many tourist resorts create suitable conditions for the spread of various intestinal diseases, typhoid, cholera, and hepatitis. Lack of forethought and ignorance result in cases of severe sunstroke and skin cancer. Inappropriate precautions result in infection by the AIDS virus, which already affects a significant percentage of the population of some countries in Africa. Governments, tour operators, airlines, and resort operators have a duty to visitors and residents alike to provide adequate information to ensure that these risks are known and minimized.

Many of the other sociocultural problems associated with tourism are related to the degree of intensity of tourism development. Although difficult to measure, there is a relationship between tourism density and the growth of local resentment toward tourism. The flow of tourists into a region increases the densities at which people live and overcrowds the facilities that tourists share with the local population. Overcrowding reduces the value of the holiday experience and creates additional strain for the resident population.

In extreme cases local people may be debarred from enjoying the natural facilities of their own country or region. Along part of the Mediterranean, for example, almost half of the coastline has been acquired by hotels for the sole use of their visitors, and in consequence the local public is denied easy access.

Issues Requiring Further Research

The literature on the sociocultural effects of tourism is quite extensive, although the majority of the contributions are concerned with specific cases in particular countries. Some of the more general contributions have been made by Dogan (1989), Dann and Cohen (1991), Smith and Brent (2001), and Reisinger and Turner (2003).

Dogan (1989) provides an interesting analysis in which he shows how the reactions of the host community to the influx of tourists and the changes that tourism brings has been quite diverse, ranging from an active resistance to the complete acceptance and even adoption of the tourists' culture patterns. He shows how the choice of strategies, deliberate or otherwise, to cope with the changes depends on both the nature of the sociocultural characteristics of the host community and the magnitude of the changes themselves. His conclusion is that even in the case of a previously homogenous community that adopts a particular response to tourism, the community will itself become diversified and groups will emerge within the community exhibiting very different responses to tourism developments.

Dann and Cohen are concerned with the contribution that the discipline of sociology can make to the understanding of the tourism phenomenon. Here, different perspectives on tourism have been adopted by sociologists, and in consequence this has lead to the emergence of a variety of approaches. Dann and Cohen believe that '. . . some of the best work in tourism has been eclectic, linking elements of one perspective with those of another, rather than opting for an exclusive point of view.'

Two major issues require the attention of sociologists.

1. There is a need for many more multidisciplinary studies where sociologists can contribute the insights of their discipline to the study of particular aspects of the tourism phenomenon or to the analysis of tourism in specific countries and regions. Here there is a clear need for work to examine the social-carrying capacity of destinations; work that must be closely linked to community-based models of tourism planning and the 'limits of acceptable change' (Saveriades, 2000). Mitchell and Reid (2001) stress the need for research into mechanisms of community integration into the planning process. Indeed, although much is written on why community empowerment is important, there is much less written on how to do it.

2. The quantification of the socioeconomic costs and benefits of tourism requires the joint efforts of sociologists and economists. At present this work is being carried out almost entirely by economists, who are not always in the best position to identify all of the phenomena requiring quantification or the appropriate weightings to apply to each (Lindberg and Johnson, 1997).

Environmental and Ecological Effects

The Environmental and Ecological Costs and Benefits of Tourism

The extent and nature of the environmental and ecological damage done by tourists is related to the magnitude of the development and the volume of visitors, the concentration of usage both spatially and temporally, the nature of the environment in question, and the nature of the planning and management practices adopted before and after development takes place. Excessive and badly planned tourism development affects the physical environment of destinations. In many areas the uncontrolled commercial exploitation of tourism has produced unsightly hotels of alien design that intrude into the surrounding cultural and scenic environment. In such cases the architectural design has been planned to meet the supposed wishes of the visitor rather than to blend into the local environment. The effects, moreover, are not solely scenic, because the waste and sewage from these developments are often discharged in an unprocessed form and pollute the rivers and seas of the holiday areas.

Poor and ill-conceived forms of tourism development also destroy irreplaceable natural environments, the true and long-term benefits of which may not have been properly evaluated. Thus, for example, marshlands and mangrove swamps, which provide both outlets for flood control and also the basic ingredients for local fishing industries, have been drained to create tourist marinas. Water resources needed by local farmers and villages have been diverted for the use of tourist hotels and golf courses, and, in some mountainous areas, forests have been depleted to create ski slopes with much resultant soil erosion, flooding, and mud slips causing substantial loss of life and damage to property.

Furthermore, the tourists themselves are often guilty of helping to destroy the surrounding environment—the more attractive a site, then the more popular it becomes and the more likely it is that it will be degraded by heavy visitation (Hillery, et al., 2001). In many areas tourists, sometimes ignorantly, sometimes deliberately, damage crops and farm equipment, frighten farm animals, and bestrew large quantities of garbage over the countryside. From one mountain alone in Great Britain during the summer months, almost a ton of litter a day (mainly discarded lunch wrappings) is brought down from the summit, whereas from the New Forest in Southern England approximately 25,000 empty bottles are retrieved each year. In other areas wildlife has been severely disturbed, coral reefs have been despoiled, and alien forms of plant life have been introduced into delicate ecosystems on the shoes and clothing of visitors.

Lest the picture appear too bleak, it should be remembered that tourism, both domestic and international, is at the same time a positive force in helping to conserve the environment of the holiday regions. In the twenty-first century, for example, new forms if tourism, such as 'clean up' tourism, are combating these problems, leaving the destination in a better environmental condition than they found it—a form of 'enhanced sustainability.' Many of the disadvantages mentioned previously can be offset by high quality planning, design and management, and by educating tourists to appreciate the environment. Tourists are attracted to areas of high scenic beauty, regions of historical and architectural interest, and areas with abundant and interesting wildlife. Some of the money spent by tourists in the region, in particular the revenue received from entry fees, can be used to conserve and improve the natural and manmade heritage (as is the case for example in the Kenyan game reserves), whereas tourism may also provide a use for otherwise redundant historic buildings.

Environmental Issues

There is obviously a need for research to examine the environmental impact of tourism, particularly in regions and environments that have been neglected in past work. Holden (2000), for example, states that research on the environmental impacts of tourism is still 'relatively immature and a true multidisciplinary approach to investigation has yet to be developed.' Butler (2000) provides a list of the research priorities in this area including:

- A need to better understand the elements that comprise environmental attractiveness and quality;
- Integration of research in the physical sciences into tourism planning and management, particularly in terms of the causes of impacts rather than their effects; and
- Assessment of 'the real impacts of tourism and the level of sustainability achieved requires in-depth longitudinal research and environmental, economic and social auditing.' This demands long-term funding commitments.

Taking the last point, environmental indicators should be developed for use in cost-benefit analysis and also to allow environmental standards to be devised at destinations to assist consumers in their choice. Manning (1999) has devised indicators of tourism sustainability to act as an early warning system and identify emerging problems. Already, the World Tourism Organization has embraced this concept and published work in the field.

It is therefore implicit in this trend that planning for tourism will be undertaken. Here the 'planning in' of the environmental, social, and cultural context of tourism at the destination (in terms of using local architectural styles, etc.) is vital. In other words, the relationship between tourism and the environment is mediated by planning and management. These tourism planning and management techniques exist and are well tried in many areas. What is necessary is for the barriers to planning and management, which exist in many areas, to be removed to allow the existing techniques to be applied effectively. This requires that an agency is willing to implement these approaches (Butler, 2000), whereas planners must also understand the role of stakeholders in operational planning and management approaches to sustainable tourism (Hardy and Beeton, 2001). On this point, Nepal (2000) stresses the need for national level policy and management issues for protection of valuable sites integrating scientific research and forging partnerships between local people, the industry, and tourism professionals. A major stumbling block here is the privatization of many public tourist agencies and the deregulation of planning in some western nations. A future issue to consider will be the development of new financing models to ensure continuity of funding for privatized agencies that perform a regulatory role.

A critical issue for the foreseeable future, therefore, will be the relationship of tourism and the environment. The environment has moved into centre stage in the debate, as evidenced by the discussion on tourism at both the 1992 Rio de Janeiro Earth Summit and the 2002 Johannesburg World Summit on Sustainable Development. Here, although the excesses of tourism development have been identified, the alliance of tourism with environmentalists to sensitize tourists to the issues is also recognised. It is this issue that forms the next section of the chapter.

Sustainable Development and Responsible Consumption of Tourism

This chapter has reviewed the key elements of the positive and negative impacts of tourism. As mentioned in the introduction, it is only in recent years that the negative 'downstream' effects of tourism on the environments, societies, and vulnerable economies have been set more fully against the tangible economic gains. Add to this the rise of environmentalism and 'green' consciousness in the mid to late 1980s, and the stage was set for a reassessment of the role and value of tourism. In part, this is also a reflection of the growing maturity of both the tourist as consumer and the tourism sector itself. In the early decades of mass tourism, short-term perspectives prevailed as the industry and public agencies attempted to cope with burgeoning demand. In the 1980s, 1990s, and early years of the twenty-first century, growth rates slowed and tourists began questioning some of the excesses of tourism development. In response, longer planning horizons are being considered and new forms of tourism advocated as industry and governments slipstream behind public opinion and media attention given to these issues.

One of the most valuable results of this reassessment has been the belated discovery of the relevance of the sustainable development concept to tourism (see, for example, Pigram, 1990; Farrell and Runyan, 1991; Bramwell and Lane, 1999; and Holden, 2000). As with many service industries, some of the most important ideas and innovations come from outside the industry or the subject area. The concept of sustainable development has a long pedigree in the field of resource management and has, at last, become an acceptable term in tourism. It has also become a debated term with definitional arguments over its meaning and operationalisation, particularly as the meaning of sustainability increasingly implies a 'triple bottom line' approach (Hardy, Beeton, and Pearson, 2002). The oft quoted Brundtland Report defines sustainability simply as 'meeting the needs of the present without compromising the ability of future generations to meet their own needs' (World Commission on Environment and Development, 1987). The concept of sustainability is central to the reassessment of the role of tourism in society. It demands a long-term view of economic activity, questions the imperative of continued economic growth, and ensures that consumption of tourism does not exceed the ability of a host destination to provide for future tourists. In other words, it represents a trade off between present and future needs. In the past, sustainability has been a low priority compared with the short-term drive for profitability and growth, but, with pressure growing for a more responsible tourism industry, it is difficult to see how such short-term views on consumption can continue. Indeed, destination 'regulations' have been developed in some areas, and already the bandwagon for sustainable development and responsible consumption is rolling. This is evidenced by a number of initiatives:

- Public agencies are issuing guidelines for the ethical consumption of tourism (see, for example, the WTO's global code of ethics for tourism).
- Industry sector organizations have developed sustainable auditing procedures for destinations (see, for example, the WTTC's 'Green Globe').
- Pressure groups and professional societies have devised codes of conduct for visitors and travelers (see, for example, the Audobon Society's 'travel ethic' and the Sierra Club's 'wilderness manners').
- The private sector is developing responsible tourism policies for the operation of their companies (a major collective project here is the

'Tour Operator's Initiative for Sustainable Tourism Development' representing 25 companies worldwide; see also individual companies such as Exodus Holidays www.exodus.co.uk).

- Tourism consumer groups are growing in number and influence (Botterill, 1991) and guides to responsible tourism are increasingly available (Mann, 2002).
- Sustainable tourism is becoming integral to tourism curricula (Jurowski, 2002).

As a philosophical stance or a way of thinking, it is difficult to disagree with the concept of sustainable tourism development and responsible consumption of tourism. But a little knowledge is a dangerous thing and some commentators have oversimplified the complex relationship between the consumption and development of tourism resources. This is particularly true of the so-called alternative tourism movement, which is lauded by some as a solution to the ills of mass tourism. Indeed, the tenor of much of the writing about alternative tourism is that any alternative tourism scheme is good, whereas all mass tourism is bad, although this is rightly refuted by Jafari (2001). Butler (1990) provides a useful characterization of the two extremes, whereas Wheeler (1991; 1992) provides telling criticism of alternative tourism. Others too warn of the ecotourism bandwagon; Beaumont (2001) is concerned that it preaches its values to the converted, whereas Ascot, La Trobe, and Howard (1998) classify deep and shallow ecotourism on the basis of commitment of the visitor.

There is, of course, a case for alternative tourism, but only as another form of tourism in the spectrum. It can never be an alternative to mass tourism, nor can it solve all the problems of tourism (Duffy, 2002). Cohen's (2002) criticism is telling. He sees forms of sustainable tourism as 'green washing,' misrepresenting the concept and using it to gain access to take over the control of natural sites or cultural practices. He also warns of issues of equity in terms of using sustainability as an instrument of power in the restriction of visitation to key sites.

A variety of issues emerge from these trends. It is important to disseminate cases of good practice in sustainable tourism, and to draw out generalities from these cases. In this way, responsible behaviour may pervade the provision and consumption of tourism and displace the more extreme calls for 'politically correct' tourism development. It must be recognised that the relationship of economics to environmental and social issues and policies in tourism is a complex one (Archer, 1996). Often economic policy is determined at the regional or national level, yet the impact of that policy is felt at the local level on environments and societies (Hough and Sherpa, 1989). Teo (2002) observes that globalisation has heightened the imperative for sustainable tourism as global process impact on tourism at the local level and are then moderated by a range of processes and power relationships that determine the success or failure of sustainable tourism.

Good models of community participation and planning in tourism are increasingly available (Richards and Hall, 2000), and in particular the notion of destination 'visioning ' is growing in acceptance as a means of communities taking control of their tourism futures (Murphy, 1985; Haywood, 1988; Ritchie, 1999; Richards and Hall, 2000; Ruhanen and Cooper, 2003). But it must also be recognised that tourism takes place in many different social and political contexts and what works in one place may need adaptation for another. From this point of view, Go (2001) is less optimistic that there has been real progress in converting the good intentions of sustainable tourism into practice.

This also applies to the borrowing of concepts and techniques from other subject areas and industries. Nevertheless, tourism has much to learn from others. In particular, techniques of environmental management, visitor planning and management, and studies of visitor/environment relationships are well developed in the recreation literature, and are just as applicable to tourism (Cooper, 1991). In particular, recreational managers are much more advanced in their use of the notion of 'capacity' than are tourism planners (Barkham, 1973; McCool and Lime, 2001), although such mechanistic planning techniques are now being questioned (Butler, 1996).

Perhaps the central issues emerging from this section are the gradual shift from short-term to longer-term thinking and planning in tourism; it is no longer acceptable for the industry to exploit and 'use up' destinations and then move on (Cooper, 1995). In addition there is an urgent need for tourism to sharpen up its terminology (e.g., alternative? responsible? soft, appropriate tourism?), to think clearly about the implications of sustainable/responsible initiatives, and to develop a code of business ethics.

Conclusions

Over the last 25 years, both the planning and marketing of tourism have been primarily orientated toward the needs of the tourist and the provision of interesting tourist experiences. This attitude has its basis first in the need of developers and operators to attract large numbers of visitors and hence ensure an adequate financial return on their investments and operations, and, second, in the desire of politicians and planners to maximize the financial benefits from tourism for their country or region. For both parties the primary concerns have been how many tourists will come, how can we attract more, and what facilities and services will they require?

Fortunately the climate of thought is changing, albeit slowly. Increasingly politicians and planners are becoming aware of the longer-term social, economic, and environmental consequences of excessive and badly planned tourism expansion. Sharpley (2000), for example, calls for national and international cooperation to facilitate the adoption of sustainable tourism-development policies. However, he notes that 'the political structure and fragmented nature of the industry suggest the political systems dedicated to equitable development and resource use are unlikely to be forthcoming.' If the adverse effects of tourism are to be prevented or remedied, it is crucial that politicians and planners become less preoccupied with increasing the number of visitors (and indeed with volume as a yardstick of success) and devote more consideration to the long-term welfare of the resident population. As Ritchie and Crouch (2003) note, it is the enhanced welfare of the local community that is the key yardstick of success for a competitive destination.

Some key questions to be considered are:

1. How many and what type of tourists does the resident population of an area wish to attract?
2. What is the optimum number of tourists that the area can support in terms of its physical, environmental, and social carrying capacity?
3. How can these tourists contribute to the enhancement of the lifestyles of the residents?

Planning for the resultant impact of tourism necessitates a careful definition of the respective responsibilities of the public and private sectors and communities. Planning should be designed to maximize the economic and social benefits of tourism to the resident population, whereas at the same time mitigating or preferably eliminating the adverse effects. In the past most of this type of planning has been remedial—it has taken place after much development has occurred. In the future, planners and communities must take a more proactive role in controlling the nature of such development in terms of stricter building and design regulations; controlled access to vulnerable sites and attractions; strict transport regulations, especially in core areas; and the use of entry fees, barriers, and designated routes for vehicles and pedestrians alike.

Tourism creates both positive and negative effects in the destination country or region. Thoughtful policy making and planning can do much to minimize or even remove the negative effects. Tourism can be a very positive means of increasing the economic, social, cultural, and environmental life of a country. The major issue now is can politicians, planners and developers, and citizens rise to the challenge and create a truly responsible, and thus acceptable, tourism industry, one which brings long-term benefits to residents and tourists alike without compromising the physical and cultural environment of the destination region.

References

Archer, B. H. 1977. *Tourism Multipliers: The State of the Art*. Cardiff: University of Wales Press.

———. 1996. Sustainable Tourism—Do Economists Really Care? *Progress in Tourism and Hospitality Research* 2(3): 217–222.

Archer, B. H., and J. E. Fletcher. 1991. *Multiplier Analysis in Tourism*: Cahiers du Tourisme, Centre Des Hautes Etudes Touristiques. Aix en Provence: University de Droit, D'Economie et Des Sciences.

Ascot, T. G., H. L. La Trobe, and S. H. Howard. 1998. An Evaluation of Deep Ecotourism and Shallow Ecotourism. *Journal of Sustainable Tourism* 6(3): 238–253.

Barkham, J. P. 1973. Recreational Carrying Capacity. *Area* 5(3): 218–222.

Beaumont, N. 2001. Ecotourism and the Conservation Ethic: Recruiting the Uninitiated or Preaching to the Converted? *Journal of Sustainable Tourism* 9(4): 317–341.

Botterill, T. D. 1991. A New Social Movement: Tourism Concern, The First Two Years. *Leisure Studies* 10(3): 203–217.

Bramwell, B., and B. Lane. 1999. Sustainable Tourism: Contributing to the Debates. *Journal of Sustainable Tourism* 7(1): 1–5.

Brunet, S., J. Bauer, T. De Lacy, and K. Tshering. 2001. Tourism Development in Bhutan: Tensions between Tradition and Modernity. *Journal of Sustainable Tourism* 9(3): 243–263.

Bryden, J. M. 1973. *Tourism and Development*. Cambridge: Cambridge University Press.

Buckley, R. 1999. An Ecological Perspective on Carrying Capacity. *Annals of Tourism Research* 26(3): 705–708.

Butler, R. 1990. Alternative Tourism: Pious Hope or Trojan Horse? *Journal of Travel Research* (Winter): 40–45.

———. 1996. Impacts, Carrying Capacity, Control and Responsibility in Tourist Destinations. *Progress in Tourism and Hospitality Research* 2(3): 283–294.

———. 1999. Sustainable Tourism: A State-of-the-Art Review. *Tourism Geographies* 1(1): 7–25.

———. 2000. Tourism and the Environment: A Geographical Perspective. *Tourism Geographies* 2(3): 19, 337–358.

Butler, R., and T. Hinch, eds. 1996. *Tourism and Indigenous Peoples*. London: International Thomson Business Press.

Cliff, S., and P. Grabowski. 1997. *Tourism and Health: Risks: Research and Responses*. London: Pinter.

Cohen, E. 2002. Authenticity, Equity and Sustainability in Tourism. *Journal of Sustainable Tourism* 10(4): 267–276.

Cooper, C. P. 1991. The Technique of Interpretation. In *Managing Tourism*. ed. S. Medlik. Oxford: Butterworth-Heinemann.

———. 1995. Strategic Planning for Sustainable Tourism: The Case of the Offshore Islands in the UK. *Journal of Sustainable Tourism* 3(4): 191–209.

Dann, G., and E. Cohen. 1991. Sociology and Tourism. *Annals of Tourism Research* 18(1): 155–169.

Dogan, H. Z. 1989. Forms of Adjustment: Socio-cultural Impacts of Tourism. *Annals of Tourism Research* 16(2): 216–236.

Duffy, R. 2002. *A Trip Too Far: Ecotourism, Politics and Exploitation*. London: Earthscan Publications.

Eadington, W. R., and M. Redman. 1991. Economics and Tourism. *Annals of Tourism Research* 18(1): 41–56.

Farrell, B. H., and D. Runyan. 1991. Ecology and Tourism. *Annals of Tourism Research* 18(1): 26–40.

Getz, D. 1983. Capacity to Absorb Tourism: Concepts and Applications for Strategic Planning. *Annals of Tourism Research* 10(2): 239–263.

Go, J. T. G. 2001. Assessing Progress of Tourism Sustainability. *Annals of Tourism Research* 28(3): 817–820.

Hall, C. M. 1994. *Tourism and Politics*. Chichester: Wiley.

——. 2000. *Tourism Planning, Policies, Processes and Relationships*. Harlow: Prentice Hall.

Hall, C. M., and J. M. Jenkins. 1995. *Tourism and Public Policy*. London: Routledge.

Hardy, A. L., and R. J. S. Beeton. 2001. Sustainable Tourism or Maintainable Tourism: Managing Resources for More Than Average Outcomes. *Journal of Sustainable Tourism* 9(3): 168–192.

Hardy, A. L., R. J. S. Beeton, and L. Pearson, L. 2002. Sustainable Tourism: An Overview of the Concept and its Position in Relation to Conceptualisations of Tourism. *Journal of Sustainable Tourism* 10(6): 475–496.

Haywood, K. M. 1988. Responsible and Responsive Tourism Planning in the Community. *Tourism Management* 9(2): 105–118.

Hillery, M., B. Nancarrow, G. Griffin, and G. Syme. 2001. Tourist Perception of Environmental Impact. *Annals of Tourism Research* 28(4): 853–867.

Holden, A. 2000. *Environment and Tourism*. London: Routledge.

Hough, J. L., and M. N. Sherpa. 1989. Bottom Up Versus Basic Needs. *Ambio* 18(8): 434–441.

Ingles, P. 2002. Welcome to My Village: Hosting Tourists in the Peruvian Amazon. *Tourism Recreation Research* 27(1): 53–60.

Jafari, J. 2001. The Scientification of Tourism. In *Hosts and Guests Revisited: Tourism Issues of the 21st Century*. eds. V. L. Smith, and M. Brent. New York: Cognizant.

Jamal, T., and D. Getz. 1995. Collaboration Theory and Community Planning. *Annals of Tourism Research* 22(1): 186–204.

Jurowski, C. 2002. BEST Think Tanks and the Development of Curriculum Modules for Teaching Sustainability Development Principles. *Journal of Sustainable Tourism* 10(6): 536–545.

Kerr, W. R. 2003. *Tourism Public Policy and the Strategic Management of Failure*. St. Louis: Elsevier.

Leitner, M. J. 1999. Promoting Peace Through Intergenerational Tourism. *Tourism Recreation Research* 24(1): 53–56.

Lindberg, K., T. D. Andersson, and B. G. C. Dellaert. 2001. Tourism Development: Assessing Social Gains and Losses. *Annals of Tourism Research* 28(4): 1010–1030.

Lindberg, K., and R. L. Johnson. 1997. The Economic Values of Tourism's Social Impacts. *Annals of Tourism Research* 24(1): 90–116.

Litvin, S. W. 1998. Tourism: The World's Peace Industry. *Journal of Travel Research* 37(1): 63–66.

Mann, M. 2002. *The Good Alternative Travel Guide: Exciting Holidays for Responsible Travelers*. Sterling: Earthscan Publications.

Manning, T. 1999. Indicators of Tourism Sustainability. *Tourism Management* 20: 179–181.

Mathews, H. G., and L. K. Richter. 1991. Political Science and Tourism. *Annals of Tourism Research* 18(1): 120–135.

Mathieson, A., and G. Wall. 1982. *Tourism: Economic, Physical and Social Impacts.* London: Longman.

McCannell, D. 1973. Staged Authenticity: Arrangement of Social Space in Tourist Settings. *American Journal of Sociology* 79: 586–603.

McCool, S. F., and D. W. Lime. 2001. Tourism Carrying Capacity: Tempting Fantasy or Useful Reality? *Journal of Sustainable Tourism* 9(5): 372–388.

Medina, K. L. 2003. Commoditizing Culture: Tourism and Maya Identity. *Annals of Tourism Research* 30(2): 353–368.

Mitchell, R. E., and D. G. Reid. 2001. Community Integration: Island Tourism in Peru. *Annals of Tourism Research* 28(1): 113–139.

Murphy, P. 1985. *Tourism, A Community Approach.* London: Routledge.

Nepal, S. J. 2000. Tourism in Protected Areas: The Nepalese Himalaya. *Annals of Tourism Research* 27(3): 661–681.

O'Reilly, A. M. 1986. Tourism Carrying Capacity. *Tourism Management* 7(4): 254–258.

Petty, R. 1989. Health Limits to Tourism Development. *Tourism Management* 10(3): 209–212.

Pigram, J. 1990. Sustainable Tourism Policy Considerations. *Journal of Tourism Studies* 2(3): 2–9.

Reisinger, Y., and L. W. Turner. 2003. *Cross-Cultural Behaviour in Tourism: Concepts and Analysis.* Oxford: Butterworth-Heinemann.

Richards, G., and D. Hall. 2000. *Tourism and Sustainable Community Development.* London: Routledge.

Richter, L. K. 1983. Tourism Politics and Political Science: A Case of Not So Benign Neglect. *Annals of Tourism Research* 10(3): 313–335.

Ritchie, J. R. B. 1999. Crafting a Value-Driven Vision for a National Tourism Treasure. *Tourism Management* 20: 273–282.

Ritchie, J. R. B., and G. I. Crouch. 2003. *The Competitive Destination: A Sustainable Tourism Perspective.* Oxen: CABI Publishing.

Ruhanen, L., and C. Cooper. 2003. The Use of Strategic Visioning to Enhance Local Tourism Planning in Periphery Communities: The Tweed Shire, Australia. *Taking Tourism to the Limits Conference.* New Zealand: Department of Tourism Management, University of Waikato.

Saveriades, A. 2000. Establishing the Social Tourism Carrying Capacity for the Tourist Resorts of the East Coast of the Republic of Cyprus. *Tourism Management* 21: 147–156.

Sharpley, R. 2000. Tourism and Sustainable Development: Exploring the Theoretical Divide. *Journal of Sustainable Tourism* 8(1): 1–19.

Smith, V. 1977. *Hosts and Guests: An Anthropology of Tourism.* Philadelphia: University of Pennsylvania Press.

———. 2001. Tourism Change and Impacts. In *Hosts and Guests Revisited: Tourism Issues of the 21st Century.* eds. V. L. Smith, and M. Brent. New York: Cognizant.

Smith, V. L., and M. Brent. 2001. *Hosts and Guests Revisited: Tourism Issues of the 21st Century.* New York: Cognizant.

Teo, P. 2002. Striking a Balance for Sustainable Tourism: Implications of the Discourse on Globalisation. *Journal of Sustainable Tourism* 10(6): 459–474.

Tisdell, C. 2000. *The Economics of Tourism*. Northampton: Edward Elgar Publishing.

Tosun, C., D. J. Timothy, and Y. Öztürk. 2003. Tourism Growth, National Development and Regional Inequality in Turkey. *Journal of Sustainable Tourism* 11(2 and 3): 133–161.

Tribe, J. 1999. *The Economics of Leisure and Tourism*. Oxford: Butterworth-Heinemann.

Tsartas, P. 2003. Tourism Development in Greek Insular and Coastal Areas: Sociocultural Changes and Crucial Policy Issues. *Journal of Sustainable Tourism* 11(2 and 3): 116–132.

Vogel, H. L. 2001. *Travel Industry Economics*. Cambridge: Cambridge University Press.

Wagner, J. E. 1997. Estimating the Economic Impacts of Tourism. *Annals of Tourism Research* 24(3): 592–608.

Wheeler, B. 1991. Tourism's Troubled Times. *Tourism Management* 12(2): 91–96.

———. 1992. Is Progressive Tourism Appropriate? *Tourism Management* 13(1): 104–105.

Whitford, M. 2003. Event Public Policy Development in the Northern Sub-regional Organisation of Councils, Queensland Australia: Rhetoric or Realisation? *Convention and Expo Summit 2003*, School of Hotel and Tourism Management, Hong Kong Polytechnic University.

Wilks, J., and S. J. Page. 2003. *Managing Tourist Health and Safety in the New Millennium*. Amsterdam: Pergamon.

Williams, J., and R. Lawson. 2001. Community Issues and Resident Opinions of Tourism. *Annals of Tourism Research* 28(2): 269–290.

World Commission on Environment and Development. 1987. *Our Common Future*. New York: Oxford University Press.

World Tourism Organization. 1980. *Manila Declaration on World Tourism*. Madrid: World Tourism Organization.

———. (1982) *Acapulco Development*. Madrid: World Tourism Organization.

6 The role of relationships in the tourist experience

Philip L. Pearce

The experience of being a pleasure traveller often poses several unexpected relationship challenges for any individual. The challenges arrive in several guises. The difficulties and rewards may include dealing with oneself and with one's familiar travel companions, of interacting with fellow travellers who are strangers, and of trying to communicate with the locals across cultural divides. These kinds of issues are of immediate concern to the travellers themselves but there can also be a management interest in these topics. Tourism industry personnel want to influence customer satisfaction and, if improving social rapport in its various forms can achieve this goal, then a commercial interest is assured. The range of relationships inherent in the tourist experience is portrayed in Table 6.1.

This chapter will describe and discuss each social interaction level depicted in Table 6.1. The greatest attention will be paid to travellers' experiences with other travellers because it can be argued that this element is the least well described in the existing literature (Yagi, 2001).

Travelling with Oneself

It is sometimes a surprise for travellers to 'discover themselves' in an exotic location. This kind of relationship with oneself as a surprising companion is described by de Botton (2002) reporting on a holiday trip to Barbados, 'A momentous but until then overlooked fact was making its first appearance: that I had inadvertently brought myself with me to the island.' The sentiments may be clearly expressed but they are not original. Two thousand years before Horace wrote, '*Coelum, non animum, mutant, qui trans mare current. (Those who cross the sea change the sky, not their soul.)*' (Pearce, 1982).

Table 6.1 Hypotheses Potentially Explaining User–User Conflict in Recreation Settings

Factor	Specific Theme	Proposition
Activity Style	Intensity	• The more intense the activity style, the greater the likelihood that social interaction with less intense participants will result in conflict.
	Status disregard	• When the private activity style contracts the status conscious activity style, conflict results because the private activity style's disregard to status symbols negated the relevance of the other participants' status hierarchy.
	Status snobbery	• Status-based intra-activity conflict occurs when a participant deserving high status must interact with others viewed as lower status.
	Status disagreement	• Conflict occurs between participants who do not share the same status hierarchies.
	Quality judgement	• The more specific the expectations of what constitute a quality experience, the greater the potential for conflict.
Resource Specificity	Respect for place	• Evaluations of resource quality: when a person who views the place's qualities as unequalled confronts behaviours indicating a lower evaluation, conflict results.
	Ownership	• Sense of possession: conflict results when users with a possessive attitude toward the resource confront users perceived as disrupting traditional uses and behavioural norms.
	Privacy of place	• Status: conflict occurs for high status users forced to interact with low status users who symbolise devaluing exclusive intimate relationship with place.
Mode of Experience	Focus	• When a person in the focussed mode interacts with one who is not, conflict results.
Tolerance for Lifestyle Diversity	Lifestyle tolerance	• If group differences are evaluated as undesirable or a potential threat to recreation goals, conflict results when group members contract one another.

Source: Jacob and Shreyer, 1980.

The implication of this unexpected discovery of self is that travellers have to deal with their own limitations and moods, their lingering concerns derived from the world they have left, and the planning of their immediate future activities. Dealing with oneself is perhaps a curious form of a social relationship but represents a traditional concern in the social psychology of leisure and travel (Mannell and Kleiber, 1997). As Bammel and Bammel (1992) suggest, classical views of the wider field of leisure that see it as the cultivation of mind, spirit, and character reinforce the view that contemporary tourists may often have to confront themselves as if they were another person and think about who they are in their social and work worlds.

The growth of qualitative methods in tourism research (Jamal and Hollinshead, 2001) offers the promise of investigating and reporting more fully how individuals deal with themselves and their emotional development during travel experiences. Such studies, which have yet to be developed in full, could consider the extent to which tourists play different roles and take on different personalities to explore their own styles (see Desforges, 2000; Murphy, 2001; Yiannakis and Gibson, 1992). In addition, more quantitative work assessing and reporting traveller moods and transient emotional states might enrich our understanding of the variability in traveller satisfaction and assessment (see Pearce, 1981).

Foster (2002) describes an innovative study directed at what travellers learn and how they perceive themselves during extended periods of travel. In a comprehensive survey of 370 youth travellers, Foster reported that more than 60 percent of all those studied perceived themselves to have improved their self-insights. The youth travellers reported themselves to be more self-confident and open minded and better able to deal with their own emotions, pressures, and stress. Although this work is built on a self-report methodology, Foster established a convincing consistency between these reported skills and parallel themes drawn from spontaneously generated Internet stories from a similar cohort of travellers. The Internet component of Foster's material was accessed by using phrases such as 'backpacker travel stories' and 'travelogues.' The resulting 95 Web pages, rich in youth traveller accounts, were coded by three researchers resulting in substantial agreement on the recurring themes. The skills of self-evaluation, independent learning, and self-awareness emerged and are reflected in such comments as:

> Whoever said 'University is the best years of life' was lying!! There's much more to learning than a diploma or degree. I learnt to be me overseas. You may wince at this cliché but I have to say t'is true!! I often wonder what I would be like as a person now if I hadn't travelled for so long on my own and learnt to live and work in different countries and experience different cultures.
>
> (Foster, 2002) (http://www.bilk.ac.uk/college/extraweb/backpack/)

Not all of Foster's respondents were actually travelling by themselves. The establishment of insights about oneself can be derived from both solo travelling and of interpersonal experiences developed with one's travelling companions. The opportunity to study the psychological and interpersonal consequences in the relationship of 'travelling with oneself' should be developed as a research topic to enrich our understanding of tourism's meaning in postmodern societies.

Other Travellers—The Role of Strangers

One source of information in the study of how travellers deal with and relate to fellow tourists who are strangers lies in the extensive literature on recreation users. This work, conducted almost exclusively in the United States, is centrally concerned with how to manage conflict between recreation users and how to set limits for the number of people in a setting.

Conflicts over use relate to and depend on perceptions of crowding. It was quickly realised in the early studies in this field that crowding was not simply about the number of people involved. Graefe and Vaske (1987), striving towards definitional clarity in this area, argued that crowding is a negative evaluation of a particular density of people. The phenomenon is therefore psychological and interpersonal rather than simply determined by observable physical parameters such as people per area.

There are three major lines of analysis in the recreation crowding and conflict literature. The first and dominant interpretive framework is referred to as goal interference theory (Jacob and Shreyer, 1980). This approach, which essentially states ten hypotheses thought to be of importance in defining user–user interaction, defines recreation conflict as 'goal interference attributed to another's behaviour.' In this approach, the style of activity, the importance attached to a particular place, the focus needed for the activity, and the broad scale tolerance of the users are the pivotal forces predicting conflict. Because so much of the subsequent work in the recreation field has built on, tested, and confirmed many of Jacob and Shreyer's hypotheses they are outlined in Figure 6.1.

There are lines of research in the recreation and park management literature pursuing many of these variables and their influence on perceived crowding and on conflict. For example, users participating in focussed activities have often been shown to report negative attitudes towards other groups in the area (Watson, Niccoulucci, and Williams, 1994). In particular there is often an asymmetry in these reactions with the non-motorised, traditional, and quieter users of the setting objecting more strongly to their motorised, newer, and noisier neighbours (Shelby, 1981;

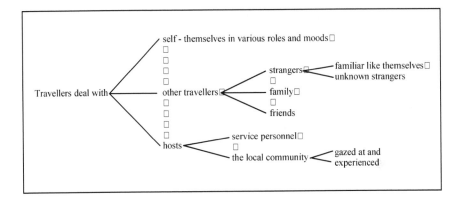

Figure 6.1:   The social players in tourist experience.

Jackson and Wong, 1982; Ruddell and Gramman, 1994; Gibbons and Ruddell, 1995; Rathmun, 1995). For example, in one of the earlier studies Shelby (1981) reported that paddling canoeists disliked motor boaters, but this negative perception was not reciprocated in the attitudes of the motor boating respondents. The structure of this finding, that is the mechanised and more recent users appearing to be less bothered by the passive, appreciative users, is consistent in studies in the recreation area in mountain and snow use settings, on beaches and along rivers, and in landscape touring and appreciation.

Additional insights concerning the important dimensions of user–user conflict are to be found in the work of Rathmun (1995). He questioned the empirical value of all of Jacob and Shreyer's categories, viewing them as somewhat overlapping and hence at times redundant. In his own studies he placed emphasis on an additional underlying dimension—the identification of being a member of an in-group or an out-group. This approach is in accordance with fundamental social psychological research on group identity and response reported in detail in the work of Tajfel (1981). This explanatory dimension will be explored further later.

A third perspective in the analysis of conflict between users was identified by Schneider and Hammitt (1995). They argued that conflict is best understood by viewing it as a process, often a series of events and perceptions leading to stressed participants and possibly a defining point of annoyance. Vaske and colleagues (1995) further observed that these defining points of annoyance do not have to be actual physical contacts involving the presence of the other group, but instead, can be social value conflicts where the idea of other people sharing the disputed space is the prime concern of the stressed group.

Although this work on recreation user–user conflict has been conducted for some years and would seem, at least initially, to be relevant to tourist–tourist encounters, there are some limitations and assumptions that warrant examination. First, the guiding principle in these predominantly North American–based studies is that larger numbers of users are not appreciated. Glasson, Godfrey, and Goodey (1995) provide a set of graphical appraisals that indicate the importance of questioning the broad applicability of the wilderness and national park–based work. They depict the relationship between user satisfaction and use levels in a number of contexts (Figure 6.2).

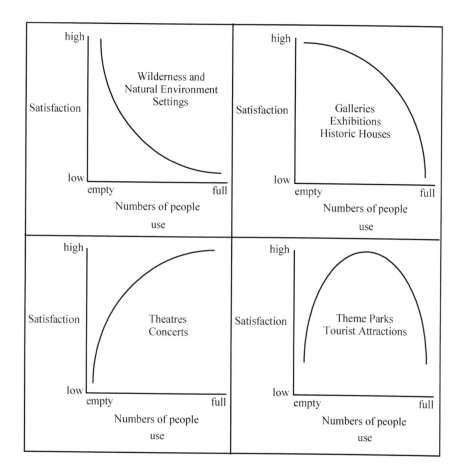

Figure 6.2:   User satisfaction and use levels (number of people).

Source: Glasson, Godfrey, and Goodey, 1995.

An important implication to be drawn from Figure 6.2 is that most of the studies discussed have actually been drawn from the first quadrant of the figure. Tourists use all of the environments depicted in Figure 6.2 so an initial caution on the applicability of the recreation literature and its findings must be exercised. Secondly, even in the first quadrant of Figure 6.2 the findings are drawn from studies of North American users. There is a mounting argument from cross-national studies of social behaviour that other cultural groups, such as Chinese, Indonesians, Koreans, and Japanese, prefer or at least tolerate group-based and high-density natural settings (Kim, 1997; Ward, Bochner, and Furnham, 2001).

A third point of commentary on the recreation findings relates to the subtly different purpose of travel associated with tourist activities. Recreational conflict appears to be particularly acute when the specific, focussed purposes of a group of people are thwarted by the actions of another group. Tourists, in many situations, are sharing the one set of goals—to see, experience, and enjoy the same setting. In this kind of scenario tolerance of the sheer presence of other people might be high. One version of this argument has been developed in some detail by Urry (1990). He used the expression 'the tourist gaze' to describe the commonality of tourists' goals in many settings. Further, he identified a romantic gaze, rich in historical Western tradition and precedent, which emphasises the value for individuals in experiencing an environment by themselves or in very small numbers of like-minded companions. Work in the recreational conflict literature may be squarely located as explicating the dimensions of user contact within the romantic gaze framework.

By way of contrast Urry also identified a collective gaze. In this style of environmental and social experience, users enjoy and indeed require the presence of others in the setting in order for it to be seen and experienced as popular, lively, successful, and socially enriching. In Figure 6.2 the third and fourth quadrants depict this kind of setting.

A final and further elaboration pertaining to the tourist–tourist encounters lies in the identification of the in-group and out-group (see Rathmun, 1995). One can raise the question of who constitutes the in-group and the out-group in a specific tourism context. For example, consider a package group of tourists from the United States walking along the Great Wall of China north of Beijing. In this context there are multiple possible out-groups present in the setting; these include North American tourists on other package tours, European tourists travelling in group arrangements, young independent Western travellers doing their own thing in seeing China, and, of course, large numbers of domestic Chinese tourists also walking the Wall. It would appear that the attitudes toward other tourists and the kinds of relationships developed may need more than one simple in-group and out-group classification to understand the developing relationships.

One such distinctive concept developed to understand tourist–tourist relationships is that of the familiar stranger (Simmel, 1950; Pearce, 1981; Yagi, 2002). In many tourism settings, and particularly in extended travel journeys, individuals repeatedly see the same other travellers. This can be illustrated by considering an international flight from Shanghai to Sydney. On checking in at the airport travellers have to wait in line with other passengers, they are then likely to see these same faces in the airport waiting lounge, and in adjacent or nearby seats during the flight. On arriving at the destination the same faces will be in the customs hall and baggage collection area. It is functional for travellers to pay some attention to these familiar strangers. They provide some guidance as to where to go, they may be people to engage in time-passing conversation, and in times of stress they may be sources of help.

Simmel (1950) reported familiar strangers in everyday urban life noting such contexts as fellow commuters, shop assistants, and patrons of favoured restaurants. Pearce (1980) noted in a quasiexperiment field study of Greyhound bus travellers in the United States that these familiar strangers were reliably more helpful on a range of small tasks to fellow travellers than were total strangers. It can be suggested that the familiar stranger is a distinctive and often frozen form of social relationship associated with but not exclusively confined to the travel experience. It is an additional mechanism, beyond those noted in the recreation literature, for understanding distinctive tourist–tourist relationships.

Yagi (2002) has noted a particular extension of the familiar stranger concept by paying attention to the obvious physical characteristics of the travellers. She observes that it is an inescapable fact of perception that such physical characteristics as race, gender, age, and dress style are readily observable by all travellers, and of course by tourist service personnel. In cross-national tourism encounters, such as when there are numerous visitors of varied nationalities in popular settings, it is likely that travellers of the same age, appearance, and nationality constitute a special kind of familiar stranger. Thus, Japanese travellers admiring the Eiffel Tower will note the presence of familiar Japanese, Germans in Australia's outback desert setting will quickly identify other Germans, and North American tourists in Egypt will be likely to hear and identify Canadian and U.S. citizens.

In a substantial program of research dealing with the relationships tourists have with other tourists, Yagi (2002) asked the question, will tourists prefer to mix with the familiar strangers of their own nationality? The studies were conducted with multiple methods. Travellers' own accounts of their experiences were accessed from Internet diaries, tourists were shown digitally altered photographs of visitors from various nationality mixes in environmental settings and focus groups were conducted to explain such preferences. The particular nationality contrasts pursued in her work were the preferences of Japanese and Western (largely Australian and U.S.) travellers toward mixing with their own and other nationalities in natural environment settings.

From the spontaneously generated travelogues provided on a range of Internet sites, Yagi concluded, using a sample of both Japanese and North American stories, that the Japanese showed consistently greater awareness of the presence of other Japanese. Sometimes a positive attitude toward these fellow travellers was expressed, but at the same time a desire to escape the confines of their own compatriots' expectations emerged.

In the studies using digitally altered photographs of different mixes of tourist appearance and density Yagi and Pearce (2002) found that Japanese travellers compared with Western travellers consistently preferred larger rather than smaller numbers of visitors in rainforest environmental settings. Perhaps surprisingly, Japanese travellers also preferred the digitally altered photographs depicting more Caucasian faces as opposed to those depicting more Asian faces in the photographs. The surprising element in this finding derives from an apparent contradiction of the preferences for one's own nationality predicted by in-group and out-group theory. For the Western travellers there were no differences in the preferences for Caucasian or Asian faces in the photographs. One explanation of these findings is that the Japanese travellers have 'Akogare' (respect, enthusiasm, and admiration) for the Western world and the greater numbers of Western faces enhances the international atmosphere of the site. This finding is congruent with Urry's analysis of the collective gaze, but extends Urry's perspective by incorporating a cross-national addition where the symbolic value of the personnel making up the crowd is important. The number of ways in which tourists may respond to other tourists is depicted in Figure 6.3.

One kind of emotional state and sequence of behaviours can be identified as noteworthy in influencing the range of responses in Figure 6.3. Armstrong (2003) observes that in time of emotional and physical stress, individuals are particularly appreciative of small acts of kindness and tenderness from others. He terms this feeling and process 'katabasis' and emphasises that it represents a vulnerability where people are confronted with loneliness and disappointment, and thus have a heightened appreciation for assistance from others. The stress of travelling has been recorded by a number of writers and Armstrong's argument that katabasis operates in tandem with positive, even ecstatic emotional episodes, is a valuable additional insight into the genesis of companionship-based tourism (see Herold, Garcia, and DeMoya, 2001).

Our understanding of stranger-based tourist relationships can be summarised by integrating the work done in the recreation settings and these more recent cross-national studies using the familiar stranger dimension. In Western countries there are strong historical and sociological forces

	Tourists seen as	Behaviours	
Positive views	Potential close friend	Friendly contact - intimacy Learn about and from them Learn about other culture	Familiar strangers ↑
	Travel companion	Partner for activities Socialise, someone to be with	
	Helper	Source of information Share costs Lend a hand	
	Security Guard	Look after possessions Prevent unwanted contacts	
	Stimulation	Improve atmosphere of destination Excitement "Marker" of good times	
Neutral perspective	Background scenery	Just there No impact	
Negative views	Stranger	Minor discomfort Something unfamiliar	
	Disturber	Noise source Adds to crowd Invades privacy Causes conflict – contributes to culture shock	
	Competitor	Competitor for accommodation, tickets, space, access to people and setting	Total strangers ↓

Figure 6.3:   The multiple perspectives tourists may have of other tourists.

predisposing travellers to experience settings, particularly natural settings, in isolation or at least small, like-minded groups. In this kind of scenario relationships with most other travellers are limited and are viewed as unwelcome intrusions because they restrict the achievement of the travellers' goals. In more purpose-built tourist attraction settings there are findings from North American studies that suggest familiar strangers may be tolerated and be useful companions. Indeed larger crowd numbers enhance the atmosphere of certain settings. For travellers of more group-oriented or collectivist cultures, the relationships with other travellers is less problematic in natural environmental settings and may be seen to enhance the appeal of the location because of the symbolic value of connoting a noteworthy site (see Kagitcibasi and Berry, 1989; Triandis, Chen, and Chan, 1998; Ward, Bochner, and Furnham, 2001).

Familiar strangers are a defining category in traveller relationships and interaction with familiar fellow travellers may include such positive roles as developing friendship, providing assistance, and aiding traveller safety and security. These relationships may be developed in times of shared positive experiences or they may arise in times of stress where katabasis operates. Less positively, tourist–tourist relationships may also degenerate into competitive and marginally hostile encounters when, as in the recreation literature, there is conflict over achieving goals and limited resources such as tickets and space. Some significant analogies between these poles of positive and negative roles for fellow travellers will be reiterated in considering traveller relationships with the members of the local community.

Travelling with Family and Friends

Regrettably much of the foundation work on tourist behaviour has unwittingly adopted a very individualistic orientation. This direction is undoubtedly linked to and driven by the dominance of questionnaire-based methodologies to explore visitor behaviour; questionnaires and surveys are typically given to and filled in by individuals and the processing of the data aggregates individual responses. Nevertheless many researchers and students of tourist behaviour in naturalistic settings will quickly recognise that many travel parties are composed not of individuals but of couples, friends, and complex family groupings. As a brief illustration of this social dimension of tourism some diverse examples can be cited. Long distance car touring in Australia is dominated by senior couples (Pearce, 1999), young budget travellers are often in small shifting friendship groups (Buchanan and Rossetto, 1997), visitors to zoos and attractions are dominated by family groups (Turley, 2001), and gay male couples comprise more than half of the U.K. gay market holidaying at home and abroad (Clift, Callister, and Luongo, 2002).

In this interconnected and social view of travel behaviours three emphases can be identified. First, the decision making about where to go on holidays is undoubtedly a complex amalgam of the motivations of and restrictions on the entire party (see Um and Crompton, 1990). Thus Moscardo and Pearce (1999) report that one cluster of visitors to a major Aboriginal cultural park in Northern Australia was not very interested in the attraction and cited their main reason for being present as 'accompanying others.' It can be suggested that this kind of tourist motivation may account for some of the moderate satisfaction scores obtained in tourist settings. The interest in this topic of 'accompanying others' and the challenge for tourism managers is to find ways to engage the interest of the whole travel party.

Travel parties and their composition also influence what people do in the site. Ryan (1992) reports that children are often the most willing participants in activities at heritage sites. Such participation may galvanise parental and adult interest and result in an extended time of visiting with some commercial implications in terms of food and souvenir purchases. In a more restrictive sense, travelling with senior members of a family or friendship group may limit participation in physically demanding activities, such as when visitors to Australia's Great Barrier Reef do not participate in snorkelling because they choose to 'stay dry' and accompany their older relatives in glass bottom boat inspections of the coral (Moscardo, 1996).

The presence of familiar faces in the form of family and friends may also exert a powerful influence on the development of the other relationships discussed in this chapter. Couples, family groups, and friendship parties are often self-sufficient in their social needs. Such self-sufficiency will limit the extent to which they fraternise with fellow travellers or seek out members of the local community for conversation and stimulation.

The third consideration pertaining to travelling with others is shared satisfaction with the experience. Unlike individual travellers, those journeying around the world or across their own region with others have a commonality of experience which they can reflect on, retell, and reinterpret as a part of their social and shared experiences. Thornton, Shaw, and Williams (1997) argue that children in particular are discerning customers and because many parents consider the satisfaction of their children to be important in the leisure context, the adult satisfaction may be influenced by the reactions of their offspring. This argument could also be extended, even though the empirical work is lacking, to other satisfaction ratings; one could anticipate that close friends should at least be somewhat influenced by the satisfaction of their travelling companions in forming their own attitudes, whereas long-term partners should demonstrate even more awareness and mutual influence in satisfaction scores. At this point, however, these links remain research propositions rather than established findings.

Travellers' Relationships with Hosts

The use of the term 'hosts' in this section of the chapter warrants a justification. Aramberri (2001) has suggested that the term should be removed from the lexicon of tourism research. He notes that its derivation and use by anthropologists writing about tourism proceeds on the basis of three features—the term connotes an implicit contract by the host to extend protection to the guest, it suggests a future reciprocity of such protection, and it implies a set of rule-following behaviours so that hosts and guests can coexist as a virtual family. Aramberri (2000) elaborates as follows:

> The host-guest paradigm cannot be used to account for most types of what is called tourist behavior. Excluded from the visual field are all of the interactions that do not take place between members of pre-industrial communities and denizens of developed societies. These are nevertheless the overwhelming bulk of tourism both domestic and international.

Table 6.1, which depicts the relationships to be explored in this chapter, does use the generic expression 'hosts,' but subdivides the term into two categories with which Aramberri would presumably be more comfortable—interaction with service providers and interaction with local community members. The presentation of information in this section simply uses the term 'host' as a convenient integrating expression for the two groups with whom tourists have contact. There is an agreement here with the argument that it is not considered appropriate to embrace the more anthropological and noncommercial use of the term 'hosts' in its traditional premodern format.

The dominant trends in the literature on tourist service personnel contact is written from the perspective of evaluating how well the service personnel perform. As Noe (1999) reports, service providers are typically evaluated on such dimensions as their reliability, the assurance they provide, the tangible aspects of their performance, and their empathy and responsiveness to client needs. These kinds of service provision evaluations have been developed by researchers such as Parasuraman, Zeithaml, and Berry (1994).

This line of inquiry is peripheral rather than central to the theme of tourists' relationships as presented in this chapter. The question can also be asked in this context of what does it mean to have a relationship with a service provider or indeed is the very term 'relationship' appropriate? The perspective adopted here is that a relationship involves multiple encounters with other people that one is able to recall and, further, the person encountered must be individually identified. The service encounters typically reported in the service quality literature essentially offer brief points of contact and many travellers would undoubtedly struggle to remember and recognise individual taxi drivers, hotel personnel, restaurant waiters, booking clerks, customs personnel, and coach drivers.

For some service providers a relationship can be considered to be a more appropriate term. For example, a tour guide who spends a day with a traveller, an interpreter or booking clerk who guides a visitor through complex travel rescheduling, and a tourist information officer who influences a day's activities may provide memorable encounters and be seen as incipient relationships. It is noteworthy that with the exception of some efforts to develop cross-cultural awareness training there is little research or analysis of how well tourists behave in these relationships (see Pearce, Kim and Lussa, 1998; Ward, Bochner, and Furnham, 2001). It would seem to be another area of potential research investigation to explore the attitudes and behaviours of different tourist market segments toward the staff and assisting personnel they encounter. To date, the research has been very much focussed on the service providers' behaviours rather than the tourists' responses.

There is one marked exception to the lack of research on relationships in tourist–local encounters. The area in question involves sexual encounters. There is widespread agreement that the relationships developed by tourists seeking sexual activities with local people is complex in terms of the motivation of the participants, the effect on the host society, and the range of relationships that develop in these situations. Herold, Garcia, and DeMoya (2001) suggest the use of the term 'companionship tourism' to help integrate the multiple relationship possibilities identified by other researchers. For example, Pruitt and Lafont (1995) noted the existence of romance tourism in Jamaica where female tourists developed relationships with the local males that included emotional involvement, courtship, and sometimes sexual intimacy. In their study it was noteworthy that indirect rather than immediate financial payments were made. By way of contrast de Alburqueque (1999) suggested that romance tourism involving female tourists was a euphemism. In his view the relationships were not romantic ones but a form of prostitution using the local beach boys. Herold, Garcia, and DeMoya (2001) reject de Alburqueque's view. They suggest that for the North American and European women travelling to the Dominican Republic the term 'consensual romantic relationships' best describes the tourist–local interaction. By interviewing both male and female tourists and male and female local participations with a female interviewer Herold, Garcia, and DeMoya (2001) reported that 'more of the women (were) motivated toward the romance end of the (companionship) tourism continuum and more of the men motivated toward the sex part of it.' More generally, McKercher and Bauer (2003) report that tourism and travel can be a unique facilitator of sexual relationships. The themes of anonymity, sensory stimulation, reduced social control, and new potential partners all act to expand the range of same sex and opposite sex encounters (Selanniemi, 2003).

On many occasions the relationships are brief and financially well defined (Opperman, 1998; Truong, 1990). The question of who is exploiting whom is not easily assessed; there are radical tourist views that the sex workers are without power, whereas others see at least some of the tourists as cautious customers, powerless to complain about any problems and controlled by the situation and experienced partners (Truong, 1990; McCormick, 1994; Ryan, 1999). The ways in which these tourist relationships are managed were portrayed in some detail by Herold, Garcia, and DeMoya (2001) in their study of the Dominican beach boys.

> The beach boys reported that they never directly ask for a specific sum of money as do female prostitutes ... Rather they use different strategies to indicate their lack of money to pay for drinks, admission to discos or taxi transportation ...
>   Another strategy is to look sad and not to talk. This throws the woman off guard because until that point the beach boy has been very friendly, smiling all the time and very talkative ...
>   The woman now quickly picks up the message that something is very wrong as he 'reluctantly' admits to having money problems.

These kinds of scams and exploitative tactics are not new or confined to the Caribbean. Cohen (1982) noted almost identical strategies in earlier studies of Thai women and Western men, Zinovieff (1991) identified similar exploitative manoeuvres in Greece (1991), du Cros and du Cros (2003) reported the use of ingratiation and flattery by young Cretan males, and Dahles and Bras (1999) identified sets of Indonesian males who 'worked' the tourists as resources to be exploited in Yogykarta.

It would be misleading, however, not to view some of these relationships as providing mutual, even if temporary, satisfaction and rewards to the participants. For Taiwanese men, Lee (2002) reports that the sexual liberation of other parts of Asia are synonymous with a better, freer lifestyle. Further as Cohen (2003) has documented, the sexually oriented tourism relationships may not always be short-lived. Cohen considered the weaknesses and strengths of marriages between Thai women and foreign men resulting from the chance tourism encounters. This relationship development represents the expressed goal of at least a subset of participants in the romance tourism category (du Cros and du Cros, 2003; Wong, 2003). Cohen's analysis noted the difficulties of such marital relationships, which included the persistent and expanding financial demands by the women on behalf of themselves and their family. The problems appeared to be the greatest when the foreigner stayed in Thailand. For some of these marriages, an initially difficult period was encountered, but a number of the relationships persisted, held together by children, common property, and growing mutual understanding.

If successful albeit infrequent marriages between tourists and local partners represent a positive pinnacle of tourist–local encounters, there are some contrasting troughs of exploitative and harmful encounters. Tourists can be targeted as victims in organised criminal attacks and assault (Chesney-Lind and Lind, 1986; Harper, 2000). The scale of this phenomenon can vary from small opportunistic attacks, such as stealing and snatching handbags and wallets, to organised terrorism against identifiable national groups such as in Bali in October 2002. The attacks may also be targeted at the elderly or identifiable groups such as gay tourists (Want, 2002). Other forms of negativity can also be identified. Exploitation of visitors by overcharging, misdirecting, and exchanging the products purchased with inferior substitutes have been reported (de Albuquerque and McElroy, 2001). Pearce, Kim, and Lussa (1998) identified that Westerners in Indonesia reported that small shopkeepers and street vendors who followed them, who touched them, and who pushed and shoved for attention were a major source of unpleasantness.

As with some of the other service and local encounters, it is perhaps overextending the ambit of the present chapter to call these forms of interpersonal contact relationships. In some senses it is likely that tourists recall these multiple minor interactions as a stereotype of the intrusive harassing vendor—a generic relationship with the locals rather than an identified personal encounter.

Conclusion

The focus of this chapter has been on the specific relationships that tourists develop during their travels. It has not considered the wider impact of these relationships on the visited community in terms of cultural change, social structure, and business performance. Many of these wider implications, together with the effects of tourist infrastructure itself, have been reviewed in studies on tourist impacts, such as in previous editions of this volume (**see** Archer and Cooper, 1998; Mercer, 1998; Pearce, 1998; Swinglehurst, 1998).

A remaining issue pertaining to the present focussed interest is the construction and development of conceptual schemes to better understand and interpret the relationships described in this chapter. Such conceptual schemes will need to be sufficiently expansive and flexible to address the full range of relationship perspectives portrayed in Figure 6.3 and expanded on in the section on companionship tourism.

There would appear to be several viable candidates for the next phase of developing our understanding of tourist–tourist and tourist–local relationships. The potential candidates include conceptualising tourist relationships as an extension of the in-group–out-group approach (Yagi and Pearce, 2002), the development of the concept of threshold and liminoid space for tourist settings (Selanniemi, 2003), innovative dramaturgical and performative accounts (Daniel, 1996; Donlon and Agrusa, 2003), and theories combining social exchange and social representation approaches

(Pearce, Moscardo, and Ross, 1996). What is certain in this area of inquiry is that relationships are pivotal to tourism, and it can be a goal of both the analytical and the managerial dimensions of tourism to enhance these interpersonal encounters.

References

Aramberri, J. 2001. The Host Should Get Lost. Paradigms in the Tourism Theory. *Annals of Tourism Research* 28(3): 738–761.

Archer, B., and C. Cooper. 1998. The Positive and Negative Impacts of Tourism. In *Global Tourism*. ed. W. Theobald. Oxford: Butterworth-Heinemann.

Armstrong, J. 2003. *Conditions of Love. The Philosophy of Intimacy*. London: Penguin.

Bammel, G., and L. Bammel. 1992. *Leisure and Human Behaviour*. 2nd ed. Dubuque, Iowa: WCB Group.

Buchanan, I., and A. Rossetto. 1997. 'With My Swag upon My Shoulder,' Occasional Paper, no. 24, Bureau of Tourism Research.

Chesney-Lind, M., and I. Y. Lind. 1986. Visitors as Victims: Crimes against Tourists in Two Hawaii Counties. *Annals of Tourism Research* 13: 167–191.

Clift, S., C. Callister, and M. Luongo. 2002. Gay Man, Holidays and Sex: Surveys of Gay Men Visiting the London Freedom Fairs. In *Gay Tourism Culture, Identity and Sex*. eds. S. Clift, M. Luongo and C. Callister. London: Continuum.

Cohen, E. 1982. Thai Girls and Farong Men: The edge of Ambiguity. *Annals of Tourism Research* 9: 403–428.

———. 2003. Transnational Marriage in Thailand: The Dynamics of Extreme Heterogamy. In *Sex and Tourism. Journeys of Romance, Love and Lust*. eds. T. Bauer and R. McKercher. Binghampton, NY: Haworth.

Dahles, H., and K. Bras. 1999. *Tourism and Small Entrepreneurs: Development, National Policy, and Entrepreneurial Culture: Indonesian Cases*. Sydney: Cognizant Communication Corporation.

Daniel, Y. P. 1996. Tourism Dance Performances: Authenticity and Creativity. *Annals of Tourism Research* 23(4): 780–797.

de Albuquerque, K. 1999. Sex, Beach Boys and Female Tourists in the Caribbean. *Sexuality and Culture* 2: 87–111.

de Albuquerque, K., and J. McElroy. 2001. Tourist Harassment. *Annals of Tourism Research* 28(2): 477–492.

de Botton, A. 2002. *The Art of Travel*. New York: PantheonBooks.

Desforges, L. 2000. Traveling the World. Identity and Travel Biography. *Annals of Tourism Research* 27(4): 926–945.

Donlon, J., and J. Agrusa. 2003. Attraction of the Naughty-Gentlemen's Clubs as a Tourism Resource: The French Quarter Example. In *Sex and Tourism: Journeys of Romance, Love and Lust*. eds. T. Bauer and R. McKercher. Binghampton, NY: Haworth.

du Cros, H., and D. du Cros. 2003. Romance, Retsina and Reality in Crete. In *Sex and Tourism. Journeys of Romance, Love and Lust*. eds. T. Bauer and R. McKercher. Binghampton, NY: Haworth.

Foster, F. 2002. The "University of Travel": Backpackers and the Development of Generic Skills. Unpublished B.Admin.(Tourism). Honours thesis, James Cook University, Townsville, Australia.

Gibbons, S., and E. J. Ruddell. 1995. The Effect of Goal Orientation and Place Dependence on Select Goal Interferences among Winter Backcountry Users. *Leisure Sciences* 17: 171–183.

Glasson, J., K. Godfrey, and B. Goodey. 1995. *Towards Visitor Impact Management: Visitor Impacts, Carrying Capacity, and Management Responses in Europe's Historic Towns and Cities*. Aldershot: Avebury.

Graefe, A. R., and J. J. Vaske. 1987. A Framework for Managing Quality in the Tourist Experience. *Annals of Tourism Research* 14(3): 390–404.

Harper, D. W., Jr. 2000. Planning in Tourist Robbery. *Annals of Tourism Research* 27: 517–520.

Herold, E., R. Garcia, and T. DeMoya. 2001. Female Tourists and Beach Boys. Romance or Sex Tourism? *Annals of tourism Research* 28(4): 978–997.

Jackson, E. L., and R. A. G. Wong. 1982. Perceived Conflict Between Urban Cross-Country Skiers and Snowmobilers in Alberta. *Journal of Leisure Research* 141: 47–62.

Jacob, G. R., and R. Schreyer. 1980. Conflict in Outdoor Recreation: A Theoretical Perspective. *Journal of Leisure Research* 12(4): 368–380.

Jamal, T., and K. Hollinshead. 2001. Tourism and the Forbidden Zone; the Underserved Power of Qualitative Inquiry. *Tourism Management* 22: 63–82.

Kagitcibasi, C., and J. W. Berry. 1989. Cross-Cultural Psychology: Current Research and Trends. *Annual Review of Psychology* 40: 493–531.

Kim, Y. J. 1997. Korean Inbound Tourism in Australia: An Analysis of Motivation and Cross-Cultural Contact. Unpublished doctoral dissertation, James Cook University, Townsville, Australia.

Lee, M. H. 2002. Male Taiwanese Attitudes to Sex Tourism. In *Asia Pacific Tourism Association Conference: APTA: Conference Proceedings*. Dalian, China.

Mannell, R., and D. Kleiber. 1997. *A Social Psychology of Leisure*. State College, PA: Venture.

McCormick, N. 1994. *Female Salvation: Affirming Women's Sexual Rights and Pleasures*. Westport, CT: Praeger.

McKercher, R., and T. Bauer. 2003. Conceptual Framework of the Nexus between Tourism, Romance and Sex. In *Sex and Tourism. Journeys of Romance, Love and Lust*. eds. T. Bauer and R. McKercher. Binghampton, NY: Haworth.

Mercer, D. 1998. The Uneasy Relationship between Tourism and Native Peoples: The Australian Experience. In *Global Tourism*. ed. W. Theobald. Oxford: Butterworth-Heinemann.

Moscardo, G. 1996. An Activities Based Segmentation of Visitors to Far North Queensland. In *Tourism and Hospitality Research: Australian and International Perspectives*. ed. G. Prosser. Canberra: Bureau of Tourism Research.

Moscardo, G., and P. L. Pearce. 1999. Understanding Ethnic Tourists. *Annals of Tourism Research* 26(2): 416–434.

Murphy, L. 2001. Exploring Social Interactions of Backpackers. *Annals of Tourism Research* 28(1): 50–67.

Noe, F. P. 1999. *Tourism Service Satisfaction*. Champaign, Illinois: Sagamore.

Opperman, M. 1998. *Sex Tourism and Prostitution*. New York: Cognizant Communication.

Parasuraman, A., V. A. Zeithaml, and L. L. Berry. 1994. Alternative Scales for Measuring Service Quality: A Comparative Assessment Based on Psychometric and Diagnostic Criteria. *Journal of Retailing* 70(3): 201–230.

Pearce, P. L. 1980. Strangers, Travellers and Greyhound Terminals: A Study of Small Scale Helping Behaviours. *Journal of Personality and Social Psychology* 38: 935–940.

——. 1981. Environmental Shock: A Study of Tourists' Reactions to Two Tropical Islands. *Journal of Applied Social Psychology* 11(3): 268–280.

——. 1982. *The Social Psychology of Tourist Behaviour*. Oxford: Pergamon.

——. 1998. The Relationship between Residents and Tourists: The Research Literature and Management Directions. In *Global Tourism*. ed. W. Theobald. Oxford: Butterworth-Heinemann.

——. 1999. The Senior Self-Drive Traveller Market. *Tourism Recreation Review*, Special issue on Aging and Tourism.

Pearce, P., E. Kim, and S. Lussa. 1998. Facilitating Tourist-Host Social Interaction: An Overview and Assessment of the Culture Assimilator. In *Embracing and Managing Changes in Tourism: International Case Studies*. eds. E. Laws, B. Faulkner, and G. Moscardo. London: Routledge.

Pearce, P. L., G. Moscardo, and G. F. Ross. 1996. *Tourism Community Relationships*. Oxford: Elsevier.

Pruitt, D., and S. Lafont. 1995. Love and Money: Romance Tourism in Jamaica. *Annals of Tourism Research* 22: 422–440.

Rathmun, R. 1995. Factors in User Group Conflict between Hikers and Mountain Bikers. *Leisure Sciences* 17: 159–169.

Ruddell, E. J., and J. H. Gramman. 1994. Goal Orientation, Norms, and Noise-Induced Conflict among Recreation Area Users. *Leisure Sciences* 16: 93–104.

Ryan, C. 1992. The Child as a Visitor. *World Travel and Tourism Review* 2: 135–139.

——. 1999. Sex Tourism: Paradigms of Confusion? In *Tourism and Sex: Culture, Commerce and Coercion*. eds. S. Clift and S. Carter. London: Cassell.

Schneider, I. E., and W. E. Hammitt. 1995. Visitor Response to Outdoor Recreation Conflict: A Conceptual Approach. *Leisure Sciences* 17: 223–234.

Selanniemi, T. 2003. On Holiday in the Liminoid Playground: Place, Time and Self in Tourism. In *Sex and Tourism. Journeys of Romance, Love and Lust*. eds. T. Bauer and R. McKercher. Binghampton, NY: Haworth.

Shelby, B. 1981. Encounter Norms in Back Country Settings: Studies of Three Rivers. *Journal of Leisure Research* 13(2): 129–138.

Simmel, G. 1950. *The Sociology of Georg Simmel*. trans. H. Woolf. New York: Free Press of Glencoe.

Swinglehurst, E. 1998. Face to Face: The Effects of Tourism on Societies Past and Present. In *Global Tourism*. ed. W. Theobald. Oxford: Butterworth-Heinemann.

Tajfel, H. 1981. *Human Groups and Social Categories*. Cambridge: Cambridge University Press.

Thornton, P., G. Shaw, and A. Williams. 1997. Tourist Group Holiday Decision-Making and Behaviour: The Influence of Children. *Tourism Management* 18(5): 287–297.

Triandis, H. C., X. P. Chen, and D. K. S. Chan. 1998. Scenarios for the Measurement of Collectivism and Individualism. *Journal of Cross-Cultural Psychology* 29(2): 275–290.

Truong, T. 1990. *Sex, Money and Morality: Prostitution and Tourism in Southeast Asia.* London: Zed Books.

Turley, S. K. 2001. Children and the Demand for Recreational Experiences: The Case of Zoos. *Leisure Studies* 20: 1–18.

Um, S., and J.L. Crompton. 1990. Attitude Determinants in Tourism Destination Choice. *Annals of Tourism Research* 17: 432–448.

Urry, J. 1990. *The Tourist Gaze.* London: Sage Publications.

Vaske, J. J., MP. L. Donnelly, K. Wittmann, and S. Laidlaw. 1995. Interpersonal Versus Social Conflict. *Leisure Sciences* 17: 205–222.

Want, P. 2002. Trouble in Paradise: Homophobia and Resistance to Gay Tourism. In *Gay Tourism: Culture Identity and Sex.* eds. S. Clift, M. Luongo, and C. Callister. London: Continuum.

Ward C., S. Bochner, and A. Furnham. 2001. *The Psychology of Culture Shock.* 2nd ed. East Sussex: Routledge.

Watson, A. E., M. J. Niccolucci, and D. R. Williams. 1994. The Nature of Conflict between Hikers and Recreational Stock Users in the John Muir Wilderness. *Journal of Leisure Research* 26(4): 372–385.

Wong, L. 2003. Island Girl. In *Sex and Tourism. Journeys of Romance, Love and Lust.* eds. T. Bauer and R. McKercher. Binghampton, NY: Haworth.

Yagi, C. 2001. How Tourists See Other Tourists: Analysis of Online Travelogues. *Journal of Tourism Studies* 12(2): 22–31.

——. 2002. Tourist Encounters with Other Tourists. Unpublished doctoral dissertation, James Cook University, Queensland, Australia.

Yagi, C., and P. L. Pearce. 2002. Tourists' Preferences for Seeing Other Tourists. In *Proceedings of First Asia Pacific Forum for Graduate Students Research in Tourism,* May 22, 2002, Macao. Hong Kong: The Hong Kong Polytechnic University.

Yiannakis, A., and H. Gibson. 1992. Roles Tourists Play. *Annals of Tourism Research* 19(2): 287–303.

Zinovieff, S. 1991. Hunters and Hunted: Kamaki and the Ambiguities of Sexual Predation in a Greek Town. In *Contested Identities: Gender and Kinship in Modern Greece.* eds. P. Loizos and E. Papataxiarchis. Princeton: Princeton University Press.

7 Alternative tourism: a comparative analysis of meaning and impact

Donald V.L. Macleod

Introduction

As a concept, 'alternative tourism' is surprisingly broad. It is fundamentally problematic when subject to analysis and brings out many emotional responses, a common feature of tourism as a subject. There is not one single or absolute definition, although there are a number of very good attempts, and many writers give a list of criteria against which it should be assessed. It remains an important issue to be dealt with, not the least because of its relationship to basic problems that human society must confront: environmental destruction, wealth inequalities, and irresponsible development, among others. It is also growing in popularity as fashions change and tourists seek different experiences. Just as it has been promoted as a 'development tool' and a means of protecting nature, so it has also been seen as an attractive way to pass leisure time without causing ecological damage.

This chapter is a critical inquiry into the character of alternative tourism and its impact, and is composed of two major sections. The first section deals with its *meaning* as can be ascertained from surveying and comparing the works of different scholars; the second deals with its *impact*, in which the influences described by various scholars are compared, including detailed case studies. Finally, the conclusion challenges the viability of the term 'alternative tourism' and proposes a new approach. It also attempts to revise our understanding of the impact of this type of tourism, critiquing earlier models and stressing the powerful influences that it has had on the environment and the host populations. Throughout this discussion problems are highlighted and suggestions are made for future research.

The Meaning of Alternative Tourism

In a paper that looked at the evolution of alternative tourism as a concept, Gonsalves (1987) charted its beginnings as a defined concept from the Manila International Workshop in 1980, although he noted that concern over tourism had become public at the World Council of Churches in 1969. In 1984 in Chiangmai, Thailand, the 44 participants of The Ecumenical Coalition on Third World Tourism (ECTWT) agreed that it was seen as a process that promotes a just form of travel between members of different communities. It seeks to achieve mutual understanding, solidarity, and equality amongst participants.

The ECTWT produced a resource book on alternative tourism and promoted models and programs. Such models included:

- Brief contacts with local people,
- Longer visits with host families and the community, and an insight into local life,
- Noncommercial learning options (study tours, work camps, exchange visits),
- Organisations or community groups in various countries concerned about third world tourism, and
- Alternative tourist travel agents in host and sending nations seeking to share rather than shield visitors from the destination's culture and problems.

Gonsalves (1987) sees the ultimate test of these alternatives in their ability to influence mainstream tourism. He cites an encouraging sign, that of the adoption of the Tourism Bill of Rights and Tourism Code by the World Tourism Organization in 1985 in response to the Penang Code of Ethics. He concludes that, 'travel, throughout history, has been a means of education, cross-cultural communication and the development of meaningful relationships. Alternative tourism considers these objectives still valid and works towards these ends.' He ended on an optimistic note, and was positive about the course and intentions of alternative tourism, a position that has more recently been subject to sceptical criticism by other writers.

For Cohen (1987), alternative tourism is not even a single general concept, but composed of two principal conceptions. First, it is seen as a reaction to modern consumerism, a counter-cultural response to mass tourism composed of such characters as the adventurer, drifter, traveller, or those looking for spontaneity or romantically searching for a lost paradise. He suggests that these types occasionally create their own cultural enclaves involving drugs and sex, treating local people as oddities, and initiating a diminution of the culture of hospitality amongst the host community. There is also the incipient creation of an alternative tourism 'establishment,' which leads to a further reduction in difference between alternative and mass tourism.

Second, it is conceived as 'concerned alternative tourism,' which is in essence a reaction to the exploitation of the third world in which the notion of a 'just' tourism arises, furthering mutual understanding and preventing environmental or cultural degradation and exploitation. In this type of tourism small groups interact with local people, and small-scale projects involving local consultation and participation are the principal means of promotion.

Cohen sees the principal quandary as being the fact that mass tourism cannot be transformed, whereas alternative tourism is too small scale to offer a realistic general option. This leads to the realisation that tourism is extremely varied and multifaceted and that criticism of mass tourism is too radical, whereas the goals of alternative tourism are set too high and are therefore unrealistic. Cohen is ultimately pragmatic, highlighting the need to reform the worst prevailing situation in mass tourism. In short, he has powerfully criticised the supposition that alternative tourism can ultimately lead to a transformation of tourism and is suspicious of the benefits that it brings. He offered a good working definition, drawing attention to two central aspects, and has added a healthy air of critical judgement.

Cazes (1989) was well aware of the ambiguity of the concept 'alternative tourism' and he likened it to the notion 'integrated,' which has been described as a 'miracle-word, a panacea concept and a mythical term.' However, he eventually provided guidelines that may be applied to six different sectorial fields:

1. *The tourist as an individual:* motivated through original aspiration, which may include active tourism (rambling, trekking), exploring, encounter travel, committed tourism (voluntary service overseas, archaeological digs), and other self-sacrificing work.
2. *The practitioners:* they do not want to be regarded as clients or consumers, and include backpackers, drifters, long-distance travellers; overall a varied group.
3. *The journey's destination:* this may be an unexplored 'virgin' location and often rests on an idealised vision of peasant societies that represent 'authentic' cultures.
4. *The type of accommodation:* 'supplementary' including camping, small local family hotels, holiday centres, village inns, private rented homes, paying guests; the dominant theme is microfacilities as opposed to massive hotels.
5. *Travel organisers and partners:* especially the nonlucrative organisations (nongovernmental organisations, mutual benefit societies), individual travel organisations; marginal or underground.

6. *The mode of insertion in the host community:* this involves a concerted effort to develop the reception of tourists wherein discourse centres on integration (economic, social, spatial, ecological, urban), local control, and auto development. A crucial factor is the prominence of the local system in overseeing the tourism.

Having critically analysed the sectorial fields, Cazes went on to deconstruct the concept of mass tourism, seeing it as a myth that represents the 'other' or 'anti-other,' a seat of harmful potentialities. Thus, alternative tourism is in actuality a discourse on difference and is fundamentally elitist. In fact, it becomes a total subversion of the dominant models on three levels:

1. *Values:* the conditions of aspiration and motivations for the journey.
2. *Process:* the quality of collaboration and partnership, cooperation and synergy between external operation and local system at different stages of the phenomenon.
3. *Forms:* social, spatial, ecological, and architectural forms are all faithful to the guiding principles of integration based on local traditional patterns and workforce.

According to Cazes, there is no perfect example that epitomises alternative tourism as described above, although the development of Lower Casamance in Senegal comes close. Further, he admits that there are dangers in idealising the concept and points to the risks of 'ghettoizing' areas and the 'museumification' of sites of interest based on an elitist interpretation.

A more straightforward definition is offered by Hitchcock, King, and Parnwell (1993) in the introduction to their edited collection, which suggests that in its purest form alternative tourism is underpinned by a number of principles:

- It should be built on dialogue with local people who ought to be aware of its effects and have political weight concerning the matter.
- It should be established on sound environmental principles, sensitive to local culture and religious tradition.
- It should be a means of giving the poor a reasonable and more equal share in the gains.
- The scale of tourism should be tailored to match the capacity of the local area to cope, measured in aesthetic and ecological terms.

The writers also noted that alternative tourism may be used to strengthen linkages between the tourism industry and other forms of local economic activity. They recognized that its promotion has led to the questioning of how tourism affects destinations and the fact that the market niche is being exploited, warning about the possibility of a green consumerism developing. However, they remained essentially optimistic, citing the case of ecotourism that can support the protection of vulnerable areas of natural beauty and scientific interest as well as to stimulate environmental awareness amongst the local population.

Continuing the theme of environmental and social sensitivity, in an article on tourism and sustainable development, Murphy (1994), using the definition offered by Krippendorf (1987) who sees alternative tourists as 'those who try to establish more contact with the local population, try to do without the tourist infrastructure and use the same accommodation and transport facilities as the natives'. He then went on to define ecotourism (a subset of alternative tourism) as occurring where the visitor contributes to the development and well being of the host ecology. Such tourists are regarded as the champions of the environment and sustainable development, and Costa Rica is cited as a country where ecotourism principles support the philosophy of sustainable development.

As is clear from the above definitions and illustrations of alternative tourism, this concept is not easily contained within neat parameters, and moreover it may be regarded as too broad to be accurately used. Further, in the opinion of Cazes, its antithesis, mass tourism, is not sufficiently well understood for an alternative to be really valid. Nevertheless, it is possible to retrieve the central aspects of the concept from the various writers, and these include contact and communication between the tourists and the indigenous population, and a desire for equality, individuality, environmental awareness, and concern. However, there are also cautionary undertones, with some writers feeling that there is an element of elitism within this type of tourism, whereas others see it as being exploited as a consumer item. One must bear in mind the need to be cautious and sceptical in imagining its impact. In addition, as tourism grows and the need for environmental responsibility increases, so the necessity for an objective and detailed understanding of the phenomenon and its influence becomes more imperative.

The Impact of Alternative Tourism

In his critique of alternative tourism, Butler (1990) plays devil's advocate, warning of the risks of passively accepting the hype surrounding it, and he compares it with the notion of 'sustainable development' in that, '[i]t can mean almost anything to anyone.' He emphasized the need to focus on the implication for destination areas, and in his attack he goes so far as to ask the question: why would anyone want to promote it? The answer, he suggests, is found in the desire of promoters and host communities for fewer negative effects on destinations and populations. This is the heart of the problem, and Butler pointed to the difficulties inherent in tourism overall, and the need to recognise it both as an industry and an agent of development and change. There is, because of tourism's fragmented and competitive nature, a need to be wary and consider the worst possible outcomes. He suggested that even the concept of 'green tourism' (ecotourism) should be treated with caution. Butler saw an element of elitism in alternative tourism, and wondered for whom it may be most 'appropriate.' He noted the correlation between the attributes of academics and the alternative tourists, and drew attention to the potential neocolonialism and ethnocentric application of their values on others.

Regarding the impact of alternative tourism, Butler draws attention to the fact that it will follow a different course than mass tourism and certain factors will assume greater significance, such as contact (visitor–host interaction), which could be of longer duration per occasion and in a more sensitive location, possibly penetrating the personal space of residents. It may also involve local people to a greater degree, use fragile resources, engender a proportionately greater leakage of expenditure, and cause political change in relation to control and development. The emphasis on contact as a precursor to change is something with which this writer is in strong agreement, as this chapter will eventually disclose, and Butler (1989) reiterates this fact by using a passage from his earlier work:

> It is generally accepted that social change and impact from tourism occur because of contact between tourists and the hosts and residents. One can therefore argue that tourism which places tourists in local homes, even when they are culturally sympathetic, and not desiring change in local behaviour is much more likely to result in changes in local behaviour in the long run than is a large number of tourists in more conventional tourist ghettoes, where contact with locals is limited, if intensive, and in, what is to locals, and tourists, clearly artificial settings.

Ultimately he suggests that the crucial question is whether alternative tourism is an appropriate form of development in its own right, and he asserts that there needs to be selective and deliberate planning and control over such development. Butler sees it as fulfilling a number of rules:

- Complementing mass tourism by increasing attractions and authenticity,
- Serving the needs of specific groups,
- Supplementing the incomes of rural dwellers on the periphery, and
- Allowing some tourism development in areas of limited capacity.

Whereas Butler writes in a generalising manner, urging caution and drawing up lists of problems and comparisons of 'hard' and 'soft' tourism,

Van den Burghe (1994) writes as a social anthropologist who has lived in a community and known it intimately over a long period of time. In his assessment of ethnic tourism in the small Mexican town of San Cristobel, he concludes that Butler and others have promoted the fact that ethnic tourism is fragile and intrinsically self-destroying unless it is carefully controlled, and needs a sensitive type of development strategy, about which he makes a number of points:

- Tourism traffic should be limited, for example not exceeding 1 percent of local population.
- The development of tourist facilities should be as invisible as possible.
- Museumization should be avoided.

Such planning should be made on a small scale by people knowledgeable about the local area. He cites the following reasons for the success of San Cristobel:

- There is paved road access but no jet airport nearby';
- The place is relatively isolated, necessitating overnight stays';
- The town is attractive, possessing 'Indianness,' a colonial ambiance, a temperate climate, and mountain scenery;
- The tourists visiting the area are nonpolluting; and
- Tourism and development are under local political control (i.e., small scale with private investment).

Van den Burghe points out that with small-scale investment there are fewer problems because with labour intensiveness there is more employment, businesses tend to be family based, and they are more flexible and more 'recession-proof' than large-scale developments where catastrophes are bigger and are often irreversible. Ethnic tourists are attracted by a lack of luxury development or access by air. They avoid consumer society and seek to get closer to local people, resisting the typical 'Club-Med' style attractions. They also tend to stay longer on less money and their spending is more likely to trickle down to the local population. Van den Burghe (1994) suggests that, 'In sheer economic cost-benefit terms, ethnic tourism is really much more profitable and beneficial to a greater number of people than it seems at first blush, it also produces less environmental and cultural pollution.'

Ecotourism is another subset of alternative tourism and was examined by Parnwell (1993) in a book on tourism in Southeast Asia. He generally supports the view that ecotourism can be environmentally beneficial. He believed that the growth of special interest tourism such as ecotourism (which includes safaris, bird-watching, wildlife photography, landscape painting, and even organised hunting trips) has 'in many instances helped to generate a greater awareness of the aesthetic value of natural ecosystems amongst both the promoters and consumers of tourism resources.'

However, in contrast to Parnwell's benign view of ecotourism, the book includes Hitchcock's (1993) rather pessimistic examination of 'dragon tourism' (involving looking at the giant lizards) on the island of Komodo, Indonesia. He revealed that despite the National Park being a success, the indigenous island population has been overlooked by the authorities and is therefore unable to participate in the new developments because of a lack of education and skills. This has occurred even though overall communications have improved, as has the macroeconomy. Hitchcock points out that there can also be problems with this type of tourism when people visit a place to observe rare creatures.

Curiously, one of the major sources of income remains the sale of goats for use as bait, though this is one of the practices that the planners had hoped to discourage. This is cause for concern because it remains unknown what effects the use of bait is having on the behaviour of the giant lizards in their natural habitat.

Research into the ecological impact of ecotourism is in its early stages, although it has been recognized that there are many problems when tourists became intimately involved with watching and pursuing wildlife, upsetting their activity patterns, intimidating animals (albeit innocently), destroying living organisms (e.g., vegetation and coral), and disturbing patterns of behaviour of both animal prey and victim (see Fennell, 1999).

Returning to the general theme of alternative tourism and its impact, the groundbreaking collection on tourism *Hosts and Guests: The Anthropology of Tourism* (Smith, 1989a) provides a brief summary of the impacts of tourism overall, while detailing economic changes as well. These changes include influences on labour, development, cash flow, foreign exchange, price inflation (especially land), and the multiplier effect. The imperialistic nature of such developments was also noted. Other impacts referred to included the rejuvenation of arts and crafts, as has happened in Bali, which were regarded as 'cultural involution' by some scholars.

Smith (1989b) considers certain cultural changes to have developed because of modernization including the transformation of traditional values and mores, the introduction of mass media, and cross-cultural understanding. She regards the modernisation of cultures through trade and globalisation as preceding or simply submerging the impact of tourism, and predicts that a worldwide cultural homogenisation is underway thereby diminishing the difference between hosts and guests. Yet she referred to the fact that tourism can accentuate negative aspects of society, such as moral decay, but at the same time also act as a bridge to an appreciation of cultural relativity and international understanding. The phrase 'alternative tourism' is mentioned briefly, and was seen as a format developed by operators featuring one-to-one interaction between hosts and guests. It was pointed out that ethnic and cultural tourism allow visitors to witness indigenous culture, which can lead to stress amongst local people if their privacy was felt to be invaded.

Smith has constructed a model of 'tourist impact upon a culture,' whereby she suggests that:

> Explorers and Elite travellers, by virtue of their limited numbers, usually make little impact upon the indigenous culture, for hotels and other services are seldom required. The Offbeat and Unusual tourist commonly stays at roadhouses or hotels that locals use, and gets about by local transportation (including the use of the school bus, for the very occasional groups who visit). The money they spend is a welcome addition, their presence is seldom disruptive and children may delight in 'talking English' with someone other than their teachers.

Stressful contacts between hosts and guests were seen as proportionate to increasing numbers, and on a sliding scale according to the volume of visitors. According to the model, those making the most impact were the charter tourists, whereas those making the least impact were the 'explorers.' The weakness of this model lies in its lack of clarification of the term 'culture' and its omission of 'contact' and 'communication' as major factors in sociocultural change. In fact, ironically, the quotation above draws attention to the interaction between offbeat or unusual tourists and the host community, a feature that is prominent in alternative tourism, and a reason for its more far-reaching potential for influencing the host community.

In the same collection of essays, Graburn (1989) also perceived mass tourists as having a greater impact on the culture of the host peoples than the youthful alternative travellers. He describes mass tourism as 'tourism of the timid (often parents of the youthful travellers) who have money and don't mind spending it, as long as they can carry the home-grown "bubble" of their life-style around with them.' Graburn explained the impact of such 'timid' tourists as: 'These tourists are likely to have the greatest impact on the culture and environment of the host peoples both by virtue of their greater numbers and by their demands for extensions of their home environments for which they are willing to pay handsomely.'

This chapter's author strongly disagrees with these assessments of the relative impact of alternative tourism and provides reasons for this later, together with examples from published ethnographic work.

In work that examined the influence of alternative tourism on a Canary Island, Macleod (1997) highlighted and pointed out the problems regarding the notion of the 'alternative tourist,' and focused on the individuals and their sense of identity as well as studying their influence on the indigenous local population. Essentially, the alternative tourists who visited La Gomera in the Canary Islands form a broad category, but they have been described as backpackers, aged between 20 and 45 years, highly educated students, or people working within liberal professions, concerned about the environment, interested in meeting the local people, and possessing a strong desire for personal freedom. Macleod was well aware of the pitfalls of creating an identifiable group and his work addressed the process of constructing identity, acknowledging the subjectivity involved, and pointing out that many tourists actually described themselves as 'alternative tourists' as well as the fact that other observers have defined them as such.

Attention is drawn to the breadth and depth of influence that this form of tourism can have on the local community in many areas of life, including the economic, sociocultural, psychological, intellectual, and environmental influences. These areas of influence are briefly summarised in detail later, using examples from research in the Canary Islands.

Economic Influence

> Rooms may be rented in the homes of local people or in purpose-built apartment blocks owned by them, thereby putting money straight into their pockets. Goods are purchased in small stores run by local people, and food and drink is consumed in outlets also run by them. In essence, many families rent out rooms and gain income from tourism-related employment. For example, one fisherman was able to sell his fish directly to restaurants serving tourists, his daughters own or work in shops selling clothes and goods to tourists, his sons work in bars and restaurants, and one son regularly works as a painter of apartment buildings. The fisherman also has two apartments in his own home that are managed by his wife, and his daughters help to clean them (Macleod, 1997).

The money earned by local people allows them to increase their spending power, creating a 'multiplier effect.' When they spend some of their earnings on purchasing other local goods or services, other merchants profit from this additional exchange of money. New business ideas introduced by tourists who have decided to settle for long periods also influence the local population. These might include T-shirt shops, craft and jewellery stores, and dolphin-watching excursion trips, all of which give local people examples of entrepreneurial ventures that they might emulate.

Sociocultural Influence

Alternative tourists mix with the local population because of their proximity in accommodation, through using local services and by communicating with landlords and their families. This often leads to friendships and in some cases, serious relationships that result in marriage. In 1991 for example, there were more than 10 such marriages in a village of 350 residents. Thus the pattern of kinship can be influenced directly, and the new members of families bring with them their own cultural behaviour in respect to parenthood and human interaction. Tourists also offer a wider possibility of sexual partners for the younger generation, especially local men, and many relationships have begun because of the propensity of local men to pursue foreign women. The community becomes more international in its composition because of the influx of foreigners who have formed relationships with locals, as well as those who choose to live and work in the area, setting up small businesses.

New work opportunities for women, through letting out rooms or working in shops and service outlets, gives them their own income and consequently, more potential for independence. In some households women have become the major earners, and the overall situation has occasionally transformed traditional gender roles within the home, as well as offering women the freedom to work and live by themselves.

Psychological Influence

Local people enter into emotional relationships with foreigners who may have different approaches to partnership and sexual behaviour. This often leads them to question their own attitudes and lifestyle as individuals. Locals become more aware of their own identity as a distinct group through continued interaction and contrast with foreign visitors, although through deeper relationships with each other, they become aware of their mutual similarities. In one rare instance a local girl began a serious relationship with a German boy. Her parents refused to accept this situation and she left her home bound for Germany. However, after some time they both returned and her parents accepted him into the family, no longer treating him as an outsider. They began to lose their deep distrust of foreigners.

Foreigners who have different ideas about how either sex can behave may challenge traditional gender roles. In turn, this may influence local people to attempt to emulate the visitors (the demonstration effect) and challenge stereotyped roles, thereby for example leading to more self-confidence and independence amongst women. This influence may be compounded by the new potential for economic freedom that women may experience through the demand for their labour in tourism-related work.

Intellectual Influence

The local population is introduced to new languages (e.g., English and German) and many have made efforts to learn them informally through contact with the tourists in shops, bars, apartments, and through friends. There is also an exchange of ideas, in which new fashions in clothing, music, and food are involved, as well as thoughts on all manner of other things. There have been a number of incidences where local people have visited a tourist's country of origin, including Germany, Austria, and Holland, through their friendships with a tourist. In some instances they have found work and stayed for a long period of time. This not only allows them an insight into what another country is like, but it also gives them a new perspective on their own country and lifestyle. One young man visited Holland with a Dutch girlfriend and lived there with her for two years while working as a builder. He recounted how it had broadened his mind and made him more understanding of foreigners. It also gave him a greater appreciation of the friendliness of his own village.

Environmental Influence

In general, German tourists on La Gomera have an interest in ecological matters. They enjoy walking around the verdant peaks of the island and travelling around the shoreline by boat. Recently, a number of dolphin safari tours have began operating on the island and some private businesses take tourists on mountain bike rides into the hills. These activities may eventually have long-term detrimental effects on the environment, but initially, they cater to the tourist's desire to enjoy the natural environment without apparently harming anything. The appreciation the tourists have for the beauty of the island and its magnificent coastline has certainly promoted a stronger awareness among the local population of their heritage. One example of this was the nomination and acceptance of the temperate rainforest (which covers 10 percent of the island) as a World Heritage Site recognised by the United Nations Educational, Scientific and Cultural Organization (UNESCO).

At one time a petition appeared in a local restaurant protesting against the construction of both roads and large apartments in the area. The petition had been signed and supported by many tourists. The whole environmental conservation concern was encapsulated in a protest by the indigenous population against the local government proposal for the 'development' of the coastline into a resort style promenade and beach. This led to a huge media discussion of tourism, development, and the character and identity of the Canary Islands, together with the importance of the natural habitat. It also became the raw material for political battles during the election campaign, and ultimately the project was abandoned.

One of the principal points to come out of this rejected proposal related to the impacts of alternative tourism. It was recognized that where tourism is already taking place, a thorough ethnographic study of a site is absolutely necessary in order to fully appreciate the influence of further development. It also emphasised the point that it is important to understand the local people and their way of life in order to realise how influential such a phenomenon can be. Macleod's study has indicated the numerous areas of human culture that are affected by tourism, and contrasts with both Smith and Graburn's concentration on economic impact and the importance of volumes of tourism traffic. These approaches reflect a general weakness in impact models because of their focus solely on economic factors in 'development' analysis. In short, a holistic analysis of potential impacts provides a more rounded and more accurate picture of how tourism can affect a community, and places greater importance on individuals, their culture, and their community.

Crick (1994), who also undertook an ethnographic study, examined international tourism in Sri Lanka. In his broad-ranging and historical examination he drew attention to the many paradoxes occurring with tourism and development, one example being the public vilification of 'hippies' and their harassment. They were used as scapegoats, were blamed for many of tourism's unsavoury qualities, and were accused of introducing bad habits such as idleness, drug taking, and nudism. He pointed out the unfairness of this campaign and the hypocrisy surrounding much of the attacks on tourism and its alleged corrupting influence, focusing only on both hippies and budget tourists. In actuality, many within the local population considered the authorities to be corrupt, and wealthy tourists linked to illegal activities. In terms of economic benefits, Crick wished to redress some general misunderstandings by pointing out that the foreign exchange from budget tourists stayed in the local economy, providing funding for private homeowners, arts and crafts workers, and owners of small cafes and shops. This contrasts with the higher spenders, whether on package tours or not, who spent most of their money on accommodation or meals before setting foot in Sri Lanka, or in establishments where there is maximum leakage of foreign exchange via profits to overseas owners or investors. Furthermore, Crick indicated other important differences between alternative and charter tourists:

> Whilst it is no doubt easy to romanticise the extent to which various types of budget travellers mix with locals, they do, in fact, enjoy a fairly positive image with some Sri Lankans precisely because they are easy-going, relaxed and often have the time to talk to local people. By contrast, there are many negative characterisations of those more affluent tourists who travel from hotel to hotel in air-conditioned luxury never stopping to speak to anyone.

Crick also speaks of the term, 'cultural pollution' attributed to tourism, a common topic of discussion in the early 1980s. He deconstructs this notion, while demonstrating the multiplicity of interpretations and attitudes towards tourism within the local community, placing the criticism of tourism into a historical context as a continuation of the slandering of Western ways.

His in-depth analysis of the 'informal' economy, in particular the informal boarding houses and 'touts,' draws attention to the number and diversity of people involved in the 'black' economy. Crick estimates that there were more than 100 such touts in the town of Kandy (Sri Lanka), mostly men in their early twenties, and notes their importance in the accommodation and shopping sectors as middlemen and guides. Through detailed accounts from individuals, one gains an insight into the culture and activity of these touts, and learns how occasionally they establish intimate relationships with tourists as well as making money off of them as well as those engaged in the tourist business. Many locals regard 'doing the tourism' as an easy and lucrative option, although it was later revealed to be an urban myth, the reality being significantly harder.

There were numerous private unregistered guesthouses in Kandy, and their owners often produced an origins 'myth,' being rather embarrassed about their involvement in the tourism business. It was excused as 'a way of keeping up' or 'something for the wife to do.' However, many went to considerable pains to acquire facilities such as toilets and showers for the prospective tourists, some even sleeping in uncomfortable situations whilst renting out their own 'spare' rooms. By so doing, it could return good money to the householder, the equivalent of a month's salary for the rental of a room for a few days. In addition, it might also provide for their children the opportunity to learn English. Those successful landlords were often subject to the envy and suspicion of their neighbours, whereas according to informants, the local people were not envious of the foreign visitors themselves.

Persistent harassment of tourists by guides often left them irritated and was a problem that led to bad feelings between the two groups. This is but one of many examples of the interactions between the hosts and visitors that do not lead to 'peace and understanding,' as is indicated throughout this book. Nevertheless, despite occasional difficulties, many local people felt that tourism was a good thing and many were able to improve their economic positions through working formally or informally with tourists.

Crick was adamant in his intent to set the record straight about those types of tourists responsible for many of the perceived problems of tourism, an industry that he saw as part of the global capitalistic pattern of development with poorer countries being dependent on the richer powers, for whom they become 'pleasure peripheries.' He suggests that it is convenient to believe that the budget tourists staying in the cheapest accommodation are those mainly involved with drugs and prostitution, but in Kandy it was quite obviously the wealthier tourists in air-conditioned cars who were being whisked away by their drivers after their rapid tour of the Temple of the Tooth to liaisons with prostitutes in expensive accommodation in or just outside the city.

Conclusion

By concentrating on a relatively small sample, rather than providing a long list of definitions, this chapter has portrayed the particularities in relative detail, which hopefully will enable the reader to recognize the similarities and overall shape of alternative tourism. In this exploration it should be apparent that alternative tourism is very much a contextual creation in terms of space and time. It is a reflection of contemporary attitudes and values within society. Hence, in a complex and changing world (ever more so with the intensity of globalisation), meanings and manifestations become more diverse. This in turn should lead to a critique of alternative tourism as a valid concept, and the need to analyse and understand the reality of its impact.

In terms of analysing the impact, alternative tourism is again subject to the prevailing values of a society in that the predominant concern over tourism's impact and development has been with the economy. Therefore, in assessing impact many academics were prone to concentrate on financial data, employment, and industrial changes, while neglecting socio-cultural, psychological, and environmental factors. An awareness of this weakness leads to a realisation of the importance of a detailed analysis and comprehensive understanding of the host community in order to fully appreciate the breadth and depth of influences that tourism can have on the lives of local residents. This further supports the need for sound ethnographic research in the host community involving both local people and visiting tourists. The conclusive findings of this study are set out next:

Meaning: Despite agreement on the content of the term 'alternative tourism,' it is overstretched to the point of being inadequate, is hazy, and is subject to parody. It has more use as a general signifier than an analytical term. One reason for this is that with changes in tourism, the boundaries between mass and alternative tourism have been disappearing. For example, group excursions to exotic locations and packaged ecotours now involve large numbers of shepherded visitors. Essentially the concept is becoming outmoded and is fragmenting into disparate subsets, the classifications of which are in serious need of revision. Instead of catch-all terms, which mean different things to different people, and eventually cease to be applicable over time, a more specific description needs to be used and rigorously defined. Such terms include ecotourism, ethnic tourism, individualistic/backpacking tourism, and adventure tourism. It is not the intention of this writer to establish a standard set of definitions, but the point should be abundantly clear that the meaning of alternative tourism has become vague and it is now an anachronism. There is a significant need to clearly define the subsets, tailoring them to changing times and conditions.

Impact: The impact of alternative tourism in its various guises has been largely underestimated by scholars such as Smith and Graburn whose models are inadequate for understanding the broader repercussions of tourism on indigenous populations. This is due to their concentration on economic impact and volume of visitors alone. The studies examined in this chapter, particularly those involving ethnographic work, demonstrate that alternative tourists have a strong influence across a broad spectrum of sociocultural and economic phenomena. This is largely due to the fact that they communicate with the indigenous population to a greater degree than do the mass or charter tourists. Alternative tourists mix with local people, occasionally forming deep personal relationships with them and exchange more than simply market goods. Even the economic impact is potentially more profound on an individual basis due to their propensity to live within the host community in private family accommodation as well as spending money on local services. New impact models need to be developed that are based on a broader range of criteria through which influence is assessed, with an emphasis on the sociocultural aspects.

The examination of impact has also highlighted the potential negative influences of tourism development. Vulnerable natural environments and human communities are at risk of being spoiled by ecotourism and ethnic tourism. These dangers are being increased by the new green consumerism; the cynical marketing of so-called alternative tours, irresponsible adventure travel, cross-cultural ignorance, and the popular belief that only mass tourism is potentially destructive.

Future research: A better understanding of the influences of tourism at the grass-roots level, partly through an awareness of the crucial part that communication plays in change and impact, can lead to a heightened awareness of how this phenomenon is affecting the world, and can have consequences for policy makers as well. It is therefore necessary that multidisciplinary discussions continue and grow, as there are risks of overspecialisation and the marginalisation of ideas and research findings in an area that so clearly deserves a broad sweep of academic approaches. More detailed ethnographic research needs to be carried out on the impact of ecotourism and ethnic tourism in order to determine their long-term effects and their breadth of influence. This research will assist in comparative analysis and offers the promise of broader insight into change. Investigations and theoretical modelling needs to be more rigorous, holistic, culturally sensitive, and people oriented if one is to understand the processes involved and alleviate problems in the future.

References

Butler, R. W. 1989. *Tourism, Heritage and Sustainable Development*. Waterloo, Canada: Heritage Resources Centre.

——. 1990. Alternative Tourism: Pious Hope or Trojan Horse? *Journal of Travel Research* XXVIII(3): 40–45.

Cazes, G. H. 1989. Alternative Tourism: Reflections on an Ambiguous Concept. In *Towards Appropriate Tourism: The Case of Developing Countries*. eds. T. V. Singh, H. L. Thevas, and F. M. Go. Frankfurt. Am Mann: Peter Lang.

Cohen, E. 1987. Alternative Tourism—A Critique. *Tourism Recreation Research* XII(2): 13–18.

Crick, M. 1994. *Resplendent Sites, Discordant Voices: Sri Lankans and International Tourism*. Chur, Switzerland: Harwood Academic Publishers.

Fennell, D. A. 1999. *Ecotourism: An Introduction*. London: Routledge.

Gonsalves, P. 1987. Alternative Tourism—The Evolution of a Concept and Establishment of a Network. *Tourism Recreation Research* XII(2): 9–12.

Graburn, N. 1989. Tourism: The Sacred Journey. In *Hosts and Guests: The Anthropology of Tourism*. 2nd ed. ed. V. Smith. Philadelphia: The University of Philadelphia Press.

Hitchcock, M. 1993. Dragon Tourism in Komodo, Eastern Indonesia. In *Tourism in South-East Asia*. ed. M. Hitchcock, V. T. King, and M. J. G. Parnwell. London: Routledge.

Hitchcock, M., V. T. King, and M. J. G. Parnwell. 1993. Introduction. In *Tourism in South-East Asia*. (ed.) M. Hitchcock, V. T. King, and M. J. G. Parnwell. London: Routledge.

Krippendorf, J. 1987. *The Holiday Makers*. London: Heineman.

Macleod, D. V. L. 1997. 'Alternative' Tourists on a Canary Island. In *Tourists and Tourism: Identifying with People and Places*. eds. S. Abram, D. Macleod, and J. Waldren. Oxford: Berg.

Murphy, P. 1994. Tourism and Sustainable Development. In *Global Tourism*. ed. W. F. Theobald. Oxford: Butterworth-Heinemann.

Parnwell, M. J. G. 1993. Environmental Issues and Tourism in Thailand. In *Tourism in South-East Asia*. eds. M. Hitchcock, V. T. King, and M. J. G. Parnwell. London: Routledge.

Smith, V. ed. 1989a. *Hosts and Guests. The Anthropology of Tourism*. 2nd ed. Philadelphia: University of Philadelphia Press.

——. 1989b. Introduction. In *Hosts and Guests. The Anthropology of Tourism*. ed. V. Smith. 2nd ed. Philadelphia: University of Philadelphia Press.

Van den Burghe, P. 1994. *The Quest for the Other: Ethnic Tourism in San Cristobel, Mexico*. Seattle: University of Washington Press.

8 The 'new pastoral industry?': tourism and indigenous Australia

David Mercer

One of the keys to realising the potential of Northern Territory tourism lies with the Territory's large Aboriginal population. Personal contacts with Aborigines is emerging as a tourism commodity especially sought after by a growing number of international visitors to Australia (Northern Territory Government, 1994).

If there is a 'wisdom' to be found in the heart of this life-world, it may lie in the often great good humour with which Aborigines entertain guests in their country, enduring and even trying to understand their guests' many and diverse fantasies about Indigenous life and culture.

—Redmond, 2002

When the Yanyuwa people of the Northern Territory in Australia classify their past, they divide it into the following phases, or 'times.' Macassan (pre-European contact), wild (first contact with Europeans), police (1890s onwards), war (World War II), welfare (1950 onward), cattle (1950s and 1960s), Gough Whitlam[1] (land rights), and this (tourist) time (Baker, 1999). The success of the cattle, or pastoral, period in particular, relied heavily on Aboriginal knowledge and labour and provided many employment opportunities. More recently, tourism has been referred to optimistically as having the potential to be 'indigenous Australia's new pastoral industry' (Ward, 2002). Each of the phases, especially the most recent 'tourist' chapter, has seen the introduction of a rush of new ideas, gender relations, and commodities, as well as diseases and community divisions, into Yanyuwa and many similar communities across northern and central Australia.

Gough first gave prominence to these issues in 1977 when he put forward a case for regarding 'tourism'—along with education, medicine, agriculture, and so on—as yet another medium for technology transfer.

1 Gough Whitlam was Australia's Prime Minister in the period 1972–1975 when Australia's first Commonwealth Department of Aboriginal Affairs was established.

Thus, in addition to novel transport, telecommunications, and image technologies, less affluent peoples in regions favoured by tourists often come to experience new food and refrigeration, construction, transportation, and finance technologies, to mention but a few obvious influences. The various impacts, however, are never uniform; neither are they always unidirectional. Increasingly, too, they are often successfully resisted (de Burlo, 1996). It is not uncommon for 'imposed' tourism ventures to founder in spectacular fashion as a consequence of failed cultural understanding. In each case the responses are different so we must beware of simplistic generalisations. Pagdin (1995) emphasizes that 'locally-affected people are not shaped passively by outside forces but react as well, at times even changing the conditions of the larger system, and that the outcome of tourism development is a negotiated process.'

Issues and Themes

Grounded in the growing body of literature on 'postmodern tourism' (Craik, 1994; Munt, 1994) and that which questions whether globalisation really has fostered cultural dialogue (Epstein, 2003), the main aim of this chapter is to illustrate some of this complexity through a discussion of the range of contemporary responses of Australia's indigenous Aboriginal and Torres Strait Islander population to the tourism phenomenon and the pressures for change.[2] It is timely to revisit this issue because, as the quotation at the start of this chapter illustrates, through such media as Lonely Planet guides[3] the Northern Territory government, and the Australian Tourist Commission,[4] the 1990s in particular has seen a strong marketing campaign based around Aboriginality as a 'tourism commodity.' As well, 2002 marked the thirtieth anniversary of the inauguration of the United Nations' (UN) 1972 Convention concerning the Protection of the World Cultural and Natural Heritage and was designated both the UN Year for Cultural Heritage and the International Year of Ecotourism. That year also saw 200 indigenous people from 19 countries participating in the International Forum on Indigenous Tourism in Oaxaca, Mexico,[5] as well as the start of an intensive, 12-month consultation process across Australia to

2 The literature on this is now extensive. See, for example, Zeppel, 1999.
3 In mid-July 2001, for the first time, Lonely Planet published a comprehensive guide to *Aboriginal Australia and the Torres Strait Islands* (Andrew, et al., 2001). The book has contributions from more than 50 indigenous Australians.
4 The Australian Tourist Commission was established through the Australian Tourist Commission Act of 1987. The Commission's main function is to increase overseas visitation to Australia.
5 The 'Oaxaca Declaration' is available from the Rethinking Tourism Project (info@rethinkingtourism.org).

develop a 10-year, strategic plan for tourism. At the time of writing that process has culminated in the production of an interim discussion document (Green Paper) entitled *A Medium to Long-Term Strategy for Tourism* (Department of Industry, Tourism and Resources, 2003a), a precursor to a final White Paper.

At the start of the twenty-first century, and in the face of enormous barriers, there are at least some indications that the descendants of Australia's original inhabitants are now successfully resisting their representation as 'exotic curios,' achieving far greater recognition of their cultural rights and insisting on meaningful consultation over the appropriation and 'marketing' of their heritage.

Such issues are central to what the prominent Australian anthropologist, Debra Bird Rose (1996), and others (e.g., Capra, 2002; Plumwood, 2003) have characterised as the 'dramatic and injurious junction' humans have now reached as a species. Rose is referring to the widespread opposition that we now encounter between ecological and human rights—an opposition that ultimately could prove fatal both for the planet and for humanity. The blunt message of such writers is that we have no choice but to take heed of the 'wisdom of the elders' and listen carefully to indigenous peoples' understandings of ecosystem functioning and place (Suzuki and Knudston, 1992). Theoretically, Australia could play a leading role in this process but only if—as in the United States, Canada, and New Zealand—the national and state governments are also prepared to cede some of their power and grant a much greater degree of indigenous sovereignty within the existing nation state. At the present time, and notwithstanding the High Court's 1992 landmark decision in *Mabo*[6] that native title could legitimately be claimed under certain, highly specific circumstances, Australia has a conservative ruling administration deeply suspicious of anything that departs from the desirable norm of a homogeneous, 'united' Australia, and there are few signs of optimism regarding significant legislative or constitutional reform under the present Commonwealth government (Hage, 1998; Neill, 2002).

In this chapter I explore a number of themes concerning the often uneasy relationship between contemporary western tourism developments and the native Aboriginal population principally, though not exclusively, in sparsely populated outback, northern and central Australia and along the nonmetropolitan littoral. 'Tourism' will be interpreted broadly here to also include the production, promotion, and marketing of indigenous paintings and artifacts (Smith, 1996). One conservative estimate is that the indigenous arts and crafts' sector is worth at least AUS$200 million per year (Whitford, Bell, and Watkins, 2001). For many remote

---

6 *Mabo and Others v. Queensland* (No. 2) [1992] HCA 23; (1992) 175 CLR 1 F.C. 92/014 (3 June 1992).

communities, the unprecedented international demand for high quality Aboriginal art in recent years has not only injected millions of dollars into often very poor settlements but has also created a new niche market for western, art-loving tourists wishing to meet the artists face to face. Not uncommonly, as at isolated Wingellina in the Northern Territory, the artistic boom was spectacular in terms of its dramatic growth and wealth creation but then effectively died just as quickly after a few short years (Rothwell, 2003).

A central focus of the discussion is the inseparability of questions surrounding tourism development and broader social justice issues concerning Aboriginal rights:

- Control over their traditional lands, practices, and cultural representations;
- Compensation for past injustices; and
- Total or partial sovereignty/self-governance (Behrendt, 2003).

Even though our main interest in this chapter is on the indigenous people of Australia, what Young (1995) calls the 'Third World in the First,' many of the ideas are also of direct relevance to other places in Oceania and the Asia-Pacific region, like Papua New Guinea and the Pacific Islands, where tourism has recently brought together peoples from vastly different cultural and economic backgrounds (Scheyvens and Purdie, 1999). Given that Australia has nine separate jurisdictions,[7] the discussion is of particular significance to other, federated states, such as Canada and the United States, where the goals and policy orientation of the national government occasionally may be in conflict with both minority native peoples and one or more subnational levels of government and where there is a strengthening indigenous rights' movement. The central problem being addressed revolves around the question of whether contemporary tourism development in Australia beyond the major metropolitan centres can be said to be economically beneficial as well as socially and culturally 'appropriate' from the Aboriginal viewpoint. This is a relatively under-researched area by comparison with the comparatively large body of marketing research literature on the perceptions, attitudes, and motivations of western travellers seeking a so-called ethnic tourism experience (Ross, 1991; Hollinshead, 1996; Harrison, 2001).

Indigenous Involvement and Interactions

Indigenous involvement in the tourism sector takes many forms, ranging from casual employment in mainstream, non-Aboriginal enterprises to

7 These are the Commonwealth government, six states and two territories (the Northern Territory and the Australian Capital Territory).

Table 8.1   Comanagement Arrangements at Australian Public and Private National and Tourist Parks

Consultation with local Aboriginal communities by the park authority
Aboriginal employment by the park authority
Park management committee with an Aboriginal minority
Park management committee with an Aboriginal majority
Park management committee with an Aboriginal power of veto
Aboriginal ownership of parks and a lease back agreement with park authority

Source: Larritt, 1993; Smyth, 2001.

total ownership and control (Mapunda, 2001). Further, there is a gradation of 'host–guest' interactions that can be categorised in terms of whether they involve low, medium, or high levels of intimacy. At one end, low level intimacy is a characteristic of the act of purchasing Aboriginal art or craft in a capital city retail outlet.[8] At the other, high level intimacy is experienced, for example, by tourists participating in small-group, extended interpretive tours on traditional lands led by indigenous tour guides (Parsons, 2002). International visitors vary markedly in terms of their comprehension of, and sensitivity toward, Aboriginal culture. In particular, conflicts and misunderstandings can occur in relation to the hunting and killing of wildlife species such as kangaroos, emus, crocodiles, and turtles. Interestingly, research consistently has found German visitors to Australia to be by far the most knowledgeable, and that understanding frequently translates into a desire to not intrude (Australian Tourist Commission, 2003).

Relatedly, at the outset it is important to grasp that there is a wide spectrum of responses on the part of the country's indigenous population ranging from complete opposition at one extreme through a variety of comanagement agreements with white Australians[9] to a commitment to indigenous-controlled and run tourism enterprises at the other (Table 8.1). That there is a wide diversity of reactions should come as no surprise, because there are considerable variations in visitor numbers and impacts between different regions and attractions, such as the highly personalised Manyallaluk Aboriginal Cultural Tours in the Northern Territory, which has only around 2000 visitors a year, whereas North Queensland's Tjapukai Dance Theatre attracts well over 100,000. The degree of historical exposure to tourism also varies markedly across this vast island continent. Indeed, contact with Europeans has been only relatively recent in

8 Increasingly, art is being sold online (see Jordan, 2000).
9 For a constantly updated reference source on negotiated agreements, see: www.atns.net.au.

north and northwestern Australia by comparison with the longer colonial encounter in the southeast. The Yolngu people of Arnhem Land in the Northern Territory, for example, had little contact with Europeans until the 1930s and have been able to maintain much of their traditional culture and customs relatively intact. Paradoxically, in the 1990s this community became the fertile breeding ground for *Yothu Yindi*, one of the most commercially successful rock groups in mainstream Australian musical history (Hayward and Neuenfeldt, 1998).

Indigenous People, 'Reconciliation' and Tourism

One of the most widely accepted definitions of the term 'indigenous' is that enunciated in 1986 by Jose Marinez Cobo, Special Rapporteur for the UN Working Group on Indigenous Populations (Cunneen and Libesman, 1995). 'Indigenous communities', he argued,

> ... are those which, having a historical continuity with pre-invasion and pre-colonial societies ... consider themselves distinct from other sectors of the societies now prevailing in those territories. ... They form at present non-dominant sectors of society and are determined to preserve, develop and transmit to future generations their ancestral territories, and their ethnic identity, as the basis of their continued existence as peoples, in accordance with their own cultural patterns, social institutions and legal systems.

Barsh (1999) has reminded us that all of the world's estimated 6,000 to 10,000 original cultures were 'indigenous' and that although most of these have long since been absorbed into modern nation states, there still exist sizeable indigenous minorities in parts of northern Europe; North, Central, and South America; Africa, Asia, and Oceania. Depending on the precise definition used,[10] Durning's (1993) estimate for the early 1990s was that there were anywhere between 190 million and 625 million indigenous people worldwide, ranging from high percentages of the national population in Papua New Guinea and Bolivia (77 percent and 70 percent, respectively) to low proportions in the United States (1 percent), Australia (2 percent), and Canada (4 percent). Almost without exception—and historically, invariably without prior consultation—promotional agencies in countries with indigenous populations use them as a marketing magnet for overseas tourists seeking an 'authentic' ethnic tourism experience. Nowhere was this more apparent than in the opening and closing ceremonies of the 2002 Sydney Olympic Games where, in marked contrast to their marginalised position in Australian society, indigenous themes were prominent (Simpson, 2002).

10 Three criteria are often used singly or together in different contexts. These are aboriginality, cultural distinctiveness, and self-identification (see United Nations' International Labour Organisation (ILO) Convention on Indigenous and Tribal Peoples, 1989).

At the same time, it has to be recognised that in many countries around the world indigenous people increasingly have come to see tourism as offering considerable opportunities in terms of reconciling some of the historical injustices that continue to plague ongoing relations between indigenous and nonindigenous people. Nevertheless, an angry 'backlash' against any attempt to deliver what are often widely interpreted as 'special privileges' to Aboriginal people has long been a common feature of the Australian political scene. In October 1985, the Commonwealth government finally recognised the legitimacy of indigenous ownership claims to that icon of Australian tourism—Uluru ('Ayers Rock')—in central Australia. Following the symbolic 'handing over' of the Rock, the government then immediately signed a 99-year leasing agreement with the local, 1400-strong Anangu community, which currently delivers approximately AUS$1000 per head, annually.[11] In some conservative circles, including the Northern Territory government of the day, this important symbolic action provoked outrage—expressed in court action and a nationwide newspaper advertising campaign—that 'land rights was totally out of control.'[12]

In both Canada and Australia, in particular, in recent years the issue of 'reconciliation' has been prominent on the political agenda. The Canadian government has now officially apologised for past injustices against its indigenous population and, through the legislated Council for Aboriginal Reconciliation (CAR), Australia went through an exhaustive, decade-long process of developing a framework for reconciliation between 1990 and 2000 (Johnson, 2002). In May, 2000, CAR presented its two final reports, *Australian Declaration Towards Reconciliation* and *Roadmap for Reconciliation*[13] to Parliament. The latter document placed considerable emphasis on the related issues of economic independence, disadvantage, rights' recognition, and sustaining the reconciliation process. On the day following the release of the reports, and in stark contrast to the Commonwealth government's position, an estimated 250,000 Australians demonstrated their support for reconciliation in a march across Sydney Harbour Bridge. The emphasis on economic independence for indigenous Australians and the potential possibilities offered by the tourism industry was in line with several of the key 'empowerment' recommendations of the earlier 1991 *Royal Commission into Aboriginal Deaths in Custody*. That Commission identified five, main tourism-related foci that appeared to offer benefits to Aboriginal communities. These were: employment (direct and indirect), investment in infrastructure (e.g., roads), the production

11 This represents 25 percent of the park entrance gate takings from approximately 400,000 annual visitors.
12 *Phillip Howard Toyne v. Paul Anthony Edward Everingham*, Supreme Court of the Northern Territory, No. 272/85.
13 See www.austlii.edu.au/other/IndigLRes/car/2000.

and sale of arts and crafts, cultural tours, and joint ventures (Executive Summary, 1993).

The mid-1990s were a time when there was more formal recognition by indigenous people themselves of the potential of tourism to aid greater cultural understanding and assist the reconciliation process. In Australia, in direct response to the findings of the *Royal Commission*, 1997 saw the release of the landmark, National Aboriginal and Torres Strait Islander Tourism Strategy. This strategy was produced after considerable indigenous input. It suggested 75 proposed actions based around three core objectives (Aboriginal and Torres Strait Islander Commission [ATSIC], 1997):

1. Remove obstacles to increased Aboriginal and Torres Strait Islander participation in the tourism industry, as investors, joint venture partners, employers (including operators), and employees;
2. Assist Aboriginal people to present their cultures to tourists in a way that is acceptable to Aboriginal communities and which also provides a valuable tourism experience; and
3. Assist Aboriginal and Torres Strait islander people in choosing how they wish to participate in the tourism industry, and building their capacity to contribute to the industry.

In both Canada and Australia, peak bodies run by Aboriginal people in the guise of Aboriginal Tourism Team Canada and Aboriginal Tourism Australia were formed in 1997 to provide leadership and for the development of indigenous tourism. These can be seen as significant developments symbolising the desire to take greater control of an industry that, in the past, had often openly exploited Aboriginal and Torres Strait Islander people.[14] and their traditional lands (Simondson, 1995). More recently in June 2000, the first ever National Indigenous Tourism Forum was held in Sydney, resulting in the formation of the 16-person, Indigenous Tourism Leadership Group. This high-level advisory group has made it clear that it now sees indigenous tourism as an integral part of the 'mainstream' tourism industry in Australia rather than a small, niche sector (Indigenous Tourism Leadership Group, 2002).

On the face of it, the potential economic benefits for what are often marginalised communities appear clear, but arguably there are also considerable social and political advantages to be gained from introducing a wider cross-section of nonindigenous people to aspects of Aboriginal lifestyles,

14 Aborigines and Torres Strait Islanders are two different ethnic groups and are distinguished as such in the Australian census. Other terms favoured by Australia's indigenous population include 'Anangu' (a central Australian term for Aboriginal people), 'Koori' (an indigenous term from southeastern Australia meaning 'ourselves'), 'Murri,' and 'Nunga'. In this chapter the term 'Aborigine' includes Torres Strait Islanders.

artistic and survival skills, and spirituality (Hinch and Butler, 1996). This is a theme that Durning (1993) has emphasised:

> Giving native peoples power over their own lives raises issues for the world's dominant culture as well . . . Indeed, indigenous peoples may offer more than a best-bet alternative for preserving the outlying areas where they live. They may offer living examples of cultural patterns that can help revive ancient values within everyone . . .

Indigenous Australia

With an area of 7.7 million square kilometres the island continent of Australia is slightly smaller than the contiguous United States, yet still has a population of only some 20 million, concentrated mainly in large urban centres along the eastern and southern seaboard. One reputable estimate is that at the time of first European contact in 1788 there were probably approximately 400,000 Aboriginal and Torres Strait Islanders living in all parts of the continent, but that within a century—decimated by disease and massacres—that number had dropped to a mere 30,000 (Bereson and McDonald, 1997).

By the late 1800s it was widely believed that it was only a question of time before the indigenous population died out completely and so they were not involved in any of the discussions leading up to formulation of the country's written Constitution in 1901. When they are mentioned in that document the language is exclusionary, and even though Aborigines and Torres Strait Islanders legally are Australian citizens in reality, many of them are profoundly marginalised, have a mortality rate that accords with the average in India or Bolivia and are, for the most part, 'citizens without rights' (Chesterman and Galligan, 1997; Mercer, 2003). Many Aboriginal communities, too, are plagued by substance abuse, domestic violence, disease, and welfare dependency—issues that are now being openly debated by indigenous leaders (Pearson, 2000; Davies, 2003). So bad are conditions in certain areas that there have been cases, such as at Garden Point in the Northern Territory, where indigenous communities have been embarrassed at the thought of tourists seeing their appalling housing conditions and so have opposed tourism developments (Altman, 1988).

One consequence of the historical belief that indigenous Australians were destined for extinction was that in many areas they were effectively written out of the history books. Recently, Clark and Cahir (2001) have argued forcefully that the Aboriginal presence needs to be reinstated in tourism landscapes. Current marketing of the historic Goldfields Tourism Region in western Victoria, for example, is almost totally silent on the rich indigenous heritage and gives the impression that settlement started only with the nineteenth-century gold rush. As well, nonindigenous controlled wildlife tourism ventures often pay scant attention to the all-important Aboriginal perspective (Muloin, Zeppel, and Higginbottom, 2001). Much contemporary advertising, too, stereotypes Aboriginal people and fails to convey the rich *diversity* of indigenous culture in Australia and the fact that, far from being ossified in the distant past, it is still highly relevant and evolving today (Ballantyne, 1995).[15] At the time of first European settlement there were an estimated 700 separate dialects of around 250 different Aboriginal languages. Even today, more than 40 indigenous languages are still spoken in the Northern Territory alone.

Despite the shameful history since colonial settlement and current social problems, in recent years the Aboriginal and Torres Strait Islander population has undergone a miraculous demographic transition and an explosive renaissance of sporting, cultural, and artistic creativity. Between the censuses of 1996 and 2001 the indigenous population, for example, increased by 16 percent, compared with the national average growth rate of only 6 percent and their numbers now approximate the estimated population at the time of first European settlement.[16] They still make up only approximately 2 percent of the total Australian population, but if the current high growth rate continues potentially there could be as many as 1 million Aboriginal and Torres Strait Islanders living in Australia by 2010 (Johnson, 2001). There are significant regional variations in their current levels of concentration. In the Northern Territory, for example, they make up a quarter of the total population of approximately 200,000. In addition, it should be noted that the vast majority of indigenous Australians live in large urban centres. Only approximately 30 percent of the population live in rural or remote areas, and the level of 'urbanisation' is rising with each census (Memmott and Moran, 2001). Given that nonindigenous market-ing invariably has equated 'authentic' ethnic tourism with the 'wild,' distant Outback, Parsons (2002) has argued that this now leaves the vast majority of '. . . Indigenous peoples in more urbanised areas with the onus of proving their own authenticity, or being encouraged by the tourism market to emulate the accepted authenticity of "The Outback Aboriginal."'

It is also clear that Aborigines have occupied Australia for approxi-mately 50,000 years and that over that time they developed a range of highly sophisticated skills for living sustainably in one of the harshest environments on earth (Colley, 2002). In some well-watered coastal areas,

15 The promotional material produced by the Aboriginal Art and Cultural Centre is an exception. Indigenous people are portrayed in active roles as tour guides rather than as passive subjects for photographs (www.aboriginalart.com.au). See Howard, Thwaites, and Smith, 2001.
16 Needless to add, defining 'Aboriginality' is not without its problems. Self-identification is commonly used in Australia, whereas in Canada and the United States registered descent has long been the norm (see Gardiner-Garden, 2003).

too, the archaeological evidence is that they were not nomadic but lived in permanent or semipermanent settlements. At Lake Condah in Victoria—currently the focus of a preparatory proposal for World Heritage listing as a cultural site—the archaeological evidence now shows more or less continuous settlement for 13,000 years, possibly making this the oldest known permanent settlement in the world. By contrast, the short period since European settlement has witnessed massive, and in many cases irreversible, degradation of the Australian environment (Flannery, 1994; National Land and Water Resources Audit, 2002). This observation alone should provide a salutary lesson that all is not well with recently introduced European land and water management practices and that maybe the time has come to listen attentively to what indigenous Australians have to teach about 'caring for country' (Howitt, 2001; Altman and Whitehead, 2003). The Gagadju people of the Northern Territory, for example, have been using 'firestick farming' as a management tool on their ancestral lands for thousands of years. After Kakadu National Park was first proclaimed in their country in 1979 they continued to burn the land in defiance of the European management regime that strongly favoured fire suppression. More recently, there has been growing recognition and acceptance of the ecological rationale for this longstanding indigenous practice (Langton, 1998; Yibarbuk, et al., 2001).

Over much of Australia indigenous ownership of land is deemed to have been obliterated by European settlement. However, in recent years, through a combination of land grants and successful native title claims, the Aboriginal-owned land base has been progressively expanding. It now comprises approximately 18 percent of Australia and has a population of perhaps 110,000 people, of whom 90 percent are estimated to be indigenous (Altman, 2001). It is likely that in the future, successful native title claims will be finalised for areas that have long been dedicated as national parks (Smyth, 2001). In passing, it is also interesting to note that, over the years, in some parts of Australia, there has been a gradual symbolic process of replacing European names of national parks with more appropriate indigenous names. Thus Ayers Rock-Mt. Olga has become Ulurua-Kata Tjuta, Jervis Bay has been renamed Booderee, and so on (Zeppel, 2001).

In the Northern Territory the farsighted Aboriginal Land Rights (Northern Territory) Act 1976, passed by a progressive Commonwealth government, granted freehold title to indigenous people over almost 50 percent of that enormous area. Given that property rights are the fundamental basis of power and control, this means that, at least in the Northern Territory, indigenous people have the ultimate power of veto over inappropriate tourism developments on their freehold land (Venbrux, 1999). This level of control, in a region that attracts almost 2 million tourists a year, is not available over much of the rest of Australia, especially in the more populous States of Victoria, New South Wales, and Queensland. However, the government of western Australia has recently signalled that it wishes to hand back to Aboriginal people the titles to 25 million hectares of national parks and state forests and then lease back the land. Already the government is negotiating such a deal with the traditional Martu people in the Pilbara region in the north of that state in relation to western Australia's largest national park, the 1.2 million hectare Rudall River National Park (Barrass, 2003).

It is also worth emphasising that the relatively high concentrations of Aboriginal people living in the northern parts of Australia are closest to the potentially huge tourism markets of Asia. Darwin airport has direct international connections into Asia and already Cairns is Australia's fifth busiest airport in terms of international arrivals.

Contemporary Tourism

Given that research in both Australia and New Zealand has found that overseas, rather than domestic, tourists constitute the main market segment interested in 'indigenous tourism' (Ryan, 2002; Ryan and Huyton, 2002; Australian Tourist Commission, 2003),[17] it is important to highlight recent, inbound visitation trends to Australia. For the last 20 years tourism consistently has been Australia's most significant service sector export industry. It currently generates approximately 5 percent of gross domestic product and provides direct employment for more than 500,000 people. Even though annual expenditure by overseas visitors (currently around AUS$17.1 billion) is less than half that of overnight domestic tourists, it still eclipses export earnings from the key mineral and agricultural commodities. In 2002 the Tourism Forecasting Council confidently predicted that by 2012 Australia could anticipate a doubling of tourists and a healthy visitation rate of approximately 10.4 million overseas visitors. But by May 2003 tourist arrivals had slumped to their lowest level for eight years and the Council had significantly downgraded its forecast to only 7.6 million by 2012. In less than two years the Australian inbound tourism sector had been subjected to no less than five major 'shocks' that had a dramatic negative impact on visitor numbers and confidence within the tourism industry. These were the terrorist attacks in New York and Bali, the collapse of Ansett airlines, the invasion of Iraq, and the SARS virus (Department of Industry, Tourism and Resources, 2003b). The Australian Tourism Export Council estimated that the two,

---

17 Research has found that up to 70 percent of inbound tourists seek an experience of 'Aboriginal Australia' when visiting the country but that only a tiny minority achieve that aim (Coulter, 1993).

latter events cost Australia AUS$2 billion in lost tourism earnings (Vergnani, 2003).

Notwithstanding these shocks, there is growing confidence that tourist arrivals to Australia will gradually recover and that, as such, there will be significant opportunities, as well as dilemmas, for indigenous tourism in the future. Visitor arrivals for the month of July 2003, registered major reductions from China and Japan, together with a lesser reduction from the United States, but strong growth from Korea, New Zealand, and the United Kingdom (Department of Industry, Tourism and Resources, 2003c).

The next section of this chapter briefly chronicles one of the most bitterly contested disputes between the non-Aboriginal proponents of a major tourism development and indigenous interests ever seen in Australia. In contrast, this is followed by a critical appraisal of a multi-award winning Aboriginal 'cultural park' in North Queensland, the Tjapukai Aboriginal Cultural Park. This attraction was mentioned briefly earlier in the chapter, but it is worthy of further consideration. These two case studies have been chosen deliberately to highlight some of the complex issues involved in any discussion of indigenous people and tourism in Australia.

Hindmarsh Island and the Ngarrindjeri People

Hindmarsh Island, or Kumerangk, as it is known by the local Ngarrind-jeri people, is a tiny island near the mouth of the River Murray in south Australia. In the 1980s a private company, Binalong Pty. Ltd., constructed a small marina there, but access was difficult and only available by ferry. Accordingly, in 1989 the company started negotiations with the enthusi-astic south Australian government of the day to upgrade the marina and associated residential facilities and construct an AUS$6.4 million bridge across the Goolwa Channel connecting the island to the mainland. In 1991 the south Australian state government agreed to become a partner in the project, which was also backed by Westpac Bank. Once it became clear what was involved, strong opposition to the proposal grew from a coali-tion of Ngarrindjeri, environmental, and church groups, the Friends of Goolwa and Kumerangk, on the grounds that fragile wetlands would be destroyed and significant spiritual values would be seriously compro-mised. In particular, the Goolwa Channel acts to protect women's tradi-tional ancestral spirits and a bridge, it was alleged by some Ngarrindjeri women, would violate the site (Bell, 1998). In protest, in April 1994, the peak national Aboriginal organization, ATSIC, threatened to withdraw AUS$1 billion in investments from the bank. Also, in July 1994, the Federal Minister for Aboriginal Affairs invoked national heritage legislation, the

Aboriginal and Torres Strait Islander Heritage Act 1984, and signed an order forbidding bridge construction, an edict that was subsequently overturned by the Federal Court on a point of law a few months later. Since that time there have been four additional state and federal government inquiries, including an AUS$1 million Royal Commission into the blocked project, as well as numerous conflicting anthropological studies and High Court appeals. One of the findings of the 1995 Stevens Royal Commission was that claims relating to 'secret women's business' had been fabricated and had no substance. Five years later the bridge was finally opened, but at a huge cost to taxpayers, the developers, and the local Aboriginal community, deeply divided over the authenticity of the 'secret women's business' claims (Simons, 2003). Indeed, in 2001 a Federal Court Judge, Justice John von Doussa, challenged the findings of the earlier Royal Commission (Ogle, 2002).

Stretching as it did over an agonising, 15 years, the Hindmarsh Island affair is a classic example of a clash of European developmentalist values, codified in the written 'logic' of Anglo-Saxon law, and indigenous values, grounded in a less precise oral tradition (Taubman, 2002). But it is by no means an isolated case. In recent years, for example, the steadily growing number of visitors to Uluru (Ayers Rock) has been fuelling mounting tensions between the Anangu people and western tourists, tourism operators, and promoters. At issue is the huge financial mismatch between what Anangu make out of tourism at Uluru by comparison with tourism operators and the lack of sensitivity shown by tourists and other nonindigenous people to sacred sites in and around Uluru Kata-Tjuta National Park. Anangu are not happy with tourists climbing the Rock and they strongly oppose the taking of photographs of certain parts of that monolith.[18] In theory, sites are protected under the Northern Territory Aboriginal Sacred Sites Act 1989, but it is only in recent years that infringements have resulted in a string of successful prosecutions (Mulvaney and Jones, 2002). The northern side of Uluru, in particular, has important women's sacred places and since 2000 strict guidelines, backed by stiff penalties, have been in place to prevent these sites from being photographed. The problem of course is that countless millions of such photographs, taken before 2000, already exist around the world in many forms,[19] and there are claims that a ban on photography over effectively 40 percent of Uluru could seriously damage tourism in Central Australia (Stewart, 2003).

18 Paradoxically, Uluru is held up internationally as one of the finest examples of comanagement for involving Aboriginal people in the protection of indigenous cultural and landscape values. In 1995 the Board of Management of Uluru-Kata Tjuta National Park was awarded UNESCO's prestigious Picasso Gold Medal for its achievements in this regard.
19 They include a famous poster of an aerial photograph of the Rock that the park authorities produced and have sold in their cultural centre since 1998.

The timing of the current 'representational crisis' at Uluru is not altogether surprising. It comes in the aftermath of years of cumulative tourism pressure and commercial exploitation, coinciding with indigenous insistence that cultural sensitivities be respected, and a related surge in litigation surrounding the protection of Aboriginal intellectual property rights (Simons, 2000). The 'Uluru model' is well known and widely praised as a classic comanagement agreement. In reality, it is deeply flawed and in need of fundamental reform (Power, 2002).

Elsewhere in Australia—in the richly-endowed rock-art Grampians-Gariwerd National Park in Victoria—the traditional owners have come up with the management 'solution' that allows tourist visitation to 10 publicised and intensively managed rock shelters but disallows access to another 100 such sites (Clark, 2000; 2002).

The Tjapukai Aboriginal Cultural Park

In many ways the Tjapukai Aboriginal Cultural Park—situated on 25 acres of indigenous-owned land at Caravonica, just outside Cairns, in far north Queensland—is an outstanding success story in terms of linking tourism innovation, cross-cultural communication, cultural revival, and employment creation for Aboriginal people. The park had its origins in 1987 with the formation of the Tjapukai Dance Theatre, which was started by a small group of indigenous dancers at Kuranda to both keep their rainforest dance traditions alive and also to perform for western tourists. As this enterprise grew and became more successful one consequence was a marked revival of interest in the Tjapukai language, which, in the early 1980s, was threatened with extinction. The Cultural Park, located on its present site since 1996, subsequently expanded and now has seven separate attractions, including History, Creation and Dance Theatres, and a Camp Village. With a staff of 100, of whom 85 are indigenous, the AUS$9 million dollar enterprise lays claim to being Australia's largest single private employer of Aboriginal people.[20] Moscardo and Pearce (1999) describe it as 'a leading player in the indigenous market place in the country' and comment that 'its dancers and staff have been central to the Australian Tourist Commission's promotion and trade show efforts.'

However, notwithstanding these positive achievements, the park project is not without its problems and contradictions for the local Djabugay people. Many of these stem from the fact that indigenous people in this area, as elsewhere in Australia, have a hybrid economy that does not always fit comfortably with the dictates of the contemporary market economy.[21] Most significantly, and in contrast to Uluru, the com-

---

20 See www.tjapukai.com.au.
21 The hybrid economy has important customary components in addition to the main elements of market and state (see Altman, 2001).

munity is a minority shareholder in the company and there is no certainty that they will ever be granted majority equity. As such, the financial benefits for the local community are not as substantial as they could be, a finding that has been a recurring theme in other research projects on Australian indigenous tourism (Altman, 1989). Further, no Djabugay occupy management positions in the enterprise and there are ongoing disputes over the presentation and representation of traditional culture. Dyer, Aberdeen, and Schuler, (2003), for example, note that boomerang making and body painting often have to be carried out with undue haste in order to match tour schedules. As well,

> Dances are adjusted periodically in response to tourist surveys to suit tourists' perception of what constitutes Aboriginal culture, resulting in the commodification of Djabugay culture whereby cultural adaptations oversimplify or homogenise 'Aboriginality.'

One example of the lack of authenticity is the regular use of didgeridoos in dance and musical performances, even though this instrument was never used by the Djabugay. The fundamental dilemma is that if the park is to continue to do well financially, it must accommodate the needs and expectations of overseas visitors.

As noted earlier, 'comanagement' is a fashionable descriptor of joint management regimes supposedly in place and 'balancing' indigenous and nonindigenous concerns at many iconic tourist sites across Australia, in addition to Tjapukai. But in many cases, upon closer scrutiny, there is a serious power imbalance in favour of nonindigenous people. Six possible relationships between Aboriginal and non-Aboriginal interests, ranked according to a hierarchy of indigenous control, were listed in Table 8.1. Across Australia, models 1 through 3 are by far the most common. But as we have seen in the case of Uluru earlier, even in the case of category 6 relationships, it does not follow that indigenous interests are always as well served as they might be.

Conclusion

Writing in 2001 Whitford, Bell, and Watkins argued forcefully that there is a need to separate the rhetoric from the reality when discussing indigenous tourism in Australia. Three years later there is no disputing that the views held by many Aboriginal people in relation to the positive aspects of tourism development are deeply ambivalent. At one extreme there have been undoubted financial gains for some individuals and communities, especially from the sale of high quality indigenous art. But by and large the evidence from the research to date is that tourism has not delivered the economic bonanza to indigenous people that was widely predicted 20 years earlier. There are also clear signs of growing frustration at the way in which Aboriginal people are often effectively disempowered in many 'comanagement' situations and also encouraged to play the role of the 'exotic other' according to the perceived dictates of 'the market.' In many instances Aboriginal people are now deciding that tourism is not something they wish to engage with, though that could change in the future if there came about a genuine commitment on the part of governments and private enterprise to demonstrate understanding of indigenous spiritual values and to involve Aboriginal people in a spirit of genuine partnership. One cautious sign of optimism in this regard is the growing movement on the part of government to gazette large tracts of land as Indigenous Protected Areas within which indigenous people can carry out their traditional land management practices and deliver ecotourism services on their own terms (Smyth, 2001). The largest such area in the country, 98,000 square kilometres in the Gibson Desert/Great Sandy Desert region, has recently been declared in western Australia.

Reconciliation between black and white Australia is one of the greatest challenges facing the country at the present time. Potentially, tourism has an important role to play in that process but only if it is planned in a context of genuine cooperation and respect. In this sense, arguably the most successful tourism ventures in Australia at the present time are not the high-profile, award-winning attractions such as Uluru and Tjapukai but the myriad small-scale, highly localised, indigenous-controlled enterprises where small groups of western tourists spend time in the bush being instructed by knowledgeable Aboriginal tour guides about 'caring for country,' deeply held spiritual beliefs, and the realities of contact history.[22]

References

Altman, J. C. 1988. *Aborigines, Tourism, and Development: The Northern Territory Experience.* Australian National University, Darwin: North Australia Research Unit.

——. 1989. Dilemmas for Aboriginal Australians. *Annals of Tourism Research* 16: 456–476.

——. 2001. *Sustainable Development Options on Aboriginal Land: The Hybrid Economy in the Twenty-first Century.* Paper No. 226. Australian National University, Canberra: Centre for Aboriginal Economic Policy Research.

22 Examples include Iga Warta, run by the Adnyamathanha community in the Flinders Ranges of South Australia, and Manyallaluk Cultural Tours and Tiwi Tours in the Northern Territory.

Altman, J. C., and P. J. Whitehead. 2003. *Caring for Country and Sustainable Indigenous Development: Opportunities, Constraints and Innovation.* Working Paper No. 20. Australian National University: Centre for Aboriginal Economic Policy Research.

Andrew, D., H. Finlay, P. Greenway, et al. 2001. *Aboriginal Australia and the Torres Strait Islands.* Melbourne: Lonely Planet.

ATSIC. 1997. *Tourism Industry Strategy.* Aboriginal and Torres Strait Islander Commission and Office of National Tourism, Canberra.

Australian Tourist Commission. 2003. *Segment Insights Pack: Market Research Intelligence on Aboriginal Tourism.* ATC, Canberra: Market Insights Unit.

Baker, R. 1999. Land Is Life: A Cultural Geography of Australian Contact History. In *Australian Cultural Geographies.* ed. E. Stratford. Melbourne: Oxford University Press.

Ballantyne, R. 1995. Interpreters' Conceptions of Australian Aboriginal Culture and Heritage: Implications for Interpretive Practice. *The Journal of Environmental Education* 26: 11–17.

Barrass, T. 2003. Native Rights for WA Parks. *The West Australian*, September 11.

Barsh, R. 1999. *Socially Responsible Investing and the World's Indigenous Peoples.* Fredericksburg, Va.: First Peoples Worldwide.

Behrendt, L. 2003. *Achieving Social Justice. Indigenous Rights and Australia's Future.* Sydney: The Federation Press.

Bell, D. 1998. *Ngarrindjeri Wurruwarrin: A World That Is, Was and Will Be.* North Melbourne: Spinifex.

Bereson, I., and D. McDonald. 1997. *Civics and Citizenship in Australia.* Melbourne: Nelson.

Capra, F. 2002. *The Hidden Connections: A Science for Sustainable Living.* London: HarperCollins.

Chesterman, J., and B. Galligan. 1997. *Citizens Without Rights: Aborigines and Australian Citizenship.* Cambridge: Cambridge University Press.

Clark, I. 2000. Sacred Sites and Feral Tourism Management: A Brief Sortie. *Historic Environment* 14: 22–26.

——. 2002. Rock Art Sites in Victoria, Australia: A Management History Framework. *Tourism Management* 23: 455–464.

Clark, I., and F. Cahir. 2001. Exclusivity in Regional Tourism Product: A Critique of 'Forgetfulness' in Regional Tourism Landscapes. Abstract in *Conference Proceedings.* Canberra: Council for Australian University Tourism and Hospitality Education (CAUTHE), Bureau of Tourism Research.

Colley, S. 2002. *Uncovering Australia: Archaeology, Indigenous People and the Public.* Crows Nest NSW: Allen & Unwin.

Coulter, B. 1993. Conference Opening. In *Indigenous Australians and Tourism: A Focus on Northern Australia.* Darwin: Proceedings of the Indigenous Australians and Tourism Conference, June.

Craik, J. 1994. Peripheral Pleasures: The Peculiarities of Post-Colonial Tourism. *Culture and Policy* 6: 153–182.

Cunneen, C., and T. Libesman. 1995. *Indigenous People and the Law in Australia.* Sydney: Butterworths' Legal Studies Series.

Davies, J. 2003. Contemporary Geographies of Indigenous Rights and Interests in Rural Australia. *Australian Geographer* 34: 19–45.

De Burlo, C. 1996. Cultural Resistance and Ethnic Tourism on South Pentecost, Vanuatu. In *Tourism and Indigenous Peoples*. eds. R. Butler and T. Hinch. London: International Thomson Business Press.

Department of Industry, Tourism and Resources. 2003a. *A Medium to Long Term Strategy for Tourism* (Green Paper). Canberra: DITR.

——. 2003b. *Forecast. The Sixteenth Release of the Tourism Forecasting Council*. Canberra.

——. 2003c. *Impact*, July.

Durning, A. T. 1993. Supporting Indigenous Peoples. In *State of the World 1993*. London: Earthscan.

Dyer, P., L. Aberdeen, and S. Schuler. 2003. Tourism Impacts on an Australian Indigenous Community: A Djabugay Case Study. *Tourism Management* 24: 9, 83–95.

Epstein, C. 2003. WorldWideWhale. Globalisation/Dialogue of Cultures? *Cambridge Review of International Affairs* 16: 309–322.

Executive Summary. 1993. *Indigenous Australians and Tourism: A Focus on Northern Australia*. Proceedings of the Indigenous Australians and Tourism Conference, Darwin, June 7–12.

Flannery, T. 1994. *The Future Eaters: An Ecological History of the Australasian Lands and People*. Chatswook: Reed.

Gardiner-Garden, J. 2003. *Defining Aboriginality in Australia*. Current Issues Brief, 10. Canberra: Department of the Parliamentary Library, Information and Research Services.

Goulet, D. 1977. *What Kind of Tourism? Or, Poison in a Luxury Package*. Working Paper Series No. 2. Montreal, Canada: Tourism Research, Department of Geography, McGill University.

Hage, G. 1998. *White Nation. Fantasies of White Supremacy in a Multicultural Society*. Sydney: Pluto Press.

Harrison, D. ed. 2001. *Tourism and the Less Developed World: Issues and Case Studies*. New York: CABI Publishing.

Hayward, P., and K. Neuenfeldt. 1998. Yothu Yindi: Context and Significance. In *Sound Alliances. Indigenous Peoples, Cultural Politics and Popular Music in the Pacific*. ed. P. Hayward. London: Cassell.

Hinch, T., and R. Butler. 1996. Indigenous Tourism: A Common Ground for Discussion. In *Tourism and Indigenous Peoples*. eds. R. Butler and T. Hinch. London: International Thomson Business Press.

Hollinshead, K. 1996. Marketing and Metaphysical Realism: The Disidentification of Aboriginal Life and Traditions Through Tourism. In *Tourism and Indigenous Peoples*. eds. R. Butler and T. Hinch. London: International Thomson Business Press.

Howard, J., R. Thwaites, and B. Smith. 2001. Investigating the Roles of the Indigenous Tour Guide. *Journal of Tourism Studies* 12: 32–39.

Howitt, R. 2001. *Rethinking Resource Management: Justice, Sustainability and Indigenous Peoples*. London: Routledge.

Indigenous Tourism Leadership Group. 2002. *Response to 'The 10 Year Plan for Tourism—A Discussion Paper.'* Canberra: Indigenous Tourism Leadership Group.

Johnson, C. 2001. The Treaty and Dilemmas of Anglo-Celtic Identity: from Backlash to Signatory. Canberra: Australian Institute of Aboriginal and Torres Strait Islander Studies, Seminar Series, May 14.

Johnson, D. 2002. *Lighting the Way: Reconciliation Stories.* Sydney: The Federation Press.

Jordan, M. E. 2000. Remote Access: Maningrida Arts & Culture and the World Wide Web. *Australian Aboriginal Studies* 1 and 2: 84–87.

Langton, M. 1998. *Burning Questions: Emerging Environmental Issues for Indigenous Peoples in Northern Australia.* Darwin: Northern Territory University: Centre for Indigenous Natural and Cultural Resource Management.

Larritt, C. S. 1993. *Aboriginal Involvement in Parks: Mootwingee National Park as a Case Study.* BA (Hons) Thesis, Melbourne: University of Melbourne, Department of Geography.

Mapunda, G. 2001. Indigenous Tourism as a Strategy for Community Development. An Analysis of Indigenous Business Initiatives in South Australia. In *Conference Proceedings.* Canberra: Council for Australian University Tourism and Hospitality Education (CAUTHE), Bureau of Tourism Research.

Memmott, P., and M. Moran. 2001. *Indigenous Settlements of Australia.* Australia: State of the Environment Second Technical Paper Series (Human Settlements). Canberra: Department of the Environment and Heritage.

Mercer, D. 2003. 'Citizen minus'?: Indigenous Australians and the Citizenship Question. *Citizenship Studies*, Vol. 7, No. 4, pp. 421–445.

Moscardo, G., and P. L. Pearce. 1999. 'Understanding Ethnic Tourists.' *Annals of Tourism Research*, 26(2): 416–434.

Muloin, S., H. Zeppel, and K. Higginbottom. 2001. *Indigenous Wildlife Tourism in Australia: Wildlife Attractions, Cultural Interpretation and Indigenous Involvement.* University of Newcastle, NSW: CRC for Sustainable Tourism.

Mulvaney, K., and J. Jones. 2002. Lightning Strikes Twice: Conflicts in Perception of Painted Images. *Australian Aboriginal Studies* 2: 27–34.

Munt, I. 1994. The 'Other' Postmodern Tourism: Culture, Travel and the New Middle Classes. *Theory, Culture & Society* 11: 101–123.

National Land and Water Resources Audit. 2002. *Australian Terrestrial Biodiversity Assessment.* Canberra.

Neill, R. 2002. *White Out. How Politics is Killing Black Australia.* Sydney: Allen & Unwin.

Northern Territory Government. 1994. *Aboriginal Tourism in the Northern Territory.* Darwin: Northern Territory Tourist Commission/Northern Territory Office of Aboriginal Development.

Ogle, G. 2002. Just When You Thought it Was Safe to Talk about Hindmarsh Island. *Indigenous Law Bulletin* 5: 16–18.

Pagdin, C. 1995. Assessing Tourism Impacts in the Third World: A Nepal Case Study. *Progress in Planning* 44: 185–266.

Parsons, M. 2002. 'Ah That I Could Convey a Proper Idea of this Interesting Wild Play of the Natives': Corroborees and the Rise of Indigenous Australian Cultural Tourism. *Australian Aboriginal Studies* 2: 14–26.

Pearson, N. 2000. *The Light on the Hill.* Ben Chifley Memorial Lecture, August 12, Bathurst, New South Wales.

Plumwood, V. 2003. Decolonizing Relationships with Nature. In *Decolonizing Nature: Strategies for Conservation in a Post-colonial Era.* eds. W. M. Adams and M. Mulligan. London: Earthscan.

Power, T. 2002. Joint Management at Uluru-Kata Tjuta National Park. *Environmental and Planning Law Journal* 19: 284–302.

Redmond, A. 2002. 'Alien Abductions', Kimberley Aboriginal Rock-Paintings, and the Speculation About Human Origins: On Some Investments in Cultural Tourism in the Northern Kimberley. *Australian Aboriginal Studies* 2: 54–64.

Rose, D. B. 1996. 'Ecological Justice for the 21st Century.' *Northern Analyst* (North Australia Research Unit) 1: 9–10.

Ross, H. 1991. Controlling Access to Environment and Self: Aboriginal Perspectives on Tourism. *Australian Psychologist* 26: 176–182.

Rothwell, N. 2003. Dust to Dust. *Weekend Australian*. August 23–24, R4–R5.

Royal Commission into Aboriginal Deaths in Custody. 1991. Final Report. Canberra.

Ryan, C. 2002. Tourism and Cultural Proximity. Examples from New Zealand. *Annals of Tourism Research* 29: 952–971.

Ryan, C., and J. Huyton. 2002. Tourists and Aboriginal People. *Annals of Tourism Research* 29: 631–647.

Scheyvens, R., and N. Purdie. 1999. Ecotourism. In *Strategies for Sustainable Development. Experiences from the Pacific*. eds. J. Overton and R. Scheyvens. Sydney: University of New South Wales Press.

Simondson, C. 1995. Tourism, Primitivism and Power: An Analysis of Some Advertising Literature of the Australian Tourism Industry. *Bulletin, The Olive Pink Society* 7(1–2): 22–27.

Simons, M. 2000. Aboriginal Heritage Art and Moral Rights. *Annals of Tourism Research* 27: 412–431.

——. 2003. *The Meeting of the Waters: The Hindmarsh Island Affair*. Sydney: Hodder Headline.

Simpson, C. 2002. Which Truth? Australian Identity—Culture and Politics. *Alternative Law Journal* 27(4): 161–164.

Smith, V. L. 1996. Indigenous Tourism: The Four Hs. In *Tourism and Indigenous Peoples*. eds. R. Butler and T. Hinch. London: International Thomson Business Press.

Smyth, D. 2001. Joint Management of National Parks. In *Working on Country: Contemporary Indigenous Management of Australia's Lands and Coastal Regions*. eds. R. Baker, J. Davies, and E. Young. Melbourne: Oxford University Press.

Stewart, C. 2003. Rock Rage: How this Monolith Disappeared from Public View. *The Weekend Australian*, August 9–10.

Suzuki, D., and P. Knudtson. 1992. *Wisdom of the Elders: Honoring Sacred Native Visions of Nature*. New York: Bantam Books.

Taubman, A. 2002. Protecting Aboriginal Sacred Sites: The Aftermath of the Hindmarsh Island Dispute. *Environmental and Planning Law Journal* 19: 14–158.

United Nations. 1989. United Nations' International Labour Organisation (ILO) Convention on Indigenous and Tribal Peoples. No. 169.

Venbrux, E. 1999. 'A glimpse of the Dreamtime': Property Rights and Tourism in the Tiwi Islands, Northern Australia. In *Property Rights and Economic Development: Land and Natural Resources in Southeast Asia and Oceania*. eds. Toon van Meijl and F. von Benda-Beckmann. London: Kegan Paul International.

Vergnani, L. 2003. Tripped Up, but Not for Long. *The Australian*, August 13.

Ward, G. K. 2002. Editorial. *Australian Aboriginal Studies* 2: 1–3.

Whitford, M., B. Bell, and M. Watkins. 2001. Indigenous Tourism Policy in Australia: 25 Years of Rhetoric and Economic Rationalism. *Current Issues in Tourism* 4: 2–4, 151–181.

Young, E. 1995. *Third World in the First: Development and Indigenous Peoples*. London: Routledge.

Yibarbuk, D. M., P. J. Whitehead, J. Russell-Smith, et al. 2001. Fire Ecology and Aboriginal Land Management in Central Arnhem Land, Northern Australia: A Tradition of Ecosystem Management. *Journal of Biogeography* 28: 325–344.

Zeppel, H. 1999. *Aboriginal Tourism in Australia: A Research Bibliography*. Report 2. Gold Coast, Queensland: CRC for Sustainable Tourism.

——. 2001. Discovering Aboriginal Australia: Making and Using Heritage Landscapes for Indigenous Tourism. In *Heritage Landscapes: Understanding Place and Communities*. eds. M. Cotter, B. Boyd, and J. Gardiner. Lismore: Southern Cross University Press.

Part Three

Changing Directions: Planning and Development Issues

Introduction

The emergence and maintenance of tourism as a dynamic rather than a static industry depends in large measure upon the adoption of a strategic approach to planning and development. The success of such an approach is largely dependent upon a systematic and structured analysis of the broad environmental factors affecting tourism demand as an essential part of the planning process. Ecotourism, tourism in support of sustainable development, tourism as a cultural expression of both hosts and guests, tourism as a reflection of 'political correctness,' are all considerations that go far beyond the traditional parameters of money, time and infrastructure.

Although tourism is generally regarded as less destructive to the environment than most other industries, nevertheless, its sheer size and widespread presence has already created negative physical and social environmental damage. Furthering the concept of sustainable development, **Murphy** and **Price** (Chapter 9) relates the notion that an inexorable relationship exists between the economy and the environment. Tourism's interest in sustainable development is logical given that it is one industry that sells the environment, both physical and human as its product. The authors contend that the integrity and continuity of these products have become by necessity a major concern of the industry . They suggest that what is now needed in tourism research and policy is a greater effort to link the academic and government interests in pursuing more sustainable tourism development with those front-line industry practitioners and the most important client, the tourist.

Some national governments such as Canada have changed their views on economic development and environmental protection, viewing them as mutually supporting rather than mutually exclusive. Such a perspective suggests that sustainable development can indeed be compatible with business objectives, and provided the appropriate safeguards, the tourism industry can continue to grow and prosper as a private business within these new parameters.

Large-scale tourism is a fact of life and the problems caused by, and associated with tourism need to be ameliorated as soon as possible. Although sustainable tourism remains an ongoing concept, nevertheless the journey toward the goal of sustainability is vital for economic, ecological and socio-cultural well-being.

The tourism lifecycle concept and the carrying capacity concept are interrelated in a manner that is both dynamic and dependent. The life cycle concept suggests that destination areas change over time, and progress through stages from introduction to decline. Although different disciplines have various meanings for it, carrying capacity embodies the idea that there is a limit to use, after which point negative effects occur.

Williams and Gill (Chapter 10) point out that like other economic enterprises, tourism is widely recognized as a change agent. With sound management, it holds the potential for being a low user of scarce resources as well as being a sustainable industry. The authors point out that effective carrying capacity management is central to tourism's continued growth and popularity. However, as a more practical and viable alternative to the concept of carrying capacity management, the chapter recommends the application of growth management planning approaches for addressing development issues in tourism destinations.

A number of tourism carrying capacity management perspectives, issues and concepts are presented. However, carrying capacity management's traditional focus on attempting to determine explicit use limits has made it a particularly difficult tool for use in a tourism management context due to too many limiting factors that hamper its use. Research suggests that traditional approaches to carrying capacity management have met with limited success in application. This is primarily due to unrealistic expectations, untenable assumptions, inappropriate value judgments and insufficient legal support systems.

On the other hand, in a growth management system context carrying capacity is linked to 'desired conditions' that best meet the goals of the area being managed. Community involvement in establishing desirable conditions is the single most important element of growth management. The focus of growth management shifts from past concerns over establishing use limits, to issues of identifying environmental, social and economic conditions desired by a community, and the creation of growth management strategies for managing tourism growth toward these ends.

Standards are documents that establish a basis, example or principle to conform to, which are linked to uniform units of measurement. Standards may be either compulsory (e.g., enforced through legislation) or voluntary **Font** (Chapter 11) discusses the development of sustainability standards from local efforts to make business improvements to becoming part of the suite of governance and regulatory tools of the global tourism industry. The proposition set forth in the chapter is that standard setting and certification are valuable tools to help bring stakeholders together.

The process of setting standards and ensuring these are met is known as conformity assessment, and provides the context to outline the development and use of sustainable tourism standards. Certification is a process whose aim is to help raise industry standards and is a policy tool to make voluntary improvements under five aspects: equity, effectiveness, efficiency, credibility and integration. The author defines each aspect and provides specific examples as applied to actual locations.

In the development of tourism strategies and policies, responsible authorities must consider the views of a number of stakeholders including industry, residents, special interest groups representing the environment and community, as well as tourists themselves. **Getz** and **Timur** (Chapter 12) examine the applicability and usefulness of stakeholder theory for developing sustainable tourism strategies and policies. Attention is given to the need for balanced input among the various stakeholder groups, including the issues of their identification, legitimization, involvement and conflict resolution.

A number of stakeholder theories are presented including a taxonomy including normative, instrumental and descriptive theories. Stakeholder theory has been applied as planning and management tools. The stakeholder framework has been applied in conjunction with the destination life cycle of tourist destinations in order to analyze stakeholder attitudes toward tourism and sustainable development.

The authors describe how stakeholder theory has been applied to sustainable tourism development, then they suggest a method of balancing the conflicting 'voices,' i.e., economic, environmental, social and cultural objectives. They suggest that creating a more participative decision-making and strategic policy-making process is the key to the stakeholder management approach.

In many developed world countries, major battles are taking place between conservationists and the tourism industry. Conservationists argue for greater environmental protection and dramatic restrictions on tourism growth. The tourism industry on the other hand seeks to upgrade and develop new facilities. They argue that it is wrong to deny businesses profits and to restrict access to tourists seeking to enjoy beautiful and accessible outdoor recreation areas throughout the world.

Should the environment have priority over humans? **Hudson** and **Miller** (Chapter 13) explore the relationship between ethics and sustainable tourism and consider how an understanding of the ethical approaches of future tourism officials can benefit their ability to effectively manage the industry in the future.

The authors conclude that highly developed countries are likely to experience greater pressure to assign rights to nature as residents are more affluent and therefore become more concerned with aesthetic issues. However, the movement for environmental protection is unlikely to proceed in less developed countries where issues of survival are more pressing. A shift to the assignments of rights of existence to nature can only come about when people are sufficiently comfortable with their own existence and do not feel threatened by, or suffer from nature being promoted.

9 Tourism and sustainable development

Peter E. Murphy and Garry G. Price

Introduction

The world is changing and experiencing shifts in social values that affect the way we act as individuals, businesses, and governments. Part of the change is an increasing recognition that past growth and development have led to some serious negative impacts on the environment. Some have been highly visible, such as shrinking water supplies or homeless garbage barges, but others have crept up on us insidiously and still remain something of a mystery, like global warming, the depletion of the ozone layer, and the loss of biodiversity.

Such economic and environmental forces led many nations, companies, and individuals to the June 1992 United Nations Conference on the Environment and Development (UNCED Earth Summit) in Rio de Janeiro. There they attempted to address a controversial agenda designed to protect the Earth's environment and to foster less destructive industrialisation and development. A binding theme of the conference was to find ways to replace the old emphasis on economic growth with a push for sustainable development (*Business Week*, 1992) but the outcomes have been limited. As was noted at the World Summit on Sustainable Development held in Johannesburg in 2002 (2002 Johannesburg Summit), 'progress in implementing sustainable development has been extremely disappointing since the 1992 Earth Summit, with poverty deepening and environmental degradation worsening' (United Nations Department of Economic and Social Affairs, 2002).

This lack of progress demonstrates that changing fundamental societal beliefs and expectations are not easy and that there are no magic steps to sustainable development. However, conferences such as those held in Rio de Janeiro and in Johannesburg are valuable contributors to an ongoing process of reassessment and one in which tourism has become involved.

In particular, the 2002 Johannesburg Summit departed significantly from previous United Nations (UN) conferences in that although 'negotiations still received the lion's share of attention, the Summit also resulted in the launch of more than 300 voluntary partnerships, each of which will bring additional resources to support efforts to implement sustainable development.' (United Nations Department of Economic and Social Affairs, 2002).

Tourism's interest in sustainable development is logical given that it is one industry that sells the environment, both physical and human, as its product. The integrity and continuity of these products have become a major concern of the industry as can be seen, for example, in The World Tourism Organization's Global Code of Ethics for Tourism and in Ecotourism Australia's Nature and Ecotourism Accreditation Program. But more articulation of the issues and options needs to be undertaken before the concept of sustainable development can move further toward physical and economic reality.

Since the first edition of this book (1994) there has been considerable academic and government interest in the concept of sustainable tourism development, but industry and consumers seem to have received less attention and to have been less vocal. Most of the reports and discussion on sustainability and tourism have come from organisations and governments, anxious to preserve resources while developing their economies (see, for example, Environment Canada's Sustainable Development Strategy 2001–2003) and from academic research and writing as in the case of articles in the *Journal of Sustainable Tourism* and in the relatively new *Journal of Ecotourism*. Much of this work has been concerned with policy issues, procedures, and implications with relatively little reference to the direct involvement and needs of the tourism industry and its principal clients, the tourists. Where studies of the industry have taken place they have generally referred to successful case practices (Hawkes and Williams, 1993) or have been condensed into generic management guides (Consulting and Audit Canada, 1995). Apart from a growing number of convenience-based samples of ecotourists and a few consulting company omnibus surveys, we do not have a clear picture of the tourists' knowledge of, or commitment to, sustainable tourism development.

What is needed now in this area of tourism research and policy is a greater effort to link the academic and government interests in pursuing more sustainable tourism development with those of front-line practitioners (the industry) and the all-important client (the tourist). If these groups could be encouraged to modify their perspectives and operate as an epistemic community—a community in which members 'share intersubjective understandings; have shared patterns of reasoning; have a policy project drawing on shared causal beliefs and the use of shared discursive practices and have a shared commitment to the application and production of knowledge' (Cinquegrani, 2002), then we could anticipate more tangible progress regarding tourism and sustainable development. Accordingly, after reviewing the growth and measurement of sustainable development to tourism this chapter will explore possible links and synergies between the works of academia and government on the one hand and the needs of industry and tourists on the other.

Growth and Definition of Sustainable Development

The need for a renewed relationship with the environment and interest in sustainable development has been building over the past 30 years. In 1972 Danella and Dennis Meadows shook the world's complacency with their book *Limits to Growth* (1972). They argued the Earth's resources and ability to absorb pollution are finite. Using computer simulations, they predicted the Earth's population and development progress would experience physical constraints within a century. After this first warning came more research and deliberation into the long-term consequences of continued industry and population expansion. This led to the publication of the World Conservation Strategy by the International Union for the Conservation of Nature and Natural Resources (IUCN, 1980), which was one of the first reports to introduce the concept of sustainable development. This was followed by the World Commission on Environment and Development (Brundtland Commission) Report in 1987, entitled *Our Common Future* (WCED, 1987), which placed the concept of sustainable development at centre stage and promoted it as a vehicle for deliverance.

The sustainable development concept is not new, but increasing pressures on the world's finite resources and environmental capacity have led to a more deliberate restatement of the philosophy, along with evolving guidelines to put it into practice. *Our Common Future* described sustainable development as 'development that meets the needs of the present without compromising the ability of future generations to meet their own needs' (WCED, 1987). This is not very different from the view that we do not inherit the earth from our forefathers but borrow it from our children, and the old philosophy that something should be left for future generations. As such, sustainable development builds on the old principles of conservation and stewardship, but it offers a more proactive stance that incorporates continued economic growth in a more ecological and equitable manner. In this regard the opening definition above is supplemented with more specific implications and guidelines throughout the WCED report.

Figure 9.1 illustrates some of the guidelines that emerged from *Our Common Future*, which in turn have stimulated further discussion at

1	Establishing ecological limits and more equitable standards	'Requires the promotion of values that encourage consumption standards that are within the bounds of the ecological possible and to which all can reasonably aspire.'
2	Redistribution of economic activity and reallocation of resources	'Meeting essential needs depends in part on achieving full growth potential and sustainable development clearly requires economic growth in places where such needs are not being met.'
3	Population control	'Though the issue is not merely one of population size but of the distribution of resources, sustainable development can only be pursued if demographic developments are in harmony with the changing productive potential of the ecosystem.'
4	Conservation of basic resources	'Sustainable development must not endanger the natural systems that support life on Earth: the atmosphere, the waters, the soils, and the living beings.'
5	More equitable access to resources and increased technological effort to use them more effectively	'Growth has no set limits in terms of population or resource use beyond which lies ecological disaster . . . But ultimate limits there are, and sustainability requires that long before these are reached the world must ensure equitable access to the constrained resource and reorient technological efforts to relieve the pressure.'
6	Carrying capacity and sustainable yield	'Most renewable resources are part of a complex and interlinked ecosystem, and maximum sustainable yield must be defined after taking into account system-wide effects of exploitation.'
7	Retention of resources	'Sustainable development requires that the rate of depletion of non-renewable resources foreclose as few future options as possible.'
8	Diversification of the species	'Sustainable development requires the conservation of plant and animal species.'
9	Minimize adverse impacts	'Sustainable development requires that the adverse impacts on the quality of air, water, and other natural elements are minimised so as to sustain the ecosystem's overall integrity.'
10	Community control	'Community control over development decisions affecting local ecosystems.'
11	Broad national/ international policy framework	'The biosphere is the common home of all human-kind and joint management of the biosphere is prerequisite for global political security.'
12	Economic viability	'Corporate environmental policy is an extension of total quality management.'
13	Environmental quality	'Corporate environmental policy is an extension of total quality management.'
14	Environmental audit	'An effective environmental audit system is at the heart of good environmental management.'
15	Triple bottom line	'Economic prosperity, environmental quality and social justice.'

Figure 9.1: Sustainable development components.

various government levels and within business. The first nine components were extracted from the WCED report and formed the basis of
Canada's early attempts to integrate this type of philosophy into its
national policy (Canadian Environment Advisory Council, 1987).

Following the WCED report other writers and agencies have added to
the list of components shown in Figure 9.1. This list is not designed to be
exhaustive but to illustrate the ongoing refinement of the concept of sustainable development and the increasing emphasis on its application. It
has been noted, for example, that the priority on maintaining ecological
diversity and distributing more productivity to developing regions
implies increased community control (Component 10), which in turn
fosters increased regional self-reliance (Rees and Roseland, 1988). Likewise, these two authors and Stanley (1992) maintain there is a need for
more international agreements and business–government partnerships
(Component 11) to direct national and individual actions. To the ecological limitations and social equity of the sustainable development philosophy must be added the concept of economic viability (Component 12)
according to the British Columbia Round Table on the Environment and
the Economy (1991).

The business community and literature have been responding to the
environmental–economic opportunities that exist within the 'greening'
process over the past ten years or so. A minority of corporations are still
in the early phase of responding to environmental problems as they arise.
The majority of corporations has established systems and programmes
to comply with the new regulations, but a further minority has moved
'beyond compliance' into a proactive mode of management. This evolutionary process is slowly leading to the complete integration of the environmental dimension into corporate strategic planning (Component 13).
To bring environmental considerations and sustainable development into
the mainstream of corporate planning requires increased accountability
and the environmental audit has been gaining credibility in this area.
Hunt and Auster (1990) contend a 'strong auditing programme' is essential to successful proactive environmental management (Component 14).

Elkington (1999) has bundled several of the earlier dimensions into his
concept of triple bottom line accounting by adding environmental and
social considerations to the more regular financial accounting concerns of
modern business. He notes the need to measure environmental impacts
in terms of new metrics such as the life cycle impacts of products and
potentially polluting emissions. Furthermore he recognises that 'if we fail
to address wider political, social and ethical issues, the backlash will
inevitably undermine progress in the environmental area' (Elkington,
1999).

As noted above, from a temporal perspective, sustainable development
should have both vertical and horizontal components. The broadening of

the definition to include consideration of the needs of future generations and of current social equity has produced a continuum of sustainability positions, a summary of which is shown in Figure 9.2.

The growing interest and support for sustainable development is not without its critics and skeptics. Some maintain that it is such a fuzzy concept that it may prove to be of little practical use in tackling the environmental issues that are emerging. However, as Figure 9.1 illustrates, the short definition of sustainable development should be viewed only as a summary goal, and that from this has evolved a series of more specific objectives and methodologies. Others consider that it is a passing fad, akin to the energy crises of the past. But this perception fails to acknowledge that evidence of environmental stress started more than 30 years ago, and instead of disappearing it has gradually increased to the point where admitted nonenvironmentalists are beginning to take notice. One author who has addressed such skepticism and doubts is George Winter (1988) who developed a listing of pros and cons for 40 issues regarding the introduction of an integrated system of environmental business management.

Some authors have criticised the fundamentals of the concept of sustainable development itself, discussing the oxymoronic nature of the term (see, for example, Huckle, 1996) and claiming that 'sustainable' (with its steady-state implications) and 'development' (with its growth implications) are mutually exclusive (Page and Dowling, 2002). According to Barkin (1996), the concept of sustainable development has created seemingly impossible goals for policy makers and development practitioners '. . . [since] present levels of per capita resource consumption in the richer countries cannot possibly be maintained much less generalized to people living in the rest of the world.'

This theme has permeated much of the recent debate on sustainable development and has contributed to the advent of terms such as 'sustainability' and 'sustainable future,' possibly in attempts to avoid emphasising the oxymoronic nature of the terms 'sustainable' and 'development.'

Relevance to Tourism

Tourism is reputed to be the world's largest industry with estimated revenues of US$3.5 trillion and hiring one worker in nine worldwide in 1995 (World Travel and Tourism Council, 1996) and with 663 million people spending at least one night in a foreign country in 1998 and with expectations that this figure will reach 1.6 billion by 2020 (World Tourism Organization, 1999). It is one industry that should be involved in sustainable development, because it 'is a resource industry, one which is dependent on nature's endowment and society's heritage' (Murphy, 1985).

Sustainability Position	Defining Characteristics
Very weak	Anthropocentric and utilitarian; growth orientated and resource exploitative; natural resources utilized at economically optimal rates through unfettered free markets operating to satisfy individual consumer choice; infinite substitution possible between natural and human-made capital; continued well-being assured through economic growth and technical innovation.
Weak	Anthropocentric and utilitarian; resource conservationist; growth is managed and modified; concern for distribution of development costs and benefits through intra- and intergenerational equity; rejection of infinite substitution between natural and human-made capital with recognition of some aspects of natural world as critical capital (e.g., ozone layer, some natural ecosystems); human-made plus natural capital constant or rising through time; decoupling of negative environmental impacts from economic growth.
Strong	(Eco)systems perspective; resource preservationist; recognizes primary value of maintaining the functional integrity of ecosystems over and above secondary value through resource utilization; interests of the collective given more weight than those of the individual consumer; adherence to intra- and intergenerational equity; decoupling important but alongside a belief in a steady state economy as a consequence of following the constant natural assets rule; zero economic and human population growth.
Very strong	Bioethical and eco-centric; resource preservationist to the point where utilization of natural resources is minimized; nature's rights or intrinsic value in nature encompassing non-human living organisms and even abiotic elements under a literal interpretation of Gaianism; anti-economic growth and for reduced human population.

Figure 9.2:   A simplified description of the sustainable development spectrum.

Source: Adapted from Hunter, 2002.

Although the tourism industry is regarded as being kinder to the environment in general than most other industries, its very size and widespread presence has created negative environmental impacts, both of a physical and social nature, in certain locations that have led to demands for a more sustainable approach to tourism. An examination of this approach is appropriate.

Sustainable Tourism Development

Over the past 20 years or so tourism has become a major part of the discourse of sustainable development, which is not surprising given the magnitude and rate of expansion of the industry; the ecological, economic, social, and cultural impacts of tourism; and, as identified by the 1992 Rio Earth Summit, the potential for tourism to help the transition to sustainable development. It can be argued that the concept of sustainable tourism emerged from the recognition of the negative impacts of mass tourism and the subsequent birth of 'green tourism' (Swarbrooke, 1999).

According to Wight (1997),

> Tourism, as it relates to sustainable development, is tourism which is developed so that the nature, scale, location, and manner of development is [sic] appropriate and sustainable over time, and where the environment's ability to support other activities and processes is not impaired, since tourism cannot be isolated from other resource activities. . . . At the heart of sustainable tourism is a set of implicit values related to striving to integrate *economic, social and cultural* goals.

This integration is illustrated diagrammatically in Figure 9.3, where Wight's three goals are seen to start to coalesce around community-based economics, conservation with equity, and integration of the environment with the economy. These, in turn, come together in the central goal of sustainable tourism.

Within any discussion of sustainable tourism development, consideration should be given to the beneficiaries of sustainable development because of the diversity of interests involved (Cater, 1994). Platteau and Gaspart (2003) continued this theme, asserting that 'communities need to evolve and be institutionally strengthened if they are to achieve the objectives of the participatory approach [to sustainable development]: economic growth, democratic governance, sustainability, equity and protection of the poor. . . . [A]s long as the grassroots are not sufficiently empowered through suitable training programs and processes aimed at making them aware of their rights and confident enough to assert them, benefits are likely to be largely preempted by local elites.'

Identification of the various perspectives of sustainable development also needs to be included in the discourse of sustainable tourism devel-

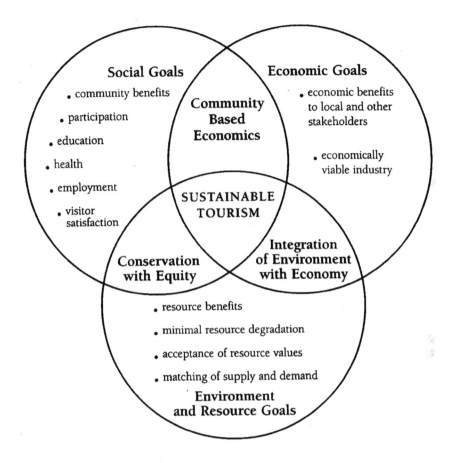

Figure 9.3: A Model of sustainable tourism values and principles.

Source: Hall, Jenkins, and Kearsley, 1997.

opment. As was asserted by Cater (1994) '[w]hat may appear to be sustainable from one point of view is unlikely to be so from another.' She further expressed the opinion that ecotourism and sustainable development 'tend to be overworked terms, neatly co-opted by political and business interests to confer an aura of respectability to [sic] their activities,' agreeing with Rees (1990) that both might be 'a laboured excuse for not departing from continued economic growth.'

Sisman (1994) also expressed a similar view, justifiably stating that 'it is surprising, post-Brundtland and post-Rio, just how many organisations have suddenly "discovered" that their policies can be made to "fit" the concept of sustainability simply by deciding their own benchmark.' He advocated 'a working partnership that blends good environmental practice and profitable business for mutual long-term advantages' in the movement toward sustainability.

Faulkner (2001) succinctly synthesised the various components of sustainable tourism, indicating that sustainable tourism development is a form of tourism that:

- Safeguards and enhances to [sic] natural and cultural assets of the destination;
- Safeguard [sic] and enhances the resident population's quality of life and life opportunities;
- Satisfies the needs and expectations of the tourist market;
- Is economically viable and achieves a return on investment for tourism operators; and
- Achieves equity in the distribution of costs and benefits of tourism between different segments of the community and between the current and future generations. That is, outcomes are considered beyond the relatively short term horizon . . . and ensure that both inter and intra generational equity is taken into account.

Currently global sustainable development and its sustainable tourism subset remain telic concepts, although effective sustainable practices might exist at a local level. Genuine sustainable development will not be reached with current global resource allocation and use. This assertion should not be seen as a refutation of the desirability of sustainable development, but rather that current practices such as the use of fossil fuels for transportation cannot be seen as sustainable. The mismatch between the theory and practice of sustainable development has produced a continuum of variants of sustainability and has elicited debate within the tourism industry and within academe on the extent to which the components of sustainable development should be applied to tourism.

Figure 9.4, illustrates the resultant continuum of views from light green variants to dark green variants. Hunter (2002) demonstrates the range of sustainable tourism options that can and have been used, thus exposing the variety of interpretations used with this concept.

Although there has been considerable debate on the concept of sustainable development, and on sustainable tourism as a consequence, relatively little attention appears to have been given to assessing sustainable practices. This is understandable given the difficulty of finding precise definitions of each, but the degree of successful implementation of principles needs to be ascertained if sound policy analysis is to occur. According to Pigram (1990),

> Sustainable tourism has the potential to become a tangible expression of sustainable . . . development. Yet it runs the risk of remaining irrelevant and inert as a feasible policy option for the real world of tourism development, without the development of effective means of translating the idea into action.

Light Green Tendencies	Dark Green Tendencies
advocate and strongly proadaptancy	cautionary and knowledge-based
benefits of tourism assumed	benefits of tourism must be demonstrated
precious view of tourism as a sector and sectoral self interest dominates	tourism need not necessarily be a component of sustainable development in an area and sectoral integration required
maintain tourism activity in existing destinations and expand into new ones	widen economic base if high dependency on tourism and engage in full proactive assessment of new tourism development
tourism products must be maintained and evolve according to market need (nature is a commodity)	natural resources must be maintained and impacts reduced (preferably minimized) where possible with products tailored accordingly (nature has existence value)
environmental action only when required and beneficial (i.e., legal obligation, to tackle specific problem, marketing benefit and cost saving)	considered as a matter of routine
narrow scope and geographical scale of environmental concern	wide range of potential and actual impacts considered beyond immediate geographical setting (e.g., hotel, complex, destination area)
disperse and dilute activity (spread)	focus and concentrate activity (confine)
industry self regulation as dominant management approach	wide range of management approaches and instruments required
introspective focus on tourism research and management literature	(more likely to re-invent the wheel)
most likely to have a direct involvement in the industry	most likely to have training in an environment-type academic discipline

Figure 9.4:   Simplified descriptions of light green and dark green variants of sustainable tourism.

Source: Adapted from Hunter, 2002.

If positive movement along the sustainable tourism continuum is to be achieved there is a need for an interdisciplinary focus, a 'consilience' of 'facts, and fact-based theory across disciplines to create a common groundwork for explanation' (Wilson, 1997). The need for a comprehensive approach also was recognised by Moldan and Billharz (1997) when they sought a common framework for comparative assessment of both problem recognition and progress made toward sustainable development. By the use of indicators they developed a comprehensive model, incorporating conflicting values, interests, and spatial and time horizons in relation to sustainable development assessment. Faulkner (2001) extended this notion to sustainable tourism development, asserting that investigation of sustainable tourism development 'requires an interdisciplinary approach, involving a balanced approach to the examination and evaluation of the social, economic and environmental impacts of tourism.'

Tisdell and Wen (1997) argued that caution should be applied to the use of indicators in the assessment of progress toward sustainability. Although recognising that the attainment of sustainable tourism is a worthy goal, they asserted that:

> the concepts involved are often quite complex and are interpreted in a variety of ways. For this reason alone, one needs to be cautious when employing these concepts. . . . They must, at least, be supplemented by deeper analysis to decide whether a tourist development is going to show long-term sustainability.

Dimensions of Sustainable Tourism Development

It is apparent from the previous discussion that sustainable development is a complex and multidimensional concept and that tourism, as a component of the process, will reflect this diversity. Seven major dimensions that reflect the general multidimensionality and interdisciplinary concerns can be discerned within the various considerations of sustainable tourism development.

The first dimension noted is the need for *resource management*, for in this crowded world with diminishing resources little can be left to chance. Second, such management needs to reaffirm that tourism is an *economic* activity, which must be capable of making a profit in order to survive and benefit the community. This is the point Porter (1991) and others have made when they say environmental legislation must leave room for individual employment and economic well being to operate within the ecological parameters. The third dimension points out the need to fulfill social obligations. This means more than intergenerational equity; it means respect for other livelihoods and customs. Such variety and heritage is a major resource for tourism in a world that is fast becoming homogenised into a global economy. A major component of environment and culture is their *aesthetic* appeal. Although the focus has often been on international markers such as world-renowned heritage sites, the aesthetic qualities of regular townscapes and general landscapes should not be overlooked.

All the earlier mentioned needs should be addressed within *ecological parameters* to sustain both the physical and human environment. Conservation of cultural legacies should not be ignored. The ecological process needs to be understood so that tourism intrusions will have the minimal impact, especially in sensitive areas like shorelines, mountains, and wetlands. The concern over maintaining our *biological diversity* is particularly germane to tourism, which thrives on the appeal of different flora and fauna along with a distinctive sense of place. Finally, the need to sustain our basic life support systems is paramount. If these basic needs are not met, then our higher level and discretionary needs like travel will fail to materialize.

Research Priorities

As in the real world, all of the previously mentioned dimensions are interrelated. This means any sustainable tourism development will involve a holistic management approach that requires integrated ecological, economic, and institutional research. Because this is a major research undertaking, some thought has been given already to categorising the scope of the problem and prioritising the research questions. In 1985 Murphy proposed an ecological model for tourism research and development. This model demonstrated the need to consider tourism as an ecological function that involved different community scales of emphasis and a balance between resident (individuals and business) and visitor (tourist and tourist industry) needs. Taylor and Stanley (1992) recommended a matrix of research priorities based on scale and time considerations (Figure 9.5).

All scales are relevant and interrelated in an ecological sense, but the pressures and issues will vary at each level. Some research questions are considered to be more pressing and have been placed under the 'now' category whereas others are either less urgent or are logical secondary steps. As Taylor and Stanley (1992) observed, all research should have a monitoring function to observe changes over time and be able to identify adjustment strategies where needed.

Scope	Now	Medium term	Long term
Site	Case studies on a variety of topics Operations Employee involvement Benefit-cost Corporate culture Environmental audit	Value of protected areas (economic, aesthetic) Willingness to pay Means of enhancing experiences Monitoring change in case studies	
Locality	Destination studies Carrying capacities: economic, social, physical Image studies	Longitudinal studies Nature of change studies	Social indicators Economic indicators Physical indicators
Region	Inventory of resources Studies of market needs and attitudes	Longitudinal studies of market needs and attitudes Measurement of benefits, costs	
Nation	Coordination Dissemination Standards	Networking Clearing house Methodologies Models, paradigms	
International	Cooperation Adaptation	Clearing house Definition of terms	

Figure 9.5:   Suggested research areas and priorities for sustainable development in tourism.

Source: Taylor and Stanley, 1992.

Measurement Issues

Although it is relatively easy to conceptualise and to proselytise about the needs for sustainable tourism development, it is far more challenging to develop an effective, yet practical, measurement process. An important issue in the Taylor–Stanley matrix is establishing the carrying capacity levels, 'the ability of a given environment to accommodate particular activities without suffering significant and irreversible damage' (Owens and Cowell, 1996) for tourism in a variety of locales and circumstances.

Initially the notion of an objective, scientific determination of an area's carrying capacity was appealing to tourism managers. However, the recognition that carrying capacity is a social construct involving a complex interplay of economic, environmental, political, and social forces means that the concept has been used little in practice (Wearing and Neil, 1999). Further, the point of view that consideration of environmental disturbance 'must be augmented by consideration of human values' (Wagar, 1964) has expanded in recent times. For example, Middleton and Hawkins (1998) asserted that carrying capacity must take into account 'factors such as tourists' behavioural patterns, facility design and management, the dynamic character of the environment and the changing attitudes of the host community.'

The literature on this subject shows carrying capacity techniques have been applied in a variety of circumstances, often clarifying and confirming levels of suspected environmental or social stress, but they leave open to discussion what it all signifies and what policy should be undertaken. A major difficulty is that carrying capacity implies the existence of fixed and determinable limits to development and that if one stays below those threshold levels no changes or deterioration will occur. We now appreciate that all changes and modifications to the environment have an incremental effect, so some degree of change must be acknowledged and accounted for at all developmental stages.

As a consequence of this recognition, several alternative approaches to the original carrying capacity concept have emerged in recent years, notably the limits of acceptable change (LAC) (Stankey, et al., 1995), (Wearing and Neil, 1999), ecological footprint analysis (EFA), and (Gössling, et al., 2002). According to Sun and Walsh (1998), 'the LAC approach is based on decisions regarding how much change is acceptable to users and managers. The VIM system highlights the importance of judgmental consideration in identifying management actions.'

This LAC approach, according to Wearing and Neil (1999), involves both resource managers and stakeholders in:

- Identifying acceptable and achievable social and resource standards,
- Documenting gaps between desirable and existing circumstances,
- Identifying management actions to close these gaps, and
- Monitoring and evaluating management effectiveness.

VIM principles, according to Wearing and Neil (1999) are:

- Identifying unacceptable changes occurring as a result of visitor use and developing management strategies to keep visitor impacts within acceptable levels;
- Integrating visitor impact management into existing agency planning, design, and management processes;

- Basing visitor impact management on the best scientific understanding and situational information available;
- Determining management objectives that identify the resource condition to be achieved and the type of recreation experience to be provided;
- Identifying visitor impact problems by comparing standards for acceptable conditions with key indicators of impact at designated times and locations;
- Basing management decisions, to reduce impacts or maintain acceptable conditions, on knowledge of the probable sources of, and inter-relationships between, unacceptable impacts;
- Addressing visitor impacts using a wide range of alternative management techniques; and
- Formulating visitor management objectives, which incorporate a range of acceptable impact levels, to accommodate the diversity of environments and experience opportunities present within any natural setting.

Although LAC and VIM principles might be applied relatively effectively at the local level, they have limited applicability on a global scale. Gössling and colleagues (2002) argued that LAC and VIM focus on changes occurring in the local environment, largely ignoring the global consequences of travel. . . . 'Existing concepts are thus insufficient to make clear statements about the sustainability of particular forms of travel or the sustainability of certain destinations.'

Gössling and associates (2002) have made a contribution to the evaluation of the environmental impacts of tourism through their EFA, a concept that uses space equivalents to calculate the appropriation of biologically productive area by individuals or nations. As has been claimed, '[t]he idea of the concept is to compare the area required to support a certain lifestyle with the area available, thus offering an instrument to assess if consumption is ecologically sustainable' (Gössling, et al., 2002).

However, despite the value of this contribution to the quest for global sustainability, there are problems with the operationalisation of the EFA concept. For example, although the environmental impact of air travel has been widely recognised (Wackernagel and Rees, 1996), the conclusion of Gössling and colleagues (2002) that 'air travel should . . . be actively discouraged' is unlikely to be implemented and, therefore, is unlikely to have any significant impact on atmospheric pollution levels.

Carrying capacity, LAC, VIM, and EFA processes examine the sustainable tourism issue from the supply side of the tourism experience, but if tourism is to be a sustainable economic proposition it cannot ignore its customers. Hence, more thought is now being applied to the demand implications of sustainable tourism development, specifically the benefits visitors are seeking and the marketing strategies that can be applied to service both the customer and the host, part of which is tourist and resident education to increase carrying capacity (Weaver and Oppermann, 2000). This contention is in accord with that of McIntosh, Goeldner, and Ritchie (1995) who asserted that '[t]ourists have responsibilities and must be educated as to their obligations and responsibilities to contribute to socially and environmentally responsible tourism.'

Murphy and Pritchard (1997) examined a model of consumers' perceived value and applied it to a tourist destination. They found that tourists had concerns about quality and price common to all consumers, but their value perceptions also varied by origin (comparison base) and season of visit (different site conditions). Hence, one can see the tourist demand for sustainable tourism development is likely to be multidimensional and culturally conditioned.

The modern interpretation of marketing has moved beyond simply promoting and selling to take into account the long-term management goals of companies and organisations. In some cases this now includes marketing to reduce consumption, as with utility companies, or to recycle, as with beverage companies. In a tourism context we see more evidence of attractions explaining to customers why certain areas are temporarily closed or out of bounds.

The broader view is provided by Mill and Morrison (1985) who noted that tourism marketing is 'a management philosophy, which in light of tourist demand, makes it possible through research, forecasting and selection to place tourism products on the market most in line with an organization's purpose for the greatest benefit.'

Such a definition has particular relevance to a sustainable development strategy. It makes marketing part of a more general management strategy and it supports the notion that marketing should balance the tourists' needs with those of the host organisation. Market research will help to identify which tourism niche is most appropriate from a business and environmental viewpoint. It can indicate a destination or business' position in the product life cycle, which could guide future marketing and development strategies.

An essential element in market research designed to assist in sustainable development initiatives is the need to monitor visitor patterns and satisfaction. Monitors are needed on an annual and seasonal basis, because the volume and type of visitor activity can vary significantly over these periods. A demonstration project on Vancouver Island, British Columbia, revealed that a basic monitoring of visitors could be achieved efficiently and at low cost through industry–destination partnerships (Murphy, 1992).

Various Tourism Markets

There is a wide variety of tourist types within the tourism market today, so much so that the term 'average tourist' has become irrelevant (Murphy, 1985). One type of tourist that has generated a lot of interest among those supporting sustainable development is the 'alternative tourist,' described by Krippendorf (1987) as those who 'try to establish more contact with the local population, try to do without the tourist infrastructure and use the same accommodation and transport facilities as the natives.' Such travellers are considered desirable market niches for those communities that are unable or unwilling to accommodate mass tourism, and they are perceived as being worthy targets because they are small in number yet often well educated and wealthy. This would appear to be a perfect match for those areas where carrying capacity could become an issue and where the host community wished to control the size of the industry.

However, alternative tourism has been criticised as being elitist and spreading tourism to areas that are not yet spoiled by tourism. One who has issued such a warning is Butler (1990). He noted that in a free society and in a highly fragmented industry it is difficult to control the numbers and types of tourist admitted to an area. Butler suggested that:

> In the short term there is little doubt that alternative tourism appears, and almost certainly is, much less conducive to causing change in destination areas than mass tourism, in part because of its dimensions and in part because of the need for fewer and smaller facilities. However, as time goes by, some factors can assume much greater significance under alternative tourism and result in greater and more serious long-term change.

Butler illustrates this by noting the intimate contact described by Krippendorf can become a social burden over time, as privacy is lost and there is nowhere to retreat from the tourist gaze. Similarly the 'backwoods' penetration by such visitors can do more environmental harm over time to these areas than the controlled mass tourism, which permits distant viewing only. What host communities need to focus on is the type or types of tourism they wish to attract and can accommodate over the long term. As Jones (1992) observed, 'some of the clues and solutions from alternative tourism can be used to inform and advise policy and practice in the development and management of mass tourism.'

Many of the observations relating to alternative tourism apply to one subset that appears particularly germane to the sustainable development movement—ecotourism. Ecotourism is based on the principles of being nature based, contributing to the quest for sustainability, being environmentally educative, and bringing local benefits (Price and Murphy, 2000). As such, ecotourists are champions of the environment and sustainable development. In Australia a joint initiative of Ecotourism Australia and the Australian Tourism Operators Network has resulted in the Nature and Ecotourism Accreditation Program (NEAP) which is designed to provide a range of benefits for nature tourism operators, ecotourism operators, consumers, protected area managers, and local communities, as shown in Figure 9.6. Such schemes are relatively easy to initiate when parties have the same goals and the numbers involved are small, but they also provide hope and direction to the application of similar strategies to a broader cross-section of the tourism industry.

In the final analysis, however, 'the most crucial contribution that applied research can make toward sustainable tourism is to show rather than say what this involves' (Sadler, 1992). As we have seen there are a growing number of advocates, sufficient paradigms, and some basic measurement techniques that should now be put into practice in order to demonstrate the feasibility of all this rhetoric. This too will be a slow process given the variety and complexity of the topic. Tourism must acknowledge also that it is not the only industry with a resource claim. In most communities there will be competition and conflict over the resources tourism desires. 'For tourism to survive sustainability, it must take a proactive leadership role in addressing the difficult challenges of integrating the needs of all user groups' (McKercher, 1993).

Tourism should be ideally suited for a leadership role in sustainable development given its multidimensional nature and private–public sector duality. Initiation of this role should be the next logical step in the evolution of sustainable tourism development, but to do so the various tourism stakeholders must pull together as an epistemic community.

Spreading the Word

Academic and government circles have been the major champions of sustainable tourism development, but if they are to be more proactive in their leadership they need to spread the word to a larger audience. Many feel the case has been made for the integration of sustainable development principles into future tourism management as illustrated by a recent article in *International Journal of Hospitality Mangement* (Manning and Dougherty, 1995). But the concept's complexity and its diverse operational requirements can be overwhelming to nonspecialists. Recognition of this fact has led the World Tourism Organization (WTO) to develop simplified guides for practitioners (Consulting and Audit Canada, 1995) and basic planning steps (Inskeep and Kallenberger, 1992). Various government and private sector agencies and academics have developed general codes of conduct to guide businesses toward more sustainable practices

Benefits to nature tourism and ecotourism operators include:

Competitive advantage in marketing nature tourism and ecotourism products (e.g., discounted advertising and logo inclusion in the Ecotourism Association of Australia's *Australian Ecotourism Guide,* logo inclusion in Tourism Queensland's *Sunlover* catalogues, logo inclusion in Northern Territory Tourist Commission motoring guides, and opportunities for cooperative advertising and logo inclusion in the Australian Tourist Commission's *Australian Tourism Source*).

Financial savings resulting from extended tenure in protected areas.

Baseline criteria for operators to determine the degree to which their product meets the standards of nature tourism and/or ecotourism.

An opportunity to promote products as genuine nature tourism or ecotourism.

A framework within which performance can be continually improved to a standard recognised as best practice.

Information on ways to improve the quality of products.

Benefits to consumers include:

A recognised means of identifying genuine nature tourism and ecotourism products.

Benefits to protected area managers *include:*

Improved practices that lead to fewer negative environmental impacts and more efficient use of natural resources.

Criteria to assist in identifying genuine nature tourism and ecotourism products.

Benefits to local communities include:

Criteria to assist in identifying genuine nature tourism and ecotourism products.

A tool to help determine a mixture of tourism activity that helps maximise benefits and minimise negative impacts.

Figure 9.6: Benefits of NEAP.

Source: Ecotourism Association of Australia, 2000.

such as the previously discussed NEAP in Australia. Furthermore, the development of government–industry cooperation is on the rise, as demonstrated by the focus of the Australian state Victoria's Strategic Tourism Plan 2002–2006, which has a clearly expressed emphasis on government–industry initiation and implementation of sustainable tourism development. These advances are evidence that government and academics are striving to broaden and simplify the sustainable tourism message and to offer some practical suggestions. However, it must be a message that diverse groups and interests are willing to heed.

Individual tourism businesses, like any other business, are often skeptical about government and academic messages that may reduce their economic viability. However, the industry leaders do recognise that long-term economic viability is intimately tied to a healthy physical and social environment. Evidence of this form of thinking can be seen in Swinth and Raymond's (1995) examination of the sports fishing industry on Yellowstone Lake. They found the development of an ecosystems management approach involving all principal stakeholders, along with an ongoing monitoring process, had saved this sports fishing attraction from the potential oblivion of the old free market economic system.

More owners and managers now appreciate the dictum that every tourist business 'needs to sell the destination first and its business second' if it is to survive and prosper. This results in a more proactive interest in the physical and social well being of all destination types.

Kavallinis and Pizam (1994) found that tourism entrepreneurs on the Greek island of Mykonos were aware of the negative environmental impacts tourism was creating and were prepared to accept their share of the responsibility. But it was also difficult to separate out the industry's individual responsibility from that of the local residents and actual tourists. So once again it would require intergroup acknowledgement and consensus to initiate a sustainable development approach.

In terms of sustainable tourism development, the consumer is often equated with ecotourists and the natural environment. This is an extremely narrow view of the potential tourist interest in sustainable tourism, because it has elitist overtones and will restrict support to a relatively small, albeit growing, market segment. It ignores the fact that exploration of ecosystems involves human habitats as well as natural ones (Murphy, 1985), and as Hall (1994) has pointed out, many of the so-called natural landscapes can seldom be separated from the cultural and economic forces that formed them.

For sustainable tourism to have the level of support it needs from the consumer, its appeal and relevance must be expanded beyond the ecotourist. There is growing evidence that the often-belittled mass tourist is showing increased interest in the local environment and social/cultural customs of their destinations. Hanauma Bay, a popular marine park just outside of Waikiki, has been overwhelmed by tourists, yet these same mass tourists have indicated their willingness to pay fees and accept limits on numbers in order to reduce the crowding and preserve the attraction of this site (Mak and Moncur, 1995). Most resorts now include the opportunity to see local culture and history in their offerings, and as the market continues to mature there will be a greater need to supplement beach and nightclub activities with more outdoor recreation and educational trips into the local area.

Bringing Stakeholders Together

If sustainable tourism development is to move from the pages of academic papers and government reports into the marketplace, it will be necessary to bring the industry and tourist stakeholders more extensively into the discussion and operationalisation of this concept. To bring about such a unity of purpose and action, sustainable tourism needs to market the concept more effectively and develop a 'more appropriate matching of markets with products' (Wight, 1993). Evidence of this can be seen in Ballantine and Eagles' (1994) examination of safari ecotourists in Africa. 'The only dissatisfaction this group found with their trip is a need for more information on conservation issues. This suggests a weakness in the interpretation programmes . . . [and] a strong interest and dedication to education about conservation issues by the tourists.' In Australia, recognition of the need to improve interpretation programmes has led to EcoGuide Certification, an industry-driven program designed to provide a number of benefits including (Ecotourism Australia, 2003):

- Certified guides who gain the advantage of an industry credential and a pathway to nationally recognised formal qualifications that will provide a defined competitive edge;
- Operators who gain a simple method of recognising quality guides, a benchmark to use for training purposes and greater product appeal through employing and promoting the use of bona fide nature and ecotour guides;
- Both guides and operators who gain an opportunity to promote guiding services as genuine nature tourism or ecotourism, providing a competitive edge for these niche markets;
- Visitors who gain a guarantee of guides who are committed to providing quality nature tourism and ecotourism experiences in a safe, culturally sensitive, and environmentally sustainable manner;
- Environmental benefits that flow from improved guiding practices that lead to fewer negative environmental and cultural impacts;

- Training providers who gain a benchmark of best practice nature and ecotour guiding; and
- A potential advantage for protected area managers, which is the ability to identify operators who employ staff with appropriate training and qualifications when reviewing permit applications in sensitive areas.

The type of marketing needed is one that emphasises education and communication along with the sales dimension. Wight (1994) correctly calls for 'the environmentally responsible marketing of tourism' and wants it to go beyond the green labelling of ecotourism to incorporate ethics and codes of practice. To go beyond the selling focus of green labelling involves marketing that stresses the synergistic qualities between a tourist's interest and visit with the product's survival and enhancement. Kotler (1988) has been one of those market researchers who has demonstrated that marketing is about more than selling. It is in fact a communications tool as expressed through its public relations function. It is now recognised as an important business component for the nonprofit sector as well, assisting in its survival and development strategies (Kotler and Andreasen, 1991).

Linking the various stakeholder groups together via marketing communications can help to sell the concept of sustainable tourism and its individual products through the element of education. Just as Disney and its numerous imitators have packaged entertainment and education, so sustainable tourism should strive to combine quality experiences with education. For some tourists, such as ecotourists, it will mean detailed explanation and exposure to the site or activity.

But these would be relatively few in number compared with those tourists who would be satisfied with a simple explanation and a 'staged' representation of the cultural or natural phenomenon. In either case the industry and governments now have a responsibility to inform tourists about their destinations and an opportunity to enhance tourists' 'sense of place' through quality interpretation and carefully designed tours and facilities.

Summary

Since the first edition of this book appeared, the need for considering sustainable tourism management has increased. The tourism industry has increased in size, while the world's resource base has remained static or declined and there has been growing competition for those resources. However, the message about sustainable tourism seems to remain largely trapped in an academic–government loop, although some industry–client initiatives are evident. This is caused in part by the relatively complex and comprehensive nature of the concept, which needs to be broken down into more manageable components and scales if it is to be adopted and appreciated on a broader scale.

This process is underway already, as indicated by the efforts of the WTO. Some individuals and organisations are beginning to spread the message that sustainable tourism involves a combination of experience, entertainment, and education. Such a change of emphasis will require more effective marketing, a marketing focus that communicates and educates to bring the major stakeholders together in a practical forum of sustainable tourism development. It is to be hoped that via such strategies the message of sustainable tourism development will reach the front lines, where it needs to be implemented. Large-scale tourism is a fact of life and the problems caused by, and associated with, tourism need to be ameliorated as quickly as possible. Although sustainable tourism development on a global scale remains a telic concept, the journey toward the goal of sustainability is vital for current and future economic, ecological, and sociocultural well being.

References

Ballantine, J. F., and P. F. J. Eagles. 1994. Defining Canadian Ecotourists. *Journal of Sustainable Tourism* 2(4): 210–214.

Barkin, D. 1996. 'Ecotourism: A Tool for Sustainable Development.' http://www. greenbuilder.com/mader/planeta/0596/0596monarch.html. Accessed August 7, 1999.

British Columbia Round Table on the Environment and the Economy. 1991. *Sustainable Communities*. Victoria, B.C.: Columbia Round Table on the Environment and the Economy.

Butler, R. W. 1990. Alternative Tourism: Pious Hope or Trojan Horse? *Journal of Travel Research* 28(3): 40–45.

Canadian Environment Advisory Council. 1987. *Canada and Sustainable Development*. Ottawa: CEAC.

Cater, E. 1994. Ecotourism in the Third World: Problems and Prospects for Sustainability. In *Ecotourism: A Sustainable Option?* eds. E. Cater and G. Lowman. Chichester: John Wiley and Sons.

Cinquegrani, R. 2002. Futurist Networks: Cases of Epistemic Community. *Futures* 34(8): 779–783.

Consulting and Audit Canada. 1995. *What Tourism Managers Need to Know: A Practical Guide to the Development and Use of Indicators of Sustainable Tourism*. Madrid: World Tourism Organization.

Ecotourism Association of Australia. 2000. *National Ecotourism Accreditation Program*. Brisbane: Ecotourism Association of Australia.

Ecotourism Australia. 2003. *EcoGuide Certification*. Brisbane: Ecotourism Australia.

Elkington, J. 1999. *Cannibals with Forks: The Triple Bottom Line of 21st Century Business*. Oxford: Capstone Publishing.

Environment Canada. 2001. *Environment Canada's Sustainable Development Strategy*. Hull, Quebec: Environment Canada.

Faulkner, B. 2001. Destination Australia: A Research Agenda for 2002 and Beyond. Paper presented at *Australian Tourism Research Institute Conference*, October 30–31, Hobart.

Gössling, S., C. B. Hansson, O. Hörstmeier, and S. Saggel. 2002. Ecological Footprint Analysis as a Tool to Assess Tourism Sustainability. *Ecological Economics* 43(2–3): 11, 199–211.

Hall, C. M. 1994. Ecotourism in Australia, New Zealand and the South Pacific: Appropriate Tourism or a New Form of Ecological Imperialism? In *Ecotourism: A Sustainable Option?* ed. E. Cater, and G. Lowman. Chichester: John Wiley.

Hall, C. M., J. Jenkins, and G. Kearsley. eds. 1997. *Tourism Planning and Policy in Australia and New Zealand: Cases, Issues and Practice*. Sydney: Irwin Publishers.

Hawkes, S., and P. Williams. Eds. 1993. *The Greening of Tourism*. Vancouver, B.C.: Centre for Tourism Policy and Research, Simon Fraser University.

Huckle, J. 1996. Realising Sustainability in Changing Times. In *Education for Sustainability*. eds. J. Huckle and S. Sterling. London: Earthscan Publications.

Hunt, C. B., and E. R. Auster. 1990. Proactive Environmental Management: Avoiding the Toxic Trap. *Sloan Management Review* 31(2): 7–18.

Hunter, C. J. 2002. Aspects of the Sustainable Tourism Debate from a Natural Resources Perspective. In *Sustainable Tourism: A Global Perspective*. eds. R. Harris, T. Griffin, and P. Williams. Oxford: Butterworth-Heinemann.

Inskeep, E., and M. Kallenberger. 1992. *An Integrated Approach to Resort Development*. Madrid: World Tourism Organization.

International Union for the Conservation of Nature and Natural Resources. 1980. *World Conservation Strategy*. Gland, Switzerland: IUCN.

Jones, A. 1992. Is There a Real Alternative Tourism? *Tourism Management* 13(1): 102–103.

Kavallinis, I., and A. Pizam. 1994. The Environmental Impacts of Tourism—Whose Responsibility Is it Anyway? The Case Study of Mykonos. *Journal of Travel Research* 33(2): 26–32.

Kotler, P. 1988. *Marketing Management*. 6th ed. Englewood Cliffs, N.J.: Prentice-Hall.

Kotler, P., and A. Andreasen. 1991. *Strategic Marketing for Nonprofit Organizations*. Englewood Cliffs, N.J.: Prentice-Hall.

Krippendorf, J. 1987. *The Holiday Makers*. London: Heinemann.

Mak, J., and J.E. T. Moncur. 1995. Sustainable Tourism Development: Managing Hawaii's 'Unique' Touristic Resource—Hanauma Bay. *Journal of Travel Research* 33(4): 51–56.

Manning, E. W., and T. D. Dougherty. 1995. Sustainable Tourism: Preserving the Golden Goose. *Cornell Hotel and Restaurant Administration Quarterly*, April.

McIntosh, R., C. Goeldner, and J. R. B. Ritchie. 1995. *Tourism Principles, Practices, Philosophies*. 7th ed. New York: John Wiley and Sons.

McKercher, B. 1993. The Unrecognized Threat to Tourism: Can Tourism Survive Sustainability? *Tourism Management* 14(2): 131–136.

Meadows, D., and D. Meadows. 1972. *Limits to Growth*. New York: Universe Books.

Middleton, V. T. C., and R. Hawkins. 1998. *Sustainable Tourism: A Marketing Perspective*. Oxford: Butterworth-Heinemann.

Mill, R. C., and A. M. Morrison. 1985. *The Tourism System*. Englewood Cliffs, N.J.: Prentice-Hall.

Moldan, B., and S. Billharz. eds. 1997. *Sustainability Indicators: Report of the Project on Indicators of Sustainable Development*. Chichester: John Wiley and Sons.

Murphy, P. E. 1985. *Tourism: A Community Approach*. London: Methuen.

——. 1992. Data Gathering of Community-Oriented Tourism Planning: A Case Study of Vancouver Island, British Columbia. *Leisure Studies* 12(1): 65–79.

Murphy, P. E., and M. Pritchard. 1997. Destination Price-Value Perceptions: An Examination of Origin and Seasonal Influences. *Journal of Travel Research* 35(3): 16–22.

Owens, S., and R. Cowell. 1996. *Rocks and A Hard Place*. London: Council for the Preservation of Rural England.

Page, S. J., and R. K. Dowling. 2002. *Ecotourism*. New York: Prentice Hall.

Pigram, J. J. 1990. Sustainable Tourism Policy Considerations. *Journal of Tourism Studies* 1(2): 3–9.

Platteau, J-P., and F. Gaspart. 2003. The Risk of Resource Misappropriation in Community-Driven Development. *World Development* 31(10): 1687–1703.

Porter, M. E. 1991. Essay—America's Green Strategy. *Scientific American* 264(3), April: 168.

Price, G. G., and P. E. Murphy. 2000. The Relationship between Ecotourism and Sustainable Development: A Critical Examination. In *Peak Performance in Tourism and Hospitality Research CAUTHE 2000 Refereed Research Papers*. ed. M. Michael. La Trobe University, Bundoora: School of Tourism and Hospitality.

Rees, N. E. 1990. The Ecology of Sustainable Development. *The Ecologist* 20(1): 18–23.

Rees, N. E., and M. Roseland. 1988. *Planning for Sustainable Development*. University of British Columbia: School of Community and Regional Planning.

Sadler, B. 1992. Sustainable Tourism and Tomorrow's Heritage: Toward Policy and Research that Make a Difference. In *Tourism-Environment-Sustainable Development: An Agenda for Research*. ed. L. J. Reid. Ottawa: Conference Proceedings of the Travel and Tourism Research Association (Canada).

Sisman, R. 1994. Tourism: Environmental Relevance. In *Ecotourism: A Sustainable Option?* eds. E. Cater and G. Lowman. Chichester: John Wiley and Sons.

Smith, E. T. 1992. Growth vs. Environment. *Business Week*, May 11: 66–75.

Stanley, D. 1992. Synthesis of Workshop Sessions. In *Tourism-Environment-Sustainable Development: An Agenda for Research*. ed. L. J. Reid. Ottawa: Conference Proceedings of the Travel and Tourism Research Association (Canada).

Stankey, G., D. Cole, R. Lucas, M. Petersen, and S. Frissell. 1995. The Limits of Acceptable Change (LAC) System for Wildernedd Planning. *General Technical Report INT-176*. Ogden, UT, U.S. Department of Agriculture, Forest Service, Forest and Range Experiment Station, p. 37.

Sun, D., and D. Walsh. 1998. Review of Studies on Environmental Impacts of Recreation and Tourism in Australia. *Journal of Environmental Management* 53: 323–338.

Swarbrooke, J. 1999. *Sustainable Tourism Management*. Wallingford, U.K.: CAB International.

Swinth, R. L., and B. C. Raymond. 1995. Sustainable Development in Practice: The Management of Yellowstone Lake for Fishing and Ecosystem Protection. *Research in Corporate Social Performance and Policy.* Supplement 1. Greenwich, CT: JAI Press.

Taylor, G. D., and D. Stanley. 1992. Tourism, Sustainable Development and the Environment: An Agenda for Research. *Journal of Travel Research* 31(1): 66–67.

Tisdell, C., and J. Wen. 1997. Why Care Is Needed in Applying Indicators of the Sustainability of Tourism. *Australian Journal of Hospitality Management* 4(1): 1–6.

United Nations Department of Economic and Social Affairs. 2002. *Johannesburg Summit 2002.* New York: United Nations Department of Economic and Social Affairs.

Wackernagel, M., and N. E. Rees. 1996. *Our Ecological Footprint: Reducing the Human Impact on the Earth.* Gabriola Island, B.C., Canada: New Society Publishers.

Wagar, J. A. 1964. *The Carrying Capacity of Wildlands for Recreation.* Society of American Foresters, Forest Service Monograph 7: 23.

Wearing, S., and J. Neil. 1999. *Ecotourism: Impacts, Potentials and Possibilities.* Oxford: Butterworth-Heinemann.

Weaver, D., and M. Oppermann. 2000. *Tourism Management.* Brisbane: John Wiley and Sons.

Wight, P. A. 1993. Sustainable Ecotourism: Balancing Economic, Environmental and Social Goals within an Ethical Framework. *Journal of Tourism Studies* 4(2): 54–66.

———. 1994. Environmentally Responsible Marketing of Tourism. In *Ecotourism: A Sustainable Option?* eds. E. Cater and G. Lowman. Chichester: John Wiley and sons.

———. 1997. Sustainability, Profitability and Ecotourism Markets: What Are They and How Do They Relate? Paper presented at an *International Conference on Central and Eastern Europe,* September 22–23, 1997. Parnu, Estonia.

Wilson, E. O. 1997. *Consilience: The Unity of Knowledge.* New York: Knopf.

Winter, G. 1988. *Business and the Environment.* Hamburg, New York: McGraw-Hill.

World Commission on Environment and Development. 1987. *Our Common Future.* Oxford: Oxford University Press.

World Travel and Tourism. Council. 1996. *Travel and Tourism.* Press Release. Brussels, Belgium: WTTC.

World Tourism Organization. 1999. <http://www.world-tourism.org/>. Accessed September 16, 2003.

———. 2003. *Global Code of Ethics for Tourism.* Madrid: WTO News.

10 Addressing carrying capacity issues in tourism destinations through growth management

Peter W. Williams and Alison Gill

Introduction

There is widespread acknowledgment of the potentially damaging relationship between increasing numbers of tourists and the escalated degradation of many tourism destinations (Hunter and Green, 1995). Embodied in this relationship is the concept of carrying capacity, which suggests an approach to management that permits growth within acceptable limits (Johnson and Thomas, 1996). Consequently it is not surprising that it has been intuitively supported by land-use planners and resource managers in many tourism regions. Despite its seemingly clear and rational intent, the actual implementation of carrying capacity management strategies has met with ongoing controversy and frustration. On the one hand, the concept of carrying capacity appeals to a recognised need to limit and control those dimensions of tourism development that may threaten the sustained use of limited resources. Simultaneously, it runs at odds with other desires for maximising opportunities for growth and realising the potential benefits associated with increased visitor use.

As a more practical and viable alternative to the concept of carrying capacity management, this chapter recommends the application of growth management planning approaches for addressing development issues in tourism destinations. It summarises the key conceptual foundations on which previous tourism and recreation carrying capacity strategies have been based, provides examples drawn from Whistler, British Columbia to illustrate the range of management tactics that can be employed to address tourism growth issues, then suggests the lessons that should be incorporated into the development of any tourism growth management strategy.

Tourism Carrying Capacity Management

Varying perspectives on carrying capacity as a tourism management tool exist. In its most traditional sense, the concept refers to the maximum number of tourists or tourist use that can be accommodated within a specified geographic destination (O'Reilly, 1986). As such, it conjures up images of a specified 'limit,' 'ceiling,' or 'threshold' that tourism development should not exceed. In a North American context, most strategies to manage tourism growth have been in controlled recreation settings such as parks and river corridors (Eagles and McCool, 2002). Some European efforts have focussed on the control of tourism expansion especially in the Alps (Godde, Price, and Zimmerman, 2000), while the management of such growth has been attempted along stretches of the Mediterranean shoreline and nearby islands (Inskeep and Kallenberger, 1992) and to a lesser extent in some Caribbean destinations (McElroy and de Albuquerque, 1996). These studies and others propose a wide variety of carrying capacity 'ceilings' that describe optimum or benchmark thresholds for tourism development in volume, density, or market-mix terms (Inskeep, 1997). Difficulties with these numerical carrying capacity limits arise when efforts are made to link them directly to the management of specific tourism impacts. Little evidence exists to suggest that by simply changing a specified carrying capacity limit, predictable changes in tourist impact will happen. Instead, the key appears to lie in how tourism use and its associated changes are managed.

From an environmental perspective carrying capacity management involves maintaining a balance between physical/ecological and visitor requirements associated with a destination area. In this context it refers to 'the maximum number of people who can use a site without an unacceptable alteration in the physical environment and without an unacceptable decline in the quality of the experience gained by visitors' (Mathieson and Wall, 1982). This implies some prior designation of preferred or desired conditions on which levels of acceptable tourism impact can be judged.

For others, tourism carrying capacity is market driven (Plog, 1991). Critical carrying capacity thresholds occur when tourist numbers approach levels that strain the capability of the destination to provide quality tourist experiences. Key indicators of encroachment on such capacity ceilings have traditionally been related to identifiable changes in market demand. Any number of physical, economic, social, environmental, psychological, or political reasons can trigger tourist apathy toward a destination. However, it is frequently assumed that when visitor perceptions of desired on-site conditions are not met, declines in tourist demand occur. Depending on the preferred conditions established by destination decision makers, actions may be taken to expand the ability of a destination to absorb tourism and rejuvenate visitor interest in the destination, or conversely constrain further development activities.

From a social perspective, carrying capacity refers to a destination's ability to absorb tourism without unacceptable negative effects being felt by local residents (Ap and Crompton, 1998; Anderdeck and Vogt, 2000). Levels at which inappropriate impacts occur are dependent on values determined by the community as opposed to the visitor. Identifying these values in a tourism destination requires considerable consensus building amongst community stakeholders (e.g., residents, developers, operators, governments). From a carrying capacity management perspective it involves identifying the desired conditions for a destination area, and deciding how to effectively manage tourism toward those ends. It is also important to recognise that community perspectives on desired conditions may change over time and in response to different planning and management approaches (Martin and Uysal, 1990; Butler, 1997). Consequently, a regular review of what is considered to be desirable and acceptable is a critical part of managing tourism from a community perspective.

New Management Directions

Carrying capacity management's traditional focus on attempting to determine explicit use limits has made it a particularly difficult tool to use in a tourism management context. There appear to be too many limiting factors that hamper its use. In particular, the concept has not been fully operationalised because of:

- Unrealistic expectations (i.e., a technique exists that can provide a magic number that identifies 'how much is too much'),
- Untenable assumptions (i.e., a direct relationship between tourism use and impact exists),
- Inappropriate value judgments (i.e., conflicts between the views of 'experts' as opposed to destination stakeholders concerning what conditions are appropriate for an area), and

- Insufficient legal support (i.e., the lack of a formally recognised institutional process to ensure management strategies are implemented and enforced) (Gill and Williams, 1994).

However, those aspects of the concept that focus on establishing desired conditions or outcomes appear to have practical value for the management of tourism destinations. This is particularly the case if they can be incorporated into broader planning processes associated with sustainable development and growth management.

When applied within planning systems that focus on managing growth for desirable and acceptable change, some components of the carrying capacity management concept offer potential. Knowledge of the consequences of exceeding desired impacts can be used to direct management policies and practices in keeping with a more sustainable tourism (Manidis Roberts Consultants, 1997). This implies the development of management guidelines that support forms of tourism that emphasise:

- Architectural character and style sensitive to an area's heritage and environment (Dorward, 1990);
- Preservation, protection, and enhancement of heritage and environmental resource quality (Bosselman, Peterson, and McCarthy, 1999); and
- Improvement to the quality of local populations' lives (Lama, 2000).

Growth Management Systems

The challenges of managing growth are especially apparent in tourism destinations. Here there are frequently several groups often with divergent views concerning growth options. They include tourists, developers, local residents, existing and proposed business operators, and the public agencies responsible for managing the environment within which all groups must operate. Depending on the specific circumstances of a community (e.g., stage of tourism development, community economic conditions, or past tourist–resident encounters), the needs of one group may take precedent over those of the others in growth management decisions (Price, Moss, and Williams, 1997). It is not uncommon, for example, to see the needs of the tourist and developer take priority over the requirements of community residents during early stages of development. Although in the short term this helps stimulate growth, long-term sustainability of the tourism industry may suffer if the quality of life of residents who require affordable housing, schools, and community facilities is not adequately addressed. However, once most of the tourism infrastructure is in place, the role of the developer may diminish and the needs of local residents and visitors may take precedence. The real possibility of such changes in priorities is what makes the establishment of fixed long-term capacity limits a particularly challenging task, and creates the need for a more flexible, systems-based approach to managing tourism growth.

In a growth management systems context, notions of carrying capacity are linked to the 'desired conditions' that best meet the goals of the area being managed. Although sensitively managing an area's unique natural and cultural resources is often central to a destination's competitive advantage in the tourism marketplace, the resource base does not determine carrying capacity. Rather it is a function of the management goals and objectives established by the community's stakeholders. If their main objective is to stabilise population growth patterns in the community, tourism's capability to contribute to that objective becomes the key growth management concern. Indicators of population stabilisation might include changes in emigration and migration levels, age, and gender structure. If job creation is identified as the community's priority objective, then indicators of the types of employment to be generated (e.g., seasonal, year round, front line, supervisory, management) by tourism development become the growth management focus. The establishment of goals and objectives determines which indicators of change become the focus of growth management and monitoring.

General goals give broad direction to the planning and management of the mountain conditions desired. Objectives offer more precise statements of the mechanisms by which the desired conditions are achieved. A general goal might be to manage the rate and quality of mountain development in order to achieve and maintain a diversified community economy. Objectives associated with this might include monitoring agricultural and tourism development to determine whether an appropriate balance between these two land uses is being maintained, or managing residential reserve areas in an attempt to ensure that employee housing supply keeps pace with this demand.

A suggested systems approach to incorporating desired destination community conditions into practical growth management practices involves:

- Developing tourism goals and objectives that mesh with the broader comprehensive plan for the destination,
- Establishing a set of performance indicators reflecting the expected objectives of tourism development,
- Implementing management strategies that direct tourism toward the achievement of the stated goals and objectives,
- Monitoring the performance of tourism development with respect to these indicators,

- Evaluating the effectiveness of the management strategies in influencing the performance of tourism with respect to these indicators, and
- Developing refined and/or new tactics for managing tourism based on the effectiveness of these techniques (Getz, 1982).

The growth management systems approach offers a distinct perspective in that it:

- Involves no identification of an ultimate limit to the number of visitors,
- Relates tourism growth and development to its effect on destination goals and objectives,
- Employs indicators of desired conditions to trigger either the implementation or adjustment to growth management strategies, and
- Reviews and modifies goal and objective priorities as destination circumstances change.

Growth Management Planning

In a North American context, carrying capacity concerns can be incorporated into the comprehensive planning agendas of most tourism destinations. A key to the success of such initiatives are growth management plans. Based on a destination's ability to articulate a vision of what community conditions and expansion rates it would like to encourage, growth management plans offer a potentially useful 'guidance system' for implementing that vision. These plans typically include policy statements, capital budgets, and specific improvement programmes that guide decision making concerning tourism expansion. Practical instruments to support identified programmes encompass public investment strategies, land-use regulations, and fiscal incentives or disincentives (Schiffman, 1989). They go beyond strictly land-use planning by incorporating control mechanisms influencing tourism and other activities within the destination.

Many tourism-dependent communities (e.g., Aspen/Pitkin County, Colorado; Jackson Hole, Wyoming; Park City, Utah; Sanibel Island, Florida; Languedoc-Rousillon, France; S'Agaro, Spain; Niagara-on-the-Lake, Ontario; and Bermuda) exhibit varying aspects of comprehensive growth management plans (Bosselman, Peterson, and McCarthy, 1999). However, there appear to be few comprehensive applications of these approaches. Whistler, British Columbia, exhibits many of what may be considered 'state of the art' growth management planning practices within its destination planning programmes. Because of its incorporation of many of the best practices occurring in other tourism destination jurisdictions, and its ongoing experimentation with such strategies, its approach to growth management is discussed here.

Whistler Case Study

Growth Management Context

Whistler is located 120 kilometres from Vancouver, British Columbia, Canada. Nestled in the Pacific Range of the Coast Mountains, the municipality encompasses an area of 12,630 hectares. Within its boundaries are found six high quality lakes, several environmentally sensitive natural areas, a variety of parks and recreation sites, an architecturally-themed and visitor-focussed commercial village, surrounding clusters of residential accommodation, as well as some limited industrial lands. Dominating the skyline of this fully incorporated resort municipality are two of North America's most highly rated and largest ski mountains, Blackcomb (2284 metres) and Whistler (2182 metres).

In 2001–2002, the full time population of Whistler was approximately 9700 residents. In that same year about 14,200 employees were needed to provide services to residents and the destination's annual inflow of 2 million tourists. The vast majority of these tourists were housed in Whistler's substantial stock of commercial hotel, condominium, bed and breakfast, and campground accommodations (13,770 bed units). In addition, these visitors were able to access the area's wide array of retail outlets, food/restaurant establishments, and bars (120,000 square metres) located primarily in the Whistler's village core (Resort Municipality of Whistler, 2003).

Whistler has evolved from a small, water-focussed summer recreation area in the 1960s, to a dynamic four-season mountain tourism destination in 2003. Its evolution to this state has been marked by several critical planning events. A special act of government incorporated the nascent destination as the Resort Municipality of Whistler (RMOW) in 1975. At that time the first Official Community Plan was established. The Whistler Village Land Company (WVLC), a wholly owned subsidiary of the RMOW, was established in 1978 to guide the development of a new village core. This placed control over the rate and direction of growth largely in the hands of the RMOW's elected Council. The Council's philosophy and intent with respect to growth was clear: to achieve the goal of creating a mountain destination of international calibre. Significant facility and amenity expansion designed to meet the demands of tourists was encouraged and approved. However, the RMOW's plans and activities were derailed in the early 1980s, when a severe recession led to the bankruptcy and eventual restructuring of the destination's governance. As part of this restructuring process, the British Columbia government took back development control of all provincially owned lands and facilities in Whistler's village core. This served to reduce the level of community input into Whistler's development, and led to an unprecedented level of tourism facility expansion. To reach the critical mass needed to have an impact in the marketplace, minimise taxation effects, support wide range of resort amenities, and recover the large public investments in infrastructure incurred prior to and during the recession period, rapid growth in Whistler was stimulated by the provincial government. As a result of these activities, by the mid 1980s, Whistler was firmly established as a major ski destination in North America. However, there was a growing recognition that this expansion was beginning to occur at a cost to other values in the destination.

Concerns over an uncertain vision of the eventual size of the resort, the protection of the quality of the environment, and the overall ability of the destination's infrastructure to handle the ever-growing levels of tourism traffic led to the development of the RMOW's first Comprehensive Development Plan (CDP) in 1988. The plan became the RMOW's policy statement and strategic guide for future development of the destination. As such, it subsequently influenced the direction and content of the RMOW's development regulations as expressed in the Official Community Plan and related by-laws.

In the process of creating the CDP, the resolution of other issues emerged as being critical to Whistler's long-term success. These concerns evolved around determining the best approaches for developing the facilities and services that would permit Whistler to achieve its all-season tourism destination status, as well as how the destination would go about providing housing and community-oriented services for a growing permanent and seasonal labour force vital to the resort's operation. Recognising the need for Whistler to have the additional summer facilities and services necessary for a truly competitive all-season resort destination, the CDP encouraged additional accommodation and related commercial development in Whistler. These expansions effectively boosted Whistler's overall accommodation ceiling to 52,600 bed units. However, the most challenging issue not directly addressed in the CDP from a growth management perspective was determining how Whistler would manage existing and future commitments to expansion without a clear appreciation of the effects of this development growth on the environment, community, and the overall quality of the resort.

By 1992, Whistler's economic circumstances had improved and the destination was firmly on its way to becoming a comprehensive year-round mountain tourism destination. As a result, the British Columbia government returned full responsibility for the allocation, development, and management of Whistler to the RMOW in that year. This event led to a more locally based and issue-specific approach to growth management, which was eventually articulated in the RMOW's revised CDP. The CDP's policies and goals reflected a fundamental shift from primarily focussing on tourism development to one that centred on the critical need to maintain and enhance the quality of the resort and the community.

Changing Goals for Growth

Initially, the primary goal guiding development in Whistler had been to achieve a level of development that would ensure a viable position in the international resort destination marketplace. Priority was placed on attracting investment to develop infrastructure and facilities serving tourists' needs. The community's approach to managing growth and development was a reflection of the unique characteristics of the area in 1988. During the 1990s, Whistler evolved from that stage and the challenge moved from developing primarily tourist amenities to a more holistic set of goals related to providing community services for residents, protecting the environment, and maintaining the quality of the overall experience for visitors (Gill, 2000).

In 2003, the development of new and internationally competitive tourist facilities is still necessary and the RMOW has embraced this challenge. However, it is now oriented toward forms of development that are aligned with a community-driven vision (RMOW, 2002). Its management focus is now firmly placed on priorities related to maintaining environmental quality, protecting the viability of the resort economy, and securing community services as opposed to more grand commitments to resort amenities and development.

The general goals specified in the RMOW's most recent CDP are to:

- Balance the environmental, economic, and social needs of the community and resort;
- Maintain the high quality of the natural and built environment;
- Encourage kinds of economic activity compatible with the resort; and
- Guide the RMOW's activities to manage growth in the resort and broader region.

Developing a Guiding Vision

The resort community's long-range view of growth management is its comprehensive resort community vision (RMOW, 2002). This community-based vision not only identifies what the priority goals for future management should be in Whistler, but it also articulates how the RMOW intends to achieve these goals. These goals are accompanied with a set of financial and business plans to ensure that the vision becomes a reality. Community support is particularly high with respect to four priorities: moving toward environmental sustainability, building a stronger resort community, enhancing the Whistler experience, and achieving financial sustainability (Waldron, Godfrey, and Williams, 1999). Each priority is supported by a number of policy directions and tasks. For each of these priorities, the business plan articulates specific programmes of action. The following examples illustrate how growth management philosophies have been incorporated into RMOW's current and proposed actions.

Growth Management Policy

The cornerstone indicator of Whistler's progress toward managing growth has historically been the community's ability to encourage appropriate forms of development that did not surpass a prescribed bed-unit ceiling. An upper limit of 52,600 bed units was established in the early 1990s as Whistler's build-out limit. It was initially established based on the capacity of the RMOW's municipal water and sewage systems to safely handle such a level of accommodation development and use. Despite its ongoing presence in Whistler's planning policies, it was not intended to be an absolute capacity limit. For instance, it was recognised that greater capital expenditures on technical support systems could expand the ability of Whistler to technically manage greater levels of development. Indeed because the establishment of the bed-unit ceiling several years ago, many enhancements to the technical capacity of Whistler's water and sewer systems have occurred.

These and other improvements in destination infrastructure capacity, as well as greater awareness of the multifaceted impacts of resort community development, have stimulated an increasingly heated political and technical debate concerning the appropriateness of this bed-unit ceiling. Growing concern is being raised by local politicians, bureaucrats, businesses, and residents about what the implications of the bed-unit ceiling will be once Whistler reaches its bed-unit capacity limit. This debate is fuelled by a growing recognition that the current ceiling will be reached in the near future. In 2002, Whistler had already reached about 88 percent of its bed-unit 'build-out' capacity (RMOW, 2003).

From a growth management philosophy perspective, 'build out' is largely a question of what the RMOW deems to be desirable, given the community's vision, goals, and capabilities to manage growth's impacts. In keeping with this viewpoint, Whistler's political and administrative leaders have cautiously adopted this growth management philosophy and are inching their way into new bed-unit ceiling territory. As of 2002, the bed-unit ceiling was increased from the once unmovable 52,600 bed-unit ceiling to a new standard of 55,159 units (RMOW, 2003).

For the most part, increments to the bed-unit ceiling standard have been guided by efforts to meet community-based priorities expressed in Whistler's vision documents. Typically they have involved 'trade offs' with real estate developers. For instance, one high profile trade off involved reallocating the number and variety of specific bed-unit types to a real estate development group in exchange for that developer providing the RMOW with a significant tract of highly valued forest lands deemed important to the community's overall environmental strategy. This trade off also included the developer providing increased school facilities deemed critical to the area's local residents and the community's vision (Gill and Williams, 2003).

Increments to Whistler's bed-unit ceiling have also been permitted in order to address the community's ongoing and escalating affordable housing challenge. In 2002, approximately 75 percent of Whistler's 14,200 employees resided in the community. However, the remaining 3500 employees had to travel to the resort community for their jobs. This commuting trend has been escalating in recent years. For both local and commuting employees, access to and the availability of accommodation units is challenging at best. As a consequence, the bed-unit ceiling is being expanded to allow a greater variety and number of bed units to be made available (RMOW, 2003).

Although the decisions were controversial at the time they were made, they were guided by overriding goals expressed in the community's vision. As such, the emphasis with respect to growth has shifted from managing numbers to addressing a broader set of impacts. Driven by the community vision statement, the RMOW's CDP outlines a wide variety of programmes designed to manage future growth toward community goals. Some of these are outlined in the following paragraphs.

Environmental Quality

Increasingly, tourists are expecting resort destinations to be set in natural environments with superior air, water, scenery, flora, and fauna attributes (Design Workshop, et al., 2002). Permanent residents are drawn to such locations for similar reasons. The RMOW has developed and is implementing policy directives that recognise that Whistler's mountain environment places unique limitations on development. The RMOW's policies with respect to land use, transportation, servicing, and other aspects of community development are consistent with the goal of protecting environmental quality. Examples of the types of growth management instruments being implemented to address environmental issues include the adoption of the Whistler Environmental Strategy and The Natural Step management system to achieve its environmental priorities. The RMOW's policies are designed to encourage environmental programmes that focus on:

- An ecosystem-based approach toward land use, including a protected area network, recreational 'greenways.' and compact, efficient urban design;

- Environmentally sustainable transportation, including a comprehensive strategy to encourage nonuse of automobiles;
- Ecoefficient water supply and waste water management programmes;
- Solid waste reduction and reuse initiatives; and
- Energy conservation practices (Waldron, Godfrey, and Williams, 1999).

Community Facilities

Development approval policies implemented in 1990s helped to ensure that Whistler had a wide array of recreational amenities. These developer-funded facilities were primarily established to meet the summer recreational needs of tourists but also served to enhance the quality of life for Whistler's permanent and seasonal residents. However, because the priority was placed on visitor-oriented amenities as opposed to more community-focussed facilities, Whistler still lacks some of the facilities that are necessary for a complete and stable community. Addressing these gaps has been incorporated into the RMOW's current policy directives with respect to future growth. Some of the approaches that are in place or being considered to address these issues include:

Affordable housing: The RMOW established a programme to ensure that a full range of housing types and prices are available throughout the Whistler municipality. An employee service charge by-law was developed to provide an ongoing fund for subsidising seasonal housing development, providing publicly owned lands at below market value for affordable housing development, and encouraging employers to develop employee accommodation. To coordinate the effective use of these funds, the RMOW established a Whistler Housing Authority (WHA). Approximately 4300 of the 17,000 employees projected to makeup Whistler's workforce at 'build out' in 2005 are expected to be housed with the assistance of the WHA. The accommodation expected to be available for these employees is intended to range from dormitory-style short-term rental units to single family homes in subdivisions. The WHA is working toward an equal split between rental and ownership tenure in these housing units (WHA, 2002). Since its inception in 1977, the WHA and its partners have succeeded in more than doubling the number of employee beds. However, it is now faced with the need for additional seasonal rental beds to supplement the existing inventory, primarily due to the projected growth in housing demand linked to the forthcoming Winter Olympic Games that will be hosted in Whistler in 2010. It is expected that the current bed-unit ceiling currently in place for Whistler will once again be escalated to accommodate this expected demand for employee bed units.

Local transportation infrastructure: The RMOW has created a programme to ensure that Whistler has a local transportation system that places an emphasis on nonauto-based modes of transportation. It intends to achieve this goal by installing bike routes and lanes as well as pedestrian routes and walking trails, consolidating air transportation service nodes at accessible community locations, and improving existing public transit services at times and locations suited to the needs of local residents. To date, Whistler's commitment to improving public transit has been especially impressive. In 2002 the local public transit system, the Whistler And Valley Transit Express System, had the highest ridership of the all British Columbia municipal programmes, carrying more passengers in each hour of service than any other bus system in the province (RMOW, 2003).

Community facilities: The RMOW community facility policies address the need for improving Whistler's cultural, educational, public safety, health and social services, and administrative capacities. It is now in the process of establishing, and in some cases implementing, specific development projects that reflect the long-term needs of the community and resort. These include the creation of an additional community recreation centre, enhanced library facilities, and an Aboriginal cultural centre.

Monitoring and Evaluation

As opportunities for further expansion and the potential cumulative effects of development increase in Whistler, the need for effective monitoring systems that gauge the effects of such development escalate. As part of the RMOW's CDP and Official Community Plan, a community and resort monitoring system has been established. This annual monitoring programme provides quantitative feedback to elected community decision makers and stakeholders on what critical changes have occurred in Whistler as a result of growth. Using information collected from a wide variety of community stakeholders and government agencies, the monitoring report:

- Collects information concerning not only changes to the natural environment, but also the 'built,' social and economic environments of Whistler;
- Communicates findings emanating from the monitoring process in an annual public report, as well as at a yearly town meeting in order to ensure the widest possible understanding of the changes happening in Whistler; and
- Is used to help solicit community feedback concerning the effectiveness of the RMOW's growth management policies.

As the sophistication of the monitoring system has increased, so has the quality of the information presented in the reports. In 2003, the monitoring reports highlighted a large range of performance measures, including:

- Salient social characteristics of the community (e.g., employment and income, school and day care enrollment, housing);
- Critical economic patterns (e.g., development permits, skier volumes, hotel and conference usage, visitor satisfaction levels, and real estate values); and
- Environmental performance activities related to maintaining protected areas, demonstrating land-use stewardship activities, building a more environmentally sustainable transportation network, water supply, and wastewater management, and material and solid waste management (RMOW, 2003).

Each year the indicators presented come closer to addressing the pressure, state, and response measures needed to more accurately judge the impact of Whistler's growth management strategies (Waldron and Williams, 2002). For instance, significant additions to the range of indicators describing the environmental component of the monitoring report were incorporated in 2002. These new indicators helped to more fully describe the community's progress in implementing land use, infrastructure, and capacity building programmes that supported Whistler's vision with respect to environmental sustainability. Specific indicators associated with ecosystem management; protected areas network development, recreation greenway, and other forms of land-use stewardship; transportation network development; water and wastewater management; materials and solid waste management; and community energy efficiency and air quality improvement were provided. Where feasible, comparison benchmarks were made with other resort communities of similar size in North America in order to provide a context for assessing Whistler's performance (RMOW, 2003).

Tourism Growth Management Lessons

The growth management concerns addressed in the preceding discussion relate to issues of growth and development found in many North American communities. The need to balance the needs of the community and visitors in tourism communities is what makes growth management particularly challenging in destinations such as Whistler. In this regard, certain distinctive features stand out as being particularly critical to the successful implementation of growth management programmes. These include the diversity and ever-changing priorities of stakeholders, the evolutionary stage of the tourist community, and the importance of maintaining a high quality resource base. What strategies are implemented typically represents the meshing of economic, social, and environmental requirements with technical, administrative, and political realities.

Stakeholder Diversity

Community involvement in establishing desirable conditions is perhaps the single most important element of growth management. Developing appropriate mechanisms to incorporate divergent views is critical for successfully establishing appropriate resident–visitor relationships (Cleveland and Hansen, 1994). A basic distinction can be made between residents and visitors, but in reality there are much finer distinctions with respect to attitudinal differences toward development (Lawrence, et al., 1993). In many tourist towns, there is a significant second-home resident population as well as seasonal employees. Each of these resident groups has very different needs in terms of housing and service amenities. Although input into the planning process from permanent residents can be accomplished through traditional means such as public meetings, incorporating the viewpoints of these other community groups is more problematic. Alternative mechanisms, such as more informal small group meetings, have been used in some instances. In conjunction with these processes, active community information and publicity programmes (e.g., via radio talk shows, newsletters, etc.) are often necessary to ensure that the perspectives of more transient and/or recent residents of the community can be incorporated into the growth management process (Gill, 1992).

In addition to residents' attitudes, it is also important to interview visitors in order to understand why they have decided to visit the destination, how well their expectations are being met and what can be done to make their stays more enjoyable. Maintaining a balance between the needs of tourists and those of all residents is critical. As many residents of tourist towns choose to live there because of perceived lifestyle and amenity factors, programmes designed to facilitate local use of tourist-focussed attractions, facilities, and services can be employed to reduce friction between residents and visitors.

Development Stage

Resort communities are extremely dynamic in character. In the early phases of development, a high investment in tourist facilities and infra-structure is necessary to reach a 'critical mass' of attractions, services, facilities, and visitors so that the destination can sustain a tourism economy. Unfortunately tourism demand is often unpredictable and subject to such problems as seasonality and aggressive competition. Development activities often entail considerable investment risk. Consequently, encouraging investment is often the primary objective in the early stages of development and destinations have often compromised the needs of the resident community to achieve this. Although in the short term this seems an appropriate course of action, there may be negative repercussions at a later date. Examples of this can be found in most tourism towns that have evolved without an employee housing policy. Although the cost of providing employee housing acts as a disincentive to early investors, failure to do so has created serious problems in many communities once land values have increased.

Environmental Quality

Many tourism regions are resource dependent. Maintaining the quality of their resources (natural and cultural) is critical to the continued success of their tourism industry. As a consequence, resource management standards and guidelines are often higher than those necessary in other settings. For instance, the capability of the sewage and water systems must be able to meet the peak loadings that characterise service use in many tourist communities. Similarly building and landscape design guidelines often reflect more stringent aesthetic goals. Identification of the desired conditions to be associated with an area's critical tourism resources is also important in establishing priorities in the event of conflicting goals. For example, in the Lake Tahoe region of California and Nevada, highest priority is given to the lake water clarity and quality, because it is the resort's most essential tourist resource.

Establishing desired conditions for the resource base is an essential step in growth management. This includes consideration of natural, cultural, and scenic resources in surrounding areas that may not necessarily lie within a municipality's borders but still affect the overall quality of the area. It is important to decide how residents and visitors feel about the desired quality of such resources prior to determining what kind of management will be necessary.

Conclusions

Research suggests that traditional approaches to carrying capacity management have met with limited success in application. This situation exists primarily because of unrealistic expectations, untenable assumptions, inappropriate value judgments, and insufficient legal support systems. As a result the concept is discussed considerably but used infrequently in tourism management contexts.

Given the inability of traditional carrying capacity management concepts and techniques to be operationalised, an alternative approach is suggested. Its focus shifts from past concerns over establishing use limits, to issues of identifying environmental, social, and economic conditions desired by a community, and the creation of growth management strategies for managing tourism growth toward those ends. In the case of Whistler, the past focus on managing for an established bed-unit capacity ceiling for growth is gradually being replaced with an approach that emphasises managing for the existing and potential effects of growth. Many of Whistler's growth management strategies are still in the early stages of development and/or implementation. Only time and monitoring will attest to their utility. However, Whistler has chosen this approach as a more workable and realistic alternative to the use of traditional carrying capacity strategies. It is designed to direct growth toward goals and conditions important to those who must live with the lasting consequences of their decisions.

References

Anderdeck, K. L., and C. A. Vogt. 2000. The Relationship between Residents' Attitudes toward Tourism and Tourism Development Options. *Journal of Travel Research* 39: 27–36.

Ap, J., and J. L. Crompton. 1998. Developing and Testing a Tourism Impact Scale. *Journal of Travel Research* 37(2): 130–138.

Bosselman, F. P., C. A. Peterson, and C. McCarthy. 1999. *Managing Tourism Growth: Issues and Applications*. Washington: Island Press.

Butler, R. W. 1997. The Concept of Carrying Capacity for Tourism Destinations: Dead or Merely Buried? In *Tourism Development: Environment and Community Issues*. eds. C. Cooper and S. Wanhill. Chichester: Wiley.

Cleveland, S., and C. Hansen 1994. Growth Management and Public Participation: A Small Town Approach Works for Sedro-Woolley. Washington. *Small Town* 24(4): 4–13.

Design Workshop, BBC Research, Brent Harley and CH2M Hill. 2002. *Characteristics of Successful Destination Resort Communities*. Whistler: Resort Municipality of Whistler.

Dorward, S. 1990. *Design For Mountain Communities*. New York: Van Nostrand Reinhold.

Eagles, P. F. J., and S. F. McCool. 2002. *Tourism in National Parks and Protected Areas: Planning and Management*. Wallingford, U.K.: CAB.

Getz, D. 1982. A Rationale and Methodology for Assessing Capacity to Absorb Tourism. *Ontario Geography* 19: 92–101.

Gill, A. 1992. Issues and Problems of Community Development in Whistler. In *Mountain Resort Development, Proceedings of The Vail Conference*. eds. A. Gill and R. Hartman. Burnaby, B.C.: Simon Fraser University, Centre For Tourism Policy and Research.

———. 2000. From Growth Machine to Growth Management: The Dynamics of Resort Development in Whistler, British Columbia. *Environment and Planning* A32: 1083–1100.

Gill, A., and P. W. Williams. 1994. Managing Growth in Mountain Tourism Communities. *Tourism Management* 15(3): 212–220, 229.

——. 2003. Corporate-Community Relations in the Tourism Sector: A Stakeholder Perspective. Unpublished paper presented at *Contrasting Ruralities: Changing Rural Economies, Societies and Landscapes Conference.* Essex, U.K.

Godde, P. M., M. F. Price, and F. M. Zimmerman. eds. 2000. *Tourism And Development in Mountain Regions.* New York: CABI.

Hunter, C., and H. Green. 1995. *Tourism and The Environment: A Sustainable Relationship.* London: Routledge.

Johnson, P., and B. Thomas. 1996. Tourism Carrying Capacity: A Critique. In *Sustainable Tourism In Islands & Small States.* eds. B. Briguglio, B. Archer, J. Jafari, and G. Wall. New York: Pinter.

Inskeep, E. 1997. *Tourism Planning: An Integrated and Sustainable Development Approach.* Chichester: Wiley.

Inskeep, E., and M. Kallenberger. 1992. *An Integrated Approach To Resort Development: Six Case Studies.* Madrid: World Tourism Organization.

Lama W. B. 2000. Community-Based Tourism for Conservation and Women's Development. In *Tourism And Development in Mountain Regions.* eds. P. M. Godde, M. F. Price, and F. M. Zimmerman. New York: CABI.

Lawrence, R. A., H. R. Hafer, P. T. Long, and R. R. Perdue. 1993. Rural Residents' Attitudes Toward Recreation and Tourism Development. *Journal of Travel Research* 31(4): 27–33.

Manidis Roberts Consultants. 1997. *Developing A Tourism Optimization Management Model (TOMM): A Model to Monitor and Manage Tourism On Kangaroo Island.* Sydney: Manidas Roberts Consultants.

Martin, B. S., and M. Uysal. 1990. An Examination of the Relationship between Carrying Capacity and the Tourism Lifecycle: Management and Policy Implications. *Journal of Environmental Managemen* 31(4): 327–333.

Mathieson, A., and G. Wall. 1982. *Tourism: Economic, Physical and Social Impacts.* Essex, U.K.: Longman.

McElroy, J. L., and K. de Albuquerque. 1996. Sustainable Alternatives to Insular Mass Tourism: Recent Theory and Practice. In *Sustainable Tourism In Islands & Small States.* eds. B. Briguglio, B. Archer, J. Jafari, and G. Wall. New York: Pinter.

O'Reilly, A. M. 1986. Tourism Carrying Capacity. *Tourism Management* 7(4): 254–258.

Plog, S. C. 1991. *Leisure Travel: Making It a Growth Market Again!* New York: John Wiley and Sons.

Price, M. F. L., A. G. Moss, and P. W. Williams. 1997. Tourism and Amenity Migration. In *Mountains of the World: A Global Priority.* eds. B. Messerli and J. D. Ives. London: Parthenon.

Resort Municipality of Whistler. 2002. *Whistler 2002: Charting A Course For the Future.* Volume 1. Whistler, B.C.: The Municipality.

——. 2003. *Resort Municipality of Whistler Monitoring Report 2003.* (Draft). The Municipality Planning Department.

Schiffman, I. 1989. *Alternative Techniques for Managing Growth.* Berkeley, California: Institute of Government Studies, University of California at Berkeley.

Waldron, D., J. Godfrey, and P. W. Williams. 1999. Implementing a Vision for a Resort Community. In *Tourism and Sustainable Mountain Development.* Berne,

Switzerland: Mountain Agenda and Centre for Development and Environment, Institute of Geography, University of Berne.

Waldron, D., and P. W. Williams. 2002. Steps Towards Sustainability Monitoring: The Case of the Resort Municipality of Whistler. In *Sustainable Tourism: A Global Perspective*. eds. Harris, R., T. Griffin, and P. Williams. New York: Butterworth-Heinemann.

Whistler Housing Authority. 2002. *Building Our Community: Whistler Housing Authority Overview 2002*. The Authority.

11 Sustainable tourism standards in the global economy

Xavier Font

Introduction

Standards are documents that establish a basis, example, or principle for firms to conform to, linked to uniform units of measurement. Compulsory standards are enforced through national legislation and industry membership requirements and tend to cover health and safety, competence standards, occupational safety, land-use planning, licensing of businesses, and consumer protection. Voluntary standards go beyond these to suggest best practice and are usually coupled with training manuals for companies to make the necessary improvements to meet the requirements. Although certification of quality in hotels has a long tradition, it has focussed on environmental concerns only fairly recently, and is now starting to consider sociocultural issues. Most programmes have developed as bottom-up initiatives with little knowledge of each other and generally operate as specific responses to manage the key negative impacts or challenges of a particular subsector in a particular location. In the last 10 years, they have moved on dramatically to become one of the buzzwords of sustainable tourism and ecotourism, considered as a potential mechanism to combat greenwashing but not without a fair share of skeptics (Morris, 1997).

This chapter will discuss the development of sustainability standards from local efforts to make business improvements to becoming part of the suite of governance and regulatory tools of the global tourism industry. The key propositions of this discussion are that standard setting and certification are valuable tools to bring stakeholders together in their sustainability efforts, and they can be part of a suite of tools to encourage improvement. At the same time it is necessary to proceed with caution and not take certification as the answer to greening the industry. This chapter outlines current developments in the sector to create a basis to critically understand and analyse key issues in the application of sustainability standards. This leads to the discussion of efforts to globalise standards, and the challenges encountered. Finally the chapter considers the range of stakeholders that can have an impact on developing standards, and hypothesises how the tourism industry could change through sustainability standard enforcement, considering both its feasibility and desirability.

Implementing Sustainability Standards

The process of setting standards and ensuring these are met is known as conformity assessment, and provides the context to outline the development and use of sustainable tourism standards (Font, 2002; Toth, 2002). First the certification body sets standards that are *industry relevant* and achievable by a proportion of the sector. Part of the process includes setting indicators that can *credibly* and *effectively* measure the standards across the range of applicants they are intended for. These indicators are then assessed by an assessor who has been deemed as competent for the task, such as someone with the necessary skills and no conflict of interest, amongst others. If the assessment is successful, the applicant is certified as meeting the standards. The certification body could be subject to a procedure of accreditation, guaranteeing that the certification body has undertaken its tasks correctly. The overall aim is that the label of this certification programme will be recognised by consumers or distribution channels, and considered as added value that leads to its acceptance in the marketplace, to support the marketing of companies that meet standards.

Reading the latest survey of 59 sustainable tourism and ecotourism certification programmes shows the patchy development that has taken place (World Tourism Organization, 2002). There are 7000 tourism products certified worldwide, and 6000 of them are in Europe. Two-thirds of the programmes are led by tourism industry associations and national government organisations (NGOs), and less often private ventures and consultancies. Governmental organisations lead approximately 20 programmes, and provide technical and marketing support to approximately 30 more. The investment for the development of ecolabels is equally spread between private, public, and private–public partnerships. Approximately 40 programmes take a multistakeholder collaborative approach to decision making and advisory roles. Nearly one-half started before 1996 and another one-half between 1996 and 2000, whereas the number of programmes having started development since 2001 runs to double figures.

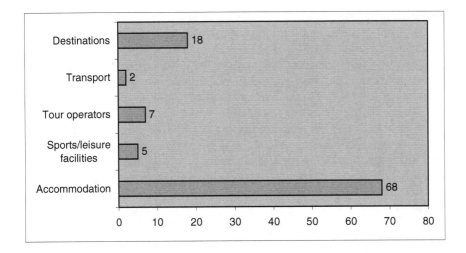

Figure 11.1:   Certification programmes by target sector (%).
Source: Font and Bendell, 2002.

Figure 11.1 paints a picture of the type of organisations undertaking certification. There are further differences across these programmes in the
nature of the companies they try to certify. To the danger of oversimplifying, European programmes focus on environmental issues in accommodation regardless of firm size, whereas developing countries focus on
a broader range of sustainability and ecotourism issues, targeting specifically small firms regardless of subsector. What is most striking is that
most standards are set for hotels (68 percent), and very few for tour operators (7 percent, in fact only four programmes), and the latter are mainly
for ecotourism ground operators, not the outbound operators in tourism-
generating countries, with access to the market. This is probably
accounted for by the fact that the impacts of hotels are generally considered to be easier to identify, more consistent across providers, and the
management unit is identifiable. Hospitality has developed advanced
tools to benchmark environmental impacts (see, for example, International Hotels Environment Initiative, 2001) that could not be conceivable
in other sectors, although Green Globe 21 (GG21) is making progress in
this respect (Green Globe, 2002). At the other end of the spectrum, tour
operators have not been the targets of certification because they rely on
suppliers to ensure the sustainability of their products; they have long
claimed they have no control over their suppliers.

The indicators used to measure standards also vary not only in contents
but also in what is measured. The most popular distinction is between

process and performance indicators (Synergy, 2000; Honey and Stewart, 2002). Process-based standards mean the company makes a commitment to improvement by putting in place management systems to ensure year-on-year progress. Progress-based standards mean different companies could perform differently and still have the same certificate, hence they are not a guarantee of sustainability. The advantage is that the system is self-updating, the standards are generic, and therefore transferable. At the other end of the spectrum, performance standards mean that the applicant has met a threshold level, which is generally defined through sector-specific benchmarks (to different degrees of sophistication). The key advantage is that they are a guarantee of basic standards. The challenges are that because industry performance changes, standards need external updating, and because the standards are context specific, they are not easily transferable across destinations.

Breadth (over depth) of standards has been used first to criticise pro-grammes only covering environmental issues and not other sustainability areas, and mainly criticising GG21 (Synergy, 2000), and interestingly then to suggest the preference of GG21 as industry-specific standards over generic ones such as ISO 14001 (Rodgers, undated). In reality the differences are fewer than first thought, and certification programmes tend to combine a number of performance criteria to ensure minimum requirements are met, with a number of process criteria to ensure the company is proactive toward making further improvements (World Tourism

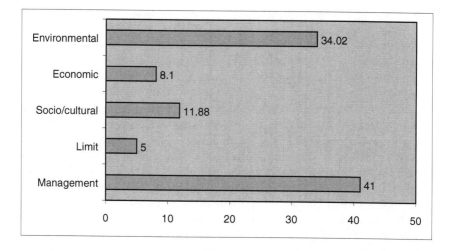

Figure 11.2: Criteria in sustainable tourism standards (%).
Source: Font and Bendell, 2002.

Organization, 2002). Just over 40 percent of the criteria in standards relate to management issues (i.e., whether the applicant has systems in place to make improvements on a number of sustainability matters), and the characteristics of the firm to be accepted as an applicant [5 percent]). The remaining 55 percent of criteria relate to specific actions or benchmarks for environmental (34 percent), economic (8 percent), and sociocultural (12 percent) criteria.

Certification as an Instrument for Sustainability

Certification as a process to raise industry standards has its advocates and critics. This section reviews the feasibility of certification as a policy tool to make voluntary improvements, under five aspects: equity, effectiveness, efficiency, credibility, and integration.

Equity refers to the fairness of an instrument, which here is considered as the ability of tourism firms to access certification. Every action, such as certification, that attempts to make an inherently inequitable market economy more transparent is likely to be tainted by that inequity. This stands out as conflictive when the main emphasis of most sustainable tourism policies is in fact to encourage a more equitable distribution of the benefits of tourism (see Chapter 21). This has sparked heated debates such as those hosted in the planeta.com e-conference on ecotourism certification. Three potential areas of inequity are considered, the cost of (1) the application, (2) implementation by tourism firms, and (3) operation of a programme.

The relative perceived high cost of certifying to a standard can be inequitable, because not all firms will have the same potential to access to being certified. Most programmes have addressed this somehow by having scaled fees, linked to turnover or size. In Costa Rica, the government has successfully subsidised first-time applications to the Certificate for Sustainable Tourism. In Australia, the Nature and Ecotourism Accreditation Program relied on paper audits to cut costs down until it revised its protocol in 2001. Although some certification programmes can provide sufficient benefits to repay the fees, and some suggest that the premise that cost is a barrier is only a myth (Toth, 2002), there are countries where the cost is prohibitive, particularly in countries without a national certification programme that have to bring in international verifiers. Yet once companies have applied the first time, they are likely to find that meeting some of the criteria make them more ecoefficient and therefore can justify further certification costs based on the savings made. There are examples of medium sized hotels that have made savings of US$40,000 per year in energy, water, and waste, which have been used to subsidise a position of environmental manager. For smaller companies, certification programmes might need to consider encouraging applications as cooperatives of small firms or as destinations. The idea here is to have a joint sustainability initiative that raises performance of the whole group, but the certification programme assesses only a percentage of the firms every year, to cut down on costs. This concept has been considered by GG21 in the certification of Hilton as a chain, and can be translated to small industry associations as well.

There are also costs from operating more sustainably and from implementing the standard (Toth, 2002). Some of these can be recouped, such as upgrading the equipment and facilities to meet the standards by, for example, buying a combined heating and power unit, or systems for wastewater reuse. Although in most locations these will be repaid in around five years through ecosavings, they require up-front capital and therefore access to credit. Then there are costs that cannot be recovered, such as stakeholder consultation, writing policies, contribution to local development, and the maintenance of environmental management systems and paper trails to mention some. For any of the mentioned to take place, the firm needs to commit staff time, and only financially sound firms will be able to do so.

Finally there are other costs that currently the applicant does not pay for and are generally subsidised by governments, donors, and NGOs, and it is expected that will continue that way (World Tourism Organization, 2003). Examples are standard setting, consultation and maintenance, verifier training, marketing, administrative costs, and quality assurance of the certification programme. These costs make certification not equitable for those governments that do not have the funds to set up their own national certification programmes or to operate low-interest loans for efficiency improvements. A number of national tourist boards have an interest in running certification programmes, but this is not their priority (Maccarrone-Eaglen and Font, 2002), whereas, in other countries, circumstances do not allow such programmes (see, for example, Bricker, 2002 on Fiji; Koch, Massyn, and Spenceley, 2002 on Kenya and South Africa, as well as the unreported failed Kiskeya Alternativa in the Dominican Republic). In the medium term their industry can become less competitive because it does not learn how to manage more sustainably, and more efficiently, although this can also take place through other policy instruments (see Chapter 21). NGOs cannot afford the start up of national programmes and instead tend to focus on particular areas of biodiversity (e.g., Smart Voyager in the Galapagos and PAN Parks in Eastern and Northern Europe's parks) or socioeconomic need (Fair Trade Tourism in South Africa).

Effectiveness is a measure of how well an instrument achieves its objectives. Ecolabels are first attracting applications from companies that

already meet the standards, and only if the core group of these companies is large enough, they have the power to change behavior in other
companies. From a global governance point of view, the fact that at
present tourism certification is resource based and incentive led, and not
market led, means that it has had little impact. The confused message
given to tourists (are we promoting an unspoiled destination or a sustainable business, and is there a difference?) has limited its power. There
are no means to control green and quasigreen claims, and customers have
limited information to discriminate between greenwashing and sound
products. Effectiveness can also be measured here against different objectives, that is, not only the number and type of firms certified, but against
the objective of advancement of the sustainability agenda. It is argued
here that in the short term the process of empowering local groups to
agree on practical methods to make local firms more sustainable is already
an achievement. However, the emphasis of certification in other sectors,
such as forestry, has focussed on closing the gap between 'very best' and
'good' practice, whereas poor forest management is little affected (Bass,
Font, and Danielson, 2001).

Efficiency is a measure of how well an instrument uses the resources
available. At present there is limited evidence of the value for money of
standard certification as a policy instrument (Rivera, 2002) because costs
are not clear and effectiveness cannot be measured. The low take-up and
high start-up costs from governments and NGOs could indicate they are
not an efficient use of resources. Most certification systems currently rely
on external funding, and would not survive without it. Blue Flag has
relied on European funds for nearly 15 years, struggling to survive when
these finished. The International Network on Fair Trade in Tourism folded
as soon as the donor grant ran out. The 'Certificate of Sustainable Tourism'
(CST) has made an impact in Costa Rica because of the government's
financial commitment to subsidise fees and provide technical know-how.
Voluntarily changing industry behaviour is a complex and long-term
process (Dewhurst and Thomas, 2003) even when most programmes
advertise the ecosavings of up to 30 percent in operational costs that can
be made from implementing the standards proposed.

Credibility and *legitimacy* refer to the extent to which an instrument is
accepted as valid by its target audience. If this is understood as market
share, then certification is not credible and legitimate, except in cases such
as the Blue Flag. If we take it as consumer demand, then the answer is
also negative, because tourists are not demanding certification. Exceptions are the cases of Blue Flag, linked to health considerations in bathing
water more than sustainability concerns, and the Nature's Best, because
of the high profile it has received in the Swedish press from the King
of Sweden giving the first certificates and being featured in television holiday programmes. If this is understood as the quality of each

certification programme and therefore value of each label, then we do not have the evidence of which are good and which are not, although this is starting to change as these are benchmarked against developing guidelines, and eventually through accreditation.

The fifth aspect of analysis of certification is its current *integration* with other instruments for sustainability. Its origin stems from the formalisation of industry awards and showcasing best practice (Synergy, 2000) and in this sense is more representative of industry practice than externally set agendas. Yet, generally, certification is integrated only with other instruments for sustainability only in as far as they are generally linked to voluntary initiatives and incentives to encourage more sustainable approaches to management. Certification does not provide a mechanism to operationalise international treaties and agreements. The fact that one-half of the ecolabels receive government support suggests it is feasible to further integrate them with government sustainability targets and for them to be used as methods to implement international agreements, as recommended by the World Tourism Organization (2003). There are limited data available on the link between national sustainable tourism policies and certification programmes to comment on the progress on this matter. Progress on integrating certification with global agendas is further developed in the next section.

Global Standards for a Global Economy

Although most certification programmes are not growing in number of applicants (only 20 percent of the medium-aged ecolabels are growing annually, according to the WTO [2002]), those that are, are doing so by becoming more global, rather than from market penetration at a national level. Global standards make sense in the marketplace. Transnational corporations can benefit from certification (Conroy, 2002), but they want to work to one standard that makes sense at corporate level regardless of operational location (Kahlenborn and Dominé, 2001). Markets want to be communicated one single meaningful message, and the current players are fighting for a voice with their small budgets (Consultancy and Research for Environmental Management, 2000). International trade rules favour international standards because these are believed to create an equal playing field that benefits competition (Bendell and Font, 2004). If certification as a process is going to make a difference in trade, it needs to come of age. This section reviews three aspects of globalisation efforts. First, it outlines the potential for certification to become a tool to implement global agreements and guidelines on sustainable tourism. Second, it reviews the growth of the current certification programmes to become regional players. Third, it presents the work of programmes aiming to have a global coverage from the outset.

There is a real challenge in agreeing on definitions of sustainable tourism and ecotourism, let alone operationalising those definitions. This is probably part of the reason why certification programmes are not used at present as tools to implement the many political statements developed in the last three decades in sustainable tourism. Ideally, a certification programme would take up the generic political agreements and make them relevant to the business unit level, considering how each business needs to operate to be within the parameters given. In 1999 the United Nations Commission on Sustainable Development made a number of recommendations with regards to seeking methods to implement amongst others Local Agenda 21, WTO's Global Code of Ethics for Tourism, and United Nations Environment Programme's Principles for Implementation of Sustainable Tourism. These are too generic to be implemented by business units, but they could be cascaded down through more detailed standards and manuals (Font and Bendell, 2002). Two examples are the development of the Blue Flag for beaches as a tool to enforce European Bathing Water Directive (Font and Mihalic, 2002) and the relaunch of the GG21 standard after the United Nations meeting (Koeman, et al., 2002). There is room to make further links; social standards in tourism do not reinforce International Labor Organization standards (Font and Harris, undated) unlike in other sectors (Andreas, Muller, Panapanaan, 2000). The technical elements of linking these general agreements to certifiable standards could be bridged; the more challenging issue would be who would have the mandate of running such programmes and where the funds would come from.

The second aspect to consider is how the current certification standards are developing to become more global, or at least regional, programmes. The model for certification in Latin America is the Costa Rican CST. Most countries in the region have signed agreements to implement national programmes to make tourism companies accountable for sustainability issues with the CST programme as a model, although the costs of starting and operating a certification programme have meant there has been little progress. CST also hoped that the WTO would offer its full support to Costa Rica in their becoming a global certification programme (Toth, 2000). However, the proposal was not accepted by The Member States of the corresponding WTO Technical Committee; instead, the Committee requested the WTO Secretariat to provide them with recommendations and guidelines on how to establish such certification systems. In Europe, the Voluntary Initiatives for Sustainable Tourism (VISIT) programme has created a federal system to raise standards amongst the current programmes, marketing more than 1000 certified accommodations to consumers in ethical trade fairs and to tour operators to include in their packages (VISIT, 2003). Blue Flag has extended outside Europe to the Caribbean and South Africa (Font and Mihalic, 2002) to become the single most popular certification programme, albeit only for beaches. All these programmes have had to reconsider the applicability of their standards, in the case of Blue Flag to other geographical conditions, in the case of VISIT to compare the work of its members in search for commonalities and best practice.

The third aspect is to consider the success of programmes that have aimed from the outset to be global, or regional. GG21 already positioned itself as a global programme from its start in 1994, and despite being one of the longest standing programmes it has achieved little market penetration worldwide, with the greatest hopes for take up being in the Asia-Pacific region, since opening offices in Australia (Griffin and De Lacy, 2002; Koeman et al., 2002). The European Union Ecolabel Award Scheme has developed environmental standards for tourism accommodation, after three feasibility studies and years of discussion, and unlikely to get high numbers of applicants because of its complex standard. Ford Foundation has supported the feasibility study and first phase of implementation of a Sustainable Tourism Stewardship Council, aiming to set an accreditation system to ensure global standards, requiring a subsidy of almost US$1 million per year once fully operational (Rainforest Alliance, 2003), not unlike accreditation in other industries. The most recent entry is the International Organization for Standardization (ISO), currently studying the desirability and feasibility of standards and other deliverables, such as guidelines, for tourism services. At the time of writing this chapter, the ISO was considering a guide outlining basic consumer requirements for tourism services, whereas the need for an ISO standard on aspects like ecotourism had received mixed responses (ISO, 2003). Lessons learned from these players are that large governance structures are costly, these programmes do not necessarily communicate to the potential applicants, and they require a further layer of organisations to help industry implement the standards.

Arguably, standards ought to be locally relevant and locally developed, to the risk of reinventing the wheel in some instances, but to the benefit of ownership and practicality (Farnworth, 2003). The main challenge is to then transform these valid exercises of local governance into tools that are meaningful beyond the resource-based approach to sustainability improvement, through a process of 'globalization from below' (Font and Sallows, 2002). There are at least two reasons for an international umbrella to support local programmes. First, the fact that applicants to programmes tend to believe that there are marketing advantages to having sustainability credentials, but small local programmes are not in a position to deliver market-led competitive advantage. Second, as more programmes are developed, and comparisons between them are made, there is a trend to consider economies of scale in some shared concerns. After a period of building trust and sharing tasks, programmes can move from a federal alliance to a position where the joint brand is likely to be more meaningful to the international markets, whereas each programme's brand is more important to the applicants. Such an umbrella structure can take the role of bridging between international agreements and local certification programmes, accrediting the processes by which each certification programme translates them to a standard that is appropriate to their location and applicants. But for all this to take place, some stakeholders need to take the initiative, and despite a range of advocates and stakeholders in standard development and certification, there are few levers for change.

Levers for Change

This section reviews some key players in the tourism industry that can accelerate or reshape the development of tourism certification, which for convenience have been divided into supply and demand.

Strategic alternatives for certification programmes are linked to market penetration, market development, product development, or diversification (Font, 2001). Having developed their governance structures, most programmes have planned to focus on marketing more than product development in the next few years (WTO, 2002). The key activities of growth from certification programmes were outlined in the previous section, and these actions are complemented by other stakeholders on the supply side groups that can incentive the up take of certification, such as governments, NGOs, and financial institutions.

Governments have been involved mainly through providing an enabling framework through ensuring a supportive environment, highlighting best practice, standard setting, institutional building blocks, providing grants or loans, and leading by example. It is expected that governments will have a more active role, as suggested in guidelines from the WTO calling for further government intervention, although these relate to governance and standard setting, and not support measures to encourage up take (World Tourism Organization, 2003). They could potentially raise their involvement by providing 'incentives' through, for example, mandatory reporting, using as evidence of statutory obligations compliance, threatening alternative measures, or financial incentives. They could also go further by making standards mandatory to gain licenses and permits or through regulation (Font and Bendell, 2002). Regulation is an aspect of particular relevance here, because of precedents set in Europe by the Package Travel, Package Holidays, and Package Tours Regulations 1992. European tour operators have been sued not only for health and safety reasons, but also for poor quality and even for 'lack of enjoyment' caused by the poor quality of tourism products (Grant and Mason, 2003). There is room for arguing that it is only a question of time until a major tour operator is sued for poor sustainability or for misrepresenting the holiday on their brochure on sustainability grounds. This could trigger a succession of events that could change the sector.

Nongovernment organisations have put pressure on distribution channels to prove the sustainability of their products, particularly to do it yourself (DIY) store giants to source all their timber from sustainable sources within a period that encouraged suppliers to change methods of production and become certified (Murphy and Bendell, 1997). NGOs have also engaged with industry to develop accreditation, such as the Marine Stewardship Council, which is now receiving preferential treatment in a number of supermarkets as part of their corporate social responsibility policies. In tourism, NGOs are active in running some certification programmes, albeit the high costs beg the question of the long-term ability to do so, and as members of the advisory boards of other programmes.

Financial institutions have taken an increasing interest in sustainability operationalised through socially responsible investments, a label to represent ethical and environmental investment criteria by banks, pension funds, and other investment organisations (Jayne and Skerratt, 2003). Good benchmark and tradable indices require companies to write policies, specific management actions, and/or reporting according to their perceived level of impact with air transport classed as high and hotel development as medium. Other similar sustainability indices managed by financial and investment groups exist. Such companies listed in those can apply for reduced rate loans from development banks and get preferential treatment in the investment portfolio of pension funds. Although in the past ethical investment screening has been undertaken internally (Jayne and Skerratt, 2003), there are attempts of linking global reporting initiative sustainability reporting to the social screening of investments (Willis, 2003), which is the overall framework for the reporting of the Tour Operators Initiative for Sustainable Development.

The supply side can provide levers for change, but for the changes to be meaningful they have to impact on the demand to ensure demand-driven, self-supporting, and financially stable certification (Toth, 2002). The demand side is broader than first could be thought, and it arguably includes not only the tourism industry as possible applicants, but also tourists and distribution channels.

Raising awareness of the tourism industry alone will not be sufficient enough incentive to increase applications. Large firms do not want to be certified as a method to attract business, but to protect their brand for public relations reasons against possible negative publicity (Conroy, 2002; see also Honey and Stewart, 2002). Multinational hotels might not perceive the need for ecolabels at present, and a Costa Rican study found that when they applied for the CST, they scored low (Rivera, 2002). If ecolabels are sold as a method to generate ecosavings, the large firms will want this to be integrated with broader management functions, such as accountancy, management systems, health and safety, and quality, not as a stand-alone product. The main challenge is for small firms. The inequities of certification arguments against rolling sustainability standards in the global tourism industry can have detrimental effects for firms that cannot access certification. There are precedents that supplier requirement of health, safety, and quality certification has gone against small companies who cannot meet the requirements (Curtin and Busby, 1999), which needs to be further explored in the context of sustainability certification.

The current demand from tourists is almost nonexistent, and surveys of latent demand have varying results, although most claim that tourists give high preference to sustainability in their purchasing and that they are willing to pay extra for sustainable holidays despite the perception that certification means higher prices (Miller, 2003; Rainforest Alliance, 2003). However there are clear differences between consumer environmental purchasing claims and actual purchasing behaviour. Few programmes can claim that their applicants increase business because of being certified (the Australian Nature and Ecotourism Accreditation Programme does; see Chester and Crabtree, 2002). The Green Tourism Business Scheme applicants have higher occupancy rates than average for Scotland but the programme is careful to note this is probably because applicants are companies that are already managing their businesses well, not because of being certified (Font and Buckley, 2001). However there are companies stating that they are more likely to have repeated visitors, or more satisfied visitors, thanks to the improvements made to be certified, but not necessarily because of being certified. For example the Green Globe 21 certification of Coconut Beach Hotel in Barbados is encouraging endangered turtles nesting, which has meant changing lighting and continuously working on customer education, but to the benefit of having a unique selling proposition that brings clients back.

Although tour operators generally consider that change will be led by consumer demand (Miller, 2001) there are pockets of activity that suggest increased corporate responsibility, in part through sustainable supply chain management (Tapper, 2001). Basically, for tour operators to claim they are sustainable, they need to know their suppliers are sustainable in the first place. Some tour operators are using environmental audits of the hotels they use, although an alternative is for tour operators to encourage hotels toward certification to cut down on the tour operator's burden of auditing. In the United Kingdom, the Travel Foundation is bringing together tour operators and other stakeholders to make outbound tourism more sustainable, and supply chain management has been listed as top priority. Elsewhere, the development of sustainability reporting indicators by the Tour Operators Initiative already considers certification of suppliers as an indicator of tour operator sustainability (Tour Operators Initiative, 2002), and a major part of the developmental work of this initiative relates to improving the sustainability of suppliers (Tour Operators Initiative, 2003) as part of a process that leads to verification (Tapper, 2003). The VISIT alliance of 10 ecolabels in Europe has demonstrated that with 1000 accommodation providers they have the beginning of a structure that allows them to target both consumers and distribution channels, and this is probably the best test of the marketplace for other regions to learn from.

Conclusions

For the last two decades, certification has been a voluntary mechanism to show high standards of performance beyond legislation. It has been thought to be a source of competitive advantage that allows a small number of firms to stand out from the average. Certification is a valid instrument to gather local stakeholders around the common purpose of defining standards to make local tourism sustainable. It is also valid to develop structures to encourage and support improvement of business units, working to a standard that will give them peer recognition, staff morale, ecosavings, and peace of mind from beyond legislation compliance, all of which make firms more competitive in the medium term. Certification in the majority of cases does not do much for increased trade; if this is to change, it needs larger economies of scale that can allow for tangible market-led benefits, such as marketing and acting as distribution channel. These economies of scale will come from a combination of addressing the international sustainability agendas, market penetration and new market development, partnerships between the current programmes, and the creation of global structures.

Certification is most suited to those countries with well-established infrastructures and the finances to support industry to reduce its impacts. It is also a tool for financially sound firms that have their basic needs covered and feel the need or desire to be more sustainable, and get recognition for it. It is not the best tool for livelihood-based economies or sectors, be it tourism, forestry, agriculture, or any other at the center of attention of certification today. Increasing the number of companies that meet these standards allows in the medium term to reach the economies of scale to produce better training for applicants, and marketing of their products. The key challenge is the potential impact this can have on those firms that are not suited to it, if it becomes a powerful tool for increased trade, or if governments and industry associations aim to enforce compulsory standards. This is a long way away, although globalising standards and the combined pressure from a number of stakeholders are heading in that direction. This has to be an enabling, carefully managed process that takes into account the moral challenges of equity.

References

Andreas, S., K. Muller, and V. M. Panapanaan. 2000. *SA8000: Corporate Social Accountability Management: A Handbook on the Implementation of the New Standard on Corporate Social Accountability Initiated by CEPAA.* Basel, Switzerland: Ellipson.

Bass, S., X. Font, and L. Danielson. 2001. Standards and Certification: A Leap Forward or a Step Back for Sustainable Development? *The Future Is Now: Equity for a Small Planet.* Volume 2. ed. IIED. London: International Institute for Environment and Development.

Bendell, J., and X. Font. 2004. Trade Standards: Towards a Sustainable GATS. *Annals of Tourism Research.* 31(1), 139–156.

Bricker, K. 2002. Planning for Ecotourism Amidst Political Unrest: Fiji Navigates a Way Forward. *Ecotourism & Certification: Setting Standards in Paradise.* ed. M. Honey. Washington: Island Press.

Chester, G., and A. Crabtree. 2002. Australia: The Nature and Ecotourism Accreditation Program. *Ecotourism & Certification: Setting Standards in Practice.* ed. M. Honey. Washington: Island Press.

Conroy, M. 2002. Certification Systems for Sustainable Tourism and Ecotourism: Can They Transform Social and Environmental Practices? *Ecotourism & Certification: Setting Standards in Practice.* ed. M. Honey. Washington: Island Press.

CREM. 2000. *Feasibility and Market Study for a European Eco-Label for Tourist Accommodations (FEMATOUR), Commissioned by the European Commission, DG ENV.* Amsterdam: Consultancy and Research for Environmental Management.

Curtin, S., and G. Busby. 1999. Sustainable Destination Development: The Tour Operator Perspective. *International Journal of Tourism Research* 1: 135–147.

Dewhurst, H., and R. Thomas. 2003. Encouraging Sustainable Business Practices in a Non-Regulatory Environment: A Case Study of Small Tourism Firms in a UK National Park. *Journal of Sustainable Tourism* 11(5): 383–403.

Farnworth, C. R. 2003. Linking Producer and Consumer: Rewarding 'More than Purely Price' Values in the Marketplace. *Ecolabels and the Greening of the Food Market Conference Proceedings.* Ed. W. Lockeretz. Boston: Tufts University.

Font, X. 2001. Conclusions: A Strategic Analysis of Tourism Ecolabels. *Tourism Ecolabelling: Certification and Promotion of Sustainable Management.* eds. X. Font and R. Buckley. Wallingford: CABI.

——. 2002. Environmental Certification in Tourism and Hospitality: Progress, Process and Prospects. *Tourism Management* 23(3): 197–205.

Font, X., and J. Bendell. 2002. *Standards for Sustainable Tourism for the Purpose of Multilateral Trade Negotiations.* Madrid: World Tourism Organization.

Font, X., and R. Buckley. eds. 2001. *Tourism Ecolabelling: Certification and Promotion of Sustainable Management.* Wallingford: CABI.

Font, X., and T. Mihalic. 2002. Beyond Hotels: Nature-Based Certification in Europe. *Ecotourism & Certification: Setting Standards in Practice.* ed. M. Honey. Washington: Island Press.

Font, X., and M. Sallows. 2002. Setting Global Sustainability Standards: The Sustainable Tourism Stewardship Council. *Tourism Recreation Research* 27(1): 21–32.

Green Globe. 2002. *Green Globe 21 Benchmarking Users Guide.* Canberra: Green Globe 21.

Grant, D., and S. Mason. 2003. *Holiday Law.* London: Thomson-Sweet & Maxwell.

Griffin, T., and T. De Lacy. 2002. Green Globe: Sustainability Accreditation for Tourism. *Sustainable Tourism: A Global Perspective.* eds. R. Harris, T. Griffin, and P. Williams. Oxford: Butterworth-Heinemann.

Honey, M., and E. Stewart. 2002. The Evolution of Green Standards for Tourism. *Ecotourism & Certification: Setting Standards in Practice.* ed. M. Honey. Washington: Island Press.

International Hotels Environment Initiative. 2001. Benchmarkhotel, http://www.benchmarkhotel.com. London: The Initiative.

International Organization for Standardization. 2003. *Annex 4 to COPOLCO 20/2003. Report to ISO COPOLCO,* ISO COPOLCO. Geneva, Switzerland: Tourism Services Subgroup.

Jayne, M. R., and G. Skerratt. 2003. Socially Responsible Investment in the UK—Criteria That are Used to Evaluate Suitability. *Corporate Social Responsibility and Environmental Management* 10(1): 1–11.

Kahlenborn, W., and A. Dominé. 2001. The Future Belongs to International Ecolabelling Schemes. *Tourism Ecolabelling: Certification and Promotion of Sustainable Management.* ed. X. Font and R. Buckley. Wallingford: CABI.

Koch, E., P. J. Massyn, and A. Spenceley. 2002. Getting Started: The Experiences of South Africa and Kenya. *Ecotourism & Certification: Setting Standards in Practice.* ed. M. Honey. Washington: Island Press.

Koeman, A., G. Worboys, T. De Lacy, et al. 2002. Green Globe: A Global Environmental Certification Program for Travel and Tourism. *Ecotourism & Certification: Setting Standards in Practice.* ed. M. Honey. Washington: Island Press.

Maccarrone-Eaglen, A., and X. Font. 2002. *Sustainable Tourism Stewardship Council Feasibility, Report for the World Tourism Organization on Consultation of Member States.* Leeds: Leeds Metropolitan University.

Miller, G. 2001. Corporate Responsibility in the UK Tourism Industry. *Tourism Management* 22(6): 589–598.

———. 2003. Consumerism in Sustainable Tourism: A Survey of UK Consumers. *Journal of Sustainable Tourism* 11(1): 17–39.

Morris, J. 1997. *Green Goods? Consumers, Product Labels and the Environment.* London: The Institute of Economic Affairs

Murphy, D., and J. Bendell. 1997. *In the Company of Partners: Business, Environmental Groups and Sustainable Development Post-Rio.* Bristol, U.K.: The Policy Press.

Rainforest Alliance. 2003. *Sustainable Tourism Stewardship Council: Raising the Standards and Benefits of Sustainable Tourism and Ecotourism Certification.* New York: The Alliance.

Rivera, J. 2002. Assessing a Voluntary Environmental Initiative in the Developing World: The Costa Rican Certification for Sustainable Tourism. *Policy Sciences* 35(4): 333–360.

Rodgers, S. undated. *Green Globe—Beyond ISO 14000 for the Travel and Tourism Sector.* Geelong, Victoria, Australia: AVTEQ Consulting Services.

Synergy. 2000. *Tourism Certification: An Analysis of Green Globe 21 and Other Certification Programs.* Godalming, U.K.: World Wide Fund for Nature.

Tapper, R. 2001. Tourism and Socio-Economic Development: UK Tour Operators' Business Approaches in the Context of the New International Agenda. *International Journal of Tourism Research* 3(5): 351–366.

———. 2003. *Contracting Sustainable Suppliers: A Stepped Approach to Supply Chain Management for Tour Operators,* Draft Report for Comments. Paris: Tour Operators Initiative for Sustainable Development.

Tour Operators Initiative. 2002. *Global Reporting Initiative Tour Operators' Sector Supplement.* Paris: Tour Operators Initiative for Sustainable Tourism Development.

———. 2003. *Sustainable Tourism: The Tour Operators Contribution.* Paris: Tour Operators Initiative for Sustainable Development.

Toth, R. 2000. *Implementing a Worldwide Sustainable Tourism Certification System.* Alexandria, Va.: R.B. Toth Associates.

———. 2002. Exploring the Concepts Underlying Certification. *Ecotourism & Certification: Setting Standards in Practice.* ed. M. Honey. Washington: Island Press.

Voluntary Initiatives for Sustainability in Tourism. 2003. http://www.yourvisit.info. Last accessed September 12, 2003.

Willis, C. A. A. 2003. The Role of the Global Reporting Initiative's Sustainability Reporting Guidelines in the Social Screening of Investments. *Journal of Business Ethics* 43(3): 233–237.

World Tourism Organization. 2002. *Voluntary Initiatives for Sustainable Tourism.* Madrid: The Organization.

———. 2003. *Recommendations to Governments for Supporting and/or Establishing National Certification Systems for Sustainable Tourism.* Madrid: The Organization.

12 Stakeholder involvement in sustainable tourism: balancing the voices

Donald Getz and Seldjan Timur

Introduction

In the development of tourism strategies and policies, it is clear that the responsible authorities or destination marketing organisations (DMOs) must take into account the views of numerous stakeholders including industry, residents, special-interest groups representing the environment and community, and even the tourists. Each stakeholder group has a different set of needs and expectations relating to a destination's performance and its sustainability goals. These different expectations may cause conflicts to arise among stakeholders, and conflicts can be extremely detrimental to the destination's competitiveness. A process of stakeholder management is therefore needed to reduce or solve conflicts, and invariably the issue of achieving a balanced perspective among stakeholder voices will have to be faced.

In this chapter, the applicability and usefulness of stakeholder theory for developing sustainable tourism strategies and policies is examined. Particular attention is given to the need for achieving balanced input among the diverse stakeholder groups, including the pertinent issues of stakeholder identification, legitimisation, involvement, and conflict resolution. Insights from three cities are presented, namely Calgary and Victoria, Canada, and San Francisco, California.

Stakeholder theory has not been used to a great extent in the tourism planning, policy, and strategy literature. However, it could be argued that to some extent stakeholder theory has implicitly been a core component in development of the sustainable tourism philosophy. Sustainable tourism aims to 'minimize environmental and cultural damage, optimize visitor satisfaction, and maximize long-term economic growth for the region' (Lane, 1994). When a destination adapts a sustainable tourism philosophy aimed to 'conserve and preserve natural and built resource base; respect and protect local culture; optimize visitor satisfaction; satisfy demands of industry, provide improved living standards and quality of life for residents' (Lane, 1994) by definition is using a stakeholder approach and 'all of the groups' that can affect or are affected by tourism development are concerned.

By adopting the sustainable tourism philosophy destinations attempt to design one development strategy that achieves the objectives of various stakeholders. The results of managing stakeholders to realise sustainable tourism development (STD) should be the establishment of destination objectives that are more balanced and long term; integrated environmental, social, cultural, and economic strategies; and effectiveness in achieving goals. In order to achieve these results, all stakeholders' interests and objectives regarding tourism development must be incorporated into the process.

Dimensions of Sustainable Tourism Development

STD, as defined by the World Tourism Organization (1998) is development that

> meets the needs of present tourists and host regions while protecting and enhancing opportunities for the future. It is envisaged as leading to management of all resources in such a way that economic, social, and aesthetic needs can be fulfilled while maintaining cultural integrity, essential ecological processes, biological diversity, and life support systems.

STD implies the need to secure the sustainability of tourism's primary resources at the destination level, and is a way of obtaining a balance between the growth potential of tourism and the conservation needs of the resource base (Lane, 1994).

Sustainable tourism strategies have several general aims (Green and Hunter, 1992; Hunter, 1995):

- To meet the needs and wants of the local host community in terms of improved living standards and quality of life;
- To satisfy the demands of tourists and the tourism industry; and
- To safeguard the environmental resource base for tourism, encompassing natural, built, and cultural components.

Because STD addresses different issues and interests, and seeks balanced tourism development where no one actor (industry, hosts, or guests) predominates, the planning, development and practice of STD requires involvement of these interested parties. Stakeholder theory has the potential to provide a framework within which STD can be delivered (McKercher, 1993; Robson and Robson, 1996).

Stakeholder Theory

The 'stakeholder' concept was introduced to strategic management by Freeman (1984) who defined it in a management and organisational context to include any individual or group who can affect the firm's performance or who is affected by the achievement of the organisation's objectives. Stakeholder theory tries to answer three general questions (Frooman, 1999):

1.   Who (or what) are stakeholders of the firm?
2.   What do they want?
3.   How are they going to get there?

In other words, stakeholders' attributes, interests, and influence are looked at respectively.

Stakeholder theory asserts that the business needs to consider the interests of groups affected by the firm. Wood and Jones (1995) argue that stakeholder theory holds the key to understanding the structures and dimensions of business and society relationships. Much of the literature using stakeholder theory suggests that it allows the organisation to consider a wider range of influencers when developing strategy, and that earlier theories of the firm do not consider all of the 'groups' that influence organisational activities (Polonsky, 1995). Stakeholder theory also differentiates between 'strategic' and 'moral' stakeholders (Goodpastor, 1991; Frooman, 1999). The strategic stakeholder literature emphasises management of stakeholders so the firm achieves its interests (e.g., Freeman, 1984; Clarkson, 1995; Rowley, 1997 cited in Frooman, 1999). The moral stakeholder literature focusses on the balancing of stakeholder interests (e.g., Donaldson & Preston, 1995; Wicks, Gilbert, & Freeman, 1994 cited in Frooman, 1999).

Normative, Instrumental, and Descriptive Stakeholder Theories

Donaldson and Preston (1995) proposed a taxonomy of stakeholder theory types, called normative, instrumental, and descriptive. Stakeholder theory is normative when it accepts that 'stakeholders are persons and/or groups with legitimate interests in a corporation' and that 'the interests of stakeholders are of intrinsic value' (Donaldson and Preston, 1995). This means that each stakeholder merits consideration for its own sake and not merely because of its ability to further the interests of some other groups, such as the shareowners. Normative stakeholder theorists argue that all stakeholders should be treated with proper respect and consideration for their own sakes (Jawahar and McLaughlin, 2001).

Stakeholder theory can also be instrumental. 'It establishes a framework for examining the connections, if any, between the practice of stakeholder management and the achievement of various corporate performance goals' (Donaldson and Preston 1995). That is, other things being equal, corporations practicing stakeholder management will be relatively more successful. According to Jones (1995), instrumental theory establishes connections between certain practices and certain end states. In other words, if you want certain results such as sustained profit, long-term growth, and so on, then carry out certain practices, such as stakeholder management process. As Berman and colleagues (1999) express it, instrumental stakeholder theory is related to what happens if managers treat stakeholders in a certain manner.

Stakeholder theory is descriptive because it presents a model to describe what the corporation is, or how organisations interact with stakeholders. 'It describes the corporation as a constellation of a cooperative and competitive interests possessing intrinsic value. It explains past, present and future states of corporations and their stakeholders' (Donaldson and Preston, 1995). In the descriptive realm, stakeholder theory is concerned about how managers actually deal with stakeholders (Berman, et al., 1999).

Finally, stakeholder theory is managerial. It does not simply describe existing situations or predict cause-and-effect relationships, it also recommends attitudes, structures, and practices that taken together constitute stakeholder management. Stakeholder management requires simultaneous attention to the legitimate interests of all appropriate stakeholders, both in the establishment of organisational structures and general policies, and in case-by-case decision making (Donaldson and Preston, 1995).

Jones (1995) stated that descriptive, instrumental, and normative stakeholder theories address 'what happens,' 'what happens if,' and 'what should happen,' respectively. Descriptive stakeholder theory is intended to describe or explain how firms or their managers actually behave; instrumental theory purports to describe what will happen if managers or firms behave in certain ways; normative theory is concerned with the moral propriety of the behavior of firms and/or their managers.

Stakeholder Management

Stakeholder management is a way of organising the firm so that it can be responsive to the concerns of its stakeholders because those stakeholders can affect the plans and activities of the firm (Husted, 1998). Freeman (1984) links stakeholder management to the stakeholders' ability to raise their voices with respect to organisational activities, and advocates that stakeholder considerations be incorporated into strategic planning approaches. Freeman proposes a four-step stakeholder management process. The first step is concerned with the identification of all relevant stakeholder groups in relation to the issue being addressed. Next, for each stakeholder group it must be determined what is their stake and how important they are. The third step is about determining how effectively the needs or expectations of each group are currently being met by the company. This is followed by the final step, which is modification of corporate policies and priorities to take into consideration stakeholder interests that are not currently met. From this perspective, corporate success depends on a stakeholder management process in which the interests and demands of stakeholders are identified and dealt with appropriately (Nasi, et al., 1997).

The aim of stakeholder management practices could be firm-centered or system-centered goals (Mitchell, Agle, and Wood, 1997). Both require broad knowledge of stakeholders. For firm-centered goals, such as survival, economic well being, taking advantage of opportunities, influencing public policy, coalition building, and so forth, managers want to know about all of their stakeholders. By contrast, for system-centered purposes, managers want an exhaustive list of all stakeholders in order to participate in a fair balancing of various claims and interests within the firm's social system.

What Is a Stakeholder?

Many definitions exist in strategic literature. Freeman's classic definition, quoted earlier, is considered to be one of the broadest (Mitchell, Agle, and Wood, 1997). In contrast, a narrower definition by Clarkson (1995) states that stakeholders are voluntary or involuntary risk bearers. Carroll (1993) said that stakeholders are 'those groups or individuals with whom the organization interacts or has interdependencies' and 'any individual or group who can affect or is affected by the actions, decisions, policies, practices or goals of the organization.' Starik (1995) suggested that the stakeholder concept be expanded to include any naturally occurring entity that affects or is affected by organisational performance. Donaldson and Preston (1995) say stakeholders are persons or groups with legitimate interests in procedural and/or substantive aspects of corporate activity.

Others defined stakeholders as groups or individuals who 'have an interest in the actions of an organization and . . . the ability to influence it' (Savage, et al., 1991). They stated that stakeholders can express interest and influence the practices of an organisation. Thus, a stakeholder qualifies if it has either power to affect the firm or a stake in the firm's performance. By these analyses, stakeholders have the potential to help or harm the company.

Clarkson (1995) suggests another definition, stakeholders are 'persons or groups that have, or claim, ownership, rights, or interests in a corporation and its activities, past, present, or future.' He classified stakeholders as primary and secondary stakeholders. A primary stakeholder group is one without whose continuing participation the corporation cannot survive; there is a high level of interdependence between the corporation and its primary stakeholders. Clarkson defines secondary stakeholder groups as 'those who influence or affect, or are influenced and affected by, the corporation, but they are not engaged in transactions with the corporation and are not essential for its survival.' Secondary stakeholders are diverse and include those who are not directly engaged in the organisation's economic activities but are able to exert influence or are affected by the organisation.

Mitchell, Agle, and Wood (1997) emphasised the need to have 'broad knowledge of actual and potential actors and claimants in the firm's environment.' In an effort to analyse how scholars working with stakeholder theory have narrowed the widely cited definition of Freeman (1984), they reviewed stakeholder concepts. They argued that narrowing the meaning of 'stakeholder' requires applying sorting criteria.

> Scholars who attempt to narrow the definition of stakeholder emphasise the claim's legitimacy based upon contract, exchange, legal title, legal right, moral right, at-risk status, or moral interest in the harms and benefits generated by company actions and that, in contrast scholars who favour a broad definition emphasise the stakeholder's power to influence the firm's behavior, whether or not there are legitimate claims.

Their review found that power and legitimacy are the core attributes of a stakeholder identification typology and added another attribute—urgency—to their stakeholder identification model. Thus, they identified three dimensions of stakeholder salience: (1) the power that a particular stakeholder group is perceived to hold, (2) the legitimacy that the stakeholder group is considered to have, and (3) the perceived urgency of the stakeholder group's demands.

Stakeholder Theory Applied to Tourism Destinations

Stakeholder theory has been applied as a planning and management tool by Sautter and Leisen (1999); Yuksel, Bramwell, and Yuksel, (1999); and Getz and Jamal (1994). Robson and Robson (1996) have applied the theory as an ethical business management tool where they argued that stakeholders should take part in decision making and stakeholder concerns, goals, and values should be included in the strategic framework of tourism businesses. Stakeholder identification and involvement has been recognised as a key step toward achieving partnerships and collaboration within tourism in the studies of both Jamal and Getz (2000) and Medeiros de Araujo and Bramwell (1999).

Ioannides (2001) applied a stakeholder framework in conjunction with the destination life cycle concept to analyse varying stakeholder attitudes toward tourism and sustainable development at different stages of destination development. Stakeholder theory has also been used as an ethical tool in sustainable tourism marketing by Walsh, Jamrozy, and Burr, (2001). The application of stakeholder theory to tourism so far has been mostly superficial, with the exception of Hardy and Beeton (2001) who applied stakeholder theory both to identify stakeholder groups and understand their perceptions of sustainable tourism.

The stakeholder concept has largely been defined in a management and organisational context, but the organisational setting of a firm and the concept of a 'destination' that is managed are somewhat similar. In this context, Ryan (2002) argued that 'destinations are also bundles of resources, like companies.' He also stated that at the strategic level 'destinations seek to configure their product, and to sustain it through adopting a mix of environmentally friendly and economically viable policies.'

However, the structure of a destination could be considered even more complex than that of an organisation, as a destination is made up of fragmented suppliers with different types of competing and complementary organisations, multiple sectors, and multiple actors (Pavlovich, 2003). One way to achieve this multisector, multiactor objective is by responding to the concerns of different stakeholders.

Applying stakeholder theory to a destination context requires incorporating stakeholder considerations into the destination's strategic tourism planning. Based on the seminal work of Freeman (1984), his four steps of stakeholder management process can be applied to tourism destinations within a sustainable tourism perspective, as follows:

1. Identify all relevant stakeholder groups in relation to STD.

Persons, groups, neighborhoods, organisations, institutions, societies, and the natural environment are entities that are generally thought to qualify as actual or potential stakeholders (Starik, 1995; Mitchell, Agle, and Wood, 1997). The tourism literature has listed many different stakeholder groups (Sautter and Leisen, 1999; Ryan, 2002; Timur and Getz, 2002). The World Tourism Organization (1993) defines major partners for STD as the industry, environment supporters, and the community or local authority.

The tourism industry creates business opportunities, jobs, income, and foreign exchange by providing an array of tourism services. These services include transportation, accommodation, food and drinks, and travel. The second partner, environment, is the basis for natural, cultural, and built (man-made) resources that the industry depends on to attract tourists. These stakeholders focus their efforts on balancing the type and extent of tourism activity against the capacity of the resources available. Finally, the host community is another participant for sustainable tourism decision making. The community is composed of residents, local government, local business organisations, and other local institutions and associations (World Tourism Organization, 1993). Swarbrooke (1999) defines the host community as all those people who live within the tourist destination. That includes those who own local tourism businesses and their association, who are employed in the tourism industry, and whose life is adversely affected by tourism in terms of air, water, and noise pollution.

2.   Determine the stake (potential interest) and importance of each stakeholder group.

The importance of each stakeholder will not be determined by their possession of critical resources, such as money, information, personnel, and so on, but in terms of their roles and contributions to STD at the destination level. The industry wants long-term growth, profitability, and new business opportunities. The importance of this group is related to a destination's level of dependency on the 'products' and services that the industry supplies. Government is concerned with the optimum use of the resources where jobs are created and resources are protected. Because the public sector has economic, social, and ecological responsibilities in developing tourism at all levels, they have important roles (Pearce, 1981; Pearce 1989; Page, 1995). The economic reasons for developing tourism are to generate new employment, diversify the economy, increase income levels, and increase revenue from taxes (Pearce, 1989; Holden, 2000). Protecting the well being of individuals and promoting cultural awareness of the destination are among the socio-cultural factors that induce the public sector to foster tourism development. The government also undertakes stewardship of the environment and tourism resources so that the agents of development do not destroy the future basis for tourism development. The community will include both people who benefit from and pay costs associated with tourism development. Their concerns will focus highly on quality of life.

Moisey and McCool (2001) stated that local residents and the tourism industry share the common goal of economic and sociocultural sustainability, whereas the economic and resource sustainability goal is shared between the tourism industry and government bodies. The goal shared between local residents and government bodies is defined as sustainable resource use and protection.

3. Determine how effectively the needs or expectations of each group are currently being met by the destination.

Numerous destination organisations exist for marketing purposes only, giving rise to what Getz, Anderson, and Sheehan (1998) called a 'policy gap.' Where industry is the dominant voice in these marketing organisations, it has to be asked who speaks for other interest groups or how other policy issues such as the environment and cultural impacts get a voice.

4. Modify the destination's tourism development policies and priorities to take into consideration stakeholder interests that are not currently met. This implies both the ability and willingness of destination organisations to act on diverse stakeholder interests as opposed to a narrow, industry-oriented mandate. It might become necessary to determine who the various stakeholders trust to represent their varied interests and formulate a balanced policy.

In summary, tourism development generates many issues within the realms of economic, social, cultural, and environmental policy domains. Economic sustainability has in many places become more important than the others, but the social, cultural, and environmental issues do not go away. Tourism is heavily reliant on cultural, natural, social, and ecological resources and the quality of resources of the destination. Tourism does affect and is affected by the environment. Tourism, being a resource-dependent industry, needs to pay more attention to the concerns of every stakeholder group and deal with them fairly. However, as it has already been discussed, each stakeholder group might approach STD from a different perspective and have different goals, which is a challenge for STD (Moisey and McCool, 2001). When each partner has a different goal for sustainable tourism, consensus building becomes a challenging process (Lane, 1994).

Figure 12.1 is a generic model showing diverse goals of major stakeholder groups toward STD. It suggests that sustainability can be reached only when stakeholder groups share goals. The size of the circles neither indicates the number of players nor the importance of stakeholders in each group. It suggests that sustainability requires involvement of all relevant stakeholders from three major clusters so that shared meaning and goals among destination stakeholders are achieved.

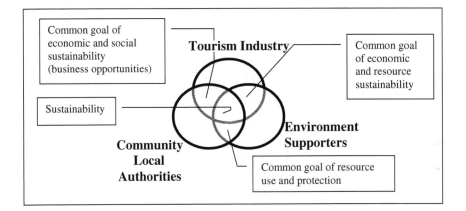

Figure 12.1: Sustainability goals of the main stakeholder groups.
Adapted from World Tourism Organization, 1993.

In an urban destination context, the industry could be the dominant player, whereas in rural and peripheral areas the local authorities or other public agency might be dominant. In highly sensitive ecological environments, a parks authority or environmental groups could be the dominant players. What we argue is that in order to achieve STD, the relative power of stakeholder groups has to be neutralised. Although collaboration of all relevant stakeholders can overcome power imbalances (Jamal and Getz 1997; Bramwell and Sharman, 1999), stakeholder theory offers a destination development approach where partnerships or relationships with very different stakeholders are built.

Stakeholder Theory Applied to Sustainable Tourism Development

Stakeholder theory allows destinations to consider a wider range of influencers when developing strategy (Polonsky, 1995). When using a stakeholder management approach destinations will be organised in such a way as to enable the optimal balancing of interests. Destinations will be challenged to create a more participative model focussed on the involvement and participation of all relevant stakeholders.

Stakeholder management offers a way of developing destinations so that it can be responsive to the concerns of its stakeholders. The stakeholder management literature is easily adaptable into a format that meets the needs of destinations, especially those faced with trying to develop a sustainable tourism policy. It asserts that destinations have duties to numerous groups and individuals, that these duties are all of equal value, and that to act in a socially, culturally, and environmentally responsible manner the claims of all these groups and individuals must be dealt with fairly. This suggests an agreed-upon 'balance' among competing claims (Humber, 2002). The stakeholder approach would ensure that all parties are identified and their positions noted. Decision making taken under these conditions is more likely to address all issues. For an example of consensus building among diverse stakeholders, using a round table process, see Ritchie and Crouch (2003).

Balancing the Voices

Achieving sustainable development requires a balance between conflicting economic, environmental, social, and cultural objectives. This ideal condition cannot be easily accomplished in a multisector, multiactor destination setting.

Balancing Process for Sustainable Tourism Development

The first step is concerned with identification of stakeholders for formulating STD policy at the destination level. The entity likely to start the process could be a DMO, a government authority, an industry leader, a visionary, or an external convener such as a consultant. This individual or organisation must already hold legitimacy, or a new group might have to be created. In either case, the initiator should not only be dedicated to the principles of sustainability but also be able to attract (even persuade) individuals and/or organisations from various stakeholder groups to participate. The initial assembled team could be called 'focal stakeholders.' It will be the responsibility of the focal stakeholders to identify other relevant stakeholders within the three clusters.

A destination's stakeholders can be grouped based on their sustainability objectives and perspectives, which may imply grouping according to destination stakeholders' existing and preferred networks. Groups focussed on economic growth may be less concerned with environmental protection or poverty of the local communities (Ioannides, 2001), hence prefer doing business with those who share the same goal. Planning for sustainability requires minimising ecological and sociocultural impacts and maximising economic and social benefits. When the definition, meaning, and/or vision of sustainable tourism is not shared among stakeholder groups, linkages among stakeholders cannot be articulated, resulting in nonsustainable solutions (Moisey and McCool, 2001).

Some stakeholders are likely to hold more resources or initially be more influential than the others, but based on STD principles and stakeholder theory consideration should be given to all, regardless of their power and access to critical resources. Three clusters or major stakeholder groups have been identified (see Figure 12.1): industry, local authorities/community, and other interest groups to represent natural, sociocultural, and environmental resources of the destination, including residents' associations. Within each major stakeholder group, every legitimate stakeholder has to be identified by that group rather than by an external agency. Stakeholders can be organisations or persons, and the numbers of each are not pertinent. Only the commonality of their voices on important sustainability issues is of concern in this process.

In other words, what is proposed is that 'legitimacy' be defined within each cluster. The notion of legitimacy could be defined as 'a generalized perception or assumption that the actions of an entity are desirable, proper, or appropriate within some socially constructed systems of norms, values, beliefs and definitions' (Suchman, 1995). Each of the three major stakeholder groups must go through an inclusive process of within-group consultations, then identify their sustainability issues and prioritise them through consensus building. Determining potential interests of each stakeholder group will complete the second step of the process.

Determining how effectively the needs and expectations of each stakeholder group are being met depends highly on the previous step, determination of each group's stake. If there are no or few relationships (including communication) within each group and between clusters then this step may not be as simple as it appears (Polonsky, 1995). Therefore, it is important that 'central' and 'bridging' organisations are identified in the second step. The former refers to organisations that have important decision-making and mediating roles, and who are the key to understanding the circulation of ideas and decisions to act collectively, particularly when the individuals are in different organisations (John and Cole 1998). The latter could be defined as organisations that facilitate exchanges of resources (e.g., information, money, etc.) between less central organisations. Bridging organisations act like 'brokers' and establish ties with less connected or isolated organisations. These organisations will either be at the intersections of existing networks within and between the three main stakeholder groups, or will have to be identified and legitimised through broad-based consultations.

The last step is to formulate or modify the sustainable tourism strategy and policy of the destination so that each stakeholder group's expectations and needs are integrated. This is the process of between-group consensus building. If destination development goals are prioritised by tourism-industry input only, then there is a lack of balance to guide sustainable tourism goals of the destination. Hence, an agency of local government might have greater legitimacy to convene and guide the process, as opposed to a DMO.

Stakeholder Views from Three Cities

Interviews were conducted to understand stakeholders' perspectives on STD in three cities: Calgary (Alberta, Canada: 15 respondents), Victoria (British Columbia, Canada: 12 respondents), and San Francisco (California: 11 respondents). Overall, 15 respondents represented industry, 10 were from government authorities/agents, and the remaining 13 represented various community organisations or institutions.

It was found that 'sustainable tourism' holds different meanings to different groups. Basically, the concept has three major dimensions: economic viability, environmental compatibility, and sociocultural compatibility. Most of the respondents used the notion of sustainability in the context of economic terms. Very few were able to provide a definition of STD that included all three basic dimensions.

When respondents were asked who should be involved in sustainable tourism policy development, there was agreement among stakeholders in all three cities that the DMO, government, and industry are the most important stakeholders. Calgary respondents emphasised the need to include government in particular to provide funding and initiate sustainability awareness and meetings. Victorian and San Franciscan respondents preferred to see their DMO and industry take the lead, rather than governmental bodies. Unexpectedly, very few respondents identified the environment and environmental supporters as one of the legitimate stakeholders.

In San Francisco all the governmental respondents identified non-governmental organizations and other interest groups to represent social, cultural, and natural resources of their city. This reflects the city's sustainable city initiative. The municipal government developed a 'Sustainability Plan for the City of San Francisco, which resulted in creation of the Department of Environment for San Francisco. In 1996 more than 350 San Franciscan community activists and others representing many city government agencies, more than 100 businesses, and academia gathered in working groups to draft a plan to achieve a sustainable society. In 1997, the goals and objectives of the sustainability plan became policy of the city and county of San Francisco (see <www.sustainable-city. organization>). It should be noted that this plan does not include a sustainable tourism policy. However, there are relevant implications to tourism businesses and activities as tourism is one of the most important economic activities of the city. Another environmentally sensitive project exists in the city's convention center.

In terms of tourism plans or STD policies, there is none in Calgary. However, the City Hall has departments for both environmental management and community-level strategies. The city's DMO (Tourism Calgary) has only a marketing mandate. In Victoria, where there is neither tourism policy nor a sustainable city development plan, the DMO (Tourism Victoria) is active in dealing with some sustainable development issues. Tourism Victoria has managed to develop tight relationships with a broad list of destination stakeholders. It seems that the strong leadership of Tourism Victoria encouraged destination stakeholders, from industry to community, to engage in partnerships for the preservation of the environment.

There was considerably more interest in sustainable tourism in Victoria than either San Francisco or Calgary, because as one of the respondents said 'with the decline in resource-based industries in Victoria, people realized the economic contribution of tourism as a significant industry and there is a growing interest.' In comparison, the interest in developing sustainable tourism in San Francisco was low. Some of the respondents believed that 'people will now (after September 11) start questioning how we can attract visitors to San Francisco, and keep earning visitor dollars. That's something new that we need to learn.' It is clear that sustainable tourism in San Francisco was more related to sustaining economic vitality of the local businesses rather than preserving or conserving the resources.

When the question of 'how to increase sustainable tourism practices' was asked, respondents from Calgary believed that practicing sustainable tourism requires cooperation and collaboration among the industry and between the industry and the government. It was also believed that enhancing communication among stakeholders is another factor in practicing more sustainable forms of tourism projects. Education of not only the industry people but also government agencies about the principles and benefits of sustainable tourism was identified as one of the ways to increase sustainable tourism practices. In addition to leadership, respondents from San Francisco highlighted the importance of management support, financial resources, and educated people in practicing sustainable projects. Respondents from Victoria suggested that sustainable tourism practices could be increased in cities by providing leadership and increasing partnerships.

Another issue raised in the interviews was that of barriers to sustainable tourism, that is difficulties facing sustainable tourism policy or development projects. Diversity within the tourism industry was identified as one of the biggest challenges. In Calgary and San Francisco there was an emphasis on the need to increase the education level of all stakeholders on the benefits of a sustainable approach in urban settings. Another significant obstacle identified in Calgary was the lack of financial resources allocated for tourism planning or STD. Respondents from Victoria believed that the fragmented nature of the industry, and hence a lack of common interests and expectations among stakeholder groups, made sustainable projects unreachable. Lack of time and clarity of goals also present a challenge to both developing and implementing more sustainable projects. To eliminate the urban STD barriers, destination stakeholders agreed on the need to come together and work with each other. One respondent from Victoria emphasised the need to involve 'shakers of the town.' Respondents agreed that these 'visionaries' are needed either to 'assemble stakeholders and put everybody on the same page' or 'explain the importance of tourism on the local economy and get community support.' Another respondent identified the value of 'learning to communicate and sharing not only resources but experiences as well' as a tool in eliminating sustainability barriers.

Conclusion

This chapter established the appropriateness and utility of stakeholder theory and stakeholder management in helping to achieve STD within a destination. A process was presented, based on stakeholder theory, as a preferred way to identify destination stakeholders, understand their perspectives and concerns, and deal with them appropriately by maintaining a balance among competing stakeholder interests. Stakeholder theorists argue that each stakeholder group, regardless of their relative power, has to be given consideration (Nasi, 1995). This explicitly defines one of the principles of sustainable development. These stakeholders must be working together to achieve sustainability goals. If a broader base stakeholder group engages in collective efforts for goal achievement, destinations will have a better chance in realising their sustainability goals.

The recommended stakeholder balancing process (following Freeman) for STD includes the following key elements:

- Commencing with or creating a legitimate focal group of stakeholders;
- Identifying relevant stakeholders *within* each of three major clusters (their numbers and relative power are irrelevant);
- Determining potential interests within clusters and prioritising sustainability issues through consensus building, first within and then between clusters;
- Determining how each cluster's expectations are met by the destination; and

- Modifying the destination's priorities, strategies, and policies to integrate each cluster's sustainability issues.

Interviews from three cities with various stakeholders illustrate that there is no one sustainable tourism definition shared by destination stakeholder groups. There are individual rather than organised efforts to practice sustainable tourism. This indicates a challenge in sustainable tourism planning and policy making because individual goals rather than shared destination goals are the norm. The question that deserves immediate attention is 'how to manage stakeholder involvement and balance their interests,' or in other words, 'how to create balance among stakeholders.' Practically, it should be asked 'how to respond to demands of both profitability and STD.' Creating a more participative decision making and strategic policy-making process is the answer implied in the stakeholder management approach. The ultimate key to balancing all the voices of diverse stakeholders is to ignore numbers and relative power in favour of a system that gives equal weight to all legitimate voices.

References

Berman, S. L, A. C. Wicks, S. Kotha, and T. M. Jones. 1999. Does Stakeholder Orientation Matter? The Relationship between Stakeholder Management Models and Firm Financial Performance. *Academy of Management Journal* 42(5): 488–506.

Bramwell, B., and A. Sharman. 1999. Collaboration in Local Tourism Policy Making. *Annals of Tourism Research* 26(2): 392–415.

Carroll, A. B. 1993. *Business and Society: Ethics and Stakeholder Management*. Cincinnati: South-Western.

———. 1994. A Risk Based Model of Stakeholder Theory. *Proceedings of the Second Toronto Conference on Stakeholder Theory*. Toronto: Centre for Corporate Social Performance & Ethics, University of Toronto.

Clarkson, M. B. E. 1995. A Stakeholder Framework for Analyzing and Evaluating Corporate Social Performance. *Academy of Management Review* 20(1): 92–117.

Clarkson, M. B. E., and M. C. Deck. 1993. Applying Stakeholder Management to the Analysis and Evaluation of Corporate Codes. In *Business and Society in a Changing World Order*. ed. D. C. Ludwig. New York: Mellen Press.

Donaldson, T., and L. E. Preston. 1995. The Stakeholder Theory of the Corporation: Concepts, Evidence and Implications. *The Academy of Management Review* 20(1): 65–91.

Freeman, E. R. 1984. *Strategic Management: A Stakeholder Approach*. Boston, Massachusetts: Pitman.

Frooman, J. 1999. Stakeholder Influence Strategies. *Academy of Management Journal* 24(2): 191–205.

Getz, D., and T. Jamal. 1994. The Environment-Community Symbiosis: A Case for Collaborative Tourism Planning. *Journal of Sustainable Tourism* 2(3): 152–173.

Getz, D., D. Anderson, and L. Sheehan. 1998. Roles, Issues, and Strategies for Convention and Visitor Bureaux in Destination Planning and Product Development: A Survey of Canadian Bureaux. *Tourism Management* 19(4): 331–340.

Goodpastor, K. 1991. Business Ethics and Stakeholder Analysis. *Business Ethics Quarterly* 1: 53–71.

Green, H., and C. Hunter. 1992. *Tourism and the Environment: A Sustainable Relationship?* New York: Routledge.

Hardy, A. L., and R. J. S. Beeton. 2001. Sustainable Tourism or Maintainable Tourism?: Managing Resources for More than Average Outcomes. *Journal of Sustainable Tourism* 9(3): 168–192.

Holden, A. 2000. *Environment and Tourism*. London: Routledge.

Humber, J. M. 2002. Beyond Stockholder and Stakeholders: A Plea for Corporate Moral Authority. *Journal of Business Ethics* 36: 207–221.

Hunter, C. J. 1995. On the Need to Re-Conceptualize Sustainable Tourism Development. *Journal of Sustainable Tourism* 3(3): 155–165.

Husted, B. W. 1998. Organizational Justice and the Management of Stakeholder Relations. *Journal of Business Ethics* 17: 643–651.

Ioannides, D. 2001. Sustainable Development and Shifting Attitudes of Tourism Stakeholders: Toward a Dynamic Framework. In *Tourism, Recreation and Sustainability: Linking Culture and the Environment*. eds. S. F. McCool and R. N. Moisey. Oxon, U.K.: CABI Publishing.

Jawahar, I. M., and G. L. McLaughlin. 2001. Toward a Descriptive Stakeholder Theory: An Organizational Life Cycle Approach. *Academy of Management Review* 26(3): 397–414.

Jamal, T., and D. Getz. 1997. Visioning for Sustainable Tourism Development: Community Based Collaborations. In *Quality of Management in Urban Tourism*. ed. P. Murphy. Chichester: Wiley.

———. 2000. Community Roundtables for Tourism Related Conflicts: The Dialectics of Consensus and Process Structures. *Tourism Collaboration and Partnerships: Politics, Practice and Sustainability*. eds. B. Bramwell and B. Lane. Clevedon: Channel View Publications.

John, P., and A. Cole. 1998. Sociometric Mapping Techniques and the Comparison of Policy Networks: Economic Decision Making in Leeds and Lille. In *Comparing Policy Networks*. ed. D. Marsh. Buckingham: Open University Press.

Jones, T. M. 1995. Instrumental Stakeholder Theory: A Synthesis of Ethics and Economic. *The Academy of Management Review* 20(2): 404–437.

Lane, B. 1994. Sustainable Rural Tourism Strategies: A Tool for Development and Conservation. *Journal of Sustainable Tourism* 2(1&2): 102–111.

McKercher, B. 1993. The Unrecognized Threat of Tourism: Can Tourism Survive 'Sustainability'? *Tourism Management* 14(2): 131–136.

Medeiros de Araujo, L., and B. Bramwell. 1999. Stakeholder Assessment and Collaborative Tourism Planning: The Case of Brazil's Costa Dourada Project. *Journal of Sustainable Tourism* 7(3 and 4): 356– 378.

Mitchell, R. K., B. R. Agle, and D. J. Wood. 1997. Toward a Theory of Stakeholder Identification and Salience: Defining the Principles of Who and What Really Counts. *Academy of Management Review* 22(4): 853–886, 959.

Moisey, R. N., and S. F. McCool. 2001. Sustainable Tourism in the 21st Century: Lessons from the Past: Challenges to Address. In *Tourism, Recreation and*

Sustainability: Linking Culture and the Environment. eds. S. F. McCool and R. N. Moisey. Oxon, U.K.: CABI.

Nasi, J. 1995. *Understanding Stakeholder Thinking.* ed. Helsinki: LSR-Publications.

Nasi J., S. Nasi, N. Phillips, and S. Zyglidopoulos. 1997. The Evolution of Corporate Social Responsiveness. *Business Society* 36(3): 296–321.

Page, S. 1995. *Urban Tourism.* London: Routledge.

Pavlovich, K. 2003. The Evolution and Transformation of a Tourism Destination Network: The Waitomo Caves, New Zealand. *Tourism Management* 24: 203–216.

Pearce, D. 1981. *Tourist Development.* London: Longman.

———. 1989. *Tourist Development.* 2nd ed. Essex: Longman.

Polonsky, M. J. 1995. A Stakeholder Theory Approach to Designing Environmental Marketing Strategy. *The Journal of Business & Industrial Marketing* 5(3): 29–46.

Ritchie, B., and G. Crouch. 2003. *The Competitive Destination.* London: CABI.

Robson, J., and I. Robson. 1996. From Shareholders to Stakeholders: Critical Issues for Tourism Marketers. *Tourism Management* 17(7): 533–540.

Ryan, C. 2002. Equity, Management, Power Sharing and Sustainability—Issues of the 'New Tourism'. *Tourism Management* 23(1): 17–26.

Savage, G. T., T. W. Nix, C. J. Whitehead, and J. D. Blair. 1991. Strategies for Assessing and Managing Organizational Stakeholders. *Academy of Management Executive* 5(2): 51–75.

Sautter, E. T., and B. Leisen. 1999. Managing Stakeholders: A Tourism Planning Model. *Annals of Tourism Research* 26: 312–328.

Starik, M. 1995. Should Trees Have Managerial Standing? Toward Stakeholder Status for Non-Human Nature. *Journal of Business Ethics* 14: 207–217.

Suchman, M. C. 1995. Managing Legitimacy: Strategic and Institutional Approaches. *The Academy of Management Review* 20(3): 571–610.

Swarbrooke, J. 1999. *Sustainable Tourism Management.* New York: CABI.

Timur, S., and D. Getz. 2002. Applying Stakeholder Theory to the Implementation of Sustainable Urban Tourism. City Tourism 2002: Proceedings of European Cities Tourism's International Conference in Vienna, Austria.

Walsh, J. A., A. Jamrozy, and S. W. Burr. 2001. Sense of Place as a Component of Sustainable Tourism Marketing. In *Tourism, Recreation and Sustainability: Linking Culture and the Environment.* eds. S. F. McCool and R. N. Moisey. Oxon, U.K.: CABI.

Wood, D. J., and R. E. Jones. 1995. Stakeholder Mismatching: A Theoretical Problem in Empirical Research on Corporate Social Performance. *The International Journal of Organizational Analysis* 3(3): 229–267.

World Tourism Organization. 1993. *Sustainable Tourism Development: Guide for Local Planners.* Madrid: World Tourism Organization.

———. 1998. *Guide for Local Authorities on Developing Sustainable Tourism.* Madrid: World Tourism Organization.

Yuksel, F., B. Bramwell, and A. Yuksel. 1999. Stakeholder Interviews and Tourism Planning at Pamukkale, Turkey. *Tourism Management* 20(3): 351–360.

13 Ethical considerations in sustainable tourism

Simon Hudson and Graham Miller

Introduction

In Banff National Park, Canada, like in many other parts of the developed world, a fierce battle is taking place between conservationists and the tourism industry. Conservationists are arguing for more environmental protection and a restriction on tourism growth, and tourism operators are seeking to upgrade and develop tourism facilities, arguing that it is wrong to restrict access and deny their businesses profits and locals and tourists the opportunity to enjoy some of the most beautiful and accessible outdoor recreation terrain in the world. Current federal policy favours the conservationists, and the new National Parks Act makes ecological integrity, not enjoyment, the primary role of Canada's national parks.

The decision by the Canadian government to give the environment priority over humans in the park is a noble one. There is a growing awareness that the natural world has limits that our current assumptions and activities are quickly exceeding. But is the decision an ethical one? Is it ethical to ignore the positive economic and environmental impacts that tourism can create, and the potentially significant contribution that tourism can make to the socioeconomic development of host and generating societies? Should the environment have priority over humans? Should we not be channelling our energies into preventing less sustainable activities like commercial logging and the transportation of heavy goods through park highways? This chapter explores the relationship between ethics and sustainable tourism and considers how an understanding of the ethical approaches of future tourism managers will benefit our ability to manage the industry in the future.

The Relationship between Ethics and Sustainable Tourism

Ethics is the study of moral philosophy and is concerned with the distinction between 'right' and 'wrong.' Clearly the world is a complex place and issues of absolute right or wrong are rare, but ethics can provide the broad disciplinary framework within which sustainable tourism can be analysed (Tribe, 2002). This is because a vital part of ethics is that of value clarification, and by examining common definitions of sustainable tourism its values emerge. However, regardless of whether we are convinced by a principles-based approach or a utilitarian view of the world, to make a decision on any topic we need to understand the issues before us. Yet, in the case of sustainable tourism, these values and our understanding have changed radically over the last 50 years, and as our understanding has changed, so has the ethical context in which past tourism managers have made their decisions.

To appreciate the importance of understanding ethics in relation to sustainable tourism, we need to consider two crucial debates that affect the successful development of the tourism industry. The first debate is thousands of years old and considers 'what is ethical,' and the second debate considers 'our view of sustainable tourism.'

What Is Ethical?

As with so many questions, the answer to the question, 'what is ethical?' depends heavily on the approach we take to answer the question. The two main approaches to ethical decision making derived from the literature are those reliant on the theories of deontology and teleology. A *deontological* approach enjoys a rich historical legacy, dating back to philosophers such as Socrates, and more recently to the work of Kant. Deontology is concerned with the idea of universal truths and principles, which should be adhered to regardless of the circumstances. Kant's categorical imperative states that a person faced with a problem should be able to respond consistently and in conformity with their moral principles and also feel comfortable with the decision being made in full view of others. A *teleological* view can be understood as 'consequentialism' (Kaynama, King, and Smith, 1996) following from the philosophical work of Jeremy Bentham and John Stuart Mill on utilitarianism. Thus, ethical decisions are made in view of expected outcomes, which eliminate the universality of decisions and subordinates principles to context.

A common expression for the two approaches would be that deontology places the means as more important than the end, whereas for teleology it is the end that justifies the means. If we go back to our original example, if the ski areas in the parks were known to be causing serious environmental damage, a deontological approach might be to close the resorts until such time as the damage could be prevented entirely. The effects of this may be unemployment for those who worked at the resorts as well as negative publicity sent to the marketplace, ultimately damaging the viability of the resorts. However, the decision to close the resorts would still be taken, because to cause environmental damage is wrong and so to solve it immediately is the correct course of action. A teleological view would be to evaluate the damage done to the environment versus the resort and the local economy and then to conduct a cost–benefit analysis to determine a course of action. The outcome may be the same as that taken by a deontologist, but the reasoning would not be made on the basis of principle but because this was the most expedient decision.

Such approaches to ethical decisions demonstrate strong ties with the concepts of corporate and social responsibility and ultimately sustainable tourism and sustainable development. Huberman-Arnold and Arnold state teleologically, 'The corporate world has seen the value of ethics in the workplace. Good treatment of those internal to the corporation as well as those external to it, and of the environment, will improve the work climate, and increase profitability backed by public approval' (2001). Preaching the alternate view, Przeclawski expresses his conviction that '. . . tourists, inhabitants and brokers should respect *fundamental values* such as human life and dignity, natural and cultural environment, family, holidays and holy places, real and suitable information, private property, freedom and observe the ethical norms connected with them' (1997). Similarly, the actions of some within the tourism industry to promote greater sustainable tourism are taken because of a belief that such actions are simply the right course of action, whilst for others, actions promoting sustainable tourism are taken because they will result in increased profits.

Related to this argument, Bowie (2001) points to a trend away from the Kantian perspective of ethics for the sake of ethics and toward a position where ethics are considered when they can produce greater profits. He cites the increase in the number of U.S. companies calculating the benefit accrued from their charitable donations, rather than just giving money to charity. Thus, ethics are seen not to have an intrinsic value, but are attractive because of their extrinsic worth. Wheeller (1993) has also argued that we support sustainable tourism because it makes us feel better, not because of a philanthropic concern for the environment. In fact he says ecotourism's impotence is its main attraction, calling it 'the perfect political fob, it soothes consciences, demands no sacrifices and allows extended holiday choice while providing an ideal shield, doubling as a marketing ploy, for the tourism industry.' However, what such a dogmatic

position ignores is that the effect of a deontological or a teleological decision can be exactly the same regardless of the reasons for which it was
taken. A decision to preserve rare species for intrinsic reasons or for extrinsic reasons still results in the preservation of rare species. Later in the
chapter we consider how managers make these decisions in order that
those decision-making processes can best be manipulated to produce a
decision of benefit to all. The following section examines the context in
which these decisions are made and the effect this has on the extent to
which decisions can be considered ethical or not.

Our View of Sustainable Tourism

From the previous discussion we know that we can take either a principled view of the world or a more pragmatic, consequentialist view, but
we need also to consider the second part of this phrase, our 'view of the
world.' The dominant view of the world will shape, and be shaped by,
our understanding of sustainable tourism and so determine the relationship between ethics and sustainable tourism. Thus, our ethical approach
to sustainable tourism depends on our view of sustainable tourism, and
although this is a more recent debate than considering our ethical
approach, it is no less important.

From the birth of mass tourism in the 1950s the tourism industry has
largely been seen as an economic panacea and mostly bereft of environmental, social, or political impact. Zierer (1952, quoted in Cohen, 1978)
states confidently, 'a notable characteristic of the tourism industry is that
it does not, or should not, lead to the destruction of natural resources.'
Convinced by the economic benefits of the industry, the World Bank was
an enthusiastic supporter of tourism development and lent nearly US$500
million to tourism projects between 1969 and 1979 (Lanfant and Graburn,
1992). Stankovic (1979) characterises the effusive views of tourism,
opining, '. . . tourism . . . can, more than many other activities, use and
valorise such parts and elements of nature as are of almost no value for
other economic branches and activities.' Bartelmus (1994) refers to this
neoclassical view as an 'empty-world' approach because of the way the
environment and humans are excluded from consideration, although such
an exploitive approach to natural resources was typical of the age before
Carson's seminal Silent Spring (Carson, 1966).

It is easy with the benefit of hindsight to be critical of the decisions
made during this period, and looking now from a time 40 years further
on we might feel that the almost total support for economic benefits was
wrong. The idea of 'moral relativism' supports the belief that decisions
are taken within a cultural context and it is unjustified for those outside
this context to criticise the ethics of the decisions made. Hence, non-

cognitivists believe that what is morally right or wrong is whatever cultural groups say it is, thus avoiding the position of one group telling another group what is acceptable. Just as moral relativists look across cultures, so it is similarly possible to look through time at the morality of decisions and avoid declaring past actions to be immoral because of what we know now. However, the problem with moral relativism is that if we accept that no cultural group has moral superiority over any other, we must also accept the immoral groups, or those morally intolerant of others, because their views carry equal weight to those of all other groups. By extension, genocide could be seen as a morally valid act because it was supported by a cultural group. Rejecting noncognitivsm and moral relativism means accepting that there are objective truths to be discovered, the problem becomes in determining what the objective truths should be based on. Many philosophers have felt that religious morality should be the foundation of any search for objective truths, and this has led easily to an anthropocentric view of the world.

Under this anthropocentric view of the world, man is placed at the centre of everything and believes that the world and all its resources are for the benefit of us. The Book of Genesis gives rise to this idea, calling on Adam and Eve to 'dominate and subdue' the earth, leading us to believe that man has been granted dominion over the nonhuman and non-sentient environment. Within this 'instrumentalist' view the value of the resources of the world is limited to the pleasure and profit they can produce for man. Concordant with this position is the opinion that resources can be substituted perfectly for each other. Thus, to leave to future generations a rich financial inheritance is of equal value to bequeathing a rich environmental legacy. Assuming this paradigm, what is 'right' is what is most beneficial for man, and the needs of the environment are not considered beyond this. Despite understanding the damage done by this approach to the environment, it is difficult to be critical of the approach taken given the moral context. There are plenty of examples in the world still where the immediate concerns of man are understandably given priority over the more distant concerns of environmental protection.

Yet, in a tourism context, the unquestioning acceptance of tourism as an economic panacea was replaced in the 1970s and early 1980s by an era of the great critique. The cautionary stance taken by the writings of the day was typified by Plog (1974) who famously observed, 'Destinations carry with them the potential seeds of their own destruction, as they allow themselves to become more commercialised and lose their qualities which originally attracted tourists.' Amongst the many epoch-marking works, Budowski (1976) and Cohen (1978) focussed on the environmental impacts of tourism; Cohen (1972), DeKadt (1979), Doxey (1975), and MacCannell (1976) the sociocultural impacts; Britton (1982) and De Kadt

(1979) the political consequences; whereas Bryden (1973) questioned the previously unchallenged economic value of tourism.

Although the critiques of the 1970s raised awareness to the potential impacts of tourism, the response adopted by the protagonists of the industry during the mid-1980s was described as 'adaptive' (Jafari, 1989). However, this promulgation of alternative forms of tourism seemed reactionary rather than adaptive and gave rise to the vilification of mass tourism (Turner and Ash, 1975; Butler, 1990; Smith and Eadington, 1992; McElroy and de Albuquerque, 1996). Mass tourism came to be synonymous with unsustainable practices, seen as being responsible for the deleterious effects of tourism on environments and societies. As a consequence, the rise of alternative tourism and 'ecotourism' were seen as the champions of a sustainable way forward with the emphasis on small-scale developments, community involvement, and the preeminence of environmental protection. This shift in thinking denotes a move from an anthropocentric ethic to an ecocentric ethic. This was a significant departure from previous thinking because man's place alongside, rather than in domination over, the rest of nature is assumed. The conservation of sentient and nonsentient beings is not just for their extrinsic value, but because they are afforded rights of existence, a recognition of an intrinsic right 'to be.' A more extreme version of ecocentrism is where the rights of the ecosystem are deemed to be more important than any single component of the system. Under such a view, the reintroduction of species to an area would be supported if it strengthened the ecosystem, even if this was at the cost of human safety, or led to a decline in numbers of a more plentiful species. However, such an ethic is felt to be out of step with current thinking, and actions taken under the direction of this ethic could be seen to be unethical against the current moral background.

The dominant approach today is arguably a second anthropocentric view of the world, described as one with a 'conservation ethic' and is perhaps the view of the world taken today by most of the international organisations such as the United Nations or the World Bank. Even the Brundtland[1] report on sustainable development can be said to have followed a conservation ethic. Under this ethic the value of nature is recognised and we seek to conserve the environment for a general benefit to mankind, not just an economic benefit. Still the economic imperative is recognised, but it is understood that a minimum amount of natural resources must be bequeathed to our children in order that the world can

---

1 The concept of sustainable development was first adopted by the U.N. World Commission on Environment and Development (WCED). The report of the WCED, *Our Common Future*, also known as the Bruntland Report after the name of its chairwoman, is a historic milestone in international environmental law because it represented the first attempt to reconcile economic development and environmental conservation through the concept of sustainable development.

continue to function and so future generations do not face problems of survival.

Within a tourism context, Hunter (1995) describes our understanding of sustainable tourism, as concerned with sustaining the tourism industry, as the 'dominant paradigm,' one where a 'tourism-centric' view is taken of sustainability. Butler (1993) characterises this interpretation of sustainable tourism as 'tourism which is in a form which can maintain *its* viability in an area for an indefinite period of time' (emphasis added). The essential element to this definition is that tourism is concerned to maintain 'its' viability over an indefinite period of time. This is clearly the definition of sustainable tourism that has been developed by those in the tourism industry, and not the definition that has crossed from the developmental literature. Although it is equally clear that a tourism industry that is not sustained is not in a position to contribute to sustainable development.

An alternative understanding of sustainable tourism is to view it in a developmental context. Butler (1993) describes sustainable tourism in this context as

> tourism which is developed and maintained in an area in such a manner and at such a scale that it remains viable over an indefinite period and does not degrade or alter the environment (human and physical) in which it exists to such a degree that it prohibits the successful development and well-being of *other activities and processes* (emphasis added).

Godfrey (1998) also identifies tourism in a sustainable development context, 'sustainable tourism is thus not an end in itself, nor a unique or isolated procedure, but rather an inter-dependent function of a wider and permanent socio-economic development process.' Under this interpretation, the most needy element of a society, whether it be the natural environment, society, culture, or finance, is what the tourism industry (and all industry) should work toward, with each element being valued equally. Despite this, Healey and Shaw (1994) believe that there is a preference for the economic over the environmental, whereas Craik (1995) places the environment above sociocultural matters for consideration. However, even if all elements of society are valued equally, it is not appropriate for tourism to necessarily contribute equally to all elements of society. Hence, tourism may be able to contribute much needed hard currency to a destination, in which case, the old interpretation of tourism as an economic panacea can be seen to promote sustainable tourism because it promotes sustainable development. Conversely, in other destinations, preservation of the natural environment may be the strongest contribution the tourism industry can make toward the development of society and here the tourism industry would be operating under a more ecocentric ethic. What is central to this understanding of sustainable tourism is that the tourism industry acknowledges itself to be a part of society and not apart from society.

By understanding the need for more sustainable development and the contribution the tourism industry can make toward this position, it is possible to assume either a teleological or deontological view of ethics. An understanding based on promoting sustainable development because it is our responsibility as stewards of the world for future generations can be achieved through more teleological means. Similarly, an anthropocentric view of the world can encourage us to pursue sustainable development, not because of the intrinsic value of the environment as an ecocentrist would hold, but because a sustainable world will make the world a nicer place to live in. Holden (2003) questions whether it is time for a new environmental ethic and reports signs of a change in the dominant ethic, evidencing the United Kingdom's 'Strategy for Sustainable Development,' which, in relation to leisure and tourism, observes, 'the environment has an intrinsic value which outweighs its value as a leisure asset.' The strategy continues to discuss the need to protect the environment for the enjoyment of future generations and so adopts a more instrumental approach. Although this change in language may appear to signal a more ecocentric approach, it is instructive that this change has happened in a developed western society where perhaps man's requirement of the environment has changed from a time when resources were to be exploited through consumption. If man is deciding that the environment has a right to exist, then arguably man is still using the environment for his purposes, albeit these purposes have changed, then the dominant view of the world could still be seen to be anthropocentric.

The reconciling of ethical approaches (deontology/teleology), a view of the world (anthropocentric/eco-centric), and our understanding of sustainable tourism (sustaining tourism/tourism that contributes to sustainable development) can be a head-spinning exercise. Yet the following section demonstrates why understanding how decisions are made and what factors influence these decisions is crucial to the ability to control the development of the tourism industry in the future.

Understanding Ethical Decision Making in Tourism Managers

The previous section shows that it is possible to be anthropocentric, teleological, and to understand sustainable tourism to be all about the advancement of the industry and yet to still be in agreement over a course of action with an ecocentric deonotologist who believes sustainable tourism means searching for how the industry can contribute to the sustainable development of society. Hence, if the industry is to encourage more sustainable practices, we need to be able to understand how the tourism managers of today and the future make decisions in order that those decision-making processes can best be manipulated to produce a benefit to all of us.

A number of 'tools' exist to control the tourism industry, ranging from market-based instruments such as taxes to more command-and-control instruments such as legislation. For a deontologist, breaking the law would contravene their view of ethics and so the legislation would be abided by almost regardless of the value of the legislation. Yet, a teleologist would consider the consequences of not abiding by the law and would weigh this against the benefits of breaking the law. If tourism managers seem to adopt a teleological approach to management, then legislation can expect to be effective only if accompanied by stringent penalties that make the outlawed behaviour not worthwhile, and hence the need to understand how decisions are made.

Malloy and Fennell (1998), Cleek and Leonard (1998), and Stevens (2001) all point to the increasing prevalence of codes of ethics employed by both the general tourism industry and the ecotourism industry as a tool to provide guidance to employees when making decisions. An important contribution in this area has been made by the World Tourism Organization, who in 1999 approved the Global Code of Ethics for Tourism that consolidated and reinforced previous recommendations and declarations on sustainable tourism. The Code aims to preserve the world's natural resources and cultural heritage from disruptive tourist activities and to ensure a fair and equitable sharing of benefits that arise out of tourism with the residents of tourism destinations. Article 3 of the Code refers specifically to sustainable development and includes some of the most innovative legal principles and environmental methods in this field (Table 13.1) (World Tourism Organization, 1999). It is also unique in that it includes a mechanism for enforcement of its provisions.

Ferrell and Skinner (1988) believe that the existence and enforcement of codes of ethics are associated with higher levels of ethical behaviour, although without the means to enforce adherence, Moore (1970) believes a code of ethics has limited meaning. The need for means of enforcement would indicate that those making decisions do not respond to the codes deontologically, but teleologically. Yet, valuable research by Malloy and Fennell (1998) declares the majority of codes to be deontological in their language. Research showing whether tourism managers did in fact apply a teleological approach to decisions would reveal deontological codes of ethics to be little more than an exercise in promoting external goodwill, whereas the opposite finding would strengthen the case for codes of ethics (Rondinelli and Berry, 2000). However, thus far there has been no tourism study to assess ethically how decisions are made by those that are subject

Table 13.1 Article 3 of the Global Code of Ethics for Tourism: Tourism, A Factor of Sustainable Tourism

1. All the stakeholders in tourism development should safeguard the natural environment with a view to achieving sound, continuous and sustainable economic growth geared to satisfying equitably the needs and aspirations of present and future generations
2. All forms of tourism development that are conducive to saving rare and precious resources, in particular water and energy, as well as avoiding so far as possible waste production, should be given priority and encouraged by national, regional and local public authorities
3. The staggering in time and space of tourist and visitor flows, particularly those resulting from paid leave and school holidays, and a more even distribution of holidays should be sought so as to reduce the pressure of tourism activity on the environment and enhance its beneficial impact on the tourism industry and the local economy
4. Tourism infrastructure should be designed and tourism activities programmed in such a way as to protect the natural heritage composed of ecosystems and biodiversity and to preserve endangered species of wildlife; the stakeholders in tourism development, and especially professionals, should agree to the imposition of limitations or constraints on their activities when these are exercised in particularly sensitive areas: desert, polar or high mountain regions, coastal areas, tropical forests or wetlands, propitious to the creation of nature reserves or protected areas
5. Nature tourism and ecotourism are recognized as being particularly conducive to enriching and enhancing the standing of tourism, provided they respect the natural heritage and local populations and are in keeping with the carrying capacity of the sites

Source: World Tourism Organization, 1999.

to the codes. Beyond understanding whether codes should be promoted, such research would enable better understanding of whether market-based instruments offered potential for progress, or if only increased legislation could force organisations into changing their preferred decision. Smith and Duffy (2003) suggest that the problem with relying on codes of ethics arises from the tendency of many businesses to interpret publicness (moral openness) solely in terms of public relations ad publicity (self-serving).

Beyond the ability to influence the direction of the tourism industry through the manipulation of tools available, we need tourism managers to be honest and explicit about the choices they are making. An understanding of ethics shows us that it is not 'wrong' to act in the belief of producing greater benefits to a greater number of people if this entails cost to some. Similarly, acting in a manner that favours man over the environment is in concordance with a considerable body of opinion and this reasoning should not be concealed. Yet, making these decision-making processes explicit will force a further evaluation of the merits of the chosen course of action. As such, continuing along a previous path without consideration will not be possible; instead decisions will necessarily become more appropriate for their constant reevaluation.

Along with the need for employees to be more explicit in their decision-making approach, the effect of organisational roles has been central to much of the debate over promoting corporate and social responsibility. This approach considers that in addition to the characteristics of the individual concerned, their decisions are functions of their roles within an organisation. The model developed by Steed, Worrell, and Garner-Steed, (1990) demonstrates the range of factors believed to impinge on the decision made by an employee (Figure 13.1). They propose that individual factors (both personality and socialisation), ethical philosophy and ideology, external forces, and organisational factors will all have an influence on ethical decision making.

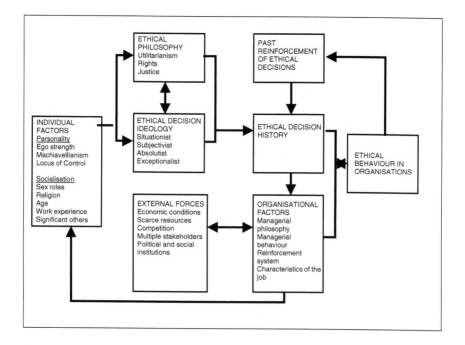

Figure 13.1: Forces influencing ethical decision making in an organisation.

Source: Adapted from Steed, Worrell, and Garner-Steed, 1990.

Table 13.2   Standards of Ethical Behaviour Applied to the Environmental Impact of Business Decisions

Standard	Behaviour
Theoretical standard	The firm will consider the environmental impact of all decisions
Practical standard	The firm will consider the environmental impact of all decisions that may significantly affect the environment
Currently attainable standard	The firm will consider the significant environmental impact of all production decisions
Basic standard	The firm will consider the legality of its decisions as they relate to existing environmental laws

Raiborn and Payne (1990) suggest exploring the outcome of the organisation's decisions and assessing them according to their degree of adherence to the four values of justice, integrity, competence, and utility. Such an approach applied in a tourism context would provide valuable data to understand what makes one organisation's approach more ethical than another and so enable the development of best practice. Table 13.2 shows how an organisation's decisions could be categorised and placed within a hierarchy, which has as its top the most moral behaviour ('theoretical standard') and ends with behaviour that is legally acceptable ('basic standard').

Producing such a framework to assess the ethicality of decisions made by tourism organisations would enable the relationship to be tested between the ethical behaviour of each organisation and independent variables. These independent variables would include the factors identified by Steed, Worrell, and Garner-Steed (1990), plus the effect of the existence of tools such as an ethical code, the existence of an ethical champion within the organisation, the severity of punishment for breaching legislation, and potentially a range of other tools.

In addition, the types of ethical dilemmas faced by tourism managers could be classified and a list of ethical principles proposed for tourism. Such principles have been developed for business in general (Josephson, 1988) and for specific fields such as marketing (Gaski, 1999) and hospitality (Hall, 1992a; Jaszay, 2002) but not for the discipline of tourism. A list of ethical principles in tourism would form a basis for ethical decision making in that field and would establish standards or rules of behaviour (the dominant ethical paradigm) within which a future tourism manager should function. Managers could be asked to describe an ethical dilemma, giving a background to the situation, the ethical choices that they had available, and the actual decision they made. Such an approach may illustrate the main constraint managers felt on their behaviour and so provide an illustration as to how to most effectively control the direction of the tourism industry.

Understanding Ethical Decision Making in Tourism Students

An outcome of the research described earlier on tourism managers would be a set of ethical scenarios that could be used for education and training purposes. In general, there is no consensus on the extent to which ethics are effectively combined with practical education in curricula, although most agree that such efforts are an important and necessary component of education (Hultsman, 1995). As we are aware, many organisations and sections of society are concerned with ethical behaviour, and the education sector is no exception.

Much research has been conducted by other subject disciplines on the level of ethics displayed by students and the way students reach decisions on ethical issues. However, research has not identified where tourism students can be positioned and how they make decisions. The tourism industry has grown to become the world's largest industry because of, or in spite of, the decisions made by managers, many of whom have not had any training in ethical decision making (World Tourism Organization, 2002). The increase in numbers of students studying tourism at university indicates that tourism managers of the future will receive a university level education, most likely at an age of continuing moral development (Piaget, 1975). Writing prophetically about the need for the accountancy industry to offer improved ethical training to its students, Cohen, Pant, and Sharp comment, 'An important role of university and early professional training is to provide professionals with the ability to recognize the ethical issues in the course of their practice, to define the norms, principles and values related to the situation, to identify alternative choices and to decide on the most appropriate course of action when such dilemmas are encountered' (2001). Whitney (1989) writing about the hotel and hospitality industries writes similarly, 'If we educators fail to address ethics in our classes we leave an important part of student education untouched. We are preparing them incompletely for careers in an industry which is becoming increasingly sensitive to ethical issues.'

Using case studies or ethical scenarios has been advocated as the most useful way of examining ethical issues and teaching ethical concepts (Hultsman, 1995; Stevens, 2001). So a useful research project would be to test the ethical dilemmas on tourism students worldwide. This would add to the limited research related to the cultural differences and similarities of ethical perspectives and decision approaches of students (Okleshen and Hoyt, 1996). The same dilemmas could be presented to tourism managers to compare and contrast responses for the two groups. Ethical responses can be examined relative to the influence of age, experience, and gender in moral and ethical development. Previous studies tend to indicate that managers have higher ethical values than students (Carroll, 1975; Freedman and Bartholomew, 1991). Indeed, in 1999, 24 students in a business ethics course at San Diego State University were dismissed from the class and put on academic probation for cheating. In response to such incidents, many schools are emphasising the need for future managers to receive ethical training. The results of greater research into the ethical positioning of tourism students and tourism managers might indicate there is a need for a discrete module on tourism ethics in the way that there are appropriate modules on ethics for would-be lawyers, doctors, accountants, and journalists.

A final by-product of testing these ethical dilemmas on students would be a standard framework for making ethical decisions specific to the tourism industry. As yet, no such framework exists and we are left to consider the appropriateness of ethical theories that have been found to be useful for other industries. It has been suggested that the teleological systems might have more application in the tourism industry because managers can be taught to compare outcomes to the various stakeholders for each possible decision and select the decision that has the best outcomes (Carroll, 1989; Khan and McCleary, 1996). Research in the area of management ethics has underscored the value of a teleological approach to ethics as a means by which to educate and learn through an understanding of the consequences of one's actions (Malloy and Fennell, 1998). Some of the models proposed for analysing ethical dilemmas are summarised in Table 13.3 and each supports a teleological approach, but the value of these to the tourism industry remains unknown.

Conclusion

Returning to our original example in Banff National Park, calling for more environmental protection and restrictions on tourism is asking for a change in environmental ethic to one where the rights of humans are placed on a more even footing with nature and with the assignment of rights to the environment. Tourism is likely to be one of the first battlegrounds where this paradigmatic shift occurs because of the extrinsic benefits of a pristine environment to the tourism industry. As such, the rights of the environment can become protected in law, as within a national park,

Table 13.3   Existing Approaches to Analysing Ethical Dilemmas

Jaszay's ethics analysis model (2002)	Blanchard and Peale's quick 'ethics check' (1988)	Hall's five-step test for ethics (1992b)
What are we trying to accomplish?	Is it legal? Will I be violating either civil law or company policy?	Is the decision legal? Is the decision fair? Does the decision hurt anyone? Have I been honest with those affected? Can I live with my decision?
Is what we are trying to accomplish ethical?		
Where do our loyalties belong?	Is it balanced? Is it fair to all concerned in the short term as well as the long term? Does it promote win-win relationships?	
Who are the stakeholders who will be affected by our decision?		
What are our decision options? (Is there a better alternative?)	How will it make me feel about myself? Will it make me proud? Would I feel good if my decision were published in the newspaper?	
Are there any ethical principles that might be violated by any of the options?	Would I feel good if my family knew about it?	
What are the consequences (positive and negative) to all the stakeholders for each option?		

and so nature's value would appear to be more intrinsic. Highly developed countries like Canada are likely to see more pressure to assign rights to nature because residents are more affluent and so become more concerned with aesthetic issues. But the movement for environmental protection is unlikely to proceed in less developed countries where issues of survival are more pressing. The shift to the assignments of rights of existence to nature can come only when humans are sufficiently comfortable within their own existence that they do not feel threatened by, or suffer from, nature being promoted. Although it may be that many Canadians have reached this position, there are undoubtedly many who do not feel that to limit the tourism industry for the protection of nature at the expense of jobs, income, and so on is a worthwhile trade.

Undoubtedly new understandings will develop as the context for decisions change and so the way we view problems facing us must change. In an increasingly complex world we can question the value of linear thinking, which believes that if button A is pressed, then B will happen. For the tourism industry with its reliance on environments and people, perhaps there is value to incorporating the more nonlinear thinking of ecologists and assuming a more adaptive style of management (Twining-Ward, 2002). There are also those who feel that until the problem is addressed on a global scale, local efforts are peripheral (Wheeller, 1993). Tourism destinations do not exist in spatial isolation, and under a tourism-centric paradigm, resources might be channelled into a destination/region to prevent or address problems, or to expand the tourism product, but the neighbouring regions could bear at least some of the cost without any financial reparation. The counter argument is that the smaller the identifiable region, the easier it is to implement strategies sustainable at that level. Thus, the Rio summit gave rise to Agenda 21 and to Local Agenda 21, which stressed the 'think global, act local' mantra.

Clearly this debate will continue. In an economically fractured society the debate will be lengthy as the richest members of society reach a point where they are able to afford to trade economic well being for environmental rights long before the poorest members of society are able to afford this luxury. As people's view of the world changes, so our understanding of sustainable tourism must change. Yet understanding the outcomes of this thought process is not sufficient, we must begin to understand how difficult decisions are made. By informing the managers of today and tomorrow about how they are making decisions then if or when we are ready to move to a new environmental ethic, the basis on which the decision is reached, will be clearly understood.

References

Bartelmus, P. 1994. Environment, Growth and Development: The Concepts and Strategies of Sustainability. London: Routledge.

Blanchard, K., and N. V. Peale. 1988. The Power of Ethical Management. New York: William Morrow.

Bowie, N. 2001. The Role of Business Ethics: Where Next? Is There a Role for Academics? *Business Ethics: A European Review* 10(4): 288–293.

Britton, S. G. 1982. Tourism and Underdevelopment in Fiji. Australian National University: Development Studies Centre.

Bryden, J. M. 1973. Tourism and Development: A Case Study of the Commonwealth Caribbean. Cambridge: Cambridge University Press.

Budowski, G. 1976. Tourism and Conservation: Conflict, Coexistence or Symbiosis? *Environmental Conservation* 3: 27–31.

Butler, R. 1990. Alternative Tourism—Pious Hope or Trojan Horse? *Journal of Travel Research* 28(3): 40–45.

———. 1993. Tourism—An Evolutionary Perspective. In *Tourism and Sustainable Development: Monitoring, Planning, Managing. Department of Geography Publication 37.* eds. R. W. Butler, J. G. Nelson, and G. Wall. Waterloo: University of Waterloo.

Carroll, A. B. 1975. Managerial Ethics: A Post-Watergate View. *Business Horizons* xviii(2): 75–80.

——. 1989. *Business and Society: Ethics and Stakeholder Management.* Cincinnati, Ohio: South-Western Publishing Co.

Carson, R. 1966. *The Silent Spring.* London: Penguin.

Cleek M. A., and S. L. Leonard. 1998. Can Corporate Codes of Ethics Influence Behaviour? *Journal of Business Ethics* 17(6): 619–630.

Cohen, E. 1972. Towards a Sociology of International Tourism. *Social Research* 39: 164–182.

——. 1978. The Impact of Tourism on the Physical Environment. *Annals of Tourism Research* 5(2): 215–237.

Cohen J. R., L. W. Pant, and D. J. Sharp. 2001. An Examination of Differences in Ethical Decision-Making Between Canadian Business Students and Accounting Professionals. *Journal of Business Ethics* 30(4): 319–336.

Craik, J. 1995. Are There Cultural Limits to Tourism? *Journal of Sustainable Tourism* 3(2): 87–98.

DeKadt, E. 1979. *Tourism—To Development?* Oxford: Oxford University Press.

Doxey, G. V. 1975. When Enough's Enough: The Natives are Restless in Old Niagara. *Heritage Canada* 2(2): 26–27.

Ferrell, O. C., and S. J. Skinner. 1988. Ethical Behaviour and Bureaucratic Structure in Marketing Research Organizations. *Journal of Marketing Research* 25: 103–109.

Freedman, A. M., and P. S. Bartholomew. 1991. Age/Experience and Gender as Factors in Ethical Development of Hospitality Managers and Students. *Hospitality Research Journal* 14(2): 1–10.

Gaski, J. F. 1999. Does Marketing Ethics Really Have Anything to Say. *Journal of Business Ethics* 18(3): 315–334.

Godfrey, K. 1998. Attitudes Towards Sustainable Tourism in the UK: A View From Local Government. *Tourism Management* 19(3): 213–224.

Hall, S. J. ed. 1992a. *Ethics in Hospitality Management.* East Lansing, Mich.: Educational Institute of the American Hotel and Motel Association.

Hall, S. J. 1992b. The Emergence of Ethics in Quality. In *Ethics in Hospitality Management: A Book of Readings.* ed. S. J. Hall. East Lansing, Mich.: Educational Institute of the American Hotel and Motel Association.

Healey, P., and T. Shaw. 1994. Changing Meanings of 'Environment' in the British Planning System. *Transaction of the Institute of British Geographers* 19: 425–438.

Holden, A. 2003. In Need of a New Environmental Ethic for Tourism? *Annals of Tourism Research* 30(1): 94–108.

Huberman-Arnold, D., and K. Arnold. 2001. Commerce with a Conscience: Corporate Control and Academic Investment. *Business Ethics: A European Review* 10(4): 294–301.

Hultsman, J. 1995. Just Tourism: An Ethical Framework. *Annals of Tourism Research* 22(3): 553–567.

Hunter, C. 1995. On the Need to Re-conceptualise Sustainable Tourism Development. *Journal of Sustainable Tourism* 3(3): 155–165.

Jafari, J. 1989. An English Language Literature Review. In *Tourism as a Factor of Change: A Socio-Cultural Study.* ed. J. Bystranowski. Vienna: Centre for Research and Documentation in Social Sciences.

Jaszay, C. 2002. Teaching Ethics in Hospitality Programs. *Journal of Hospitality & Tourism Education* 14(3): 57–63.

Josephson, M. 1988. Teaching Ethical Decision Making and Principled Reasoning, Ethics: Easier Said Than Done. Winter. 27–33.

Kaynama, A., A. King, and L. W. Smith. 1996. The Impact of a Shift in Organizational Role on Ethical Perceptions: A Comparative Study. *Journal of Business Ethics* 15(5): 581–590.

Khan, M. M., and K. W. McCleary. 1996. A Proposed Model for Teaching Ethics in Hospitality. *Hospitality & Tourism Educator* 8(4): 7–11.

Lanfant, M., and N. H. Graburn. 1992. International Tourism Reconsidered. The Principle of the Alternative. In *Tourism Alternatives: Potential and Problems in the Development of Tourism*. ed. V. Smith. Philadelphia: University of Pennsylvania Press.

MacCannell, D. 1976. *The Tourist: A New Theory of the Leisure Class.* London: Macmillan Press.

Malloy, D. C., and D. A. Fennell. 1998. Codes of Ethics and Tourism: An Exploratory Content Analysis. *Tourism Management* 19(5): 453–461.

McElroy, J. L., and K. de Albuquerque. 1996. Sustainable Alternatives to Insular Mass Tourism: Recent Theory and Practice. In *Sustainable Tourism in Islands and Small States: Issues and Policies*. eds. L. Briguglio, et al. London: Pinter.

Moore, W. E. 1970. *The Professions: Roles and Rules.* New York: Russell Sage Foundation.

Okleshen, M., and R. Hoyt. 1996. A Cross Cultural Comparison of Ethical Perspectives and Decision Approaches of Business Students: United States of America Versus New Zealand. *Journal of Business Ethics* 15(5): 537–549.

Piaget, J. 1975. The Moral Judgement of a Child. In *Social Behaviour and Experience*. eds. H. Brown and R. Stevens. Buckingham, U.K. Milton Keynes: Open University Press.

Plog, S. 1974. Why Destinations Areas Rise and Fall in Popularity. *Cornell Hotel and Administration Quarterly* 14(4): 4, 55–58.

Przeclawski, K. 1997. Deontology of Tourism. In *Tourism Development: Environmental and Community Issues*. eds. C. Cooper and S. Wanhill. Chichester, U.K. John Wiley and Sons.

Raiborn, C. A., and D. Payne. 1990. Corporate Codes of Conduct: A Collective Conscience and Continuum. *Journal of Business Ethics* 9: 879–889.

Rondinelli, D. A., and M. A. Berry. 2000. Environmental Citizenship in Multinational Corporations: Social Responsibility and Sustainable Development. *European Management Journal* 18(1): 70–84.

Smith, M., and E. Duffy. 2003. *The Ethics of Human Development.* London: Routledge.

Smith, V. L., and W. R. Eadington. 1992. *Tourism Alternatives: Potentials and Problems in the Development of Tourism*. Philadelphia: University of Pennsylvania Press.

Stankovic, S. M. 1979. A Contribution to the Knowledge of the Protection of Nature and Tourism. *Tourist Review* 34(3): 24–26.

Steed, E., D. Worrell, and J. Garner-Stead. 1990. An Integrative Model for Understanding and Managing Ethical Behaviour in Business Organisations. *Journal of Business Ethics* 9: 233–242.

Stevens, B. 2001. Hospitality Ethics: Responses from Human Resource Directors and Students to Seven Ethical Scenarios. *Journal of Business Ethics* 30(3): 233–242.

Tribe, J. 2002. Education for Ethical Tourism Action. *Journal of Sustainable Tourism* 10(4): 309–324.

Turner, L., and J. Ash. 1975. *The Golden Hordes: International Tourism and the Leisure Periphery.* London: Constable.

Twining-Ward, L. 2002. Monitoring Sustainable Tourism Development: A Comprehensive, Stakeholder-Driven, Adaptive Approach. PhD dissertation. University of Surrey.

Wheeller, B. 1993. Sustaining the Ego. *Journal of Sustainable Tourism* 1(2): 121–129.

Whitney, D. L. 1989. The Ethical Orientations of Hotel Managers and Hospitality Students: Implications for Industry, Education, and Youthful Careers. *Hospitality Education and Research Journal* 13(3): 187–192.

World Tourism Organization. 1999. Approval of the Global Code of Ethics for Tourism, <www.world-tourism.org/projects/ethics/principles.htm>. Accessed April 11, 2003.

——. 2002. Tourism Highlights. <http://www.world-tourism.org>. Accessed September 3, 2003.

Part Four

Places and Products: Marketing and Consumer Issues

Introduction

The provision of high-quality, creative, relevant and meaningful experiences are the most critical challenge facing the visitor industry today. Consumer perceptions concerning the quality of their own individual tourism experiences and the actual quality of the tourist resource are central issues in tourism management. Leisure destinations offer products that have gotten stale and too commercial, resulting in declines in tourist arrivals. In addition, all tourism organizations are in the service business, but only those organizations that focus on service excellence as the cornerstone of their operations will be sustained.

Product development specialists in marketing departments of consumer companies often discuss the six magic words that define their quest, i.e., *Find a need and fill it.* **Plog** (Chapter 14) suggests that in a mature market such as travel, a variant of this phrase is required. Specifically, the goal would be to *Find a segment and target it.* The formula for success is two sided—the segment must be clearly identified and the travel product(s) offered must focus on their travel interests.

The task of targeting segments has become increasingly difficult over time since travel is now a mature industry with all of its associated problems of stiff competition, multiple competitors in similar categories, pricing pressure and slower growth. The search for new segments has become more prominent in the travel industry in recent years, offering proof of the increasing maturity of the industry.

The author identifies and reviews a number of travel segments in the chapter that are commonly discussed among travel suppliers, travel agencies and the travel media. He describes in some detail those elements that constitute travel segments including market size, travel patterns, spending on leisure travel, vacation leisure activities, motivations for travel, and both demographics and psychographics. However, he warns that these travel segments are obviously not all inclusive. He states that the potential for new groupings is relatively unlimited, but market size should always be a consideration.

Taylor and **Chesworth** (Chapter 15) question the overemphasis or principal concern tourism has placed on consumption rather than on the consumer. Little systematic attention has been directed toward gaining a greater understanding of the tourist and his participation patterns and travel habits. The concept of styles of travel may be useful in developing a body of knowledge about tourism consumers. Styles of travel is defined as the way people perceive, organize and execute travel. Two types of information are important when measuring styles of travel: the incidence of travel and the way people think about the travel they take.

In addition to identifying travel styles, this chapter reflects the impact of global events on tourism such as terrorism, economic recession, human and animal disease outbreaks, and the invasion of Iraq. Each of these events has had a major impact on the propensity to travel as well as individual's travel styles.

The use of both travel incidence and travel style data can provide a greater understanding of international tourism, and when these two data sets are examined at the same time, the fact of change will be accompanied by the direction of change. The implications of such data should not be overlooked as a means of improving knowledge of both the markets and the opportunities for increased consumer satisfaction.

Tourist typologies have primarily resulted from consumer segmentation marketing studies conducted during the 1970's which used among other variables, lifestyle criteria. According to **Dolnicar** (Chapter 16), the logical starting point is the insight that consumers are heterogeneous, differing in many respects including their product preferences. The chapter discusses and illustrates a number of different approaches taken in empirical tourism market segmentation, and raises conceptual, practical and methodological problems in this context.

Although market segmentation in tourism has become a common tool in strategic marketing, there remains many unresolved issues that may cause segmentation solutions to be anything between patently absurd to strategically invaluable. The author poses a series of questions that managers should ask when attempting to understand the market and the consumer.

Faulkner (Chapter 17) argues that because tourism demand is highly discretionary, a strategic approach to tourism marketing is essential for long-term effectiveness. The current international preoccupation with advertising among tourism promotion agencies may well be counter productive to sustained visitor growth and can progressively undermine any competitive tourism advantage currently enjoyed by a destination area.

Focusing on planning and development in Australia, the author emphasizes that the factors influencing demand for tourism are highly dynamic and he discusses a strategic approach to marketing Australian tourism as being essential to long-term effectiveness.

Finally, **Morgan** (Chapter 18) looks at the future of established seaside tourist resorts, especially those along the Mediterranean coast. He argues that most such resorts are homogeneous, and as such have begun to lose some of their appeal to the public, resulting in a loss of market share. As the decline stage in the product lifecycle concept nears since they are no longer in favor with the travelling public, established resorts face the decision to either let their facilities die gradually, or to somehow rejuvenate these aging resources. He considers the new markets open to established resorts, while warning of the ever increasing, discriminating tourist.

The author provides a brief history of seaside resorts and describes the conditions that have led them to first be established, then become homogeneous. Changing economic and demographic factors as well as product maturity have influenced tourists holiday decisions. The adoption curve is used to illustrate how such facilities have also fallen out of fashion since, as they no longer attract either innovators or allocentrics, the general public begin to look for other destination options.

The adoption curve as related to tourist destinations is presented and an example is given that indicates how Mediterranean beach resorts have ceased to attract 'innovators' and allocentric tourists because they become dissatisfied and move on. As a means of helping overcome this problem, a tourist or eco-tax strategy to provide sufficient financial resources for government to help offset the impact of tourism on the environment is presented. The controversial nature of such a tax is discussed and the author suggests a number of unresolved questions on such a scheme.

14 Targeting segments: more important than ever in the travel industry

Stanley C. Plog, Ph.D.

Perspective

By now, just about everyone who earns a living in travel knows that its constant growth since the end of World War II has vaulted it into the lofty position as the largest industry in the world. And it has occupied that spot for several years (Scott, 2000). Because it continues on an upward climb, except for temporary market disruptions (war, regional terrorism, disease outbreaks, and a soft economy), it should be able to make that claim for at least most of the current decade. Its size exceeds the fields of health services, technology, agriculture, automotive, and a number of other major industry categories that, at one time, were significantly larger. When this author completed his first travel study in the late 1960s, the industry placed from eighth to twelfth in size, depending on how it was measured (Behavior Science Corporation/BASICO, 1967). By the mid 1990s, it was sometimes referred to as the largest industry when entertainment was included as part of a broader *travel and entertainment* category. That is no longer required. Travel claims the top spot without including expenditures for movies, dining out (when not travelling), and related items.

The amazing growth of travel has resulted in another characteristic that is not recognised as often. In spite of its still bright future, it has become a mature industry. That fact has consequences for those intent on choosing it as a career or hoping to start a new business venture. Mature industries have certain characteristics in common. These include:

1. *Slower growth*: New industries, or those still in their early stages, typically enjoy extraordinarily high growth rates. That growth drops dramatically as the industry saturates the market and fewer new customers can be identified. An example of this is technology (software and computers). At one time, it grew at five times the rate of the gross domestic product (GDP) of the United States. Now the best it can hope for in the future under the best of circumstances is double the rate of the GDP, according to Carly Fiorina, CEO of Hewlett-Packard (*Forbes*, 2003). When personal computers became affordable for the home market, new software manufacturers often doubled or tripled revenues each year. Growth would typically settle down to still phenomenal rates of 50 percent or more each year for these companies, but that curve also declined in time. Now many in the technology industry feel glad if they can forecast more than single digit revenue growth in their updated five-year plans, whereas other companies falter and some go out of business.

    Because of the requirement for huge investments in infrastructure development (airports, highways, hotels, support services, etc.), travel could never hope to reach the lofty growth levels of some industries. However, developing countries that offer a good product can expect early annual increases in tourism of up to 20 percent. Most mature destinations around the world, in contrast, will enjoy no more than strong single digit increases (6 percent to 8 percent) year over year, and more likely about one-half that amount in time. Travel has matured and this fact must play into the strategies of all travel-related companies.

2. *Multiple competitors in similar categories*: Lofty growth rates become an open invitation for new entrants to join the fray. More and more people want to be part of the action. New companies appear regularly, some with strong financial backing. Travel shows those characteristics. For a period of time, startup airlines appeared by the dozens in the United States, and to a lesser degree in Europe and elsewhere in the world. This occurred during the late 1970s and into the 1990s. Each identified an underserved market, the initial investors thought, but the vast majority failed. They did not foresee the challenges facing new competitors in a mature industry. The formation of new tour and travel package companies followed an even more vigorous path. But most don't recognise the difficulties of facing off against well-established, financially stable, large tour operators who are able to adapt to a changing competitive environment. Few of these start ups manage to become profitable or financially solvent. CEOs of hotel chains not infrequently get invitations to form new hotel companies and, in spite of hotel companies gobbling up competitors, a proliferation of brands has occurred. But, again, few made themselves into

recognisable, preferred brands. All of this leads to a greater number of players in every segment of the travel industry. That trend will continue, but on at a slower pace. This author has counselled with a number of start-up travel suppliers, and many have not listened to cautionary advice because their enthusiasm blinds them to the realities of the marketplace.

3. *Pricing pressure*: Competition leads to an obvious consequence— pricing pressure. In order to grow a company, or protect market share when competition increases, established companies drop their prices. For a time after deregulation of the U.S. airline industry in 1978, major carriers were able to protect their well-honed variable pricing models (charge business travellers more than leisure travellers) and make strong profits. However, a few discount airlines and start-up carriers ultimately discovered a new formula for success. The new kids on the block have managed not only to survive but to grow and achieve greater profitability than the high cost major airlines. In the United States, Southwest, Jet Blue, Air Tran, ATA, and a couple of other low-cost, low-fare airlines will soon account for about 40 percent of market share. Their growth has been a greater contributor to the huge losses and bankruptcy filings of major airlines early in the twenty-first century than the September 11, 2001, terrorist attacks on the New York World Trade Center and the Pentagon, or the economic downturn that began in the late 1990s and continued into late 2003. Almost every segment of the travel industry throughout the world now feels strong pressure to reduce costs in order to remain competitive in a fast changing world.

4. *Increased difficulty for new entrants*: In new emerging industries that are experiencing rapid growth, there's room for almost everyone, whether the ideas are sound or half-baked. Inefficient operators can usually get by because of high demand. But, as competition increases, even good ideas fall victim to marketplace vagaries because major competitors answer new challenges with a vengeance by deep discounting or offering added value services. Young start-ups cannot match these offers because they lack deep financial pockets. Travel increasingly fits this model. Most parts of the industry have major players that will try to snuff out competition before it can get a foothold and grow into a significant threat.

5. *A search for segments*: As growth becomes more problematic, companies that originally served the broad market now begin to search for new segments that may have been overlooked previously. New entrants especially must concentrate on ferreting out niches that large competitors have ignored. In either case, the company that first identifies a viable segment or picks up on a growing trend hopes to become a market leader in its specialty area and assume a position of

leadership and dominance. If the market segment turns out to be a winner, then a company will try to expand the segment or identify other niches to build an even bigger base for company growth. Although the concept of a segment implies a small group, many newly identified target groups can be quite large in size. They simply have not been identified before.

The search for new segments has become more prominent in the travel industry in recent years, offering proof of the increasing maturity of the industry. This discussion reviews six segments that are commonly discussed among travel suppliers, travel agencies, and travel media as offering good opportunities for growth and profits. The market size, travel patterns, spending on leisure travel, activities pursued while on vacations, motivations for travel, demographics, and psychographics for each group are described in material that follows. The review concludes with a summary profile of each segment to aid in a conceptual understanding of how best to target each group. And the segments are compared with trends and patterns exhibited by the travel market in general to show how they differ from the average. The segments reviewed include:

- Adventure travellers,
- Budget travellers,
- Family travellers,
- Gay travellers,
- Luxury travellers, and
- Baby boomer generation.

Not included in this analysis are travel segments related to personal sports, such as golfers, tennis players, downhill skiers, and cross country skiers. These segments are reviewed in a recently completed book by the author on marketing leisure travel (Plog, 2004). Without going into detail, travel agencies and travel packagers that serve golfers and downhill skiers can make good money. Those that focus on tennis players and cross country skiers will have difficulty. Quite obvious in what has been presented so far is that this discussion concentrates on the leisure market. Business travel has many common attributes throughout the world and does not have the growth potential of the leisure market. Businesses cut back on travel during the economic downturn in the early part of the twenty-first century and have discovered new, acceptable substitutes for some portions of corporate travel. And how important is leisure travel? In almost every nation, it dominates travel patterns. In the United States, it comprises 72 percent of all trips; business travel only 28 percent (NFO/Plog, 2003).

Source of Data

Information supporting the concepts presented in this chapter comes from the 2003 American Traveler Survey (ATS). ATS is a very large, annual survey conducted by NFO/Plog Research (more than 10,000 completed surveys) since 1995. Based on a random sample of all U.S. households, it collects extensive data on a broad range of leisure and business travel patterns, allowing the opportunity to observe trends over time. Although it focusses on the U.S. market, the trends it discovers are mirrored in many developed countries throughout the world. The author no longer has a direct association with Plog Research (the company was acquired by NFO Worldwide in 1996) but continues to cooperate with its research staff on various matters. Data are collected from the ongoing household panel of nearly 2 million households developed by Plog Research's parent company, NFO Worldwide. The panel is structured to be representative of all U.S. households by matching current census criteria quite exactly.

Except for the baby boomer group, the segments reviewed in this article are self-defined by ATS survey participants. In the survey, respondents identified the segments that apply to them as travellers. This approach allows overlap between segments in a manner that reflects the marketplace. Thus, a budget traveller could also qualify as an adventure traveller, or a family traveller, and/or a gay traveller. For this reason, totals across the segments add to more than 100 percent. Budget and luxury groups tend not to overlap, however. The baby boomer segment is defined by age (i.e., anyone born between the years 1946 and 1964). Allowing overlap also tends to wash out potential differences between groups because the same people appear in more than one category. In spite of that fact, true differences emerge between the groups, as will be seen. Also, the adventure travel segment really consists of two markets—soft adventure and hard adventure—both of which primarily take place outdoors. Hard adventure trips usually involve more vigorous activity, with more of the trip planned and experienced personally without support from a travel provider. And there could be some degree of personal risk of injury. Soft adventure is less physically active, usually includes more support services (such as a van to pick up straggling cyclists on a tour of the fall colors in New England, hotel accommodations at night instead of sleeping in a bedroll, etc.). However, because the two groups tend to overlap to a considerable degree (hard adventure travellers also take many soft trips), the two groups are combined into a single segment for purposes of this analysis. Based on these criteria, the size of each segment in the adult travel marketplace is:

- Adventure travellers: 15 percent,
- Budget travellers: 41 percent,

- Family travellers: 55 percent,
- Gay travellers: 2 percent,
- Luxury travellers: 10 percent, and
- Baby boomers: 51 percent.

The two dominant segments, family travel and baby boomers, hardly seem like segments because of their size. However, both receive considerable attention among travel marketers for a couple of reasons. Boomers travel for leisure far more than their parents did a generation ago. With that segment continuing to grow during the current decade, the question arises about whether this market is as good as other smaller specialty niches. That topic is addressed in this article. The viability of the family market is a subject of continuing debate but a number of professionals suggest that it has strong potential for increased growth and development. For example, magazines that target families work hard at presenting the case that family travel is a large and growing market in order to attract travel advertisers. But, with families facing large financial commitments and parents not yet at their earnings peaks, the question remains as to whether it is a profitable segment for most travel providers. The remaining segments truly represent smaller segments (niches). Luxury travellers have long been recognised as good clients. They provide high profit margins, but the segment's limited size means that only a few in the travel business can serve their needs. The gay market has received a considerable amount of attention over the recent couple of years because of greater acceptance of gays in all walks of life. Current offerings include gay cruises, tours, resorts, and a range of packages. Although small in size, is it worth the effort for selected companies to consider targeting this group? Whatever segment is considered, the basic questions remain the same for any company wanting to expand its reach into specialty markets. Which groups do they believe they can reach effectively through marketing and promotion programmes, and which of these groups can provide opportunities for growth and profitability? This discussion addresses the topic of the characteristics and marketing viability of each of the groups.

Segment Travel Patterns

A first indication of differences in travel characteristics can be seen in Table 14.1. In all data presented here, a trip is defined as 'requiring an overnight stay.' It shows the percentage who have taken domestic and international trips in the past 12 months, and the percentage planning trips within three years. Several points are obvious in the chart.

Table 14.1   Travel Characteristics (percentage visited in last 12 months; plan trip in next 3 years)

Type of Trip	Total	Adventure Travellers	Budget Travellers	Family Travellers	Gay Travellers	Luxury Travellers	Baby Boomers
Visited U.S. Destination	71	81	80	79	71	86	76
Visited Int'l Destination	14	26	17	14	21	32	16
Planning U.S. Trip	65	79	75	73	77	81	69
Planning Int'l Trip	25	46	32	26	49	49	28

- The majority of all segments travel domestically, but with significant differences. Gays equal the average for the total population, whereas all other groups exceed it. International travel shows more dramatic differences, with the luxury market exceeding all others (as would be expected) and adventure travellers in second place. Note that gays demonstrate a pattern of strong increased interest in future domestic trips, and an even more dramatic increase in planning future international trips. This market, small as it may be, shows strong potential for growth.
- The baby boomer market is considered to be golden by most professionals in the travel field. Its size, propensity to travel, and the fact that populations in developed countries around the world continue to age, place it high on most travel marketers' lists of groups they want to attract. However, it measures only slightly above averages for the total population on the characteristics measured (i.e., visits to domestic and international destinations and planned trips).
- Budget travellers, surprisingly, take more trips domestically and internationally than the population as a whole, and are also planning more future trips. In contrast, the family market concentrates more on domestic travel and measures at average for international travel.

The patterns noted here will, to some extent, continue as other information is presented on their travel habits and motivations.

Table 14.2 provides specific information about the characteristics of the most recent leisure trip. Note that:

- The luxury market, as would be expected, leads on all characteristics—amount spent in total, per diem expenditures, number of nights away, and number of activities on the trip.

Table 14.2   Characteristics of Last Trip

Characteristic	Total	Adventure Travellers	Budget Travellers	Family Travellers	Gay Travellers	Luxury Travellers	Baby Boomers
Nights Away	6.4	7.3	5.9	6.4	6.2	7.6	5.6
Amount Spent/ Last Trip	$1788	$2236	$1640	$1764	$1758	$3547	$1919
Amount Spent per Day	$279	$306	$278	$276	$284	$467	$343
No. of Activities on Trip	4.7	6.8	5.0	4.8	6.8	7.5	4.9

- Adventure travellers place a strong second, however, on most characteristics, spending more than average and taking relatively longer trips (nights away).
- The baby boomer market stands out in an important way. It spends fewer nights away from home than average, but its per diem expenditures measure second only to the luxury market. Thus, boomers truly offer good opportunities for travel providers because of the size of the market (51 percent of total travellers) and the amount they spend when travelling. That market will continue to grow in importance during the next decade. The Travel Industry Association estimates that boomers will have '$2 trillion in buying power by 2007' in the United States (*Los Angeles Times*, 2003).

The number of trips by transportation mode follows a similar pattern, as can be seen in Table 14.3. Luxury travellers take the most trips, whether by air or car, followed by adventure travellers. But Table 14.3 also points out that gays tend to be heavier air travel users, an important point in considering the value of any segment. Those who travel by air also rent more hotel rooms because of fewer visits to friends and relatives; sign up for more rental cars; and book more packages, tours, and cruises. The family travel market measures lowest compared with other segments on total trips (along with boomers), and much lighter on air travel (also along with boomers). Families simply cannot afford as much air travel because of the need to buy an average of four air tickets, not two, and their continuing financial obligations from raising their children.

Another way to determine the relative value of a segment is to examine the degree to which its trip taking is spread throughout the year, rather than concentrating on the most heavily travelled summer months. The desired goal for most travel providers should be to serve niches that travel almost as frequently in the fall and spring as they do in the summer. And, if they also take frequent trips during winter months, that provides a

Table 14.3 Number of Trips (by transportation mode)

Transportation Mode	Total	Adventure Travellers	Budget Travellers	Family Travellers	Gay Travellers	Luxury Travellers	Baby Boomers
Airline (U.S.)	1.9	2.5	2.3	1.9	2.6	2.8	1.9
Car (U.S.)	3.4	4.1	3.4	3.4	3.2	4.4	3.3
Other (U.S.)	0.1	0.1	0.1	0.1	0.1	0.2	0.1
Airline (International)	0.1	0.2	0.1	0.1	0.2	0.3	0.1
Total Trips*	4.0	5.1	4.0	3.9	4.7	5.8	3.9

*Categories do not add cumulatively because multiple modes can be used on the same trip.

Table 14.4 When Taken Trips (percentage in each season)

Season	Total	Adventure Travellers	Budget Travellers	Family Travellers	Gay Travellers	Luxury Travellers	Baby Boomers
Spring (Mar/Apr/May)	50	56	51	50	61	62	51
Summer (Jun/Jul/Aug)	70	72	71	72	70	72	72
Fall (Sep/Oct/Nov)	58	63	59	55	69	65	57
Winter (Dec/Jan/Feb)	46	53	46	45	56	59	44

significant bonus. The reason is obvious. Travel agencies, airlines, tour operators, resorts, and leisure destinations often have difficulty meeting summer demand. During off seasons, however, they frequently beg for customers. Off-season travel has gradually increased over the past four decades as resorts and destinations become more effective in their marketing approaches, but travel providers still have a need to fill empty beds during soft times. Table 14.4 summarises the percentage of each segment that took at least one trip during each of the four seasons of the year. Based on the criteria of spreading their trips more equally throughout the year, the best segments are the luxury group, gay travellers, and those who seek adventure trips, in that order. Seasonal differences in the amount of travelling among these 3 groups vary only by 13 percent to 19 percent. These segments also travel more during the lowest season of the year—the winter months. In contrast, the budget travel market, families, and boomers show a much larger difference in seasonal variation with a 25 to 28 point spread. Thus, these groups can cause problems for travel providers that need to keep their operations going on a year-round basis.

Trip Planning and Booking

Knowing about information sources used by various segments in planning trips can help to target these groups efficiently and effectively. Table 14.5 provides an overview of the primary categories used regularly by each group. It offers some interesting insights. Except for turning to travel agencies, gays use more information sources than any other group. They go to the Internet quite often (75 percent), and also rely heavily on recommendations from friends (62 percent). But they also select various print sources and call toll free numbers regularly. Apparently they are more concerned about ensuring that all facets of their trips meet their needs. Luxury travellers place second in use of multiple sources and the highest percentage of this group (33 percent) turn to travel agents to help them plan trips. Adventure travellers, who tend to vary their vacation experiences from year to year, also rely on travel agents quite often to help them plan their next venture, and they also search the Internet to get answers to many of their questions. Budget and family travellers, along with baby boomers, tend to search less for travel information than those in other niche groups.

In booking trips, the Internet has been growing dramatically in importance in recent years, a fact widely known in the industry. Again, gay travellers lead the pack, with 58 percent booking at least one portion of their trip on the Internet in the past 12 months, compared with 54 percent for luxury travellers, 51 percent for adventure travellers, and less than one-half for the remaining segments (46 percent for boomers, 44 percent for budget travellers, and 41 percent for the family market). As a result, Internet advertising, especially on travel sites, should be considered an important part of most marketing programmes targeting each of these groups.

Table 14.5 Information Sources Used in Trip Planning (percentage using source)

Sources	Total	Adventure Travellers	Budget Travellers	Family Travellers	Gay Travellers	Luxury Travellers	Baby Boomers
Travel Agency	22	27	22	20	25	33	24
Internet/Tech.	45	57	49	45	75	60	52
Friends/Relatives	42	45	44	44	62	43	38
Print Sources	40	50	45	40	52	51	44
Toll Free Numbers	34	37	36	35	49	46	40

Travel Motivations

In targeting these markets, it is important to understand the reasons why each group likes to travel. The ATS questionnaire includes a set of 14 travel-related motivations and asks respondents to select from the list the ones that apply to them. This information appears in Table 14.6. The data indicate that:

- All groups tend to measure above average for the total population (stronger reasons to take trips), as indicated by the fact that they give higher rankings to nearly every item. The highest rated selection in all cases is the 'chance to relax and get rid of stress.' Luxury travellers

Table 14.6 Why I Like to Take Vacations (percentage selecting motive)

Reason	Total	Adventure Travellers	Budget Travellers	Family Travellers	Gay Travellers	Luxury Travellers	Baby Boomers
Get Rid of Stress	70	74	72	72	71	79	76
Time with Spouse	60	59	61	71	40	63	63
Enjoy no Schedules	59	66	63	59	67	71	61
See/Do New Things	56	76	62	55	72	71	57
I Feel Alive/Energetic	33	53	37	33	38	53	33
Gain Perspective	31	47	35	31	43	45	34
Like Being Waited on	24	25	26	25	26	41	25
Have Time for Friends	23	25	23	24	28	22	24
Learn History/Culture	23	36	25	22	31	31	24
Important Part of Life	21	40	23	20	27	43	22
Romantic Time	21	30	23	20	23	39	22
Like Solitude/Isolation	16	21	18	15	22	20	19
Enjoy Being Outdoors	14	22	16	14	12	15	14
Enjoy Physical Tests	10	20	10	9	13	13	10

and adventure seekers in particular select more motivations as important for them than do other groups. An opportunity to spend time with a spouse and the lack of schedules and commitments are next in order of importance for the population, in general. Collectively this configuration points to the fact the most people seek the chance to unwind and recharge their psychic batteries on a leisure trip.

- Adventure travellers stand above other segments in their dual interest in an active vacation experience and in also wanting to participate in culturally related activities. Related to the active portion of their trips, they achieve highest scores on such items as seeking 'a chance to see and do new things,' 'I feel alive and energetic when I travel,' 'I like to be outdoors,' and 'I like to test my physical abilities with an outdoor adventure.' Their strong interest in culturally based experiences is evidenced by wanting to 'gain knowledge of history and of other cultures,' and a desire to experience vacations that help to 'gain perspective on life.'

- Luxury travellers show some similarities to the adventure group in that they also measure well above average on all items except seeking 'time for friends' when travelling. More than any other group, they believe that travel helps to reduce stress that is part of their lives. Although not their top rated item, they rank above other groups in 'It's nice to have others serve and wait on me.' In general they demonstrate a high level of energy, enthusiasm, and interest in the world around them when they travel.

- Gay travellers present a very unique profile. They also place getting rid of stress as their most important motivation, and they demonstrate an interest in the world in which they live by measuring strongly on wanting to see and do new things and in their desire to gain personal perspective when they travel. Having time with friends is more important for them than for other groups or the general population. Interestingly, they also measure highest in seeking a sense of solitude and isolation. Surprisingly, 40 percent express a desire to spend more time with a spouse. This reference may include a current partner or a spouse from an earlier marriage because some had led heterosexual lives at one time.

- The family market, more than other groups, believes that travel provides a welcome opportunity to spend more time with one's spouse. And, as would be expected, they seek the opportunity to get rid of stress, probably caused by the commitments and problems of raising children. But they measure lower than other groups on all items related to a need to gain perspective or to experience an active and energetic vacation—a consistent finding in all of the author's research. On most dimensions, however, they measure at average levels for the total population.

Table 14.7   Importance of Taking Vacations (average on 10-point scale)

	Total	Adventure Travellers	Budget Travellers	Family Travellers	Gay Travellers	Luxury Travellers	Baby Boomers
(10 = Most important)	7.3	8.6	7.9	7.7	7.8	8.7	7.5

- The budget market and boomers lack distinctive profiles, measuring at average levels on most dimensions. Broad-based marketing programmes could capture the attention of both groups.

The ATS also asks respondents to indicate, on a 10-point scale (10 = most important), the importance they place on leisure travel in their lives (Table 14.7). Although all groups rate it strongly (7.5 and above), luxury travellers and the adventure group rank it highest (8.7 and 8.6, respectively). Those who are more price conscious (budget travellers) also score well above average (7.9 versus 7.3 overall), indicating that vacation trips are important to them, even if they spend less and participate in fewer activities than most segments. The gay market and family travellers are close behind in the importance they give (7.8 and 7.7, respectively). Boomers place last at 7.5, only slightly above the importance assigned to travel by the overall market.

Demographic Characteristics

Demographic groupings define most marketing plans. Travel providers generally target higher income groups that have sufficient income to use their services. Age also becomes a factor. Tour companies, cruise lines, resorts, and other travel companies provide products that appeal to certain age groups. The question arises, then, as to how these segments differ on age, income, education, and marital status. It can be assumed that the luxury segment will have the highest income. A common assumption also is that they are older because income usually correlates with career advancement. Table 14.8 provides this summary and also includes a useful measure not commonly included as an analytic tool—household wealth. The greater the assets of a household unit, the more likely they will travel because they have extra resources when needed, independent of annual income. A good case in point is retired couples. Income may be 60 percent or lower than what it was when either or both spouses were employed. However, high equity allows them to pursue leisure travel

Table 14.8   Demographic Characteristics

Characteristic	Total	Adventure Travellers	Budget Travellers	Family Travellers	Gay Travellers	Luxury Travellers	Baby Boomers
Age (Mean)	50	45	46	46	42	46	48
Percentage Male	45	50	42	42	78	45	47
Marital status (%)							
Married	69	61	69	81	18	66	75
Single	14	24	16	7	68	21	11
Wid/Div/Sep	17	15	15	12	14	13	14
Percentage Completed College	30	36	32	32	41	40	34
Household Income (in thousands)	$57	$65	$56	$60	$57	$91	$70
Household Assets (in thousands)	$350	$447	$285	$351	$672	$906	$416

nearly at will. Table 14.8 confirms some expectations but also provides some unanticipated results.

- All segments exceed household income for the population in general. The luxury group, as would be expected, earns considerably more than any other segment. However, boomers, who fall behind on some travel dimensions, place second in income. Thus, they have income to travel even more than they currently do, but their travel motivations are not as strong as some other segments. The budget group measures lowest on income, as would be expected, with gays slightly above them. But a second demographic characteristic makes the gay group a more viable target for marketing programmes than might at first be considered (see next point). The remaining segments place between these groups.
- Marital status follows patterns that would be expected. Overall, about 7 out of 10 persons in the population are married, with the family market having the largest percentage and gays placing well below average, as would be expected. However, a hidden conclusion lies in the data. Because most gays are single, their reported household income is based on one wage earner, not two. But, when they travel, they usually go in pairs. Thus, they would pay for only one-half of the cost of a trip and can actually afford to put more money into their travel arrangements than might be projected on the basis of their income. This conclusion is bolstered to some degree in examining household wealth. Their *household equity is second only to the luxury group*. Considering that their assets also are measured for only one

person, not two, it indicates that they rank well above average (per person) in this table. Gays offer a good potential to increase their travel spending. Adventure travellers place second in household asset value, with the budget group at the bottom.

- Age provides some additional surprises. Little spread exists between the niche groups. Boomers are somewhat older and gays are the youngest. And all are younger than the total population. But *the luxury group is the same age as most segments*, not older as might be expected based on their higher incomes and greater assets. Thus, this is a group that has been financially successful earlier than average in life and is able to enjoy a grander lifestyle when they travel.

Segment Profile Summary

Although this chapter has minimised the amount of data presented, it still can be difficult to come to clear conclusions about the relative viability of the six segments reviewed. This section presents a summary, examining each segment separately. The presentation is from the bottom up (i.e., the least desirable segment to the most desirable). The purpose is to provide additional understanding to travel providers about which groups might fit best in their marketing plans, and what kinds of programmes could offer the greatest appeal.

First, some points for clarification. In making comparisons, it should be remembered that today's populations travel far more often and more internationally than generations preceding them. Leisure travel has grown at a compounded rate since the end of World War II. Thus, all comparisons between groups can be judged only on a relative basis. Segments that rank last in this list of six venture forth more often than the generation that returned home after World War II. As a result, almost all niche markets are viable as targets to some travel providers. Second, targeting segments (niches) generally provides greater opportunities for initial success than launching a programme designed to appeal to the broad market. Established companies typically dominate the mass market making it difficult for new entrants that lack the financial and strategic resources to offer an effective challenge. However, the limited size of some segments also means that it is possible that a diminishing number of potential new customers will occur at some point. Therefore, segment marketing must almost always include plans to add new segments at some point to ensure continued revenue growth. Continued success requires constant adaptation to new challenges and opportunities.

Table 14.9 offers a different kind of summary. It is meant to be conceptual, not statistical. It provides a quick way for the reader to determine

Table 14.9   Segment Summary (conceptual presentation*)

Category	Adventure Travellers	Budget Travellers	Family Travellers	Gay Travellers	Luxury Travellers	Baby Boomers
Market Size (total %)	15	41	55	2	10	51
U.S. Travel (no. trips)	+	+	+	=	++	+
Int'l Travel (no. trips)	++	–	=	–/+**	+++	+
Amount Spent (travel)	++	–	=	+	+++	+
Nights Away from Home	++	–	=	=	++	–
Amount of Air Travel	++	+	=	+	+++	=
Total No. Trips Taken	+	=	=	+	++	=
Travel in 4 Seasons	+	=	=	++	++	=
Use Multiple Information Sources	+	=	=	+++	++	+
Travel Importance (7.3 average)	8.6	7.9	7.7	7.8	8.7	7.5
No. of Travel Motivations	+	=	=	+	=	=
Seek No-Stress Vacations	+	=	=	=	+	+
Household Income	+	=	=	=	+++	++
Household Assets	++	–	=	++	+++	+

*+, ++, and +++ are degrees above average to total population; = is average; – is below average.
**Current international travel for gays is below average; planned future international travel above average.

the viability of each of the segments reviewed. Plus, minus and equal signs compare each group to the average for the population, not to each other. A single plus (+) indicates the group is somewhat above average on that dimension. Double and triple pluses point to even stronger differences. Similarly, minus signs, presented as (–) indicate below average characteristics. And, equal signs (=) indicate average characteristics, again compared with the population at large.

Budget Travellers

No surprises here. It would be expected that budget travellers would rank at the bottom for consideration in marketing plans among the six segments reviewed. With average income, fewer household assets, and average age, they have been less successful in their careers than members of other segments reviewed. So why even consider them as viable targets, especially because few companies with which this author has consulted have ever developed programmes for this group? Well, there are an awful lot of them around. A total of 41 percent identify themselves as budget travellers, a huge slice of the market. And they do travel, even internationally. Their motivations for travel measure high, and they are above average on the number of U.S. trips taken and air travel. The importance of this market can be seen in the number of roadside motels and family restaurant chains that focus on this group.

Like most people, their need for vacations rests on the desire to get away from daily stress, avoid schedules, and spend more time with a spouse or family. Even budget travellers want the same sense that they have left town to do something special and recharge their psychic batteries. Marketing programmes to this group often achieve success by emphasising *value added features*, such as kids sleep free at hotels/motels, free in-room television, half price second entrees at restaurants, one price includes all rides at theme parks, and so on. And, it is important to stress the value of these features to convince them that they have gotten a good deal. The important point is that this group should not be taken for granted. Good marketing strategies always require careful thought, planning, and execution.

The Family Market

Perhaps no group, in the author's experience, gets more attention as a segment and is touted as offering greater potential for development than the family market. The travel trade press, parts of the consumer media, and speakers at travel conferences regularly suggest that its potential is extraordinary. They point to the enormous size of the segment (55 percent of all travellers, according to ATS data presented in this discussion), and the continuing need for families to get away together. Some travel groups that serve them have become billion dollar enterprises. But, as pointed out earlier, the types of companies that achieve success are relatively limited. These include theme parks, movie theaters, arcades, low-priced motels, and family-oriented (moderate-priced) restaurants. But even these groups face the problem of seasonality. How can revenues be sustained during the nine months of the year when families do not travel because school is in session? Disney added adult instructional programmes at its Disney World location in Orlando without much success. Several hotels in Las Vegas added family fare, including a theme park within the grounds of the MGM Grand and live action shows for children at Treasure Island to increase summer traffic. But most of these were dropped. MGM converted the theme park to convention space and Treasure Island shows, although still active, have not developed a family market.

The good news is that families want to travel. Their travel interests measure well above average for the total population, and they also take more domestic trips than most. On the bad news side, they often stay with friends and relatives when they leave home, spending few dollars on hotel rooms. They also use travel agents less, and do not exceed population averages for air travel, international trips, number of trips, or days away on each trip. And, the old unsolvable problem of seasonality creates difficulty for destinations and travel providers about how to create demand for shoulder months and off seasons.

The most common travel motives dominate their interests. Like most people, they feel a strong need to relax on a trip, get rid of stress, enjoy quiet moments with a spouse, spend more time with children, get involved in activities different than what they do while at home, and especially to avoid schedules. Destination marketing that emphasises this kind of vacation experience will have a better chance of success. And, families particularly like packages that include a number of elements for a single price. It implies value (very important to them) and convenience, making the entire trip seem reasonably priced and more convenient. It's a large market, but consider the risks before entering. Even more important, destinations and other travel providers that offer multigenerational activities will do best. One of the most difficult challenges facing families is the need to satisfy the different interests of their mixed aged children, preteens, and teenagers, on the same trip.

Gay Travellers

The gay travellers group also has received considerable attention within the travel industry in recent years, and a number of companies now have programmes targeting the gay community. Gay resorts, gay cruises, gay tours, and gay travel packages appear regularly. And travel agencies located in gay communities have long searched out places where gays will not feel out of place or uncomfortable. In this case, the interest of major travel suppliers in the gay market seems justified. Overall, this group travels at relatively average levels, but the amount that they travel has grown over the years and they demonstrate the largest increase in wanting to take future trips. And, very important and typically over-looked when examining demographic data, their household income and amount spent on travel usually reflect that of one person, not two as is the case for married couples. But when they travel, they usually include a partner. Therefore, when computing per diem and total trip spending, the numbers given often should be doubled to include the amount spent by a partner. This makes them good niche targets, as some in the travel industry suggest. The down side of this conclusion is the extremely small size of the segment—about 2 percent among those who travel.

Although getting rid of stress and not worrying about schedules measure strongly as travel motives, like others, their profile differs to some degree from other groups. They seek unique trips where they can see and do different things than what they are accustomed to while at home, and they also hope to gain new perspective from exposure to other countries and their peoples. Similarly, many want to learn more about the history and culture of places they visit, with a strong desire to be able to share these experiences with a travel companion. The message about this segment is positive. The difficulty is knowing how to reach them effec-tively in a media intensive world that targets mass populations, not small niches.

Baby Boomers

As a segment, boomers changed the world. From the time they were infants to when they entered the work force, formed families, and became empty nesters, this huge segment impacted most major industries. Now it's their turn to impact travel. Since they graduated from high school, boomers have pushed along the travel bulge like no other group. A trip to Europe became almost a right of passage into adulthood. They toured the world with few dollars in their pockets and little concern about their futures. As they matured, they kept on travelling at a rate much higher than generations preceding them. Now travel companies salivate because, as boomers increasingly reach the empty nest stage, they can now pursue their long-standing interests in leisure travel to a degree not possible while raising a family. They have equity and income to go where they want to and when they want to. As a segment, the data suggest that they measure only slightly above average on travel propensity and related characteristics. But that hides the obvious fact that they now contribute heavily to what is the average (51 percent of the travel population). Few travel providers or destinations can achieve great success by ignoring this group.

Their travel profile includes that they take more domestic and international trips than most, have an above average interest in travel, and have the income and household equity to pursue their interests with relative freedom. More than most they take trips to get rid of stress, enjoy a quiet and relaxing time with a spouse, and gain new perspective on the world around them. Because they are so well travelled, they consciously seek new places to visit that often are off the beaten path. This sense of discovery invigorates them and they return home feeling refreshed and ready to take on the daily challenges of their active and full lives. The primary message, however, is that many travel offerings designed to attract smaller segments will also appeal to subsegments of this group. Their broad interests and travel propensity make them ideal targets for a variety of companies. But usually only well-established travel organisations have sufficient financial strength and depth of research intelligence to develop new programmes that will successfully withstand the heat of intense competition from other travel providers.

Adventure Travellers

The adventure traveller segment also receives a lot of attention by travel prognosticators. In this case, they have it right. Those who like a dose of adventure added to their trips make excellent targets for marketing programmes. They take more domestic trips than average, and stand out even more in the amount of international travel they pursue. They spend considerably more while away, take longer trips, and have household income and personal assets well above the norm. The importance they place on travel measures is very high, and they are also more likely to get away during the off season. Their interest patterns reflect very active minds and energetic lifestyles. They not only choose to participate in more activities on their trips than any other group, but they have a strong intellectual curiosity as well. They want to explore new places and meet new and different kinds of people, preferring to select a different destination each year rather than returning to the same old places. The benefits of targeting this group are multiple.

As was mentioned, the group includes hard adventure and soft adventure travel. Most travel providers and destinations should focus on the soft adventure market for several reasons. This group wants more services included as part of their travel arrangements. As a result, they spend more on each trip and especially on the kinds of services that the travel industry provides. Hard adventure types are likely to go to places lacking in hotels and restaurants and, therefore, require little back up or assistance. And, as the boomer population ages, with smaller population segments following behind, more strenuous types of vacation packagers will face declining sales in the future. Further, and most important, the amount of soft adventure travellers outnumbers hard adventure travellers by about four to one. These advantages should not be ignored. One final point: the market for adventure travel, especially soft adventure, is larger than indicated here. Fifteen percent of the population identify themselves as adventure travellers. But, when data are examined, about one-fourth of the population takes soft adventure trips each year. This segment deserves a closer look.

Luxury Travellers

A stand-up comic during the Borsch-belt era used the line, 'Folks, let me tell you. I've been rich and I've been poor, and being rich is better.' Data certainly confirm that little observation. Any group that successfully penetrates this segment will enjoy multiple benefits. Superlatives describe their travel characteristics. They take the most trips and longer trips among the segments reviewed, both domestic and international, go to more distant places, and are more likely to fly than go by car as compared with other groups. They also use travel agents more in spite of the fact that they make use of multiple information sources to plan each trip than any group. With the highest household incomes and the greatest personal assets, they have the freedom to pursue all travel interests.

To the uninformed, it might seem that this group most often would seek relatively inactive travel arrangements. We usually associate wealth with advancing age and sedentary lifestyles. As was noted, however, they are the youngest segment reviewed. And, when they travel, they are second only to adventure travellers in the number of activities pursued and the strenuousness of these activities. Further, they measure above average on nearly every travel motive measured. More than any group, they feel a need to get rid of stress, and avoid any semblance of schedules or commitments while away from home. Their active minds lead them to seek out and participate in new experiences, meet new and interesting people, and learn about history and culture of places they have read about. And travel also provides a chance to be more romantic and alone with a loved one. Because they measure highest on the importance that they assign to travel in their lives, they also return more often to travel agents for help in planning upcoming trips. A better segment cannot be found. The only problem is that the segment is relatively small. At only 10 percent of the total market, competition for this elite group will always be intense. And any company that achieves success with them can count on imitators. Excellent service and follow through are prerequisites to achieving service to the high-end market. And serving their needs requires offering them more choices to satisfy their diversity of interests than is true for any other segment.

Final Thoughts

Product development specialists in marketing departments of consumer companies often talk about the six magic words that define their quest— *Find a need and fill it.* In a mature market, such as travel, perhaps a variant of that phrase is required. Specifically, the goal would be to *find a segment and target it.* The formula for success obviously is two sided—the segment must be identified clearly and the travel products offered must focus on their travel interests. That task becomes increasingly difficult over time because travel is now a mature industry with all of its associated problems of stiff competition and slower growth. But, good ideas will always rise to the surface if they have been planned, researched, and marketed properly. Travel has an important advantage over most other industries with which it can be compared. It is an exciting and challenging field to the point that many people refuse to leave it even when they could make more money doing something else. Selling televisions or pursuing a career as an accountant somehow does not seem as exciting or challenging as becoming involved in leisure travel. And people who enjoy what they do for a living are more likely to achieve personal success. The psychologic rewards of pursuing a travel career often outweigh some of its disadvantages.

The segments identified in this discussion obviously are not inclusive. The potential for new groupings is almost unlimited. But market size should always be a consideration. Some clients have asked this author to look at the viability of segments that are so narrowly defined that the opportunity for success is slight. One client hoped to target high-income families interested in adventure travel. The small size of the market (about 1 percent of the population), the fact that families would only consider an adventure trip every three or four years, the difficulty of satisfying everyone on the same trip (wife, husband, and different age and different sex children), and the high cost of media to reach this group combine to make it a nonstarter. Another client hoped to target high-income boomers who would like to participate in Antarctic vacations aboard an ice breaker ship. But most of the same problems exist, with the added difficulty that, as the baby boomer group ages, it will pursue less strenuous, more comfortable lifestyles. This summary is presented not to discourage the development of new travel products, but with the hope that putting more effort into researching and understanding a market segment in advance will increase the rate of successful new ventures. Because of the broad diversity of the kinds of people who travel, the industry can accommodate new ideas very rapidly. Smart people will always find a road to success, even if some of their ideas may seem somewhat off the wall at times. Travel welcomes all newcomers—the naïve, the smart, the aggressive, and even the somewhat timid! There's room for all if good thinking and planning are done upfront.

References

Behavior Science Corporation/BASICO. 1967. *New Markets for Air Travel.*

Fiorina, C. 2003. As quoted in *Forbes, We Did It* August 11, 2003, p. 77.

Los Angeles Times. 2003. As reported on 24 August 24, p. F-6.

NFO/Plog Research. 2003. American Traveler Survey. Syndicated annual survey.

Plog, S. C. 2004. *Leisure Travel: A Marketing Handbook*. Upper Saddle River, N.J.: Pearson/Prentice-Hall.

Scott, J. ed. 2000. *Travel Industry World Yearbook: The Big Picture*. Spencertown, New York: Travel Industry Publishing Company.

15 Travel styles

Gordon D. Taylor and Nancy E. Chesworth

Introduction

In the second edition of *Global Tourism*, the need to place the consumer at the heart of tourism was stressed. In order to understand the consumer, a coordinated ongoing global measurement process was seen as a basic step. At any stage of development information is vital to all destination areas. An international approach to data collection and analysis was recommended as the best solution.

This chapter has been revised to reflect the impact of terrorism, economic recession, disease outbreaks in cattle and humans, and the invasion of Iraq. Each of these events has had an impact on the propensity to travel and on the previously identified travel styles. The revised chapter has three parts: a summary of the information presented in the previous edition, a discussion of the impact of global events on tourism, and some thoughts on research and the future. The basic tenets of the original chapter are used here as the introduction to the new chapter.

Part One

Tourism researchers have traditionally focussed on measuring consumption and economics related to travel. Measures such as expenditures per day, number of visits, number of trips, and the like reflect the concern with economic impact and consumption.

Little consistent effort has been made in developing a basic understanding of the consumer. A body of consumer knowledge based on empirical evidence is needed in order to thoroughly examine the phenomenon of tourism, and the place of the consumer as tourist. A number of questions can be hypothesised to provide a sense of direction in developing a better understanding of the consumer.

1. What proportion of the population of a country travels and how frequently?
2. How is this proportion changing over time, if it is indeed changing?
3. Who are becoming travellers and who are ceasing to be?
4. Is the proportion of travellers in a population uniform by sex, age, education, income, and other standard sociodemographic measures?
5. For those people who travel, do they all think about travel the same way or can succinct groups in the population be described based on this thought process?
6. If such groups can be described, are they unique to individual countries or do they occur on a wider basis?
7. Are these groups consistent or do they change over time?

The seldom used concept of styles of travel can be useful as a way of thinking about the kind of analysis needed to answer these questions and to develop useful concepts related to understanding the travelling consumer. For the purpose of this discussion, travel style is defined as the way people perceive, organise, and execute travel. Two streams of information are included within this definition:

1. The incidence of travel and
2. The way people think about the travel that they do.

To illustrate the above, empirical data from several sources will be examined to:

1. Determine the incidence of travel in two countries and indicate the type of information that can be derived from incidence data,
2. Describe and classify segments of travellers, and
3. Examine changes, if any, that may have taken place over time.

Incidence of Travel

The incidence of travel is the proportion of the population of an area that travels. For practical purposes, the examination of the empirical data will be limited to a minimum age of 14 in one case and 15 in the other. Trip purpose is limited to pleasure travel. It should be noted that an international agreement on limiting factors would be required in order to make the data comparable internationally. Data on the incidence of travel are inconsistent. This is unfortunate because the incidence of travel is one of the most important measures of the consumption of travel; the characteristics of the consumer; whether the market is growing, declining, or remaining constant; and how fast changes are taking place. It is also the best measure of who is in the travel market, and of who is entering and leaving it. Together with frequency of trip data, it is also the basis for differentiating the heavy and light users of travel.

Data Sources
The data used to illustrate the incidence of travel are drawn from the annual German Travel Analysis and the biennial Canadian Travel Survey. Both of these studies consistently measure travel intensity. The German study conducted since 1970 is based on 6000 interviews of those over the age of 14. Since 1990 the survey has included all of unified Germany. The Canadian study covers the population age 15 years and older and includes 6000 households.

Analysis
Both surveys asked respondents if they had taken a holiday trip in the period preceding the survey. The German study clearly showed consistent growth in the proportion of the population that had taken at least one five-day holiday trip. Analysis of the data performed for *Stern* magazine concluded that: 'at all levels of income consumers with higher education are at the advantage' (*Stern*, 1983). Thus education level is an essential aspect of travel incidence.

In Canada similar growth was noted; however, nonmetropolitan areas had a higher incidence of travel within Canada, whereas metropolitan areas showed a higher incidence of foreign travel. Again, incidence of travel increased with levels of education and household income.

Discussion
By not using this type of data, a rich resource for understanding tourism in its broadest sense and determining where tourism fits into the economic and social priorities of populations is being missed. The relationship between travel incidence and standard of living by country may indicate future trends in travel. The movement of certain groups in and out of the travel market in times of economic recession may also be of significant interest.

Travel Philosophy

A concept of travel philosophy has been developed by Tourism Canada as part of market segmentation research resulting in travel styles segments. The segmentation process is based on the following assumptions:
   There are recognizable groups in the population based on:

1.   How people organise and value travel (i.e., how people think about travel);
2.   Benefits sought from specific pleasure trips; and

3. Activities, interests, location, and facilities required to realise the benefits sought from specific pleasure trips.

Data Sources

Market research studies conducted by Tourism Canada in the 1980s and 1990s provided the data for this section. Three studies were involved:

1. Attitudes of West Germans to Canada as a holiday destination,
2. Canadian Tourism Attitudes and Motivation Study, which was included in the Canadian Labour Force Survey, fall, 1983, and
3. Pleasure Travel Markets to North America.

The Pleasure Travel Markets study included the following countries at various times: Australia, Brazil, France, Hong Kong, Italy, Japan, Mexico, Singapore, South Korea, Switzerland, United Kingdom, Venezuela, and West Germany. The studies were based on 50-minute in-home interviews with those who had taken a long haul vacation in the preceding three years, or who intended to take such a trip in the next two years.

Analysis

The study of West German attitudes to Canada resulted in the emergence of four segments:

1. The uninspired fellow traveller, 33 percent;
2. The busy sightseeing tourist, 20 percent;
3. The comfort-loving relaxation vacation, 26 percent; and
4. The globetrotter adventurer, 21 percent.

That the largest segment was not very interested in travel was surprising. There were indications that this segment accompanied the Group 4 adventurers on holidays. The critical point is that they were taken along on holidays by other people and were not individually motivated. Thus, they are not a market that could be targeted for travel.

The Canadian Tourism Attitudes and Motivation Study for 1983 eliminated questions for respondents who had not travelled in the preceding 12 months. Four segments emerged from the entire sample of those who had travelled in the previous 12 months:

1. Planned adventurer, 31 percent;
2. Casual traveller, 27 percent;
3. Low-risk traveller, 24 percent; and
4. Stay-at-home, 18 percent.

The fourth group was composed of those who did not see travel as part of their lifestyle, did not enjoy travel, and travelled very little. It is likely that every population contains a group that is essentially outside of the travel market. This group should be included from time to time in segmentation studies so the underlying characteristics can be studied.

Eliminating the stay-at-home group from the analysis leaves three groups that resemble the groups that were developed for the overseas markets. They are:

1. Planned travel, 37.5 percent;
2. Independent travel, 33.5 percent; and
3. Reluctant travel, 29 percent.

In order to establish a common terminology for travel philosophy segments, the names used in this report differ from those used in the original reports. The term 'planned travel' replaces 'package travel,' although package travel is a major component of the segment. Independent travel describes those who make their own travel arrangements. They avoid guided tours and packages. Reluctant travel describes a group for whom travel is not a priority. When they travel, they leave arrangements to someone else.

The study of Pleasure Markets to North America involved 13 different countries studied between 1986 and 1990, four of them on two occasions. The three philosophy segments noted previously have been recognised in all of the countries. Hence, the groups are transnational and transcultural. However, they do not exist in all countries in the same proportions. The countries can be divided into three groups depending on which group is the largest in each country. Germany and Switzerland each appear in two of the groupings because the two groups are of the same size.

1. High independent travel:
   France (two studies);
   United Kingdom (two studies);
   Australia, South Korea, Switzerland.
2. High planned travel:
   Brazil, Germany (1989), Hong Kong, Italy, Singapore, Venezuela.
3. High reluctant travel:
   Germany (two studies), Japan, Switzerland.

In the United Kingdom, France, and Germany some slight shifts in the proportions were observed. However, with only two points in time studied, these changes are interesting but cannot be considered a trend.

Discussion

On the basis of the evidence available, the three philosophy segments appear to be relatively stable. Further study is required to determine whether significant shifts in the structure of travel markets are occurring. Further study is also needed to see whether countries with recent entries into the international travel market as origins develop the pattern of the older, established markets.

In the older markets, one-third of travellers prefer to travel on their own terms, another one-third wants as many of the unknowns removed as possible before travel, and a final one-third is not really keen on travel. Each of these groups requires a separate style of marketing approach. The industry response to their travel needs should reflect the different ways they look at travel.

Conclusion

The fact that some universals in travel segments are emerging highlights the need for international cooperation in developing much-needed research in travel segments. There is need for international agreement on:

• The type of survey to be performed,
• The questionnaire content,
• The methodologies of administration, and
• The analysis.

An international approach to the development and classification of multisegments will be required if target marketing and future product lines are to be relevant and relative to future market segments. A priority is to find a fast means of identifying the various groups.

The use of both travel incidence and travel style data makes possible a greater understanding of tourism on an international basis. The opportunity to develop comparable data worldwide would provide a means of monitoring changes in travel markets, which is vital to the process of adapting tourism marketing to change. When incidence and style are analysed at the same time, the fact of change will be accompanied by the direction of change. Tourism cannot afford to overlook the implications of these data as a means of improving knowledge of the markets and of increasing the opportunities for customer satisfaction.

Part Two

At the time the 1998 chapter was written, tourism had enjoyed a number of years of sustained growth and the market looked relatively stable. It was assumed that uninterrupted growth would continue. Occasional downturns in tourism resulting from terrorist incidents since the 1970s have been relatively short lived. Coshall (2003) found that destinations that are highly attractive to travellers from the United Kingdom experience rapid recovery after a crisis.

The economic impact of terrorism on destinations has been discussed in a number of studies (Enders, Sandler, and Parise 1992; Sonmez 1994) and is usually the focus of most travel news articles following a terrorist incident. Although acts of terrorism are seldom aimed directly at tourists, the image of destinations where such acts occur is negatively affected in the mind of potential travellers. Bramwell and Rawding (1996) found that image is a major determinant of destination choice. Richter and Waugh (1986) indicated that declines in tourism demand predictably follow terrorist events, even if tourists and the tourism industry are not involved. In a study of the effects of terrorism in Israel, Pizam and Fleischer (2002) concluded decreased travel to Israel was more the result of the frequency of terrorist acts than their severity. However, Krakover (2000), also studying the impact of terrorism on travel to Israel, found that the more severe the event, the greater the drop in demand, especially in international tourism.

Many of the studies noted previously indicated that the negative impact of a terrorist event can last up to nine months. The fact that tourism has been able to recover from terrorism and violent events indicates that such acts do not remain long in memory. Mansfield (1996) indicated that the rate of recovery is directly related to the effectiveness of crisis management and careful analysis of travel trends, aided by price cuts and marketing efforts.

At this writing, two years after the attack on the World Trade Center, there are few people on the planet who are not aware of the enormous impact of that event on tourism. As a result, the economic importance of tourism has achieved marked attention in the media and among governments, many of which had previously ignored, underrated, or misunderstood the impact of tourism on their countries. Expectations were that tourism would recover, albeit slowly. When recovery did not happen in the summer of 2002, it was assumed that tourism would return to previous levels in the summer of 2003. The bombing in Bali, invasion of Iraq in March 2003, the SARS outbreak, a continuing decline in the U.S. economy, and an unusually hot summer in Europe, however, served to heighten the fears of international tourists and particularly the already nervous American public, so that predicted increases in international travel did not materialize. Few seem to remember that tourism had clearly begun to decline in the United States by the summer of 2001, due to a downturn in the U.S. economy following the crash of technical stocks and several high profile bankruptcies.

Warnings that all was not well with tourism had been raised earlier. Taylor (1996) noted:

> Tourism faces new and increasingly complex challenges. That fact is indisputable. How tourism adjusts and reacts to these challenges will determine whether tourism flourishes or withers in the next century. The nature of these challenges and of the initial responses to them are beginning to be identified. The identification process must move ahead rapidly because it is clear that tourism cannot continue to do business as it has in the past. Research must play a key role in this process.

That the challenges would appear so quickly and so dramatically was not anticipated. The new century brought with it a period of unprecedented change. The events in the early years of the twenty-first century have hit the travel industry with a devastating series of blows. Headline stories of layoffs, financial losses, and bankruptcy proceedings are common. The question must be raised—will tourism revert back to its late twentieth-century characteristics or have such fundamental changes occurred in such a short period of time that the knowledge and understanding gained a few years ago may now be out of date? The events that have brought tourism to its current state of apparent disarray are well known:

1. The Hoof and Mouth Disease outbreak in the United Kingdom, 2001, 9/11, and the after effects of regulations and inspections;
2. The SARS panic of April 2003 and the continuing fear of another outbreak of this disease;
3. The discovery of Mad Cow Disease in one cow in Western Canada, May 2003, and the continuing problem of banned beef imports from Canada;
4. Natural catastrophes such as the unprecedented heat wave in Europe, floods in China, monstrous forest fires in North America, and hurricanes in North America in late summer and early fall 2003;
5. The Iraq War that began in March 2003 and the continuing unrest in Iraq and other parts of the Middle East;
6. The August power outage in eastern North America; and
7. The hotel bombings in Bali and Jakarta, Indonesia.

The list could go on, but certainly the widespread nature and variety of events within a relatively short period of time must be unprecedented in world history. These events, terrorism, war, disease, and natural catastrophes, have been damaging in their own right. Modern communication has provided the people of the world with front row, centre seats at all of them on an ongoing 24/7 basis. The news coverage has been nonstop, each event has been broadcast to the world with all of the colour, hoopla, and noise of a championship football game. There have been play-by-play announcers, colour commentators, expert opinion, and highly probing question sessions.

Under normal circumstances, a terrorist incident is seen on television a limited number of times. However, footage of the collapse of the World Trade Center towers in particular, was ubiquitous. Broadcast for several days, coverage of the destruction saturated all venues of media. On some networks, it was possible to see the towers fall multiple times in the course of an hour. Consequently, millions of people have possibly viewed the scene of the impact and collapse hundreds of times each. This dramatic and frightening sight is undoubtedly permanently engraved in the memory of millions.

The fact that these events and the problems arising from them are an ongoing issue, constantly brought to the attention of the public, are reflected in a series of headlines that give a flavour of the problems of tourism from 2001 to 2003:

1. Residents of SARS-Hit Areas Targeted in Tourism Drive (*e-Turbo News*, August 1, 2003).
2. Airlines Filling Seats but Profits Still Grounded (*e-Turbo News*, August 1, 2003).
3. The Challenge of Living in New York (Elinore Garely, *e-Turbo News*, August 15, 2003).
4. France's Version of Shock and Awe (Dave Brown, *The Ottawa Citizen*, June 14, 2003, p. C1,C4).
5. Asia Geared to Fight SARS as New Case Emerges (*e-Turbo News*, September 11, 2003).
6. Jakarta Blast Might Have Been Directed against US Interest (*e-Turbo News*, August 5, 2003).
7. American Tourists Deserting Europe (King Housego, *e-Turbo News*, August 8, 2003).
8. Eye for an Eye—Terrorist Threat (*e-Turbo News*, August 7, 2003).
9. Tough Security in US May Deter Tourists Too (*e-Turbo News*, August 29, 2003).
10. SARS to Affect Tourism for Years (Kristine Gaff, *The Ottawa Citizen*, p. D1, D2, July 7, 2003).
11. Shrinking Pie in the Sky? (*e-Turbo News*, October 6, 2003).
12. A Drought of Foreign Tourists (*Business Week*, July 15, 2002).
13. 9/11—Two Years Later: Hotels, Tourism Still Struggling (*Naples Daily News*, September 23, 2003).
14. Terror's Toll on Tourism Tallied (*Las Vegas Review-Journal*, September 22, 2003).

How will the constant reminders of the events of the past several years, and the continuing fear of further terrorism, alter the attitudes and choices of the tourist consumer, if at all? The travel styles most affected by terrorism and the ongoing threat of more terrorism, although not researched, can be surmised to some extent by examining those segments suffering the greatest losses since September 11, 2001. Obviously, the airline segment has been most affected, and high-end hotels, restaurants, car rental agencies have also seen a marked drop in patronage, for the most part due to the reduction of business travel. Planned, package travel has also been hard hit. Motorcoach tours, and other forms of large group travel, have experienced a high rate of cancellation. The cruise industry has responded by taking ships to the passengers by opening new ports so passengers do not have to fly. Rumours that independent travellers, especially backpackers, are travelling in numbers similar to those of 2000 are unconfirmed. However, a survey by BedandBreakfast.com revealed the bed and breakfast sector experienced an 8 percent increase since September 11, 2001.

At one extreme some tourist destinations may become fortress areas—the modern version of the castle in the middle ages. In many countries resorts are already 'exclusive'—off limits to residents of the area other than to work. Other areas are striving to avoid the fortress type development, working to incorporate tourism into the community and to develop alternative forms of tourism.

Will the tourism consumer of tomorrow, if not today, look for a 'big box' type of development, for the sake of safety, security, and the image of luxury? Or will the consumer search out a 'small box' area in hope of finding adventure and the intimacy of a more realistic, authentic environment? Will some look for one type and some for the other? Will the seeking be consistent or will those looking for a big box on one occasion desire a small box on another depending on the travel experience and satisfactions sought?

Like the giant discount store Wal-Mart or the corner store—the two groups are not necessarily mutually exclusive. The tourist can be in one today and the other tomorrow but they will not seek a big box experience in a small box area. Will the big box be seen as more secure, hence preferable in troubled times?

Several possible consumer groups can be hypothesised from this thinking:

1. Big box only,
2. Big box mainly but small box on occasion,
3. Small box only,
4. Small box mainly but big box on occasion, and
5. A 50–50 split between big and small box.

The consumers classified into these categories will not remain in a category for long periods. As life situation, life stage, needs, and desires change and as the security outlook changes, the consumer may well move from one category to another. The situation will require constant monitoring and the groups must never be seen as being forever—they will change in composition and in experience sought.

Part Three

A Changed Industry?

The travel industry spent a great deal of time and money, wisely we might add, in the second half of the twentieth-century on sophisticated research into the critical characteristics of many travel markets. This information lead directly to marketing and development activities designed to provide the visitor with a highly satisfactory experience and the industry with a profit. The knowledge base of tourism was expanded and this additional information was adopted quickly by the industry.

Events in the early years of the twenty-first-century have hit the travel industry with a devastating series of blows. There are severe problems with tourism markets as a result of the events outlined earlier. The question must be asked—will tourism revert back to its twentieth-century characteristics or have such fundamental changes occurred in a very short period of time that the knowledge gained a few years ago may now be out of date? A research programme that would seek to provide the information required in order to develop a solution is needed.

The problem that must be faced is have these events altered the very nature of tourism. The research hypothesis that must be tested can be stated in two ways:

1. The events of 2000 through 2003 have had little long-term effect on the health of the tourism industry, or
2. The events have fundamentally affected tourism markets and new understandings of how they will respond in the future are needed.

The hypothesis stated should be tested. The outcome of that testing will determine the nature of further studies that may be required. A small task force should be established before any major research effort is launched. The task would be to arrive at a more precise definition of the key elements that should be measured.

Changed Tourists?

In all of the public discussion that has taken place as a result of the disasters, the concern has been with the effect on the industry—

transportation, accommodation, food, attractions, and so on. There has been practically no mention of the effect on the tourist. What has the tourist lost or gained by any travel plan changes required in response to the events? There is a great opportunity to develop an understanding of tourists and changes, if any, on tourists' travel styles. For too long research has concentrated on the business side of tourism with very little regard for the tourist. There have been some very useful studies conducted but all too often the critical measurements that were desired were the effect on the means (the travel industry) and not the end (the individual tourist).

A quote (Taylor, 2002) from the foreword to Claire Gunn's recent book on tourism planning suggests that:

> The end product of tourism is a satisfied customer. Without a succession of satisfied customers the product will wither and die. All of the pieces of a tourism destination whether it is at the local, area, or regional level are but the means to that end. . . . It is true that tourism has significant economic benefits, but the continued success of tourism depends upon the level and sustainability of visitor satisfaction.

The basic response of the tourism industry has been to spend large sums of money on additional promotion, and the immediate outlook is for requests for larger and larger promotion budgets. The effect of the current world conditions has been the apparent loss of visitor satisfaction—the capability of the industry to cater to the known needs of tourists has not been altered. What has changed is the willingness of many tourists to travel. The lack of visitors has resulted in loss of business, and that loss has brought about massive layoffs, bankruptcies, and so on. We need to take a close look at various groupings of tourist to determine how they have been affected by the events of the last two to three years and how any problems created can be overcome. In addition to testing the hypothesis, the opportunity exists to examine the impact of the events noted on the tourist and the tourists' travel styles. Several approaches to investigating changes in tourists' attitudes, motivations, motivators, and consequent travel styles are suggested in the following hypotheses:

1. People who experience less exposure to television and other media are more likely to travel,
2. Experienced, adventurous 'small box' travellers are more likely to travel mass 'big box,' and
3. Travel styles have shifted, showing more reluctant travellers than previously.

Certainly it would seem prudent to ear mark a small portion of the funds being spent to encourage travel to the hardest hit destinations in an effort to test the hypotheses laid out. There is a great opportunity to develop a greater understanding of the world's tourist markets, how they react to real or perceived disasters and does the reaction change over short and long periods. Action cannot be delayed if advantage of the current situation is to be taken to expand our knowledge of tourism markets and how they react to changing conditions.

An International Task Force

In our view an international task force should be established to carry out the research programme. The task force must be seen to be a true task force; it must be established, come together, do its job, and disband. It must be representative of all aspects of tourism but it is to be a research-oriented body, able to design, undertake, analyse, and prepare reports that include clear action proposals. It will use its own expertise and that of consultants.

The role of existing organisations is critical. The Travel and Tourism Research Association, the World Tourism Organization, the Pacific Asia Travel Association, the International Association of Scientific Experts in Tourism, the European Association for Tourism and Leisure Education, and others must be involved in the development of the task force but none of them must be in control or seen to be in control.

A wide range of interests on the supply side from the major business concerns to the extreme sustainability viewpoint will need to be represented on the task force. The problem will be how to get tourists involved. Because tourists are to be at the centre of the work, the role of tourists must be very transparent.

The approach of the task force must be nonjudgmental on the reasons for the problems that have been identified. The role of the force is to see the degree to which tourism (from the tourists' view) has been changed by these events. Are the changes likely to be permanent or short lived or will there be a noticeable if not radical change? Will tourism revert back to the twentieth-century model if no further major incidents occur? The guiding light must always be the assurance that tourists can obtain the satisfactory experience that they seek.

It is not our function to develop a plan of work. All we can do is point to the necessity of the task force approach. We recommend a task force because it can be structured to take in a wide range of interests. The problems may have to be examined through several prisms. Business and pleasure are two obvious breaks, but within each there are major differences as there are major differences between them.

To whom will the task force be accountable? The key to the success of the work of the force is accountability. The tasks must be seen to have a practical outcome in the first instance. They must have an impact on public and private policy. Accountability is a critical issue. The task force cannot be seen to be without accountability, yet it cannot be seen in a subservient role. Adequate financing and staff are necessary to enable the task group to do its work unimpeded. The source of funds must allow the force to function independently, otherwise credibility and accountability are forfeit.

The academic community must play a key role. The task force could be located at a university or college and be accountable to it. An academic institution would be involved in the work of the group as well as providing a home and discipline.

Two possible approaches are suggested. One is to actively research what has happened and what is happening to tourism, secondly, observe and record what is happening, and discover whether trends are being established. Both approaches are needed and likely others will become apparent as the work progresses. There must be a management attitude that the work of the group can change direction and purpose quickly if circumstances warrant.

The process of establishing and operating the task force would seem to require four stages:

1. Define objectives, develop terms of reference and staffing levels, and set budgetary limits;
2. Establish task;
3. Do its work; and
4. Report and disband.

When completed, the work of the proposed task force will provide direction for the industry, clarification of the impacts of the events discussed earlier on the industry and especially on the tourist. If tourism is to thrive and prosper, meaningful research will lead the way.

References

Bramwell, B., and L. Rawding. 1996. Tourism Marketing Images of Industrial Cities. *Annals of Tourism Research* 23(1): 201–221.

Coshall, J. T. 2003. The Threat of Terrorism as an Intervention on International Travel Flows. *Journal of Travel Research* 42: 4–12.

Enders, W., T. Sandler, and G. F. Parise. 1992. An Econometric Analysis of the Impact of Terrorism on Tourism. *Kyklos* 45: 531–554.

Krakover, S. 2000. Estimating the Effects of Atrocious Events on the Flow of Tourism in Israel. In *Tourism, War, and the Commemoration of Atrocity.* eds. G. Ashworth and R. Hartman. New York: Cognizant Communication.

Mansfield, Y. 1996. Wars, Terrorism and the Middle East Factor. In *Tourism, Crime and International Security Issues*. eds. A. Pizam and Y. Mansfield. Chichester, U.K.: John Wiley and Sons.

Pizam, A., and A. Fleisher. 2002. Severity versus Frequency of Acts of Terrorism: Which Has a Larger Impact on Tourism Demand? *Journal of Travel Research* 40: 337–339.

Richter, L. K., and W. L. Waugh. 1986. Tourism Politics and Political Science: A Case of Not So Benign Neglect. *Annals of Tourism Research* 10(3): 313–315.

Sonmez, S. F. 1994. An Exploratory Analysis of the Influence of Personal Factors on International Vacation Decisions Within the Context of Terrorism and/ or Political Instability Risk. Doctoral dissertation. The Pennsylvania State University.

Stern. 1983. The German Holiday Maker—Projections to 1990. *Stern Magazine*, Hamburg, August, p. 14.

Taylor, G. D. 1996. A New Direction. *Journal of Travel and Tourism Marketing* 5(3): 253–264.

——. 2002. Foreword. In *Tourism Planning: Basics, Concepts, Cases.* 4th ed. ed. C. A. Gunn. New York: Taylor & Francis.

http://www.bedandbreakfast.com. Accessed September 11, 2002.

Pleasure Travel Markets to North America, published by Tourism Canada, Ottawa:
   (a)   Full reports for individual countries:
         — France, Japan, United Kingdom, West Germany, 1986
         — Switzerland, Hong Kong, Singapore, 1987
         — Australia, Brazil, Italy, Mexico, 1988
         — France, Japan, united Kingdom, West Germany, 1989
         — South Korea, Venezuela, 1990
   (b)   Highlights reports for all countries studied in a year.

16 Empirical market segmentation: what you see is what you get

Sara Dolnicar

Introduction

Tourism is just like any other industry. Although it offers intangible, perishable services, is characterised by global competition, and is threatened or strengthened by political developments, it is just like any other industry with regard to the most fundamental market characteristic: customers have certain ideas of what they are looking for (preferences), and they choose the offer that best meets their preferences. It is therefore crucial to thoroughly understand what ideas customers have about the vacation of their dreams, the honeymoon to remember for a lifetime, or the adventure trip that still gets adrenaline pumping in their veins when they flip through the photos. As an organisation or a tourist destination, it is important to understand customers' ideas in order to be capable to design offers that best match the consumer preferences and thus increase sales, possibly even satisfaction and consequently the probability of repeated purchase of the same tourism product.

This sounds like a very simple and straightforward task for tourism management (i.e., understand the preferences of potential customers). It would indeed be very simple and straightforward if individuals were all the same. If they would share a common view, the same picture about the vacation of their dreams, one perfect tourism product would be designed and marketed.

The complexity of the problem increases dramatically when it is acknowledged that consumers differ in their preferences: different individuals have different ideas about how they imagine their ideal vacation. For tourism management this means that it becomes necessary not only to understand one set of preferences, but a number of different ideal tourism products: the wild Australian adventure with a touch of real danger for the young, single male tourist; the quiet and relaxing spa holiday for the retired couple; or the five-day Europe sightseeing bus tour for culturally ambitious groups of Japanese.

The fact that individuals differ in their perception of the perfect vacation implies that there is a lot of variety, or heterogeneity, in the tourism marketplace. Heterogeneity that challenges the market research skills of tourism destinations and organisations: those destinations or organisations that see what the market, and the many submarkets or market segments, want will be able to attract those individuals and thus 'get what they see,' thereby making them their customers. By doing so, they automatically gain competitive advantage over other destinations and organisations that do not understand market preferences, mostly because they do not bother to look, thus underestimating the importance of thorough market research in the tourism industry. Destinations or tourism organisations that do not see consumer preferences, and the continuing development of these preferences put themselves at risk of competitors stealing their customers: those competitors who see clearly and offer what the markets or particular segments require.

The starting point of this chapter is the insight that consumers are heterogeneous. They differ in many regards, including their product preferences, and understanding those differences leads to the capability to make the best possible catering arrangements for particular needs, thus gaining competitive advantage in the marketplace. The aim of the chapter is to discuss and illustrate different approaches taken in the area of empirical market segmentation in tourism and to raise conceptual, practical, and methodological problems in this context. The chapter provides a discussion of empirical market segmentation, which means that an empirical data set (typically resulting from a tourist survey) represents the basis. Purely conceptual derivation of market segments or tourist typologies is not treated. Given this aim, readers should be provided with an overview of empirical market segmentation in tourism and realise how much unexploited potential for improvement remains in this area.

Causes of Variety

Clearly, consumers are not different in every single aspect. They have many things in common (for instance, one-half of the consumers are female) but they differ in other ways. The differentiating characteristics are of interest in the context of market segmentation. These represent the causes of variety or heterogeneity in the marketplace and, consequently, are the main focus in the identification or construction of market segments. Sometimes one single characteristic or segmentation criterion is sufficient to discriminate between relevant segments. Other times a number of characteristics are used simultaneously to group customers into segments. This would then be referred to as a segmentation base (Wedel and Kamakura, 2002).

Anything that is useful to management can be used as a segmentation criterion or segmentation base. The most typical criteria and segmentation bases are the following:

- *Sociodemographic:* Typical sociodemographic criteria used in market segmentation include gender, age, education, or income.
- *Geographic:* In tourism geographic segmentation is probably the most common concept in the area of destination management with the country of origin of tourists functioning as the segmentation criterion.
- *Behavioural:* Typical behavioural information includes vacation activities, choice behaviour, general vacation habits (e.g., how often do tourists go on vacation, how long do they stay, etc.), expenditures, and similar pieces of information.
- *Psychographic:* Travel motivations probably represent the single most popular psychographic segmentation base. Other criteria in this group would include guest satisfaction or lifestyle statements.

The borders between these bases of segmentation criteria are fuzzy. Therefore, different authors use different classification schemes. But this is not a conceptual problem. It is only a matter of preference in systematising criteria.

Although it has been claimed that psychographic criteria outperform sociodemographic groupings of customers, the usefulness of each of those groups of criteria is entirely dependent on the purpose of the study. Therefore it seems unreasonable to make general recommendations regarding the best choice of segmentation criteria.

Standard Approaches

Two standard approaches are known in empirical market segmentation:

One is referred to as *a priori* segmentation (Mazanec, 2000) or commonsense segmentation. This approach implies that tourism management is aware of the consumer characteristic(s) that can be used to split all tourists into managerially relevant groups. For instance, if a family hotel is being designed, it is clear *a priori* that customers will be adults with children. Choosing the segmentation criterion of 'having children' is thus a commonsense decision that is managerially highly useful in this case. Why would management want to design a family hotel and then try to attract single couples?

The second standard procedure in tourism market segmentation is called *a posteriori* (Mazanec, 2000), or *post-hoc* (Wedel and Kamakura, 2002) or data-driven (Dolnicar, 2002a) segmentation. In this case it is not quite so obvious which characteristic of the consumers might be most useful to group tourists. Because it is not obvious, data from consumers has to be collected and explored. Through systematic exploration of data, a number of different groupings will become apparent, from which management can choose the single most useful one. The best grouping is thus known only *a posteriori* or *post-hoc* (after exploring data) and is derived in a data-driven manner rather than resulting from a commonsense selection of a consumer characteristic.

Examples of a priori/Commonsense Segmentation

In 2000, the Austrian Business Chamber decided that their hotel star grading criteria needed to be revisited to shift from a product-oriented perspective to a market-oriented view. The future criteria for categorising hotels into one- to five-star accommodation facilities should reflect the needs and expectations of the respective customers.

This problem is a typical commonsense segmentation task: the total market of tourists has to be split into segments according to the hotel star category they typically chose. This is clear in advance and it is also clear that the market will thus be divided into precisely five groups of customers: people who choose to stay in five-star hotels, four-star hotels, three-star hotels, two-star hotels, and one-star hotels.

A large-scale empirical survey was conducted in order to determine which hotel attributes matter (Dolnicar and Otter, 2003) as well as the particular needs and desires of each one of the segments. The sample size amounted to 614 respondents (selected using a hypothesis-oriented quota sampling technique accounting for season, country of origin, city or noncity destination, business or vacation travel purpose, and star grading categories). The interviews each took about 15 minutes and were conducted in the hotels the respondents stayed at.

From this empirical data set relevant insights could be deducted. For instance, it was found, that there were significant differences between guests staying in different hotel categories: the brand signal 'number of stars' was relevant for 6 percent of the one-star, 16 percent of the two-star, 28 percent of the three-star, 34 percent of the four-star, and 38 percent of the five-star guests indicating that the signalling function of the star categories effects the decision reached by potential customers in a different way. Managerially, this finding means that five-star hotels have a powerful tool in their possession for attracting customers by informing them about the star category, whereas for a one-star hotel it would be a waste of effort to communicate the category, because only 6 percent of tourists include this information in their decision making process. The contrary applies to prices: about 80 percent of customers of one- and two-star hotels actively seek for price information when deciding on their accommodation, 67 percent of the three-start-hotel guests require this information, 55 percent in the four-star, and 27 percent in the five-star category. The implications of this significant—but not very surprising—difference leads to the debate of whether or not the hotel star category criteria should impose price ranges on hotels. Another very practical difference is that one-fifth of the five-star hotel guests directly inquire during their hotel decision-making process whether or not a sauna and a gym are offered. This has direct consequences for product design to optimise satisfaction of the needs of this particular segments. Further differences were found with regard to perceived risks, expectations, disappointments with prior hotel experiences, and many more. As a result of this study, the Austrian Business Chamber was provided with the precise descriptions of all five segments, including the information in which the differences are statistically significant. This was used as a basis for the redesign of the hotel star-grading system criteria.

A second commonsense segmentation that resulted from this same empirical study was to investigate specific needs of business travellers (Dolnicar, 2002b). Again, the choice of the criterion to define the market segment (in this case the purpose of travel had to be business) is chosen in advance. For instance, a hotel that is catering to business travellers will gain more insight into the market only by looking at the segment of business travellers than by exploring the needs of individuals choosing certain hotel categories.

Although this example illustrates the concept of commonsense segmentation, its functioning and managerial usefulness, the simple most typical commonsense segmentation in the tourism industry at destination levels is to form market segments based on the country of origin. In Austria, for example, the national tourism organisation conducts a three-yearly large-scale guest survey. One of the standard reports resulting from this survey is the detailed description of tourists from different nations. This is a grouping that is not only known in advance but also does make a lot of practical sense, because countries of origin differ in languages and cultural backgrounds and thus typically require separate treatment.

As illustrated in the examples above, *a priori*/commonsense segmentation basically requires two steps:

1. The selection of the criterion that is used to split up the customers (choice of hotel category, country of origin), and
2. Description of the resulting segments based on empirical market data and including statistical testing of differences.

This procedure is widely used and represents the most common kind of market segmentation practically applied in tourism.

Further examples published in academic journals include the following: Baloglu and McCleary (1999) contrast the way visitors and nonvisitors of a destination perceive the image of this region; Goldsmith and Litvin (1999) compare heavy users and light users, a very typical approach in commonsense segmentation; Kashyap and Bojanic (2000) explore differences between business travellers and holidaymakers; Smith and MacKay (2001) investigate how age groups differ in remembering pictures used in advertising; Israeli (2002) studies destination perception differences between disabled and nondisabled visitors; Klemm (2002) focusses on one ethnic minority in the United Kingdom and describes their vacation preferences; McKercher (2001) explores differences between tourists staying at one destination and those who only travel through; Meric and Hunt (1998) profile the ecotourist; Court and Lupton (1997) construct groups of different levels of intention to revisit a destination and investigates differences; and Arimond and Lethlean (1996) form segments based on the kind of site rental taken at a campground.

Examples of a posteriori/post-hoc/Data-Driven Segmentation

Interestingly, from a strict perspective of pure data-driven segmentation, very few such studies exist. Most of the studies of this nature fit into the combined category described later.

A pure example of data-driven segmentation is provided by Bieger and Lässer (2002) who group the Swiss population into market segments. The basis for segmentation is a set of travel motives. The reason why this is one of the few pure data-driven segmentations lies in the fact that typically a preselection of respondents is made before the data-driven task is initiated. This approach, however, represents a combination of commonsense (preselection) and data-driven segmentation. Studies of this nature have dramatically increased in popularity over the past decades, although practical implementation in tourism industry still remains limited.

A data-driven example is briefly described here to illustrate the concept. It is concerned with the grouping of culture tourists (preselection with regard to primary motivation for the trip) according to their vacation activities (Dolnicar, 2002c). The analysis is based on data from the Austrian National Guest Survey conducted in 1997/1998 including a total of 10,203 personal interviews. This example was selected because the Austrian National Guest Survey provided an excellent data basis for data-driven segmentation (i.e., large number of potential segmentation bases and a high sample size). The subsample of cultural tourists that was included in this segmentation study (these respondents stated that their main motivation to travel is culture or city tourism) amounted to 2492. The aim was to construct segments of cultural tourists with distinct vacation activity patterns. For this purpose, several activity statements from the interview were used as segmentation base: participation in organised excursions, undertaking excursions, shopping, sightseeing, visiting museums, exhibitions, theatre, musical, opera, visiting festivals, concerts, and visiting local and regional events. A behavioural segmentation solution with nine segments was chosen because it emerged as the most stable solution and was managerially interpretable. These segments render plausible interpretations and the external validity is high; this means that there are significant differences between the segments with regard to additional descriptive information that was not used in the grouping process itself. One of those segments will be described here. It was named the 'individual culture explorers.' The vacation activity profile of this group is shown in Figure 16.1, where the columns represent the percentage of members of this particular segment who agree to undertake those activities during their stay, and the black horizontal lines show the average participation in those activities among all cultural tourists. If the column and the horizontal lines are very similar, as is the case for sightseeing, the segment under inspection is not very distinct as compared with the average cultural tourists visiting Austria. The more the two values differ, as in organised bus trips as shown in Figure 16.1, the more distinct and unique a market segment is. The segment profile provided thus shows that the segment of *individual culture explorers* is very characteristic because all members, without exception, shop and visit museums and exhibitions. On the other hand, bus trips and excursions do not appeal to this segment at all. This particular data-driven segment could be an excellent target group for museums.

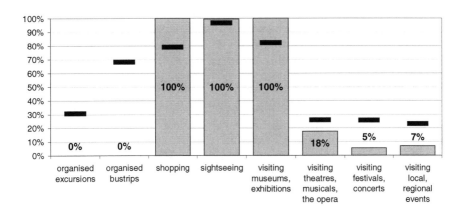

Figure 16.1:   Vacation activity profile of the individual culture explorers.

Source: Dolnicar, 2002.

In addition to the vacation activity profiles used to define market segments, a number of additional pieces of information about these individuals are available from the Austrian National Guest Survey. It can be used to examine the external validity of the segmentation solution derived from the data. A valuable insight can be gained from this examination: if the segments differ only in the vacation activities and nothing else, they might be of questionable practical value. External validity, however, gives management the security that segments actually represent different groups of individuals, if they differ in several aspects, even those that were not used to group them. Consequently, such segments are reasonable targets for separate marketing action.

Individual culture explorers, for instance, significantly differ from other cultural tourists with regard to numerous managerially relevant pieces of information: they visit Austria more frequently in winter than other segments do, and they value cultural offers significantly more than other segments, a fact that is reflected in the highest level of expenditures per person per day for entrance fees to cultural attractions.

Such a data-driven segmentation can be of great value to businesses involved in providing or organising cultural attractions in Austria. It enables managers to choose which segment to focus on. In this case, the individual culture explorers would be highly attractive given their pattern of activities and their willingness to spend a lot of money to visit cultural attractions.

As illustrated in this example, data-driven segmentation requires at least three steps given that an empirical data set is available even though it is more favourable to design the survey based on the following segmentation needs:

1. The selection of the criterion that is used to separate customers. In this case information is multivariate; it contains more than one question of the questionnaire. In the culture tourism example the criterion used were eight questions on vacation activities people engaged in during their stay.

2. Data analysis with an appropriate algorithm avoiding a number of typical mistakes made in the context of data-driven market segmentation (Dolnicar, 2002a).

3. Interpretation of the segments and testing of the validity of the solution. Although data-driven segmentation has been increasingly used in tourism research, industry has not fully adapted this approach yet—probably because it is methodologically more complex and conceptually less intuitive than commonsense segmentation. However, it has a sunny wide: adopting *a posteriori* approaches represents an excellent opportunity to extract more information about the market than the competitors and, consequently, to gain competitive advantage.

Further examples of combined commonsense and data-driven segmentation studies published in academic tourism journals in the past include the following: Silverberg, Backman, and Backman (1996) split nature-based tourists into benefit segments; Dodd and Bigotte (1997) preselected winery visitors and grouped them according to demographics in a data-driven manner; Formica and Uysal (1998) used visitors of a cultural–historical event in Italy as a starting point and investigated psychographic segments on the basis of their motivations; Kastenholz and Gordon (1999) studied benefit segments among visitors to rural areas; and Moscardo and colleagues (2000) chose the visitors of friends and relatives and study segments based on behavioural patters. Focussing on senior motor coach travellers as preselection of tourists, Hsu and Lee (2002) constructed segments based on motor coach selection criteria. Dolnicar and Leisch (2003a) searched for vacation segments among winter tourists in Austria. Again, the above list is by no means comprehensive, but it provides the reader with further relevant sources in the area of data-driven market segmentation in tourism.

Unasked Questions, Fundamental Misconceptions, and Ignored Dangers

Unasked Questions and Fundamental Misconceptions

Unasked Question 1: What Is the Commercial Benefit of Market Segmentation?

To the author's knowledge the crucial question regarding the benefits of market segmentation remains uninvestigated in tourism research. Typically, market segments are revealed or constructed and the resulting groups are described. The single most crucial criterion for the usefulness of a segmentation solution is, whether choosing a segmentation strategy based on those segments actually increases tourism revenues at a destination or profit in tourism industry. This is seldom mentioned.

Unasked Question 2: Do Market Segments Change over Time?

In the case of commonsense segmentation, it is typical to study on a yearly basis the changes that take place in the market. For instance, are Japanese tourists spending more money, travelling more, travelling further, or staying longer than they did last year? This is a very important question to ask because the market changes constantly and missing market changes means not seeing which preferences need to be met. In the area of data-driven segmentation this question remains widely unasked. Typically, one segmentation solution is computed at one point in time. The grouping of tourists is then used as basis for strategic marketing and is usually not questioned either in view of its usefulness or with regard to possible changes that might be occurring over time. Such a limited approach can be dangerous. It means that management takes one glimpse at the market and then instantly shuts their eyes again. A simple recommendation of how data-driven segments can be monitored over time was provided by Dolnicar and Leisch (2003b).

Unasked Question 3: How Does Market Segmentation Interact with Product Positioning and Competition?

Market segmentation is only one of three building blocks in strategic marketing. Market segmentation studies typically do not treat all three areas as integrated and strongly associated. For instance, the most attractive market segment is not a good choice for a destination if another destination is strongly perceived in this particular way already, and therefore competition would be too intense. Such integrated issues reflect on the segmentation choice but are typically ignored while segmentation is treated as an independent and isolated area of strategic marketing. Mazanec and Strasser (2000) suggested an integrated framework to conduct market research and analysis simultaneously for all those areas.

Misconception 1: There Are True, Real Groups among Tourists that Need to be Revealed

The most fundamental misunderstanding in the area of market segmentation is an implicit assumption of tourism management: segments are clearly distinct entities that exist naturally among individuals. It is assumed that any segmentation of tourists, be it commonsense or data-driven reflects a true and real existence of groups that are clearly separated. From the author's experience in segmenting tourism data sets for one decade now, this is an illusion. Rarely is there an empirical data set in which individuals form homogeneous groups that are clearly and distinctly separated from other homogeneous groups. Consumer heterogeneity is an individual phenomenon. As such, all grey shades exist and most groupings of such individuals into market segments represent an artificial task. Market segments are constructed, not revealed. This has never been discussed in the scientific community, where the focus of development lies on methodological improvements of segmentation techniques. However, the view regarding the underlying assumption about the occurrence or nonoccurrence of natural groups of tourists has been implicitly mentioned. It shows the transition from the strict revelation of true groups among individuals toward the acceptance of artificiality of market segmentation. Frank, Massy, and Wind (1972) stated that the purpose of taxonomic procedures is to describe *natural groupings* in empirical data sets. Myers and Tauber (1977) referred to market segments within

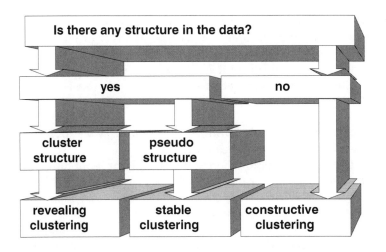

Figure 16.2:   Conceptual data-driven segmentation framework.
Source: Dolnicar and Leisch, 2001.

the field of segmentation research as clearly defined natural groupings of people. Consequently, the goal of the segmentation process is to identify these natural groupings. Two decades later, Mazanec (1997) did not assume the existence of natural segments, consequently implying that homogeneous groups have to be constructed rather than found. Wedel and Kamakura (2002) agreed with this latter assumption, and they claimed that market segmentation involves *artificial groupings* of individuals that are constructed for best possible targeting action. A framework to increase transparency with regard to the underlying segmentation concept was proposed by Dolnicar and Leisch (2001) that distinguishes between three data-driven segmentation settings, as illustrated in Figure 16.2.

The fundamental idea of this framework is to ask two questions about the empirical data:

1. Is there any structure in the data at all?
2. If yes, is this structure real cluster structure or is it data structure of other nature?

No matter what the answers to these questions are, it is managerially useful to segment the market. But the underlying concepts are entirely different: in the case of *revealing clustering*, true clusters are found, in the case of *stable clustering*, segments can be repeatedly identified although clear border lines between the segments do not exist. And finally, if no structure exists in the data, it is still better to construct artificial groups (*constructive clustering*) that include members similar to each other rather than to address all tourists on the planet in an identical manner. In any case, this framework is a useful structural guide for improved managerial understanding of the market structure, which is the basis for their long-term strategy.[1]

Misconception 2: The Software/the Algorithm Will Provide the Answer to the Segmentation Problem

In data-driven segmentation there is a wide misconception that exposing empirical data to a clustering algorithm (typically the Ward's clustering if hierarchical procedures are favoured by the researcher or *k*-means clustering if partitioning techniques are chosen) will result in *the* answer. This is not the case because each grouping computation might result in a different solution. This makes systematic exploration so important. Although there will always be some kind of a numeric result emerging from a computation, this is neither the only nor the best possible grouping that can be found. Algorithms impose structure on data; they do not simply look at data in a neutral objective manner. It is important for segmentation researchers and tourism managers to acknowledge this fact.

Ignored Dangers

Although most of the unasked questions and fundamental misconceptions represent ignored dangers as well, this section aims at pointing out a few dangerous habits of data-driven segmentation that have emerged through the many years of applied data-driven segmentation in tourism and tourism research. This was investigated in detail by Baumann (2000) and Dolnicar (2002a). The main points of these studies include:

Ignored Danger 1: Exploring Empty Space

It is crucial for any data-driven segmentation study to be based on data of sufficient sample size given the number of variables included as the segmentation base. In the majority of segmentation studies in tourism research, this is not the case. The number of variables used defines the dimensionality of space. More variables mean increased space in which groups are searched for. If, for instance, ten travel motive statements are used to group tourists, the space that is explored is ten dimensional. It takes a lot of respondents to fill that space sufficiently to actually find patterns or groupings. The best protection against this danger is commonsense. More formalised security is provided by Formann (1984) who

---

1 A methodological toolbox for answering the questions that help to classify which segmentation concept is required for a particular data set is presently being developed.

suggests the minimal sample size to include no less than 2^k cases (k = number of variables), preferably $5 \cdot 2^k$ if respondents answered the questions with *yes* or *no* (binary answer format).

Ignored Danger 2: Using Inappropriate Distance Measures for the Data

In tourism research it has become a standard procedure in guest surveys to use ordinal data scales, five- or seven-point scales that are ordered and indicate the strength of agreement or the strengths of guest satisfaction. Such data scales are not suitable for the standard distance measures implemented in clustering algorithms, mostly Euclidean distance. By applying distance measures for other data scales, assumptions are made. Assumptions that most probably are not satisfied in the case of ordinal data and Euclidean distance especially the critical assumption of equal intervals between the answer categories. To illustrate the general ignorance toward this problem, two-thirds of tourism segmentation studies use ordinal data and practically all of the authors who mention which measure of association underlies the computations use Euclidean distance. By so doing, the value of the collected market data is overestimated and the segmentation results thus do not mirror only pure market information.

Ignored Danger 3: Unquestioned Data Preprocessing

A standard clustering ritual has emerged over the years in tourism research that involves conducting factor analysis before clustering the data. This is a dangerous habit if applied in an uncritical manner. Typically, the variance explained by the retained factors is approximately 50 percent, meaning that the price researchers pay for reducing the number of variables is that they literally throw away one-half of the information they have collected from the marketplace. Neither factor analysis nor standardisation procedures should be used as part of some standardised segmentation procedure. They should be applied only if there is a good reason to do so, for instance the standardisation of different answer formats for different survey questions. The danger of uncritical preprocessing lies in constructing a segmentation solution in a transformed space, a space that has little to do with the initial market information collected from potential visitors.

Ignored Danger 4: The Number of Segments

In the case that true clusters do not exist in the empirical data used to construct a market segmentation solution (these include stable and constructive clustering in Figure 16.2), the decision of how many segments to construct influences the results in the most dramatic way. For example, grouping tourists into two segments based on vacation activities will lead to one highly active market segment and a rather passive, relaxation-oriented segment. If, however, the same tourists are grouped into ten segments, the active tourist will be further subdivided in segments with particular interests: for instance, culturally active and sports-oriented tourists. The number of clusters therefore most strongly influences the results. Although many researchers have studied this problem in the past, there is no simple solution (Dimitriadou, Dolnicar, and Weingessel, 2002). But ignorance is certainly the worst solution. The minimum requirement for a properly conducted segmentation study therefore is to investigate whether certain numbers of clusters render more stable results, basically representing a measure of internal validity. If this is not the case, a wide variety of solutions has to be constructed and explored in detail before one specific solution is chosen as the basis for an organisation's or destination's long-term strategy.

Conclusions (Critical Questions for the Informed Tourism Manager)

In tourism, market segmentation has developed to become a very common tool in strategic marketing. However, as this chapter aims at illustrating, there are still many unresolved issues in the area that can cause segmentation solutions to be anything between utterly absurd to strategically invaluable. Segmentation is a long-term building block of organisation success and as such represents one of the most critical managerial decisions. For these reasons it is most important for tourism managers to invest a lot of time and thinking into their segmentation solution and critically question it.

A few questions that could help a manager in doing this might be the following:

- Do I need to search for segments? Which benefits do I expect from treating different tourist groups differently?
- What is the purpose of my segmentation?
- Keeping this purpose in mind, what are segmentation criteria or segmentation bases that are relevant in this context?
- Are there single segmentation criteria that are known and guaranteed to split the tourists into relevant segments? In this case, commonsense segmentation is sufficient.
- Which segmentation base is relevant and should be explored in an attempt to identify or construct market segments?
- Which one of the many possible data-driven market segmentation solutions is managerially most useful? If the market research company

conducting the study claims there is only one true solution, consider switching to another market research company.

- Are the resulting market segments valid, either because they can be revealed repeatedly or because they differ with regard to additional information about the tourists?
- Which segment or segments are the best matching targets for the offer my organisation or destination can make?
- Which segments are most appropriate targets considering product positioning and competition knowledge?
- Does a chosen segment change over time?

Understanding the market, understanding the consumer, and the variety among consumers remains a rich source of competitive advantage in tourism. However, the amount of readily available market data is constantly increasing. Computers and statistical software packages are becoming standard marketing tools. And new marketing graduates are learning the art of data exploration in the core subjects of their degree. Consequently, understanding the market will soon be a prerequisite of organisational or destination survival in the highly competitive global tourism marketplace. Market segmentation makes use of the understanding of systematic variety among customers and as such represents a powerful tool for success. It functions like a magnifying glass for managers willing to look at the market, and invest some time into exploring it. And if they take the time to look, they are likely to 'get what they see.' If they do not, their competitors might.

References

Arimond, G., and S. Lethlean. 1996. Profit Center Analysis within Private Campgrounds. *Journal of Travel Research* 34(4): 52–58.

Baloglu, S., and K. W. McCleary. 1999. U.S. International Pleasure Travelers' Images of Four Mediterranean Destinations: A Comparison of Vistors and Nonvistors. *Journal of Travel Research* 38(2): 144–152.

Baumann, R. 2000. *Marktsegmentierung in den Sozial- und Wirtschaftswissenschaften: eine Metaanalyse der Zielsetzungen und Zugänge.* Vienna: Vienna University of Economics and Business Administration.

Bieger, T., and C. Lässer. 2002. Market Segmentation by Motivation: The Case of Switzerland. *Journal of Travel Research* 41(1): 68–76.

Court, B., and R. Lupton. 1997. Customer Portfolio Development: Modeling Destination Adopters, Inactives, and Rejecters. *Journal of Travel Research* 36(1): 35–43.

Dimitriadou, E., S. Dolnicar, and A. Weingessel. 2002. An Examination of Indexes for Determining the Number of Clusters in Binary Data Sets. *Psychometrika* 67(1): 137–160.

Dodd, T., and V. Bigotte. 1997. Perceptual Differences among Visitor Groups to Wineries. *Journal of Travel Research* 35(3): 46–51.

Dolnicar, S. 2002a. Review of Data-Driven Market Segmentation in Tourism. *Journal of Travel and Tourism Marketing* 12(1): 1–22.

———. 2002b. Business Travellers' Hotel Expectations and Disappointments: A Different Perspective to Hotel Attribute Importance Investigation. *Asia Pacific Journal of Tourism Research* 7(1): 29–35.

———. 2002c. Activity-Based Market Sub-Segmentation of Cultural Tourists. *Journal of Hospitality and Tourism Management* 9(2): 94–105.

Dolnicar, S., and F. Leisch. 2001. Knowing What You Get—a Conceptual Clustering Framework for Increased Transparency of Market Segmentation Studies. *Abstract Proceedings of the Marketing Science*, 88.

———. 2003a. Winter Tourist Segments in Austria: Identifying Stable Vacation Styles for Target Marketing Action. *Journal of Travel Research* 41(3): 281–193.

———. 2003b. Tracking Posteriori Market Segments Over Time. *CD Proceedings of the 32nd EMAC Conference.*

Dolnicar, S., and T. Otter. 2003. Which Hotel Attributes Matter? A Review of Previous and a Framework for Future Research. In *Proceedings of the 9th Annual Conference of the Asia Pacific Tourism Association (APTA).* Volume 1. eds. T. Griffin and R. Harris. Sydney: University of Technology Sydney.

Formann, A. 1984. *Die Latent-Class-Analyse: Einführung in die Theorie und Anwendung,* Beltz: Weinheim.

Formica, S., and M. Uysal. 1998. Market Segmentation of an International Cultural-Historical Event in Italy. *Journal of Travel Research* 36(4): 16–24.

Frank, R., W. Massy, and Y. Wind. 1972. *Market Segmentation.* Englewood Cliffs, N.J.: Prentice-Hall.

Goldsmith, R., and S. Litvin. 1999. Heavy Users of Travel Agents: A Segmentation Analysis of Vacation Travelers. *Journal of Travel Research* 38(2): 127–133.

Hsu, C., and E. Lee. 2002. Segmentation of Senior Motorcoach Travelers. *Journal of Travel Research* 40(4): 364–374.

Israeli, A. 2002. A Preliminary Investigation of the Importance of Site Accessibility Factors for Disabled Tourists. *Journal of Travel Research* 41(1): 101–104.

Kashyap, R., and D. Bojanic. 2000. A Structural Analysis of Value, Quality, and Price Perceptions of Business and Leisure Travelers. *Journal of Travel Research* 39(1): 45–51.

Kastenholz, E., and P. Gordon. 1999. Segmenting Tourism in Rural Areas: The Case of North and Central Portugal. *Journal of Travel Research* 37(4): 353–363.

Klemm, M. 2002. Tourism and Ethnic Minorities in Bradford: The Invisible Segment. *Journal of Travel Research* 41(1): 85–91.

Mazanec, J. 1997. Segmenting City Tourists into Vacation Styles. In *International City Tourism: Analysis and Strategy.* eds. K. Grabler, G. Maier, J. A. Mazanec, and K. Wober. London: Pinter Cassell.

———. 2000. Market Segmentation. In *Encyclopedia of Tourism.* ed. J. Jafari. London: Routledge.

Mazanec, J., and H. Strasser. 2000. *A Nonparametric Approach to Perceptions-Based Market Segmentation: Foundations.* Berlin: Springer.

McKercher, B. 2001. A Comparison of Main-Destination Visitors and Through Travelers at a Duel-Purpose Destination. *Journal of Travel Research* 39(4): 433–441.

Meric, H., and J. Hunt. 1998. Ecotourists' Motivational and Demographic Characteristics: A Case of North Carolina Travelers. *Journal of Travel Research* 36(4): 57–61.

Moscardo, G., P. Pearce, A. Morrison, et al. 2000. Developing a Typology for Understanding Visiting Friends and Relatives Markets. *Journal of Travel Research* 38(3): 251–259.

Myers, J., and E. Tauber. 1977. *Market Structure Analysis*. Chicago: American Marketing Association.

Silverberg, K., S. Backman, and K. Backman. 1996. A Preliminary Investigation into the Psychographics of Nature-Based Travelers to the Southeastern United States. *Journal of Travel Research* 35(2): 19–28.

Smith, M., and K. MacKay. 2001. The Organization of Information in Memory for Pictures of Tourist Destinations: Are There Age-Related Differences? *Journal of Travel Research* 39(3): 261–266.

Wedel, M., and W. Kamakura. 2002. *Market Segmentation. Conceptual and Methodological Foundations*. Boston: Kluwer Academic Publishers.

17 Developing strategic approaches to tourism destination marketing: the Australian experience

Bill (H.W.) Faulkner

Introduction

The emergence and continuation of tourism as a dynamic and viable industry is dependent on the adoption of a strategic approach to destination planning and marketing. The hallmark of such an approach is the inclusion of a systematic and structured analysis of broader environmental factors affecting tourism demand as an integral part of the planning process. Equally, as an adjunct to this approach, the ongoing evaluation of the strategies adopted is essential to ensure programmes that become ineffective or counter-productive are identified and replaced. The dynamics of the strategic planning process can thus be likened to the 'natural selection' of programme activities.

Although it can be argued that this approach is necessary in any domain of human activity, it is particularly applicable to the tourism field because of the highly discretionary nature of tourism demand, and its consequent sensitivity to both transitory shocks and long-term trends in the broader environment. A full appreciation of these factors is essential if public sector tourism organisations and private sector tourism enterprises are to exploit new opportunities as they arise and adapt to potentially threatening changes.

Although the above may appear to be a mere statement of the obvious to many readers, the approach advocated is either not generally applied, or it is applied only in a partial sense. This point is developed by referring to the case of public sector tourism marketing in Australia, where there has been a focus on advertising at the expense of a more balanced strategic approach. It would appear that, although the Australian experience may not necessarily be typical in this regard, it is at least widespread.

In considering these issues, we begin with an overview of the essential ingredients of the strategic approach and highlight symptoms of this approach not being applied in the Australian situation. Elements of the marketing perspective are then discussed in order to bring into focus specific aspects of tourism destination marketing that are relevant to the application of the strategic approach in this setting. A model describing factors affecting tourist arrivals at a destination is used as a backdrop for reviewing the dynamics of the Australian inbound market and, in the process, attention is drawn to the range of environmental factors that have a bearing on the effectiveness of marketing programmes. The current status of tourism destination marketing in Australia is then reviewed in order to elaborate on the key facets of the strategic approach and, finally, the argument for including evaluation procedures as a routine component of the strategic planning process is outlined.

Essential Ingredients of the Strategic Approach

For the purposes of this analysis, the strategic approach is regarded as involving the following essential ingredients:

- A comprehensive and integrated plan of action for an enterprise organisation.
- A clearly enunciated set of goals and objectives that provide the focus for the plan of action. These will reflect the corporate view of what is essential for the long-term effectiveness and survival of the organisation and its product.
- The establishment of systems for monitoring and evaluating progress toward goals, objectives, and targets specified in action plans.
- An approach to planning which explicitly reconciles the inherent competitive advantages and limitations of the organisation (or its product) with the challenges (opportunities and threats) of the environment.

The development of the latter aspect of the strategic approach usually involves what is referred to as SWOT analysis—(i.e., strengths, weaknesses, opportunities, threats) (Johnson and Scholes, 1984). SWOT analysis includes an assessment of existing, and anticipated, opportunities and threats within the environment. Its main purpose is to determine whether or not, in the light of emerging environmental conditions, the weaknesses of an enterprise, product, or destination have the potential to undermine its long-term survival. If this is so, those weaknesses will need to be remedied. Alternatively, the enterprise may have certain strengths that may put it into an advantageous position for exploiting new opportunities.

In the Australian context there are several symptoms of a general lack of strategic thinking in tourism. First, there is a prevailing 'boom and gloom' mentality, with dramatic shifts between the extremes of optimism and pessimism reflecting a tendency to overreact to short-term events and developments. Secondly, there is an inclination to rely on 'gut feelings' and anecdotal evidence as a basis for making decisions, rather than drawing on readily available objective research. It is human nature to assess a situation in a way that reinforces our preconceptions and prejudices. The first impression is therefore often reinforced by selectively drawing on anecdotal evidence that tells only part of the story. Then, when more soundly based research contradicts what has become the conventional wisdom, it is the research that is questioned rather than the conventional wisdom. Finally, following on from the previous point, there is a parsimonious attitude to investment in research. This is reflected in the data presented in Table 17.1, which reveals a disproportionately low level of investment in tourism research by the public and private sectors, relative to other industries.

The first two symptoms, in particular, reflect the incomplete picture of the environment affecting tourism held by many decision makers. That is, the assessments they make are not balanced by an appreciation of the full range of factors influencing trends in tourism. This point is considered in more detail subsequently when public sector tourism marketing in Australia is examined more closely. Aspects of the third symptom, relat-

Table 17.1 Research and Development in Australia by Industry, 1990/1991

	Share of GDP % (A)	Share of total R&D expenditure % (B)
Industry		
Agriculture	4.3	14.2
Mining	4.6	7.0
Manufacturing	15.3	32.1
Transport/communications	7.2	22.4
Tourism	6.6	0.3

Sources: (A) ABS Cat. No. 5306.0 and BTR estimates; (B) Cat ABS. No. 8104.0 (Faulkner, Peace, Shaw and Weiler, 1994, Table 2, p. 16)

ing to the lack of commitment to research, are also considered in this context.

Tourism Marketing in Perspective

Most analyses of tourism marketing (see, for example, Greenley and Matcham, 1971) highlight distinguishing features of the tourism product by referring to such characteristics as:

- Intangibility (product cannot be seen, touched, tasted, or sampled before purchase).
- Perishability (production is fixed in time and space and the product cannot be stored for future use).
- Heterogeneity (it is difficult to achieve standardisation to the extent that is possible in mass-produced goods).
- Inseparability (the act of production and consumption is simultaneous).

Although this approach may have been useful for pin-pointing characteristics of the tourism product that have a bearing on the marketing process, in these respects tourism is in fact no different from services in general. Furthermore, Middleton (1983) and others (for example, Wyckham, Fitzroy, and Mandry, 1975) have argued that services are not really distinguishable from goods in terms of these dimensions in any case.

Whatever one's position on the issues in this debate, there are two features of tourism that have a fundamental bearing on the subject of this paper, but which are neither emphasised nor generally recognised in the literature.

First, tourism is an amalgam of complementary services that are destination specific. Although Medlik and Middleton (1974) and Jeffries (1971), for instance, recognise the 'amalgam' characteristic, they do not specifically emphasise, or spell out the implications of, tourism being destination specific.

The implications of this from a marketing point of view are that some emphasis has to be placed on promoting the destination, rather than individual elements of the amalgam per se. Also, because the organisation of the services at a particular destination is fragmented, a considerable amount of coordination is required in this process. The need for this coordination has resulted in government intervention (Gilbert, 1990), and in fact the main role of the public sector in tourism development (in Australia if not in all countries) has focussed on generic marketing of regions, states, and the country as a whole.

To appreciate the second prominent feature of tourism marketing that is most relevant to the point of this paper, it is necessary to go back to the classical 'four Ps' framework (i.e., product, price, promotion, and place) attributed to McCarthy (1981). Using this framework, tourism marketing is described as being:

- The process of identifying the needs and propensities of the consumer (or, more specifically, different segments of the consuming public),
- Developing or modifying the product in accordance with the needs of identified target markets,
- Devising mechanisms for facilitating awareness of, interest in, and access to the product, and
- Translating the above into sales through distribution networks, pricing mechanisms, and so on.

However, given that the attractions or attributes of a destination are relatively fixed, there is a considerable element (at least in the short term) of adjusting consumer wants to the product. We thus have a typical chicken-and-egg situation in the marketing process, which was explicitly recognised by Kottler (1961) more than 30 years ago when he pointed out that 'marketing's short-term task is to adjust consumers' wants to existing goods, but its long-term task is to adjust the goods to the customers' wants.' Of course, when considering tourism we should substitute 'products' for 'goods,' because this statement clearly applies across the board to both goods and services.

The problem with public sector tourism agencies in Australia, and probably the world over, is that they have become fixated on the short-term aspect of tourism marketing by putting all their efforts into packaging regional icons into images designed to appeal to consumers in advertising programmes. This process usually involves some marketing research (group sessions, sample surveys, market segmentation analyses, etc.), which is used to identify those features of the product that have an affinity with the attitudes and preferences of consumers. However, as a consequence of the emphasis on advertising programmes, agencies have lost sight of the fact that consumer decisions occur within the context of a range of broader environmental factors. These factors impact on the propensity of specific market segments to make discretionary expenditures, and they influence the trade off between tourism and other outlets for leisure activity that must also be taken into account.

A strategic approach to marketing therefore requires a more rigorous analysis of these contextual factors than has been generally carried out to date. To elaborate on this point, an outline of what constitutes the environmental (or contextual) factors is provided in the following section. It provides the background required for the analysis of recent developments in public sector tourism agencies in Australia, which leads to the conclusion that they have become preoccupied with a tactical, as opposed to a strategic, approach.

The Dynamics of the Australian Inbound Market

For the purposes of elaborating on the strategic considerations that need to be taken into account in tourism marketing, we will examine the dynamics of the inbound market. The range of factors influencing the market is described in Figure 17.1, where a distinction is made between:

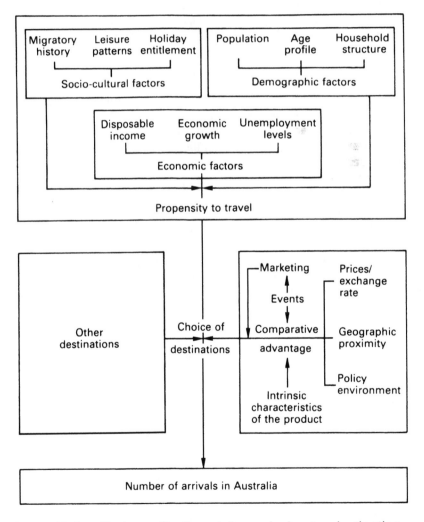

Figure 17.1: Factors affecting visitor arrivals at a destination.

- Factors that affect the propensity of populations to travel; and
- Factors that affect the comparative advantage of the destination question and, therefore, the potential for it to be chosen as a place to visit.

At this point it is important to note that the model has been for illustrative purposes only. It is not intended to provide a comprehensive or exhaustive coverage of all factors at this stage, although it could be construed as having the potential to provide a heuristic framework for doing so in the longer term. Again, examples from the Australian situation will be used for clarification purposes.

Considering the factors that affect the propensity to travel first, one of the main sets of variables relates to *economic factors*. The general health of the economy, as reflected, for instance, in gross domestic product (GDP), has a bearing on:

- Disposable incomes, and therefore the ability and preparedness to spend on discretionary items such as travel. The significance of this variable is reflected in the fact that, according to Middleton (1983), three-quarters of world travel in the 1980s was generated by the 20 countries with the highest per capita disposable incomes. The distribution of incomes within the population is also important because this will influence the proportion of the population who have sufficient income to travel.
- The general health of the economy also affects unemployment levels, which in turn have a fundamental influence not only on the size of the population with the disposable income required for travel, but also on the overall confidence of the market to spend in this area. High unemployment generates uncertainty within individuals about their future income-earning capacity, and thus reduces their preparedness to spend on discretionary items such as travel.

The significance of economic growth, and its bearing on tourism through its effect on disposable incomes, unemployment levels, and general consumer confidence is highlighted in Figure 17.2. The trend in visitor arrivals to Australia over the past 20 years reveals only three periods when arrivals actually declined—1975, 1983, and 1989. All these reversals coincided with periods of general worldwide economic downturns. The more pronounced reversal in 1989 reflects the additional effects of other contributing factors, such as:

- Time-switching effects associated with the 1988 World Expo in Brisbane and the Australian bicentennial celebrations,
- The appreciation of the Australian dollar,
- An Australia-wide domestic airlines pilots dispute, and

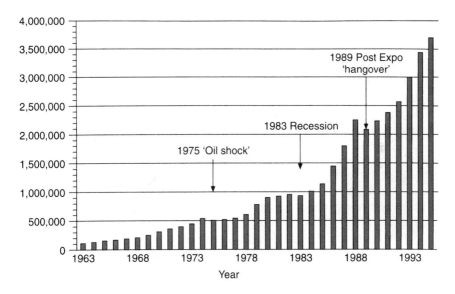

Figure 17.2:   Short-term arrivals in Australia, 1963–1991.

- An increasing proportion of holiday visitors in the Australian inbound market, which has the effect of making the market more volatile because of its increasingly discretionary nature (Faulkner, 1990).

The second set of factors affecting propensity to travel relate to *demographic factors* such as the size, age profile, and family structure of the population:

- After taking into account disposable incomes and the distribution of incomes, the actual size of the population is obviously critical in determining the number of travellers that can be generated by a particular market.
- Aging populations often generate more travel owing to the higher proportion of retirees who not only have more free time at their disposal for travel, but also have relatively high disposable incomes despite being income poor.
- Household structure has a bearing on the nature of demand through its influence on household disposable incomes through, for example, the incidence of double income households with no kids (DINKS) and the free time available for holidays (e.g., DINKS have an inclination for short breaks because of the work commitments of partners and the difficulty of arranging concurrent leave).

The third set of factors affecting propensity to travel relate to the *socio-cultural background* of the population. Relevant factors include:

- The migratory history of the population, which will have a bearing on travel to the extent that it generates visits-to-friends-and-relatives traffic, and
- Institutional factors, such as holiday entitlements, affect the amount of free time a population has at its disposal for travel vis-à-vis other leisure pursuits.

For instance, travel for Japanese is constrained by them having only two weeks annual leave.

Because population and wealth are two of the more easily measurable and potent factors affecting the potential of individual markets, various markets are classified in terms of these two factors (Figure 17.3). Here each country has been plotted according to its population (on the vertical axis) and GDP per capita (on the horizontal axis). If it is assumed that wealth takes precedence over the size of the population, then each group's potential to generate visitors can be ranked in accordance with the numbering system adopted in the graph. Thus, for instance, China is a low generator of overseas travellers despite its huge 1.1 billion-person population because fewer of its people can afford to travel.

If we look at how each market has performed in terms of the number of arrivals in Australia (Table 17.2), however, we can see that there are a number of anomalies:

- Japan has almost double the number of arrivals compared with the United States, despite these two countries being in the same group.
- The United Kingdom stands out as having up to 10 times the number of arrivals of other countries in its group.
- Singapore, New Zealand, and Hong Kong registered more arrivals than most of the wealthier and larger countries in the previous group.
- New Zealand is among the top three inbound markets despite its being one of the smallest countries.

To address these apparent anomalies, we need to look at the second set of factors in the model—factors affecting the *competitive advantage* of Australia vis-à-vis other destinations. These include such factors as:

- Geographical proximity, which in turn affects costs of getting to Australia in terms of both time and money, the level of inconvenience associated with time zone adjustments, and what the geographers refer to as intervening opportunities.
- Comparative prices of various aspects of the product, which, in turn, can be influenced by relativities between countries in wages, price

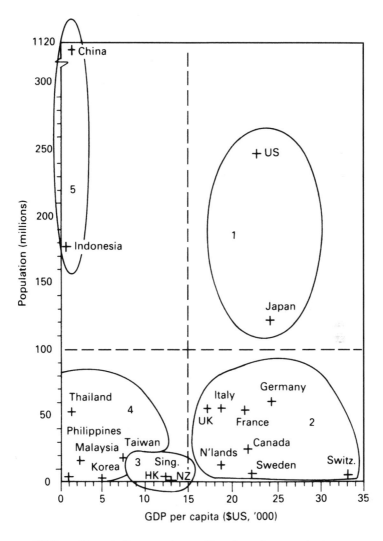

Figure 17.3: Population and wealth of major markets.

inflation, and exchange rates. The policy environment in the destination can have a profound effect on its competitiveness. The microeco-
nomic reform agenda in Australia has enhanced its competitiveness
as a destination through the impact of deregulation on the price and
quality of domestic airline services. However, despite this and other
reforms, many aspects of the Australian product continue to be
uncompetitive in terms of price (Commonwealth Deptartment of
Industry, Science and Technology, 1996). In particular, Australia's

Table 17.2   Visitor Arrivals from Major Market Groups

Group	Country	Arrivals in 1995 (000s)
1	USA	304.9
	Japan	782.7
2	Germany	124.2
	France	35.2
	Canada	58.4
	Switzerland	35.3
	Netherlands	34.5
	Italy	36.8
	Sweden	22.4
	United Kingdom	347.9
3	Singapore	202.4
	New Zealand	538.4
	Hong Kong	131.4
4	Taiwan	152.0
	Korea	168.0
	Malaysia	108.2
	Thailand	81.3
	Philippines	27.0
5	China	42.6
	Indonesia	135.0

weak position competing against Asian destinations stands out in this analysis.

- The political stability of a country will affect its attractiveness as a destination to the extent that this influences safety considerations. The decline in Fiji's inbound market during and after the 1980s political coup provides an example of this effect, as does the more recent impact of the Gulf War on world travel in general.
- As we have seen in the recent history of inbound travel to Australia, events such as the 88 Expo can have a profound short-term effect on visitor numbers. They can also have a longer term promotional effect. The staging of the 2000 Olympics in Sydney has been broadly endorsed as a major coup for the tourism industry because of its potential to have this effect.

Given that Australia is a long-haul destination for most countries, international airfares make up a substantial proportion of the total cost of visiting this destination. The effect international airfare fluctuations can have on visitor numbers is highlighted in Figure 17.4, which shows a peak in arrivals to Australia from the United States coinciding with the height-

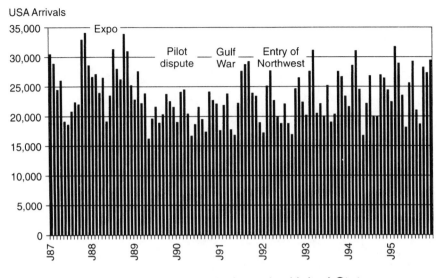

Figure 17.4: Short-term arrivals from the United States.

ened competition on the U.S.–Australian route that accompanied the entry of Northwest Airlines. This figure also highlights the response of the U.S. market to the 1989 World Expo in Brisbane.

The two remaining factors that affect the competitive position of a destination are the natural and man-made attributes (or intrinsic characteristics) that affect its appeal as a place to visit, and the effectiveness of the marketing of the destination. Advertising and promotional activities are fundamental catalysts by virtue of the role they play in stimulating the overseas markets' awareness of, and interest in, travelling to the destination.

In the analysis of inbound markets in terms of wealth and population, we noted several anomalies. These anomalies become somewhat more understandable if we take into account just one of the more readily quantifiable factors referred to earlier as contributing to comparative advantage—geographical proximity. When we superimpose the geographical proximity factor on the earlier classification based on population and wealth, as in Figure 17.5, it can be seen that most of the anomalies exceed expectations because of their greater geographical proximity to Australia.

What stands out in this sort of analysis is the impression of transience in the factors affecting demand. It seems that the combination of variables that is most influential varies in time, with each variable (or set of variables) coming into play periodically as some threshold is reached, which represents the point at which the market becomes sensitive to the

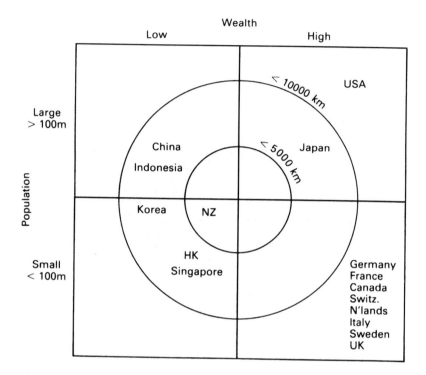

Figure 17.5:   Geographical proximity of major markets.

variable in question. If this is the case, then it is little wonder that empirical studies fail to agree on a common set of dominant variables (Crouch and Shaw, 1990). This suggests that constant surveillance and analysis of all these factors are necessary if the dynamics of the market are to be properly understood.

Public Sector Tourism Marketing in Australia

The previous model highlights the need to analyse macro-level factors affecting tourism demand in order to provide a context for other aspects of marketing research. Indeed, the analysis of these factors is essential for establishment of a truly strategic approach for two specific reasons:

• Such analyses provide the basis for identifying, and therefore targeting, those markets that exhibit the greatest potential to travel, and

- In evaluating the effectiveness of promotion programmes, variables that affect the response of markets, but are less susceptible to manipulation through the advertising process, must be taken into account.

In reviewing the progress of public sector marketing in Australia toward the satisfaction of these requirements one would have to conclude that, at best, we have had mixed success. There have been some positive developments, which represent a tentative step in the right direction, but progress beyond this point has faltered, owing to a shift in priorities toward an all-consuming concentration of resources on advertising.

On the positive side, the establishment of the Australian Bureau of Tourism Research (BTR) in 1987 resulted in the concentration of state and commonwealth resources to create the critical mass required for an effective research programme. Also, through this initiative, a more coordinated approach to tourism research at the national level has been established. Systems for monitoring the levels and characteristics of tourist activity have been upgraded and progress has been made in the analysis of factors affecting demand, especially through work carried out on the development of forecasting models. This work has been extended recently through the establishment of the national Tourism Forecasting Council, which adds a consultative dimension to the forecasting process. In line with the BTR's designated role of promoting the more effective use of research in tourism development, it has been instrumental in fostering the adoption of a strategic approach by making government and industry more aware of the importance of a firm research foundation in the planning and management process.

In general, marketing research carried out by government tourism bodies has consisted mainly of market segmentation studies aimed at calibrating advertising activities and, incidentally, to provide input to product development. Tracking studies have also been carried out for the purposes of gauging the immediate effect of individual advertising campaigns on changing the awareness of, and interest in, the product. Meanwhile, some satisfaction surveys have been conducted from time to time. These surveys have not always involved the degree of methodological rigor that would justify the conclusions drawn from them.

The recognition of the influence of contextual factors has been to some extent forced upon the commonwealth and state tourism agencies by their respective departments of finance and treasuries. The simplistic attribution of growth in tourism numbers directly to advertising campaigns, without reference to other factors, is no longer accepted as a credible justification for continued public funding of tourism promotion (Faulkner and Shaw, 1992). Such pressure was instrumental in the conduct of a more rigorous evaluation of the Australian Tourist Commission's (ATC) programme (Australian Tourist Commission, 1991), which featured a detailed analysis of contextual factors (Crouch and Shaw, 1990). Crouch (1994) has since extended this work by using a meta-analysis–based approach to isolate the key independent variables that have been used in the analysis of international tourism movements.

Despite the impetus that the ATC initiative could have provided, there remains a general insensitivity to the level of commitment to research, which is essential to the development of a truly strategic posture. Indeed, as mentioned previously, the prevailing trend among public sector tourism agencies in Australia is toward the concentration of resources on advertising programmes at the expense of research. This phenomenon has been referred to as 'advertising fundamentalism' (Faulkner, 1991), the rationale of which appears to hinge on the following proposition that 'gaining the competitive edge in the quest for maximising market share resides in the manipulation of consumer awareness and choice through advertising programs. In the context of limited funding and the high cost of maintaining electronic media exposure, therefore, the diversion of funds from research and other areas is justified.'

Although it is plausible that an increased commitment to advertising will increase market share, this will occur only if these programmes are integrated with a broader strategy encompassing product development and the effective identification and targeting of potential market segments. Also, the impacts of advertising and the marketing programme as a whole need to be continuously monitored and evaluated so that deficiencies can be remedied and adjustments made in response to changing circumstances. Therefore, without a sound research basis for these aspects of the marketing process, the destination marketing organisation's stewardship of the overall marketing programme is akin to 'flying blind.'

Systematic Evaluation as an Integral Component of the Destination Marketing Process

From the discussion in the previous section, it might be concluded that a considerable investment in research is an essential prerequisite for the development of a truly strategic approach to tourism destination marketing, and research has a two-fold role in this context. First, research is necessary to assess the current state of affairs and scan the environment in the manner necessary to carry out a destination SWOT analysis and, in the light of this, devise marketing plans for the future. Second, research is necessary to evaluate the impacts of these plans and thus provide a basis for identifying deficiencies and devising measures to remedy these.

The approach to the evaluation phase to date, however, has been distorted by the tendency for this activity to be carried out largely as a

response to external demands for accountability, rather than as a consequence of any recognition of its importance as an integral part of the planning process. A piecemeal and fragmented approach to evaluation has
therefore prevailed, with the high profile/high cost elements of marketing programmes being the focus of attention and the timing of the evaluation being governed by the periodic concerns of other agencies, rather
than the continuous requirements of internal programme management.
Within this environment, the full potential of evaluation as an integral
part of the destination marketing plan development and management
process is yet to be realised.

A framework for the comprehensive evaluation of destination marketing programmes is provided in Figure 17.6. Here, the evaluation process
is depicted as comprising four basic layers of activity:

- The programme review stage, where the appropriateness of organisational objectives is assessed, and the key strategies (media advertising, direct marketing, travel writer programmes, etc.) are identified.
  Associated targets around which the marketing programme is structured are also noted as benchmarks for considering outcomes.
- The performance monitoring phase involves the measurement of the
  output of each element of the programme in terms of various performance indicators (number of inquiries generated, coupon responses,
  column inches generated, etc.).
- The causal analysis phase carries the previous activities a step further
  by attempting to establish linkages between outputs and responses
  in the marketplace. At one level, we may employ such techniques
  as tracking studies and conversion studies to quantify immediate
  impacts, whereas market share analyses might be used to map longer
  term market trends with a view to identifying longer term effects. At
  another level, multivariate analysis or experimental methods might be
  applied in an effort to distinguish market reactions specifically attributable to the programme from those associated with the effects of
  broader environmental factors such as those discussed earlier in this
  chapter.
- Finally, the cost–benefit analysis stage is essentially concerned with
  establishing whether or not the costs incurred in implementing the
  programme are outweighed by the benefits derived from any increase
  in visitor arrivals that is achieved.

A more detailed review of the methods involved in the development of
this approach to evaluation appears in Faulkner (1997), where the underlying rationale for its application is also described. Briefly, there are two
key points regarding the limitations of evaluation methodologies and the
strategic planning process that warrant mention at this point:

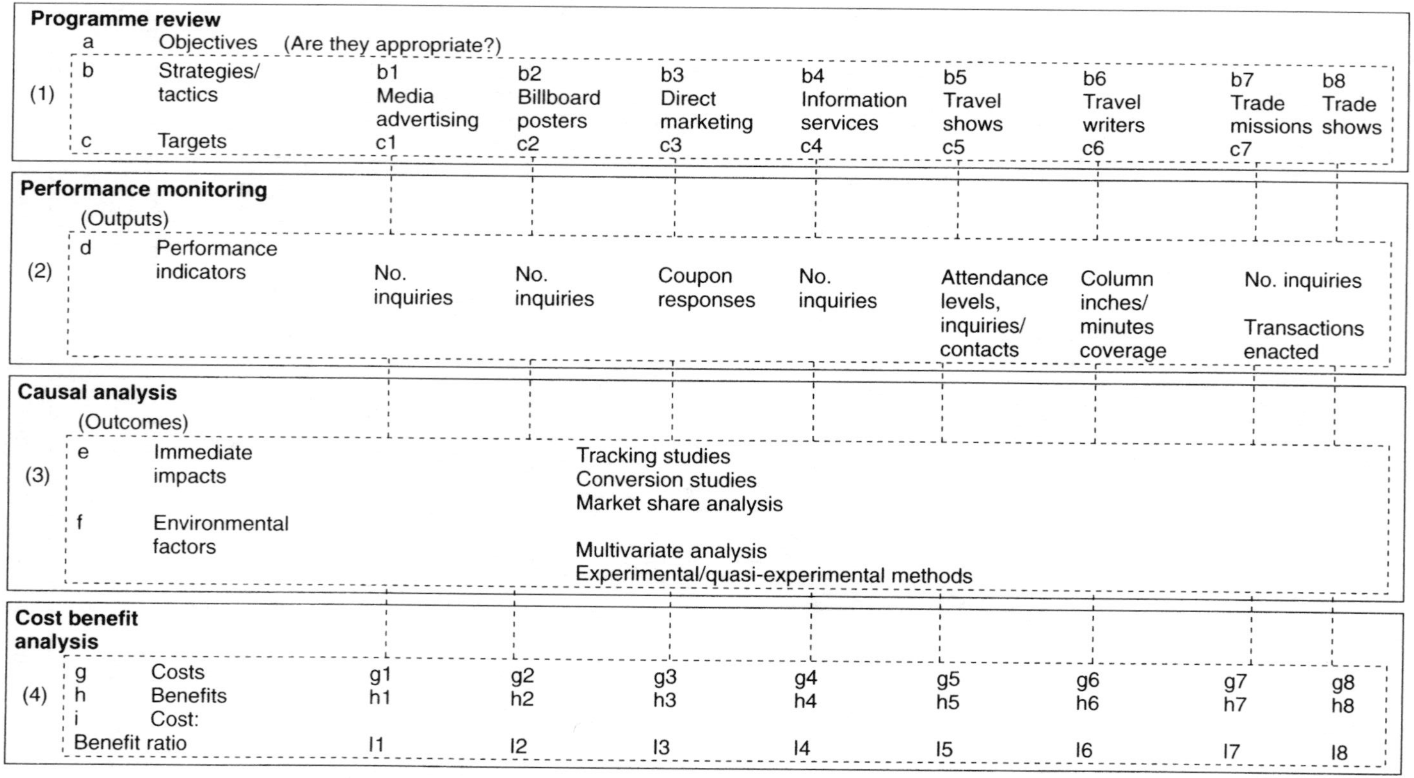

Programme review

		b1 Media advertising	b2 Billboard posters	b3 Direct marketing	b4 Information services	b5 Travel shows	b6 Travel writers	b7 Trade missions	b8 Trade shows
a	Objectives (Are they appropriate?)								
(1)	b	Strategies/ tactics							
	c	Targets	c1	c2	c3	c4	c5	c6	c7

Performance monitoring
(Outputs)

(2)	d	Performance indicators	No. inquiries	No. inquiries	Coupon responses	No. inquiries	Attendance levels, inquiries/ contacts	Column inches/ minutes coverage	No. inquiries · Transactions enacted

Causal analysis
(Outcomes)

(3)	e	Immediate impacts	Tracking studies · Conversion studies · Market share analysis
	f	Environmental factors	Multivariate analysis · Experimental/quasi-experimental methods

Cost benefit analysis

(4)	g	Costs	g1	g2	g3	g4	g5	g6	g7 · g8
	h	Benefits	h1	h2	h3	h4	h5	h6	h7 · h8
	i	Cost: Benefit ratio	I1	I2	I3	I4	I5	I6	I7 · I8

Figure 17.6:   Framework for destination marketing evaluation.

- Destination marketing programmes encompass a range of activities that represent a small proportion of the extensive array of factors that influence international tourism flows. Although some of these factors are quantifiable and can therefore be taken into account in conventional forms of analysis, many potentially important variables have been excluded because adequate data is not available and/or they are simply not quantifiable. We can, therefore, only ever expect to isolate the impacts of marketing and other contributing factors in a partial sense.
- Also, whatever techniques are applied in the evaluation process, they will each be deficient in some respect and the interpretation of results will be subject to certain caveats. This problem resulted in the ATC (1991) adopting a 'weight of evidence' approach to the evaluation of its programmes, whereby several parallel studies involving methodologies with different sets of strengths and weaknesses were involved. Thus, collaborative results produced by a combination of these studies imply a higher level of confidence to the extent that the limitations of one technique might be compensated by the strengths of another. The framework described in Figure 17.6 represents an extension of this approach in the sense that it provides a more systematic and coherent methodology.
- Attempts to attribute market trends to specific marketing initiatives are further compounded by the fact that many of the variables and events influencing tourists' decisions in general, and the relative attractiveness of the destination in particular, are simply beyond the control of destination marketing organisations. There are two implications of this. First, whatever criteria are adopted as indicators of success in the marketplace, caution must be exercised in the extent to which outcomes are attributed specifically to marketing activities. Some outcomes are achieved as the consequence of a fortuitous (or unfortunate) convergence of random events irrespective of the actions of destination marketing organisations. Second, no matter how sophisticated the forecasting methodologies on which strategic planning may be based, the environment in which we operate is essentially chaotic and the only certainty is that the unexpected will happen. Accordingly, a flexible approach to strategic planning is necessary, with environmental scanning and evaluation being constant ingredients of this process. As an integral part of this approach, a repertoire of contingency plans should be in place so that the organisation can respond more promptly to unexpected threats and opportunities as they arise (Faulkner and Valerio, 1995).

In the Australian context, the advertising fundamentalists will appear to be vindicated in the short term, as growth in the inbound and domestic tourism sectors in the early to mid-1990s has continued in response to improving international and domestic economic conditions, and the inbound market in particular continues to be boosted by the growth of nearby Asian economies. The extent to which increased visitation levels are actually attributable to the emphasis on advertising will therefore be open to question, and will certainly not be verifiable if research functions remain underresourced. More importantly, however, problems will be encountered in the future as the effectiveness of longer term (i.e., strategic) planning is jeopardized by the insufficient research input to both the analysis of emerging trends and the evaluation of previous methods. We are therefore prone to repeating the mistakes of the past.

Conclusion

The basic proposition of this chapter has been that the analysis of the contextual or environmental factors affecting tourism demand is an integral part of the more strategic approach to tourism marketing, which is so essential for long-term effectiveness. Equally, more rigorous and systematic evaluations of marketing effectiveness are required to complement this approach. The trend toward advertising fundamentalism (at the expense of the commitment to research) among tourism agencies in Australia is therefore inconsistent with the development of the strategic marketing approach and will be counter-productive in the longer term.

From an Australian point of view, this trend will progressively undermine any competitive advantage its tourism product either currently possesses or has the potential to develop in the future. Of course, this will occur only to the extent that other countries, which provide alternative destinations, are not also falling into the 'advertising fundamentalism' trap.

It seems highly likely, however, that the failure to adopt a truly strategic approach is not unique to Australia. On an international scale, therefore, the implications of this phenomenon go beyond simply the effect it may have on the competitive advantage of individual countries vis-à-vis others. The real problem is that the prevailing approach to tourism development and marketing has the potential to stifle the emergence of tourism as a dynamic and sustainable force in many economies.

References

Australian Tourist Commission. 1991. *Evaluation of the Australian Tourist Commission's Marketing Impact.* Sydney: Australian Tourist Commission.

Commonwealth Department of Industry, Science and Technology. 1996. *Australian Tourism: Is it Price Competitive*. Tourism Occasional Paper No. 4. Canberra: Australian Government Publishing Service.

Crouch, G. I. 1994. The Study of International Demand: A Survey of Practice. *Journal of Travel Research* 32(4) (Spring): 41–55.

Crouch, G. I., and R. N. Shaw. 1990. Determinants of International Tourist Flows: Findings from 30 Years of Empirical Research. *Proceedings of 21st Annual Conference of the Travel and Tourism Research Association*. June 10–14. New Orleans, La.

Faulkner, H. W. 1990. Swings and Roundabouts in Australian Tourism. *Tourism Management* 11(1): 29–37.

———. 1991. The Role of Research in Tourism Development. *Tourism Update* (Bureau of Tourism Research). September qtr: 2–3.

———. 1997 forthcoming. A Model for the Evaluation of National Tourism Destination Marketing Programs. *Journal of Travel Research* Vol. 35(3) (Winter): 23–32.

Faulkner, H. W., and R. N. Shaw. eds. 1992. The Evaluation of Tourism Marketing Campaigns. Occasional Paper No. 13. Canberra: Bureau of Tourism Research.

Faulkner, H. W., and P. Valerio. 1995. Towards an Integrative Approach to Tourism Demand Forecasting. *Tourism Management* 16(1): 29–37.

Gilbert, D. 1990. Tourism Marketing: Its Emergence and Establishment. In *Progress in Tourism, Recreation and Hospitality Management*. Volume 3. ed. C. Cooper. University of Surrey.

Greenley, G. E., and A. S. Matcham. 1971. Problems in Marketing Services. *European Journal of Marketing* 17(6): 57–64.

Jeffries, D. 1971. Defining the Tourism Product: Its Significance in Tourism Marketing. *Tourist Review* 26(1): 2–5.

Johnson, G., and K. Scholes. 1984. *Exploring Corporate Strategy*. Englewood Cliffs, N.J.: Prentice-Hall.

Kottler, F. H. 1961. *Marketing Management Analysis, Planning Control*. Englewood Cliffs, N.J.: Prentice-Hall.

McCarthy, E. J. 1981. *Basic Marketing: A Management Approach*. 7th ed. Homewood, Ill.: Irwin.

Medlik, S., and V. T. C. Middleton. 1974. The Tourism Product and Its Marketing Implications. *International Tourism Quarterly* 28–35.

Middleton, V. T. C. 1983. Product Marketing—Goods and Services Compared. *Quarterly Review of Marketing*, Summer: 1–10.

Wychkam, R. G., T. Fitzroy, and G. D. Mandry. 1975. *European Journal of Marketing* 9(1): 59–67.

18 Quality and sustainability in established destinations: who pays?

Michael Morgan

Global Tourism

On May 25, 2003, the centre-right People's Party was elected to power in the Spanish Autonomous Region of the Balearic Islands and immediately announced that it would abolish the tourist tax introduced by its left wing predecessor Partido Socialista Obrero Español (PSOE) the previous year. This ended an experiment that once again had made the Balearic Islands the focus of debate on the future development of established mass-market beach resorts.

This chapter will use the controversy over the tourist, or 'eco-tax,' to review the underlying issues. The Balearic Islands, Mallorca, Ibiza, Minorca, and Formentera, contain archetypal examples of mass-tourism resorts described in earlier editions of this book as 'homogenous products.' They grew rapidly in the 1970s and 1980s but by the 1990s were facing the problems of maturity—in the face of widening competition they were no longer perceived as offering the quality of holiday now expected by an increasing informed and experienced public. In response the Islands introduced a programme of infrastructural and environmental improvements subsequently copied throughout Spain and other beach resorts. Backed by partnerships with hotels and tour operators in a concerted public relations effort, this appeared to succeed in reestablishing the Islands as the leading Mediterranean resorts in the key British and German markets. The Calvia region of Mallorca was one of the first local authorities to introduce a comprehensive sustainable tourism strategy in response to the 'Local Agenda 21' resolution of the 1992 Rio Earth Summit.

However, with continuing expenditure needed to maintain the over-burdened infrastructure and retain a competitive edge, the Islands Council needed additional income. The eco-tax was their answer to the question of how the quality systems and sustainable policies, which many writers say are essential to the future of resorts, are financed in practice.

Why Tourist Resorts Tend to Become Homogenous Products

The factors that explain the homogenised nature of tourist resorts are still powerful. What Spain experienced in the 1970s, other regions, for example the newly formed Indonesian province of Banten, are struggling to control today.

Core Benefits

One of the first principles of marketing is that people buy benefits and not product features (Kotler, 1988). The physical features and facilities of the resort, its transport links, and the multinational network of tour operators and travel agents through which it is sold are all simply the means of 'delivering the desired satisfaction' (Kotler, 1988). In the case of beach tourism this is commonly described as Sun, Sand, and Sea, which in terms of benefits means warmth, recreation, relaxation, and an escape from the routines of working life. Some versions add other Ss to the list, such as sangria (or spirits) and sex, reminding us that holidays also satisfy social needs, and that one of the functions of the resort is to provide an environment where normal social inhibitions are suspended for the duration of the holiday. For many beach tourists the precise destination where they obtain these benefits is of secondary importance.

Tangible Features

The tangible features of the resort develop from its core attractions of a beach, safe bathing, and a warm climate. Hotels within walking distance of the sea, preferably with a sea view, are essential. Cafes for refreshment in the heat of the day, and bars and nightspots for socialising in the warm nights soon follow. Shops develop to serve the needs of the tourists for souvenirs, beachwear, games equipment, cosmetics, and gifts. It is inevitable that the land use of resorts follows predictable patterns distinct from normal residential and commercial developments (Lavery, 1971) with a recreational business district—'a seasonally oriented grouping of restaurants, novelty and souvenir shops' (Stansfield and Rickert, 1970).

Packaging and Distribution

These Mediterranean resorts are packaged by Northern European tour operators with very little emphasis on their geographical location. As Goodall and Bergsma say, 'The mass tour operator is marketing a holiday brand image emphasising the quality of service of that operator and in which the image of a holiday in a given destination is unlikely to figure prominently' (Goodall and Bergsma, 1990). Instead they are sold as a composite destination known as Summersun, or as tribal enclaves inhabited by like-minded tourists, normally segmented by age—Club 1830, Twenties, Young at Heart, Golden Days, and so on. These very successful products sell by delivering the core benefits more effectively or more cheaply than their competitors. The local culture, scenery, history, and architecture are optional excursions or a once-a-week folkloric floorshow in the hotel. As the operators control the marketing channels, the individual hotels and the destination tourist board have little influence on how the resort is presented in brochures and advertising.

International Markets, Global Products

The hotels and other facilities may be managed by local companies, but the style of their services is deliberately international. A hotel in Spain with British, German, Scandinavian, Italian, and Spanish guests tries to cater for all tastes with buffet meals and multilingual entertainment. The success of the Palma-based Grupo Sol, with 140 hotels from Bali to Venezuela, run on this multinational formula seems to support Levitt's (1983) famous assertion on the globalisation of markets, which is that 'The world is becoming a common marketplace in which people—no matter where they come from—desire the same products and lifestyles.' If the price is right, says Levitt, 'they will take highly standardised world products . . .' including, one might add, purpose-built high-rise resorts with a standardised nightlife based on Coca-Cola, Budweiser, and 'dance' music.

Economies of Scale

The successful growth of tourism in the post-World War II period has indeed been price led, based on the tour operators' ability to deliver hitherto inaccessible warm-climate destinations at prices affordable by the vast majority of people in Northern Europe (and North America). To do this, the operators have needed to achieve economies of scale on charter flights and large allocations at resort hotels.

These low prices depended on the operators negotiating low rates from the hoteliers, which in turn were made possible by low wage levels and favourable exchange rates. As a result tourists were given three-star quality at prices that would hardly pay for a guesthouse in their own countries. This further encouraged the growth in the overseas market at the expense of the domestic market especially in Britain.

Standardised Building Methods

To benefit from the rising demand for large numbers of beds at low prices, local hoteliers have had to employ standardised building methods and plot ratios more reminiscent of London or Manhattan than of their own vernacular architecture.

It is too easy to condemn architectural styles in the resorts when buildings in the same styles were being built with the same disregard for the historical and cultural environment in most towns and cities of the world at the time. The growth of mass tourism coincided with an era of architecture advanced in technology but limited in aesthetics. Functional simplicity was preferred to ornamentation and disguise, straight lines and rectangles to curves and ovals—admirably honest in theory, cheap to implement, but monotonous in result. The spa resorts of the eighteenth-century and the seaside towns of the nineteenth were equally mass produced and homogeneous in architecture, but the crescents of Bath have to modern eyes an elegant charm we have not yet learnt to discern in the towers of Benidorm.

The reaction against such resorts can be seen as part of a wider post-modernist revolt against functionalism and internationalism in style. When the heir to the British throne described a modernist design for an extension to London's National Gallery as 'a monstrous carbuncle on the face of a well-loved friend,' he could have been articulating many a tourist's reaction to the overdevelopment of his favourite holiday area.

Yet when they were developed the high-rise resort hotels symbolised to the local business community not only profit but prestige, modernisation, and an alluring Americanised lifestyle.

Quality Assurance

This symbolism also worked for the tourist. Standardised products promoted globally with a strong brand identity do not succeed only on price advantage. Their instantly recognised style and logos promise a standard quality, reassuring amid the unfamiliar imagery of locally produced goods and services. To quote two recent advertising slogans, 'You're never far from a Hilton,' or 'If Thomsons do it, do it. If Thomsons don't do it, don't do it.'

For a tourist making his or her first visit to a country, the modern architecture and the multinational logos of the hotels promise an enclave of familiarity and security in a strange and threatening world. Around the hotels, smaller businesses, often run by ex-patriots, offer a similar reassurance in the form of British, American, or German style bars, cafes, and supermarkets.

In some resorts, this sense of the tourist district as a safe enclave is only too accurate. Tourists in some African resorts and European and American cities are warned not to venture away from the hotel on their own. In others, such as beach resorts on the North African coast there is literally nowhere to go—the nearest 'real' indigenous settlements being an hour or more away. The resort, or even the individual hotel with its pool replacing the crowded and polluted beach, is self-contained, like a permanently moored cruise liner from which the 'passengers' disembark only for organised excursions.

New resorts in the Caribbean and Far East are designed specifically as integrated resort developments (Stiles and See-Tho, 1991) with a range of sporting and social facilities such that the guest need not leave the site for the duration of the holiday, a concept pioneered by holiday centres such as Butlins in the United Kingdom and the French Club Mediterranee. These take the concept of the brand image replacing the destination image to the logical extreme, but the same characteristics of self-contained uniformity are shared by many more conventional resorts.

Why Has this Formula Succeeded in the Past?

This formula works very successfully as long as the tourist's prime concern is for relaxation and recreation in a warmer climate among people they feel comfortable with. The very artificiality of the resort enhances the sense of the holiday as a break from the real world. The familiar symbols in a warmer climate create a relaxed mood in which the normal social inhibitions are suspended. The 'British Pub' stays open all night, plays loud music, shows nonstop action videos, and garlands you with paper streamers. You are neither in Britain nor Spain but Never Never Land. The 1980s music and fashioned tastes have changed, but new generations of young people have sought the same hedonistic escapism in a series of resorts from Magaluf, Ibiza, Ayia Napa, and Faliraki.

The function of the destination in this holiday experience is primarily to provide the warm climate and the low prices based on lower wage costs and favourable exchange rates. It also gives the holiday an exotic background, often experienced as superficially as that of a themed bar or restaurant at home. It is made tangible in souvenirs of the local national stereotypical symbols—famous buildings, wildlife, or local customs—that bear little relation to the content of the holiday. Often they are not relevant to the particular region, as with the ubiquitous flamenco dancing dolls in regions of Spain far from Andalucia. These souvenirs and gifts help to give the tourist status on his or her return home from the exotic destination.

Growth of the Tourism Market in the 1980s

In the growth market of the 1980s, tourist resorts proliferated. New markets of first generation tourists took advantage of the short jet flights and low prices to escape the uncertainties of the Northwest European climate for their annual holiday. The boom was experienced not only in Spain but also throughout the Mediterranean.

Newer destinations were added to operators' programmes and new resorts built to cater for the demand. This led to the rapid development of previously untouched coastline in places like the Turkish coast into 'high density, low grade holiday townships, lacking not only visual attraction but also basic services' (Economist Intelligence Unit *International Tourism Reports*, 1989). The Algarve in Portugal is another area often cited as a recent victim of overdevelopment, having failed to learn the lessons from the development of the Spanish Costas (Barrett, 1989).

In the meantime the established areas of Spain went on increasing the accommodation stock, 70,000 beds being added, for example, in Majorca between 1986 and 1990 (Morgan, 1991).

This growth primarily from the United Kingdom was fuelled by the low prices commented on earlier. In 1986 the leading U.K. tour operator, Thomson, reacted to the first signs of market saturation and potential loss of market share with a dramatic series of discounts, sparking off a long price war with its main competitors. The result was volume growth at the expense of profit margins, which led to mergers and bankruptcies wiping out several leading tour operators, including, in 1991, Thomson's main rivals the International Leisure Group. However, a new rival, Airtours, emerged and the price-led competition continued for most of the next decade. A new wave of price-led development is currently being experienced by some European towns and cities near secondary airports chosen by low-cost airlines. Although the city short break market has different tastes, the temptations the sudden growth in demand offers for speculative and unplanned development, leading to the loss of local distinctiveness, are fundamentally the same.

In the short term, price wars benefit the tourists and the resorts, but the reduction in profitability affects the hoteliers as well as the tour operators. In Spain, particularly, the tourist industry was at the same time experiencing rising wage and other costs as the nation's standard of living rose in the era of democracy and European community membership. Compared with its emerging competitors it was no longer a cheap destination, a process later accelerated by the entry of Spain into the Euro currency zone.

There was therefore a lack of capital for refurbishment and renewal of the accommodation stock. As Fayos Sola (1992) writes of the Valencia region, 'the huge expansion of hotels at the beginning of the 1970s has not enjoyed adequate continuity or renovation. The approximately 900,000 hotel beds on offer are still concentrated in hotels with three star rating or less, and suffer from a high rate of obsolescence.'

As long as the tourists kept coming, there was no perceived problem, except in the minds of a sensitive elite who were not the target market of resorts like Valencia's Benidorm. The complacency was well expressed by Farrell (1982), writing of another tourist enclave on the other side of the world, 'Outsiders and insiders alike point to Waikiki as a design disaster—yet the generally rising occupancy rates suggest that far from being repelled, tourists come back in greater numbers.' This attitude also helps to explain the lack of any product differentiation strategy in these resorts during the period of growth.

The Crisis of the Early Nineties

Toward the end of the 1980s, tourism to the established Mediterranean resorts appeared to show signs of decline leading the travel industry in both sending and receiving countries to reconsider their strategies. The details are now history, and are well documented in earlier editions of this book and other articles (Morgan, 1991; 2000). The underlying issues remain a threat to the established resorts and lie at the heart of the decision to introduce an eco-tax (Balearic Islands Government Web site www.ecotaxa.org in Salguero Gomez, 2002):

> Tourism has essentially been based on a standardised product, offering good quality and value for money, and for years practically the only resources used to establish the product have been the sun and the beach. For just over a decade, however, the tourist seeking the sun and beach has given way to the tourist who wants a more active holiday, and who places a heavier demand on the choice of destination. This has in turn coincided with the expansion of tourist products in other Mediterranean countries,

such as Turkey, Bulgaria, Tunisia, Croatia and Egypt, which with their lower costs and less exploited resources, could represent serious competition for the Islands.

Product Maturity

An increasing number of destinations offered the same sun sand and sea resorts formula as Spain, with the advantage of added novelty and status. The success of the travel industry in taking the risk out of foreign holidays had lowered the 'involvement' of the tourist in his annual holiday decision. As a consequence, it no longer required what consumer behaviourists call 'extended problem-solving' but instead was guided by 'variety-seeking behaviour' (Engel, Blackwell, and Miniard, 1990). If all the resorts are basically similar, the tourist is more likely to try a different one each time in a search for variety. If the new destination offers the status of a long-haul holiday at a competitive price, the appeal is even stronger.

The concept of the product life cycle was adapted by Butler (1980) to apply to tourism areas. The difference is that in manufacturing industry, products that reach the decline stage of their life cycle can be discontinued or completely redesigned and relaunched. Neither option is available to an established resort. You cannot 'close' Magaluf or Salou. Too many jobs and too much capital are at risk. Nor can any one organisation 'redesign' a resort that is the result of years of interaction between private and public sector tourist undertakings and the local community.

Demographic Factors

The generation now buying family holidays (25 to 45 years age group) had grown up taking the annual Mediterranean holiday for granted. They were therefore less apprehensive than their parents about foreign travel. They were likely to have stayed in education longer and are more likely to speak a foreign language. They had also grown up with the car and wanted the benefits of mobility on holiday. They are health conscious and fitter, more interested in sports and 'extreme' activities such as windsurfing and its variations. They are also seeking to satisfy the need for self-fulfilment by learning or experiencing something new while on vacation. Tourism is one of the leading edges of Pine and Gilmore's (1999) 'experience economy' in which competitive advantage is gained by offering a unique, memorable, and transforming experience. The permanently moored cruise liner type of resort was therefore less attractive to them than a motoring tour based on a self-catering cottage or villa.

The influence of these trends could be seen in the way that independent holidays have continued to grow, fuelled recently by the Internet and by the rise of low-cost flights by new budget carriers and seat-only offers from charter airlines.

Changing Perceptions and Expectations

With increased competition from rising destinations and the greater sophistication of the tourist, differentiation of the resort product is now at last being recognised as essential (Fayos Sola, 1992). It is also being realised that the quality of the product, that is the fit between the tourist's expectations and experience (Parasuram, Zeithaml, and Berry, 1985) had fallen due to three main factors tackled in the Islands programmes in the early 1990s: lack of refurbishment, growing environmental awareness, and problems with bad behaviour in the resorts.

Lack of Refurbishment
The public spaces and the hotels have had to be refurbished and improved to meet contemporary tastes and expectations.

Environmental Awareness
There has been a response to the increase in environmental awareness in Britain and most notably in Germany where a survey noted that 80 percent of tourists said that an intact environment was important in choosing their holiday destination (Studienkries fur Tourismus und Entwicklung, 1997). That is not to say that the average beach tourist is a dedicated ecologist looking for sustainable tourism. What has happened is that stories in the popular media had made him or her aware of the threat of pollution and disease in Mediterranean resorts, of poor standards of hygiene, and fire safety in holiday hotels, and so the names of the popular resorts had become associated with overcrowding and overdevelopment—half-finished hotels and noisy dusty construction sites (Astles, 1989). Well-publicised environmental campaigns such as Calvia's Local Agenda 21 strategy have helped to improve the image of the islands.

Bad Behaviour of Tourists
The price war years have produced a phenomenon known to the British press as the Lager Lout. Encouraged by cheap discounted fares and holiday packages targeted at the teen and twenty market, large numbers of young British Scandinavian and other North Europeans flocked to the big resorts with their all-night disco bars. The resorts gained a reputation for drunkenness, drug taking, promiscuity, noise, and fights, exaggerated, they would argue by sensational coverage in the media. Successive Mediterranean resorts have sought to curb the excesses and restore their appeal to wider markets.

For all these reasons the established Spanish resorts, although retaining a price advantage, were no longer perceived as value for money compared with their newer competitors.

Out of Fashion?

The concept of the adoption curve (Rogers, 1962) is relevant here. New products, such as destinations, are first bought by a relatively small group of 'innovators' who are attracted by the idea of trying something new and different. These people set the trend or fashion, which is copied first by 'early adopters,' then by the majority and latterly by the 'laggards' who adopt only the most tried and commonplace products. Plog (1974) sees the diffusion in terms of psychological types; he considers that the allocentric or outward looking type who is interested in discovering the world and the people outside his previous experience will be the first to seek out new and different destinations, whereas the psychocentric or self-focussed type prefers the familiarity of established destinations where he or she feels 'at home.'

It is clear that the Mediterranean beach resorts have ceased to attract the innovators and allocentric tourists. What is worrying the tourist industry is that even the majority, mid- to psychocentric tourists, are becoming dissatisfied and ready to move on.

The tourist and the tour operator can move on to newer, more distant destinations, switch to other types of holiday, or revert to domestic tourism. The established resorts remain. Tourism, which is responsible for 70 percent of the Mallorca's employment, is as much a monoculture as any third world cash crop, and communities that depend on it are just as vulnerable to fluctuations in world demand. Indeed the success of tourism had led to a movement of labour away from the land and a decline in the traditional agricultural base of the islands' economy.

Newer resorts could save expense and problems in the long term by balancing the need to desire to grab the benefits of tourism with the need to control some of the most obvious environmental consequences from the start. An optimist would argue that the growing environmental awareness in the major tourism originating nations makes this task easier than it was for the resorts that developed in the 1970s and 1980s.

Addressing the Problems

The initial programmes of refurbishment undertaken in the Balearics and subsequently elsewhere were explained in detail in earlier editions. The strategy can be summarised using Ansoff's matrix:

- Market Penetration (existing products and markets)
  - Improve the public and private sector facilities in the established resorts to meet the growing expectations of the tourists.
- Product Development
  - Extend the season through winter activity programmes.
  - Encourage quality development through stricter building regulations.
- Market Development.
  - Target new markets such as the domestic Spanish market and Eastern Europe.
  - Target new segments through golf, water sports, nature, and cultural tourism.
- Diversification.
  - Develop business tourism through facilities for meetings, incentives, conferences, and exhibitions.

The eco-tax strategy was a continuation of the same objectives and will be used here to identify the issues. The key objectives were set out in a statement on a special Web site: www.ecotaxa.org.

> To keep the Islands' tourist product *competitive* and at the same time guarantee its *sustainable development* requires a great effort on the part of the Balearic institutions and it is an effort in which *co-operation* is expected from the sector that will in the end also benefit from the *improvement in quality*. This principally means investing in environmental conservation, the framework within which the tourist industry develops.

With insufficient resources available from the state it is essential to find additional finance to implement the policies . . . without taking a short-term risk of irreversibly damaging the economic environmental balance.

In brief, the tax of around 1€ per person per night was to be collected by the accommodation providers. Rather than going to the general exchequer, proceeds were to be hypothecated to a Tourist Area Restoration Fund. This was to be used to finance four types of project to:

1. Redesign and restore tourist areas;
2. Recuperate resources and open rural spaces;
3. Revalue heritage features with social, cultural, and tourist relevance; and
4. Revitalise agriculture as a financially competitive activity.

The detailed programme is shown in Table 18.1 (Salguero Gomez, 2002, based on www.ecotaxa.org).

In addition, the socialist government abandoned plans for road improvements, building instead a new rail line in Mallorca linking inland towns with the captal Palma, refused planning permission for marinas and golf courses, and further tightened the regulations on hotel and apartment development.

Table 18.1 Activities of the Tourist Areas Restoration Fund

- Redesign and restore tourist areas
- Modification of access to eliminate traffic problems along seafronts
- Build dissuasive car parks
- Declassify development land in tourist centres
- Build sports and cultural facilities
- Network for reuse of treated water
- Improve public transport
- Adapt tourist town centres into areas for pedestrians
- Rationalise the building development model by demolishing obsolete buildings
- Create green areas and install public seating and lights
- Signpost for tourists

Recuperate resources and open rural spaces
- Conservation of nature reserves and areas of ecological and scenic interest
- Recuperate paths for trekking and excursions
- Create infrastructures of environmental interpretation
- Restore the natural heritage (wetlands, dunes, marine reserves . . .)
- Maintain traditional agricultural activities and local crafts

Revalue heritage features with social, cultural, and tourist relevance
- Restore monuments
- Provide cultural and congress facilities
- Install signpost and lighting in heritage resources, restoration work
- Conserve archaeological sites
- Recuperate traditional architecture
- Open centres for the diffusion of traditions and ethnographical values (salt flats, quarries, local fiestas, oil presses, etc.)

Revitalise agriculture as a financially competitive activity
- Recuperation of the countryside
- Recuperation and conservation of the rural heritage
- Installation of sales outlets for the autochthonous products of the Balearic Islands

Source: Salguero Gomez, 2002, adapted from www.ecotaxa.org.

The Principles Behind the Tax

The eco-tax can be seen as a case of a government intervening in the economy to correct a market failure to address its externalities (Pigou, 1938, cited by Kahn, 1998), in this case the cost of natural resources and the value of environmental damage (Holden, 2000). This abstract concept was given concrete expression by the Balearic minister for tourism. Companies that are investing the profits they make in Majorca abroad must realise that this money is made here and must be spent here in improving facilities and boosting new markets (Alomar, 2002).

It is an application of the 'polluter pays principle' of European Union regional policy. 'Public financing of environmental policy is in most cases to be avoided as it should be financed by the polluters themselves as far as they can be identified' (Europa Web site, quoted in Salguero Gomez, 2002). The growth of tourism puts pressure on the local environment through increased water and energy consumption, traffic congestion, and land use. The water table in Mallorca fell 90 metres between 1975 and 1999 (Tourismus auf Mallorca, quoted by Salguero Gomez, 2002). An environmental group warned that the potential value of tourism could be severely damaged by the destruction of natural resources, soil erosion through development, and fire risks through deforestation and high population density in the dry summer period (GBODN, 2002).

It also raises the question of the role of the public sector in tourism development. Is it simply one of quality regulation, promotion, and facilitation of an industry that is essentially a private enterprise, or does it have a responsibility to take a longer strategic view than the profit-focussed private sector is able to take?

Criticisms of the Eco-Tax

The tax was set at 1€ per person per night, but there were variations according to the type and category of establishment. The top categories (five-star hotels and aparthotels and four-key tourist apartments) paid 2€, whereas the lowest categories (one- and two-star hotels, and one-key apartments) paid 0.5€. Holiday campsites and agrotourism (farmhouse) establishments were also charged less. Although this was intended to be progressive—charging the rich more—in practice it was regressive. As Salguero Gomez (2002) points out, the tax paid is a lower percentage of the total holiday expenditure for those in five-star hotel than those in the four- and three-star categories. Although research in Germany suggested that resistance to the tax was greater in lower income groups, youth, lower income families, and retired people, it could be seen as discriminating in favour of more up-scale markets, a subtle tactic to reposition the Islands.

When the tax was introduced, some hotels chose not to pass it on to the customers in the form of higher charges, instead absorbing it and accepting reduced profit. The hotels adopting this policy were mainly the international chains with high volume business with package tour operators. In many case rates had been agreed on well before the tax was announced. The result could be seen as discriminating against the smaller independent hotels that could not afford not to charge their customers.

If these variations can be seen as distorting the market within the Islands, the effect on the competitive position of the Islands in the total Mediterranean beach tourism market was even more controversial. This effect has as much to do with perceptions as with the reality. It could have been seen as the equivalent of paying the price of a beer a night to help the local environment. Instead it received condemnation by the tourism industry on the islands and in the main originating markets. This was then taken up by the media, for example, in a campaign by Bild Zeitung to get its readers to e-mail the King of Spain in process. As a result of the publicity, Peter Rothwell, chief executive of TUI, the largest tour operator in Germany and Great Britain, claimed: 'Tourists have been choosing to travel to other Spanish destinations to avoid paying' (Templeton, 2003).

The issue then became a political one. Just before the local elections in April 2003, the Spanish Deputy Prime Minister, Rodrigo Rato, a member of the People's Party, blamed the policies of the Balearic Islands Socialist government for a fall in visitor numbers and in the Islands market share, with a resulting threat to jobs. 'The Balearic government has damaged the local economy and the facts and figures are for all to see' (Carter, 2003).

The Impact of the Tax

The extent to which this is true is debatable. The performance of the tourist industry in resorts and regions is heavily dependent on global economic, social, and political factors. The recovery of the Spanish resorts in the late 1990s, though no doubt enabled by the resort refurbishment programmes described earlier, was also partly due to the collapse of Yugoslavia as a destination during the Balkans wars and a sense of insecurity about the Eastern Mediterranean as a whole, and partly the result of the buoyant economy in Britain. Similarly, the slowdown of the German economy had begun to affect visitor numbers to the Balearics by 2000, before the tax was introduced.

Although German numbers had continued to decline, arrivals from the United Kingdom to Mallorca, Ibiza, Menorca, and Formentera were up 8 percent in 2002 with predictions of a further 5-percent increase in 2003. The outgoing administration received only five complaints about the tax (Templeton, 2003). It did not help the PSOE that the election was held just after a poor Easter period when numbers were down because of the Iraq war and bad weather in the islands.

Even the political acceptability of the tax is still debatable. Despite vociferous opposition from local business interests, the PSOE, which was the driving force behind the eco-tax, increased its share of the vote and lost power only because of a decline in support for its coalition partners.

The Unresolved Questions

The Balearic Islands continue to provide a fascinating case study of the central issues in global tourism, particularly those relating to the future of the established resorts. In contributions to previous editions of this book, I suggested that they offer a number of lessons for newly developing resorts to avoid the mistakes of the past. It is truer than ever to repeat that the pressures that led to those mistakes still exist.

Avoid overdependence on particular markets, or on tourism at the expense of other industries and agriculture. When the tourism market is more volatile than ever as a result of terrorism and its consequences, this is obviously desirable. Nevertheless, the Balearics have not demonstrated any evidence of moving to a posttourist economy, unless the growing number of permanent foreign residents is part of this process.

Do not lose control of the distribution channel. Pressure from the major tour operators played a big role in the demise of the eco-tax. Regrettably individual resorts cannot penetrate international markets effectively without the aid of intermediaries in the target countries. As East (1990) pointed out, the best way to sell a holiday hotel or resort in a foreign market is to make sure it is in a tour operator's brochure. It is too soon to judge whether the Internet has yet shifted the balance of power to the hotels and airlines or simply created new virtual intermediaries.

Maintain and enhance the quality of the resort facilities. As the Balearic Islands government realised, this requires investment that in a price-led low-profit-margin industry can be difficult to generate on purely commercial grounds. It also requires development controls that are still politically difficult to impose.

It is nevertheless the public-sector tourism authorities with their concern for the economic and social benefits of tourism to the whole community who have been responsible for most of the initiatives to refurbish the established resorts. In attempting to rectify the consequences of a previous lack of investment and effective planning controls, the Islands have had some success.

As we have seen, such measures incur considerable costs. What remains unresolved is how these costs are to be met:

- From a targeted and hypothecated tax such as the eco-tax?
- From general taxation?
- From borrowing for capital investment funded by the return such investment may bring in the future through increased competitiveness?

Sustainable development in tourism, as in any industry, is almost universally accepted as a theory. The case of the Balearic Islands suggests that implementing it in practice is not going to be so easy.

References

Alomar, C. 2002. Interviewed in *Majorca Daily Bulletin WTM Special*. November 11, 2002.

Astles, R. 1989. Overseas Package Holidays, Where Next? *Leisure Intelligence* 2: 43.

Barrett, F. 1989. On the Algarve Road to Ruin. *The Independent*, July 22, 45.

Butler, R. 1980. The Concept of a Tourism Area Life-Cycle *Canadian Geographer* 24: 5–12.

Carter, H. 2003. Interview with Roderigo Rato. *Majorca Daily Bulletin*. April 23.

East, M. 1990. Business Update. *Travel News*. December 7, 7.

Engel, J., R. Blackwell, and P. Miniard. 1990. *Consumer Behaviour*. 6th ed. Orlando: Dryden Press.

Farrell, B. 1982. *Hawaii, the Legend that Sells*. Honolulua: University of Hawaii Press.

Fayos Sola, E. 1992. A Strategic Outlook for Regional Tourism Policy—The White Paper on Valencian Tourism. *Tourism Management*. March, 45–49.

Goodall, B., and J. Bergsma. 1990. Destinations as Marketed in Tour Operators Brochures. In *Marketing Tourism Places*. ed. Ashworth, C. and B. Goodall. London: Routledge.

Group Balear î Defensa de la Naturalesa. Dades urbanístiques I ambientals de l' any 2000, Group Balear. Palma, Mallorca. n.p.

Holden, A. 2000. *Environment and Tourism*. London: Routledge.

Kahn, J. R. 1998. *The Economic Approach to Environmental and Natural Resources*. Orlando: Dryden.

Kotler, P. 1988. *Marketing Management, Analysis, Planning, Implementation and Control*. 6th ed. Englewood Cliffs, N.J.: Simon and Schuster.

Lavery, P. 1971. *Recreational Geography*. David and Charles, Newton Abbott.

Levitt, T. 1983. The Globalisation of Markets. *Harvard Business Review*. May/June, 92–102.

Morgan, M. 1991. Dressing Up to Survive, Marketing Majorca Anew. *Tourism Management*. March, 15–20.

——. 2000. Calvia, Mallorca Case Study. ETUP *Resort Management in Europe* London: Continuum Books, 26–36.

Parasuram, A., V. Zeithaml, and L. Berry. 1985. A Conceptual Model of Service Quality. *Journal of Marketing*. Vol. 49 (Fall), 41–50.

Pine, B. J., and J. H. Gilmore. 1999. *The Experience Economy*. Boston: Harvard Business Press.

Plog, S. C. 1974. Why Destination Areas Rise and Fall in Popularity. *Cornell Hotel and Restaurant Administration Quarterly*, Vol. 14, 55–58.

Rogers, E. M. 1962. *The Diffusion of Innovation*. New York: Free Press of Glencoe.

Salguero Gomez, E. 2002. *The Balearic Eco-Tax: An Evaluation of the Effects on the German Market*. Masters diss. European Tourism Management, Bournemouth University (unpublished).

Stansfield, C. A., and J. E. Rickert. 1970. The Recreational Business District. *Journal of Leisure Research* 2(4): 213–225.

Stiles, R., and W. See-Tho. 1991. Integrated Resort Development in the Asia Pacific Region. *Travel and Tourism Analyst* 3: 27–37.

Templeton, T. 2003. A Kick in the Balearics for Eco-Tax. *The Observer*. 6.

Studienkries fur Tourismus und Entwicklung. 1997. 'Fremdes verstehen.' *Sympathie Magazin*. (34), Ammerland, Selbstverlag.

Part Five

Bureaucracy and Procedure: Geopolitical and Policy Issues

Introduction

This chapter deals with a somewhat different planning and development issue, the role of government incentives in tourism. **Wanhill** (Chapter 19) suggests that historically, governments have intervened in order to both assist and regulate private sector tourism development. Due to the complex nature of tourism, it is improbable that the private sector can satisfy completely government policy objectives fostering a balance between host and guest benefits. Incentives are viewed as policy instruments that can help ensure cooperative development between the private and public sectors. The rationale for sustainable development is the alleviation of absolute poverty and the replacement of renewable natural and cultural resources.

A classification system of government incentives is presented including financial incentives and investment security. Rationales for each incentive are presented as well as a series of graphic information presented to illustrate the impacts of such incentives on the total amount of investment provided. Finally, in order to assess the effectiveness of the tourism project (from government's perspective), benefit analyses are discussed and illustrated examples are provided.

The author concludes by describing conflicts that frequently appear in national tourism policies. He states that incentives are policy instruments that may be used to correct for market failure and to insure a development partnership between the public and private sectors. From this perspective, the goal of sustainable development is the alleviation of absolute poverty and replenishment of the natural resource base.

Some type of government intervention is necessary, since on their own, market economies will not produce sustainable tourism. Such facilitation often takes the form of policy objectives that are intended to produce a balance of resources that meet the needs of visitors while at the same time benefiting the host community.

The mix of politics, culture and questions of social identity raise important issues addressed by **Burns** (Chapter 20). Similar to globalization, tourism is a set of cultural, economic and political phenomena, and its meaning and application are often both ambiguous and uncertain.

The author suggests four themes that frame the discussion of critical issues of tourism and culture at a global level and which frame the structure of the chapter: cultural politics; social identities; contested culture; and mediated culture. These themes that are explored form the common threads which lead to helping place tourism and globalization in context.

The chapter argues for the view which holds that tourism is a complex construction making up a powerful interface between cultures and societies. Despite the differences between politics, identity and culture, the confluences between them constitute a measured framework for discussion on the future sustainability of tourism. Such a framework indicated that social life, work, business, the environment and culture can be organized differently that the dominant economic models that prevail today.

The selection by **Bramwell** (Chapter 21), examines the myriad issues that must be considered when government officials initiate the process of selecting sustainable tourism policy instruments. It provides a description of some conceptual foundations behind these issues, and provides specific examples in order to illustrate the pragmatic implications of these issues for policy instruments. Preferences for policy instruments must be based upon moral and political assessments as well as economic evaluations.

The author points out that policymakers must consider the entire range of tourism policy instruments as well as the mix of those instruments. He suggests that when selecting policy instruments, government officials often demonstrate ideological or political bias, thereby favoring certain types of instruments over others. Ideally, policy makers must assess both the strengths as well as the weaknesses of specific instruments, together with the effect of ideology, social values, ethics, politics and economics on those assessments.

The intent of the chapter is to help facilitate assessments of specific policy instruments in different situations and to demonstrate how ethics, social values, economics, ideology and politics can affect their use.

The next chapter in this section deals with the political role of gender as seen by **Richter** (Chapter 22), as it relates to tourism. Gender differences in tourism throughout history are reviewed, areas of tourism research which have politically important gender issues are explored, and trends in political organizations and tourism that may effect emerging gender distinctions are presented. The main theme here is that women are not regarded as equal or given the dignity and respect that men are in the tourism industry. Some inequities include women's wages are usually lower, seasonal, part-time or minimum. The chapter also discusses the prospects for policy change toward allowing women to become equal partners in all aspects of the tourism industry.

As an employment and ownership sector, a rationale is provided for prostitution, and arguments for sex tourism are explained. Examples of gender differences in marketing, souvenirs and attractions are also provided. Marketing, linking tourism with sex is rampant throughout the industry, souvenirs continue to promote women as sex objects, and destination attractions remain male dominated preserves.

The bulk of the financial control of both the private and public tourism sectors lies in the hands of men. Right or wrong, women have always been perceived as particularly appropriate for 'front line' tourism positions due to their assumed more social and hospitable skills. However, women holding public office have consistently demonstrated a disproportionate concern for areas such as health, social welfare and concern for the environment, which the tourism industry has tended to downplay or ignore. Thus, if women achieve greater access to management and public policy positions, their greatest impact may well be in those tourism areas where they have traditionally had the least control or influence.

Crisis management in tourist destinations is the theme of the work of **Aktas** and **Gunlu** (Chapter 23). These destinations, if they are to remain viable over time must adapt to changing market trends and prepare strategic plans dealing with anticipated potential changes. However, when destination areas are unprepared for changes in demand or supply, especially if they arise without warning, they may have profound, long-term negative effects.

The authors provide a description of the nature of crisis, and offer a typology of crises that relates to tourist destinations. The prevailing approach toward crisis classification of events is to place them in two categories, either those that arise externally or those that are self-inflicted. These are further split into groups of disasters and management failures brought about by physical, social, political or economic environments.

Contingency plans that can deal with the potential effects of crises in tourism destinations are an essential part of management planning. Such planning cannot prevent a harmful event, but can serve as a guide for managing its aftermath. The chapter offers a basic checklist for tourism destination crisis management including damage assessment, and provides actual examples of such management in a number of world countries.

19 Role of government incentives

Stephen Wanhill

Introduction

The undoubted growth in the economic prosperity of the major industrial countries together with the travel revolution brought about through holidays with pay, lower international transport costs in real terms, and information technology has seen world tourism grow to a truly global business. Thus the worldwide significance of the sector as a mechanism for economic development has meant that it is an investment opportunity that few governments can afford to ignore. However, defining a tourist's journey, whether for leisure or business purposes, is quite complex. The tourist trip has a number of characteristics, namely:

- The trip is not a single product.
- It is made up of components supplied by a variety of organisations with different objectives and different economic structures.
- Success is the delivering of the right mix of components to satisfy the demands of the visitor.
- This delivery requires coordination and cooperation.

From this, it may be seen that tourism is a multifaceted product. It includes accommodation, transport, restaurants, shopping facilities, attractions, entertainment, public infrastructure support, and the general way of life of the host community. Thus, the essence of successful tourism development is a partnership between the various stakeholders in the activity of tourism to satisfy the requirement to provide a balanced range of facilities to meet the demands of visitors in a sustainable way. Because the tourism sector does not control all those factors that make up the attractiveness of a destination and the impact on the host population can be considerable, it is necessary that the options concerning the planning of tourism should be considered at the highest level of government and the appropriate public administrative framework put in place.

In this manner, governments around the globe have intervened to assist and regulate private industry in the development of tourism because the practicalities of economics dictate that the market system has to operate under certain parameters in order to have any success. Thus, the market mechanism and governance should not be seen as mutually exclusive activities, but rather complementary so as to signal the appropriate way forward for the sector. For example, tourism in Mexico began as a totally private sector activity. Its growth was limited in size (largely in the area of Acapulco), the product on offer was generally poor, and developments were unplanned. To counteract this, the government of Mexico created FONATUR in 1974 for the purpose of developing resorts, and funded the organisation from oil revenues and World Bank loans.

Where the line is drawn in partnership development between the public and private sectors depends on the prevailing economic and political and social policies of the country. The private sector may have many reasons for investing in tourism: on the one hand, there are foreign tour operators and leisure companies always looking to reap the benefits from the appeal of a new and exciting destination being placed onto the international travel market, whereas, on the other, there are many attractions at tourist destinations that have grown out of their owner's special interest or hobby. But in the long run, private operators must be concerned with the viability of their investments through generating an ample surplus to sustain the capital employed. As a rule, the greater the importance of tourism to a country's economy the greater is the involvement of the public sector and the stimulus the government is prepared to give to encourage investment, to the point of having a government ministry with sole responsibility for tourism. It is often the case that the planning powers with respect to tourism are devolved to local government, whereas the executive arm of government is transferred to a quasipublic body in the form of the national tourist administration (NTA).

Market Failure

The case for public sector involvement in tourism rests on concepts of market failure, namely that those who argue for the market mechanism as the sole arbiter in the allocation of resources for tourism are ignoring the lessons of history and are grossly oversimplifying the heterogeneous nature of the product. The early growth of the seaside resorts during the latter half of the nineteenth century, as, for example, in the United Kingdom, was the result of a partnership between the public and private sectors (Cooper and Jackson, 1989; Cooper, 1992). The local authorities invested in the promenades, piers, gardens, and so on, while the private sector developed the revenue-earning activities that enhanced the income of the area and in turn increased property tax receipts for the authorities.

Embodied in the tourist product are goods and services that are unlikely to be provided in sufficient quantity by the market mechanism. The market fails because of the existence of items within the tourist product that everyone can enjoy in common and that are equally available to all, which implies nonrivalry in consumption. These are public goods; their principal feature is that they are nonexcludable, resulting from the lack of or incompleteness of property rights. If the good or service is to be provided at all, it may be consumed by everybody without exception, and without charge at the point of use. There are also merit goods, whose consumption the state wishes to encourage because they yield wider benefits that cannot be retained by private businesses themselves and would lead, therefore, to underprovision. The upshot is that the single-minded pursuit of private profit opportunities within tourism may be self-defeating, as many older resorts in the Mediterranean and elsewhere have found to their cost (Plog, 1973). The outcome may not be the integrated tourism development that distills the essence of the country in its design, but a rather crowded, overbuilt, and placeless environment with polluted beaches that is totally out of keeping with the original objectives set by the country's tourism policy. For example, the major hotel developments that took place in the resorts of southern Spain during the 1960s and early 1970s were completed under laissez faire expansionism with little consideration given to planning or control. In general, the public infrastructure was overloaded and this has only been put right from the second half of the 1980s onward. New moves have taken place to refurbish the resort centres to give more 'green' space in the form of parks and gardens, and remove obsolete hotel structures. What is clear is that the complex structure of the product lends itself to the fact that in any tourism development programme there is often a marked difference between private and social benefits and cost.

The precise nature of a country's stance on tourism investment is determined by the kind of development the government is looking for and what role it envisages for the private entrepreneur. A markedly contrasting policy from the past is the case of Eastern European countries before 1990, where most of the emphasis was on social tourism, which allowed the population to benefit from subsidised holidays through workers' organisations and central government provision. Currency movements were arranged on a country-to-country basis through the form of bilateral swaps. The success criteria were based on visitor numbers and most tourist facilities were heavily subsidised. This has now changed as these countries have modernised their economies along market lines prior to joining the European Union and the common monetary regime of the

Euro. African countries have recognised the importance of tourism for conservation. By giving wildlife an economic value, funds are generated to support game reserves, preserve endangered species, and help eradicate poaching. Many Caribbean countries have strong views about the wisdom of developing casinos for tourists, because of the possibility of criminal involvement and also on moral grounds. In some cases, there are separate funding schemes for particular ethnic groups, for example, the Maori in New Zealand and the Sami in Sweden. Particular sectors may also be singled out for support: craft workers are important for the provision of souvenirs, so special provision has been made for them in New Zealand through the Arts Council.

Tourism Objectives

Incentives given by governments for tourist developments are the instruments used to realise the objectives set by the country's tourism policy. A list of strategic objectives that are commonly found in tourism plans is shown in Table 19.1. It is important from the outset to ensure that strategic objectives do not conflict with each other and that incentives offered to investors are compatible with those same objectives. Too often governments talk of tourism quality yet measure performance in terms of numbers. Common examples of policy objectives that are most likely to be at variance with each other are:

- Maximising foreign exchange earnings versus actions to encourage the regional dispersion of overseas visitors;
- Attracting the high-spend tourist market versus policies to continually expand visitor numbers;
- Maximising job creation through generating volume tourist flows versus conservation of the environment and heritage; and
- Community tourism development versus mass tourism.

Nevertheless, it must be pointed out that it is no longer considered acceptable in political terms that these objectives should be achieved at a cost to the environment or by adversely affecting the host community.

Thus sustainable development has become a high profile concept in any tourism strategy. This has been formalised through a set of defining rules, namely:

- *Weak sustainability:* This demands maintenance of the total capital stock, but permitting, in the very weak case, the free substitution of natural capital for man-made capital. In the weak case, this is allowed only up to a certain level and subject to minimum ecological constraints.

Table 19.1   Strategic Tourism Policy Objectives

Develop a tourism sector that, in all aspects and at all levels, is of high quality, though not necessarily of high cost.

Encourage the use of tourism for both cultural and economic exchange.

Distribute the economic benefits of tourism, both direct and indirect, as widely and to as many of the host community as feasible.

Develop tourism in a sustainable way so as to preserve cultural and natural resources. Facilitate this through architectural and landscape designs that reflect local traditions.

Appeal to a broad cross-section of international and domestic tourists through policies and programmes of site and facility development.

Maximise foreign exchange earnings to ensure a sound balance of payments.

Attract high-spending, 'up-market' tourists.

Increase employment.

Aid peripheral regions by raising incomes and employment, thus slowing down or halting emigration.

- *Strong Sustainability:* The requirement here is for maintenance of the natural capital so that substitution is permitted only between one form of natural capital and another, subject to various ecological constraints. The very strong version advocates the perpetuation of the status quo, so no substitution is permitted, which rules out economic growth other than that based on human well being from using renewable resources alone.

Very weak sustainability implies that the net present worth of an investment must be greater than the net present worth of any environmental effects generated. Weak sustainability requires the same rule but includes the implementation of compensatory environmental projects to the extent that the sum of any negative environmental effects of the proposed project over its lifetime, subject to threshold levels, is counteracted. Strong sustainability follows the same rule, but does not permit the natural capital stock to be depleted at any time during the life of an investment.

Unfortunately, for political reasons, governments often want the tourism sector to meet multiple and various objectives, thus the question of the environment becomes a difficult one to maintain when it threatens to be a drag on the economy in matters of employment creation. Weak sustainability is the only practical policy rule in these circumstances. Cast in this light, tourism policy as exercised by the NTA is not usually one of maximising but rather one of optimisation subject to the constraints imposed by the directions dictated by the selected objectives.

Classification of Incentives

Bodlender (1982) and Jenkins (1982) have considered the variety of incentives that are available in tourism, and these may be broadly classified as follows (Wanhill, 1999):

- Financial incentives;
- Reduction in capital costs;
- Reduction in operating costs; and
- Investment security.

Financial Incentives

The objective of financial incentives is to improve returns to capital so as to ensure that market potential, which is attractive to developers and investors, may be turned into financially sound projects. Where there is obvious market potential, the government may only have to show its support for tourism by providing the necessary conditions for investment security by removing any difficulties facing outside investors. Such a situation occurred in Bermuda during the early 1970s and so, in order to prevent overexploitation of the tourism resources, the Bermuda government imposed a moratorium on large hotel building (Archer and Wanhill, 1980).

The impact of financial incentives on the amount of investment is illustrated in Figure 19.1. The schedule SS represents the supply of investible funds, whereas D_1D is the schedule of returns to capital employed. D_1D slopes downward from left to right as more and more investment opportunities are taken up—the declining marginal efficiency of investment. In the initial situation, equilibrium is at e_1 with the amount of investment being I_1 and the internal rate of return i_1.

Conditions of market failure imply that the community benefits from tourism investment are not entirely captured in the demand function D_1D. Optimal economic efficiency is where the demand function that includes these externalities D_2D, intersects the supply curve at e_3, yielding a return i_3. To achieve this, the government now implements a range of financial incentives, which, in the first instance, has the effect of raising the internal rate of return per unit of capital to i_2, moving the marginal efficiency of investment schedule to D_2D. The new return i_2 equals $(1 + s)i_1$, where s is the effective rate of subsidy. If the amount of investible funds available for tourism is limited at I_1, then the impact of incentives serves merely to raise the return to investors by raising the equilibrium point to e_2. The loss to the government treasury is the area $i_1e_1e_2i_2$, which equals the gain to private investors, so there is no net economic gain to the community.

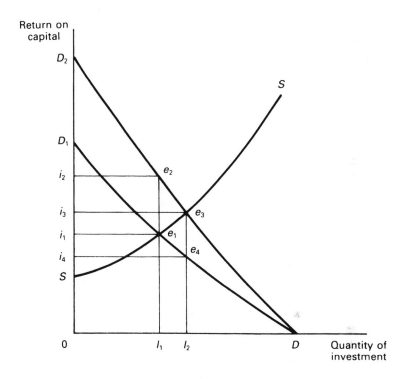

Figure 19.1:   Financial incentives on capital.

There is no doubt that many countries have been forced by competitive pressures for foreign investment into situations that are similar to those mentioned earlier. Countries can become trapped in a bidding process to secure clients and as a result the variety of financial incentives multiplies together with an escalation of the rates of benefit, without evaluating their necessity or their true cost to the economy.

Given that the supply of investment funds is responsive or elastic, the net effect of an incentives policy is to expand the amount of tourism projects to I_2, setting the rate of return at i_3, and the equilibrium point at e_3, which is the target level. In this situation the net gain in returns to tourism developers is $i_3I_2 - i_1I_1$, which is equal to the sum of the areas $i_3e_3e_1i_1 + I_1e_1e_3I_2$. The cost to the treasury is $s\ i_4I_2$, which, in turn, is equal to the area $i_3e_3e_4i_4$.

The private opportunity cost of the investment funds is the area under the supply curve, $I_1e_1e_3I_2$, whereas the public willingness to pay for correcting the externality is the area $I_1e_2e_3I_2$: subtracting the two areas gives a net gain represented by the area $e_2e_3e_1$.

The alternative to stimulating the demand is to increase the supply of investible funds. In Figure 19.1, this may be shown by a shift in the supply function to the right, which reduces the cost of capital to the private sector, thus permitting the marginal project to earn an internal rate of return of, say, i_4, and generating the optimal level of investment I_2. Typically, governments attempt to do this by establishing development or investment banks, arranging special credit facilities or constituting tourism development corporations. The economic rationale for this is that governments are usually able to borrow at lower rates than the private sector, because they have ultimate recourse to taxation to cover their debts. In the case of less developed countries (LDCs), finance may be obtained from international banks and multinational aid agencies on favourable terms. The counter arguments to adopting supply-side investment strategies are twofold. First, there is concern that government actions should not displace or 'crowd out' capital funds from other private investments, which could do equally as well, and second, the wider objectives of governments may generate institutional inefficiencies (and in some cases corruption) in the allocation of investment funds, which will frustrate progress toward I_2. These arguments have found expression in macroeconomic policy through restrictions on government borrowing and the privatisation of state enterprises, but equally beg the question as to the extent to which existing capital market mechanisms are suitable for achieving tourism policy objectives. In practical terms, the implementation of financial incentives is often a combination of both demand and supply initiatives.

It is important to note that there are frequent instances where it is gross uncertainty, as in times of recession, rather than limited potential that prevents the private sector investing. In such situations the principal role of government intervention is to act as a catalyst to give confidence to investors. Thus public funds are able to lever in private money by nature of the government's commitment to tourism and enable the market potential of an area to be realised.

Reduction in Capital Costs

Incentives to reduce capital costs may include capital grants, 'soft' loans, equity participation, provision of infrastructure, provision of land on concessional terms, and tariff exemption on construction materials. Capital grants are cash payments, which have an immediate impact on the funding of the project, as do matching benefits in kind such as the provision of land or facilities. They are usually preferred by investors because they are one-off transactions involving no further commitment and therefore are risk free. From the standpoint of the authorities they are relatively easy to administer. For small businesses, grant aid is often most appropriate, because they usually have substantial debt already and are in no position to lever in more.

'Soft' loans are funds that are provided on preferential terms. At their most simple they may be the granting of interest rate relief on commercial loans. Beyond this the government will normally have to put aside loan funds and create a development agency to administer them. Worldwide, the common features of most 'soft' loans relate to generous interest rate terms, extended repayment periods, creative patterns of repayment, and usually some restriction of the debt/equity mix so as to ensure that the project is not too highly geared in terms of loan finance, which makes it vulnerable to downturns in the market. In some instances loans may be tied to specific sources of supply; this is very common in country-to-country (bilateral) aid programmes.

Creative repayment patterns are methods designed to counter the risk profile of the project or the nature of the cash flow over the project's life. Thus a tourist project, such as an attraction, which may be particularly vulnerable in its early stages, may be given a moratorium on all repayments for several years. Alternatively a hotel in which the greater part of the cash flow accrues in the second half of the loan term may be granted 'balloon' financing in which the principal is paid back toward the end of the term so as to ensure greater freedom of operation during the initial years of the investment.

Bodlender and Ward (1987) point out that providing loan funds for tourism is more acceptable politically than the provision of grants. The argument in favour of loans rests on the fact that the funds will be recycled and the cost to the treasury will be only the preference element. This is not a rational argument, because all incentives have a grant component. For example, in the mid–1980s any hotel of international standard in New Zealand, which had a minimum of 100 rooms, could apply for a 10.5 percent grant in lieu of a 22 percent first year depreciation allowance. Major tourism development projects could get 48 percent grant-in-lieu of the first year depreciation allowance on specified items. Thus it is always possible under conditions of reasonable certainty to prepare a loan scheme that will bestow exactly the same present worth as a cash grant and vice versa. In a world of uncertainty the grant is risk less, whereas the loan plan becomes part of the risk environment of the project. Any risk premium attached to this environment will differ from project to project, so that the equivalence of the preferential element of the loan and the capital grant can no longer be assured. The instance under which the loan is chosen in preference to the grant would correspond to the situation where the investor is unable to raise the capital funds over and above the grant from elsewhere. This demands the question as to the cause of the inability to raise funds. It may be because of matters of investment security and then it is up to the government to give the necessary guarantees.

Equity participation involves the public sector investing in the commercial aspects of tourism development with the private sector. The extreme case is where governments themselves set up a tourist development corporation and take 100 percent investment in revenue earning activities such as hotels, which are traditionally regarded as the preserve of the private sector. Examples around the world have included New Zealand, Malaysia, India, Egypt, and many African countries, as well as Mexico mentioned earlier, but the rising trend toward market economics since the 1980s has led states increasingly to divest themselves of trading operations that could be undertaken by the commercial sector.

Perhaps more than any other economic sector, the development of tourism involves the exploitation of real estate. In many countries, the state owns considerable tracts of land and by providing sites on concessional terms the government may be able to attract the investors that best match its tourism policy objectives. The worth of such sites to investors is reinforced by the provision of the necessary construction works, such as access roads, and utilities (water and energy supplies).

Reduction in Operating Costs

To improve operating viability governments may offer direct and indirect tax exemptions, a labour or training subsidy, subsidised tariffs on key inputs such as energy, special depreciation allowances, and double taxation or unilateral relief. Indirect tax exemptions cover such items as wavers on import duties for materials and supplies, exemption from property taxes, licenses, and value added tax. The latter is a tax on labour and payments for capital in use, whether capital is in the form of debt or equity (Jensen and Wanhill, 2002). Concessions in respect of import duties and other fees are common incentives offered to foreign investors.

Exemption from direct (income or profits) taxes through 'tax holidays' and special depreciation allowances have meaning only when the project is profitable (hence viable because debt charges are normally deductible), and therefore over the hurdle of initial start-up risks. Tax holidays and reduced profit tax rates are some of the most popular forms of incentives given to new tourism projects and, more recently, are especially noticeable in the packages offered to investors by the expanding Eastern European and the Commonwealth of Independent States (CIS) regions: their approach has been to offer tax holidays from two to five years after the first year's profits have been recorded, whereas such holidays have tended to be between five and ten years for developments in LDCs. After the expiration of a tax holiday, governments may offer reduced rates of income or profits tax to international firms, depending on:

- The amount of profits invested locally;
- How much foreign exchange is generated;
- Improved economic linkages through purchases from domestic suppliers; and
- Staff training undertaken by the firm.

Depreciation allowances and tax holidays are often used in tandem, thus a five-year tax holiday may be followed by special depreciation allowances. The latter may vary from permitting the organisation to write off its assets to its best advantage over an eight-year period, to providing a substantial initial allowance of 20 percent to 30 percent of the capital cost and a normal 'wear-and-tear' allowance thereafter. The effect of special depreciation allowances is to defer tax payments, which amounts to an interest-free tax loan from the government (Bloom and Mostert, 1995). This favours longer term investments, because the longer the life of the capital asset, the greater is the present worth value of the tax loan. A further fiscal boost may come from the provision of an investment allowance (also known as a tax or investment credit), which is not merely tax postponement analogous to accelerated depreciation, but a tax reduction through being able to write off, say 30 percent of the initial capital, without affecting the tax value of the asset for depreciation purposes. Investment allowances favour assets that are replaced frequently, allowing the firm to take advantage of the tax savings.

The matter of a labour subsidy is indicative of the employment creation objective in tourism development. Factor subsidies can alter the choice of technology in the supply process. One criticism of capital subsidies is that they will tend to promote a capital-intensive structure whereas the emphasis is on generating jobs. A labour subsidy will always improve employment opportunities whereas the effects of a capital subsidy are indeterminable. This aspect is illustrated in Figures 19.2 and 19.3.

In Figure 19.2 the effect of a capital subsidy is to move the relative factor price line from FF_1 to FF_2. This moves the business on to a higher level of output as given by the shift from isoquant O_1 to isoquant O_2. In this instance both the amount of capital and labour employed increases from OK_1 to OK_2 and OL_1 to OL_2, respectively. But for Figure 19.3 the impact of the subsidy is to greatly increase the use of capital at the expense of labour. It was with this in mind that the Trade and Industry Committee of the U.K. House of Commons (1985) recommended that, on an experimental basis, the U.K. government should pay a grant of 30 percent of the employment costs of tourist facilities remaining open for one month longer than the previous year.

As a rule, tourist authorities counter the contrasting effects of subsidising capital by giving priority in funding to employment-creating

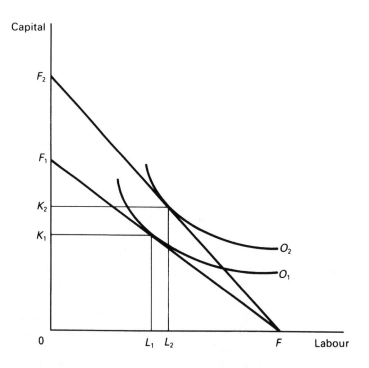

Figure 19.2:   Positive impact of capital subsidies on employment.

projects. A ready method of doing this is to tie the amount of grant to the number of full-time equivalent (FTE) jobs (Wanhill, 2000). The latter allows for the fact that a good number of tourism jobs are often part time or seasonal. This presumes an element of discretion in the awarding of incentives, which is not always possible when they have been laid down by legislation and are therefore automatic.

Tourism projects involving hotel developments are high users of energy, particularly where there are climatic extremes, such as in tropical areas where there is a need for air conditioning or in colder climes where the requirement is for continual heating. In these circumstances, energy use and management becomes a key element in the operating budget of the hotel. Large hotel corporations have always been able to negotiate energy prices with suppliers, but where the energy supplier is a public utility, as is the case in many newly emerging destinations, then the government is able to offer the additional incentive of reduced tariffs to strengthen the profitability of the business.

Double taxation and unilateral relief are country-to-country or single country agreements to ensure that multinational investors are not taxed

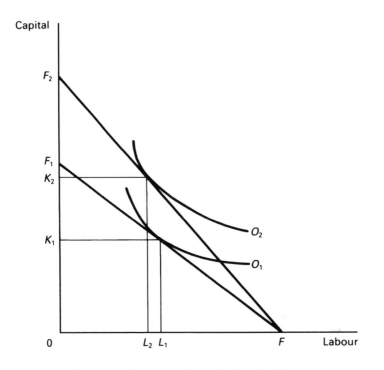

Figure 19.3:   Negative impact of capital subsidies on.

on the same profits in different locations. Suppose a company controlled in Country A trades in Country B through a permanent establishment in the latter country, it will pay tax on its trading profits both in Country A and Country B, but if there is a double taxation agreement between these countries, then a tax credit in respect of Country B's tax will be allowed against Country A's tax. If there is only unilateral relief, the company will be entitled to offset its tax liability elsewhere against tax payable in Country B.

Investment Security

The objective of providing investment security is to win investors' confidence in a sector that is very sensitive to the political environment and the economic climate. Action here would include guarantees against nationalisation, ensuring the availability of trained staff; free availability of foreign exchange; repatriation of invested capital, profits dividends, and interest; loan guarantees; provision of work permits for 'key' personnel; and availability of technical advice. To support these actions, there is the broader issue of the government's support for tourism. This may be demonstrated by marketing and promoting the region, particularly abroad, reducing administrative delays, simplifying the planning process, easing frontier formalities, initiating liberal transport policies, and so forth.

Clearly, without the confidence in the government to set the right economic climate for the tourist sector to prosper, investment incentives on their own may be of limited value in attracting outside funds or mobilising domestic investment in tourism. To counter bureaucratic inefficiency, complicated administrative processes and the lack of transparency in the legislation affecting foreign businesses, together with frequent modifications to the legislation, some governments, notably in countries looking to become new tourist destinations, such as in Eastern Europe and the CIS, have established 'one-stop-shop' agencies to ease the path of foreign investors, as well as including 'grandfathering' clauses in the legislation, which exempt foreign enterprises from unfavourable legal changes for up to ten years. For similar reasons, a good deal of World Bank lending, particularly in Africa, has gone toward structural adjustment policies to set the economic framework within which market-oriented projects may function.

Implementation

In implementing a tourism investment policy the government has to decide to what extent incentives should be legislated as automatic entitlements, as against being discretionary awards. It has already been noted that automatic incentives may give too much money away, when what is required to ensure that the treasury receives maximum benefit from its funds is the application of the concept of additionality. The latter seeks to provide financial support or the equivalent benefits in kind to the point where the developer will just proceed with the project.

The implication of additionality is an ideal situation where all incentives are discretionary and therefore offered selectively. The legislation would be fairly general, empowering the ministry responsible for tourism to offer loans, grants, tax exemptions, and equity investment as it sees fit. Such legislation is embodied, for example, in the U.K. 1969 Development of Tourism Act. The granting of incentives to prospective developers would be in accordance with ministerial guidelines. The latter should be regularly reviewed in response to the level of tourism activity and changes in policy. These guidelines may include statements giving priority to certain kinds of tourism projects that, for example, provide specific benefits to local communities, extend the tourist season, enhance the range of tourist facilities at the destination, offer full-time employment, give access to disabled visitors, attract both domestic and foreign visitors, and preserve the landscape. In sum, discretionary incentives allow tourist agencies to:

- Switch sector priorities with the object of encouraging new developments, modernization, and achieving a balanced development of tourist facilities in specific locations;
- Supporting projects that have high income and employment-creating potential;
- Selecting projects that have most chance of success, and are socially and environmentally sustainable; and
- Adjusting the money awarded to oblige the applicant to meet any investment specifications in respect of type, quality, and quantity.

To have only discretionary incentives, however, is a counsel of perfection. Competition for tourism investment often requires countries to legislate for automatic financial help in order to attract investors in the first instance. Some countries may legislate for all the incentives discussed here, others for a subset of them. Many countries have been guilty of copying the incentive legislation of their neighbours without any real grasp of the meaning of this legislation.

The appropriateness of the various financial incentives available depends on understanding the nature of the business risk and the likely returns of the tourist sector, as well as the ability of the country to afford them. Thus developing countries may find themselves in no position to offer grants or cheap loans. It is well known that part of the business risk in tourism projects lies in the fact that services are nonstorable (a hotel bed unsold is lost forever) and in demand being generally seasonal. This implies that peak demand determines capacity (unless capacity is regulated by planning legislation in order to preserve amenity value) so that the sector is always facing excess capacity at other times, which inculcates a certain reluctance amongst banks and other financial institutions to lend to the tourism sector, particularly because they often experience difficulty in appraising the financial viability of both tourism products and the managers of projects. As a rule, to control costs, government treasuries are against giving blanket reductions in general taxation, because it is difficult to prevent them applying to 'old' capital as well as new investment. The emphasis on incentives is their ephemeral nature for the purposes of providing the foundation for new projects to establish themselves.

An important trend is the growing interest in community tourism development, which has generated in the developed world, though less so in LDCs because of limited capital markets, a switch of emphasis away from large automatic grants to attract inward investment projects, toward small companies and indigenous development (Wanhill, 2000). The promotion of small firms is on the basis that they provide the community structure for entrepreneurship and job creation, and should ideally be a business that is flexible in terms customising products to customers, adapting production techniques to the essentials of place, and in respect of networking. However, what is necessary here is an action programme to augment investment incentives in order to create the right business environment for small firms, so that they might improve their quality, diversity, competitiveness, and profitability. To be specific, a programme of this kind could be structured around the following priorities: targeting small business finance, upgrading standards, improving communications channels, and raising the level of market intelligence.

Cost Structures

Not always apparent is the dominant cost structure in the sector. Typically, tourist projects have a high operating leverage, which implies a high level of fixed costs arising out of the initial capital investment and low operating costs. This makes pricing difficult, because operating costs are no longer a reliable guide as to what to charge, and also results in businesses that are very sensitive to variations in demand. The problem is illustrated in Figure 19.4, where it is assumed that there are two projects that have exactly the same revenue line R and breakeven point BEP. However, one project has a high operating leverage as shown by the cost line C_1, and the other a low operating leverage represented by C_2. The possible outcomes of these two projects are shown by Q_1, Q_2, and Q_3. Suppose Q_3 sales are achieved, it is clear that the project with the high operating leverage makes substantially more profit than the other. This is represented in Figure 19.4 by the difference between the revenue and cost schedules, where it may be seen that $DF > DE$. On the other hand, if the outcome is Q_1 sales then the project with the cost structure C_1 will make large losses, $AC > AB$. Thus a 1 percent variation in load factors on aircraft may be critical to the profitability of tour operators, and when things do go wrong the consequences are often spectacular. The nightmare scenario for governments is where a major tour operator collapses either depriving its millions of customers of previously arranged holidays or leaving them stranded abroad.

In addition to the above, it has already been indicated that tourism at the destination end is extensive in its use of land and property. This tends to induce elements of real estate speculation, but the nontransferability of assets such as hotels or tourist attractions to other uses hinders their worth as a property investment. Add to this the seasonality of demand, which

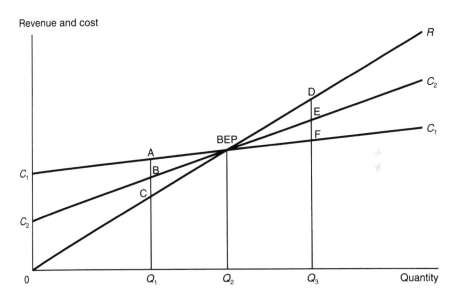

Figure 19.4: Effects of operating leverage.

produces irregular cash flows, and it is not surprising that financial institutions view tourism projects as risky investments. So if the objective is to improve viability, then the preferred form of financial incentives are those that reduce capital costs (Wanhill, 1986).

In the light of this emphasis on capital costs, the term 'viability' has a distinct role in the financial evaluation of tourism projects and the award of discretionary incentive in the form equity purchase, soft loans, or grants. In the first instance, the scheme must be feasible, in that it is capable of generating a surplus of revenue over its operating costs. Viability, however, has to do with servicing the capital investment; it depends on the interest rate, which can fluctuate considerably by virtue of government policies, the funding package for the capital involved, and methods of repayment. These concepts are presented in Figure 19.5. As before, R is the revenue line and C the total cost schedule attributable to running the project in a given year. The line C^* represents the cost of operation excluding the provision for capital payments. At a level of V_2 visitor days the project is feasible, because it produces a surplus BC over C^*, but it is not viable because there is a gap AB in the funds available to service the capital. To the left of D the project is neither viable nor feasible and conversely for point E. The object of giving investment incentives is to ensure that the programme becomes viable, either by moving the C line down to B at V_2 visitor days or reshaping the project to expand the market to V_3 visitor days or some combination of the two.

Revenue and cost

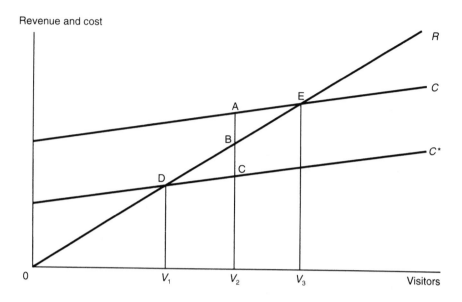

Figure 19.5: Viability of tourism projects.

Evaluation

It is well known that tourism is a demand-led sector whose influence pervades many different sectors of the economy. There is no single industrial classification called tourism, so the starting point for evaluating tourism projects, from the government's perspective, is to measure the economic impact of tourist spending and derive appropriate multipliers, in particular income and employment multipliers. Tourists come to a destination for many reasons so if the requirement is to establish the worth of a project that has been assisted through public funds, the first step is to establish the criteria for assessment.

Benefit Analysis

Suppose that there exists a tourist destination with two attractions and a seaside. Visitors are surveyed at both attractions and on the beach to ascertain what motivated them to come to the destination. Total spending at the destination (T) amounts to expenditure at Attraction X (T_x) plus expenditure at Attraction Y (T_y) plus all remaining expenditure (R). The pull factor (reason for visit) for Attraction X is a. For Attraction Y the pull factor is b, leaving $1-a-b$ as the significance of the beach. It follows therefore that attributable tourist expenditure by drawing power is:

$$\text{Attraction } X = aT_x + aT_y + aR$$
$$\text{Attraction } Y = bT_x + bT_y + bR$$
$$\text{Seaside} = (1 - a - b)(T_x + T_y + R)$$
$$T = T_x + T_y + R$$

The local tourist board has put public money into Attraction X and so wishes to evaluate its worth in terms of its contribution to tourist spending and employment in the area. The benefits of Attraction X *(B)* are the difference between with and without the project. The without situation is:

$$\text{Attraction } X = 0$$
$$\text{Attraction } Y = bT_x + bR$$
$$\text{Seaside} = (1 - a - b)(T_y + R)$$
$$T_w = (1 - a)(T_y + R)$$

Hence

$$B = T - T_w = T_x + a(T_y + R) \tag{1}$$

If the visitors to Attraction X would have come to the area anyway then the benefits would simply be T_x.

Employment Effects

The benefits shown in equation (1) are in two parts. The first term on the right hand side is on-site expenditure and the second, off-site expenditure. The amount of off-site expenditure attributable to the attraction depends on its ability to generate additional visitors. Hence, this may be termed the visitor additionality factor. The application of employment multipliers per unit of tourist spending to equation (1), either on an FTE or employment headcount basis, will give the gross employment *(E)* generated by the project. These multipliers are calculated so as to measure the direct employment effects of the project, the indirect effects arising out of intermediate purchases made by the project and the induced effects on the local economy as a result of the respending of local incomes derived from the project, and similarly for off-site expenditure. Thus:

$$E = T_x e_x + aOe_o \tag{2}$$

where e_x is the employment multiplier appropriate to the attraction, O is the sum of off-site expenditure $(T_y + R)$ and e_o the required employment multiplier. However, equation (2) ignores any demand diversion from elsewhere in the area. This is termed displacement and in this respect it is important to define the boundary of the project. As observed by Johnson and Thomas (1990):

> In the case of the economy as a whole it is sometimes argued that all expenditure, and consequently employment, is diverted and there is in effect a zero-sum game. This point is of some importance from the point of view of public bodies providing funds. Local authorities and the Treasury for example might have very different views on what is the net impact because they are concerned with different reference areas.

At a national level this argument assumes that market forces are moving the economy toward full employment equilibrium so that public investment expenditure is simply displacing private funds in the capital market. Similarly, the operation of the project is displacing demand in the same or related product markets and likewise in the labour and property markets. In reality economies do get stuck at a level of Keynesian unemployment disequilibrium and one of the major objectives of regional policy is to 'kick start' a demand deficient economy so as to raise the level of output through the multiplier process. This discussion does not imply that displacement should be neglected so that policy decisions are made in terms of the gross effect only, but merely raises the issue that the logic of the crowding out effect ends up with a 'do nothing' policy.

If d is the proportion of locally diverted demand (or demand diverted from other assisted projects) in equation (1), then, from equation (2), net employment is:

$$N = E - dE = (1 - d)(T_x e_x + aOe_o) \qquad (3)$$

Equation (3) forms the core of the basic evaluation model, which can be used to judge in employment terms the return to public funds given to the project by way of the whole range of incentives discussed earlier. As an example, consider the data presented in Table 19.2. The total on-site and off-site expenditure arising from the project is \$28,056,000. Visitor surveys have shown that only about 12 percent of staying visitors came to the destination because of the existence of the attraction. As is to be expected, this percentage is much greater for day visitors and local residents. From equation (1):

$$B = \$9,520,000 + 0.12 \times \$14,470,400 + 0.9 \times \$2,464,000$$
$$+ 1.0 \times \$1,601,600 = \$15,075,648$$

It is known that the attraction creates 87.5 FTEs directly on-site and so the relevant addition to this number is the employment generated by the indirect and induced effects of on-site expenditure. Using the appropriate FTE

Table 19.2   Calculating the Employment Impact of an Attraction

	On-Site Expenditure	Off-Site Expenditure
Markets		
Stay	$2,475,200	$14,470,400
Day	2,760,800	2,464,000
Local Residents	4,284,000	1,601,600
Total	9,520,000	18,536,000
Visitor Additionality		
Stay	Not applicable	12%
Day	Not applicable	90%
Local Residents	Not applicable	100%
Displacement		
Stay	0%	0%
Day	30%	30%
Local Residents	70%	70%
FTE Multipliers per $10,000 of Visitor Expenditure		
Direct	0.0683	0.0561
Indirect	0.0368	0.0349
Induced	0.0053	0.0053
Total	0.1104	0.0963

multipliers in Table 19.2, the number of jobs is $(0.0368 + 0.0053) \times$ $9,520,000 \div \$10,000 = 40.1$. Off-site jobs created amount to $0.1078 \times$ $(\$15,075,648 - \$9,520,000) \div \$10,000 = 53.5$.

Thus the value of equation (2) is:

$$E = 87.5 + 40.1 + 53.5 = 181.1 \text{FTEs}.$$

So far the analysis has only measured gross FTEs generated by the attraction. The net figure has to account for the displacement factors given in Table 19.2. Suppose that the evidence indicates that there will be no displacement of staying visitors because the attraction is providing them with more 'things to do' but there will be a 30-percent diversion of day visitor spending and 70 percent for local residents. It could be argued that there should be a 100-percent displacement of local resident demand, but, although this may be a good working assumption in that residents have many opportunities to spend in the local area, it does imply that there is no flexibility in residents' leisure spending budgets. Using the information on expenditure in Table 19.2, the weighted overall displacement factor is 0.3724, hence the solution to equation (3) is:

$$N = 181.1 - 0.3724 \times 181.1 = 113.7 \text{ FTEs.}$$

It is this number of FTEs that is traded against the estimated grant element of the incentives offered, in order to give the cost to public funds of job creation.

The core model given by equation (3) is capable of further adjustment to take into account factors such as project additionality; business displacement, differential impacts on the local labour market, and externalities. Incentive legislation used in the United Kingdom is hedged about with the concept of additionality. As stated before, this lays down the criterion that a grant (or loan) would be forthcoming only if the project would not proceed without it. Assessment of this position by project officers involves considerable subjective judgment about the likely future behaviour of the investor and in practice requires the investor to sign a document to the effect that the funds are a necessary condition for the project to go ahead. In reality there are degrees of project additionality, because the investment could have gone ahead at a later date, on a smaller scale, or at a lower quality. If a numerical value can be placed on such assessments then they can be included in the model. The difference between 100 percent project additionality and observed additionality in any postevaluation monitoring is known as the 'deadweight' element in the funding process, because it is money that is not required for the project to proceed. Similarly business displacement may arise in several ways: the funded project crowds out a competing investment opportunity, the investment replaces an existing business on the same site, or the project may result in a property move to a new site, leaving the old site vacant.

Replacement of an existing business may have a beneficial effect if there is a quality and cost improvement that raises long-term viability. Many assisted tourist projects have been built on derelict sites and have therefore resulted in a net improvement. Differential impacts on the labour market relate to the use of unemployed as opposed to people already in jobs; improving the skills of the work force, full-time, part-time, and seasonal jobs; the male/female ratio; local people versus outsiders; and so on. Externalities would account for the agglomeration benefits arising by virtue of the synergy of one project with another and its linkages with the rest of the economy to ensure a balanced growth of facilities at the destination in order to meet the many and changing needs of visitors. However, as the model moves through increasing levels of sophistication so data requirements spiral upward. Given that data sources are imperfect and there is always pressure on time, the practical effect of this is to increase the level of economic assumptions made, which in turn downgrades the robustness of the core model presented in equation (3).

Conclusions

Around the globe governments have intervened to assist and regulate the private sector in the development of tourism. This is because the complex nature of the tourist product makes it unlikely that private markets will satisfy a country's tourism policy objectives to produce a balance of facilities that meet the needs of the visitor, benefit the host community, and are compatible with the wishes of that same community. Incentives are policy instruments that can be used to correct for market failure and ensure a development partnership between the public and private sectors. The extent of public involvement depends on the economic philosophy of the government. The trend toward pure market-led economics since the 1980s has led to a clawback of state involvement and the questioning of incentives as mechanisms more likely to lead to market distortions. This is in total contrast to the concept of sustainable development, which challenges the ability of private markets to improve the distribution of income and protect the environment.

The baseline scenario for sustainable development is the alleviation of absolute poverty and the replenishment of the resource stock so that at a minimum no one generation is worse off than any other. The spillover benefits of tourism are well known, and, more than any other sector, tourism deals with the use of natural and cultural resources. The lessons of the past indicate that it is unwise for the state to abandon its ability to influence the direction of tourism development either through the provision of finance or through legislation. The short-term gains sought by capital markets are often at odds with the long-term sustainability of tourism environments. Moreover, when dealing with small tourism businesses, there may be a range of concerns and the authorities may want to ensure viability by trying to implement a variety of instruments through a multitasking action programme.

References

Archer, B., and S. Wanhill. 1980. *Tourism in Bermuda: An Economic Evaluation.* Hamilton: Bermuda Department of Tourism.

Bloom, J., and F. Mostert. 1995. Incentive Guidelines for South African Tourism: Implications and Challenges in the Context of Developing Socio-Political Trends. *Tourism Economics* 1(1): 17–31.

Bodlender, J. A. 1982. The Financing of Tourism Projects. *Tourism Management* 3(4): 277–284.

Bodlender, J. A., and T. J. Ward. 1987. *An Examination of Tourism Incentives.* London: Howarth & Howarth.

Cooper, C. 1992. The Life Cycle Concept and Strategic Planning for Coastal Resorts. *Built Environment* 18(1): 57–66.

Cooper, C., and S. Jackson. 1989. Destination Life Cycle: The Isle of Man Case Study. *Annals of Tourism Research* 15(3): 377–398.

Jenkins, C. L. 1982. The Use of Investment Incentives for Tourism Projects in Developing Countries. *Tourism Management* 3(2): 91–97.

Jensen, T., and S. Wanhill. 2002. Tourism's Taxing Times: VAT in Europe and Denmark. *Tourism Management* 23(1): 67–79.

Johnson, P. S., and R. B. Thomas. 1990. The Economic Impact of Museums: A Study of the North of England Open Air Museum at Beamish. Proceedings of a Conference on *Tourism Research into the 1990s*. University of Durham, December.

Plog, S. 1973. Why Destinations Rise and Fall in Popularity. *Cornell H.R.A. Quarterly* 13–16.

Trade and Industry Committee. 1985. *Tourism in the UK*. Vol.1. Session 1985–1986. London: HMSO.

Wanhill, S. 1986. Which Investment Incentives for Tourism? *Tourism Management* 7(1): 2–7.

———. 1999. The Economic Aspects of Location Marketing. In *Economic and Management Methods for Tourism and Hospitality Research*. eds. T. Baum and R. Mudambi. Chichester: Wiley.

———. 2000. Small and Medium Tourism Enterprises. *Annals of Tourism Research* 27(1): 148–163.

20 Social identities, globalisation, and the cultural politics of tourism

Peter M. Burns

Introduction

The potent mix of politics, culture, and questions of social identity raises important issues for the present volume and its concern with a rapidly changing world. Just like globalisation, tourism is a set of cultural, economic, and political phenomena, its meanings and applications loaded with ambiguities and uncertainties (Franklin and Crang, 2001). The rapid growth of cyber media and new destinations have exposed tourists to a bewildering array of images and potentials and the travel industry with critical issues on a scale hitherto undreamt.

Such matters cannot be simply dismissed in neo-Marxist fashion as the crude determinacy of market-led images. It would be a caricature to imagine place and space being occupied only by passive consumers in the role of tourists and a congenial, compliant local population. Tourism is simply too important and valuable to be so dismissed. As a multilayered, complex global phenomenon, tourism deserves a more nuanced analysis than the familiar binary divisions ('left-right,' 'good-bad,' 'right-wrong,' and indeed 'hosts-guests') can provide. Regarding the critical issues of tourism, it can reasonably be assumed that the industry is well aware of the environmental impacts and many companies are taking serious steps, in cooperation with international institutions such as the United Nations Environmental Program and World Tourism Organization to address issues of physical sustainability. Environmental awareness is clearly on the tourism business agenda. However, although a plethora of social scientists have spent decades dealing with social issues of tourism, there is very little evidence to suggest that cultural sustainability in the form of harmonious relationships between host communities, especially in poorer parts of the world, tourists, and the supplying tourism business sectors has gained the same level of importance as the physical environment, or indeed the same level of support as animal protection (Tricia Barnett, Tourism Concern, personal communication). Within this context, underpinned by the fact that globalisation does not simply 'impact' upon ossified local cultures but interweaves them into the changing global situation, four themes emerge to frame the discussion on the critical issues of tourism and culture at a global level and which will help structure the present chapter:

Cultural politics: where culture becomes political as increased competition among travel firms forces them to seek further for more undiscovered destinations, or to reinvent existing destinations (Hall, 1998) and their populations according to the latest market intelligence reports on consumer trends.

Social identities: perceptions of race, nation, and ethnicity can engender a simplistic view of 'Other' (Said, 1978), creating a global problem of new forms of discrimination, racism, and exclusion when juxtaposed with (a) the commercially constructed identities used in the travel industry and (b) the social realities of local peoples at the destination.

Contested culture: as the private and local, backstage space sought after by tourists in their search for the authentic is violated by their presence (Boissevain, 1996). And, contested in the sense that local people may comprise groups or minorities who disagree with tourism or feel excluded from the identity on display (Richter, 2001).

Mediated culture: culture becomes mediated as locals, academics, planners, and managers seek solutions to some of these problems, especially in the context of transforming political economies and postmodern and postcolonial conditions cultures (Higgins-Desbiolles, 2003).

These four aspects, together with a final reflexive section to bring the threads together into some cohesive conclusions, form the chapter, which commences with a brief contextualisation for tourism and globalisation.

The Context: A Globalisation Continuum?

Often missing in the discussions on globalisation is the notion of exclusion, not so much who is 'in' the global village but who is irrelevant. The excluded comprises regions and nations who do not fit the profile of potential consumers of producers, such as large parts of Africa, which, after the cold war implosion, no longer hold the attention of the superpowers (or the one remaining super power) as their capacity for being objects in cold war surrogacy disappears along with the dismantling of political systems of opposition that characterised the global situation between the early 1950s and mid-1990s. On the other hand, the right-wing writers John Micklethwait and Adrian Wooldridge (2000) in defending their book on 'the hidden promise of globalization' in which they praise George W. Bush's grasp of globalisation and dismiss concerns over Disneyfication, McWorld, and Cocacolonisation as being feared only 'wherever Chablis is drunk,' said quite specifically that 'Globalization does not involve the triumph of any particular culture at the expense of another. It opens people's minds to an unprecedented range of ideas and influences. And it encourages cultural mixing on an unprecedented and thoroughly admirable scale.' Monica Amor's (1998) essay on the kind of 'in-between' or 'liminal' worlds inhabited by the self- or socially excluded provides another position bringing together a number of conflicting perceptions on globalisation,

> In the twenty years since Edward Said, in his landmark study Orientalism, framed debates about cultural identity and the construct of the Other, there have been extraordinary worldwide political, economic, and social realignments; massive migrations and displacements of peoples; and the development of a seemingly borderless electronic communications network. At the same time, there have been intense and often violent, reassertions of the particularities of cultural, ethnic, and religious identification.

Although Amor's discussion is about art, her references to 'cultural nomads' and cultural resistance in the face of homogeneity hold resonance for students of tourism.

These three sets of values veer, just like the variety of definitions of globalisation, between triumphalism and cynicism. The two ends of this continuum on globalisation are captured in the political commentator Thomas Friedman's phrase 'the Lexus and the Olive Tree.' In his view on the politics of progress, one-half the world is 'dedicated to modernizing, streamlining and privatizing their economies in order to thrive' (Friedman, 2000). The other one-half hug the olive tree as a dichotomous symbol of traditional values (and local, anchored identities), which effectively impede progress by reifying and idealising an imagined past (where things were more connected and doors never locked) to the extent that progress is seen as a threat to social identity. Journalistic reflections such as Friedman's may not pass the 'scientific' test, but they provide helpful insight and capture the zeitgeist (the kind of social mood of the moment) that underpin the more theoretical perspectives such as to be found in the work of Roland Robertson, an early writer on the sociology of tourism.

Among Robertson's (1992) propositions for globalisation is that the world, pressured by global products and globalised consumerism, is becoming the same. 'Less differentiated' as Brewster and Tyson (1991) termed it, the 'homogenized world system' cited by Robertson (1992), or Levitt's (1983), is undergoing a 'converging commonality.' Alongside these converging trends are paradoxical divergences of power and culture. Most significantly, by power, moving toward metropolitan centres of capital and knowledge (creating an economic schism between rich and poor) coupled with a cultural shift whereby 'societies are converging in some respects (mainly economic and technological), diverging in others (mainly social relational)' (Robertson, 1992). Robertson (1992) also argued that globalisation can be characterised as 'compression of the world,' furthering Marshall McLuhan's (1960) earlier and optimistic concept of 'the global village' (for an update on this, see Boniface and Fowler, 1993). Dunning (1993) also identifies this trend 'as the cross-border interchange of people, goods, assets, ideas and cultures becomes the norm, rather than the exception, so our planet is beginning to take on the characteristics of a global village.' However, these latter views deny that the tendency toward a 'global village' (even when used as a metaphor for instant communications) is almost solely the territory of like-minded elites. It is they who have access to the electronic superhighway and who communicate with each other across the globe surrounded by seas of poverty, inhabited by those who do not communicate outside their own reference groups. Even with the electronic revolution, there are still parts of the globe that remain 'uninformed and lacking in "adequate" and "accurate" knowledge of the world at large and of societies other than their own (indeed of their own societies)' (Robertson 1992).

Cultural Politics: Framing the Narratives

Cultural politics happen at the intersection between culture and power, the space where civil society meets the body politic; culture, power, and politics are not simply inseparable, but are elements of the same amorphous whole that form societies and identities. For complex societies, especially those with contested or multiple identities, cultural politics will also refer to the ways in which power relations and systems of production frame and maintain the various layers of culture.

The relationship between tourism and the cultural politics at a destination is a complex one. It involves the way in which appropriated local cultures are represented in brochures and other media (Dann 1988; 1996). Oftentimes, it means creating a 'cutesy,' nonthreatening native backdrop to the leisure-holiday experience—a constructed identity within the global culture of international tourism (Franklin, 2003). In accepting this premise, we also have to accept the dichotomous and yet synchronous processes of localisation and globalisation as being inseparable (Turner, 1994).

This approach suggests that it is possible to examine tourism not as a true 'object' that science progressively uncovers, but as an historically produced discourse (Torgovnick, 1990) present as the global meshes with and locks into the local, the local–global nexus as Burns (2001), among others, has termed it. Cultural politics are then affected by both internal and external factors. In other words, culture would change anyway. In this, Wood (1993) is right in asserting that there is no such thing as a 'pristine culture' waiting to be smashed. Aspects of culture (including material culture in the form of souvenirs) are bought into the tourism system through spatial, temporal, and above all, political arrangements. For this reason a clear understanding of the cultural politics of tourism is essential in discussing tourism and globalisation.

However, the narratives arising out of the tourism, culture, and political nexus present something of a conundrum. Each of the positions, in their own way, starts from the somewhat simplistic premise that culture is somehow tangible. But, where a plural society collides with tourism even the 'ownership' of culture might be in dispute. An alternative reading might question, in the way that Wood (1993) seems to, the absoluteness of 'other' cultures. It might be that globalisation has created such ambivalent, yet powerful, modes of production (especially in the case of tourism) that the idea of an independent culture existing outside the framework of globalising cultural politics becomes a contradiction. When travel firms use the notion of 'unique culture' in their advertising media for exotic destinations, they are promoting a constructed culture that exists for the brochure, which is linked to the international tour company, which in turn is linked to global networks of workers, suppliers, and tourists (Sassen, 1998). The local people may cooperate in this enterprise because it might be in their best economic interests so to do (Enloe, 1989). The point also needs to be made that anthropology and mass tourism, just like mechanical image making, photography, share a common spatial and temporal background from late nineteenth-century technology and colonialism to the present time. During this period anthropologists and tourists alike discovered the 'pristine' cultures ironically noted by Wood (1993) and, in a sense, turned them into MacCannell's (1992) 'ex-primitives.'

This section has discussed the multiplicity of linkages and interconnections among states, societies, and economic enterprises that make up the postmodern and postcolonial world (Narotzky, 1997). The process by which events, decisions, and activities in one part of the world can come to have significant consequences for individuals and communities in quite distant parts of the globe (Gardner and Lewis, 1996), especially where their identities have been framed and put up for show by tourist companies following a commercial activity. The following section takes these arguments to their next logical step by framing them more clearly against the notion of social identity.

Social Identities: Moments of Tourism

As Marie-Françoise Lafant so eloquently asserted in the introduction to the edited book on tourism and identity, *International Tourism: Identity and Change,* the idea of building a social identity in a postmodern world of instant communication and travel without 'abutting it against the identity of others' (Lanfant, Allcock, and Burner, 1995) is an impossibility. Issues of representation and commoditisation create fundamental problems for tourism. Representation (in a metaphoric sense) without consultation is a phrase normally associated with politics, but for tourism there are an unimaginable number of cases where representation (in the literal, visual sense) of Other, for example, in tribal dress, in markets, as servants, as harmless, decorative background material to visual travelogues or advertisements for travel (Dann, 1988) can take place as a sort of cultural appropriation without reciprocal benefit or understanding (Crick, 1996; Franklin, 2003). The argument here is that although more developed nations have cultural stereotypes (such a the various countries of Europe, northern versus southern states in the United States, etc.) that are constructed through jokes or history or simply fiction, these are not the only ways in which such advanced places are known. Lesser developed countries have neither the political or economic clout that allows them to negotiate beyond the exploitation of culture as a tourism resource. Neocolonial analysts (Bianchi, 2002) would point toward the power of language (Pidginization or Creolization), whereas antiglobalists cite the dominance of global brands and cultural celebrities. However, in a curious way, it was Pidgin and Creole that enabled a quick entry into global networks at the turn of the nineteenth-century and culture at the local level, as expressed through and by tourism, that provides a modern day counterbalance to cultural dominance.

The role of commoditisation and social identity in tourism has been extensively discussed (Greenwood, 1989; Franklin, 2003) and many commentators agree that cultural reproduction at a local level for global markets emphasises shallow and fleeting 'moments of tourism,' where exchange is based on money for vulgarised culture. However, as with most things touristic, the solution (nor even the description of the problem) is not so simple. Such negative interpretations (even acknowledging the awfulness of airport art; Dorfles, 1969) have to be balanced against the possibility for the nexus of culture and tourism as a form of

identity booster that can play a pivotal role in leading people to rediscover or reinforce their identity through traditional dance, crafts, and arts
(Stanton, 1989; Bricker, 2001). For example, since the collapse of the Soviet
Union, where unique, ethnic, tribal, or national identities were subsumed
into the notion that all citizens were 'Soviets,' traditional forms of dress,
dancing, and other folkloric customs have combined with tourism to
boost (along with a resurgence in national languages) pride in the newly
emerging independence and freedom (Burns, 1998).

Meaghan Morris (1995, italics and parentheses in original) captures the
dichotomous essence of these arguments very well.

> Wherever tourism is an economic strategy as well as a money-making activ-
> ity, and wherever it is a policy of state, a process of social and *cultural* change
> is initiated which involves transforming not only the 'physical' (in other
> words the *lived*) environment of 'toured' communities and the intimate
> practice of everyday life, but also the series of relations by which cultural
> identity (and therefore difference) is constituted for both the tourist and the
> toured in any given context.

However, the other side to the cultural coin is that identity is being
changed 'at home' for tourists from the postindustrialised world (Lanfant,
1995) as work becomes displaced from the centre stage of modern social
structures (economy, technology, occupational systems) with egocentric-
ity in the form of increased concern for self-actualisation and a generalised
diffusion of the leisured class coming to dominate the sociocultural milieu
(Selwyn, 1996a). These moments of tourism (epitomised in Europe by
the hastily snatched city break from the likes of Lastminute.com or
Travelocity.com) do serve MacCannell's (1976) (contested) thesis on the
tourist that 'somewhere, . . . in another country, in another lifestyle, in
another social class, perhaps, there is a genuine society.'

Having discussed the roles played out in tourism that help construct
some aspects of social identities it can be seen that the commercial nature
of these constructions mean that although cultural encounters might be
synchronous, tourism in its globalised form also comprises a series of
encounters that are, in effect, 'moments of tourism' and reflect fragmenting societies that somehow lack a unifying ethic framed by the type of
contested culture described in the next section.

Contested Cultures: Collision, Collusion, and the Fusing of Histories

If it is argued that culture (and nostalgia) can be appropriated as a
resource by the tourism sector, tourism needs to be understood in terms

of contested cultures, created by (a) the collision of local realities and globally driven commercialism and (b) the collusion between state and the tourism sector to construct social identities and to fuse (and perhaps, muddle) histories. For a prime example of this we need look no further than Jerusalem where culture has been contested by three major religions (Christian, Jewish, and Islam) that have engaged in violent resistance and contestation for the past millennia. This example is not so extreme as might at first be thought. In modern times, each of the faiths has blurred the distinction between religious pilgrim and secular tourist to create a tourist infrastructure that, in effect, seeks to legitimate their respective moral authority over the Holy city. Tourists become pawns in a cultural–political chess game (Aziz, 1995; Wahab, 1996).

The idea of contested culture as a type of discourse has its roots in Marxist and postcolonial studies, which acknowledge that societies are unequally divided along class, gender, and generational lines and that the struggle to resist or resolve these issues are bound by varying interpretations of culture and lingering colonial power relationships (the colonisation might be metaphorical rather than literal). Resistance in all forms ranging from passive to violent exists because the people of the destinations are drawn into the confluences of multiple relations, such as between governmental institutions and civil society; tour operators, tourists, and local populations; and more directly between visitors and visited. This milieu provides the backdrop against which the relations become discursive and fragmented causing local relationships with the global to reconfigure. These reconfigurations will affect both modes of production and representation.

At least two central questions arising from the constantly reconfiguration of tourism, culture, resistance, and globalisation remain unanswered: How do minority groups 'read' tourism? and What cultural identities are included and excluded from particular constructions of tourism? The answers are unlikely to be found in the formulaic responses to tourism by governments and market makers or reductionist approaches to tourism's analysis such as to be found in Graburn's (2001) simplistic (and somewhat elitist) assertions that 'secular ritual' provides a general theory for all forms of tourism. Such interpretations of tourism are one sided and do not allow for its complexities. For example, culture in tourism can be contested, such as when a national government uses assumed postures on racial harmony or multiculturalism or simply by excluding reference to certain groups to promote a constructed worldview. For example, before the political turmoil of the 1988 military coups in Fiji, ethnic Indians (making up some 47 percent of the population) were virtually excluded from brochures that featured smiling native Fijians. Morris (1995) refers to this as 'manufacturing traditions for tourism' and goes on to describe how the Singapore tourist authority regularly emphasises the country's 'diverse ethnic traditions . . . in ways that change how actual cultures of ethnicity are henceforth to be lived. Toured communities are increasingly required by the state to live out their (manufactured) ethnicity for the gaze of the others' (italics in original). Morris (1995) also reminds us that 'it is misleading to assume that the toured [hosts at a destination] mat be treated as victims of a process beyond their control.' From the foregoing, it can be seen that the discussion about culture, globalisation, and tourism is important because of what the 'collision, collusion and fusing of histories' that tourism development eventually produces (taking account of the structures that arise from planning: entrepreneurial, social, governmental): a confused situation in which, as Selwyn (1996a) puts it, there is a need to:

> Distinguish between the myths and fantasies of tourists (authentic in some senses as these may be), on the one hand, and politico–economic and socio–cultural processes, on the other, there may in the end, as Baudrillard (1988) has warned, be no way out of the eventual wholesale Disneyfication of one part of the world built on the wasteland of the other.

There is a parallel to be drawn here with the iconoclastic stance of both Selwyn and Baudrillard (as cited by Selwyn in the quote above) and the politico–socio–economic notion of the 'Brazilianisation' of society whereby the top few become fabulously wealthy, whereas the bottom few exist in abject poverty. In the case of Britain, Hutton (1995) described this as a 30/30/40 society 'with 30 per cent of adults either unemployed or economically inactive, 30 per cent in jobs where one way or another tenure is insecure—and only 40 per cent who have tenure . . . which could be regarded as reasonably secure.' And yet these nihilistic views toward culture take no account of either the enjoyment taken from tourism or the dynamism added to local cultures as they interact on a bigger stage.

What remains within the contested cultural borders of social identities, which are central to the notion of the cultural politics of tourism, is the question of how local identity is compromised in the face of tourism promotion (whether from inside or outside of national boundaries), a question that leaves us with a major paradox: the assumption that minority (or poor) cultural groups are vulnerable, a generalisation that does not always stand up to close examination.

Mediated Culture: *The Local–Global Nexus?*

Dean MacCannell (1992) has argued that the 'empty meeting grounds' of tourism have not only supplied new conditions for the appropriation and conversion of tangible objects and intangible elements of culture into commodities, but that tourism is a postmodern, organic system that provides no alternative to itself, almost a synonym for Fukuyama's 'The End of History' (1992) as cultures come together forming a bland, homogenised whole. But in a sense, this does not account for the ways in which culture is mediated in various ways and by diverse agencies including the individual. The resulting mediated culture and meanings inform, but are constantly morphing and reconfiguring. Thus, far from the claims of the end of culture that can be inferred from the writings of Greenwood (1989), MacCannell (1992), Selwyn (1996b), and Wood's (1993) analysis of culture and tourism, which rely on identifying and understanding systems, argue that 'The central questions to be asked are about process, and about the complex ways tourism enters and becomes part of an already on-going process of symbolic meaning and appropriation.'

Such systems and processes will include not only a supply-side point of view framed by the notion of culture-as-attraction but also less-than-passive responses to mediating culture on the part of local peoples and industries. Culture is mediated from both sides of the equation assigning multiple meanings. In the hybrid culture of tourism (that is to say at the local–global nexus) the aim should be for institutions, civil society, and (for the purpose of the present chapter) the tourism industry to weave a social fabric that allows culture to be mediated for commercial purposes (thus creating economic opportunities), whereas at the same time reinforcing mutual respect and mutually beneficial relationships. In recognising that relationships and social identities across the globe are being changed and hybridised at a rapid pace, Peggy Teo (2002) has suggested that tourism research 'has neglected to incorporate the discourse surrounding globalization' going on to remark that 'too often, research on sustainable tourism points to a managerial approach.'

Having presented the last of the four themes that helped frame the discussion on culture, tourism, and globalisation, the next section summarises the key points and raises some critical issues.

Critical Issues: Substantive Implications

The present chapter has attempted (not always successfully) to strike a balance between the antiglobalisation, antichange perspective and the other side of that particular coin, which seems to view unfettered markets as a particular salvation. From the four preceding themes, we can make the following summary (Table 20.1).

The critical issues arising then can all be found in the overarching problem: the approach to research on this topic. There still remains a rift between academics (in the field of social sciences) who still tend to view

Table 20.1   Critical Issues: Some Substantive Implications

Cultural Politics	Representation of local cultures is a political act
	Localisation and globalisation are inseparable
	The cultural narratives of destinations are ambivalent and cannot exist without reference to tourism
	Multiple relationships mean multiple narratives; inevitably some will be stronger than others
Social Identities	Social identity is a global 'project' that has some parallel to appropriation of Other
	Difference is synchronously emphasised (as toured Other) and homogenised (as local culture is drawn into networks of global social behaviors and consumption patterns)
	Tourism can be expressed as a series of superficial encounters resulting from a desire on the tourists' side for self and for economic opportunity on the receiving side
Contested Cultures	There is a collision between local realities (expressed through social and economic ambitions) and globally driven capitalism
	The collusion between the state and the tourism sector can construct social identities that exclude minorities considered inappropriate to the image of tourism at particular destinations
	Histories of sending and receiving populations become intertwined, fused, and muddled
Mediated Culture	The mediation of culture need not necessarily lead to homogenisation (the 'end of history' approach) but rather hybridisation (whereby cultures learn and adapt from each other)
	Tourism can be read as a historically produced discourse
	The challenge of mediating culture for tourism in a global context lies in finding appropriate responses to the shift away from state capitalist structures (as found in many developing countries) to the more ambivalent, borderless culture of corporate capitalism

tourism with suspicion and the industry (and academics in marketing, management, and economics) who see tourism either simply as business or as panacea. Both sides, from time to time get it wrong on local cultures, either from a patronising 'stop the world' perspective or from a simplistic 'markets rule' point of view that fails to allow for the complexities and the need to develop beneficial relationships to underpin social responsible attitudes toward commerce.

Any analysis of tourism must take account of the structures that frame the relationships between nation-states and global markets. Susan Strange (1988), in the context of her work on the international political economy, identified these structures as security; production, finance, and knowledge. In all of this, the key question is, as Strange asks, *cui bono?* (Who benefits?). Balaam and Veseth (1996) describe why this seemingly simple question is fundamental:

> Asking this question forces us to go beyond description to analysis. To identify not only the structure and how it works, but its relationship to other structures and their role in the international political economy [an understanding which] therefore becomes a matter of holding in your mind a set of complex relationships and considering their collective implications.

The idea of 'collective implications' is one that holds great resonance for tourism and is one to be borne in mind when considering the cultural politics of tourism taking into account tourism's role in development and in fostering the rights and aspirations of the local communities. Tourism has a role in the legitimisation and affirmation of cultures through principles of beneficial relationships, autonomy, and self-determination. Tourism strategies can positively contribute to civic pride and positive social identities by helping develop decision-making capacity; creativity; solidarity; pride in their traditions; and rightful attachment to their place, space, and identity.

Conclusions: Tourism and the Local–Global Nexus

This chapter has focussed on social identities and representation at the local–global nexus and generally concludes that tourism and its alternatives must articulate a vision of both the present and a possible future based on inclusive ('collective' being a little far fetched) aspirations. If tourism is to have a positive effect on culture it must go well beyond the creation of infrastructure and the improvement of material conditions to strengthen local cultures and languages.

This chapter has argued for a view of tourism as a complex construction constituting a powerful interface between cultures and societies that is organised within a global framework, but which takes place very much at a local level. The fragmented and ephemeral nature of tourism, together with the definitional paradoxes has meant that its growing presence has not generated the same level of social movements in parts of the world where other forms of capitalism (such as GM crops, footwear, and clothing manufacturing) have been heavily criticised, even in the form of public demonstrations some of which are organised at a global level. In a sense, this could be more to do with the fragmented nature of the industry at the local level and that vast parts of the operational aspects and indeed staff fall under the tourist gaze, thus creating a level of self-regulation regarding working conditions. Despite their precariousness, the confluences between cultural politics, social identities, contested culture and mediated culture constitute an alternative analytical framework for discussions on the future sustainability of tourism in the broadest context. This framework shows that social life, work, business, nature, and culture can be organised differently than the dominant economic models that prevail in much of the tourism debates.

The approach to tourism analysis from the perspective of the cultural construction of the locality can be seen in terms of the defense of local modes of production and tradition as articulated by many social scientists. From the perspective of government institutions, there is room and the need for creative thinking and policy-making alternatives that create frameworks for beneficial interaction with the 'rest of the world.' From the tourism industry perspective, it is time for them to take on the challenge of working with a far greater range of social factors at the destinations they do business with, from social movements to progressive academics and international/local national government organisations (NGOs).

Although the gap between academy and industry remains, the spaces of encounter and debate are increasing and ways for academics, business people, NGOs, local people, and their representatives in government to reflect on, and support alternative frameworks for tourism development that are emerging rather than wait for a universal theoretical solution to the problems arising from the cultural politics of tourism that clearly acknowledge the need to stop thinking about cultures as though they were stuck in time and space.

References

Amor, M. 1998. Liminalities: Discussions on the Global and the Local. *Art Journal* 57(4): Winter 28–49.

Aziz, H. 1995. Understanding Attacks on Tourists in Egypt. *Tourism Management* 16(2): 91–95.

Balaam, D., and M. Veseth. 1996. *Introduction to the International Political Economy.* New Jersey: Prentice Hall.

Baudrillard, J. 1988. *Selected Writings.* Cambridge: Polity.

Bianchi, R. 2002. Sun, Sea and Sand: And a Sense of Spectral Danger. *Times Higher Educational Supplement.* July 26th: 16.

Boissevain, J. 1996. Problems with Cultural Tourism in Malta. In *Sustainable Tourism in Mediterranean Islands and Small Cities.* eds. C. Fsadni and T. Selwyn. Valetta: MEDCAMPUS-EuroMed.

Boniface, P., and P. Fowler. 1993. *Heritage and Tourism in the 'Global' Village.* London: Routledge.

Brewster, C., and S. Tyson. eds. 1991. *International Comparisons in Human Resource Management*. London: Pitman.

Bricker, K. 2001. Ecotourism Development in the Rural Highlands of Fiji. In *Tourism and the Less Developed World: Issues and Cases*. ed. D. Harrison. Walingford: CABI.

Burns, P. 1998. Tourism in Russia: Background and Structure. *Tourism Management* 19(6): 555–565.

———. 2001. Brief Encounters: Culture, Tourism and the Local–Global Nexus. In *Tourism in the Age of Globalisation*. eds. S. Wahab and C. Cooper. London: Routledge.

Crick, M. 1996. Representations of International Tourism in the Social Sciences: Sun, Sex, Sights, Savings, and Servility. In *The Sociology of Tourism: Theoretical and Empirical Investigations*. eds. Y. Apostolopoulos, S. Leivadi, and A. Yiannakis. London: Routledge.

Dann, G. 1996. The People of Tourist Brochures. In *The Tourist Image, Myths and Myth Making in Tourism*. ed. T. Selwyn. Chichester: Wiley.

Dann, G. M. S. 1988. Images of Cyprus Projected by Tour Operators. *Problems of Tourism* 3(41): 43–70.

Dorfles, G. 1969. *Tourism and Nature: The World of Bad Taste*. New York: Bell.

Dunning, J. 1993. *The Globalization of Business: The Challenge of the 90s*. London: Routledge.

Enloe, C. H. 1989. *Bananas, Beaches & Bases: Making Feminist Sense of International Politics*. London: Pandora.

Franklin, A. 2003. *Tourism: An Introduction*. London: Sage.

Franklin, A, and M. Crang. 2001. The Trouble with Tourism and Travel Theory? *Tourist Studies* 1(1): 5–22.

Friedman, T. 2000. *The Lexus and the Olive Tree*. London: Harper-Collins.

Fukuyama, F. 1992. *The End of History: And the Last Man*. London: Penguin.

Gardner, K., and D. Lewis. 1996. *Anthropology, Development and the Post-Modern Challenge*. London: Pluto.

Graburn, N. 2001. Secular Ritual: A General Theory of Tourism. In *Hosts and Guests Revisited: Tourism Issues of the 21ˢᵗ Century*. eds. V. Smith and M. Bryant. New York: Cognizant.

Greenwood, D. 1989. Culture by the Pound: An Anthropological Perspective on Tourism as Cultural Commoditization. In *An Anthropology of Tourism*, ed. V. Smith. Philadelphia: University of Pennsylvania Press.

Hall, M. 1998. Making the Pacific: Globalization, Modernity and Myth. In *Destinations: Cultural Landscapes of Tourism*. ed. G. Ringer. London: Routledge.

Higgins-Desbiolles, F. 2003. Engagement and Resistance through Indigenous Tourism. Conference Paper. *Tourism Identities*. University of Brighton. September 10–11.

Hutton, W. 1995. The 30/30/40 Labour Market. *The Jobs Letter*. No. 30., 15 December. New Plymouth Taranaki, N.Z.

Lanfant, M.F., J. et al ed. 1995. *International Tourism: Identity and Change*. London: Sage.

Levitt, T. 1983. The Globalization of Markets. *Harvard Business Review* 6(3): 92–102.

MacCannell, D. 1976. *The Tourist: A New Theory of the Leisure Class*. New York: Shocken Books.

———. 1992. *Empty Meeting Ground: The Tourist Papers.* London: Routledge.

McLuhan, M. 1960. *Explorations in Communication.* Boston: Beacon Press.

Micklethwait, J., and A. Wooldridge. 2000. *A Future Perfect: The Challenge and Hidden Promise of Globalization.* New York: Times Books.

Morris, M. 1995. Life as a Tourist Object in Australia. In *International Tourism: Identity and Change.* eds. M.-F. Lanfant, J. Allcock, and E. Bruner. London: Sage.

Narotzky, S. 1997. *New Directions in Economic Anthropology.* London: Pluto.

Richter, L. 2001. Where Asia Wore a Smile: Lessons of Philippine Tourism Development. In *Hosts and Guests Revisited: Tourism Issues in the 21st Century.* V. eds. Smith and M. Brent. New York: Cognizant.

Robertson, R. 1992. *Globalization: Social Theory and Global Culture.* London: Sage.

Said, E. 1978. *Orientalism: Western Concepts of the Orient.* London: Routledge and Kegan Paul.

Sassen, S. 1998. *Globalization and its Discontents: Essays on the New Mobility of People and Money.* New York: The New Press.

Selwyn, T. ed. 1996a. *The Tourist Image: Myths and Myth Making in Tourism.* London: Wiley.

———. 1996b. Tourism, Culture and Cultural Conflict. In *Sustainable Tourism in Mediterranean Islands and Small Cities.* eds. Fsadni and Selwyn. Valetta: MEDCAMPUS-EuroMed.

Stanton, M. 1989. The Polynesian Cultural Center: A Multi-Ethnic Model of Seven Pacific Cultures. In *Hosts and Guests: The Anthropology of Tourism.* ed. V. Smith. Philadelphia: University of Pennsylvania Press.

Strange, S. 1988. *States and Markets: An Introduction to International Political Economy.* New York: Basil Blackwell.

Teo, P. 2002. Striking a Balance for Sustainable Tourism: Implications of the Discourse on Globalization. *Journal of Sustainable Tourism* 10(6): 459–474.

Torgovnick, M. 1990. *Gone Primitive: Savage Intellects, Modern Lives.* Chicago: University of Chicago Press.

Turner, B. 1994. *Orientalism, Postmodernism and Globalism.* London: Routledge.

Wahab, Salah. 1996. Tourism and Terrorism: Synthesis of the Problem with Emphasis on Egypt. In *Tourism, Crime and International Security.* eds. A. Pizzam and Y. Mansfeld. London: John Wiley.

Wood, R. 1993. Tourism, Culture and the Sociology of Development. In *Tourism in South East Asia.* eds. M. Hitchcock, V. King, and M. Parnwell. London: Routledge.

21 Interventions and policy instruments for sustainable tourism

Bill Bramwell

Introduction

There is growing recognition that market economies on their own will not produce tourism activities that promote sustainable development and that some government interventions are necessary. Government interventions are guided by policies and are implemented using policy instruments, which are the specific mechanisms or tools employed to put policy into practice. Public authorities are faced with an extensive array of policy instruments to implement sustainable tourism. These instruments include zoning to control development or to limit tourist access to sensitive areas, dissemination of codes of conduct to encourage more sustainable behaviour, taxing of energy use and waste treatment services to prompt enterprises to save scarce resources and reduce pollution, and public provision of traffic management infrastructure to reduce congestion and pollution in tourist areas. All such instruments for sustainable tourism are interventions by government that alter what would otherwise happen. When instruments are being selected, it is important to consider the complete range of instruments and to select a mix of them that in the particular circumstances is likely to meet the overall policy objectives.

The selection of policy instruments by policy makers is, however, only partly a 'technical' question based on identifying which instruments will achieve the desired results most effectively. It is also essentially a moral and political choice that is influenced by diverse economic and societal pressures. Yet much of the tourism planning literature leaves the impression that the choices are primarily technical ones. Hall (2000) recently complained that 'tourism planning is still presented as being primarily a technical issue and not a political problem.' This emphasis in the tourism literature on 'technical' evaluations of policy instruments should not be allowed to mask the moral dilemmas; the competing beliefs, values, and ideologies; and the political choices that lie at the heart of both policy making and sustainable development. As Hughes (2002) contends, 'In plain terms, the solution of the environmental crisis of tourism does not rest solely with scientific management.' It is essential to consider the politics that affect the selection of policy instruments, including the economic pressures of capital accumulation and the inequalities in power relations that influence these choices (Bramwell, 2003). But it is also important to examine the potential consequences of different policy instruments for society and culture, for the environment and economy, and for various affected actors. It is necessary to understand these potential consequences so that political debate can be more informed and policy makers might be better placed to meet their desired objectives.

Public interventions for sustainable tourism will be unsuccessful if inappropriate instruments are used. The use of unsuitable mechanisms is one reason why '[d]espite the acceptance of sustainable tourism as a desirable alternative to more predatory modes of development, a gap commonly exists between policy endorsement and policy implementation' (Pigram, 1990). A policy instrument can contribute to this gap because there may be unrealistic expectations about its potential to deliver against overall objectives. There is a further potential gap between the policy intention and what the instrument actually achieves. Often policy makers fail to recognise potential problems in implementation. For instance, many problems stem from the consequences of cultural and political circumstances that are unforeseen or ignored, including an inability or unwillingness to adopt or enforce policy measures.

This chapter examines some of the potential implications for the economy, society, and environment and for the affected actors that need to be considered when public authorities are selecting sustainable tourism policy instruments. It also describes some conceptual foundations behind the implications of these interventions. Policy makers would be helped if the tourism literature included more comparative evaluations of the strengths and weaknesses of different policy instruments in specific situations. In this context, the chapter examines a range of issues to consider when making such comparisons. It also argues that comparisons of instruments in environmental economics have tended to concentrate on only a few of these issues and give little consideration to the importance of social values, ethics, and politics. Finally, the chapter discusses how preferences for policy instruments are based on moral and political evaluations, and the case is made for an interdisciplinary approach to the critical examination of policy instruments.

Sustainable Tourism

Selecting policy instruments for sustainable tourism requires an understanding of the principles of sustainable development and of tourism within this. Although sustainable development is a fundamentally contested concept with many potential interpretations, there are certain principles or ideals underlying this concept that are identified particularly often in the literature (Bramwell and Lane, 1993; Local Government Management Board [LGMB], 1993). Of course there are many parties who will refute or object to some or all of these principles:

- *Resources:* It is increasingly argued that the health and integrity of natural, man-made, and human resources is critical to future well being, and that this depends on how these resources are treated. It may be suggested that the stock of environmental resources must be conserved and that this implies minimal use of nonrenewable resources and minimal emission of pollutants. Sustainable development is often seen as being concerned with the viability not only of the environment but also of economic, cultural, and social resources.
- *Futurity:* This relates to the well being of future generations, so that they benefit from resources, opportunities, and choices at least as good as those inherited by the current generation.
- *Equity:* Some argue that there should be fairness in the distribution within society of the economic, social, cultural, and environmental benefits and costs of human activity. These equity considerations may be depicted as closely related to sustainable development in at least four ways. First, because it tends to be disadvantaged social groups who bear the brunt of the negative costs of human activity, and, second, it is argued that poverty encourages unsustainable lifestyles, based on a clamour for quick returns to meet immediate needs. Third, the effects of policies depend on people's wealth, and this is seen clearly with policies that involve high charges for the use of resources and so tend to exclude poorer people. And, lastly, it is considered hard to justify caring about fairness to future generations without extending this concern to people in society today.

Several of these principles are contained in Eber's (1992) proposal that tourism can contribute to sustainable development when it 'operates within natural capacities for the regeneration and future productivity of natural resources; recognises the contribution that people and communities, customs and lifestyles, make to the tourism experience; accepts that these people must have an equitable share in the economic benefits of tourism; and is guided by the wishes of local people and communities in the host areas.'

The sustainable tourism literature also suggests certain principles for policy development by government, and presumably these might guide the use of specific policy instruments (LGMB, 1993). One such principle is that deciding on and implementing policies requires wide participation, partnerships, and cooperative action by all affected groups in society. Community participation, for example, is generally seen as necessary for sustainable tourism planning (Singh, Timothy, and Dowling, 2003). Another common proposition is that policies should be integrated with each other, based on recognition of the interdependence of issues and policies, such as for tourism, employment, and transport (Hall, 2000). Third, it is sometimes indicated that because of practical constraints it is necessary to set achievable short-term targets for improvement, and that these targets should be raised steadily upwards over time. Such progressive target setting might help to secure progress in the right direction and to maintain momentum.

At times certain principles for policy choice by government are also suggested in the literature of sustainable tourism, and these too are relevant for policy instrument selection (LGMB, 1993). One such principle is that where there is uncertainty about the consequences for natural, man-made, or human resources of a particular course of action, it is necessary to be cautious and to avoid taking risks. This 'precautionary principle' is suggested as necessary to reduce the chance that actions will produce irreversible damage to resources and quality of life. Another principle for policy choice that may be proposed is that, because certain demands to use resources are unsustainable and should not be met, then policies and related instruments need to be designed to reduce or redirect these unmeetable demands. A third ('polluter-pays') principle sometimes suggested is that those who cause damage to scarce resources generally should pay for the damage, and in this way they are penalised for harmful actions and are encouraged to alter their behaviour.

Whatever principles or ideals of sustainable tourism are put forward, inevitably they are both fraught with ambiguity and also counsels of perfection. For example, implementation is highly problematic because of the numerous interested parties with diverse beliefs and aims and also due to the constraints involved with the operation of the market and pressures of capitalist development. It is also the case that too often public authorities adopt sustainable tourism ideas with only a fairly confused view of what they might entail and of how they will apply them in practice. These difficulties may encourage skeptics to dismiss the approach altogether. However, others may contend that, despite the problems, it is still important for policy makers to strive for sustainability ideals.

Types of Policy Instruments

Policy instruments for government use in order to promote sustainable tourism may be categorised into four types. An understanding of these categories helps clarify what issues to consider when selecting policy instruments to apply in specific circumstances. The four types are used in the subsequent discussion.

- *Government encouragement* through information, education, and general persuasion directed at operators, tourists, or communities in tourist areas in order to encourage them voluntarily to adopt more sustainable behaviour. This would include interpretation at publicly owned sites about damaging visitor activities or government-assessed 'green' ratings for tourism businesses adopting environmentally friendly practices (Font and Buckley, 2001; Font, 2002). A moral appeal using information may help change behaviour, particularly if the harmful actions are largely the result of ignorance.
- *Government financial incentives* that alter the prices facing businesses, tourists, or host communities for environmentally or culturally damaging or beneficial behaviour. They may be taxes or subsidies intended to make some resources more or less expensive than others, so that activities change in consequence. Examples are fees for entry to natural or cultural sites and local tourist taxes designed to raise revenue for environmental work or to control visitor pressure by deterring visitors, and also charges for water consumption by hotels that are intended to encourage water conservation. Subsidies offer positive incentives, such as by providing payments to hotels that introduce energy-saving techniques (Hunter and Green, 1995). In many countries agricultural producers are given subsidies to protect ecologically sensitive areas under their control, and often these areas are important tourism resources (Briassoulis, 2002).
- *Government expenditure* on actions taken directly by government or state-owned agencies, such as spending on public transport, land purchase, and conservation measures in national parks, and on community development initiatives and waste management.
- *Government regulations* that either prohibit or require particular courses of action and are backed by the law, but which do not involve a financial incentive or direct government expenditure. These policy instruments compel tourism businesses or tourists to comply, with non-compliance likely to involve judicial punishment (Jacobs, 1991). For instance, there may be specified environmental quality standards and land-use zoning regulations in a tourist area. Included in these might be fixed standards for the maximum number of beds per hectare

and maximum number of hotel rooms and hotel building height in resorts. As well as restrictions on land use, there could be limits to the discharge of certain pollutants and restrictions on contracts between tour operators and hoteliers (Nijkamp and Verdonkschot, 1995).

Issues in Selecting Policy Instruments

There are many specific forms of public policy instrument within each of the four types outlined previously. It is useful to identify the potential implications that need consideration when selecting instruments to suit local conditions (Sinclair and Stabler, 1997; Van der Duim and Caalders, 2002). The following framework of selected potential implications or issues is an adaptation and extension of one developed by Jacobs (1991) for general environmental instruments.

Effectiveness

The issue of effectiveness concerns the degree to which a specific public policy instrument is likely to meet the policy objectives of sustainable tourism (Tribe, et al., 2000). Among related considerations are the certainty that an instrument will deliver against objectives, the speed of delivery, and the instrument's flexibility of response to changing circumstances.

Policy instruments based only on encouragement through information and education are likely to have the least certainty of achieving sustainable outcomes because they depend on people understanding and accepting the information and responding voluntarily. For instance, despite publicity that noisy airboat rides across the wetland habitat of the Big Cyprus National Preserve in Florida disturb wildlife and cause distress to nesting birds, many visitors still see taking a ride across the swamp as an ecologically friendly activity (Shackley, 1996). But information and education initiatives have several advantages. For example, although published codes of conduct may help protect environmental resources, they can also provide security for the visitor and maximise the quality of his or her experience. In addition, such policies can encourage tourism businesses, visitors, and host communities to understand what is damaging, which may lead them to avoid this harmful behaviour in the long term. Encouragement to voluntary actions is also advantageous if it encourages these groups to be proactive in taking responsibility for initiating change (United Nations Environment Programme [UNEP], 1995).

There tends to be greater certainty that nature tourism operators will respond to public exhortations to conserve environmental resources when there are only a few operators in a destination and when there is a close coincidence of their interests with those of the environment. In these circumstances cooperation and self-enforcement between all the operators to behave responsibly may be easier (Forsyth, Dwyer, and Clarke, 1995). Steps can be taken to increase the certainty that education programmes about resource conservation will be effective. Thus, environmental codes of conduct for tourism may be more effective if they are developed after wide consultation and are well publicised (Genot, 1995). In Finland, codes of conduct for tourism were developed by a working group chaired by the Finnish Tourist Board and including representatives from the Finnish Rural Tourism Group, Ministry of Environment, National Board of Water and the Environment, Finnish Municipal Association, Association of Rural Centres, and the Finnish Association for Nature Protection, and this was later enlarged to include industry representatives. A publicity campaign accompanied the dissemination of the codes (UNEP, 1995). Governments that commit to codes of conduct might also increase compliance by monitoring and reporting on performance against standards set out in the codes. The Australian government integrated sustainable development objectives into its National Tourism Strategy, with the industry body, Tourism Council Australia, adopting similar guidelines in its code of conduct and performing regular monitoring of responses to the code (Harris and Leiper, 1995; Turner, 1995; UNEP, 1995).

The certainty of achieving sustainable tourism objectives may be greater when government regulation instruments are used. These require certain behaviour and are backed by law. For instance, access zoning with quantitative limits to the number of visitors allowed to enter socially or environmentally pressured areas has the potential advantage of relatively precise and predictable impacts. Such zoning may take the form of quantitative limits on cars allowed into a park or on boats permitted to visit a coral atoll (World Tourism Organization/UNEP, 1992; Forsyth, Dwyer, and Clarke, 1995). However, such government regulations usually depend on effective monitoring, enforcement, and judicial punishment to be fully successful. It should not be assumed that behaviour will change once laws are enacted, even in countries that have relatively strong legal traditions and institutions. One reason is that enforcement requires energy and resources, and there will be other calls on these resources. Furthermore, there will always be people whose interests lie in not having environmental policies enforced. Mak and Moncur (1995) describe how a smoking ban was imposed at Hanauma Bay Nature Park in Hawaii in order to stop cigarette butts from littering the beach and contaminating the water in the bay, but park staff were told not to confront violators and the Honolulu police were very reluctant to cite violations. In addition, even if regulations are enforced, there may be ingenious means to get around them. For example, the Honolulu Department of Parks and

Recreation introduced restrictions on tour vehicles from dropping off visitors at the Hanauma Bay Nature Park in an attempt to reduce degradation of the natural environment and the quality of the visitor experience. However, tour operators circumvented these restrictions by bussing their customers to a nearby shopping centre or to residential neighbourhoods and contracting with taxi companies to shuttle passengers to the park (Mak and Moncur, 1995).

With government financial incentives, the certainty of meeting sustainable tourism objectives depends greatly on setting charges or subsidies at appropriate levels. In order to change public behaviour, charges or subsidies must be sufficiently high to either choke off demand or encourage preferred behaviour. Before setting a charge or subsidy it is important to have reliable information on how it will affect demand or supply, but such information is not easily obtained and so in practice, adjustment of charges or subsidies often involves much 'trial and error.' Responses to charging or subsidy levels in other regions or countries may provide some indication, although each case is likely to be different and necessitates local research. But even information from other situations may be unavailable. As Laarman and Gregersen (1996) state, for the use of higher fees for visits at peak times to nature tourism areas, 'evidence on off-peak pricing to shift use patterns is inconclusive, possibly because even "high" fees have been modest in most cases to date.'

Another influence on the effectiveness of a policy instrument in a specific situation is the extent to which it has the potential to tackle the full scope of the problem. For example, in the Galapagos Islands of Ecuador, varied instruments have been used to control damage by visitors, but Steele (1995) argues there have been very few controls on the total number of visitors despite this being the wider cause of many problems.

The effectiveness of instruments is also affected by any indirect benefits or costs that they may have. In the case of a pricing system at a site, this may be intended to raise revenue for site management and conservation but there may be other valuable, indirect visitor management benefits. It can ensure that all visitors go through an entry procedure and at this point they are given necessary information, personal contact is made between site staff and visitors, and visitors realise that someone is on duty as a deterrent to irresponsible behaviour. People going through the entry point might then also realise the site is valuable and appreciate what they are paying for (Gale and Jacobs, 1987). A proposed increase in site entry fees may have the indirect benefit that this requires forecasts and its implementation may lead to monitoring and evaluation to determine actual impacts. These activities provide profiles on visitor numbers, composition, and likes and dislikes, and these profiles are useful for visitor management and improving the visitor experience (Laarman and Gregersen, 1996).

Administrative Cost

Policy instruments vary in their cost to public authorities in implementing them. For instance, tourist taxes that rely on multiple points of collection, such as at tourist accommodation in a region, can involve the public authority in relatively expensive policing activities. In the case of entrance fees to control visitor numbers or raise income for conservation work, these can be very expensive to collect, especially when there are few visitors and many entry points. However, these costs may be reduced by modifying the specific form of charging mechanism. Instead of collecting charges at all entry points, visitors could be required to purchase a permit in advance at one place, such as with the issue of camping permits for national parks in Queensland, Australia (Tisdell, 1995). Alternatively, indirect charging for car parking rather than access itself could be introduced and collected using automatic ticket machines that issue tickets for display in car windows. Charging for car parking using automatic ticket machines is used at some countryside sites in Wales to offset some site management and maintenance costs of local government and of bodies such as Forest Enterprise and Welsh Water (Broom, Bramwell, and Beard, 1995).

Motivational Effect

Consideration needs to be given to whether public policy instruments provide a continuing incentive to businesses, visitors, and host communities to behave in more sustainable ways (Carter, 2001). For instance, do policies for tourism operators encourage them to continue to reduce their harmful pollution emissions or to innovate with the development of less damaging technologies? Here government regulation may be less effective than charges or taxes, because regulations require polluters only to meet specified standards, whereas financial incentives can encourage them to continue reducing their pollution in order to gain further cost reductions.

Administrative 'Workability'

Policy instruments need to be considered in relation to their administrative 'workability' and institutional acceptability. This involves such issues as the simplicity, ease, and cost in time required to set up, administer, monitor, and police specific policy instruments. If a scheme is very complex or time consuming, or has no clear sense of ownership for the institution to be tasked with administering it, it is much less likely to be workable.

Distributional Impact and Equity

Policy instruments intended to develop more sustainable tourism will differ in their distribution of positive and negative impacts between individuals, social groups, and geographical areas. These distributional outcomes are affected by such factors as the choice of target group, whether intervention influences access to resources by ability to pay, and by how any revenues raised are redistributed. As discussed earlier, sustainable tourism approaches often give prominence to creating more equitable distributions. However, there is always some inequality in the outcomes from specific policy instruments, and there are also many different concepts of distributional equity to consider (Kasperson and Dow, 1991; Hay, 1995). Clearly, evaluations of what is an acceptable distributional impact have to be made within an ethical and political context.

The effects of policy instruments on distributional outcomes between different tourists is one consideration. With pricing proposals, for example, poorer people may be unable to purchase at the same level, and what they do purchase may still represent a larger proportion of their income than for higher income groups. To counter such regressive effects, charges may be reduced for categories of visitors such as children, students, and retired persons. In the case of public information initiatives based on moral persuasion among tourists, these may have a disadvantage in that those who respond to the moral arguments will carry the burden of this policy, whereas those who respond less well will enjoy the benefits of others' restraint but escape their share of the burden.

Sustainable tourism policies often emphasise the importance of equitable outcomes for residents living in tourist areas. Spatial instruments of zoning and national park designation are often used to protect ecological resources, but the distributional consequences for people living within or adjacent to these must also be a prime consideration.

In the case of government expenditure on national park designation and management, this can exclude local residents from areas that formerly had provided them with resources such as grazing, hunting, or construction materials. The Maasai nomadic pastoralists of the Ngoro Ngoro Conservation Area in Tanzania have been denied access to their traditional grazing lands and it has been suggested that they have experienced a consequent decline in living conditions over the past 20 years (Cater, 1995). In Kenya, wildlife reservations were carved out of lands previously used by 'traditional' pastoral peoples, denying them of invaluable herding and agricultural resources and in some cases fishing rights. Another potential source of conflict between the demands of Kenya's wildlife-based tourism and the well being of local people is that the wild animals can be a menace to livestock, crops, and people living in surrounding areas (Sindiga, 1995). Local communities can pay a heavy price for supporting wildlife protection areas, and thus it can be argued that at a minimum the management plans and policy instruments should take into account the provision of an alternative resource base, as well as potential compensation (Shackley, 1996). One approach to this issue is to share revenues from park entry fees with local communities. The Kenya Wildlife Service has adopted such a programme, starting with the Amboseli National Park and the Maasai Mara National Reserve in 1989, with the main beneficiaries being landowners and local authorities in wildlife dispersal areas outside parks or reserves. However, the revenue-sharing programmes in Kenya have sometimes generated unrealistic expectations without clear revenue-sharing guidelines, because it has not been specified who is to be compensated, or how much is to be paid and when (Berger, 1996; Shackley, 1996). Another problem is that the money ceded to local authorities in Kenya does not necessarily help the local people who are affected (Sindiga, 1995). These issues are important for equity and also for conservation, because local communities are much more likely to continue to support park and reserve objectives if they are seen to assist in people's development. Without an economic incentive, local communities may not take responsibility for land management and might choose land uses that are incompatible with conservation (Berger, 1996).

Respect for Cultural Differences

Much thinking about resource management instruments is based on dominant cultural approaches in western society, emphasising competition rather than cooperation as well as the supremacy of individualism rather than communitarianism and of 'scientific' knowledge rather than traditional, local-level, or 'indigenous' knowledge. More generally, the thinking often reflects first world values of materialism, consumerism, and scientific rationalism. Such resource management approaches can easily ignore crucial issues of cultural consent, self-determination, and respect for cultural differences. It is also often forgotten that local or indigenous cultural traditions may provide valuable solutions to problems of resource misuse in an area, particularly because these can involve cultural and institutional constraints on self-interested behaviour that damages the collective interest.

No doubt many practical applications of sustainable tourism ideas in both developing and industrialised countries have emphasised 'scientific' approaches. However, even if it is recognised that other cultural approaches and traditions should be respected much more fully, this still leaves complex and difficult questions unanswered. When resources are threatened, should their management be based on promoting indigenous approaches and reviving traditional local-level institutions, or should indigenous approaches be integrated with 'scientific' resource management systems and policy instruments? Some people may see the latter as often inappropriate, because the approaches are based on fundamentally different ways of viewing resources. However, a number of commentators argue that there is often potential for useful interplay between scientific and indigenous resource management systems, although it must be recognised that there are marked imbalances in power both within and between the involved groups (Berkes, 1989; Bromley, 1992). Such ideas are also now being discussed in the tourism literature (Hughes, 1995; Briassoulis, 2002). It must also be remembered that local communities may not always decide to develop their resources in a sustainable manner, and this is not only because of the proven capacity of others to use these communities to exploit their own resources (Adams, 1990).

Freedoms and Fairness

The use of policy instruments for sustainable tourism will affect the property rights or the decision rights of individuals or groups in society, whether actual or perceived. These consequences for property rights or decision rights might be considered to infringe the freedoms of individuals or groups and therefore be seen as unfair. Property rights in the sense used here are not bestowed automatically with ownership of property, but rather as with decision rights, they are allocated by society. Sometimes these are formally enshrined in law and sometimes they are informally constituted through public opinion. These popularly constituted and accepted rights evolve and change over time as societal values and circumstances change. Policy instruments will differ in their consequences for property and decision rights and in the perceived fairness of these consequences for different individuals and groups. These effects need to be an important consideration when selecting policy instruments. Clearly, such decisions about rights, freedoms, and fairness are affected by ethics, values, ideology, and politics (Harvey, 1992).

Decision rights will be altered if, for example, a public authority introduces charging for access to a tourist area in order to raise revenue for local conservation work. Tourists may consider public access to the countryside or heritage areas to be intrinsically a 'good thing' for society and individuals, and to be a decision right that should be available without charge and with very few other restrictions. In Britain, for example, there is a strong tradition that countryside access should be free and unimpeded (Ramblers Association, 1994). Tourists may also consider they have already paid the government for local conservation work through their taxes. Consequently, new charges for access to a rural or heritage area may be perceived as a harmful and unfair loss of the decision rights of tourists.

Such objections to access charges for conservation potentially might be overcome by schemes for tourists to make voluntary contributions for this work. In the English Peak District a scheme was introduced for voluntary contributions to fund conservation work that was linked to the purchase of various tourist services (Bramwell and Fearn, 1996). Such schemes give tourists the opportunity to take greater direct responsibility for the adverse effects of their visit, but it is possible that some tourists will feel under moral pressure to contribute, thereby reducing their perceived decision rights.

Political Acceptability

Policy instruments may be proposed by government officials as appropriate, only for the proposals to be defeated by politicians on the grounds of political acceptability because they may be unpopular and may affect their political survival. Officially adopted policies may be changed by politicians for similar reasons. For instance, Ioannides (1995) describes how the president of the Republic of Cyprus sought to stall his waning popularity by amending certain strict zoning regulations in environmentally sensitive parts of the island in order to appease local landowners. A policy tool for sustainable tourism has more chance of being implemented if it is acceptable to interest groups and individuals who are directly affected and also to the general public. Questions about liberty and fairness are obviously important for political acceptability, as are more pragmatic considerations of how easy it will be to implement the instrument.

Certain practical considerations may increase the political acceptability of an instrument. For example, its acceptability may increase if it has been developed in consultation with those likely to be affected by it and also with those who will be responsible for implementing it. Instruments may also need to be introduced with a pilot stage in order to demonstrate their suitability. The Tir Cymen scheme in Wales, involving payments to farmers for countryside conservation and management and for public access provision, was piloted in three areas in order to test it in practice, and this also meant that initial costs were more predictable (Broom, Bramwell, and Beard, 1995). Acceptability may also increase if a new instrument is accompanied by information about it being communicated clearly to those affected, so that they may be more likely to understand it and potentially less likely to be resentful and dissatisfied. Timely announcements and education about a scheme are important. For instance, Jim (1989) argues that the introduction of a scheme to ration access to natural areas by the use of prior reservation and permits must have sufficient advance notice and good publicity, otherwise visitors will arrive at the destination in ignorance, only to be refused entry and to be totally unprepared for the disappointment and with no alternative plan.

Compatibility and Balance between Policy Instruments

In general, public policy instruments for sustainable tourism will be used in combination. The mix of instruments employed should be carefully matched to the particular policy objectives. For example, policy makers need to identify optimal combinations of instruments that will reinforce each other in particular circumstances in order to achieve the intended objectives. Thus, a tax on pollution by tourism facilities may well need to be supported by information and educational provision for operators concerning operational practices and new technologies that can reduce pollution.

When selecting an appropriate balance between policy instruments it is essential to consider the overall balance between the four types of instruments: government encouragement of voluntary changes in behaviour, government financial incentives, government expenditure on actions taken directly by public authorities, and government regulations. Decisions on this balance will be influenced by attitudes to the extent to which government needs to require parties to change their behaviour as distinct from encouraging them to volunteer to do this of their own volition. These decisions will also reflect attitudes to the extent to which government should intervene in the operation of the market in a market-based economy. In this context it is important to recognise the considerable economic pressures on governments to encourage economic growth due to the dynamics of capital accumulation and globalisation, and the policies pursued for tourism are often those most suited to the economy and industry rather than to broader objectives of sustainable development. Views about the mix of policy instruments may be affected by economic pressures, ethical considerations, social values, ideology, and politics, as well as by practical experience.

Although the operation of the market in capitalist societies may not always be incompatible with aspects of sustainable tourism, it will normally require significant assistance for it to increase sustainability. There are a number of reasons for this. For instance, the market is not very effective at protecting resources that cannot easily be bought and sold, such as clean air, natural habitats, public spaces, landscapes, and views, despite these being essential resources for sustainability. The market is also generally poor at distinguishing and giving priority to more sustainable over less sustainable ways of achieving particular outcomes. It tends to create problems of resource depletion, income inequality, and limited concern for the collective rights of the community. Despite these major shortcomings, the market has certain advantages. In particular, it can be effective at encouraging economic development, responding quickly to changing market conditions, providing incentives, and at encouraging innovation. Excessive or insensitive government intervention in the operation of the market potentially can hold back economic development, stifle initiative, and impose too much bureaucracy.

A balanced mix of government instruments for sustainable tourism is likely to include an important role for information, education, and persuasion in changing behaviour. Butler (1991) argues that educating all concerned with tourism—the industry, the public sector, local populations, and the tourists—'is still the best key' for developing more sustainable tourism, and that 'in the long term it is probably the only solution which is likely to be broadly successful.' Education and persuasion potentially can encourage parties to take more responsibility and to be proactive in initiating change, and it can avoid more costly or authoritarian government interventions. Information provision can demonstrate that parties may be able to gain advantages from more sustainable forms of development. For example, it could help tourism businesses to see the potential commercial advantages of sustainable approaches, such as opportunities for reducing raw material and waste disposal costs, developing new services and products, improving the working environment for staff, and for enhancing their appeal to more environmentally aware consumers (Goodall, 1995). Public education and persuasion might also contribute to the overall climate of civic responsibility, which can make it possible to institute new policies and make it easier to administer and enforce them.

Despite the advantages of government education and persuasion, on their own they are very probably insufficient to produce substantial change and they will need to be combined with policy instruments based on more direct government intervention. In practice there are major constraints on self-regulation. For example, in capitalist economies the intense commercial pressures to gain immediate economic returns mean that tourism businesses usually focus on the short-term requirement of producing a healthy annual balance sheet, and this severely restricts the potential for sustainable practices (Josephides, 1994; Forsyth, 1996). The so-called green consumers may also have little influence over the traditional package holiday because it is very difficult for them to determine whether a holiday is a relatively sustainable product, and they are not encouraged to have a deep commitment to a destination area because they are there only for a short period (Hunter and Green, 1995). And most tourists are unlikely to seek out information on specific environmental issues before booking a holiday; they are often very cost conscious; and they may be more likely to forget ethical issues when they are on holiday as they seek to relax and enjoy themselves.

Conclusions

This analysis has sought to identify the potential implications to be considered when selecting sustainable tourism policy instruments. The range of moral, political, and economic issues will influence the choice of instruments. An understanding of these implications is helpful for assessments of the comparative merits of different instruments in different contexts. It is important that policy makers consider the complete range, and also the appropriate overall mix, of instruments, and that they recognise that the issues are context specific.

Policy makers would be helped if the tourism literature included more comparative evaluations of the strengths and weaknesses of different policy instruments in particular circumstances. Such comparative work is perhaps discouraged by disciplinary boundaries, with, for example, particular interest among geographers in instruments using spatial boundaries, such as zoning and national park designation, and among economists in instruments that alter prices most directly, such as taxes, subsidies, and entrance fees. Despite this, growing numbers of economists have begun to compare instruments for environmental protection. However, many policy makers are unfamiliar with this literature, which draws on environmental economics. One reason for this low familiarity is that the literature often requires prior understanding of neoclassical economic theory and techniques. Although the abstract economic arguments in some of these studies can be useful, it may be even more helpful to policy makers if there was more practical research on how different instruments have actually worked in practice. Different emphases between some economists and policy makers may help explain why, 'while economists often see charges as a way of regulating demands for tourism resources . . . , practical policy makers often see rules and regulations governing resource use as more appropriate' (Forsyth, Dwyer, and Clarke, 1995).

Some policy makers and academics are also uneasy that much literature on environmental economics depends on assumptions about social behaviour from neoclassical economics with which they disagree. As Redclift (1993) argues, 'Economic frameworks and methods are founded upon an a priori commitment to a particular model of human nature and social behaviour.' In the neoclassical model social behaviour is seen as essentially instrumental and intended to achieve the maximum utility for each individual. This means that the tastes and preferences of individuals are considered a 'given,' and the underlying social commitments that determine how we use the environment are unexamined. The assumptions in neoclassical economics mean aspects of human behaviour are not questioned, and this may encourage a gap between policies and their implementation as people fail to respond as expected. Unease about neo-classical economic theory also arises from how environmental concerns are incorporated into its analysis. This is achieved by environmental resources being given monetary values either by theoretical analysis or by opening new markets for environmental resources so that they are priced and the prices affect how businesses and consumers behave toward them. Critics contend this ignores the ethical basis of environmental policies and that consumers' concerns and preferences are not necessarily reflected in their behaviour. Furthermore, placing monetary values on environmental resources to ensure their survival is a dangerous game because if such an economic argument fails then there is no justification for saving these resources.

The task for policy makers in selecting policy instruments is complicated by political and ideological biases favouring certain kinds of instruments over others. Although governments may talk 'green,' in practice they may well give priority to weaker policies and related instruments that suit the interests of economic growth and the tourism industry over those of environmental protection and sociocultural diversity. Thus government preferences for direct public regulation or else self-regulation in tourism may well be guided more by politics and ideology, and by the dynamics of capital accumulation, than by concern to have a balanced approach. The British government's commitment to neoliberalism and market-based policies during the 1980s and early 1990s, for example, led to a strong preference for financial instruments directly affecting market prices, such as taxes, subsidies, and charging. This was reflected in an increasing emphasis on financial incentives to farmers for countryside conservation and recreational access (Bishop and Phillips, 1993). However, a strong political commitment to one group of instruments can prejudice assessments of the effectiveness of particular policy tools in achieving greater sustainability in specific circumstances.

This chapter is intended to facilitate assessments of the strengths and weaknesses of specific instruments in different situations, and to show why ethics, social values, economics, ideology, and politics will affect their use. Future critical evaluation of interventions and of related policy instruments associated with sustainable tourism objectives would benefit from the use of interdisciplinary approaches in which ideas and methods from a number of fields of study in the social sciences are combined. Each subject specialism tends to have its own concerns in relation to policy instruments: the focus of political science is on power, conflict, and legitimacy; and the preoccupation of economics is with the examination of the production and consumption of goods and services and also with efficiency. These emphases and their related lexicons can act as barriers to dialogue across and between the disciplines. A hybrid or interdisciplinary approach to interventions for sustainable tourism might be better placed to explain decisions about policy instruments. It may well also help in assessments of their implications for efficiency, equity, effectiveness, and legitimacy, and also in terms of their connections with flows of knowledge, power, and resources and with diversity and scale.

References

Adams, W. M. 1990. *Green Development. Environment and Sustainability in the Third World.* London: Routledge.

Berger, D. J. 1996. The Challenge of Integrating Maasai Tradition with Tourism. In *People and Tourism in Fragile Environments.* ed. M. F. Price. Chichester: Wiley.

Berkes, F. ed. 1989. *Common Property Resources. Ecology and Community-Based Sustainable Development.* London: Belhaven.

Bishop, K. D., and A. A. C. Phillips. 1993. Seven Steps to Market—Development of the Market-Led Approach to Countryside Conservation and Recreation. *Journal of Rural Studies* 9(4): 315–338.

Bramwell, B. 2003. The Policy Context for Tourism and Sustainability in Southern Europe's Coastal Regions. In *Coastal Mass Tourism: Diversification and Sustainable Development in Southern Europe.* ed. B. Bramwell. Clevedon: Channel View.

Bramwell, B., and B. Lane. 1993. Sustainable Tourism: An Evolving Global Approach. *Journal of Sustainable Tourism* 1(1): 1–5.

Bramwell, B., and A. Fearn. 1996. Visitor Attitudes to a Policy Instrument for Visitor Funding of Conservation in a Tourist Area. *Journal of Travel Research* 35(2): 29–33.

Briassoulis, H. 2002. Sustainable Tourism and the Question of the Commons. *Annals of Tourism Research* 29(4): 1065–1085.

Bromley, D. W. ed. 1992. *Making the Commons Work: Theory, Practice and Policy.* San Francisco: Institute for Contemporary Studies.

Broom, G. F., B. Bramwell, and C. Beard. 1995. *Paying and Charging for Access to the Welsh Countryside.* Bangor, Wales: Countryside Council for Wales.

Butler, R. W. 1991. Tourism, Environment, and Sustainable Development. *Environmental Conservation* 18(3): 201–209.

Carter, N. 2001. *The Politics of the Environment: Ideas, Activism, Policy.* Cambridge: Cambridge University Press.

Cater, E. 1995. Environmental Contradictions in Sustainable Tourism. *Geographical Journal* 161(1): 21–28.

Eber, S. ed. 1992. *Beyond the Green Horizon: Principles for Sustainable Tourism.* Godalming, U.K.: World Wide Fund for Nature.

Font, X. 2002. Certification Systems and Standards in Tourism. *Annals of Tourism Research* 29(3): 869–870.

Font, X., and R. C. Buckley. eds. 2001. *Tourism Ecolabelling: Certification and Promotion of Sustainable Development.* Wallingford: CABI.

Forsyth, T. 1996. *Sustainable Tourism: Moving from Theory to Practice.* Godalming, U.K.: World Wide Fund for Nature.

Forsyth, P., L. Dwyer, and H. Clarke. 1995. Problems in Use of Economic Instruments to Reduce Adverse Environmental Impacts of Tourism. *Tourism Economics* 1(3): 265–282.

Gale, F., and J. M. Jacobs. 1987. *Tourists and the National Estate: Procedures to Protect Australia's Heritage.* Canberra: Australian Government Publishing Service.

Genot, H. 1995. Voluntary Environmental Codes of Conduct in the Tourism Sector. *Journal of Sustainable Tourism* 3(3): 166–172.

Goodall, B. 1995. Environmental Auditing: A Tool for Assessing the Environmental Performance of Tourism Firms. *Geographical Journal* 161(1): 29–37.

Harris, R., and N. Leiper. 1995. Commonwealth Department of Tourism: The National Ecotourism Strategy. In *Sustainable Tourism: An Australian Perspective.* eds. R. Harris and N. Leiper. Chatswood, Australia: Butterworth-Heinemann.

Hall, C. M. 2000. *Tourism Planning: Policies, Processes and Relationships.* Harlow: Prentice Hall.

Harvey, D. 1992. Social Justice, Postmodernism and the City. *International Journal of Urban and Regional Research* 16: 588–601.

Hay, A. M. 1995. Concepts of Equity, Fairness and Justice in Geographical Studies. *Transactions of the Institute of British Geographers* NS 20: 500–508.

Hughes, G. 1995. The Cultural Construction of Sustainable Tourism. *Tourism Management* 16(1): 49–59.

———. 2002. Environmental Indicators. *Annals of Tourism Research* 29(2): 457–477.

Hunter, C., and H. Green. 1995. *Tourism and the Environment: A Sustainable Relationship?* London: Routledge.

Ioannides, D. 1995. A Flawed Implementation of Sustainable Tourism: The Experience of Akamas, Cyprus. *Tourism Management* 16(8): 583–592.

Jacobs, M. 1991. *The Green Economy: Environment, Sustainable Development and the Politics of the Future.* London: Pluto Press.

Jim, C. Y. 1989. Visitor Management in Recreation Areas. *Environmental Conservation* 16(1): 19–32.

Josephides, N. 1994. Tour Operators and the Myth of Self-Regulation. *Tourism in Focus.* Winter 1994. London: Tourism Concern.

Kasperson, R. E., and K. M. Dow. 1991. Developmental and Geographical Equity in Global Environmental Change: A Framework for Analysis. *Evaluation Review* 15(1): 149–171.

Laarman, J. G., and H. M. Gregersen. 1996. Pricing Policy in Nature-Based Tourism. *Tourism Management* 17(4): 247–254.

Local Government Management Board (LGMB). 1993. *A Framework for Local Sustainability.* Luton: U.K.: Local Government Management Board.

Mak, J., and J. E. T. Moncur. 1995. Sustainable Tourism Development: Managing Hawaii's 'Unique' Touristic Resource—Hanauma Bay. *Journal of Travel Research* 33(4): 51–57.

Nijkamp, P., and P. Verdonkschot. 1995. Sustainable Tourism Development: A Case Study of Lesbos. In *Sustainable Tourism Development.* eds. H. Coccossis and P. Nijkamp. Aldershot: Avebury.

Pigram, J. J. 1990. Sustainable Tourism—Policy Considerations. *Journal of Tourism Studies* 1(2): 2–9.

Ramblers Association. 1994. *Access Payment Schemes: A Response to a Discussion Paper by the Countryside Commission.* London: Ramblers Association.

Redclift, M. 1993. Environmental Economics, Policy Consensus and Political Empowerment. In *Sustainable Environmental Economics and Management: Principles and Practice.* ed. R. K. Turner. Chichester: Wiley.

Shackley, M. 1996. *Wildlife Tourism.* London: ITBP.

Sinclair, M. T., and M. Stabler. 1997. *The Economics of Tourism.* London: Routledge.

Sindiga, I. 1995. Wildlife-Based Tourism in Kenya: Land Use Conflicts and Government Compensation Policies over Protected Areas. *Journal of Tourism Studies* 6(2): 45–55.

Singh, S., D. J. Timothy, and R. K. Dowling. Eds. 2003. *Tourism in Destination Communities.* Wallingford: CABI.

Steele, P. 1995. Ecotourism: An Economic Analysis. *Journal of Sustainable Tourism* 3(1): 29–44.

Tisdell, C. 1995. Investment in Ecotourism: Assessing Its Economics. *Tourism Economics* 1(4): 375–387.

Tribe, J., X. Font, N. Griffiths, et al. 2000. *Environmental Management and Rural Tourism and Recreation.* London: Cassell.

Turner, A. 1995. Tourism Council Australia. In *Sustainable Tourism: An Australian Perspective.* eds. R. Harris and N. Leiper. Chatswood, Australia: Butterworth-Heinemann.

United Nations Environment Programme (UNEP). 1995. *Environmental Codes of Conduct for Tourism.* Technical Report 29. Paris: United Nations Environment Programme, Industry and Environment.

Van der Duim, R., and J. Caalders. 2002. Biodiversity and Tourism. Impacts and Interventions. *Annals of Tourism Research* 29(3): 743–761.

World Tourism Organization and United Nations Environment Programme (WTO/UNEP). 1992. *Guidelines: Development of National Parks and Protected Areas for Tourism.* Madrid: World Tourism Organization.

22 Exploring the political role of gender in tourism research

Linda K. Richter

Gender and tourism have something in common when it comes to political analysis: Neither was taken seriously by political scientists as important subjects of political inquiry until relatively recently. Recognition of variations in political behaviour between men and women became a subject of research only after the second world war and public policy studies of either tourism or gender issues are less than 25 years old in the United States.

Gender studies have developed a rich literature in that time. Tourism, although gradually attracting more attention by social scientists, continues to lack sustained political study. In most cases, researchers stumble onto tourism inadvertently when they are exploring something else. Surprisingly, it was the Christian Church in Asia that perhaps earlier than any other institution recognised the political importance of tourism.

Today, however, in the church and within several other forums linkages are also being made between gender and tourism. Church and peace and justice groups are looking at the issue of international tourism's impact on the exploitation of women and children and on labour, education, and development issues. In each issue, gender differences exist. *Annals of Tourism Research*, a refereed social science journal, devoted a special issue to the relationships between gender and tourism (Swain, 1995). Even in women's studies and international relations texts, new connections are being made between gender and tourism. One of the best such analyses is Cynthia Enloe's *Bananas, Beaches, and Bases* (1989). It explores not only the gender differences in opportunity structure, but also the substantial evolution of travel and tourism roles.

What this discussion will do is suggest areas of tourism research in which there are politically important gender issues and speculate about how trends in tourism and political organisations may affect the gender distinctions that have emerged. But first some definitional clarification is appropriate.

There are dozens of ways to define the study of politics, but one both pithy and pertinent is that of American political scientist Harold Lasswell. He said politics is 'who gets what, when and how' (1936). Knowing if and how tourism differently affects men and women would seem the very essence of studying the politics of gender and tourism.

But if tourism is like almost every other policy issue to which a gender analysis has been applied, the sexes do not begin with a level playing field. Thus, to Lasswell's definition, it would be prudent to add Michael Parenti's addition 'and who already has what' (1977). Richter would add 'and who cares' (1991a). The factual discussion of the topic can take us only so far; attention also needs to be given to the perceptions, intensity, and salience of the issue to individuals and groups of varying resources and commitments.

The political relationship of gender to tourism is not static but rapidly evolving. The elite-driven policy sector is increasingly opening up to more claimants for influence—in gender terms that process has meant increased access to and impact on women. That represents a marked departure from the historical gender differences *vis-a-vis* tourism.

Gender Differences in Tourism: An Historical Perspective

'Until the sixteenth century to be a woman, travel, and remain respectable one had to be generally either a queen or a pilgrim' (Robinson, 1990). Travel has had a different contextual meaning for men than for women until very recent times. Travel meant conquest, wars, crusades, exploration, trading opportunities, hunting, trapping, fishing, and commerce. Overwhelmingly, that was the public sphere of men in contrast to the global tendency to assign the private sphere of home and family to women. To the extent women participated, they did so as a vital support system for missionary work, immigration, imperial adventures, diplomatic support, or 'civilizing the frontier.'

By the nineteenth-century, travel had come to be seen as a value in its own right. The Grand Tour of Europe was the capstone to an affluent young man's education. Travel was a scarce resource eagerly sought that enhanced a young man's economic and political prospects even as it broadened his tastes. It augmented a man's prestige but it diminished a woman's reputation.

For women, education generally was seen as having much less utility and was characteristically confined to music and the domestic arts. Travel was irrelevant unless it functioned to support family goals or was justified for religious pilgrimage or health considerations. Unchaperoned travel of single women until the mid-twentieth-century compromised marriage prospects and was not seen as a positive reflection on the woman's intellect and sophistication, but as betraying a certain lack of modesty and propriety. In western societies, women were seen as requiring the protection of men from the dangers posed by other men, particularly when venturing beyond family and friends.

In general, in Asian and Middle Eastern societies, the assumptions were quite different though the solution similar. Women were considered sufficiently lusty and unreliable that family honor required their early marriage and sustained surveillance. In China, the practice of footbinding assured that affluent women would contribute to their husband's status by their absolute inability to labour, let alone travel except by palanquin! By being economically useless and dependent, they demonstrated their husbands' ability to afford such idleness.

Thomas Cook launched his famous travel-based empire in Europe intent on providing reliable, properly escorted tours for curious women eager to transcend home and earth—albeit respectably. It would be another 100 years before the travel industry began to cope with the needs of female business travellers!

There were always female mavericks who travelled with gusto with and without spouses and entourages. Their exploits are only beginning to be rediscovered. As Mabel Crawford remarked in 1863, 'If the exploring of foreign lands is not the highest end or the most useful occupation of feminine existence, it is at least more improving, as well as more amusing than crochet work' (Morris, 1993). Not all would agree. Most press accounts of the day viewed them with disdain as 'globe trotteresses' and dismissed their considerable insights as irrelevant. It was not until 1892 that the Royal Geographic Society admitted women. In the United States it would be more than 30 more years before women were allowed in The Explorers Club. Women by that time had set up their own Society of Women Geographers (Tinling, 1989)! But for most women of means, travel adventures were not on the horizon.

Women's accounts of their travels have differed markedly from men. Women have had greater access to the women and children in other societies than have men, and their accounts, as a consequence, offer more of a sense of family customs. Men, as might be expected, were more apt to comment on political affairs, the impact of European ideas, and the state of technology (Blunt, 1994; Tinling, 1989).

Not just travel, but even at home the very notion of leisure time was one enjoyed by men long before women. The weekend, for example, meant far less of a change in activity for women than for men. As Rybczynski notes in *Waiting for the Weekend*, 'The proper place for proper women was the home—public leisure was exclusively a male domain' (Rybczynski, 1991).

Gender Differences in Employment and Ownership

Men and women not only have historically been socialised to view travel from very different perspectives, but there continues to be a division of labour by gender at all levels of the travel and tourism hierarchies (Steiger and Wardell, 1995).

Let's consider 'who already has what.' United Nations' statistics tell us that although women do two-thirds of the world's work, they get one-tenth of the world's income and have one-hundredth of the world's property (Johnson, 1983). Comparable statistics focussed on the travel and tourism industry do not exist, but inequality appears nonetheless to be the norm in most sectors.

The tourism sector taken as a whole (and its boundaries are still open to dispute) is small scale. In the United States, for example, more than 95 percent of tourism-related businesses are quite small. Women dominate travel agency ownership and are the majority of travel agents (Richter, 1991b). They may also play an important role as producers of crafts, art, and other services for the tourist trade (Swain, 1993). In fact, within the United States women make up 52 percent of the employment in travel and tourism in contrast to 44 percent of industries in general (Edgell, 1993).

In monetary terms, however, men control the major sectors of the tourism economy. There are few women owners of airlines, railroads, major destinations (except Dolly Parton's Dolly World), hotel chains (former inmate Leona Helmsley's empire is an exception), car rental companies, and travel magazines. Even female travel writers are scarce—Jan Morris being a notable exception and having established her reputation first as a male.

Nationalists in developing countries bemoan the perils of tourism turning their country into a nation of waiters and bellhops because of largely male-dominated foreign control (Barry, Wood, and Preusch, 1984; English, 1986). The real bottom of the hierarchy, however, are the chambermaids, restaurant help, and laundresses. They get few tips and have the least dignified positions (Enloe, 1989). Female cooks and waitresses tend to be found in the lowest paid parts of the food sector. Although cooking is historically a female task in most societies, it becomes an overwhelmingly male niche in the fancier restaurants where salaries and tips are substantial. That these disparities are not obvious is probably because women in the tourist sector are doing what they traditionally do as unpaid labour in the home (Richter, 1995).

In summary, although women do have access and employment disproportionately to men in the travel sector, these positions tend to be available—as indeed, they are to minorities—because they are seasonal, part-time, or minimum wage. They also are in the least organised sectors of the travel labour market. Thus, the answer to 'who already had what' is that women have the majority of the jobs at the base of the tourism employment hierarchy; men have almost all of the jobs at the middle and top (Enloe, 1993).

Prostitution

'Sex tourism is not natural or endemic, but rather the result of decades of political choices and accidents' (Leheny, 1995). One employment sector, prostitution, once almost exclusively female, has become unenviably open to men and boys. Although most countries have prostitution—legal or not—certain destinations have become inextricably linked with sex tourism, such as Thailand (nicknamed 'Thighland' in some circles), the Philippines, Sri Lanka, and Brazil (Barry, Bunch, and Castley, 1984; Holden and Horleman, 1983; Leheny, 1995; Richter, 1989a; Sereewat, 1983; Thanh-Dam, 1983). The numbers are boggling. Estimates of the numbers of women and child prostitutes range from 350,000 to 1 million in the Philippines alone. Thailand is presumed to have at least that many, thousands of whom are virtual slaves from Burma (Thomas and Jones, 1993). Prostitution is not an employment decision for thousands who are coerced, kidnapped, or sold into prostitution. Huge numbers of women, particularly from countries like the Philippines, find themselves involuntarily in what is referred to as the 'entertainment industry' (Caul and Youngblood, 1996; Esplanada, 1996; Rosca, 1995). Although most prostitutes are female, a growing gay and pedophilia market exploit men and young boys (ECPAT, 1992), particularly in countries like the Philippines and Sri Lanka, (Rogers, 1989; Rosca, 1995). In any case, the customers are almost exclusively male. Females buying the 'escort plus' services of black males in the Caribbean are not unknown (Pruitt and Lafont, 1995), but the sex tourism industry revolves around the fantasies of men and is owned and controlled by men. Women work for men, not vice versa, when it comes to the provision of most sexual services.

The disproportionately male tourist traffic in Asia and Africa continues, but those seeking sex at their destination have changed their behaviour somewhat. To protect themselves, men seek out children or young prostitutes from countries without a reputation for AIDS. Thus, the number of children involved in tourism soars and the incidence of AIDS among them does as well.

Explaining Sex Tourism

Many things combine to link sexual activity with tourism. By its minimum definition, a tourist is someone staying overnight at least 100 miles from home. The anonymity of being away from friends, business associates, and relatives offers opportunity for discreet extramarital sexual liaisons without the emotional, long-term commitment of an affair. It combines a sense of kinky adventure with intimacy in a strange location.

Two interesting arguments are advanced by those more sanguine about sex tourism than is this writer. Both place the responsibility not on the men but the morals and attitudes of women. One line of reasoning is that prostitution is the world's oldest profession, and that in many of the travel markets where it is most explicit, concubinage has been its domestic equivalent for centuries.

This argument does not face the very different conditions associated with prostitution in a touristic context. Regularly patronising a prostitute or supporting a concubine were much less dangerous for the men and women involved than the transient and fleeting associations now taking place. The legalisation and institutionalisation of prostitution in such places as Australia and Las Vegas, have in fact been a response to the robberies, murders, drug dealing, and health problems associated with unregulated prostitution. It is also a way to tax a lucrative industry and get kickbacks from the licensing of prostitutes.

The second argument places the blame for sex tourism on the women's movement! Instead of women staying in their place, they have demanded equality. Instead of unshackling their inhibitions, they have become pickier about the men with whom they will mate! Imagine, the women's movement did not define itself the way some men wanted. Pro-choice was extended not only to abortion but to coupling! This argument was actually made in a supposedly serious research paper this writer reviewed. It purported to explain why Australian males went on sex trips to Thailand. Supposedly, they needed to do some male bonding and be with some feminine women after contending with increasingly uppity Australian women, corrupted by the women's movement!

Not only is it insulting to suggest such fragile egos in Australian men, but it is also a curious argument to suggest that a bid for equality among Australian women naturally will result in the exploitation of other women! Nor does it appear to be a sufficient explanation for sex tourism from Japan where the women's movement is almost microscopic, or pedophilia tours from Germany where presumably the children are no more aggressive than anywhere else!

So who cares? Increasingly, groups are organising against sex tours, the exploitation of children, and the health and safety issues attached to each. One of the most active of these groups is End Child Prostitution in Asian Tourism (ECPAT, 1992) which is moving on child prostitution issues in scores of countries. They have already had some success.

Realistically, they have their best chance of success in terms of controlling child prostitution through stiff fines and sentences for the customers and parents of such abused children. The global network against such exploitation offers some support to governments long on good intentions but short on will. AIDS may be a more effective antidote to misplaced ardor than government action, but advertising, family fares, and destination development that sell nonsexual activities are all options that more and more groups may sponsor.

As AIDS and other sexually transmitted diseases spread like wildfire throughout poor nations, the response of governments has varied widely. Some European countries have prosecuted men involved in child prostitution in third world countries. The Philippines since the overthrow of dictator Ferdinand Marcos in 1986 has taken numerous, albeit not very successful, steps to shut down sex tours, prosecute pedophiles, and clean up tourist areas (Contours, 1996; Sherwill, 1996). Some nations now require proof of a negative AIDS test for nontransit tourists. Contrast that with Thailand, where authorities permitted AIDS to go unchallenged for years rather than risk depressing tourism, Thailands' number one industry (Hall, 1994; Shenon, 1992). Cuba, like Thailand, has no legal prostitution but rather an enormous illicit industry (Darling, 1995). Unlike Thailand, Cuba quarantines AIDS victims, moving swiftly to control spread of the disease. Recently, however, the Thai government has tried to attract female tourists in an effort to refashion Thailand's tawdry image. 'Women Visit Thailand Year' in 1992 was an attempt to attract the increasing numbers of Japanese women going abroad. Indications are that it was successful (Leheny, 1995).

Gender Differences in Marketing, Souvenirs, and Attractions

Theoretically, the appeal of combining sex with tourism should be the same for both sexes, but it is not. Whether we ascribe the differences to biological propensities, socialisation, or opportunity structure, an industry providing a sexual ambiance and sexual favours to male clients creates a potentially hostile environment for female clients. Yet, because males control the industry and particularly its marketing and promotion, the expectations of linking sex with tourism are everywhere. Handsome, flirtatious men are not what the ads offer. It is women, alone or with other women, and often in remote natural settings or in a serving role, as in hotel and airline ads. Intact families, older people, and children are not pictured in most advertisements.

In fact, advertising encouraging whole families to travel is the exception, although industry analysts predict more of this as aging baby boomers bring children along on vacations, spawning children's versions of Club Med or their own cruise activities. In general, men who bring their wives on business trips are sold romantic, second honeymoon experiences. Women, on the other hand, are promised physically pampering environments with excellent shopping!

Until recently, the older woman traveller has been virtually ignored in the marketing research, although evidence suggests she may be a much more active and economically important element than anticipated (Hawes, 1988). This is not surprising. The industry generally has been both myopic and sexist in its assumptions about what women need and want, despite the fact that women make the majority of the decisions regarding discretionary travel (Maruff, 1993; Smith, 1979; Tunstall, 1989). Recently, tours have been mushrooming that are exclusively for women. They range from theater tours for sorority alums to trekking expeditions in the Himalayas.

Marketing has also focussed on the older traveller, who is increasingly important demographically and is disproportionately female. Elderhostel, Earthwatch, and other research-cum-travel groups are attracting a huge, well-educated generation with disposable income. Nor is this group confined to the United States and western Europe. Korea and Taiwan lifted their barriers in the last decade to men of military age travelling abroad, but there are also significant numbers of female group travellers going abroad from these countries (Militante, 1993).

As women have increasingly become more of the travel market, the industry response has adapted in some curious ways consistent with male orientation and female concerns. The general advertising has become a bit subtler, but prostitution services have become less small scale, more entrepreneurial. Visa and Mastercard are accepted for a dazzling array of itemised sexual services from virtually any racial ethnic group one desires. Presumably routinising such services will encourage less hassling of women in general, and women travelling alone in particular. It will also encourage men to patronise services controlled by other men. In the age of AIDS and herpes, men get some assurances that the women they buy will be inspected and presumed healthy. The women, of course, get no such protection from their clients!

Women business travellers, then, are just as likely to be interacting professionally with men who are buying the sexual favours of other women. Still, some studies show that U.S. female business travellers find the pace less difficult than male counterparts (Del Rosso, 1992). One is tempted to suggest they get more sleep than those buying sexual services, but the answer is more complicated. Women away from home are removed from the traditional tasks of the household, cleaning, cooking, and caring for children, whereas male travellers on the road have laundry, meals, and mending they would not usually have at home.

The male-controlled industry offers increasingly better protection for the growing numbers of female business travellers. Thus, there is greater attention to security in the issuance of keys, better locks, and more attentive service in restaurants. Hair dryers, skirt hangers, and bubble baths are also more likely to be included in hotels, be it for clients or their female guests. That women still feel vulnerable is suggested by their much greater use of room service for meals.

Gender and Souvenirs

Another area where gender differences emerge with respect to tourism is in the selling of memories through postcards and souvenirs. Semiotics has demonstrated that those in control show us an image of 'the other' that is congruent with the dominant group values, their expectations, and their goals. For example, we can now look back with some amusement, tinged with horror, at the way early travel writings described non-Western societies. The more lurid the tales from Asia, Africa, and the American frontier of cannibals, sacrifices, savages, and bare-breasted maidens, the easier it was to rationalise imperial 'civilizing' adventures.

The United States was not immune. President McKinley reportedly declared in 1898 that he was annexing the Philippines 'for our little brown brothers for whom Christ also died.' This ignored the fact that the Philippines after 350 years of Spanish rule were already 85 percent Catholic! Travel brochures often encourage the traveller to expect friendly pampering. One widely promoted Caribbean advertisement had a staff of black cooks, maids, bellmen, drivers, and so forth with trays of food and flowers out waist deep in the ocean offering these goodies to a white couple lounging on a rubber raft. Gender was not the issue but racial and economic dependency; however, in postcards, brochures, and souvenirs the gender dimension, like that of race, is well worth exploring.

Under Philippine dictator Ferdinand Marcos, the tourism slogan was 'Where Asia Wears a Smile' and the advertising promised 'a tanned peach on every beach' (Richter, 1982). Nude or scantily dressed women are the staple of many postcard shops. To its credit, the Philippines under President Aquino was one nation that dramatically changed its government marketing of tourism (Richter, 1988). Indonesia, on the other hand, sells pictures of nude tribal people (both male and female) and penis sheaths at its Biak airport shop. The exploitation of native peoples is so much easier after you take away their dignity.

In Hawaii, this is taken a step further. Authentic Hawaiians are not even pictured, but usually some generic Polynesian-cum-Filipino-Japanese mix deemed sexier for North American and European markets. Blond, blue-eyed women are more apt to be the erotic subjects of advertising targeting the Japanese!

Even the United States permitted its government tourist office to promote one of its Caribbean territories with giant buttons saying 'TRY A VIRGIN . . . island.' Happily, it evoked an appropriately negative response when called to the attention of the Coalition on Third World Tourism and the Caribbean Council of Churches (Richter, 1989b).

In 1984, a new product hit the market with the editorial approval of the Honolulu Star Bulletin—'scratch and sniff' postcards. Scratch the females pictured and they give off scents of the flowers of Hawaii. Someone once said, 'No one ever went broke underestimating the taste of the American public!' Similarly, there would not be a shortage of sexist souvenir kitsch should one try to collect it. In sculpture, be it marble, wood, or terracotta, in pictures on black velvet or canvas, in virtually any medium, so-called airport art flourishes. Often, when human beings are the subject, they are sexually explicit female renditions.

Gender and Attractions

although women figure prominently in advertising, postcards, and souvenirs, they are sadly neglected in cultural and historical tourism destinations supported by taxpayers' money. Battlefields do not celebrate those who nursed the soldiers; galleries seldom provide showcases for female talent; museums may feature fashions from an era or the dresses of First Ladies, but they seldom recall the daring adventures or courage of women. Statues recall war heroes, 'forefathers' not 'foremothers,' male 'founders' of towns (not their invisible spouses). In the United States the Statue of Liberty, the Madonna of the Plains, and monuments to the frontier woman occasionally remember women as a category, rarely the specific woman.

It was not until the 1980s that a museum of women's art was opened in Washington, D.C., with private donations. It was not until the 1990s that the cornerstone was laid for a memorial to U.S. women veterans and an impressive sculpture added to the Vietnam War Memorial to belatedly acknowledge the service of women in Vietnam. Even one of the most beautiful tourist sites in the world, the Taj Mahal, although built as a crypt for a woman, is remembered as a testament to Emperor Shah Jahan's love! Thus, the impact of tourism continues to socialise generations to the importance of what men have done while women are ignored or immortalised on postcards, nutcrackers, and t-shirts.

Prospects for Policy Changes

Will 'who gets what, when and how' change as more women enter the workplace, as the numbers of both men and women travelling accelerate? Probably. But the prospects for greater balance in gender control are mixed.

The vast bulk of the financial control of the private tourism sector is in the hands of men. That is almost equally true of the public sector. Government policy makers, be they political appointees or career bureaucrats, are overwhelmingly male. The U.S. example illustrates this point. The executive branch is overwhelmingly male at the policy-making levels (GS 16–18). Only two of the President's cabinet officials in 1992 were female, along with five percent of the Senate. Forty-seven of the fifty states are headed by male tourism directors (Richter, 1985). In 1992 Richter was the only female among the 15 members of the National Travel and Tourism Advisory Board. In 1992, however, women in leadership included the United States Secretary of Commerce and the head of United States Customs. The Philippines was unusual in 1992 and again in 1996 in having a female Secretary of Tourism. The Aquino role model accelerated a pattern already more pronounced there: more women in the poorly paid public sector versus more men in the private sector, but at least the women are often in positions of influence.

Women have been perceived as particularly appropriate for 'frontline' tourism positions because they are assumed to be more social and more hospitable than men. In fact, in the Philippines, the euphemism for tourism prostitute is a 'hospitality girl.' Zulfiqar Ali Bhutto, former Prime Minister of Pakistan, actually saw tourism as a new sector that would be ideally suited to women, whose employment and social uplift were a priority with him. For that very reason, among others, tourism was seen as a force of corruption and pollution among conservative forces in Pakistan and within other Islamic cultures. Christian churches in Asia, the Pacific, and the Caribbean would be inclined to agree. In the Maldives, a tiny Muslim nation in the Indian Ocean, only men are allowed to work at the tourist resorts that are on separate islands physically isolated from the rest of the population (Richter, 1989a).

Ideological forces now sweeping the globe are encouraging less national planning, more devolution of power, greater privatisation of industry including the privatisation and deregulation of the tourist industry. These forces may create an industry more susceptible to market forces but it may deprive further those with the least influence and political access. Equity, systemic justice and the public interest, which were seldom well served by the tourist industry before, may have an even greater struggle in the days ahead (Richter, 1991a; b).

As this writer has noted elsewhere:

> The primary reason why US tourism policy has not taken a more holistic approach to tourism is because of its fixation on tourism as a revenue-producing activity rather than as an important facet in improving the quality of life by reducing stress, enhancing education, instilling variety, and contributing to shared family experiences. While concern for revenue is reasonable since tourism generates billions in federal, state and local taxes, such a perspective ignores the nonmonetary features of tourism policy and the not so easily quantified monetary costs of tourism development. Unlike much of the industrialised world, which also appreciates tourism's economic impact, the United States and its policy has not moved beyond the profit motive to a consideration of the role of leisure in the promotion of health, reduction of crime, reward of labour, or the importance of travel as an information medium (Richter, 1991b).

On the other hand, the antigovernment fever that has gripped not only the United States but countries around the globe may argue for a stronger role for the ultimate political outsiders—women. However, there are many reasons to assume that class, race, religious and ethnic loyalties will continue to be more salient than gender. What we do know is that women in public office have shown a disproportionate concern for social welfare and environmental issues, for the issues of health, women, and children—all areas toward which the unfettered tourism industry has on many occasions been overly cavalier (Darcy, Welch, and Clark, 1987). Thus, if women achieve more access to representative institutions and public policy positions, current research suggests they will have an impact on tourism in specifically those areas where women have had least control and influence. Stronger worker safety, wage, health, and family leave laws might be anticipated.

A phenomenon as massive as tourism and a variable as basic as gender cannot be discussed thoroughly in this brief space. Clearly, however, there are numerous evolving dimensions of this relationship that deserve further scrutiny. Once we acknowledge that tourism has been marginalised and trivialised as a research subject and requires careful analysis, it is a logical next step to explore its impact in the context of such a central variable as gender.

References

Barry, K., C. Bunch, and S. Castley. 1984. International Feminism: Networking Against Female Slavery. New York: International Women's Tribune Centre.

Barry, T., B. Wood, and D. Preusch. 1984. *The Other Side of Paradise: Foreign Control in the Caribbean.* New York: Grove Press.

Blunt, A. 1994. *Travel, Gender and Imperialism: Mary Kingsley and West Africa.* New York: Guilford Press.

Caul, M., and R. L. Youngblood. 1996. Structures of Imperialism and the Exploitation of Women and Children in the Philippine Entertainment Industry. A paper presented at the Fifth International Philippine Studies Conference. Honolulu, April 14–16.

Contours. 1996. Philippines Targets Foreign Syndicates to End Flesh Trade. *Contours* 7(5): March.

Darcy, R., S. Welch, and J. Clark. 1987. *Women, Elections and Representation, Longman.* New York.

Darling, L. 1995. Havana at Midnight. *Esquire* (May): 96–104.

Del Rosso, L. 1992. Study Shows Women Handle Business Travel Better Than Men. *Travel Weekly* July: 30–31.

ECPAT. 1992. Children in Prostitution: Victims of Tourism in Asia. Conference Statement. End Child Prostitution in Asian Tourism, Bangkok.

Edgell, D. 1993. World Tourism at the Millennium. Washington, D.C.: U.S. Dept. of Commerce, 18.

English, P. 1986. *The Great Escape: An Examination of North-South Tourism.* Ottawa: North-South Institute.

Enloe, C. 1989. *Bananas, Beaches, and Bases: Making Feminist Sense of International Politics.* Berkeley: University of California Press.

———. 1993. *The Morning After, Sexual Politics at the End of the Cold War.* California: University of California Press.

Esplanada, J. 1996. Women Sold in Body Parts. *Philippine Daily Inquirer* 1, 6.

Hall, C. 1994. *ASEAN: 6-in-1 Tropical Paradise? Tourism in the Pacific Rim*, Australia: Longman.

Hawes, D. K. 1988. Travel-Related Lifestyle Profiles of Older Women. *Journal of Travel Research* (Fall): 22–32.

Holden, P., and P. Horlemann. eds. 1983. *Documentation: Tourism, Prostitution, Development.* Bangkok: Ecumenical Coalition of Third World Tourism.

Johnson, S. 1983. Women and the Quest for Justice. A speech given at Kansas State University, April 29.

Lasswell, H. 1936. *Politics: Who Gets What, When, and How?* New York: McGraw-Hill.

Leheny, D. 1995. A Political Economy of Asian Sex Tourism. *Annals of Tourism Research* 22(1): 380–381.

Maruff, P. 1993. Fledgling Women's Movement in Korea. *Asia Travel Trade* (March): 20–21.

Militante, G. 1993. Japanese Women are Going Places. *Asia Travel Trade* (March): 17–19.

Morris, M. ed. with L. O'Connor. 1993. *Maiden Voyages.* New York: Vintage.

Parenti, M. 1977. *Democracy for the Few.* New York: St. Martin's Press.

Pruitt, D., and S. Lafont. 1995. For Love or Money, Romance Tourism in Jamaica. *Annals of Tourism Research* 22(1): 422–440.

Richter, L. K. 1982. *Land Reform and Tourism Development: Policy-Making in the Philippines.* Cambridge, Mass.: Schenkman.

———. 1985. State-Sponsored Tourism: A Growth Field for Public Administration. *Public Administration Review* (November–December): 832–839.

———. 1989a. *The Politics of Tourism in Asia.* Honolulu: University of Hawaii Press.

———. 1989b. Action Alert. *Contours* 4(4): 4.

———. 1991a. Political Issues in Tourism Policy: A Forecast. In *World Travel and Tourism Review.* eds. D. Hawkins and J. B. Ritchie. United Kingdom: CAB International.

———. 1991b. The Impact of American Tourism Policy on Women. In *Gender Differences.* ed. M. L. Kendrigan. Colorado: Greenwood Press.

———. 1995. Gender and Race: Neglected Variables in Tourism Research. In *Change in Tourism: People, Places, Processes.* eds. R. Butler and D. Pearce. London: Routledge.

Robinson, H. 1990. *Wayward Women: A Guide to Women Travellers.* London: Oxford University Press.

Rogers, J. 1989. Tourism and Child Prostitution. *Contours* 4(2): 20–22.

Rosca, N. 1995. The Philippines Shameful Export. *The Nation* (April): 522, 524, 526–527.

Rybczynski, W. 1991. *Waiting for the Weekend.* London: Viking Penguin.

Sereewat, S. 1983. Prostitution: Thai-European Connection. World Council of Churches. Geneva, Switzerland.

Sherwill, P. 1996. Nailing Johns. *World Press Review* (January): 13.

Shenon, P. 1992. After Years of Denial Asia Faces Scourge of AIDS. The *New York Times,* November 8, A1.

Smith, V. L. 1979. Women: The Taste-Makers in Tourism. *Annals of Tourism Research* 6(1): 49–60.

Steiger, T., and M. Wardell. 1995. Gender and Employment in the Service Sector. *Social Problems* 42(1): 91–123.

Swain, M. 1993. Women Producers of Ethnic Arts. *Annals of Tourism Research* 20(1): 32–51.

———. 1995. Gender and Tourism. *Annals of Tourism Research* 22(1): 247–266.

Thanh-Dam, T. 1983. The Dynamics of Sex Tourism: The Case of Southeast Asia. *Development and Change* 14: 533–553.

Thomas, D., and S. Jones. eds. 1993. A Modern Form of Slavery: Trafficking of Burmese Women and Girls into Brothels in Thailand. *New York: Asia Watch* 15–16.

Tinling, M. 1989. *Women into the Unknown.* New York: Greenwood Press.

Tunstall, R. 1989. Catering for the Female Business Traveler. In EIU Travel and Tourism Analyst, No. 5, 26–40.

23 Crisis management in tourist destinations

Gurhan Aktas and Ebru A. Gunlu

Introduction

A tourist destination, if considered as a dynamic organism constantly adjusting its tourist offers to changing market trends, can secure its place in the competitive tourism environment only through close scrutiny of emerging trends, and the use of strategic plans prepared according to anticipated changes. The problem, however, arises when the destination gets caught unprepared by changes in both the demand and supply sides, especially if they arise in a short period without warning but with damaging effects on the industry. Unless the destination management network addresses such threats to the effective functioning and maintenance of the industry sufficiently, promptly, and in a collaborative manner, the market advantages of the destination may be severely damaged and may require a long period before full recovery from negative image perceptions among potential visitors is achieved.

Although changes in the tourism market vary from changing consumer wants, needs, and expectations to newcomer destinations with adventurous offers challenging the tourist package of traditional destinations, the most severe and sudden fall in tourism demand is often a result of 'destination crises.' Although associated aptly with hospitability, pleasure, and entertainment, tourism is arguably one of the foremost income-producing sectors, which cannot escape the adverse, and often long-term, effects of incidents like violence, scandals, and conflicts either in its operating environment or in generating markets. In fact, the fragmented nature of the industry makes the eradication of crisis-causing factors difficult. Crises occurring in one of the subsectors of the industry such as the accommodation, transportation, or attraction sectors may soon cause a domino effect across the destination, resulting in diminished profitability. Similarly, as the effectiveness of the industry relies on the interdependence and harmony of all economic sectors existing at a destination, a crisis threatening any of these sectors and degrading the credibility of the destination in the minds of potential visitors, can be detrimental for tourism to such an extent that the industry might be the last one of the revenue-generating sectors to recover from the damage.

Worse is the situation where tourist destinations have little or no control over crisis-causing factors engendered in an external environment. International human transaction and communication are the inevitable prerequisites of success for tourist destinations competing in the international tourism market. Therefore, although the existence of the industry depends on the volume of visitors attracted from generating markets through business deals established between tourism organisations operating in different countries, crises surfacing on the other side of the world, can soon acquire a *global* characteristic harming the industry worldwide. In fact, it has been global crises such as the September 11 terrorist attacks on the United States and the Asian financial crisis that have caused much controversy and growing interest in crisis management theories and their application to tourism destinations among tourism practitioners and academicians in the recent past.

Although crisis management has been an established research field in business and managerial sciences since the early 1970s (Keown-McMullan, 1997), it is still a relatively new concept to tourism with much effort needed to investigate various topics including types of crises in tourist destinations, the impacts of such events on the tourism industry, the response of the industry to different crises types, and cooperation among industry stakeholders during crises situations (Faulkner, 2001). In addition to the manifold crisis-causing factors stemming from the fragmented nature of the industry, the *perishable* characteristic of tourist products that they cannot be stocked and sold later when demand reaches precrisis levels, requires the acknowledgement of systematic and effective policy planning during difficult times in order to counteract downturns in demand as immediately and accurately as possible. As suggested by Faulkner, only through developing a theoretical and conceptual framework on the concept and learning from previous case studies comprehensively investigated by academicians will practitioners gain guidance on how to respond to crises and how to develop unique recovery strategies for different crises in individual destination settings. In spite of the existing gap in the literature, the existing research embraces subjects including the definition and classification of crises (Tarlow and Muehsam, 1996; Pizam, 1999; Faulkner, 2001; and Glaesser, 2003), the impacts of crises on tourism (Prideaux, Laws, and Faulkner, 2003), terrorism and tourism (Wahab, 1996; Wall, 1996; Leslie, 1999; Mansfeld, 1999; Sonmez, Apostolopoulos, and Tarlow, 1999; and Goodrich, 2002; Pizam, 2002), natural disasters and tourism (Durocher, 1994; and Huang and Min, 2002), marketing tourist destinations in difficult times (Gonzales-Herrero and Pratt, 1998; Beirman, 2002; 2003; and Hopper, 2002), tourism in postcrisis

(Anson, 1999; and Richter, 1999), and the operation of tourism organisations in crisis situations (Cavlek, 2002; Stafford, Yu, and Armoo, 2002; and Henderson, 2003).

The universal ground established by the existing research on crisis management in tourism is that the issues safety and security can no longer be neglected during the formulation and presentation of tourist offers and that tourism authorities should acknowledge the importance of crisis contingency plans to be prepared in conjunction with strategic destination development and marketing plans. In today's world, no matter how strict security and safety measures are, tourist destinations cannot completely be protected against manifold threats including wars, terrorist attacks, natural disasters, and epidemics. Therefore, vacationing in a destination that has not acquired an unsafe image is one of the main concerns of most visitors during the decision-making process. Contingency plans prepared with the joint effort of all industry stakeholders can help destinations respond to crisis situations and overcome their adverse effects accordingly and promptly before they cause further damage and lack of confidence in the destination among potential visitors.

The Nature of '*Crisis*' and Types of Crises in Tourist Destinations

Despite the anonymous consensus in the academic literature on the need for widespread implementation of crisis management theories in the tourism industry, which is considered to be especially sensitive to crisis situations mainly due to its international and fragmented nature, there seem to be varying approaches toward defining crisis. In his study aiming to construct a generic model for tourism disaster management, Faulkner (2001) distinguishes 'crises' from 'disasters.' According to the author, although the root cause of crises is self-inflicted through problems caused by inept management structures and practices, disasters refer to situations where a destination, in the context of tourism, experiences unpredictable catastrophic changes over which it has little control. The author further states that it is not always easy to identify certain events as disasters or crises because of the difficulty of assessing the factual reasons behind what actually causes damage. The 1999 Izmit earthquake, for instance, led to nearly 20,000 deaths and destruction of more than 300,000 buildings in the surroundings of this industrialised city in Turkey with severe impact on the tourism industry nationwide. Only following the earthquake did the Turkish government revise the construction regulations to protect buildings against disasters such as earthquakes and the laws on optional property insurances (Beirman, 2003). Therefore, the fact that buildings collapsed simply because they lacked an architectural integrity needed, given the country's history of earthquakes, can be argued to be as damaging as the catastrophe itself.

In addition to management failures grouped under crises, and catastrophic disasters from the influence of external factors, Prideaux, Laws, and Faulkner (2003) add another group of events, namely 'trends,' which interrupt the tourism industry. Trends, for which the warning signals are more predictable than those for crises and disasters, include such events as low fertility rates and ageing population in developed countries altering the characteristics of tourism market segments, global warming threatening the environment and climate conditions of tourist destinations, shortage in energy resources, increasing world population, political and economic unions among countries leading to the development of new trading schemes leaving nonmembers with unfavourable market positions, and emerging consumer trends resulting from globalisation. The authors further state that, although trends do not have the shocking effect of crises and disasters, they still need to be managed through systematic planning in order to mitigate any potential disruption.

The prevailing approach toward the classification of events with damaging impact on the tourism industry is, however, to assemble them under the main notion of crisis (Sonmez, Apostolopoulos, and Tarlow, 1999; Stafford, Yu, and Armoo, 2002; Beirman, 2003; and Glaesser, 2003). In such classifications, events, which either arise externally or are self-inflicted, are considered to be crises and are then split into groups of disasters and management failures engendered by the physical, social, political, or economic environments of tourist destinations. Rather than defining the main reason what caused the event, this approach strives for the explanation of those elements that determine when situations develop into deteriorating crises. These elements are (Keown-McMullan, 1997; Faulkner; 2001):

A triggering event: Crises are a result of an unexpected event or a flow of events evolving in a short period and with potential to cause significant change, challenging the existing structure or survival of the crisis-struck tourist destination.

Threat and damage: The crisis-triggering event is so significant in its impact that it would cause panic and loss of control among those directly affected and would pose a threat to the effective functioning of the destination, with some short-term damage experienced instantly.

Need for action: In order to overcome long-term effects, crises require urgent and expert action through cooperation of key authorities and the industry stakeholders.

If a given destination were to experience an event with the characteristics listed, one way of determining the type of crisis would be to look into its

Table 23.1   Crisis Types in Tourist Destinations

	Damaging Effect of the Crisis			
	'Minimal'			'Maximum'
Origin of the Crisis	Crisis in the Competitors	Crises in the Generating Markets		Crisis in the Destination
Scope of the Crisis	Local	Regional	National	International
Duration of the Crisis	One-Time	Repetitive with Intervals		Consecutive and Ongoing
Motive of the Crisis	Technological/Environmental/Sociocultural/Economic/Political			

origin, scope, duration, and motive. As Table 23.1 shows, a crisis can occur in a destination, in its competitors, or in the visitor generator markets. From the perspective of their scope, crises can be split into local, regional, national, and international crises, whereas the duration of the situation reveals whether it is a one-time, repetitive, or ongoing problem. Finally, the motive refers to the main reason behind the crisis and can be sociocultural, technological, environmental, economic, or political.

As noted, crises, by their very characteristic, have some sort of deteriorating impact on destinations and deter potential visitors from purchasing the tourist products on offer. However, it is also clear that not all crisis types would lead to similar consequences, but differ from each other according to the scope and extent of the damage caused. International crises, for instance, understandably have greater potential to disrupt the industry across the world, whereas a negative event on a local scale could be toned down reasonably easily through sufficient policies before the affected destination returns to operate on precrisis visitor figures and tourism income levels. Nevertheless, the distinction between different crises types is not always clear cut. The September 11 attacks on the United States, for example, were unprecedented in the country's recent history and can be considered as a one-time event. But the attacks soon gained an international concern partly because they were politically driven terrorist attacks followed by military actions against Afghanistan and Iraq. Furthermore, the attacks were carried out using airplanes, which are directly associated with the tourism industry in the minds of potential travellers, thus raising concerns over the security of airline passengers. Therefore, although Table 23.1 provides some insight into the varying effects of categorised crises, it should be regarded as only a key to different crisis types. The real-life incidents may be complex and intriguing events demanding a cross-sectional analysis of different types.

In the light of the previous information, it is broadly accepted that political threats, including wars, terrorist attacks, coups d'état, and international conflicts, cause more severe and long-term damage to tourist destinations than other forms of crises, especially if their effects spread internationally (Pizam, 1999; Sonmez, Apolstolopoulos, and Tarlow, 1999; Cavlek, 2002). Acts of terrorism on tourists and visitor attractions, meantime, do not only impede the flow of visitors to the affected locality during and shortly after the crisis, but also harm its perceived image as a safe destination for years to come. Pizam (1999) explains the selection of tourists and tourist destinations as targets of terrorism because of their high visibility and exposure to the international media and the intention to impair the main income-earning industry of those traditional tourist destinations. Some examples to the jeopardising outcomes of wars and terrorism regarding the development and growth of the tourism industry include the cases of Egypt, Israel, Northern Ireland, and the United States (Wahab, 1996; Wall, 1996; Anson, 1999; Leslie, 1999; Mansfeld; 1999; Goodrich, 2002; and World Tourism Organization, 2002).

Politically motivated threats are followed by economic, sociocultural, environmental, and technological crises with relatively smaller degrees of disruption for tourist destinations. However, one cannot overlook the interrelated duration and scope of each crisis type, which determines the actual level of damage. Policy makers first need to clarify whether the emerging crisis is expected to be of temporary or long lasting. Beirman (2003) gives the example of a man killing 35 tourists with an automatic rifle at the historical site of Port Arthur in Tasmania in 1996 as a one-time crisis. Although the case led to a fall in demand in the destination, the marketing process initiated following the event helped the destination to recover rapidly from the adverse effects. In contrast, the ongoing conflict between Israel and the Palestinians and serial terrorist acts occurring in major cities still prevents the Israeli tourism industry from reaching what could otherwise be achievable targets (Mansfeld, 1999).

Second, the scope of a crisis needs to be examined. As mentioned earlier, the September 11 attacks were of a one-time nature, but they inhibited the tourism industry on an international scale. The degree of shocking effect and the political significance of an event can attract wide media coverage where information is dispersed across the world in a matter of seconds and can immediately construct negative image perceptions among potential visitors whose travel behaviour can be altered against those destinations concerned.

Finally, the crisis emerging in a tourist destination can clearly be more harmful than a crisis in generating markets or competitor destinations. In fact, destinations can benefit from the crisis difficulties of their competitors to an extent that the market share lost by those in trouble can be grasped by others. Those market segments, which previously booked or were considering a trip to the crisis-struck destination, can be attracted to other destinations through timely marketing activities emphasising the safety and crisis-free status of their vacation spots. The impact of a crisis in a generating market on a given destination, meanwhile, varies according to the significance of the market for the tourism industry. If the generating market has the largest share of incoming visitors or accounts for the largest tourism income for the destination, the tourism industry could experience severe decline in its growth regardless of its crisis-free position. The policies for the revival of inbound tourism should then focus on attracting supplementary or new potential market segments until the main market segment recovers from the crisis and generates visitors for the destination.

Before examining crisis contingency plans and crisis management teams within the concept of tourism in the following sections, it is important to note here that crises do not always cause negative impacts on tourist destinations, but can also be considered as turning points along the manifold phases of destination development (Keown-McMullan, 1997). As Beirman (2003) notes, through time, the scenes of past crises, such as wars, crimes, or natural disasters, can become tourist attractions in their own right, whereas effective management of a crisis and appropriate marketing efforts during and after crisis periods, supported by exclusive media coverage, can turn an unknown locality into a popular tourist destination.

Crisis Management and Contingency Plans in Tourist Destinations: How Necessary is it to Be Ready?

It is the very nature of a crisis to emerge as a shock, which later evolves into a situation threatening the effective functioning of tourist destinations, if not demolishing their tourism industry altogether. Therefore, any specific event predicted long before it occurred, and for which necessary action had been taken by the relevant authorities to eliminate its potentially undermining impact, can hardly be considered a crisis. The difficult managerial task is to prepare urgent and exclusive action plans for those situations, whose warning signals and damaging effects are difficult to foresee. Along with their surprise factor, crises in tourist destinations are further complicated events to manage and plan for, because of the necessity of cooperation among manifold parties striving for recovery and dealing with victims ranging from residents to potential visitors, from organisations operating in the destination to international organisations working with the destination, and finally, from employees working in the industry to those working in the complementary industries. This, as a result, requires tourism authorities, planners, and stakeholders to respond to crises systematically and to consider multifaceted solutions.

The initial rationale of preparedness, therefore, is related to 'the actual and perceived damages' of crises. The ramifications of crises are mostly negative in their effect, therefore the tourism industry needs to work toward protecting or rebuilding the destination's image as a safe and attractive vacation location while reestablishing the industry's functionality through aiding tourism organisations during their economic recovery (Sonmez, Apostolopoulos, and Tarlow, 1999). As the authors further note, crisis management and contingency plans cannot prevent a harmful event, but they can serve as a guide for managing its aftermath. Along with the actual physical and economic damage caused by catastrophic or disastrous events, a crisis-struck destination may suffer from the perceived damage among potential visitors induced by exaggerated media coverage, which could consequently harm the destination's image severely. No matter how distant the crisis occurred from major tourist spots and how trivial its impact was on the tourism industry, the destination could lose its appealing image if the negative event gets primetime coverage on television or if it reaches the front page of newspapers. This explains why some countries, where information and communication networks are not fully free, but are under the stern control of governments, still tend to censor the information on off-putting events in order not to weaken the well being of their tourism industry and not to discourage potential market segments from visiting their destination. Although information distribution is not repressed by governments in most countries, crisis management helps authorities assess the damage correctly and provide the existing and potential visitor markets with unbiased and accurate information circulated both by the destination itself and selected media.

Another purpose of being prepared is associated with 'the environment of panic and chaos' generated by crises. A destination caught unprepared by a crisis can face numerous conflicts, disorder, and stress among the industry players. Not knowing how to respond to the extraordinary and sudden downfall in their business may lead stakeholders to search for scapegoats. Destination-wide authorities, meantime, may show reluctance to take responsibility for recovery, because the situation gets too complicated too soon. Spontaneous decision making would put the credibility of the destination in jeopardy and could further worsen the adverse impact of the crisis through quick-fix solutions underestimating long-term damage. On the contrary, the establishment of crisis management teams and the preparation of contingency plans in advance help tourist destinations distinguish which sequential steps to follow during a crisis situation, equip each stakeholder with appropriate responsibility and control over the recovery process, and take immediate action in coordination. This way, a prestructured recovery process is accomplished rationally and promptly, whereas probable chaos is excluded.

Moreover, no matter how recognisable a crisis may seem, each is different in its root cause, scope, and duration, and hence requires 'a systematic and pertinent planning process.' Also, specific variations on uniform crisis management guidelines need to be made according to the individual characteristics of destination settings. The establishment of crisis management teams, the use of marketing tools to boost recovery, and the assignment of responsibilities among the stakeholders could differ even in those destinations struck by the same crisis. As Richter (1999) emphasises there is no single recovery model that can be applied to all crisis situations. Tourist destinations are compelled to design their own way of responding to a negative event following a thorough analysis of how the event happened, what the main causes were, and how severely it will affect the tourism industry.

Finally, being prepared is a more cost-effective approach to dealing with recovery and response during times of turmoil than not having a contingency plan. Uncertainty and panic engendered by crises may lead to irrational wastes of time and resources, whereas crisis management would help shorten the recovery process with damage ameliorated efficiently and collaboratively. The problem arises, however, as to the selection of crisis types for different tourist destinations and as to equipping the tourism industry with appropriate crises management teams and plans. It would clearly be unreasonable and costly to prepare detailed contingency plans for every possible negative event. Instead, tourist destinations should assess and categorise different crisis forms by using forecasting techniques and according to the probability of occurrence and potential damage ascribed to each crisis type. As Prideaux, Laws, and Faulkner (2003) state, the employment of risk scenarios is one way of predicting a range of events and developing alternative action plans based on the characteristics and previous experiences of each destination. For example, a destination with a history of earthquakes should take necessary precautions to monitor, assess, and recover from similar disasters, whereas its organisation network and physical structure should be upgraded in order to minimise expected postcrisis damage. Along with recognition of highly probable crises identified according to the scale of probability, tourist destinations are also advised to be primed for such events, which, though are less likely to emerge, would cause a significant shift in the tourism business. Stafford, Yu, and Armoo (2002) give the terrorist attacks on the U.S. mainland as an example to low-probability crises with high-impact on the industry.

The basic checklist of crisis management for tourist destinations, meantime, could be as follows:

Establishment of a Crisis Management Team and Preparation of Contingency Plans

- Launch a crisis management centre;
- Select the key stakeholders as members of the crisis management team;
- Analyse several risk scenarios and propose contingency plans for highly probable and most damaging crisis forms;
- Define roles and distribute responsibility among crisis management team members;
- Organise training sessions for tourism organisations, destination authorities, and local residents on how to respond to crises;
- Test the contingency plans with simulation exercises;
- Encourage individual tourism organisations to establish their own crisis management teams and to prepare contingency plans in line with the destination-wide plans; and
- Formulate back-up contingency plans.

Identification of the Crisis

- Monitor the social, economical, physical, and political environments of the destination on a regular basis in order to determine vulnerability toward possible crises;
- Detect warning signs;
- Entrust the crisis management team with the recovery process;
- Determine the type of the crisis;
- Measure probable damage; and
- Activate the contingency plan immediately.

Response to the Crisis and Minimisation of Its Adverse Effects

- Ensure consistency and commitment to the decisions made by the crisis management team and to the practiced contingency plan;
- Establish an effective chain of communication between the crisis management team, the industry, and public authorities;
- Support tourism organisations through providing guidelines for their operations during crises;
- Run frequent safety inspections and ascertain the well being of visitors and local residents through necessary precautions taken to ensure destination-wide security;
- Provide existing and potential visitors and residents with an adequate amount of information on the crisis and its likely effects, and restore their confidence in the viability of the destination and the crisis management team in charge;
- Regularly notify tourism organisations located outside the crisis zone, but work with the crisis-struck destination about the current situation; and

- Learn from destinations that experienced similar situations and ask for assistance from national/international consultancy organisations, if necessary.

Marketing Crisis-Struck Destination

- Compose and distribute press releases to the media;
- Arrange regular press conferences;
- Provide a special section within the crisis management centre to deal with inquiries;
- Establish a one-voice approach among the industry stakeholders when providing information to the media on the crisis and how the destination is coping;
- Assure potential visitors about the safety of the destination following the recovery; and
- Make use of appropriate marketing tools to promote the destination after recovery.

Monitoring Recovery and Analysing the Crisis Experience

- Measure the success of the contingency plan used and make alterations to the existing structure of the crisis management team if necessary; and
- Review and revise contingency plans regularly.

In addition to the suggested steps to crisis management, it is crucial that crisis management teams should be relaunched according to the changing physical and managerial environments of the destination, whereas contingency plans should be considered as flexible guidelines rather than strict rules, which can be adjusted according to both the reviewed strengths and weaknesses of the destination and the crisis type experienced. Moreover, a crisis may not pose a threat solely to the tourism industry, but it may put the destination with all of its economic and administrative functions at risk of collapse. In such difficult times, interdependence and partnerships among organisations ranging from police forces to municipalities and from trade associations to labour unions become critical. This is why tourism and subsector (e.g., accommodation and transportation sectors) contingency plans should be considered as a component of destination-wide plans and why the priorities in recovery should be given to those most severely damaged aspects of the area. The following sections provide further insight into damage assessment and marketing in crisis-struck tourist destinations.

Damage Assessment and Crisis Recovery in Tourist Destinations: Who Is Responsible for Recovery?

Today, the variety of destinations and the many product packages offered in the international tourism market provide potential visitors with a broad range of holiday alternatives. The fierce competition forces destination planners and marketers to consider every possible way to improve and differentiate their tourist offer to gain market advantages. The perceived quality, image, price, and packaging of a tourist destination play an important role throughout the decision-making process of travellers. More importantly, tourists often expect to be at ease on vacations and give priority to their own safety, relaxation, and enjoyment. Therefore, it would be imprudent to predict growth in demand in crises-ridden destinations until they recover from the negative occurrences and restore their image. The fall in demand and the scale of the damage, meantime, depend on several factors including the scope, origin, motive, and duration of the event.

Huang and Min (2002) note that the 1999 earthquake in Taiwan resulted in an evident decline in visitor figures with the reconstruction and renovation costs of tourism operations totaling approximately US$155 million in the Sun Moon Lake tourist area, in addition to tragic loss of human lives and property across the island. Similarly, Hopper (2003) states that the combined effects of the foot and mouth crisis and the September 11 attacks hit the tourism industry in London in 2001, accounting for 10 percent and 11 percent drop in visitors and spending, respectively, in comparison with the previous year. The loss in tourism business of the city was estimated at around US$1.8 billion, and full recovery is not expected in the short term. Finally, Goodrich (2002) investigates the adverse effects of the September 11 attacks on the U.S. economy and reveals that the estimated cost of the recession triggered by the tragedy is approximately US$105 billion. The author further analyses the damage caused in subsectors of the tourism industry and adds that the airline industry with an estimated business loss of up to US$ billion, suffered most with regard to sales revenues.

Although the previous examples indicate striking economic impacts and costs of crises on tourist destinations, the wreckage of a crisis-struck destination may become further repellent with long-term effects of the impaired image, anxiety among tourism organisations to work with the destination, and the devastated stakeholders hesitating to operate in the destination. Therefore, although it may not always be possible to measure the overall damage quantitatively and monetarily, the fall in demand and visitor expenditure is considered to be the main reflectors of negative occurrences on destinations. However, crisis management teams should regularly assess how potential visitors, governments of main visitor generator markets, and international tourism organisations perceive the safety, quality, and well being of the destination and its tourist offers. The recovery process should aim to establish a sound balance between winning back visitors, upgrading and reconstructing the tourism infrastructure and suprastructure, and assuring the interested parties about the accomplished recovery with regained standards in service quality and reformed image of the destination.

The unanimously accepted way of determining how tourist destinations are adversely affected by events is to cross-examine cyclical phases of crises, namely precrisis, crisis, and postcrisis stages (Cavlek, 2002; Henderson, 2003). The process is cyclical, because it is believed that destinations move from crises to restored postcrisis environment provided that necessary and sufficient recovery management and planning are performed by crisis management teams. The postcrisis period is then linked to the precrisis, because destinations revise and upgrade their contingency plans for potential future threats. The shift in the tourism businesses during crises can be compared with precrisis levels, whereas the initial aim during postcrisis is to return the industry to similar levels before further gains can be made.

Proactive planning should be performed throughout the crisis cycle in order to minimise damage. The aim during the precrisis period, as noted previously, is to prepare possible risk scenarios, whereas weaknesses of the destination is reduced to optimum levels through infrastructure and suprastructure improvement, law enforcement of higher security maintenance and regular official inspections of sanitation, and safety in both the destination and its tourist organisations. At this stage, the leading public and private authorities are expected to provide guidelines on how to prepare the destination for crises and how to operate during difficult times. As Pizam (1999) states, the industry stakeholders need to work in cooperation with governments, law enforcement agencies, visitors, residents, complementary business sectors, and the international community to prevent the destination from possible negative occurrences. Frequent training to educate tourism staff, residents, and visitors is also crucial at this stage.

Although it is the crisis management team that is in charge during the crisis phase, the recovery at the postcrisis stage again requires collaboration among various parties ranging from public and private authorities to the leading associations of all income-generating industries existing in the destination. Although no single authority on its own can be expected to provide solutions to problems caused by a crisis, it is often governments who steer the joined efforts of numerous organisations and launch special public units and centres to accelerate recovery. Sonmez, Apostolopoulos, and Tarlow (1999) cite special policing departments established in various countries to eradicate tourism-related crime, violations, and terrorism as an example to such purpose-founded organisations.

The task of governments does not only entail administrative leadership during crises, but also involves the responsibility of financing difficult times via incentives, grants, and loans to organisations in trouble and also through spending public money to refurbish and restore public spaces and services. Although the scope and duration determines the overall cost of a crisis, governments should be especially careful in planning the right amount of their budget for such unexpected expenses and in funding budget deficits caused by the crisis with additional taxes and price increases in public services. In fact, because a crisis itself becomes a discouraging factor influencing the preferences of potential visitors against the destination, an increase in tourist products and services could hardly be considered a strategy to revive the industry soon after the crisis. On the contrary, product discounts and cheaper package offers should be considered to amend the disadvantageous market position of the destination and to win back visitors.

Whether it is a public or private authority that takes the leading responsibility of the organisation for crisis management, crises are the times when consistency and determination becomes crucially important. Therefore, unless the whole situation is caused or has been worsened by inept management, the opposition raised toward governments and their policy approach would only further foster the damage and not the recovery. One should not forget that the prompt adaptability of the destination and its tourism industry to the new crisis-generated environment depends on the mutual understanding of the needs and expectations of the stakeholders and crisis management teams mainly orchestrated by governments.

Although the comparison of precrisis and postcrisis phases provides an insight into how badly the industry was affected at home, the assessment of the changing market positions of competitor destinations after the event could shed more light onto the real damages experienced by the host destination from the perspective of marketing. In Figure 23.1, seven destinations are shown as examples to how a crisis in one destination can influence the others, with the direction of the arrows representing growth or decline in their tourism businesses. As the only location in the crisis environment, Destination A experiences downfall in tourism until the situation becomes normal again. The effects of the crisis can also spread to other destinations, even though they may have no relation to crisis-causing factors. Although the tourism industry in Destination D is adversely affected by the crisis, Destination C benefits from the current situation by attracting visitors who may have been initially considering a trip to Destination A or D. Cavlek (2002) cites the war in Kosovo in 1999 to spreading effects of crises. Although the war in Serbia lasted three months, its impact on the neighbouring countries and even in remote places like Greece and Turkey was felt. Croatia, which is argued to be the destination that suffered the most, had a 15-percent drop in international arrivals in 1999, although prewar forecasts were suggesting a rise of about 30 percent for the same year.

Competitor destinations (i.e., Destinations X, Y, and Z in Figure 23.1) that manage to free themselves both from the root cause of the crisis and its spreading effects are not expected to experience undesirable repercussions on tourism. The growth in the number of their visitor and in their

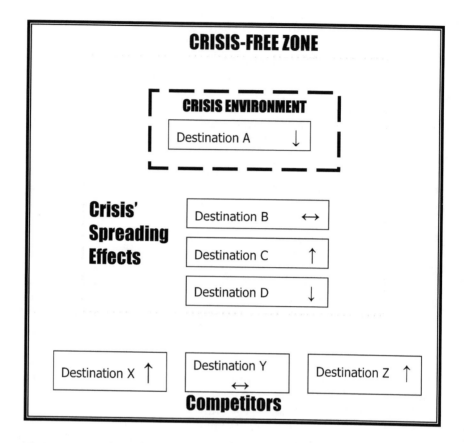

Figure 23.1:   Crisis Types in Touris Destinations.

tourism income depends on how they turn the crisis to their advantage through marketing activities emphasising their safety, quality, and crisis-free status, and the substitutability of their tourism offer vis-à-vis the one offered by the destination in crisis. Those who succeed in attracting the market segments lost by Destination A will have an increase in visitors (i.e., Destinations X and Z), whereas some others may retain their expected market position with neither significant growth nor decline in demand generated by the overall situation (i.e., Destination Y).

Communicating among the industry, residents, and potential visitors during and after the recovery process through systematic and well-planned marketing activities is required to restore the image of the destination in crisis impaired by the crisis itself, travel advisories, and warnings issued by the governments of generating markets, the marketing efforts of competitors, and, in some cases, exacerbated media coverage. Marketing activities launched during and following the full recovery of the destination should give accurate and consistent messages on the situation and the reinstated tourist offer of the destination, but remaining weaknesses should not be concealed. As Beirman (2003) emphasises, destinations should be careful that recovery programme and marketing activities be ethical and offer a truthful assessment of the crisis situation, the failure of which may provide short-term gains, but in the long run, may harm the reliability of the destination authorities, reflecting negatively on the credibility of the tourism industry.

Short-, medium-, and long-term plans should be prepared and implemented sequentially with a consistent balance between them. Redirecting marketing efforts, usually toward regional and domestic markets, is a common approach to return tourism business to normal gradually before existing and new international market segments are targeted again. Familiarization trips for intermediates and tourism journalists; constantly updated Internet Web pages, press conferences, newspaper, and television ads; product discounts; repackaging of the tourist offers; complementary offers and competitions with the prize of a vacation in the destination; and public relation activities are among the most widely used marketing tools during difficult times. As Faulkner (2001) notes, destinations planning their marketing activities innovatively can benefit from the transformational opportunities that arise from crises and acquire potential positive outcomes to counteract the initial damaging effects. Through effective and dynamic marketing and management, a crisis-struck destination may regain its precrisis state or achieve a totally new and more vigorous tourism business with the crisis becoming a catalyst for improvement.

Conclusion

Various types of crises ranging from terrorist attacks to the involvement of political parties in national scandals may cause a fall in supply and demand in many sectors. Although the impact of some crises is felt only in the location where they occurred, the globalised business environment of today often causes many crises to spread their postevent effects all around the world. As tourism relies on international human and business transactions, it is arguably among the most severely crises-damaged industries. Tourism organisations should be well-equipped to deal with crises emerging both in their host community and in the generating markets.

Despite the recent interest among tourism academicians on crisis management and contingency planning in tourism, there is still a need for further research on a variety of topics including methodological developments in studying crisis situations, comparative studies of effective and less effective responses to tourism crises, distinctions between differing damaging impacts of crisis situations, positive and negative outcomes of crises in host destinations and their competitor destinations, the use of forecasting methods in predicting the impacts of crises on tourism, investigations on varying effects of marketing tools to restore crisis-impaired images of tourist destinations, the causes of regional and international spreading of crises, and development of new theoretical and practical insights into crisis management in tourist destinations.

References

Anson, C. 1999. Planning for Peace: The Role of Tourism in the Aftermath of Violence. *Journal of Travel Research* 38(1): 57–61.

Beirman, D. 2002. Marketing of Tourism Destinations During a Prolonged Crisis: Israel and the Middle East. *Journal of Vacation Marketing* 8(2): 167–176.

——. 2003. Restoring Tourism Destinations in Crises: A Strategic Marketing Approach. Oxon: CABI.

Cavlek, N. 2002. Tour Operators and Destination Safety. *Annals of Tourism Research* 29(2): 478–496.

Durocher, J. 1994. Recovery Marketing: What to Do After a Natural Disaster. *The Cornell Hotel and Restaurant Administration Quarterly* 35(2): 66–71.

Faulkner, B. 2001. Towards a Framework for Tourism Disaster Management. *Tourism Management* 22(2): 135–147.

Glaesser, D. 2003. *Crisis Management in the Tourism Industry.* Burlington: Butterworth-Heinemann.

Gonzales-Herrero, A., and C. B. Pratt. 1998. Marketing Crises in Tourism: Communication Strategies in the United States and Spain. *Public Relations Review* 24(1): 83–97.

Goodrich, J. N. 2002. September 11, 2001 Attack on America: A Record of the Immediate Impacts and Reactions in the USA Travel and Tourism Industry. *Tourism Management* 23(6): 573–580.

Henderson, J. 2003. Communicating in a Crisis: Flight SQ 006. *Tourism Management* 24(3): 279–287.

Hopper, P. 2002. Marketing London in a Difficult Climate. *Journal of Vacation Marketing* 9(1): 81–88.

Huang, J. H., and J. C. H. Min. 2002. Earthquake Devastation and Recovery in Tourism: The Taiwan Case. *Tourism Management* 23(2): 145–154.

Keown-McMullan, C. 1997. Crisis: When Does a Molehill Become a Mountain. *Disaster Prevention and Management* 6(1): 4–10.

Leslie, D. 1999. Terrorism and Tourism: The Northern Ireland Situation—A Look Behind The Veil of Certainty. *Journal of Travel Research* 38(1): 37–40.

Mansfeld, Y. 1999. Cycles of War, Terror and Peace: Determinants and Management of Crisis and Recovery of the Israeli Tourism Industry. *Journal of Travel Research* 38(1): 30–36.

Pizam, A. 1999. A Comprehensive Approach to Classifying Acts of Crime and Violence at Tourism Destinations. *Journal of Travel Research* 38(1): 5–12.

———. 2002. Tourism and Terrorism. *International Journal of Hospitality Management* 21(1): 1–3.

Prideaux, B., E. Laws, and B. Faulkner. 2003. Events in Indonesia: Exploring the Limits to Formal Tourism Trends Forecasting Methods in Complex Crisis Situations. *Tourism Management* 24: 475–487.

Richter, L. K. 1999. After Political Turmoil: The Lessons of Rebuilding Tourism in Three Asian Countries. *Journal of Travel Research* 38(1): 41–45.

Sonmez, S., Y. Apostolopoulos, and P. Tarlow. 1999. Tourism in Crisis: Managing the Effects of Terrorism. *Journal of Travel Research* 38(1): 13–18.

Stafford, G., L. Yu, and A. K. Armoo. 2002. Crisis Management and Recovery: How Washington, D.C., Hotels Responded to Terrorism. *The Cornell Hotel and Restaurant Administration Quarterly* 43(5): 27–40.

Tarlow, P., and M. Muehsam. 1996. Theoretical Aspects of Crime as They Impact The Tourism Industry. In *Tourism, Crime and International Security Issues.* ed. A. Pizam and Y. Mansfeld. Chichester: John Wiley & Sons.

Wahab, S. 1996. Tourism and Terrorism: Synthesis of The Problem With Emphasis on Egypt. In *Tourism, Crime and International Security Issues.* ed. A. Pizam and Y. Mansfeld. Chichester: John Wiley & Sons.

Wall, G. 1996. Terrorism and Tourism: An Overview and An Irish Example. In *Tourism, Crime and International Security Issues.* ed. A. Pizam and Y. Mansfeld. Chichester: John Wiley & Sons.

World Tourism Organization. 2002. *The Impact of the September 11th Attacks on Tourism: The Light at The End of The Tunnel.* Madrid: World Tourism Organization.

Part Six

People, Places, Things: Alternate Issues

Introduction

As tourism continues to expand its role as the world's largest industry, it also encourages the proliferation of academic research focused both on highly specific segments and impacts of tourism, and on the larger philosophical implications of this phenomenon. Tourism dramatically influences the entire range of economic, cultural, environmental, and even political values that in some combination constitute the modern world.

Coles, Duval and **Hall** (Chapter 24) propose that tourism, as an established field of academic enquiry has been conspicuously absent from recent discipline-based efforts toward understanding the range of mobilities prevalent in globalised environments, and in large measure has failed to embrace similar levels of theory building. While there is considerable lateral movement to tourism, there is a lack of vertical theoretical integration with wider perspectives of mobility.

The purposes of this chapter are first, to examine and draw out existing conceptual linkages between tourism and temporary mobilities. As such, tourism is presented as a temporary form of mobility, and is therefore roughly analogous in both scope and meaning to other forms of movement such as travel to second homes, return migration and emigration. Second, a more grounded approach in the chapter is to survey forms of tourism that have precipitated from enhanced global mobility and the creation of extended networks of kinship and community.

The chapter raises arguments that attempt to characterize a new approach to tourism that is based broadly on various forms of temporary mobilities. The authors conclude that some tourists' world view and motivations might be explained within a broader context of mobility, including migration and social connections to particular locales and destinations.

Industrialized countries are changing from the traditional production economy to an information-based economy. Tourism-related activities have been classified as convenience services. At the national level, tourism's future success may well depend on the ability of each country to educate not only tourism employees, but also tourists and destination area residents about each other's culture in order to better understand and appreciate one another. According to **Go** (Chapter 25), continued prosperity in tourism will depend largely on well-educated people who are able to think, weigh and judge crucial issues in addition to providing quality tourist services.

The evolution of tourism education is presented, and the suggestion is made that tourism thinking has passed through two distinct stages: (1) the early 1940's-1970's pragmatic concerns of educators for such things as career preparation and placement, and (2) beginning in the early 1980's, a shift from the pragmatic to the academic, emphasizing research and methods of enquiry. However, the 1990's are seen as a period of transformation brought about by social change, concern for the environment, a global economy, and rapid advancements in technology.

The dual forces of technology and globalization will raise the competency demanded for all positions in the tourism industry and turn effective education into a competitive necessity. Industry, government and academic institutions must recognize that productivity and quality gains are derived from increased employee skills and knowledge. These value-added skills must continue to be developed if the tourism industry is to survive.

The author relates the importance of tourism education for developing countries, as well as the necessity of broadening the intellectual scope of tourism programmes in developed nations. Such education must be firmly grounded in solid academic principles.

The final section of the chapter concludes with a discussion of how investments in global e-learning holds the potential to contribute to the formation of emergent communities which may result in sustainable, high quality tourism.

Ryan and **Trauer** (Chapter 26) concentrate on the socio-demographic changes that have occurred in the past few decades and extends these changes into the immediate future. While the consequences of such changes are somewhat speculative, nevertheless, they are often foreseeable and may be planned for. Such changes are not independent of wider social and technological trends, as a symbiotic relationship often exists between all of the drivers for change itself.

When considering trends within tourism and experiential mobility, socio-cultural factors or psychographics, specifically those related to the lifestyle concept are generally thought to be more influential in shaping the demand for tourism than socio-economic indicators. This is apparent within the ageing population since they are just as heterogeneous as other age groups, not only with regard to education, income and professional status, but also in reference to differences in their previous travel and leisure patterns and experiences.

The authors conclude that tourism has been about travel. However, they suggest that in the twenty-first-century it will increasingly take on the characteristics of the 'nomad.' As the century unfolds, they see three major forces impacting travel: the ageing of the population in wealthy countries with developed economies; migration from the less developed to those developed nations, and developments in information technology that will draw tourism into a nexus of technology, entertainment and travel.

The concluding chapter of this volume **Dwyer** (Chapter 27) discusses the ways in which drivers or trends (the global economy and globalization, natural resources and environment, science and technology, and demographics) will affect the global tourism industry over the decade. A number of important change agents, both on the supply and demand sides of tourism are identified and discussed.

Changes present significant challenges to tourism education. The content of tourism marketing, planning and policy subjects must reflect an awareness of long-term trends. Future industry leaders must possess the knowledge and skills to enhance organizational competitive advantages through strategy formulation and implementation in a dynamic, ever changing world.

24 Tourism, mobility, and global communities: new approaches to theorising tourism and tourist spaces

Tim Coles, David Timothy Duval, and C. Michael Hall

Introduction

In the past decade, a number of social science disciplines have engaged in debates of both local social complexity and, by extension, global social connections. Cultural and media studies, for example, have interrogated global media pathways in order to tease out representations of culture, the self, and social practice. Sociologists and anthropologists (although both would likely object at the conceptual lumping) have sought to trace social relationships and identities that often span multiple localities (Lee, 2003). Along with scholars in development studies and political studies, some human geographers have also attempted to trace the influences of globalisation in the production and consumption of global labour, consumer goods and social practice. Similarly, many migration scholars have approached the movement of people from a transnational perspective, as opposed to the more rigid classification of origin–destination models (King, 2002). Unfortunately, although some criticism of theoretical excess has recently emerged, 'Tourism,' as an established field of academic enquiry (as opposed to lowercase 'tourism' as the phenomenon under scrutiny), has been conspicuously absent from recent discipline-based pushes toward understanding the range of mobilities prevalent in more-or-less globalised environments and has not embraced, at least to any great extent, similar levels of theory building.

Tourism is often characterised (and thus, represented) as bipolar investigations of contemporary human travel (Franklin and Crang, 2001). One end is represented by social science-based research into, for example, host–guest relationships, tourist typologies, and traveller motivations. At the other end are those studies with a strong business and managerial orientation. Their scope is inclusive of hospitality and recreation-based investigations of quality, satisfaction, and even marketing (Franklin and Crang, 2001). Neither end has made a serious attempt to connect studies at the microlevel with global movement. In other words, although there is considerable lateral movement to Tourism, there is a lack of vertical theoretical integration with wider perspectives of mobility. Research agendas in Tourism that are inherently based within social science enquiries into understanding how travel is positioned within the human condition need to take hold of higher-level theories of mobilities as opposed to the existing structured, middle-range theories of motivation, decision modelling, and even destination image that, although useful, do little to bridge fairly substantial gaps in our knowledge of tourism as a representation of contemporary social systems (see Hall and Williams, 2002). Tourism must be willing to formulate a coherent approach to understanding the meaning behind the range of mobilities undertaken by *individuals*, not tourists. The basis of this chapter, therefore, forms somewhat of a response to Franklin and Crang's (2001) suggestion that '. . . perhaps tourism should search for links with other mobilities such as commuting, mobile labour markets, migration and Diasporas.' In this respect, the conceptual maturing of understanding issues relating to global mobilities, as represented in fields of migration, sociology, human geography, and anthropology, provides a useful toolkit with which a more fluid and social answer to the question of why people travel, and the extent to which their travel can often best be characterised as temporary mobility, can be answered.

The purpose of this chapter is two-fold. In the first instance, existing conceptual linkages between tourism and temporary mobilities are drawn out. Tourism is, in essence, presented as a temporary form of mobility, and as such is roughly and conceptually analogous in scope and meaning to other forms of movement (e.g., travel to second homes, return migration, emigration). By extension, a new conceptualisation and theoretical approach applied to Tourism would consider relationships to other forms of mobility. Second, a more grounded approach in the chapter is to survey forms of tourism that have precipitated from enhanced global mobility and the creation of extended networks of kinship and community. Several parallels and affiliations that exist between tourism and other aspects of mobilities as represented in the social science literature are discussed. Considered, then, are those concepts central to the study of migration, transnationalism, and diasporas as forms of transitory mobility and movement, and how these are linked to issues of production and consumption. In concluding this conceptual survey, it is suggested that tourism might be conceptualised from the perspective of global, regional, and local mobilities and flows.

Tourism and Contemporary Mobilities

Tourism is still categorised, and its flows still measured, by raw statistical data. Decisions are made and celebrations held based almost exclusively on recent arrival statistics. Unfortunately, such an approach fails to recognise the position of tourism as one of a number of forms of leisure-oriented mobility. There is often little statistical or intellectual overlap with other fields concerned with mobility such as transport, retailing, or migration. In one sense, this limitation has already started to be recognised by the World Tourism Organization, which has begun to identify the category of day tripping as a form of tourism behaviour. The inclusion of same-day travel 'excursionists' within technical definitions of tourism clearly makes the divisions between what constitutes leisure, recreation, and tourism extremely arbitrary, and there is increasing international agreement that 'tourism' refers to all activities of visitors, including both overnight and same-day visitors (United Nations, 1994). Given innovations in transport technology, same-day travel is also becoming increasingly important at widening spatial scales, and is exemplifying space–time compression. This emphasises the need for those interested in tourism to address the arbitrary boundaries between tourism and leisure, and tourism and migration. Tourism therefore constitutes just one form of leisure-oriented temporary mobility, and it constitutes part of that mobility, both being shaped by and shaping it (Hall, Williams, and Law, 2004).

Drawing on geographical understandings of spatial interaction, spatial diffusion, and time geography, Hall (2003; 2004a; 2004b) has posited a model of mobility that seeks to integrate tourism with other forms of mobility through representing the total number of trips (interactions) over plasticised delineations of time and space (Figure 24.1). Tourism is therefore seen as a leisure-oriented component of a continuum of mobilities that stretch from commuting and shopping through to what is usually categorised as migration. Such a representation of tourism clearly seeks to explicitly connect tourism not only with other discussions of mobility in the social sciences, but also to integrate macroscale and microscale understandings of mobility. Moreover, such a conceptualisation assists in further integrating research on the leisure dimensions of other forms of mobility such as second homes (e.g., Coppock, 1977; Hall and Müller,

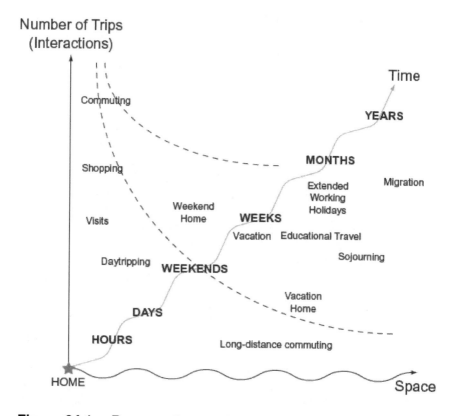

Figure 24.1: Representing tourism mobilities in time and space.
Source: Adapted from Hall, 2004a; 2004b.

2004), mobility of the highly skilled (OECD, 2002), travel for overseas work experience (Mason, 2002), and educational travel (Kraft, Ballatine, and Garvey, 1994) with that of tourism mobility.

From a more macroperspective, tourism mobility is connected to broader empirical research on spatial interaction and diffusion models. Spatial interaction models are used to predict spatial choices reflected in flows of goods or people between origins and destinations, expressing trade offs between the accessibility of alternative destination opportunities and the perceived intrinsic 'attractiveness' of these opportunities. Such models have been heavily used in retail shopping planning and predictive capacities with respect to expenditure patterns and can be generated with rather basic data such as population, travel times (or distances between settlements), and retail floor space. These gravity models, with respect to human mobility, have been in development since the 1880s, when they were applied to migration behaviour (Ravenstein, 1885; 1889). The friction of distance—the decay of interactions such as trips and communication over space—is well recognised in the social sciences but its implications have, arguably, been only lightly touched on in tourism studies (Hall, 2004a). Arguably, this may be because of some of the issues that arise out of the study of distance-decay curves. For example, although such curves may be empirically identified, 'it is not clear to what extent their form depends on the model structures used to replicate them' (Robinson, 1998). Moreover, the nature of the relationships between interaction, mass (population size), and accessibility are inherently complex. Nevertheless, they provide useful macrolevel descriptions of mobilities and have a substantial predictive component to them, so much so that Hall (2004a) argues that such time–space accessibility lies at the heart of understanding the destination life cycle.

Models of spatial interaction and diffusion are a collective representation of individual mobilities or time–geographies. Time–geography examines 'the ways in which the production and reproduction of social life depend upon knowledgeable human subjects tracing out routinised paths over space and through time, fulfilling particular projects whose realisations are bounded by inter-locking capability, coupling and steering constraints' (Gregory, 1985). Based on the work of authors such as Hägerstrand (1967a; 1967b), Carlstein, Parkes, and Thrift (1978), Thrift (1977), and Pred (1981a; 1981b) time–geography has been influential in seeking to understand individual space–time patterns as well as underlying significant developments in social theory such as Giddens' (1984) notion of structuration.

According to Giddens (1984), '[t]ime-geography is concerned with the constraints that shape the routines of day-to-day life and shares with structuration theory an emphasis upon the significance of the practical character of daily activities, in circumstances of co-presence, for the constitution of social conduct,' while also stressing 'the routine character of daily life' connected with features of the human body, its means of mobility and communication, and its path through the 'life cycle'. Significantly, however, time–geographies were not related to tourism, which was seen as being an occurrence outside that of the routine, a perspective that continues to the present day in much tourism writing. For example, Aronsson (2000) argues, '[W]e are prisoners in the present-day time-space structure that we have created for our lives, we often use the free time we have in the evenings, at week ends and during our holidays to change this state of affairs through, for instance, a change of environment or, if you will, a change of time-space.' Similarly, Wang (2000) observes that tourism is 'a kind of social action which distances the paramount reality' both in time and geography and in terms of culture. Yet such perspectives fail to acknowledge the extent to which space–time compression has led to fundamental changes to individual's space–time paths in recent years.

The routinised space–time paths of those living in 2004 are not the same as those of people living in 1984 when Giddens was writing or even more so in the 1960s when Hägerstrand was examining daily space–time trajectories. Instead, because of advances in transport and communication technology, for a substantial proportion of the population being able to travel long distances to engage in leisure behaviour (what one would usually describe as tourism) is now a part of their routine activities.

People's travel time budgets have not changed substantially, but the ability to travel further at a lower per-unit cost within a given time budget (Schafer, 2000) has led to a new series of social encounters, interactions, and patterns of production and reproduction as well as consumption. The locales in which this occurs are sometimes termed destinations, and represent a particular type of lifestyle mobility that, when it occurs away from the home environment, is usually termed 'tourism' (Hall, 2004b). Just as significantly, space–time distanciation through both tourism and changes in communication technology have provided for the development of often dense sets of social, cultural, and economic networks stretching between the two ends of the mobility spectrum from daily leisure mobility through to migration and thereby promoting the development of transnational communities in which movement is the norm. It is to such communities that this chapter will now turn.

Tourism and Transnational Communities

A logical extension of the relationship between different forms of mobility such as tourism and migration is the consideration of the social and cultural ties that migrants build in multiple localities. Although migration has historically incorporated somewhat linear characterisations involving rather simplified 'origin–destination' dichotomies, there has been new recognition in the past few decades of the social ties that are maintained between not only the origin and destination but often other localities. Investigations of the 'betweenness' of migrant belongings (e.g., Fortier, 2000; Duval, 2004a) represents a new strand of migration research. The past decade has seen a new shift toward the adoption of a transnational approach to explaining globalised, interconnected migrant identities. Remaining 'connected' is precisely where tourism fits within a transnational framework. Of interest, then, is how transnational social ties (Vertovec, 1999) can be juxtaposed with temporary mobility/tourism. Such conceptual linkages introduce, therefore, instances where significant overlap with Tourism can be identified.

Despite the conceptually crowded landscape of definitions of transnationalism in the social science literature (Kivisto, 2001), many use, as their general frame of reference, the notion that transnationalism is a broad conceptual base through which migrant identities are viewed. Despite what appears to be a rather crowded conceptual landscape—witness in the literature discussions centring around transnational migration circuits (Rouse, 1992), social fields (Faist, 2000), activities (Portes, 1999), and communities (Portes, Guarnizo, and Landolt, 1999)—the transnational experience emerges as the dominating theme in the attempt to rationalise and explain the multiple identities and social ties that arise as a consequence of migration. Layton-Henry (2002) might argue that such connections should not necessarily be cognitive: 'Transnationalism requires more than just the fact of international migration. It requires evidence of people leading dual lives, living in two cultures and making a living through continuous regular contact across national borders.' In various research centred on migrants, emigrants, and the processes of social adaptation and adjustment, transnationalism is used as a sweeping conceptual framework that attempts to make clear the interconnected social experiences that defined the migration experience (Basch, Schiller, and Blanc, 1994). For example, Spoonley (2000) notes that transnationalism incorporates linkages between situated communities and their (as an organic analogy) place of origin. As such, for Spoonley (2000), transnationalism means 'that significant networks exist and are maintained across borders, and, by virtue of their intensity and importance, these actually challenge the very nature of nation-states. . . .'

A transnational framework of analysis within Tourism would allow for the recognition of interconnected social networks and the resulting movement between and among multiple localities. In other words, such interconnected transnational networks mean that movement, or temporary mobility, by transnational actors is perhaps another means by which tourism can be viewed. Such social networks and linkages could very well, in reality, account for a significant amount of global tourism, especially when viewed in the context of migrant mobilities (Duval and Hall, 2004). Examples include the temporary movement of Italian migrants from Perth (Baldassar, 2001) or Britain (Fortier, 2000) to Italy, or children of Tongan migrants living in the United States (Lee, 2003). These would suggest that such temporary mobility is inherently influenced by previous migration and thus would perhaps be better examined in the context of transnational identities.

The reality, however, is that very little tourism literature has explored the tourist in the context of transnational behaviour (see Duval, 2004b). There are several instances in the transnational literature where Tourism, if such individuals were exposed to a familiar instrument of empirical research stemming from Tourism, would identify a tourist. In their study of Viet Kieu attitudes toward travelling back to Vietnam from Australia, Nguyen and King (1998) found that many who do travel stay with family and friends. Layton-Henry's (2002) research among African-Caribbeans in Birmingham uncovered wide networks incorporated formal homelands. Byron's (1994; 1999; see also Byron and Condon, 1996) study of migrants from the tiny island of Nevis residing in Leicester suggested that a considerable amount of travel took place between the United Kingdom and the Caribbean. Nearly three-quarters of Byron's respondents had travelled to the Caribbean at least once since migrating to Britain. Over time, it seems, and with enough funds saved, visits to friends and relatives in the Caribbean were made possible. Duval's (2004b) research among Eastern Caribbean migrants in Toronto uncovered similar travel patterns and suggests that some trips were being made out of familial obligation. As well, questions regarding the notion of 'home' (Duval, 2004c) and the relationship between temporary mobility and permanent return have been raised (Duval, 2002). In their study of French migrants from Guadeloupe and Martinique, Condon and Ogden (1996) found substantial circular movement that was of 'great significance for the decision-making process in relation to [permanent] return.'

Presentations of the transnational linkages designed to reaffirm social and familiar relationships are common in the migration literature, especially where second-generation (and even third-generation) migrants are concerned. Smith (2001) found that second-generation Mexican youth living in New York City travel back to the parents' hometowns on holidays. Lee's (2003) ethnographic study of Tongan migrants living overseas revealed that many embark on return visits, but the reality is that the cost of such travel is prohibitive for some. Yet although some would sell vehicles in order to return for a special occasion, others return much more frequently. Interestingly, returning visitors to Tonga are, as Lee (2003) reports, 'shocked by negative attitudes towards them.' In her analysis of online bulletin boards, Lee (2003) found a young Tongan woman who experienced significant problems as a temporarily returning migrant: 'When I first went to Tonga about 3 years ago ALL the girls even some of my cousins were calling me names and talking shit about me because like, I didn't know jack bout Tongan language . . . Tongan culture . . . nothing.' Duval (2004b) found similar sentiments among Commonwealth Eastern Caribbean migrants living in Toronto. What is interesting is that the level of reception reserved for those temporarily mobile migrants returning home is not unlike the more negative feelings levied toward western tourists in some situations.

Diasporas, Tourism, and Production

Transnational communities exist in quite abstract spaces and settings. Within such communities social relations are mediated and negotiated across extended networks that transcend borders and frontiers. Family and kinship ties bind community members from state to state. As the previous section has demonstrated, this condition of spatial displacement precipitates two immediate and distinct forms of travel and tourism. Friends and relatives are visited in the extended community both back in the 'homeland' from whence the migrant's family originated, as well as in other global locations occupied by the group. Sikhs in Britain, for example, not only travel back to the Punjab to visit their extended families and sites of religious and secular pilgrimage, but they also journey to visit relatives in such countries as Canada, the United States, and Singapore (Tatla, 1999).

With its origins in the Greek words for 'dispersion' and 'through' (Helmreich, 1992), the word 'diaspora' has often been used to describe these diffuse transnational communities bound by a common perception of their origins. Dominicans living in New York form part of the wider Dominican diaspora (Itzigsohn, et al., 1999), whereas those claiming Scots ancestry in New Zealand, South Africa, Australia, and the United States often claim membership of the wider Scottish diaspora. Diaspora is a highly contested term (Mitchell, 1997; Shuval, 2000; Werbner, 2002; Braziel and Mannur, 2003). At its most basic, the term describes groups of people scattered across the world but drawn together as a community by their actual, perceived, or imagined common bonds of ethnicity, culture, religion national identity, and sometimes race. For Braziel and Mannur (2003), 'diaspora suggests a dislocation from the nation-state or geographical location of origin and a relocation in one or more nation-states, territories or countries.' Although diasporic communities vary greatly, Cohen (1997) contends that, irrespective of their historical trajectories and experiences, all 'acknowledge that the "old country"—a notion buried deep in language, religion, custom or folklore—always has some claim on their loyalty and emotions.' Clifford (1997) has, in contrast, noted that diasporic *routes* are as crucial in identity formation as the (geographical) *roots*. For this reason, although they share the same 'basic' historical origins, Greek-Americans and Greek-Australians will inevitably have distinctive identities because of their differing experiences of migration and of their life in the host country.

This albeit highly truncated discussion should not obscure the fact that diasporas are not homogenous entities, and they are driven by often deep and complex internal cleavages. Notwithstanding interdiasporic and intradiasporic variations, diasporas precipitate five modes of travel and tourism inspired by the collision between their migrational histories (their 'routes'), their attachment to the 'home' country (their 'roots'), and their experiences of and in the host country (their 'routine') (Coles and Timothy, 2004). Perhaps most predictably, diaspora tourists travel back to their original, ancestral homeland in search of their roots and family background (e.g., Bruner, 1996; Stephenson, 2002). More systematic, highly structured journeys of self-discovery focussed on the search for tangible artifacts of forebears have also been termed 'genealogical' (Nash, 2002), 'family history,' or 'ancestral' tourism (Fowler, 2003). The second mode represents the first in reverse as residents of the original 'homeland' travel into the diaspora, whereas the third involves intradiasporic travel to the far-flung destinations beyond 'home' occupied by diaspora(s). Fourth, spaces of transit in the scattering process along diasporic trajectories may assume sacred importance and motivate trips. Ellis Island and the Statue of Liberty have become popular sites of pilgrimage for many European-Americans to pay homage to their forebears and their migrational achievements. As Ioannides and Cohen (2002) highlight, spaces of transit are not necessarily restricted to points of entry or departure. Former neighbourhoods and ethnic enclaves, such as the Lower East Side of New York, that functioned as precursors to wider dispersion throughout the United States have popular appeal to many Jewish-Americans in search of their ancestors' routes. Just as diasporic communities adapted to life in their host societies through distinctive home spaces, in time they also produced distinctive vacationscapes, some of which endure today. Jewish-Americans on the eastern seaboard of the United States patronised the Catskill Mountains as a retreat (Ioannides and Cohen, 2002), whereas the early investment in the resort of Sosua in the Dominican Republic was from the capital of exiled Jews from Germany.

What this broad typology infers is that diaspora tourism is often a far more complex exercise than merely visiting friends and relatives, or independent travel inspired by diasporically focussed guidebooks (see Gruber, 1999). Instead, diaspora tourism often requires more organised and systematic modes of production (Coles and Timothy, 2004). Packages are designed and visitor attractions are developed for the particular edification of diaspora tourists (Coles, 2003a; Cohen, 2004; Collins-Kreiner and Olsen, 2004). Public as well as private sector stakeholders have recognised that diasporas are potentially big business, and that they present the opportunity for some destinations to develop the highly localised, truly unique selling propositions that are often so sadly lacking (Coles, 2003b). For instance, based on VisitScotland's diasporic strategy documentation (Scottish Tourist Board, 2001), Morgan, Pritchard, and Pride (2002) note that there are 28 million people worldwide who claim Scottish ancestry. If only a fraction of them could be enticed to make an extra visit to Scotland, there would be a substantial increase in the volume and value derived of tourism. In partnership with Lufthansa and in cooperation with the German National Tourist Board and the Israel Ministry of Tourism, TAL Tours, a New York–based tour operator, offered six packages variously involving destinations in Germany and Israel to Jewish-Americans (TAL Tours, 2001). These ranged in price from US$2995 to US$3795 in 2002. The Hungarian State Tourism Office in the United States ran a 'Routes to your Roots' promotion in the late 1990s exhorting Hungarian-Americans to 'retrace your Hungarian routes in the year of Hungary's millennium' (Hungarian National Tourist Office, c.1999). As part of its commitment to diaspora tourism (Scottish Tourist Board, 2001), the London office for VisitScotland, the national tourism organisation for Scotland, promoted Scotia Travel's relatively cheap (£299) three-night, fly–drive holiday that encouraged visitors to '. . . . get closer to your roots on the unique Outer Hebridean Isle of Harris, where it's possible to trace your Hebridean ancestors . . .' (Scotia Travel, 2001).

Although the experiential aspects of diaspora tourism have been frequently read, supply-side discourse has been relatively uncommon. As Klemm (2002) notes, one reason for this imbalance is that ethnic minority groups (and hence diasporic communities) are invariably viewed as elements of tourism products rather than market segments that purchase holidays. Beyond a mapping of diaspora tourism products and experiences, one of the critical issues raised by commentators, but as yet to be fully explored, is how commodification of diaspora functions and the possible practical and conceptual implications and outcomes of the process. Diasporas are imbued with rich cultural capital by virtue of their formation and contemporary conditions (see van Hear, 1998). The question is how to obtain best value from this capital and how to release the value most effectively.

Given the complexity of diasporic spaces, places, narratives, and forms in individual destinations that could be embedded within dedicated products and experiences, auditing diasporic cultural resources is a logical first step in potential product development (Ioannides and Cohen, 2002). Different segments within diasporic communities and their demands must be recognised by producers. As Gruber (2002) notes of 'the needs, knowledge, and expectations of widely varied [Jewish] target audiences. . . .', '[w]hat works for some targets may deeply offend or alienate others.' To this end, Collins-Kreiner and Olsen (2004) note the plurality of vacations that are sold by Jewish travel agents and tour operators over the Internet. Their nine categories of products range from heritage tours to Jewish singles' tours. Although the Internet may be an obvious mechanism for promoting diasporic tourism because diasporic communities are often strengthened by their existence in hyperspace, Morgan, Pritchard, and Pride (2002) suggest that diaspora tourists can be reached by cost-effective, nontraditional methods such as database marketing and public relations as well as informal word of mouth (see Cohen, 1999). Notwithstanding, work on tourism marketing to British-Asians suggests that more comprehensive, intelligent, and dedicated approaches are required by major tour operators and travel agents to acknowledge, engage with, and increase business from, as yet unrealised demand from non-European ethnic markets in the United Kingdom (Klemm, 2002).

The imbalance between experiential accounts and those concentrating on supply-side aspects of diaspora tourism is a curious one and one not without obvious significance. As argued previously, experiences of visiting friends and relatives at 'home' and in the diaspora are identity-forming exercises. Whether enjoyable reaffirmations of membership of the extended community or tense, uncomfortable encounters with distant, diffident relatives, diasporic travel and tourism shape an individual's self-perception as well as social relations throughout transnational networks. In turn, these will inevitably impact on future travel decision making in terms of how visits manifest and articulate self- and/or group identity, whether to make a visit or not, and if so who to visit, when to visit, and what destinations or attractions will be visited. Conceptually, although they have as yet been mostly overlooked, it is crucial to recognise that the same types of feedbacks associated with experiences of 'informal' diasporic tourism are predictable, and indeed often intended, outcomes of deliberately constructed products. Cohen (2004) describes how historical narratives are purposely produced, varied according to group backgrounds, and presented to young people in educational tours that are designed to mediate explicitly Jewish identities through direct contact with diaspora heritage. Identity may be moderated, however, in far more subtle ways. Jewish-(German)-American package tours to Germany (and Israel) may be read as representing the fusion of present and former Jewish landscapes with mainstream promotional themes, the commercial realities of tour operating, and the desire among tourists for a combination of recreation and self-discovery (McKercher and du Cros, 2002). 'Jewish-themed' vacations result, but the challenge is to understand both how these hybridised narratives are understood, interpreted, and fed back into contemporary Jewish-American identities. Moreover, diasporic identity is more fluid than many producers realise. In turn, more complex identities may be mediated, which producers will have to acknowledge in order to reinvent diaspora tourism products. Thus, diasporic travels in all their guises, not least tourism, function to maintain, mediate, and moderate dynamic, restless, evolving, fluid communities, although the mechanics involved are only partly sketched out. Such diasporic communities also provide challenges for not only how we understand travel and tourism mobility but also how we understand the concept of home (Duval, 2004c). Indeed, second home purchase may be used within some diasporic and transnational communities as a means of maintaining complex social and place relationships over space and time.

The traditional notion of the location of second homes as being a distinct expression of a national identity that takes place within national boundaries has clearly changed (Hall and Müller, 2004). Müller's (1999) research on German second home owners in Sweden for example, clearly indicates the transnational nature of second home ownership in Europe, a situation clearly reinforced in studies of second home and retirement migration elsewhere in Europe (Hall and Williams, 2002). Such transnational second home movements are not uniquely European. In North America the significance of 'snowbirding' has meant the seasonal migration of many Canadian retirees, as well as American retirees from the northerly states, to Florida, the southwestern United States and, increasingly, Mexico. In Australia, the Gold and Sunshine Coast resort areas near Brisbane both receive significant amounts of New Zealand retirees during the New Zealand winter in an Antipodean version of snowbirding. Undoubtedly, such large-scale movement has significant longer term implications for national and transnational identities that are only beginning to be recognised (Duval, 2002; 2004b). Yet many of the broader agreements surrounding free trade and human mobility, such as those found within the European Union or Asia-Pacific Economic Cooperation (APEC), are serving only to encourage further transnational second homing. It is likely that even given the increased regulation of human mobility for some nationalities as a result of security concerns, that the capacity of wealthier individuals in the developed world to engage in transnational second homing will not only continue relatively unhindered but may even be further encouraged by some regions seeking inward investment (Hall and Müller, 2004). Changes in mobilities and locales, as discussed earlier in the chapter, will have substantial implications for tourism.

Conclusion

The earlier discussion highlights specific examples from the broader literature on mobility in which transnational linkages are manifested in the form of travel and, in some cases, tourism. The chapter also stresses that individual space–time trajectories are shifting leading to greater social and economic interaction in various, often transnational, domains, or what Giddens (1984) prefers to 'call the regionalization of time-space: the movement of life paths through settings of interaction that have various forms of spatial demarcation.' What has been highlighted is the fact that multiple localities spawn temporary movement that is inherently culturally influenced and predicated by previous emigration/migration as well as other forms of economic, social, cultural, and political constraints. Such movements often involve individuals located within a broader diasporic identity who embark on temporary movement to a specific locality that represents an alternative 'home' as a social construction and for the purpose of maintaining social threads between communities. Transnationalism and other understandings of contemporary mobility, then, would seem to have much to offer Tourism.

The arguments raised in this chapter can be seen as an attempt at characterising a new approach to Tourism that is based broadly on various forms of temporary mobilities, but more specifically within the frameworks offered in other social science disciplines that incorporate complex and global scapes and flows (Urry, 2000). An approach toward tourism as form of temporary mobility is perhaps useful for understanding how communities, particularly global communities, are formulated, retasked, reimaged, repositioned, and ultimately (re)packaged. For tourism as a form of temporary mobility, this would also suggest that tourism, or the touristic consumption of space and place, incorporates rather limited periods of movement (as opposed to permanent migration). At the same time, however, temporary mobility in the form of tourism may feature embedded social meanings that are inherently similar to the social process designation that has come to dominate metatheories of migration as well as new understandings of the routinisation of extended time–space trajectories for those individuals who lead mobile leisured lifestyles.

Although the purpose of this chapter has been to suggest several ways in which Tourism might benefit from conceptual and theoretical arguments relating to mobilities, it should be emphasised, however, that a particular format of mobility has been stressed. The vast majority of studies of tourism delineate tourists moving through rather fixed space; that is, tourists move from one destination to another. Each destination, in turn, is characterised sociopolitically, and thus travel is often represented as being 'to' a particular place such as a country, region, or city. Such a model of mobility, to which Kauffman (2002) might affix the model designation of areolar, is inherently rigid and thus inflexible at explaining patterns of movement. Some forms of tourism feature strong linkages to migration, transnationalism, and diaspora, yet at the same continue to incorporate some elements normally associated with tourism studies, namely production, consumption, and marketing. A more appropriate characterisation, therefore, might be one in which a rhizomatic approach (Kauffman, 2002) is used to understand the tourism/migration nexus, then, might feature the temporary mobility of individuals and involving localities that are off shoots of a central locality (a node) but nonetheless retain connections to that locality. Such an approach might speak to the general degree of (temporary) displacement (Kaplan, 1996) built into the system of mobilities worldwide.

At the same time, it should be noted that many studies of migration, transnationalism, and diasporas either fail to take into account, or offer only passing mention of, the degree to which travel and temporary mobility is an integral part of linking social spaces, locales, stations, and networks. Interestingly, Guarnizo (1997), in seeking to extrapolate the borderless nature of identities and cultural patterns, purposely excluded those whom he called 'the most obvious transnational migrants;' that is, 'those who shuttle back and forth for short working periods abroad and *visiting migrants temporarily in the country*' (emphasis added).

It would, therefore, seem rather appropriate to conclude that some tourists' world view and motivations might be explained within the broader context of mobility, including migration, and social connections to particular destinations and locales. Contemporary tourism is itself a synthesis, the resolution of a dialectic that has formed new forms of migration, movement, place associations, and life structures, yet contemporary Tourism must work toward constructing an epistemological and methodological toolkit that allows for fuller investigations of the issue presented in this chapter. Recognition of the place of tourism within the context of mobilities goes some way toward a theoretical grounding, but the kinds of topics addressed earlier should be embedded in the mainstream curriculum more fully, especially if Tourism is to be centred on contemporary issues and current moments.

References

Aronsson, L. 2000. *The Development of Sustainable Tourism.* London: Continuum.

Baldassar, L. 2001. *Visits Home: Migration Experiences between Italy and Australia.* Melbourne: Melbourne University Press.

Basch, L., N. Glick Schiller, and C. Szanton Blanc. 1994. *Nations Unbound: Transnational Projects and the Deterritorialized Nation-State.* New York: Gordon and Breach.

Braziel, J. E., and A. Mannur. eds. 2003. *Theorizing Diaspora: A Reader.* Malden: Blackwell Publishing.

Bruner, E. M. 1996. Tourism in Ghana: The Representation of Slavery and the Return of the Black Diaspora. *American Anthropologist* 98: 290–304.

Byron, M. 1994. *Post-War Caribbean Migration to Britain: The Unfinished Cycle.* Aldershot: Avebury.

———. 1999. The Caribbean-Born Population in the 1990s Britain: Who Will Return? *Journal of Ethnic and Migration Studies* 25(2): 285–301.

Byron, M., and S. Condon. 1996. A Comparative Study of Caribbean Return Migration from Britain and France: Towards a Context-Dependent Explanation. *Transactions of the Institute of British Geographers* 21: 91–104.

Carlstein, T., D. N. Parkes, and N. J. Thrift eds. 1978. *Timing Space and Spacing Time.* London: Edward Arnold.

Clifford, J. 1997. *Routes: Travel and Translation in the Late Twentieth Century.* Cambridge: Harvard University Press.

Cohen, E. H. 1999. Informal Marketing of Israel Experience Educational Tours. *Journal of Travel Research* 37(3): 238–243.

———. 2004. Preparation, Simulation and the Creation of Community: Exodus and the Case of Diaspora Education Tourism. In *Tourism, Diasporas and Space.* eds. T. E. Coles and D. J. Timothy. London: Routledge.

Cohen, R. 1997. *Global Diasporas: An Introduction.* London: Routledge.

Coles, T. E. 2003a. Tourism, Diaspora and the Mediation of Vacationscapes: Some Lessons from Enticing Jewish-Americans to Germany. *Espaces, Populations, Sociétés,* 2: 327–340.

——. 2003b. Urban Tourism, Place Promotion and Economic Restructuring: The Case of Post-Socialist Leipzig. *Tourism Geographies* 5(2): 190–219.

Coles, T. E., and D. J. Timothy. eds. 2004. *Tourism, Diasporas and Space.* London: Routledge.

Collins-Kreiner, N., and D. Olsen. 2004. Selling Diaspora: Producing and Segmenting the Jewish Diaspora Tourism Market. In *Tourism, Diasporas and Space.* eds. T. E. Coles and D. J. Timothy. London: Routledge.

Condon, S. A., and P. E. Ogden. 1996. 'Questions of Emigration, Circulation and Return: Mobility between the French Caribbean and France, *International Journal of Population Geography* 2: 35–50.

Coppock, J. T. ed. 1977. *Second Homes: Curse or Blessing?* Oxford: Pergamon.

Duval, D. T. 2002. The Return Visit-Return Migration Connection. In *Tourism and Migration: New Relationships Between Production and Consumption.* eds. C. M. Hall and A. Williams. Dordrecht: Kluwer.

Duval, D. T. 2004a. Conceptualising Return Visits: A Transnational Perspective. In *Tourism, Diasporas and Space: Travels to Promised Lands.* eds. T. E. Coles and D. J. Timothy. London: Routledge.

——. 2004b. When Hosts Become Guests: Return Visits and Diasporic Identities in a Commonwealth Eastern Caribbean Community. *Current Issues in Tourism,* 6(4): 267–308.

——. 2004c. Mobile Migrants: Travel to Second Homes. In *Tourism, Mobility and Second Homes: Between Elite Landscape and Common Ground.* eds. C. M. Hall and D. Müller. London: Channelview Publications.

Duval, D. T., and C. M. Hall. 2004. Linking Diasporas and Tourism: Transnational Mobilities of Pacific Islanders Resident in New Zealand. In *Tourism, Diasporas and Space.* eds. T. E. Coles and D. J. Timothy. London: Routledge.

Faist, T. 2000. Transnationalization in International Migration: Implications for the Study of Citizenship and Culture. *Ethnic and Racial Studies* 23(2): 189–222.

Fortier, A.M. 2000. *Migrant Belongings: Memory, Space, Identity.* Oxford: Berg.

Fowler, S. 2003. Ancestral Tourism. *Insights,* March 2003: D31–D36.

Franklin, A., and M. Crang. 2001. The Trouble with Tourism and Travel Theory. *Tourist Studies* 1(1): 5–22.

Giddens, A. 1984. *The Constitution of Society: Outline of the Theory of Structuration.* Berkeley: University of California Press.

Gregory, D. 1985. Suspended Animation: The Status of Diffusion Theory. In *Social Relations and Spatial Structures.* eds. D. Gregory and J. Urry. London: Macmillan.

Gruber, R. E. 1999. *Jewish Heritage Travel: A Guide to East-Central Europe.* Northvale, N.J.: Jason Aronson Inc.

——. 2002. *Virtually Jewish: Reinventing Jewish Culture in Europe.* Berkeley: University of California Press.

Guarnizo, L. E. 1997. The Emergence of a Transnational Social Formation and the Mirage of Return Migration among Dominican Transmigrants. *Identities* 4(2): 281–322.

Hägerstrand, T. 1967a. *Innovation Diffusion as a Spatial Process.* trans. A. Pred. Chicago: University of Chicago Press.

——. 1967b. On the Monte Carlo Simulation of Diffusion. In *Quantitative Geography, Part 1: Economic and Cultural Topics.* eds. W. L. Garrison and D. F. Marble. Evanston, Ill.: Northwestern University Press.

Hall, C. M. 2003. Tourism and Temporary Mobility: Circulation, Diaspora, Migration, Nomadism, Sojourning, Travel, Transport and Home. Paper presented at International Academy for the Study of Tourism Conference. June 30–July 5. Savonlinna, Finland.

——. 2004a. Space-Time Accessibility and the Tourist Area Cycle of Evolution: The Role of Geographies of Spatial Interaction and Mobility in Contributing to an Improved Understanding of Tourism. In *The Tourism Area Life-Cycle.* ed. R. Butler. Clevedon: Channelview.

——. 2004b. *Tourism.* Harlow: Prentice-Hall.

Hall, C. M., and D. Müller. eds. 2004. *Tourism, Mobility and Second Homes: Between Elite Landscape and Common Ground.* Clevedon: Channelview Publications.

Hall, C. M., and A. Williams. eds. 2002. *Tourism and Migration: New Relationships between Production and Consumption.* Dordrecht: Kluwer.

Hall, C. M., A. M. Williams, and A. Law. 2004. Tourism: Conceptualisations, Institutions and Issues. In *Companion to Tourism.* eds. A. Lew, C. M. Hall, and A. M. Williams. Oxford: Blackwells.

Helmreich, S. 1992. Kinship, Nation and Paul Gilroy's Concept of Diaspora. *Diaspora* 2(2): 243–249.

Hungarian National Tourist Office (HNTO). undated, c.1999. *Routes to your Roots. Retrace your Hungarian Roots in the Year of Hungary's Millennium.* New York: HNTO.

Ioannides, D., and M. W. Cohen. 2002. Pilgrimages of Nostalgia: Patterns of Jewish Travel in the United States. *Tourism Recreation Research* 27(2): 17–25.

Itzigsohn, J., C. D. Cabral, E. Hernandez Medina, and O. Vazquez. 1999. Mapping Dominican Ttransnationalism: Narrow and Broad Transnational Practices. *Ethnic and Racial Studies* 22(2): 316–339.

Kaplan, C. 1996. *Questions of Travel: Postmodern Discourses of Displacement.* Durham: Duke University Press.

Kaufmann, V. 2002. *Re-thinking Mobility: Contemporary Sociology.* Aldershot: Ashgate.

King, R. 2002. Towards a New Map of European Migration. *International Journal of Population Geography* 8: 89–106.

Kivisto, P. 2001. Theorizing Transnational Immigration: A Critical Review of Current Efforts. *Ethnic and Racial Studies* 24(4): 549–577.

Klemm, M. 2002. Tourism and Ethnic Minorities in Bradford: The Invisible Segment. *Journal of Travel Research* 41: 85–91.

Kraft, R. M., J. Ballatine, and D. E. Garvey. 1994. Study Abroad or International Travel? The Case of Semester At Sea. *Phi Beta Delta International Review* 4: 23–61.

Layton-Henry, Z. 2002. Transnational Communities, Citizenship and African-Caribbeans in Birmingham. Working Paper, ESRC Transnational Communities Programme (WPTC-02-07), www.transcomm.ox.ac.uk.

Lee, H. M. 2003. *Tongans Overseas: Between Two Shores.* Honolulu: University of Hawaii Press.

Mason, P. 2002. The 'Big OE': New Zealanders Overseas Experiences in Britain. In *Tourism and Migration: New Relationships between Production and Consumption.* eds. C. M. Hall and A. M. Williams. Dordrecht, Kluwer.

McKercher, B., and H. du Cros. 2002. *Cultural Tourism. The Partnership Between Tourism and Cultural Heritage Management.* Binghampton: Haworth Press.

Mitchell, K. 1997. Different Diasporas and the Hype of Hybridity. *Environment and Planning D: Society and Space* 15: 533–553.

Morgan, N., A. Pritchard, and R. Pride. 2002. Marketing to the Welsh Diaspora: The Appeal of *Hiraeth* and Homecoming. *Journal of Vacation Marketing* 9(1): 69–80.

Müller, D. K. 1999. *German Second Home Owners in the Swedish Countryside: On the Internationalization of the Leisure Space.* Umeå: Kulturgeografiska institutionen.

Nash, C. 2002. Genealogical Identities. *Environment and Planning D: Society and Space* 20(1): 27–52.

Nguyen, T. H., and B. E. M. King. 1998. Migrant Homecomings: Viet Kieu Attitudes Towards Traveling Back to Vietnam. *Pacific Tourism Review* 1: 349–361.

Organization for Economic Cooperation and Development (OECD). 2002. *International Mobility of the Highly Skilled.* Paris: OECD.

Portes, A. 1999. Conclusion: Towards a New World—The Origins and Effects of Transnational Activities. *Ethnic and Racial Studies* 22(2): 463–477.

Portes, A., L. E. Guarnizo, and P. Landolt. 1999. The Study of Transnationalism: Pitfalls and Promise of an Emergent Research Field. *Ethnic and Racial Studies* 22(2): 217–237.

Pred, A. R. 1981a. Social Reproduction and the Time-Geography of Everyday Life. *Geografiska Annaler* 63B: 5–22.

———. 1981b. Production, Family, and Free-Time Projects: A Time-Geographic Perspective on the Individual and Societal Change in 19th Century US Cities. *Journal of Historical Geography* 7: 3–6.

Ravenstein, E. G. 1885. The Laws of Migration. *Journal of the Royal Statistical Society* 48: 167–227.

———. 1889. The Laws of Migration. *Journal of the Royal Statistical Society* 52: 214–301.

Robinson, G. M. 1998. *Methods & Techniques in Human Geography.* Chichester: Wiley.

Rouse, R. C. 1992. Making Sense of Settlement: Class Transformation, Cultural Struggle, and Transnationalism among Mexican Migrants in the United States. In *Towards a Transnational Perspective on Migration: Race, Class, Ethnicity, and Nationalism Reconsidered.* Annals of the New York Academy of Sciences, Vol. 645. eds. N. Glick Schiller, L. Basch, and C. Szanton Blanc. New York: New York Academy of Sciences.

Schafer, A. 2000. Regularities in Travel Demand: An International Perspective. *Journal of Transportation and Statistics* 3(3): 1–31.

Scotia Travel. undated, c. 2001. *Hebridean Connections.* Halifax, N.S.: Nova Scotia Department of Tourism and Culture.

Scottish Tourist Board. 2001. *Genealogy Tourism Strategy & Marketing Plan.* Edinburgh: STB.

Shuval, J. T. 2000. Diaspora Migration: Definitional Ambiguities and a Theoretical Paradigm. *International Migration* 38(5): 41–55.

Smith, R. C. 2001. Comparing Local Level Swedish and Mexican Transnational Life: An Essay in Historical Retrieval. In *New Transnational Social Spaces: International Migration and Transnational Companies in the Early Twenty-First Century.* ed. L. Pries. London: Routledge.

Spoonley, P. 2000. Reinventing Polynesia: The Cultural Politics of Transnational Communities. Working paper (WPTC-2K-14). Transnational Communities Research Programme, Institute of Social and Cultural Anthropology, University of Oxford, U.K.

Stephenson, M. 2002. Travelling to the Ancestral Homelands: The Aspirations and Experiences of a UK Caribbean Community. *Current Issues in Tourism* 5(5): 378–425.

TAL Tours. German National Tourist Board, Israel Tourist Board, Lufthansa. undated, c. 2001. *Germany and Israel, 2001–2002.* Valley Stream, N.Y.: TAL Tours.

Tatla, D. S. 1999. *The Sikh Diaspora. The Search for Statehood.* London: UCL Press.

Thrift, N. J. 1977. Time and Theory in Human Geography, Part 2. *Progress in Human Geography* 1: 23–57.

United Nations. 1994. *Recommendations on Tourism Statistics.* New York: United Nations.

Urry, J. 2000. *Sociology Beyond Societies: Mobilities for the Twenty-First Century.* London: Routledge.

van Hear, N. 1998. *New Diasporas. The Mass Exodus, Dispersal and Regrouping of Migrant Communities.* London: UCL Press.

Vertovec, S. 1999. Conceiving and Researching Transnationalism. *Ethnic and Racial Studies* 22(2): 447–462.

Wang, N. 2000. *Tourism and Modernity: A Sociological Analysis.* Oxford: Elsevier Science/Pergamon.

Werbner, P. 2002. The Place Which Is Diaspora: Citizenship, Religion and Gender in the Making of Chaordic Transnationalism. *Journal of Ethnic and Migration Studies* 28(1): 119–113.

25 Globalisation and emerging tourism education issues

Frank M. Go

Introduction

'Tourism enabled people to move beyond the mentality of 'being tied to one location' and encounter other "thought worlds." In essence, tourism is about the time–space compression of societies, as the result of "diminishing costs and increasing ease of international travel for purposes of leisure, by enabling increasing numbers of people from nearly all Western social classes . . ." to 'escape their routine environment and experiences"' (Held, et al., 1999).

In many countries around the world, tourism education and training curricula focus on the workforce, which is responsible for planning, marketing, and delivering of quality service and maintaining productivity to keep the tourism sector competitive. Education is the act or process of imparting knowledge. Training may be defined as the process of bringing a person to an agreed standard of proficiency for responsibilities through practice or instruction. Both education and training are communicative and interactive in nature, that is, both bring about developmental transfer of concepts, methods, and models from the initial context of learning to the context of the classroom and on to the professional career context, where knowledge and competencies are applied in particular tasks.

The education and professional tourism career interface 'lies at the very heart' (Airey, 1998) of the issues, challenges, and the opportunities for education and professional careers in tourism (Gee, 1980; Hawkins and Hunt, 1988; Bratton, Go, and Ritchie, 1991; EIESP, 1991; Parsons, 1991; Go 1994; 1998). It provides a focus for dilemmas, such as, how to develop sustainable, high-quality growth. And whether the latter should be accomplished by conservation, preservation (Plog, 1998), or innovation

(e.g., appropriately product–market matching, which emphasises education and communication along with sales) (Wight, 1993; 1994, cited by
Murphy, 1998). It also feeds the debate about the aims of tourism courses,
in particular their content, context, and delivery process.

Should tourism, for instance, be defined as specialism (Pearce, 1993)?
Or would it make more sense to view the tourism field in a much broader
context, for example, as a 'toolbox' to help us put into perspective the
global challenges of the new millennium. One study (http://nafsa.org/
press), titled 'Securing America's Future: Global Education for a Global
Age,' prepared by the National Association of Foreign Student Advisers
(NAFSA) suggests that the terrorist attacks of September 11, 2001, 'sealed
the case' for global education and imposed an urgent demand on Americans to foster their 'international knowledge and skills.' The current
armed conflict in Iraq further reinforces NAFSA's suggestion that Americans 'were blindsided by their ignorance of international threats' and that
the future competitiveness and national security could be undermined in
the United States by citizens' lack of 'global skills.' NAFSA urges government, higher-education institutions, and the private sector to increase
opportunities for U.S. students to study abroad to enhance, amongst
others, 'their global foreign-language proficiency, comprehension of international problems, and broader awareness of multicultural issues in all
fields.'

Improved global education is essential for all those who wish to make
informed decisions: citizens and both the private sector stakeholders and
the public sector (destination). The former has relevance, for instance,
in regard to the diffusion of knowledge about alternatives in the resident–tourist relationship through education–community information,
which may influence resident perception (Pearce, 1998). It can help buyers
and vendors to make better decisions in relation to the delivery of tourist
services. In that sense a durable competitiveness does not reside as much
in today's competencies and knowledge. Rather the realisation that a
developmental transfer of education and knowledge and competencies
represents a dynamic mechanism for continuous improvement (Haywood
and Maki, 1992).

Today's decision makers, both in the private and public sector, cannot
assume that the rate of change in tourism markets, products, technologies, competitors, and tourism destinations, which occur at an increasingly rapid pace, are only temporary disruptions. Instead they are
confronted with the effects of informational capitalism (Castells, 2000),
which have resulted in a blurring of boundaries and the rise of flexible
production systems (Volberda, 1998). The knowledge needed to compete
under conditions of complexity is 'becoming more diverse as markets
converge and industries collide' (Sawhney and Prandelli, 2000). The
rapid rate of knowledge obsolescence in a world where complexity rules

means the need of increased 'knowledge socialization and flexibility and risk reduction of autonomous knowledge production' (Sawhney and Prandelli, 2000).

The focus of this chapter is on how the education-employer interface (Haywood and Maki, 1992) appears to emancipate in the global context toward the rise of communities of creation, which include the knowledge of partners and customers to manage the process of distributed innovation (Sawhney and Prandelli, 2000). The emergence of communities of creation is particularly relevant in the European Union (EU), which strives for sustainable, high-quality tourism development and growth. Beside developing the needed knowledge internally or buying it in the market, the communities of creation provides an alternative for parties 'to innovate and modify practices in order to solve common problems' (Botterill, 1996). Provoked by the environmental dynamics and the notion that a firm's critical resources for survival may extend its boundaries, knowledge-driven alliances have become popular. The advantages of such alliances are amongst others, gaining expertise in new product development, speeding up cycle time, and mitigating risk.

In the distributed cognition view, information and communication technology (ICT) become central to the way individuals and organisations in trans-sector partnership networks construct meaning, make sense to themselves and their environment (Weick, 1995), and change the way organisations compete (McFarlan, 1984). In short, ICT makes feasible the coordination and control of the process of developmental transfer of knowledge and competencies within a network approach, which is relevant to sustainable, high-quality tourism practice. The purpose of this chapter is to explore whether Web-based distributed, cooperative learning within creative communities can add value to the education-employer interface and by extension to other stakeholders, including the host society.

This chapter is divided in three sections. The first chronicles the evolution of tourism education and the research platforms that underpin it and signal an epistemological shift toward dialectical, relational, and integrative approaches in tourism education. The second comments on globalisation and explores particularly how the EU, in response to the former, tries to support destination stakeholders to identify the 'right' partnerships that complement their own core competencies. The final section then concludes with a discussion of how investments in global e-learning hold potential to contributions to the formation of emergent communities, which represent a crucial, intermediate level to connect individual knowledge and organisational learning, both for purposes of exploration and exploitation resulting in sustainable, high-quality tourism (Bogenrieder and Nooteboom, 2003).

The Evolution of Tourism Education

What abilities and concepts should a tourism education programme impart? This review positions tourism education against the stakeholder (buyer/vendor) and destination (host/guest) relationship, because their conduct determines the structure of the tourism phenomenon. Tourism education, that is the act or process of imparting knowledge of this mutual relationship and the factors that change it, is key to understanding the evolution of tourism phenomenon. Tourism education evolved through the 'pioneer phase,' the 'rationality phase,' and recently, entered the third phase of 'value-adding partnership networks.'

The Pioneer Phase (1940s–1970s)

Professors Hunziker and Krapf started their investigations in tourism research and education in Switzerland during the 1940s and are recognised as early pioneers of tourism studies. Among Swiss social scientists there seemed to have been an awareness of the need to extend the tourism research horizon (Kaspar, 1994). It took until the 1970s before Anglo-American academics began to map the uncharted waters of tourism studies in earnest. Medlik and Burkart, who were affiliated with the University of Surrey, took the lead in Britain, whereas Clare Gunn of Texas A&M University and Robert McIntosh of Michigan State University were among the early pioneers of tourism education in the United States. The early pioneers of tourism studies had to cope with significant challenges, in part, of their own making, because, 'in nearly all cases [tourism education programmes were] developed as a result of academic enterprise rather than industrial demand' [and] 'certain segments of the tourism industry seemed to accept specific academic qualifications' (Christie-Mill, 1978). These findings, which are based on an analysis by Lawson's (1974) comparative study 'Teaching Tourism: Education and Training in Western Europe' serve as an important reminder that tourism education in the 1970s and 1980s was primarily educator driven. Furthermore, Lawson's comparative analysis of newly introduced tourism courses in Western Europe paid considerable attention to the ongoing concern expressed by tourism educators for highly pragmatic matters, particularly the career placement of students and tourism career path development.

The Rationality Phase (1980s–1990s)

The rationality phase of tourism education was heralded by a coedited review by Jafari and Ritchie (1981) of the state of the art of the rapidly expanding field of tourism education. It shifted the focus of tourism education from the pragmatic to the academic level. By expanding the scope of tourism education, the authors attempted in particular to reach the following objectives:

- To place tourism in a broader context and identify major concerns before defining tourism education and curriculum content;
- To examine alternative disciplinary approaches to the study of tourism; and
- To focus on a number of critical issues in tourism education.

Among the key observations Jafari and Ritchie made regarding the gaps in tourism research, which they perceived to possess both weaknesses and opportunities in terms of the lack of empirical research on which to base the design of tourism curricula, were the:

- Conceptualisation and design of tourism courses and programmes by individual educators in relative isolation as opposed to groups of educators representing various educational institutions.
- Highly vocational nature of the manuscripts submitted for publication received from North American sources, compared with other geographical regions such as Europe, where tourism 'is conceptualized in much broader terms.'

This viewpoint on the interdisciplinary nature of tourism studies led to the increased recognition that tourism education and research are inextricably intertwined.

Communities of Creation Phase (Turn of the Century Onward)

In a globalised world an essential aspect of foreign tourists, but also refugees and migrants, is that their networks reach out into the wider realm of transnational space. The creation of this new social reality implies that the centre of gravity has shifted from the stable environments that characterise nation-states to 'a broader ... "culture" ... with no clear cut distinctions' (Urry, 1996). The 'de-materialization' of assets, such as, information and capital, lead to a multidimensionality of reconfiguration opportunities. Because 'dematerialized assets,' are almost completely 'liquid,' they can be present at almost any place at any time. It led Appadurai (1990) to suggest the need for the mapping of human activities in transnational space in terms of 'mediascapes,' 'ethnoscapes,' 'finanscapes,' and 'technoscapes.' In this context, enterprises are being transformed from hierarchical and complex organisations with simple jobs, to more decentralised and network-oriented organisations, with more complex jobs. It has significant consequences for how we approach the tourism phenomenon (Wahab and Cooper, 2001). Not as a new model, but rather as process toward ever-improving practices, which are organised through complex interlocking networks both within and across different thought worlds of business, culture, and education/research. Whilst the first and second phases of tourism education may be characterised as rather 'inward-looking' and 'location-bound,' the third phase of tourism education represents an epistemological shift toward dialectical, relational, and integrative approaches, in a global context. The latter builds on 'contributory disciplines' (Hall, 1998), away from "'traditional positivist methods' that were blinding scholars" (Echtner and Jamal, 1997; Ryan, 1997). It has resulted in the rise of a permeable system, with ever-changing boundaries, which balances on the borders of 'the closed hierarchical model of innovation and the open-market-based model,' which Sawhney and Prandelli (2000) have coined a 'community of creation.'

Tourism Research Platforms

Sustainable, high-quality tourism development depends on the diffusion of knowledge and competences. Presently, the relevant theory is fragmented, which impedes both research and tourism education development, 'as well as the legitimacy of tourism studies' (Echtner and Jamal, 1997). Typically, a solid tourism curriculum depends on tourism research. The latter can be positioned within Jafari's (1990) 'four tourism research platforms: the Advocacy, Cautionary, Adaptancy and Knowledge-based Platforms,which have emerged chronologically, but without replacing one another.'

The Advocacy Platform and the Cautionary Platform

The Advocacy Platform and Cautionary Platform are treated together, because both focus on the development and growth of tourism and the impacts of tourism on the physical/social environment upon which it depends. An example of the Advocacy Platform is the metaphor of tourism as employment creator. For instance, the EU has featured it in its 'European Tourism New Partnerships For Jobs' initiative (1998). It has put the sector 'at the forefront, both as a driver of change and as a respondent' (Wahab and Cooper, 2001). In contrast, the Cautionary Platform came about, and is sustained, by the explosive tourism growth, which caused a stream of publications that stereotyped tourism as an 'irrational,' heterogeneous, rent-exploiting, partially industrialised sector that is very difficult to coordinate, let alone to govern (Tremblay, 1998). Amongst others, it resulted in opposition to 'mass-tourism' and a growing concern for the developing countries, in part, through tourism education (Theuns, Leo, and Go, 1992).

The Adaptancy Platform

The Adaptancy Platform concentrates on forms of tourism development and growth (Wahab and Pigram, 1997). Put differently, the primary objective of most sustainable tourism research studies has been to suggest which policies might help minimise the negative consequences of tourism development and activity through appropriate resource planning and management. In short, sustainable tourism is equated with sustainable resource use. As a result, much of the literature is concerned with appropriate site management or visitor management techniques, embodied in approaches such as 'Environmental Management Systems' (Tribe et al., 2000). Thus, although environmentally and economically justifiable, both the first and second platform treat tourism largely in isolation from the other factors that constitute its social, environmental, and economic dimensions.

The Knowledge-Based Platform

The Knowledge-Based Platform aims to study tourism as whole and strives for the formation of a scientific body of knowledge in tourism, while maintaining bridges with other platforms (Echtner and Jamal, 1997). Within the tourism sector, networks and partnerships represent the predominant mode of organising and coordinating and controlling exchange relationships within value-adding partnerships. Following Johnston and Lawrence (1988) we define a value-adding partnership as a set of interdependent stakeholders, destinations, and institutions of higher education, which cooperate closely to manage the development, transfer, and application of both knowledge and competencies, in order to realise sustainable, high-quality tourism at the lowest possible costs. The number and variety of networks have been accelerating as witnessed by the proliferation of publications on the various aspects of interorganisational relationships (Nohria and Eccles, 1992; Gulati, 1995). As a consequence of globalisation and the spread of information systems, interorganisational relationships increasingly occur in the context of international projects and international tourism development.

Three key factors contribute to the geographical distribution of tourism networking and value-adding partnerships. First, multinational companies become increasingly decentralised and operate on a global scale. Furthermore, from May 2004 onward the single European market in which international companies and supranational organisations operate, will be given a further impulse to the integration of the European continent. Both these developments shall require improved education (Witt, 1998) and distributed project work (Kumar and van Fenema, 1997). Second, on the supply side, outsource activities have become a cost-effective way to organise tourism business processes. Third, ICT advances enable the emergence of online communities as a new form of distributed society.

Presently, there are two types of gaps that impede 'cross-border' thinking and acting and the attainment of a semblance of coherence in colocated tourism development. First, 'sustainable, high quality tourism development' remains a contested concept (Wall, 1997; Sharpley, 2000). The tourism stakeholders, destinations, and higher education represent different thought worlds, perceptions, expectations, and experiences, which influence the growth of understanding and decision making in relation to curriculum development and delivery. Second, most tourism education is discipline based (marketing, sociology, anthropology, economics, geography, psychology), therefore, it is primarily focussed on the first three research platforms as opposed to the application of theories, methods, tools, and resources within a multidisciplinary knowledge framework (Ritchie, 1988).

An ICT-supported tourism Knowledge Platform would represent a new type of information-sharing system that could combine multidisciplinary views and numerous complex communication and coordination mechanisms and activities around a unity of purpose: to jointly achieve sustainable, high-quality tourism. Despite their growing importance in knowledge management and electronic business, the topic of ICT for platform support receives only limited attention in tourism education today.

Information and Communication Technology

After digesting the literature on social changes in relation to the tourism context (Go and Haywood, 2003), we conclude that much of the time researchers are locked into a debate, steeped in ideologies, that amount to two sides of the same coin. On one side is an eclectic group of advocates (Bell, 1988; Piore and Sabel, 1984; and Castells, 1989) who have utopian faith in the power of new technology. These technosocial scientists 'proclaim a new society,' wherein the combination of the information society and free market forces will deliver humanity from the mundanities of everyday work, liberate us from bureaucratic incompetence, and lead to a more prosperous future. Juxtaposed to this view are those such as Harvey (1985), Giddens (1985), and Habermas (1962) who opine that technology and unbridled market forces are making us work harder and faster, destroying human connections and our neighbourhoods. They 'place emphasis on continuities' and 'argue that the form and function of information is subordinate to long established principles and practices.'

Despite their obvious ideological differences, these viewpoints suggest that exogenous forces are reshaping society and the evolution of tourism development. The complexity of tourism development calls into being the need for the coordination of activities by myriad stakeholders and, by extension, ICT. Therefore, the increasing importance of ICT and corresponding organisational transformations as drivers of change should become a point of attention in tourism education. It is important to underscore in this regard that it is not ICT itself that drives change, but rather the way such technologies cause incremental shifts in social adaptation to fit successfully into the organisation of our every day work, consumption, and leisure life (Lash and Urry, 1994). 'Information and communication systems' are, like tourism, 'embedded in a global net' (www.cognizantcommunication.com) and the relationship between ICT and tourism poses many challenges to social scientists. For example, it is one of the major driving forces behind the 'explosive' increases in the volume of tourist information available and among the main reasons that consumers face complexity (Govers and Go, 2004). Furthermore, in the postmodern era tourist demand has become more fragmented and less predictable. Travellers are demanding greater product variety customised to their unique requirements, anywhere, any time. It leads to a situation where managers and policy makers must make decisions on much shorter notice, with information that cannot be easily verified and realise that the potential penalty cost is high. Major developments in information and communication technology, including telecommunications, knowledge-based systems, and database management system, have provided organisations with systems to support their decision-making process (Wierenga and Ophuis, 1997). At the same time, the integration of many networked electronic devices result in new kinds of interaction with technology into our personal domains. On different occasions, the same tourist demonstrates different types of buying and leisure behaviour and seeks for vendors who respond in a personal manner (Prahalad and Ramaswamy, 2000). In this regard the tourist is becoming increasingly a cocreator of the content of his or her own script, which is translated into trip-related experiences, during the delivery stages of the tourism channel.

In this framework ICT become central to the way individuals and organisations in transsector value-adding partnership networks construct meaning, create a competitive edge, and make sense to themselves and their environment (Weick, 1995) through the coordination of information (Kumar and van Fenema, 1997). ICT makes feasible the coordination and control of information over vast distances. Given its critical importance in coordination, ICT serves as a source of competitive advantage. Under conditions of informational capitalism (Castells, 2000), the rate of change in tourism markets, products, technologies, competitors, and tourism destinations occur at an increasingly rapid pace. Therefore, a key issue is how to enhance the absorptive capacity of actors to acquire and link internal and external knowledge.

The information revolution has resulted in a blurring of boundaries in the tourism sector and the rise of flexible production systems. From a 'boundary' perspective (Tulder, 1999), which may be classified as an emerging paradigm with synthesising characteristics, it raises a key issue regarding the perceived identification in distributed groups and the potential for conflict. But conceptions of intercontextual conflict represent not necessarily a negative force. If combined with common sense, intercontextual conflict can be effectively used for learning and the strengthening of identity (Wetlaufer, 2000).

However, the human participation and coordination of common sense plays within increasingly more and different social and cyber networks. It implies confrontation on a daily basis with contrasting worldviews, many of which can be characterised as emotional, leaving a mental imprint. Therefore, to promote more intercontextual collaboration, people need a support system such as computing that integrates the micro and macro dimensions of everyday life. Specifically, methodological approaches, that help them cope with our high-speed culture, including mobility, fast paced, polyscriptedness, and parallelisation of experiences such as jogging with a Walkman and include travel motivation in relation to our every day life world, including work, community, and family life (Jamal and Lee, 2003). The latter results in polyinclusive patterns of human behaviour (Figure 25.1) and may be categorised as taking place in material space (e.g., physical environment), informational space (e.g., online representations), mental space (e.g., perceived image), and social space (e.g., sharing experiences with others). Interaction in these spaces or worlds leads to complex, if not chaotic, patterns but also novel opportunities (Go and Fenema, 2003).

The information revolution coincides with a demographic time bomb epitomised by an aging population that will affect labour, consumer, and tourist markets. It shall place significant pressure on incumbent higher education systems in order to transform from a supply-driven education approach to a demand-driven education approach. It implies the transfer of responsibility for learning from educator to learner, based on polyinclusive patterns of human behaviour.

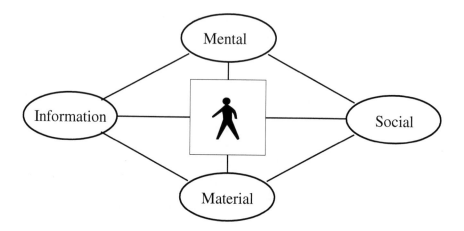

Figure 25.1: Polyinclusive patterns and hedonic consumption experiences.
Source: Go and Fenema, 2003.

Contested Space

Globalisation may be defined as 'a process (or set of processes) which embodies a transformation in the spatial organisation of social relations and transactions—assessed in terms of their extensivity, intensivity, velocity and impact—generating transcontinental or interregional flows and networks of activity, interactivity, and the exercise of power.' . . . 'As economic, social and political activities are increasingly "stretched" across the globe they become in a significant sense no longer primarily or solely organized according to territorial principle' (Held et al., 1999).

In the 'Age of Globalization,' tourism has become 'an ideological framing of history, nature and tradition' with 'the power to reshape culture and nature to its own needs' (MacCannell, 1992, as cited by Wahab and Cooper, 2001). Global tourism is characterised by opposing ideologies. It is a contested space in which a multitude of tensions and competing demands are played out, often reflecting wider political, cultural, and economic differences and conflicts (Clark et al., 1994). It might also be seen as a value constellation (Normann and Ramirez, 1993), for instance, by those who use ICT as the enabling factor for more coordination within the tourism channel and boundary crossing 'to benefit from the new media-enabled creativity, diversity, and agility' (Sawhney and Prandelli, 2000). In the latter context, the 'locus of innovation is no longer within the firm', but rather a collection of members, who through their participation in a creative community foster the process of distributed innovation. For instance, small and medium-sized enterprises (SMEs) in tourism, which need access to media (Smith, 1998), may decide to connect with the latter in a shared opportunity arena (Sawhney and Prandelli, 2000) around focal themes, such as Citizenship and Consumption, Cultural Policy and Industrial Policy, Convergence and Fragmentation, and Identity and Diversity (www.lboro.ac.uk/research/changing.media). Such collaboration enables participants to gain insight and knowledge of business procedures (Smith, 1998), which are relevant to the development of sustainable, high-quality tourism.

Citizenship and Consumption

From a historical perspective, 'the rise and the fall of the public sphere' (Habermas, 1962) has witnessed the rise of conflict between the forces aimed at commercialisation of all sectors of society and forces trying to maintain and expand democracy. In the industrialised countries, a combination of factors, including urbanisation, rising incomes, and access to education, have contributed to the growth of consumption and international tourism development during the past decades. The explosive growth of tourism has led to pressure on local resources with a limited contribution for the elevation of the economic status of host communities. It caused an all too familiar stream of negative reactions, which stereotyped tourism as a sector that is 'irrational,' heterogeneous, rent—exploiting, and partially industrialised (Tremblay, 1998). Despite the enormous variety of categories of organisations and agencies in terms of their respective activities, purpose, and direction, it has essentially resulted in two underlying ideological perspectives: the 'antiglobalists' and the 'advocates of globalisation.'

According to this tradition, the so-called antiglobalists are represented by, amongst others, Klein (2000) and Hertz (2001) who hold that global tourism undermines the cultural discourse and causes an increase of power and capital in the hands of few, as evidenced by mergers and acquisitions of transnational corporations and banking conglomerates. The antiglobalists have raised concerns about environmental quality and the need for environmental planning (Ashworth, 1991). The antiglobalist ideology raises a political issue of import, namely, whether tourism will be in the future 'uncloaked as a despoiler of destinations and a harbinger of adverse social change' (Cooper et al., 1993).

On the other hand, advocates such as Leadbeater (2002) and Legrain (2002) represent the perspective that globalisation presents an unrivalled opportunity to reduce the barriers to economic growth, enhance access to other cultures, and enhance business performance. They view Klein and Hertz as pessimists.

Cultural Policy and Industrial Policy

The advances of ICT have profound effects on society, including space–time compression (Lash and Urry, 1994), the death of distance (Harvey, 1985), and time–space distantiation and, as a consequence, the disembedding of social activities from place (Giddens, 1990). The creation of value-adding networks depends to a significant extent on the ability to shape policy and understand which encompasses both cultural policy and industrial policy perspectives. For instance, urban heritage represents an interpretation of history by a range of users whose view on the value proposition of urban heritage differs substantially (Orbasli, 2000). From a cultural policy perspective it is important to note, that transnational tourism corporations (TNCs) operate in world markets and have a major influence on (foreign) tourist streams. In that sense, especially Western consumer culture, for example, does not leave the local (non-Western) culture untouched, because the local population is confronted with visitors who think and behave differently (van Rekom and Go, 2003). Furthermore, TNCs push global competition and 'international bench-marking drive up the standards and the quality of the domestic tourism industry' (Wahab and Cooper, 2001), including SMEs. In turn, tourist destinations represent an important environment for tourism firms, for example in terms of labour and infrastructure provision, rules, and regulations. Knowledge of this mutual relationship of cultural policy and industrial policy is necessary to comprehend the decision-making process, weigh and judge its outcomes, and learn from both success and failures. In that sense Plog's (1998) plea is significant. 'Our environment talks to us, but too often we don't listen. It cries out for help—for protection from the destruction imposed by uncontrolled development . . . Perhaps the ultimate solution must come from travelers themselves. Educate them about the benefits of preserving and enhancing destinations and they will become more ecologically sensitive.'

Convergence and Fragmentation

Networking has caused the convergence of several media-related industries, including broadcasting and motion pictures, publishing and print, computing (Shapiro and Varian, 1999), and more recently, the cable and telecommunications industry. Convergence manifests itself also on another level of classification, for example, according to 'content,' 'delivery,' and 'distribution.' At the boundaries of the various media industries new products and services emerge. Examples are educational programmes, games, video-on-demand, and publishing-on-demand. Simultaneously, fragmentation has become a way of everyday life in the postinformation age, because we often have an audience only the size of one. Everything from newspapers, to products and pricing can be personalised (Shapiro and Varian, 1999). But it also raises the issue of whether the ICT revolution widens the digital divide. Later on we will return to this issue.

Identity and Diversity

Gobal signs and symbols, including, McDonald's and Sheraton hotels, have led to basic shifts: from local to global images, from public to private institutions, and in the sources of cultural identity. Young people all over the world, when they have the means tend to adopt global trends and fashions, rather than remaining loyal to their cultural heritage. Under such conditions, if the local community's tendency for assimilation with the global culture has been determined, a decision can be made as to how to preserve the local community's identity, that is, if there is a need for such measures (van Rekom and Go, 2003). An educational programme aimed at the host community may be a persuasive communication approach in order to educate the local community (Pearce, 1998). For example, since September 2002, the British Department of Education and Skills has joined forces with businesses, the Association for Citizenship Education, the Citizenship Foundation, the Institute for Citizenship, charities, and schools to introduce and develop a teacher's resource packet 'to support active citizenship in the classroom and community' (www.community.barclays.co.uk). The packet offers a range of materials that encourage pupils to explore particularly three main strands of citizenship: 'rights and responsibilities,' communities and identities' (local, national and global), and 'democratic process and government' (www.dfes.gov.uk/citizenship). The emerging diversity of society demands a more flexible approach. The diffusion of e-content offers society new opportunities, for example, when adopting e-government and a life-long learning approach to education.

European Union at the Crossroads

The European tourism sector contributes 12 percent of gross domestic product and accounts for 13 percent of total employment or 28 million jobs. Therefore, it is of great economic importance to the EU. However, as a result, in part, of intense global competition the European tourism brand is losing its market share, whereas tourism continues to grow worldwide. Without new initiatives, this trend is likely to continue. What are the challenges to improve European's tourism competitiveness as well as the conditions and means to capitalise on the opportunities for growth? The so-called High Level Group on Tourism and Employment identified the following perceived challenges (Anon., 1998):

- Activate tourism businesses, especially SMEs that make up the bulk of the industry to meet the increasing demand of tourists for high-quality, personalised tourist services.
- Improve the business environment by strengthening the functioning of the European single market through the simplification of regulations for businesses and provision of training and information technology on industry cooperation.
- Modernise and improve the efficiency of tourism-related infrastructures, especially the insufficient interoperability of Europe's transport network and of information technology systems put up barriers for tourists and SMEs in terms of user-friendly access.
- Upgrade human resources in tourism as a consequence of the refocussing of core competencies, 'de-skilling' of tasks in some sub-branches of tourism, and the need to create new professional profiles for meeting tourists' needs and preferences.
- Encourage the sustainable development of tourism because it adds value and attractiveness to the destination; provides a marketing asset in view of the greater sensitivity of tourists to environmental problems; contributes to reduce costs; and creates further opportunities for new products, new services, and new jobs.

The mentioned challenges have led the Tourism Unit of the Enterprise Directorate-General to take a number of initiatives, which aim to promote the flexible integration of knowledge domains and have so far developed largely independently of each other. These are, first, to increase the interaction within value-adding partnerships, which use the historic and natural assets to satisfy the demands associated with leisure and business travel. Second, policies that support the mobilisation of existing centres of competence for the generation and transfer of knowledge and skills and monitoring of tourism. Finally, the planning, promotion, and intervention are aimed at ensuring that the sector is moving toward sustainable, high-quality tourism and competitive businesses. It is difficult to assign simple labels to each of these fields let alone bridge the potential and perceived gaps between the myriad different 'thought worlds' within the private tourism sector, public destinations, and education.

In essence, there are three broad approaches to the development of links to promote developmental transfer of knowledge and competencies (Botterill, 1996).

1. First, an arm's length's approach with both sides taking entrenched positions, critical of each other;

2. A cooperative approach 'in which specific projects are found to be mutually beneficial and where there is minimal change to existing practices of either party;' and
3. A 'strategic alliance approach' in which parties 'jointly seek to innovate and modify practices in order to solve common problems'.

Presently, the majority of stakeholders apply either the first or second approach. Those who adopt a strategic-alliance approach often struggle with its implementation, because their incumbent organisation models are inadequate to coordinate cultural, social, and commercial interaction within complex, transsector networks (Tilman et al., 2003). Strategic alliances often fail because of a lack of a common context of experience. Therefore, there is an urgent need for a model that enables 'participants to socialize knowledge developed in specific context,' which links business, destination, and higher education (Sawhney and Prandelli, 2000) for the purpose of cooperative, distributed learning.

Life-Long Learning

Reflecting on the complexity within society, the rise in expectations of higher education within business and society, and the decline of public funding for education has caused the European Council to call for the introduction of a new approach to education and training. It has resulted in many countries in traditional 'education' being replaced with 'life long learning,' a process whereby the national institutional structure and location of formal education is being replaced by a wider, more decentralised, and demand-oriented format of learning both internal and external to the educational institutions. In particular, the Feira European Council and the Memorandum of Lifelong Learning (LLL) Web site have defined life-long learning as 'all learning activity undertaken throughout life, with the aim of improving knowledge, skills competence, within a personal, civic, social and/or employment-related perspective' (http://europa.eu.int/comm/education/life/index.html).

Life-long learning is concerned with 'all learning activity undertaken throughout life.' Viewed from the perspective of 'activity theory,' diversity in learning experience and capacity is considered an enrichment of the learning process (www.edu.helsinki.fi/activity/6a).htr). Translated to the employer–education interface, it represents a potential for stakeholders to cogenerate knowledge and produce valid results. Currently, activity theory is evolving toward the development of conceptual tools to understand dialogue, multiple perspectives and voices, and networks of interactive activity systems (Blake and Go, 2002). Therefore, the command-performance market approach based on a Taylorist tradition is being replaced by a new context that may be referred to as organisations that are made up of 'decision making teams.' The concept of decision-making teams can be characterised as Vennix (1996) suggests:

- Flat organisations with few hierarchical levels;
- Networked organisations with responsibilities delegated to self-supporting business units, self-controlling teams, or autonomous task groups. Control and accountability are organised through performance (output) rather than by presence or activity;
- Close, but flexible, synchronisation between parts of the primary process, resulting in 'just in time' production and lean organisations in which minimal stock is kept and characterised by flexible human resource management; and
- Operation in anywhere and anytime working environments.

Decision-making teams survive by learning from different viewpoints of their members and developing a shared perspective. Team learning presupposes social and communication skills (e.g., soft or people skills), initiative, entrepreneurship, flexibility, and reasoned risk taking. Furthermore, it implies a need to transform from the current emphasis on control within a single organisational context to the coordination of interfacing between learning communities in the extended enterprise. The extent to which tourism stakeholders and destinations in selected different countries are conducive to Internet-based opportunities can be measured through the e-readiness indicator (see Table 25.1) (http://www.eiu.com).

Table 25.1   E-Readiness Rankings

E-Readiness Raking (2002)	Top Ten	Score (max.: 10)	E-Readiness Ranking (2001)
1	United States	8.41	1
2	Netherlands	8.40	10
3	United Kingdom	8.38	3
4a	Switzerland	8.32	11
4b	Sweden	8.32	6
5	Australia	8.30	2
6	Denmark	8.29	9
7	Germany	8.25	12
8	Canada	8.23	4
9	Finland	8.18	8
10a	Singapore	8.17	7
10b	Norway	8.17	5
	Verschil in ranking van 1–10	0.24	

Table 25.2   E-Readiness Indicators

E-Readiness Factors	Weight	Netherlands	United States	Highest Ranking
Connectivity and Technology Infrastructure	25%	7.38 (8)	7.38	Singapore (8.21)
Business Environment	20%	8.82 (1)	8.63	Netherlands (8.82)
Consumer and Business Adoption	20%	8.65 (4)	8.6	Austria (9.05)
Legal and Policy Environment	15%	<8.60 (Not in top ten)	<8.60 (Not in top ten)	Australia (8.85)
Social and Cultural Infrastructure	15%	9.00 (6)	9.25	United States (9.25)
Supporting E-Services	5%	<8.50 (Not in top ten)	9.25	United States (9.25)

Exploiting the formidable opportunity of life-long learning implies the need for restructuring, which in turn requires a broad understanding of the institutional arrangement, in which the exchange relationships in the tourism sector and the tourism education interface are embedded. It requires, furthermore, knowledge of the mixture of forms of coordination and governance mechanism that would be most effective to establish a 'sense of control' within intraorganisational and interorganisational partnership networks. It raises an important question: What kind of configuration of relationships would serve the simultaneous, ongoing competition and collaboration within value-adding partner networks, so as to allow for the attainment of shared competitive advantages? (see Table 25.2)

Summary and Potential Future Directions

How the world has changed from Descartes' proposition, 'I think therefore I am.' to the current 'We participate, therefore we are.'—John Seely Brown, Chief Scientist of the Xerox Corporation

The 'convergence of telecommunications and computing' and the prospects of intraorganisational and interorganisational links (Webster, 1999) enable the coevolution of creating, exploiting, and leveraging joint opportunities within a value constellation. At the same time, we have seen how the majority of tourism stakeholders and destinations struggle with the implementation of managing distributed innovation in tourism markets across the EU. At the same time higher education must respond on various fronts, that is to say, significant changes in full-time and part-time education and learners who have special needs such as foreign students. Therefore, the benefits of using Web-based media should be investigated to bridge any potential misalignment between higher education and employment opportunities. We assume it will bring about the interorganisational flows, change, and processes (Weick, 1995) that better resemble the dynamism of tourism and enable stakeholders to respond to market-driven needs for convenience, accessibility, and affordability.

Historically, academic programmes, including those in tourism education, have been rooted and governed by national policies. Knowledge transfer continues to take place within a single context, for example, an academic discipline or organisation, which often lead to 'compartmentalised thinking.' Because of exogenous forces educational systems shall have to become more demand oriented. Under the latter regime, programme heads, designers, and deliverers must take into account the different approaches of academics and business practitioners (see Table 25.3) (Jenkins, 1980).

Table 25.3   Approaches of Academics and Business Practitioners

	Academics	Practitioner Tourism Researchers
Knowledge (explicit/tacit)	Advance knowledge and understanding of the subject	Work in a contractual, project-specific, and profit-driven environment
Information Dissemination	Disseminate information through teaching, publications, and conferences	Disseminate information through project-specific reports, plans, and studies that are commissioned and have a limited circulation
Sphere of Influence	Educate and influence students, academics, and the industry	Aim to develop their expertise to secure further work

Source: Jenkins, 1980.

The application of Web-based learning environments provides an appropriate platform to bridge gaps between the representatives from academia and business through the flexible organisation of learning. Forsblom and Silius (2002) identify four distinct categories in the application of Web-based technology that are relevant to the concept of adding value in the context of the tourism employer–education interface. It affords the opportunity to improve the quality of knowledge transfer, develop learning and communication skills, and increase the interaction between stakeholders within a community of learners. In the next decade, Web-based learning will cause professionals throughout the world in business, government, education, and competence training to experiment, exercise, and evaluate new theories, techniques, and tools. It represent a critical success factor to generate, transfer, and apply competencies and knowledge in value-adding networks to achieve sustainable, high-quality tourism. However, Forsblom and Silius (2002) note that value in one context should not be generalised to all contexts.

Flexible Organisation of Learning

The emerging e-economy implies the need for flexible forms of formal education in networks, which connect business, higher education, and tourism destinations. The global corporate e-learning market is projected to exceed US$23.1 billion by 2004, compared with US$1.8 billion in 1999. In short, the new forms of interenterprise partnership render obsolete the incumbent structures and lead to flexible responses, which are characterised by a network of interactions (Bloch and Pigneur, 1996).

Flexible forms of organisation (Volberda, 1998) are typically engaged in a process of continuous, cooperative learning within knowledge-driven alliances. It is a difficult task because learning across boundaries involves the interacting with the invisible assets of one's partners. Within the context of the education–employer interface this development leads to integrative approaches and the adaptation of the distributed cognition view. It is based on developmental transfer, which has its roots in cultural activity theory (Engestrom, 1987). It redefines the unit of analysis of cognition and learning as a collective activity system mediated by cultural artifacts (tools and signs) as well as rules, community, and division of labour. In the latter view, significant learning processes are achieved by collective activities. Meaningful transfer of learning takes place through interaction between collective activity systems. Such transfer takes the form of negotiation and exchange between different cultures.

Web-based learning communities represent an important instrument for bringing different distributed cultures, including tourism stakeholders, together on the destination level (Murphy, 1998). In the tourism education context, the challenge is to define a type of collaborative inter-action, in which both activity systems (individuals and organisations) can jointly identify and create mutually relevant 'boundary objects' (Star, 1989), which benefit both.

The crossing of boundaries increases the participants' perceived poten-tial for risk. It therefore demands a reliable, flexible structure such as Web-based learning to support participants to cross the gaps that they may encounter during their learning process. Web-based learning may be defined by remote, not necessarily physical, mediated interaction (Forsblom and Silius, 2002). Although learning always takes place in a physical context, Web-based learning offers a flexible form of organisa-tion enabling users to access situational learning and experiential teach-ing approaches. It complements the more traditional didactic methods that are part of a social science–based tourism education. A Web-based learning approach gives users an opportunity to apply behavioural skills in a context-oriented environment and enriches the learners' under-standing of themselves and their abilities and increases their own self-confidence to perform the myriad tasks expected of them by potential employers. Working in project teams is an example of context-dependent, situational learning (Anon., 2001).

Flexible organisations operate in global space, which is characterised by polysemic or heteroglot properties (Styhre and Engberg, 2003). In this context, Kumar and van Fenema (1997) distinguish five barriers that stakeholders must bridge to connect: geographical distance, possibly time zone differences, cultural differences, infrastructure differences, and gov-ernance differences.

First, there is a physical gap as a result of geographical distance. Tourism involves multiple sites, such as point of origin, stopover, and des-tination. Second, time zone differences may constrain cooperative learn-ing activities. Third, people with different cultural backgrounds may participate in the delivery of services, including attractions, accommoda-tions, information, and promotion, and create cultural gaps. Fourth, in-formation and mobility infrastructures may differ from place to place, thereby leading to a technical gap. Finally, because tourism development and management involves multiple organisations, each with its own aes-thetics and ethical values, procedures, and policies, the political challenge of sustainable, high-quality tourism development and growth could involve a governance gap.

Quality Improvement of Knowledge Transfer: Designing Learning Environments

The transnational and transsector integration of economic activity is often at odds with existing governance structures and tourism education systems that are closely tied to national territories. In contrast, knowledge generation, transfer, and application occur increasingly within 'global space' and in value-adding partnerships. Following Johnston and Lawrence (1988) we define a value-adding partnership as a set of interdependent stakeholders, which cooperate closely to manage the development, transfer, and application of both knowledge and competencies in order to realise sustainable, high-quality tourism at the lowest possible costs.

Lately, Communities of Practice have attracted the attention of researchers, businesses, and educational institutes. Communities of Practice are groups that share a concern, a set of problems, or a passion about a theme, and who may search to better their understanding of their given knowledge and expertise area through the interaction on an ongoing basis. Web-based tools and virtual communities provide an appropriate environment to connect people from all over the world at any time and any place to 'develop, leverage and disseminate knowledge on a world wide basis, and foster an environment in which inter-country learning can occur' (Moore and Birkinshaw, 1998). Forsblom and Silius (2002) view 'the carefully designed and pedagogically appropriate learning environment essentially as a community of learners where communal learning and culture and the active process of the learner becomes real.' It raises a central question: What principles and practices will lead to the design of a pedagogically appropriate community of learners and the development and updating of materials in Web-based environments? Although the concept of virtual communities renders the notion of strict colocated knowledge development obsolete, Fenema and Go (2003) opine, however, that successful virtual communities enable their members to connect material, social, information, and mind space in order to make sense to themselves and their environment.

Development of Learning and Communication Skills in Web-Based Environments

The conventional neoclassical approach in economics no longer suffices to explain the origins of competitiveness in international tourism. It has given ground to other, interdisciplinary explanations of economic institutions that aim to cooperate with trading partners and customers to create knowledge. Although distributed cooperative learning offers exciting opportunities for actors to capitalise on the creativity of trading partners and customers, it requires that stakeholders at both the practice and theory side of tourism to reexamine the mechanisms they apply to govern the transfer of knowledge. We have discussed how learning communities should be designed to bring distributed knowledge together around a common interest for innovation purposes. The latter is 'the output of a synergistic interplay between individual contributions and social interactions' (Sawhney and Prandelli, 2000). It means that learning communities must resolve the dilemma (and many others) of how to maintain a wise and renewing balance between the forces of social inclusion and social exclusion. Earlier in the chapter we raised the issue whether the ICT revolution widens the Digital Divide. The ILO's 'World Employment Report, 2001: Life at Work in the Information Economy' indicates how informational capitalism and its inherently knowledge-based nature allows lower income cities and regions to 'leapfrog' stages in traditional economic development through investment in human resources. It implies the need for individuals and organisations to develop and maintain skills directed at participation and socialising, knowledge sharing, and argumentation in a multidisciplinary manner (Sawhney and Prandelli, 2000; Forsblom and Silius, 2002). To improve access to the Web (more than half of its users originating from markets where English would be a second language), language barriers can be removed. Human language technologies, such as ICT applications, are available that harness the naturalness and intelligence of everyday language usage in a digital context.

Innovative Use of Information and Communication Technology

The field of knowledge sharing is 'characterized not by the centrality of knowledge or information, but rather how knowledge is used to generate, transfer and apply knowledge in a cumulative feedback loop between innovation and the uses of innovation' (Castells, 2000). Therefore, one must test and evaluate if, and to which degree, knowledge sharing within learning communities has contributed to meet the objective of achieving sustainable, high-quality tourism in a particular destination. Particularly, did the instrument (Web-based learning) that was applied result in added value? If so, for whom?

The application of the concept of the incubator affords the opportunity for testing and evaluation (Go, Lee, and Russo, 2004). For instance, research conducted in the United States suggests that incubators have been very successful at growing companies at high survival rates at low public costs. In North America the most common sponsors of incubators are academic institutions (25 percent), government (16 percent), economic development organisations (15 percent), and for-profit entities (10 percent). In 2001 alone, North American incubators assisted more than 35,000 start-up companies that provided full-time employment for nearly 82,000 workers and generated annual earnings of more than US$7 billion. At the end of 2002, there were about 3000 business incubators worldwide, with 1000 in North America, up from 587 in 1998, 1000 in Europe, and 1000 in the rest of the world. Every 50 jobs created by an incubator generate another 25 jobs in the community.

Investment in tourism business incubation within the EU could create learning communities, which capitalise on the distributed creativity of partners and customers. These learning communities would recognise a key EU principle of social inclusiveness by affording opportunities for diverse needs, for instance through SME development.

References

Airey, D. 1998. Exploring Links Between Education and Industry. Paper presented at the Association of Tourism Teachers and Trainers Tourism Education Exchange. London: University of Westminster. February 5.

Anon. 2001. *European Tourism New Partnerships for Jobs, Conclusions and Recommendations of the High Level Group on Tourism and Employment.* Brussels: Commission of the European Communities.

——. 1998. *e-learning-Designing Tomorrow's Education.* Brussels: Commission of the European Communities.

Ashworth, G. J. 1991. *Heritage Planning.* Groningen: Geo Pers.

Appadurai, A. 1990. Disjuncture and Difference in the Global Culture Economy. In *Global Culture.* ed. M. Featherstone. London: Sage.

Bell, D. 1988. The World in 2013. *Dialogue* 81(3): 3–9.

Blake, C., and F. M. Go. 2002. Stimulating E-Learning in Europe: A Supply Chain Approach. *The New Educational Benefits of ICT in Higher Education.* Conference Proceedings. Rotterdam: Erasmus University and University of Twente.

Bloch, M., and Y. Pigneur. 1996. The Extended Enterprise: A Descriptive Framework, Some Enabling Technologies and Case Studies. Proceedings of the 2nd International Conference Network Organisation Management.

Bogenrieder, I. and B. Nooteboom. 2003. The Emergence of Learning Communities: Conceptual Considerations. Unpublished paper. Rotterdam: Erasmus University, Rotterdam School of Management.

Botterill, D. 1996. *Making Connections Between Industry and Higher Education in Tourism, NGL Guideline No 5.* London: National Liaison Group.

Bratton, R. D., F. M. Go, and J. R. B. Ritchie. 1991. *New Horizons in Tourism and Hospitality Education, Training and Research.* Calgary: University of Calgary.

Castells, M. 1989. *The Informational City: Information Technology, Economic Restructuring and the Urban-Regional Process.* Oxford: Blackwell.

——. 2000. The Information Age: Economy, Society and Culture. *The Rise of the Network Society.* Vol. I. 2nd ed. Oxford: Blackwell.

Christie-Mill, R. 1978. *Tourism Education: Its Development and Current Status with Special Reference to Selected Segments of Tourism-Related Industries in Michigan.* East Lansing, Mich.: Department of Administration and Higher Education, Michigan State University.

Cooper, C., J. Flechter, D. Gilbert, and S. Wanhill. 1993. *Tourism Principles & Practice*. London: Pitman.

Echtner, C. M., and T. B. Jamal. 1997. The Disciplinary Dilemma of Tourism Studies. *Annals of Tourism Research* 24(4): 868–884.

Echtner, C. M., M., M. Charlotte, and T. B. Jamal. 1997. The Disciplinary Dilemma of Tourism Studies. *Annuals of Tourism Research* 24(4): 868–883.

EIESP. 1991. *Education for Careers in European Travel and Tourism*. A Study Commissioned by the American Express Foundation. Paris: European Institution of Education and Social Policy.

EU. 1998. European Tourism New partnerships for Jobs Conclusions and Recommendations of the High Level Group on Tourism and Employment. Brussels: European Commission, Directorate General XXIII.

Fenema, P. C., and F. M. Go. 2003. Dispersed Communities: Weaving Collective and Individual Life, Fact and Fiction, Mediated and Direct Spatial Experiences. Paper presented at the Workshop *Knowledge Sharing Under Distributed Circumstances*. Amsterdam: September.

Forsblom, N., and K. Silius. 2002. What Is the Added Value of Web-Based Learning and Teaching? The Case of Tampere University of Technology. *The New Educational Benefits of ICT in Higher Education*. Conference Proceedings. Rotterdam: Erasmus University & University of Twente.

Gee, C. Y. 1980. Professionalization and Travel Industry Education. *The Journal of Hospitality Education* 4(2): 71–84.

Giddens, A. 1985. *Contemporary Critique of Historical Materialism, Vol. II: The Nation State and Violence*. Cambridge: Polity Press.

——. 1990. *The Consequences of Modernity*. Cambridge: Polity Press.

Go, F. 1994. Emerging Issues in Tourism Education. In *Global Tourism The Next Decade*. ed. W. Theobald. Oxford: Butterworth-Heinemann.

——. 1998. Emerging Issues in Tourism Education. In *Global Tourism*. 2nd ed. W. Theobald. Oxford: Butterworth-Heinemann

Go, F., and K. M. Haywood. 2003. Marketing of the Service Process: State of the Art in Tourism, Education, and Hospitality Industries. In *Classics Reviews in Tourism*. ed. C. Cooper. Clevedon: Channel View.

Go, F., R. M. Lee, and A. P. Russo. 2004. e-Heritage in the Globalizing Society: Enabling Cross-Cultural Engagement through ICT. *Information Technology & Tourism, Vol. 6*. Elmsford, N.Y.: Cognizant Communication Corp.

Go, F. M., and P. C. Fenema. 2003. Moving Bodies, Separating Mind and Body, A Matter of Mind over Matter. Paper presented at the EGOS Conference. Copenhagen: Denmark. July 3–5.

Govers, R., and F. Go. 2004. Deconstructing Destination Image in the Information Age. *Information Technology & Tourism, Vol. 6*. Elmsford, N.Y.: Cognizant Communication Corp.

Gulati, R. 1995. Does Familiarity Breed Trust? The Implications of Repeated Ties for Contractual Choice in Alliances. *Academy of Management Journal* 38(1): 85–112.

Habermas, J. 1962. *The Structural Transformation of the Public Sphere: An Inquiry into a Category of Bourgeois Society*. trans. Thomas Burger, with F. Lawrence. Cambridge: Polity Press.

Hall, C. M. 1998. Editor's Introduction. *Current Issues in Tourism* 1(1): 1.

Harvey, D. 1985. *The Urbanization of Capital.* Baltimore: John Hopkins University Press.

Hawkins, D. E., and J. D. Hunt. 1988. Travel and Tourism Professional Education. *Hospitality and Tourism Educator* 1(1): 8–14.

Haywood, K. M., and K. Maki. 1992. A Conceptual Model of the Education/Employment Interface For the Tourism Industry. In *World Travel and Tourism Review Indicators, Trends and Issues.* Vol. 2. ed. J. R. B. Ritchie, D. E. Hawkins, F. Go, and D. Frechtling. Wallingford: CAB International.

Held, D., A. McGrew, D. Goldblatt, and J. Perraton. 1999. *Global Transformations.* Cambridge: Polity Press.

Hertz, N. 2001. *The Silent Takeover Global Capitalism and the Death of Democracy.* London: Heinemann.

Jafari, J. 1990. Research and Scholarship: The Basis of Tourism Education. *Journal of Tourism Studies* 1(1): 33–41.

Jafari J., and J. R. B. Ritchie. 1981. Toward a Framework for Tourism Education. *Annals of Tourism Research* 8(1): 13–34.

Jamal, T., and J. H. Lee. 2003. Integrating Micro and Macro Approaches to Tourist Motivations: Toward an Interdisciplinary Theory. *Tourism Analysis* 8(1): 47–60.

Jenkins, C. L. 1980. Education for Tourism Policy Makers in Developing Countries. *International Journal of Tourism Management* 1(4): 238–242.

Jenkins, C. 1999. Tourism Academics and Tourism Practitioners: Bridging the Great Divide. In D.G. Pearce and R.W. Butler, eds. *Contemporary Issues in Tourism Development.* London: Routledge.

Johnston, R., and P. R. Lawrence. 1988. Beyond Vertical Integration—The Rise of Value Adding Partnerships. *Harvard Business Review* 88: 94–101.

Kaspar, C. 1994. Tourism Research: Achievements, Failures, and Unresolved Puzzles. *44th AIEST Congress Proceedings.* St. Gall: Association of Scientific Experts in Tourism.

Klein, N. 2000. *No Logo.* London: Flamingo.

Kumar, K., and P. C. van Fenema. 1997. Barrier Model: Towards a Theory of Managing Geographically Distributed Projects. Rotterdam: Erasmus University (Management Report No. 46(13)).

Lash, S., and J. Urry. 1994. *Economies of Signs and Space.* London: TCS.

Lawson, M. 1974. *Teaching Tourism.* London: British Tourist Authority.

Leadbeater, C. 2002. *Up the Down Escalator: Why the Global Pessimists are Wrong.* London: Penguin.

Legrain, P. 2002. *Open World: The Truth about Globalisation.* London: Abacus.

McFarlan, F. W. 1984. Information Technology Changes the Way You Compete. *Harvard Business Review* (May–June): 98–103.

MacCannell, D. 1992. *Empty Meeting Grounds, The Tourist Papers.* London: Routledge.

Moore, K., and J. Birkinshaw. 1998. Managing Knowledge in Global Service Firms: Centers of Excellence. *Academy of Management Executive* 12(4): 81, 92.

Murphy, P. E. 1998. Tourism and Sustainable Development. In *Global Tourism.* ed. W. F. Theobald. Oxford: Butterworth Heinemann.

Nohria, N., and G. E. Eccles. 1992. *Networks and Organizations: Structure, Form and Action.* Boston: Harvard Business School Press.

Normann R., and R. Ramirez. 1993. From Value Chain to Value Constellation. *Harvard Business Review* (July–Aug): 65–77.

Orbasli, A. 2000. *Tourists in Historic Towns.* London: E & FN Spon.

Parsons, D. 1991. The Making of Managers Lessons From an International Review of Tourism Management Education Programs. *Tourism Management* 12(3): 197–208.

Pearce, P. 1993. Defining Tourism as a Specialism: A Justification and Implications. *TEORUS International* 1(1): 25–32.

Pearce, P. L. 1998. The Relationship between Residents and Tourists: The Research Literature and Management Directions. In *Global Tourism.* 2nd ed. W. Theobald. Oxford: Butterworth-Heinemann.

Piore, M., and C. Sabel. 1984. *The Second Industrial Divide: Possibilities for Prosperity.* New York: Basic Books.

Plog, S. C. 1998. Why Destination Preservation Makes Economic Sense. In *Global Tourism The Next Decade.* ed. W. Theobald. Oxford: Butterworth Heinemann.

Prahalad, C. K., and V. Ramaswamy. 2000. Co-opting Consumer Competence. *Harvard Business Review* 30: 1, 83–77.

Ritchie, J. R. B. 1988. *Alternative Approaches to Tourism Teaching.* Paper presented at the Teaching Tourism Into the 1990's Conference. July 19–22. Surrey, U.K.: University of Surrey.

Ryan. C. 1997. Tourism—A Mature Discipline? *Pacific Tourism Review* 1(1): 3–5

Sawhney, M., and E. Prandelli. 2000. Communities of Creation: Managing Distributed Innovation in Turbulent Markets. *California Management Review* 42(4): 24–53.

Shapiro, C., and H. R. Varian. 1999. *Information Rules A Strategic Guide to the Network Economy.* Boston: Harvard Business School Press.

Sharpley, R. 2000. Tourism and Sustainable Development: Exploring the Theoretical Divide. *Journal of Sustainable Tourism* 8(1): 1–19.

Smith, V. 1998. Privatization in the Third World: Small Scale Tourism Enterprises. In *Global Tourism The Next Decade.* ed. W. Theobald. Oxford: Butterworth Heinemann.

Star, S. 1989. The Structure of Ill-Structured Solutions: Boundary Objects and Heterogeneous Distributed Problem Solving. In *Readings in Distributed Artificial Intelligence 3.* eds. L. Gasser and M. N. Huhns. Menlo Park, CA: Morgan Kaufmann.

Styhre, A., and T. Engberg. 2003. Spaces of Consumption: From Margin to Centre. www.ephemeraweb.org 3(2): 115–125.

Theuns, H., Leo, and F. Go. 1992. Need Led Priorities in Hospitality Education for the Third World. In World Travel and Tourism Review Indicators. Trends and Issues. Vol. 2. ed. J. R. B. Ritchie, D. E. Hawkins, F. Go, and D. Frechtling. Wallingford: CAB International.

Tilman, H., T. van de Vecht, G. de Vink, and D. Wijnands. 2003. Competentieprofiel Manager Toerisme. Deventer, Netherlands, Saxion.

Tremblay, P. 1998. The Economic Organization of Tourism. *Annals of Tourism Research* 25(4): 837–859.

Tribe, J., X. Font, N. Griffiths, et al. 2000. *Environmental Management for Rural Tourism and Recreation.* London: Cassell.

Tulder, R. 1999. The Boundaries of Redrawing Organizations. In *Redrawing Organizational Boundaries.* Rotterdam: Erasmus University.

Urry, J. 1996. Post Modern Society and Contemporary Tourism. In *Tourism and Culture: Global Civilization in Change.* ed. W. Nuryanti. Yogyakarta: Gadja Mada University Press.

van Rekom, J., and F. M. Go. 2003. Cultural Identities in a Globalizing World: Conditions for Sustainability of Inter Cultural Tourism. In *Conference Proceedings. Global Frameworks and Local Realities: Social and Cultural Identities in Making and Consuming Tourism.* ed. P. Burns. Eastbourne, U.K.: University of Brighton.

Vennix, J. A. M. 1996. *Group Model Building Facilitating Team Learning Using System Dynamics.* Chicester: Wiley.

Volberda, H. 1998. *Building The Flexible Firm: How to Remain Competitive.* Oxford: Oxford University Press.

Wahab, S., and C. Cooper. 2001. *Tourism in the Age of Globalisation.* London: Routledge.

Wahab, S., and J. J. Pigram. 1997. *Tourism, Development and Growth: The Challenge of Sustainability.* London: Routledge.

Wall, G. 1997. Sustainable Tourism—Unsustainable Development. In *Tourism, Development and Growth: The Challenge of Sustainability.* eds. S. Wahab and J. Pigram. London: Routledge.

Webster, F. 1999. What Information Society? In *The Media Reader: Continuity and Transformation.* eds. H. Mackay and T. O'Sullivan. London: Sage.

Weick, K. E. 1995. *Sensemaking in Organizations.* London: Sage.

Wetlaufer, S. 2000. Common Sense and Conflict. *Harvard Business Review* (Jan–Feb) 78(1): 114–124.

Wierenga, B., and P. A. M. Oude Ophuis. 1997. Marketing Decision Support Systems: Adoption, Use, and Satisfaction. *International Journal of Research in Marketing* 14: 275–290.

Witt, S. F. 1998. Opening of the Former Communist Countries of Europe to Inbound Tourism. In *Global Tourism.* ed. W. F. Theobald. Oxford: Butterworth-Heinemann.

26 Aging populations: trends and the emergence of the nomad tourist

Chris Ryan and Birgit Trauer

Introduction

In the forthcoming decades of the twenty-first century the only certain thing is that tourism will face change. This change can emanate from a number of different directions—technological, social, political, and economic. In some instances the source of change may occur as something seemingly unexpected, such as that of September 11, 2001, when terrorists crashed United Airlines Flights 11 and 175 into the World Trade Center. In other cases the changes may be developmental, but for all that, the current direction or rate of change may be uncertain. For example, can technological change based on virtual reality become a commercially valid option that stimulates the senses into simulations so apparently real that the fantastic journey might yet take place in our own homes? Or is it simply a question of when such technologies will be on the market? For how much longer can the airlines of the world depend on the present patterns of aviation fuel supply at prices acceptable to the mass market? Are there the equivalent aeroengine technologies to the electric car, to the use of vegetable-based fuels, or the dreamt of source of hydrogen–oxygen–derived power that can be extracted from water? To these and similar questions the answers are speculative, dependent on varying degrees of optimism about human creativity, technological skills, and economic structures that may facilitate or inhibit the development of new products that, in turn, can change market structures within comparatively short times, and in such a process make or break the existing patterns of commercial power.

But there is one powerful source of change that sends long-term warning signals of transitions yet to occur. That source is demographic change. This chapter concentrates on the sociodemographic changes that have occurred in the last few decades and extends these into the immediate future. Although the consequences of such changes are in some ways no less speculative that those associated with technology, economics, and politics, they are foreseeable and no less important for all that they can be planned for. Equally these changes are not independent of wider social and technological trends. Indeed a symbiotic relationship between all of these drivers for change exists, as is evident from the history of the last half of the twentieth century.

Societal development and sociodemographic changes have always had an impact on mobility and migration. This is not likely to be different in the twenty-first century (Rojek, 1997; Opaschowski, 2001). However, traditionally mobility has been seen as possessing two facets: that for basic needs such as work, education, and housing is conventionally contrasted with mobility based on a desire to be away from home for pleasure; the latter being mobility of touristic nature (Urry, 1996). Alongside nomads of work place and relationship changes in a global economy, tourism has produced 'tourism nomads,' nomads in search of something different in a temporary home away from home (Opaschowski, 2001).

Yet tourism has been referred to as the 'experience industry' (Pine II and Gilmore, 1999) of the twenty-first century and is part of a societal framework that includes:

- Sociopolitical agendas (policies, legislation, and/or tradition providing for freedom and rights to travel);
- Economic concerns (local and global);
- Environmental issues (local and global);
- Socioeconomic aspects (age, gender, education, income, professional status/work, household structure, and time budget); and
- Sociocultural factors (lifestyle, values, and beliefs).

All these are important when considering trends within tourism and experiential mobility. However, sociocultural factors or psychographics, specifically those of the lifestyle concept, are generally thought to be more influential in shaping the demand for tourism than the previously domineering socioeconomic and demographic indicators (Born et al., 2000; Ryan, 2003a). This is no more apparent than within the aging population that is just as heterogeneous as other age groups, not only with regard to education, professional status, and income, but also with reference to their differing prior travel and leisure experiences. From the differing conceptual perspectives of Born and colleagues (2000) 'Ein Leben lang, ein Leben lang' (life long, life long); Dimanche, Havitz, and Howard (1991), (enduring involvement); or Bordieu, 1986 ('habitus'), individual travel behaviour when older does not differ much from that undertaken in younger years. Although intervening health and fitness factors may cause some change in how an activity is undertaken, the fundamental nature of the activity remains constant. Consequently the tourism products required for the future cohorts of the over 60 age group may need to be different from those of past cohorts of a similar age.

Nonetheless, it is proposed in this chapter that psychographic profiles are dependent on social experiences and opportunities that are determined to a large degree by wider social changes that have as their base demographic and economic changes in a reiterative process. Social trends determine attitudes that in turn have social consequences. Although psychographics are pertinent for a better understanding of tourism markets, the consistency of such profiles may be uncertain in a state of significant demographic and social change. This chapter argues that such changes are upon us. The text will initially describe those trends, speculate on future implications for the tourism industry for the period of the next decade, and advance an argument that the nomadic tourist of the future will be more embedded in a mobility derived from migration and changing social and job patterns that embrace serial relationships.

The Scale of Demographic Change

In 1900 just four percent of the U.S. population was over the age of 65 years, and in 1950 it was 8 percent. In 2000 it was 13 percent and by 2040 it is expected to be more than 20 percent (Centre for Strategic and International Studies, 2000). Europe and Japan are 'graying' even more rapidly. By 2050 those older than the age of 80 years are expected to equal or surpass those younger than 20 years in Germany, Japan, and Italy if current trends are sustained. On such trends Germany's working age population could, in the next five decades, fall by 43 percent, France's by 25 percent, Italy's by 47 percent, and Japan's by 36 percent (Centre for Strategic and International Studies, 2000).

In 2001, in his key note address to the Second Plenary of the Commission on Global Ageing, I.K. Gujral, former Prime Minister of India stated that 'Global ageing . . . is a trend that is fundamental, irreversible and . . . is transforming the world.' Mr. Gujral highlighted the problems, particularly in a developing world, of developing policies to take care of the elderly, while forecasting a possible scenario that 'an ageing world will be world in a slow and protracted economic decline.' For him the means through which such a scenario could be defeated was by means of globalisation, technology, and the free movements of people.

Thus the signs of significant population change and movements are already upon the world. Dataquest (2003), in a review of issues relating to Information Technology (IT) and outsourcing, stated that the future world movement 'isn't even about visas, rules and a few jobs. It's about immigration, the services economy and a new world in the making, and the churn that goes with it.' It was noted that in Australia, the United States, the United Kingdom, the Netherlands, Germany, and India the proportion of the residential population that was foreign born was 21 percent, 10.5 percent, 8 percent, 9 percent, 9 percent, and 2 percent, respectively. That this situation arises is not unexpected given economic disparities in the world and the differences between developed and developing countries and their age profile as shown in Table 26.1. Table 26.1 demonstrates the significant differences that exist between the third world, developing, and developed economies of the world, and by implication the linkages between economic development and age distribution

Table 26.1 Population—Age Distribution in Selected Countries (2000)

Country	Percentage of Population Aged 0–14 Years	Country	Percentage of Population Aged 15–64	Country	Percentage of Population Aged Over 65
Uganda	50.9	Singapore	75.3	Monaco	22.4
Gaza Strip	49.7	Northern Mariana Islands	74.8	Italy	18.6
Marshal Islands	49.1	British Virgin Islands	72.7	Greece	18.1
Congo	48.2	Qatar	72.1	Japan	18.0
Niger	47.9	Hong Kong	71.6	Spain	17.4
Chad	47.8	South Korea	71.0	Guernsey	17.3
Sao Tome and Principe	47.3	Macau	70.9	Sweden	17.3
Burkina Faso	47.3	Bosnia and Herzegovina	70.6	Isle of Man	17.2
Benin	47.2	Liechtenstein	70.5	Belgium	17.1
Ethiopia	47.2	Czech Republic	70.3	Germany	17.0
Mali	47.2	Russia	70.2	Bulgaria	16.9
Zambia	47.1	Trinidad and Tobago	70.2	France	16.3
Yemen	47.0	Slovakia	70.1	Portugal	15.8
Mayotte	46.6	Taiwan	70.0	United Kingdom	15.8
Burundi	46.5	Thailand	69.9	Switzerland	15.5

Source: NationMaster.com. Accessed September 2003.

within populations. The figures are arguably so startling that little commentary is required.

With reference to tourism, then, for the most part, as is readily demonstrated by reference to World Tourism Organization statistics, tourist flows mirror much else that exists in patterns of world trade, namely the majority of passenger movements are primarily between the more advanced economies. Consequently much of the remainder of this chapter will concentrate on those trading nations with particular reference to the English-speaking world and the demographic trends that exist among them. In all cases, those trends are of an aging population.

The Nature of Sociodemographic Change from the 1950s—The Case of Developed Economies

In the 1960s with the emergence of Business and Management Schools in Universities and the development of marketing as an academic discipline, a popular way of defining market segments was by reference to life stage within a life cycle of family change (Kotler, 1980). The stages were characterised by the young being dependent on their parents, then maturing, becoming independent of their parents, subsequently marrying, and then having children of their own. These too would eventually leave home and the parents would then live out the remainder of their lives until one partner died, leaving a 'survivor' until he or she too died. In the 1960s, with a postwar baby boom, the teenage or youth market emerged as possessing importance because, although incomes were limited, freed from parental burdens and mortgages, discretionary spending on leisure tended to be high. In addition, it was a period when comparatively small proportions of the 18- to 25-year-old age group went to university, and thus full-time employment with an accompanying income was high among this group. With the advent of a long period of economic growth by the end of the 1970s and into the 1980s, the 'empty nester' stage began to increasingly attract the attention of those promoting products and services. According to conventional life-cycle theory, a couple in their early 50s would have high levels of disposable discretionary spending resulting from a combination of being at their peak earning power and no longer having to meet large costs. For such a couple, the formerly dependent children would be adults with their own concerns away from home, the family home would be mortgage free, and the couple would still feel young and fit enough to travel and garner the benefits of past labour. In the United Kingdom the emergence of holiday companies like Saga Holidays and various winter sun programmes offered by major holiday companies like Thomsons among others were testament to the existence of this group. In other English-speaking countries similar phenomena were observed. The 'snow birds,' elderly Canadians, would drive their motor homes south to escape the winter, whereas in Australia similar groups headed north to the motor home and camp sites of the Northern Territory to enjoy the warmth of a tropical dry season.

However, the period of the last half of the twentieth century was not only a period of demographic change of the aging of the baby boomers in Europe and North America, and the emergence of youth-oriented populations in other parts of the world, but of immense social change. Table 26.1 provides some evidence of demographic profiles and reveals a division between the mature and developing economies in terms of age profiles, but it also needs to be noted that the social trends that emerged in the developed economies have begun to be imitated by other parts of the world. The cynic might note that the best form of contraception is wealth, as those with financial resources become less dependent on children as insurance against a poverty-stricken old age, and furthermore wish to better enjoy material things without the necessity of continuous child rearing and parenting. Consequently with improving income family size began to fall, with for example, the average size of household in the United Kingdom falling from more than 3 persons in 1950 to 2.4 in 2002 (National Statistics, U.K., 2003).

A combination of economic growth and increases in personal income and family wealth, and changing expectations has created significant changes in patterns of family life. Possibly the first of these changes that began to emerge in the mature economies of the first world was the change in divorce laws that were initiated in the 1960s and 1970s. One consequence of this is that in many countries a ratio of approximately three to one exists where for every three marriages that occur in a year, one divorce is taking place. In addition, among the marriages that take place, an increasing percentage in many countries includes one spouse who has been previously been married. Yet a further factor is that many such couples proceed to have children from a second marriage, while possibly still having responsibility for children from the first marriage. For such people, the empty-nester stage may become delayed by a decade or longer.

However, other changes have delayed the empty-nester stage for both those who do or do not divorce. Some of this change has arisen from the demand for more highly skilled work forces that has seen the participation rates in higher education climb significantly from the 1960s. In that decade, in many European countries, about only 5 percent of the 18- to 25-year-old cohort went to university, though many others undertook some form of technical training. In 1950 there were only 68,000 university students in Britain (Halsey, 1961). However, with the declining importance of the primary and secondary industrial sector as economic drivers in many economies, educational systems based on the apprenticeship system also declined. Instead there emerged a growth in demand for qualifications gained by full-time study provided by a tertiary education system that itself experienced significant growth in the last quarter of the twentieth century. New universities were created in many countries under governmental policies that stressed the need for new skills that were required for the emergent economies based on service provision in the areas of social welfare, education, financial and legal services, administration, and information technology among others. Consequently, by the commencement of the twenty-first century the participation rate in university education by those in the 18- to 25-year age group was about 35 percent to 40 percent in many English-speaking countries, whereas in others like, for example, South Korea, the figure was in excess of 80 percent. Much of this growth has occurred particularly in the last decade of the twentieth century.

A number of consequences emerged from this. First, young people are dependent on their parents for much longer periods of time than in the past. Second, the income earning capacity enjoyed by past generations of young people was delayed by approximately five years. Third, arguably a societal tendency toward age cohort socialisation is reinforced and past intergenerational mixing in many work and social environments was and remains diminished or delayed until the late twenties. Fourth, although the youth market remained important because leisure spending by this age group remained high, attention began to switch toward an older age group of young professional people in their later twenties as the main source of trends and fashion. It was this age group that achieved independence from home while remaining comparatively free from high costs associated with family and home ownership (partly because of a trend toward later marriage, particularly among those with tertiary education qualifications).

Associated with the investment of time and effort involved in tertiary education and the emergence of an economy based on a service sector that demanded high levels of interpersonal skills, another important change was that of the role of females. Female participation in university education increased both proportionately and in absolute numbers so that whereas in the 1960s in a country like the United Kingdom, females accounted for approximately 40 percent of the university student population, by 2001 females accounted for approximately 55 percent of that university population (Higher Education Statistics Agency, 2003). Consequently the expectation of females changed from one of having a career determined primarily by family needs to one based on professional skills. As a result both the years of marriage and child bearing were delayed, and the average age of having a first child in many advanced economies rose from the early to the late twenties. Delayed marriage and child bearing also meant that many females had developed careers that they were reluctant to abandon, whereas such jobs also produced the means by which to pay for child care. Family size declined to the point that in many economies of the first world the birth rate has dropped below the level required to sustain current population size. This has given rise to debates about optimum population levels (Hollingsworth, 1996) and what levels of migration may be required to support a future aging population.

By the end of the twentieth century other features had also emerged. First, there was an emergent trend for some young people of both genders to eschew marriage, adopting lifestyles of serial temporary liaisons where each retained their own asset base. For example, in the United Kingdom in 1971 about one-quarter of all males and one-fifth of all females were single. In 2002 the respective percentages were 34 percent and 26 percent; an increase not solely explicable by age profile, divorce, and delayed marriage. Second, social tolerance of different lifestyles to that of the conventional nuclear family meant that homosexual and lesbian partners were able to live more openly as a couple. Third, the emergence of neoclassical economic policies that required flexibility of working patterns combined with the different work expectations of those under the age of 40 years, meant that by the end of the twentieth century people began to perceive careers that involved considerable degrees of job and geographical movement. Part-time work became a reality if not a choice for many who might simultaneously have more than one such job. For many under the age of 25 years, with changes in policies relating to fee structures for university education in many countries like the United Kingdom and New Zealand, the period of university education became extended beyond the three full-time years common in the 1960s. First, there was a need to pay increasing student fees as government funding of universities became insufficient to sustain past modes of operation, and thus students began working careers with part-time jobs. Second, as cohort participation in university education increased, a need for postgraduate qualifications began to emerge in order to gain the better paid posts associated with corporate careers. It can also be noted that education also impacts on choice of marriage partner and hence lifestyles (Halpin and Chan, 2003). Third, increasing numbers of what have been termed the Generation X and dot.com generations began to accept learning careers of gaining formal tertiary qualifications via extended periods of time that combined both study and work, and for whom flexible working patterns and little expectation of extended careers with a single employer have become the norm. Arguably this latter change in expectations is but part of a wider process toward expectations of more instant rewards in at least psychological terms if not monetary. In short, if work is not proving to be satisfactory then one simply changes employer, even if that means changing place of abode.

However, although this is evidence of a significant change, some contrary evidence is beginning to emerge that reinforces the notion that the trends of the last 30 years or so toward what might be termed a more hedonistic and self-centred society introduced during the 1960s might itself be challenged from within. In Germany, according to an attitudinal study by the B.A.T. Forschungsinstitut [Research Institute], of 2000 people age 14 years and older, the younger generation now aspires again to marriage, children, and family at a higher rate than in the 1980s and 1990s This suggests demographic changes in the future, although only of slow nature. It appears that the younger generation wants to have it all, fun and family life, as the increasingly negative responses to the statement 'One can be happy also without marriage, children and family' demonstrate (1994: 46 percent, 1999: 45 percent, 2003: 37 percent). Already in 1999, the B.A.T. Research Institute suggested an attitudinal change, commenting that 'in unsettled times the wish for peace and safety (or a sense of belonging) increases' (B.A.T.-Freizeitforschung, 2003). Similarly in the United States the National Center for Chronic Disease Prevention and Health Promotion (2002) has reported higher levels of abstinence from sexual intercourse among teenagers, representing again a potential change in social attitudes.

A further consideration was that of increasing family wealth through home ownership. Although this factor was more important in English-speaking countries than on Continental Europe where home rental was more common, it is a factor that is beginning to establish itself in non-English cultures. One reason for this that emerged in the first part of the twenty-first century was the slow down in economic growth that resulted from the downturn in the American economy after the Asian financial crisis of 1998, September 11, 2001, the SARS epidemic of 2003, and global uncertainty. Investors found that the stock markets of the world drifted while interest rates also fell to their lowest levels for decades. Consequently both commercial and private investors found a safe haven in property, especially in areas of population growth. To some extent the rising property prices were also fed by changing policies by financial lenders, who, at a time of falling interest rates, were able to make some money by extending the period of the loan and also by being prepared to make easier the purchase of second properties for rental purposes for those able to make such investments.

However, the concept of a home-owning democracy was well established in the immediate postwar boom of the 1950s in the English-speaking world. By the end of the twentieth century one consequence was that a new home-owning generation of postwar boomers was beginning to not only own their own property, but also inherit the properties of their parents upon their death. Data provided by the U.K. Inland Revenue service derived from death duties provides evidence of just how significant a change this became in a comparatively short period. The numbers of individuals whose estates are being notified for purposes of probates varies dependent on tax laws, but in the United Kingdom these have remained relatively constant throughout the 1990s. In 1992–1993 approximately 18,000 people paid inheritance tax, in 2002–2003 the number was approximately 25,000 people. The values of estates have risen significantly in this period and in 2000–2001, 173,837 residential properties to the value of £15,755 million were bequeathed (Inland Revenue, 2003). Hence family wealth has been increasing for a significant percentage of the population, even though other factors have increased costs of living in terms of education and health through needs to pay for these services where once the majority (at least in those societies modeled on social-democratic welfare policies) found public sector provision sufficient.

As demonstrated in Table 26.1, many of these changes noted contributed to and were aided by an underlying demographic change that was the aging of the population in many western economies; a pattern that is beginning to be repeated in the more successful Asian economies like that of Japan. This in its turn has brought about change in social policy. First, governments have sought to increase the retirement age, fearful of the cost of sustaining pensions for an age group that is likely to live longer than its predecessors. Indeed, in some countries like Australia and New Zealand, it is no longer compulsory to retire upon reaching a certain age—in short, employees can elect to continue working so long as they are capable of performing to the satisfaction of their employers. Second, governments are seeking means by which the costs of care of the elderly are more fully met by families, thereby threatening the acquisition of inherited wealth. Indeed, some commentators have referred to a 'squeezed generation' in that the baby boomers of the 1950s are finding that they have to finance the educational needs of their offspring and the care of their parents as a consequence of the retreat of the state from past social commitments to these age groups. Third, in the long term, both governments and employers are beginning to express concern about the worker to nonworker ratio, in that those paying tax will become a smaller proportion of the total population, whereas those drawing on government expenditure might well increase. This has turned attention to migration policies that, for the most part, tend to favour the better educated from the developing countries, thereby arguably imposing more stress on those economies as many of its more skilled workers seek work in the higher wage economies of the developed world. At the same time it creates a more diverse social and ethnic mix in the host economies.

Implications for Tourism

As a consequence of these changes a number of potential implications for the tourism industry exist. These include changes in the nature of demand for the products and services that the industry offers, and for the manner of supply of such products. It can also be argued that a number of these implications are already making themselves felt and that the industry has begun to respond to some of the changes, but more radical solutions may be required within two decades.

The Demand for Products and Services—Meeting the New Demands

It is evident that the conventional family life cycle as usually envisaged in the early 1960s marketing literature has undergone a transformation into a more complex pattern of family life. One immediate implication is that the market is far more heterogeneous today. Indeed, it can be argued that concepts of market segmentation are of limited use in an emergent world of the experiential economy. Traditionally marketing theory has reinforced the dominance of the consumer and the importance of knowing what the market wants, but the market of, if not today, potentially of the future comprises individuals with individual wants. These wants are composed of necessities and desires, and to a large extent the tourism industry operates in the latter dimension, albeit in a postmodern world of choice and dedifferentiation the desire can often become a necessity for a given lifestyle thought essential by the consumer. These desires are often expressed in experiential terms couched in the language of transitory experience. Thus novelty, fun, adrenalin highs, immediate satisfactions, escape, and serial romances are among the 'products' wanted by the tourist. 'Funology' is becoming an accepted word (Bythe, 2003). If the tourist is a modern day explorer of new experiences, loyalty to product or place is replaced by loyalty to self. The industry is increasingly becoming adept at supplying a promise to a market primarily characterised by a wish to adopt any new experience being offered. The emphasis is arguably changing from demand to the nature of supply. Although it is true that certain products possess consumers primarily characterised by specific age, income, or gender, the suppliers of that product can often cite examples from a wide range of ages and personalities who consume their product. For example, in New Zealand bungee jump operators find that although their market is primarily composed of young backpackers, they can also provide examples of much older people and those with physical handicaps also testing themselves by jumping off high platforms and bridges. Equally, not all young backpackers go bungee jumping. The market is therefore defined by the product supply—that is the product defines the experience and those wishing to possess the experience buy the product.

This is not to declare the death of the consumer as king. Obviously if no one found the experience appealing then bungee jumping would cease to be a financially viable product. However the authors suggest that image formation is important and propose an amendment to the tourism system of Leiper (1990) by attributing an important role to the media. They adopt Prentice and Andersen's (2003) argument that the tourist is not always in search of the new, but rather, they suggest, is seeking to act out a role that has become familiar to them through the media, which role is attractive to them in that it defines and activates desired self-image.

The linkage between media and tourism will become closer and symbiotic, and indeed both are arguably part of the entertainment business. This is arguably demonstrated best by the theme park and the interweaving of cinema, technology, and tourism that is illustrated by, for example, the Terminator 3 Show at Universal Studios Theme Park in Los Angeles. But it is also shown by the deliberate marketing of Tourism New Zealand in promoting New Zealand using themes from the successful film trilogy, *Lord of the Rings* and its deliberate seeking of ties with the *Discovery Channel* in order to obtain images of New Zealand in 'normal' television viewing shows. Product placement in films includes the placement of place in images to create associations of place for viewers that might be derived from fantasy. The authors argue that, in adventure tourism, although the place may be new, the role of participant in 'adventure' is not—the tourist having seen the images many times on film and television, thereby creating different sources of expectation and satisfaction.

It is evident that these new demands will increasingly be defined not by sociodemographic group membership, but by self-defined concepts of self, both real and imagery. This is not, however, to say that age profile is without importance, in that arguably age becomes in part a proxy for degrees of entertainment information technology 'savvy.' In many senses, those in the western world who are reaching their sixth decade are the first of the mass entertainment media generation, in that it is they who have been exposed to daily television from their early years. It was their generation that created the terminology of the 'global village.' They have seen the advertising and become sophisticated users of advertising for their own uses. Those who are now in their twenties and thirties have become used to definition of self through the use of brand names in a way not chosen by their elders. Today's preteens and early teens are arguably the first real generation of the Internet and are perhaps the first for whom a global village exists in a hyper-reality where they play games linked to friends with whom they communicate daily, whether their friends are in the United States, United Kingdom, Mongolia, Thailand, or wherever. Equally their world is one of instant interaction through Web pages designed to appeal to and be used by individuals in individual ways. This perhaps is the first generation for which issues of dedifferentiation between objective and subjective worlds may not be a matter solely of academic debate. Already, concerns are emerging about obesity and a lack of fitness among the young, which is being attributed to long hours spent in front of the computer screen (but then previous generations spent time in front of television sets).

Consequently it is perhaps not surprising that tourism, that most fantastical of all industries, responds by increasingly promising the authentic. A quick search of three Web sites found that New Zealand is pure and green, Australia is unique, and Canada asks you to discover its true nature. Whereas in the past tourism offered a promise of escape from what was often postulated as an anomic society (Krippendorf, 1989), a society where the individual was bound to a world of work determined by technology, today new technologies become shaped to the individual and hence the promise of tourism becomes one of offering a new promise, a new escape. But what will be the nature of that promise? Boniface (2001) has argued that a new, dynamic tourism will be premised on Zen-Buddhist principles of an awareness of self in relation to nature, culture, and heritage, and it is notable that these have become 'buzz words' in the emergent tourism products of the late twentieth and early twenty-first century, most notably in 'ecotourism.' More cynical commentators have queried such trends. Ryan (2003b), in a review of Boniface's work, notes the sustained sex and booze products found in mass hedonistic resorts; Wheeller (2002) has long queried what for him is a hypocritical notion inherent in ecotourism that travel to the unspoilt areas of the world is a means of protection of natural environments, whereas researchers like Becken and Simmons (2002) have argued that ecotourism and adventure products are often associated with the highest levels of pollutant emissions.

What therefore of the future demand for tourism given these social, technological, and population trends? It is possible to discern some trends that will be of emerging importance in the next decade. These include a growing demand for travel from independent and often solo female travellers, the importance of value for money, growth in the luxury market segment, *the growth of fantasy—'Nations Lite,' home trotting, and labour costs.*

A Growing Demand for Travel from Independent and often Solo Female Travellers

This trend of female travellers is already emerging but will grow. There are more female executives who will need to engage in business travel. There are more single, well-educated, affluent urban-based women who will have travelled as students, engaged in adventure tourism, are confident, and will want recognition. Additionally, single female travel by divorced women will continue to rise. These demands will not only be those already being recognised by the hospitality industry (for example safety in hotel car parks, full-length mirrors in rooms, use of room service for in-house meals) but for products and services more appropriate for females. In the adventure sports, manufacturers have begun to produce female-oriented sports shoes, wind surf harnesses and sails, ski equipment, and so on. The issue is in what form will this new demand express itself? There is a literature that has described the emergent 'romance' tourism of 'rent-a-dreadlock' beach boys (Pruitt and LaFont, 1995) and the Shirley Valentines (Wickens, 1994). It is notable that escort agencies now offer males and not simply for the gay market. But although the Chippendales and Australian Manpower shows are part of the entertainment business, they remain marginal and not mainstream, and so too tourism demands for sex and romance are unlikely to become mainstream but will increasingly be commercial and aimed at other than the teen market.

On the other hand tour operators are already responding to the emergent single female market with adventure and long-haul holidays being established with every expectation that the market will continue to grow (for example, see Adventure Women, which commenced operations in 1982 and specialises in adventure holidays for women over the age of 30 years, www.adventurewoman.com). Ryan (2003a) has noted literature relating to the growth of the single woman traveller market.

The Importance of Value for Money

Although groups characterised by high incomes available for leisure spending such as childless couples, single professional people, and gay and lesbian market segments will continue to grow in importance, family groups will continue to dominate much of the holiday industry product. This market segment will be better educated than in the past and will have a personal history of travel acquired during early adulthood, and the acquisition of a lifestyle that they will wish to perpetuate as they grow older and take on responsibilities of parent hood and home ownership. They may also become time constrained because of competing demands of work and matching work time with school holiday periods. The movement toward shorter holidays in place of the long summer break has often been noted, but another factor in this scenario is the squeeze on family incomes. Although household incomes may be higher than before, so too is expenditure as working couples in turn finance child care, sustain young adults financially through university, and meet higher household capital good expenditures and running costs. Consequently, while wanting holidays the search becomes one for value for money. Thus the trend that has seen the demand for good three-star accommodation outstrip that for higher rated accommodation will continue. Pricing will become more important in terms of attracting family markets and will need to balance an equation whereby price is used as a indicator of quality with a need to be affordable and yet profitable. Generally it can be argued that it is not in the interest of operators to simply discount, and hence price/product packaging will become even more essential. Family group 'offers,' loyalty schemes, corporate packaging, Internet-based pricing, holiday package pricing, pricing based on time of not just year but of week—all these mechanisms will become more important meaning even more emphasis on yield management in the future. Some product suppliers will react against this by offering 'simple—what you see is what you get' pricing structures, but these will very much be based on 'no-frills—basic product' services like those offered by 'no frills' airlines.

In short, the market place will become more complex as it responds to individual demands. It is also a market place that will see more business to consumer sales and the conventional distribution channel will be stressed as product suppliers seek to protect margins by engaging in commission-free sales, even where such sales might involve other agencies in the chain. Consumers will thus be faced with a myriad of more 'value for money products' but also with a need for search time to find those products. Hence, although the product may be price effective the client may also find another cost is that of paying for travel agency services.

Growth in the Luxury Market Segment

Although the future market place will be the increasingly heterogeneous, and even whilst many seek value for money at the lower and middle segments of industry provision, the demand for luxury accommodation and experiences will also grow. First, there is simply a growing number of the well to do. From the emergent middle classes of India and China there are emerging new numbers to join their western counterparts. Second, the number of childless couples and consequently high discretionary income groups are expected to increase in number. Third, an increasing number will be looking for that once in a lifetime experience as a result of inheriting wealth from prior property-owning generations. In consequence this market will still tend to be dominated by those of middle and older age groups, and thus again, bearing in mind the aging population noted previously, again this aging process gives a reason for believing that the market for the more discerning able-to-afford-a-higher-priced-product will grow in numbers.

However, this market segment will be looking to combine luxury with relaxation and natural settings and a beneficiary of this will be the luxury lodge market segment. Island settings, settings in places of scenic beauty, combined with privacy, discretion, safety, and high levels of service will be a growth sector. In addition, it is an older generation that seeks to maintain outdoor and sporting activities, albeit perhaps less risky than those sustained in their youth, and hence sports/keep-fit provision will be of importance (Wopp, 2003).

The Growth of Fantasy—'Nations Lite'

Fantasy has often been associated with tourism and its epitome is arguably the theme park that combines echoes of carnival with technology to produce worlds of escape into rides and childlike fun. However, an emergent trend is what Trendwatching.com has termed 'Nations Lite': defined as a 'light version of a country or society, like a Diet Coke, stripped of annoying "features" like crime, bad weather and excessive taxes. Which leaves the good things like sun, nice villas and glittering shopping malls' (Trendwatching.com, 2003). Trendwatching.com identifies developments in the United Arab Emirates as examples of such 'Nations lite'—nominating in particular 'The World Islands' development by the Nakheel Corporation. This project will comprise a series of 200 islands positioned to represent the globe and share some similarities to the countries they represent. It is also noted that Dubai International Airport is one of the fastest growing airports in the world and in 2003 was being expanded at a cost of US$4.1 billion.

To some extent such developments are not new—being in the tradition of Disney's Celebration in Florida, Portmeirion, or indeed developments like that of La Manga in Spain. What is new is the increasing self-containment of such resorts—in part havens of safety where access to the world can be controlled by the degree to which the tourist wishes to view CNN or the BBC World Service.

Home Trotting

The increasing numbers of migrants will create a high demand for travel and imported goods. London, in 2003, is home to 300,000 Australians and 100,000 Russians among other ethnic groups—all of whom wish and will probably travel to visit friends and family back home, while also wishing to retain a flavour of home such as pickled fish (Trendwatching.com, 2003). The tourist of the future may well be more of a nomad moving from temporary home to past home to future home, where holidays, business, and personal identities become increasingly associated with movement and collection of places.

Labour Costs

Given the demographic trends one aspect that will impact significantly on the tourism industry will be the availability and cost of labour. The industry is traditionally a large employer of labour, particularly in some sectors, of comparatively young aged people. It will need to compete for labour and hence this will impact on wage levels, and thus it can expect its labour force to be both age and become better paid. Like other industries it will need to find means by which technology can replace human labour and the Accor F1 accommodation formula might be repeated to higher degrees than is the present case. The counter-balance to this scenario is the increased use made of labour derived from the developing countries that appeared in the left hand column of Table 26.1. Investments in education and training are likely to increase and corporations will intensify their relationships with education and training providers even more; both in an attempt to obtain labour and, second, in schemes designed to offer career enhancement, training, and rewards to already employed staff.

Conclusions—The Emergence of the Tourist as Nomad

Tourism has been about travel—arguably in the twenty-first century it will increasingly take on characteristics of the nomad. Traditionally the nomad moved from one to another area, 'home' being that place where he or she was located. Home was and will become located within self as a memory of those different places and the events that occurred there. As the first part of the twenty-first century unfolds, three major forces will impact on travel—the aging of the population in the wealthy countries of the developed economies, migration from the less developed to those developed nations, and developments in information technology that will draw tourism into a nexus of technology, entertainment, and travel. As those in the west age they will seek the benefits of the sun, will have inherited wealth, and will buy their holiday properties in cheap housing areas by coastal strips in warm climates in places that are perceived 'safe.' Those of working age will see their careers as ones of movement between countries and not simply within countries. The market will increasingly be heterogeneous based on changing tourist roles, which include not simply those listed thus far in the literature but also that of tourist as migratory worker. As a migratory worker the tourist will hop back to the place of birth and family but eventually will accrue a worldwide network of friends and perhaps lovers; the nomad will have serial places and serial relationships that need to be sustained over the Internet and in person. Such nomads will operate at different levels of income, but all will seek travel as part of a new global society of work and leisure. The world will be more fluid and societies will change to reflect that.

Yet, in writing this, there are also alternative scenarios that are possible. The western world (and the Asian world that has adopted its model of technological-based economic growth) faces challenges to its hegemony. It is challenged by a rise in alternative ideologies that have given rise to terrorist actions that have provoked far greater reactions from the United States than anything that occurred in the 1970s and 1980s—if only because terrorist action has shown itself capable of inflicting death on the American mainland. The scenarios described imply that the world did not change on September 11, 2001, that American policies and society did not transform itself, and that the Bush presidency is not an augur for long-term change with all that might imply for global politics. The scenario assumes continued plentiful energy supply, or that a world does not accelerate into environmental problems due to inaction on Kyoto and all that it represents. In short, to repeat the opening paragraph, some changes are foreseeable, others are less so. In short, contrary to Fukuyama's 1992 thesis, perhaps history is far from dead because fundamental principles still remain uncertain, if only perhaps, the tourist, by definition, defies the possibility of 'the last man' as described by Fukuyama (1992).

References

British American Tobacco (BAT)-Freizeitforschung. 2003. *Bestaendigkeit: Der neue Jugend-Trend. Wachsende Sehnsucht nach Ehe, Kindern und Familie.* Hamburg, Germany: British American Tobacco.

Becken, S., and D. G. Simmons. 2002. Understanding Energy Consumption Patterns of Tourist Attractions and Activities in New Zealand. *Tourism Management* 23(4): 343–355.

Boniface, P. 2001. *Dynamic Tourism.* Clevedon: Channel View Publications.

Born, A., A. S. Middendorf, W. Perl, et al. 2000. *Tourismus in Einer Alternden Gesellschaft.* Europaeische Gemeinschaft, Europaischer Sozialfond, Gemeinschaftinitiative ADAPT, Gelsenkirchen.

Bordieu, P. 1986. *Distinction.* London: Routledge.

Bythe, M. A. ed. 2003. Funology—From Usability to Enjoyment—Human Computer Interaction. New York: Kluwer Academic Publishers.

Centre for Strategic and International Studies. 2000. *Global Ageing Initiative.* Washington D.C.: Centre for Strategic and International Studies.

Dataquest. 2003. Backlash-II: It's not about the Money. Dataquest Resource Center. www.dqindia.com/content/top_stories/103052902.asp. Accessed September 4, 2003.

Dimanche, F., M. E. Havitz, and D. R. Howard. 1991. Testing the Involvement Profile (IP) Scale in the Context of Selected Recreational and Tourist Activities. *Journal of Leisure Research* 23(1): 51–66.

Fukuyama, F. 1992. *The End of History and the Last Man.* Harmsworth: Penguin.

Halpin, B., and T. W. Chan. 2003. *Educational Homogamy in Ireland and Britain: Trends and Patterns.* Sociology Working Papers, No. 2003–06. Oxford: Department of Sociology, University of Oxford.

Halsey, A. H. 1961. British Universities and Intellectual Life. In *Education, Economy and Society: A Reader in the Sociology of Education.* eds. A. H. Halsey, J. Floud, and C. A. Anderson. London: Collier-MacMillan.

Higher Education Statistics Agency. 2003. UK University Population Statistics. London: Higher Education Statistics Agency.

Hollingsworth, W. G. 1996. *Ending the Explosion: Population Politics and Ethics for a Humane Future.* Santa Ana, Calif.: Seven Locks Press.

Inland Revenue. 2003. *Table T12.8 Inheritance Tax. Tax Statistics 2002.* London: Inland Revenue.

Kotler, P. 1980. *Marketing Management: Analysis, Planning, Control.* 4th ed. Englewood Cliffs, N.J.: Prentice-Hall.

Krippendorf, J. 1989. *The Holidaymakers: Understanding the Impact of Leisure and Travel.* London: Heinemann.

Leiper, N. 1990. *Tourism Systems—An nterdisciplinary Perspective.* Palmerston North: Massey University, Department of Management Systems.

National Center for Chronic Disease Prevention and Health Promotion. 2002. Youth Risk and Behaviour Surveillance Systems Report. *MMWR* 28(51): SS54.

National Statistics, U.K. 2003. *Social Trends.* Report No. 33. London: National Statistics.

Opaschowski, H. W. 2001. *Tourismus im 21. Jahrhundert, Das gekaufte Paradies.* Hamburg: B.A.T. Freizeit-Forschungsinstitut GmbH.

Petermann, T. 1999. *Entwicklung und Folgen des Tourismus.* Available at <http://www.itas.fzk.de/deu/itaslit/pewe99b.htm>. Accessed September 5, 2003.

Pine II B. J., and J. H. Gilmore. 1999. *The Experience Economy: Work is Theatre and Every Business a Stage.* New York: Harvard Business School Press.

Prentice, R., and V. Andersen. 2003. Festival as Creative Destination. *Annals of Tourism Research* 30(1): 7–30.

Pruitt, D., and S. LaFont. 1995. For Love and Money: Romance Tourism in Jamaica. *Annals of Tourism Research* 22(2): 419–440.

Rojek, C. 1997. Indexing, Dragging and the Social Construction of Tourism Sights. In *Tourism Cultures.* eds. C. Rojek and J. Urry. London: Routledge.

Ryan, C. 2003a. *Recreational Tourism: Demand and Impacts.* 2nd ed. Clevedon: Channel View Publications.

———. 2003b. Review of Boniface, Dynamic Tourism. *Tourism Management* 24(6): pp. 719–720.

Trendwatching.com. 2003. Trendwatching.com Newsletter—Global Consumer and Marketing Trends. *Nations Lite.* September. Available at www.trendwatching.com/newsletter/newsletter.html.

Urry, J. 1996. *Sociology Beyond Societies, Mobilities for the Twenty-First Century.* Routledge: London.

Wheeller, B. A. 2002. *Egotourism. Ten Years On and Worse Than Before?* Keynote address, Ecotourism, Wilderness and Mountains. Department of Tourism. University of Otago. August 27–29.

Wickens, E. 1994. Consumption of the Authentic: The Hedonistic Tourist in Greece. In *State of the Art.* eds. A. V. Seaton, C. L. Jenkins, R. C. Wood, et al. Chichester: Wiley.

Wopp, C. 2003. No Sports! Von Wegen! Ein Wissenschaftlicher Blick of Trendsportarten und Tourismusentwicklung. *Wirtschaft Osnabrueck-Emsland*, No. 5.

27 Trends underpinning global tourism in the coming decade

Larry Dwyer

Because tourism is essentially integrated with other sectors in the economy, global tourism trends cannot be considered in isolation from key drivers that will shape the world of the future. Key drivers can be grouped under four headings: the global economy and globalisation, natural resources and environment, science and technology, and demographics. Each driver or trend will have varying inputs in different regions and countries. This chapter discusses the way in which these drivers will affect the global tourism industry over the decade. Important change agents on both the supply side and the demand side of tourism are identified and discussed. The chapter will conclude with a discussion of the resulting challenges to tourism education.

Introduction

Over the last decade, the Asia Pacific region has been the fastest growing tourism region in the world. . . . The future outlook is bright for the tourism sector, and the region is expected to maintain a high rate of growth well into the next century (Singh, 1997).
Global tourism will continue to grow rapidly for at least the next 20 years (Cetron, 2001).

Forecast in 1995 to grow at an annual average rate of 4.1 percent until 2020 at least (World Tourism Organisation, 2003), the reality today is that the tourism industry worldwide has been reeling from a series of events that has called into question its very existence, at least in the types and forms that have evolved to date. These events, including September 11, 2001, the bombings in Kenya and Bali, SARS, and the Iraq war, have impacted both the demand for tourism services and their supply by providers. On the demand side, potential travellers have become much more fearful of travel and more conscious of security and safety issues than in any other period of history. Travel numbers are down globally as many potential travellers adopt a 'wait and see' attitude to travel bookings. Many countries that were experiencing an above-the-world-average rate of growth in tourism demand, will, in 2003, experience their third consecutive year of negative growth. On the supply side, except for low-cost airlines, the aviation sector is ailing badly together with all sectors dependent on long-haul traffic. Hotels have occupancy levels that cannot be sustained and many are closing down and the attractions sector is suffering low numbers as, generally, are restaurants, travel agents, and tour operators. 'Do-it-yourself' is becoming more fashionable for mature and experienced travellers (World Tourism Organisation, 2003). The losses experienced by suppliers are creating barriers to new investments in the industry. In every sector there are business closures, job losses, and a feeling of malaise.

Will tourism resume its growth path? The answer is a definite 'yes' but its form will be different. It is evident that human beings will always wish to fulfill their needs to explore, to fantasise, to experience, to learn, to wonder, and to wander. Although such needs remain unfulfilled by alternatives to tourism, people will wish to travel in order to satisfy these types of needs.

What form will tourism take in the future? Many commentators have prepared lists of top 10 or 15 trends/critical issues in tourism (PATA, 1999; Yesawich, 2000). Such lists contain the usual suspects—technology, globalisation, changing travel motivations, environmental awareness, and so on. These lists make interesting reading, but in most cases they lack coherence. The reader gains no sense of the wider social, demographic technological, environmental, political, or other forces underpinning the projected changes; their implications for different stakeholders (e.g., tourists, industry, community, government); or the relative impact of the different factors on the different industries that have links with tourism.

Various scenarios of world futures are being advanced (Hammond, 1998; Held et al., 1999; Glenn and Gordon, 2000). The National Intelligence Council (NIC), in close collaboration with U.S. Government specialists and a wide range of experts outside the government, has worked to identify major drivers and trends that will shape the world of 2015 (NIC, 2000). The international system in 2015 will be shaped by seven global drivers and related trends: population, natural resources and the environment, science and technology, the global economy and globalisation, national and international governance, the nature of conflict, and the role of the United States. These trends will influence the capacities, priorities, and behaviour of states and societies and thus substantially define the international security environment. For present purposes we include the role of national and international governance and the role of the United States in our discussion of globalisation and 'conflict' in our discussion of barriers to globalisation.

Thus, four key drivers may be highlighted: (1) the global economy and globalisation, (2) natural resources and environment, (3) science and technology, and (4) demographics.

In examining these drivers, several points should be kept in mind:

- No single driver or trend will dominate the global future.
- Each driver will have varying impacts in different regions and countries.
- The drivers are not necessarily mutually reinforcing; in some cases, they will work at cross-purposes.

Taken together, these drivers and trends set the context in which the tourism industry may be expected to develop over the coming decade. They provide a flexible framework to discuss and debate the future.

The Drivers and Trends
The Global Economy and Globalisation

The networked global economy will be driven by rapid and largely unrestricted flows of information, ideas, cultural values, capital, goods and services, and people (i.e., globalisation). Dynamism will be strongest among so-called emerging markets—especially in the two Asian giants, China and India—but will be broadly based worldwide (NIC, 2000).

Economic growth is the main determinant of tourism flows. The projected dynamic world economy will provide the basis for increased outbound and domestic tourism. Tourism is now seen as an affordable commodity to be enjoyed by all who choose to engage in a variety of leisure pursuits. The prospects for continued economic growth underpin the World Tourism Organization (WTO) 2020 forecasts of sustained tourism growth in South America and the Asia Pacific in excess of the world average (World Tourism Organization, 1999).

The Trend: Dynamism and Growth

Five factors will combine to promote widespread economic dynamism and growth and associated with this, an increased demand for tourism experiences:

1. *Political pressures for higher living standards.* The growing global middle class now 2 billion strong is creating a cycle of rising aspirations, with increased information flows and the spread of democracy giving political clout to formerly disenfranchised citizens.

2. *Improved macroeconomic policies.* The widespread improvement in recent years in economic policy and management has set the stage for future dynamism. Inflation rates have been dramatically lowered across a wide range of economies. The abandonment of unsustainable fixed exchange rate regimes in Asia and the creation of the European Monetary Union (EMU) should contribute to economic growth.

3. *Rising trade and investment.* International trade and investment flows will grow, spurring rapid increases in world gross domestic product. Opposition to further trade liberalisation from special interest groups and some governments is unlikely to erode the basic trend toward expansion of trade. International capital flows, which have risen dramatically in the past decade, will remain plentiful, especially for emerging market countries that increase their transparency.

4. *Diffusion of information technology (IT).* The pervasive incorporation of IT will continue to produce significant efficiency gains in the developed economies. But the absorption of IT and its benefits will not be automatic because many countries will fail to meet the conditions needed for effective IT use (i.e., high educational levels, adequate infrastructure, and appropriate regulatory policies).

5. *Increasingly dynamic private sectors.* Rapid expansion of the private sector in many emerging market countries along with deregulation and privatisation in Europe and Japan should spur economic growth by generating competitive pressures to use resources more efficiently. The impact of improved efficiencies will be multiplied as the information revolution enhances the ability of firms around the world to learn 'best practices' from the most successful enterprises. Indeed, education will be determinative of economic success over the decade at both the individual and national levels. The globalising economy and technological change inevitably place an increasing premium on a more highly skilled labour force. Labour mobility will increase as Internet Web sites allow people to find work in different parts of the world. There will be great demand for people with language skills and ability to work in different cultures. The tourism industry may be expected to play an important role in maintaining this demand.

Possible Brakes to Growth

Economic liberalisation and globalisation entail risks and inevitably will face constraints, some of them potentially highly disruptive. Economic downturns may occur from situations such as a recession in the United States, Europe, and Japan caused by failing to manage their demographic challenges; China and/or India failing to sustain high growth; emerging market countries failing to reform their financial institutions; and global energy supplies suffering a major disruption. In addition, the trends toward free markets and deregulation will allow financial markets to overshoot, thereby increasing the possibility for sudden reversal in sentiment, and exposing individual countries to broad swings in the global market. Any of these could trigger a financial crisis. At the same time, increased trade links and the integration of global financial markets will quickly transmit turmoil in one economy regionally and internationally. Disputes over international economic rules are also likely. The Asian financial crisis revealed differences among countries regarding global financial architecture (NIC, 2000). As emerging market countries continue to grow, they will seek a stronger voice in setting the terms of international economic governance. A lack of consensus could at times make financial markets skittish and undermine growth.

Countries and regions most at risk of falling behind economically are those with endemic internal and/or regional conflicts and those that fail to diversify their economies (NIC, 2000). The information revolution will make the persistence of poverty more visible, and large regional differences will remain. Within countries, the gap in the standard of living also will increase. Even in rapidly growing countries, large regions will experience low growth relative to others.

Trends in the global economy will influence market shares of tourism-generating markets, globally, regionally and within domestic destinations, with implications for the types of products developed by the tourism industry.

The Challenge for the Tourism Industry

Economic trends imply increasing competition in the tourism and hospitality industries over the coming decade resulting in:

- Increased competition between destinations worldwide (between established markets and from new markets);
- Increased competition between domestic destinations; and
- Increased competition between firms within a destination.

At the destination level, the increased competitive environment has implications for destination management organisation, destination marketing, destination policy, planning and development, human resource development (education and training), environmental management, as well as for the strategic management of firms comprising the industry. In light of the increasingly competitive situation in many regions, traditional methods of marketing a destination to the masses has yielded to more focussed marketing segmentation strategies and themed campaigns (Singh, 1997). Although the focus on the economic contribution from tourism will remain, at the same time, destination managers may be expected to become increasingly concerned with achieving sustainable outcomes from tourism developments. The emphasis on linking destination competitiveness with sustainability will continue (Dwyer and Kim, 2003; Ritchie and Crouch, 2003).

At the firm level, there has already been a shift to giving priority to profitability over volume growth with its implications for strict cost management, a reorientation of activities toward more profitable markets, and greater flexibility of supply to meet changing consumer expectations (World Tourism Organization, 2003). Multinational corporations have also expanded operations in recent years as governments have deregulated their economies, privatised state-owned enterprises, and liberalised financial markets and trade. This trend is expected to continue. It is predicted that tension will exist between the desires of governments to maximise the economic impact of tourism by retaining expenditures within destinations, and within the local region and the desires of global multinational groups to repatriate franchise, distribution, management fees, and various other forms of earnings to parent companies overseas (PATA, 1999). Local ownership of tourism and hospitality facilities and particularly, the sourcing of inputs locally, help to maximise the economic contribution of tourism to a destination, and it is likely that increasing attention will be paid to such matters.

Economic trends are likely to support an extension of U.S. influence throughout the travel and tourism industry. The most visible signs of U.S. presence are movies, fast food chains, hotels, airlines, theme parks, credit card companies, media, and Internet distribution technology. Over the next decade, prominent signs of a U.S. presence will grow globally, but particularly throughout Pacific Asia through equity deals, management, and franchise contracts. Branded hotels will have support from image marketing and networking power. As branding gains strength, the unbranded may find themselves increasingly isolated from other industry stakeholders. Because tourism is a high-profile industry, the response from local communities could well be unpredictable, especially in places where such images are not popular (PATA, 1999).

Associated with the increasing competitiveness of the industry is a realisation of the benefits of forming strategic alliances. This is occurring in both the public sector as national tourist organisations (NTOs) form alliances and also in the private sector. The conditions for successful alliances have not been studied sufficiently to date. As access to databases becomes critical and direct marketing progresses, these alliances will drive the industry. There is an expectation that joint promotions and alliances between NTOs and the private sector will create a stronger collective tourism product that will increase arrivals and enhance tourism growth. However, the benefits of collaborative promotion activity are not assured (Dwyer, 2003).

As trade and investment liberalisation continues so also will the liberalisation of air transport. Traditionally, countries have safeguarded their national flag carriers in order to protect them from foreign competition. However, the situation is changing as governments realise that such restrictive policies are counter-productive to tourism. Liberalisation of air transport is increasingly recognised as enhancing trade and tourism growth. It will to lead to more multilateral open skies agreements between countries. In the Asia Pacific region, liberalisation of aviation policies have also sparked the creation of new carriers and subsidiaries of major carriers such as Silkair (Singapore), Dragonair (Hong Kong), and Sempati (Indonesia). This trend should continue to develop new routes to secondary destinations, especially in China, Indonesia, Thailand, and Malaysia, in order to serve the emerging and growing tourism market in secondary cities (Singh, 1997).

Natural Resources and Environment

According to the NIC (2000) report, the global economy will continue to become more energy efficient through 2015. Traditional industries, as well as transportation, are increasingly efficient in their energy use. Moreover, the most dynamic growth areas in the global economy, especially services and the knowledge fields, are less energy intensive than the economic activities that they replace. Energy production also is becoming more efficient. However, by 2015 nearly one-half of the world's population, more than 3 billion people, will live in countries that are 'water stressed' (i.e., have less than 1700 cubic metres of water per capita per year), mostly in Africa, the Middle East, South Asia, and northern China. This is likely to constrain tourism developments at these destination areas.

Contemporary environmental problems will persist and in many instances grow over the next decade. With increasingly intensive land use, significant degradation of arable land will continue as will the loss of tropical forests. Developing countries will face intensified environmental problems as a result of population growth, economic development, and rapid urbanisation. Topics in need of greater attention include air pollution, acid rain, loss of forests, depletion of the ozone layer, waste disposal, toxic chemicals in food and water, soil erosion, extinction of species, pollution of beaches, oceans, reservoirs, and waterways. Concern for the indoor environment will also spread as new regulations will control the quality of indoor air, the effects of building materials, conservation of water, and energy savings (Cetron, 2001).

Given the promising global economic outlook, greenhouse gas emissions will increase substantially. The depletion of tropical forests and other species-rich habitats such as wetlands and coral reefs will exacerbate the historically large losses of biological species now occurring, thereby reducing the supply of the world's natural tourism assets.

Global warming will challenge the international community with consequences such as melting polar ice, rises in sea levels, and increasing frequency of major storms. The Kyoto Protocol on Climate Change, which mandates emission-reduction targets for developed countries, is unlikely to come into force soon, or without substantial modification. Even in the absence of a formal treaty, however, some incremental progress is likely to be made in reducing the growth of greenhouse gas emissions (NIC, 2000).

At this point, the question is not whether industries and lifestyles will change to accommodate the environment, but how radically they must change, how quickly they must act, and how much it will cost. However, this will not be an easy transition. As the United States continues to resist changes, which could retard its economy, and developing countries assert their right to the same energy-consuming polluting luxuries the industrialised economies have long enjoyed, the controversy over environmental issues will only grow in the years to come.

The Challenge for the Tourism Industry

The successful preservation of environmental, cultural, and social assets is becoming increasingly important as the goal of sustainable tourism development becomes more internalised by decision makers in both the private and public sectors. Perhaps, travel and tourism's main problem will be the environmental impact of other polluting industries within, or proximate to, destinations. The best example of this is climate change. If sea levels rise significantly as a result of climate change, the ensuing economic, social, political, and environmental turmoil will affect tourism flows generally, in addition to the immediate effects associated with submerged destinations (Lohmann, 2001).

Increasing visitation is placing significant pressures on the social and environmental carrying capacities of many destinations. Local tourism industries must be mindful of the effects of pollution on the tourism experience and advocate mechanisms for environmental protection. Demands for still more environmental controls are inevitable, especially in relatively pristine regions. Increasing demand for nature-based tourism is placing ever greater pressure on fragile environments.

If tourism development is to be sustainable, a harmony with community values is crucial. Tourism planning must be integrated with community planning. New attractions, special events, and festivals are likely to seek to integrate resident and tourism market support. This implies that resident perceptions of tourists must be understood for different destinations.

Tourism businesses have a vested interest in protecting the natural, social, and cultural environments that draw tourists, but many lack the long-term vision of adopting environmentally appropriate management strategies. Tourism operators may be expected to better appreciate the increasingly recognised fact that today, 'green' business can increase profits and equates to 'good' business. However, it does appear that consumers and investors reward those firms that address environmental concerns and social injustices (Olsen, 2001). The emergence of the 'triple bottom line approach' to sustainable development, with widespread adoption worldwide, will help tourism/hospitality firms integrate social, environmental, and economic information into managerial decision making (Sauvante, 2001).

Science and Technology

In the transportation field, improved technology in both aviation and surface travel may be expected to result in greater speed, frequency, comfort, safety, availability of information, access, and cost efficiencies that reduce price (Seekings, 2001). A decade ago, few predicted the profound impact of the revolution in IT. Looking ahead another decade, the world will encounter more quantum leaps in IT and in other areas of science and technological change.

The Challenge for the Tourism Industry

Although the price of aviation and surface transport has generally fallen in real terms, Seekings (2001) has flagged the concern that governments are becoming increasingly reluctant to provide financial support for transport infrastructure, or to subsidise noneconomic state-run or state-supported transport services. Any change in the price of transport products relative to nontransport products will have an adverse impact on visitor flows.

Virtually all aspects of tourism and hospitality organisations in all sectors are being dramatically changed by new technology. Tourism and hospitality firms must meet the challenges and opportunities offered by technological advances if they are to achieve and maintain a competitive advantage.

The literature on tourism IT has grown and matured over the years since the first major writings occurred only a decade ago. The themes that have developed, in somewhat of a chronological order, are application of IT to enhance operations in travel firms; special considerations for small and medium enterprises; destination management systems; IT applications to strategic management and decision making; the travel distribution system, travel advising, and trip planning systems; marketing and marketing research applications; Internet, Intranet, and Extranet; mobile technologies; virtual communities; and virtual realities (Sheldon, 2003). For each of the themes there are substantial challenges posed to tourism operators, large and small.

The tourism industry generally does not take an active role in developing or adapting new technology. Despite the proliferation of new technologies, the industry is often reluctant to adopt new methods and tools. Moreover, many sectors of the tourism industry have failed to benefit from information and communications technology development because of substantial barriers to technology uptake. These barriers include the high proportion of small businesses in the sector, the high cost of investment, and the lack of applications specifically developed for the less industrialised sectors of tourism. The emergence of e-commerce and online technologies presents enormous opportunities for tourism enterprises, intermediaries, and destination managers to expand markets and to improve efficiencies in product delivery and communications management (Frew, 2000). The Internet has changed the way consumers purchase goods and services. Expanding the marketplace, dealing with more channels, and selling to a larger number of buyers in different market segments will increase the importance of yield management for optimal use of capacity and revenue maximisation (Affolter, 2001).

What we do not know about the science and technology revolution, however, is staggering. We do not know to what extent technology will benefit or further disadvantage disaffected national populations, alienated ethnic and religious groups, or less developed countries. These are all primary factors that are all capable of destabilising the tourism industry globally.

Global new technologies compete with tourism by delivering new forms of entertainment in or near consumer's homes. Because technology and communications are continually changing the way we live, life-long learning will become essential. Members of the generation now entering the labour force can expect to have several entirely separate careers before their working days are over (Cetron, 2001). With each new career, old skills become obsolete and individuals are forced to learn anew. Tourism providers will more easily and more often form strategic partnerships offering complementary products. Small and medium sized businesses will be forced to take a more strategic approach doing business, and new mediators on the market will assist in doing so.

The Internet makes it possible for small businesses throughout the world to compete for market share on an even footing with market leaders (Willmott and Graham, 2001). This is particularly advantageous in the tourism industry where overwhelmingly, small firms dominate industry numbers. Tourism and hospitality firms must meet the challenges and opportunities offered by technological advances if they are to achieve and maintain a competitive advantage.

Demographics

Several types of demographic variables are changing in ways that influence future demand for tourism and the specific types of tourism experiences that will be preferred. These variables include:

- Changing social structures;
- Population, health, and aging;
- Changing work patterns;
- Values, aspirations, and expectations; and
- Influence of generations X and dot.com.

Social Structures

Social structures, community aspirations, business activities, family, and individual values are experiencing profound global change. At the same time, populations are aging, people have more flexible work structures, and consumer expectations are changing along with their legal rights in respect to products and services purchased.

Because consumers will increasingly have access to information about pricing and customer satisfaction through the Internet, the consumer marketing battle is likely to see a halt in price competition as well as a shift of emphasis on service improvement.

Population and Aging

In both the advanced and emerging market economies, increased life expectancy and falling fertility rates result in an aging population. In some developing countries, these same trends will combine to expand the size of the working population and reduce the youth bulge, thereby

increasing the potential for economic growth. However, a high proportion of youth will be destabilising, particularly when combined with high
unemployment or communal tension. Many older people wish to enjoy
the same activities and entertainment that they enjoyed in their youth,
and they have more disposable income to spend on those activities. With
above average wealth and relatively few demands on their time, the
elderly will make up an ever larger part of the tourism and hospitality
market (Willmott and Graham, 2001). The industry will prosper provided
they cater to their needs for special facilities and services. More retirees
will travel off season, tending to eliminate seasonality associated with the
industry (Cetron, 2001).

Changing Work Patterns

The proportion of self-employed individuals will grow over the next
decade. Because their business travel will be self-funded, it is to be
expected that business travellers will become more price sensitive than
previously. Further, the distinction between work time and holiday time
will increasingly become blurred (Willmott and Graham, 2001). This phenomenon is likely to lead to growth in the no frills aviation and hotels
sectors. It also implies that the industry can no longer segment travellers
into the traditional categories of business, leisure, or group. As Connolly
and Olsen (2001) argue, provision of a 'digital infrastructure' by accommodation providers is an essential competitive tool for the future.

Forecasters once imagined that computers would make it possible to
cut the work week and provide more leisure. Instead, the opposite has
happened. Companies have downsized, often dramatically, leaving more
work to be done by fewer people both in the workplace and also at home.
In the United States, workers spend more time at work than they did a
decade ago. European executives and other nonunionised workers face
the same trend. In this high-pressure environment, single workers and
dinks (double incomes, no kids), are increasingly desperate for any
product that offers to simplify their lives or grant them a taste of luxury
(Cetron, 2001).

Values, Aspirations, and Expectations

In developed countries, further growth of 'time poor' but 'money rich'
people will entail a high demand for short-time holidays. Two-earner
households want and can afford buying top quality goods and services.
Small, affordable luxuries such as restaurant meals are increasingly substituted for absent leisure. Multiple shorter vacations spread throughout
the year will continue to replace the traditional two-week vacation

because of time constraints and job insecurities. This may give travel service providers the opportunity to offer seamless, stress-free packages, reversing somewhat the trend to independent travel (Wilmott and Graham, 2001). This implies that industry suppliers must become more flexible in catering to tourists' changing needs (Butler and Jones, 2001). Holiday patterns too appear heading in that direction. Holidays were once purely recreational but in the last decade have moved into physical and mental rejuvenation. Spiritual rejuvenation is quite likely to be next including increased 'religious tourism.'

Consumers are becoming more interested in self-improvement as part of the tourism experience with an emphasis on health, well being, education, skill development, and cultural appreciation. In developed countries, the demand for luxurious 'weekend getaways' has grown rapidly. All-inclusive holidays are demanded by a large number of people with needs for complete relaxation and relief from the pressures of work. The increasing dominance of technology in people's lives also promotes this trend. Rain forests, wilderness areas, oceans, and other unpolluted regions provide a unique and necessary chance to escape from keyboards and cell phones. As the world's supply of pristine natural environments dwindles and the demand for them increases, their price will increase compared with mass tourism experiences.

Increasing Influence of Generation X and dot.com

These are the sons and daughters of the post-World War II baby boomers. They are increasingly entrepreneurial and are starting new businesses at an unprecedented rate. They prefer to own a business rather than being employed by others as an executive. They have little or no loyalty to their employers, to established political parties, or even to branded products. They have been variously described as 'irreverent,' 'individualistic,' and 'egocentric.' They are skeptical of marketers. However, they are extremely experimental, willing to try new products, foods, and attractions, but too impatient to give a second chance to a product or service that fails to satisfy initially (Cetron, 2001). Brand names associated with high quality are thought more desirable, especially if far from home. However as Olsen (2001) argues, the price of loyalty will be superior products that add real and significant value to the tourist experience.

Generations X and dot.com will be major customers for tourism and hospitality services in the future, and the industry will have to learn to market to them appropriately. They will also be the industry's future employees. This is both good and bad because they are well equipped for work in an increasingly high-tech world but have little interest in their employer's needs and little job loyalty. They also have a powerful urge to do things their way (Cetron, 2001).

The Challenge for the Tourism Industry

There is an increasing awareness in the industry of the importance of skilled personnel to deliver quality services to customers. However, only a small proportion of tourism businesses invest in tourism education and training for their employees. Managers, both home and abroad, are becoming increasingly aware of the importance of possessing knowledge of 'best practice' management, marketing, accounting/finance, and computing activities as investment decisions are increasingly market driven and removed from the political process.

The main challenge for the tourism industry is to develop products and services that meet the changing needs of the consumer. Change in consumer values means that tourists will increasingly want to undertake new experiences, interact with the community, and learn about a destination at more than a superficial level. Several emerging special-interest markets may be identified including senior tourism, cultural tourism, health tourism, nature-based tourism, cruise tourism, and wine tourism, among others.

Safety/Security Issues

Clearly, the world tourism industry is experiencing a substantial change in the perception, if not the reality, of the risks assumed in travel. The current crisis in world tourism requires both demand-side and supply-side responses for its resolution. On the supply side, governments and tourism operators need to address the specific concerns relating to tourist safety and security. These issues concern all tourism product suppliers, large and small. On the demand side, tourists need to be assured that concern for their safety is paramount and that all appropriate measures are being taken in this respect. In essence, tourists need greater assurances of quality, safety, and well being. Rising prices in many sectors seem to be inevitable in the medium to longer term. Occupational health and safety issues have been recognised as extremely important. To the extent that safety considerations promote a trend to 'enclave' or ghetto' tourism, wherein the tourist is insulated from local populations, the achievement of truly 'sustainable' tourism development may therefore be frustrated.

Implications of Trends for Tourism/ Hospitality Education

These types of changes present challenges to tourism and hospitality education. The content of tourism/hospitality marketing, planning, and policy subjects needs to reflect an awareness of these longer term trends. Future industry leaders will be those who have the knowledge and skills to enhance organisational competitive advantages via strategy formulation and implementation in a difficult, dangerous, dynamic, and diverse world. Students need to understand the relevance of various business disciplines in helping organisations achieve and maintain competitive advantage by creating strengths in functional business areas. This includes the need to have a sound knowledge of computer information systems, e-commerce, and use of IT in order to achieve that competitive advantage.

Principles and practices of sustainable tourism should be placed firmly into course curricula. Students in tourism and hospitality management need to understand the roles that individual establishments can play in achieving sustainable tourism development (e.g., 'think globally, act locally'). They must have an understanding of the techniques for assessing and valuing the impacts of operating decisions. An understanding of the 'triple bottom line approach' to evaluation of managerial decision making will become increasingly important to tomorrow's managers. An understanding of the different types of impacts of tourism and their significance, as well as skills in formulating strategies to maximise the net benefits to society, is crucial for policy making at all levels.

Tourism and hospitality education must prepare students to play a leadership role in an industry that is undergoing rapid changes on both the demand and supply sides. The new breed of managers emerging in the tourism and hospitality industries must have the knowledge, but more importantly, must have the adaptive capabilities to apply that knowledge in contexts of change. Such capabilities mature within organisations that 'embrace change and foster learning cultures' (Connolly and Olsen, 2001). Given the safety and security issues that will continue to comprise a background to tourism, students must have knowledge of risk management, crisis management, and contingency planning. Tourist operators must become more sophisticated 'crisis managers' and the education they receive should promote this objective.

There are researchers who argue for a change of 'paradigm' from a traditional perspective to one based on a recognition of the 'chaos' in which much of the industry development is taking place. An alternative view is that in the context of change, it is important that students be instructed in decision-making tools that can aid 'best practice' management in different tourism and hospitality sectors given different situational conditions. This type of information can provide a knowledge-based platform for innovation in tourism management, planning, and policy. It also requires the development of management and planning frameworks for ensuring that the industry adapts to, and takes advantage of, changing global conditions. It also requires that students understand systems, models, tools, and technologies to improve the competitiveness and sustainability of both tourism enterprises and the destination as a whole. It requires instructors to enhance student's problem-solving ability by emphasising the role of theory in helping to solve real world problems in dynamic contexts. It is student's problem-solving ability as well as the ability to think 'proactively' rather than 'reactively' that will help them as future managers to achieve competitive advantage for their organisations.

Conclusion

The types of change taking place in the global tourism industry present both challenges and opportunities to public and private sector organisations around the world as they seek to achieve a sustainable tourism industry comprising organisations that have a competitive advantages over their rivals.

Tourism does have a future but it will develop, both on the supply side and the demand side, consistent with wider economic, social, cultural, political, technological, and environmental trends affecting all nations. A major challenge for tourism and hospitality education and training is to convey to students the nature of these 'environmental influences' and their implications for sustainable tourism development. Students must understand the role that they play if they are to add value to their organisations and promote the achievement of sustainable outcomes.

References

Affolter, D. 2001. The Tourism Marketplace: New Challenges. In *Tourism and Hospitality in the 21ˢᵗ Century*. eds. A. Lockwood and S. Medlik. Oxford: Butterworth-Heinemann.

Butler, R., and P. Jones. 2001.Conclusions, Problems, Challenges and Solutions. In *Tourism and Hospitality in the 21ˢᵗ Century*. eds. A. Lockwood and S. Medlik. Oxford: Butterworth-Heinemann.

Cetron, M. 2001. The World of Today and Tomorrow: The Global View. In *Tourism and Hospitality in the 21ˢᵗ Century*. eds. A. Lockwood and S. Medlik. Oxford: Butterworth-Heinemann.

Connolly, D., and M. Olsen. 2001. An Environmental Assessment of How Technology is Reshaping the Hospitality Industry. *Tourism and Hospitality Research* 3(1): 73–93.

Dwyer, L. 2003. Cooperative Destination Marketing: Revisiting the Assumed Economic Impacts. *Pacific Tourism Review* 6(2): 95–106.

Dwyer, L, and C. W. Kim. 2003. Destination Competitiveness: Determinants and Indicators. *Current Issues in Tourism* 6(3): 369–413.

Frew, A. 2000. Information and Communications Technology Research in the Travel and Tourism Domain: Perspective and Direction. *Journal of Travel Research* 39(November): 136–145.

Glenn, J. C., and T. J. Gordon. eds. 2000. *State of the Future at the Millennium.* American Council for the United Nations University

Hammond, A. 1998. *Which World? Scenarios for the 21st Century: Global Destinies, Regional Choices.* Washington, D.C.: Island Press.

Held, D., A. McGrew, D. Goldblatt, and J. Perraton. 1999. *Global Transformations: Politics, Economics and Culture.* Stanford Press.

Lohmann, M. 2001. Coastal Resort and Climate Changes. In *Tourism and Hospitality in the 21st Century.* eds. A. Lockwood and S. Medlik. Oxford: Butterworth-Heinemann.

National Intelligence Council. 2000. *Global Trends 2015: A Dialogue about the Future with Nongovernmental Experts.* National Foreign Intelligence Board, December. www.cia.gov/cia/publications/globaltrends2015/index.html.

Olsen, M. 2001. Hospitality and the Tourist of the Future. In *Tourism and Hospitality in the 21st Century.* eds. A. Lockwood and S. Medlik. Oxford: Butterworth-Heinemann.

Pacific Asia Tourism Association. 1999. 21 Issues & Trends That Will Shape Travel and Tourism in the 21st Century. Pacific Asia Tourism Association, www.PATA.org.

Ritchie, J. R. B., and G. Crouch. 2003. *The Competitive Destination: A Sustainable Tourism Perspective.* Wallingford: CABI Publishers.

Sauvante, M. 2001. The Triple Bottom Line: A Boardroom Guide. *Directors Monthly* 25(11): November 2–6.

Seekings, J. 2001. Transport: The Tail that Wags the Dog. In *Tourism and Hospitality in the 21st Century.* eds. A. Lockwood and S. Medlik. Oxford: Butterworth-Heinemann.

Sheldon, P. 2003. Tourism Information Technology. In *International Handbook of International Tourism Economics.* ed. L. Dwyer, P. Forsyth, and Edward Elgar. London: Edward Elgar.

Singh, A. 1997. Asia Pacific Tourism Industry: Current Trends and Future Outlook. *Asia Pacific Journal of Tourism Research* 2: November Vol. 2, No. 1, pp. 89–99.

Willmott, M., and S. Graham. 2001. The World of Today and Tomorrow: The European Picture. In *Tourism and Hospitality in the 21st Century.* eds. A. Lockwood and S. Medlik. Oxford: Butterworth-Heinemann.

World Tourism Organization. 1999. *Tourism 2020 Vision.* Madrid: WTO.

——. 2003. *WTO World Tourism Barometer.* 1(1) 2.

Yesawich, P. 2000. Ten Trends Shaping the Future of Leisure Travel. *Hotel and Motel Management* 215(19): 26–27.

Name Index

Subject Index